Latin Prayer

Latin Prayer

Aspects of Language and Catholic Spirituality

David Birch

Rivo Torto @ Drouin : Pax et Bonum

CONTENTS

ABBREVIATIONS

CITATIONS

ACKNOWLEDGEMENTS

I | INTRODUCTION 17

II | NOMINATIVE PRAYER 41

III | VOCATIVE PRAYER 73

IV | ATTRIBUTIVE PRAYER 109

V | IMPERATIVE PRAYER 155

VI | TRANSITIVE PRAYER 193

VII | PURPOSIVE PRAYER 227

VIII | INSTRUMENTAL PRAYER 265

IX | SOCIATIVE PRAYER 301

X | INDICATIVE PRAYER 341

CONTENTS

XI | SUBJUNCTIVE PRAYER 389

XII | DISPOSITIONAL PRAYER 431

XIII | EXPERIENTIAL PRAYER 487

XIV | AFTERWORD 549

APPENDIX: ACCENTING AND PRONUNCIATION

BIBLIOGRAPHY: REFERENCES

BIBLIOGRAPHY: LITURGICAL LATIN

Copyright © 2022 by David Birch

All rights reserved. No part of this book may be reproduced in any manner whatsoever without written permission except in the case of brief quotations embodied in critical articles and reviews.

First Printing, 2022.

All royalties from this book will be donated in full to the Benedictine monks of Notre Dame Priory, Colebrook, Tasmania, Australia. For additional donations please go to: https://www.notredamemonastery.org/helpus

Book design consultant Khairi bin Razaai
Cover photograph courtesy of Simon Knott (Ipswich, UK)

Rivo Torto @ Drouin
Pax et Bonum

Pro Priore et Monachis
a Coenobio Dominae Nostrae de Cana Colebrook
Vere Moventur Audacissime

ABBREVIATIONS

The book titles for the *Vulgate* abbreviated here are taken from the version used throughout this book: the *Vulgate, Douay-Rheims* and *Knox* side by side text at http://catholicbible.online/

1 Io	*Epistola I Ioannis* (John)
1 Reg	*Liber I Regum* (1 Kings -1 Samuel)
1/2 Cor	*Epistola I/II ad Corinthios* (1/2 Corinthians)
1/2 Par	*Liber I/II Paralipomenon* (1/2 Chronicles)
1/2 Pe	*Epistola I/II Petri* (1/2 Peter)
1/2 Thess	*Epistola I/II ad Thessalonicenses* (1/2 Thessalonians)
1/2 Tim	*Epistola I/II ad Timotheum* (1/2 Timothy)
2 Reg	*Liber II Regum* (2 Kings - 2 Samuel)
abl	ablative
Ac	*Actus Apostolorum* (Acts of the Apostles)
acc	accusative
act	active
adj	adjective
adv	adverb
Apc	*Apocalypsis Ioannis* (Apocalypse of John)
b	born
BVM	Blessed Virgin Mary
c	circa
C	Century

Cat	*Catechism of the Catholic Church* (2019 2nd edition)
Catechismus	*Catechismus Catholicae Ecclesiae* (1994 *editio typica*)
cf	compare
Col	*Epistola ad Colossenses* (Colossians)
comp	comparative
conj	conjunction
Cov	Coverdale
CPDV	*Catholic Public Domain Version*
d	died
dat	dative
dep	deponent
det	determiner
Dn	*Prophetia Danielis* (Daniel)
DR	*Douay-Rheims Bible*
Dt	*Liber Deuteronomii* (Deuteronomy)
Ecc	*Ecclesiasticus* (Sirach)
Eccle	*Liber Ecclesiastes* (Ecclesiastes)
ed/s	editor/s
eg	for example
Eph	*Epistola ad Ephesios* (Ephesians)
et al	*et alii* (and others)
et seq	*et sequens* ('and following years')
Ex	*Liber Exodus* (Exodus)
Ez	*Prophetia Ezechielis* (Ezechiel)
f	feminine
Fr	Father
fut	future
Gal	*Epistola ad Galatas* (Galatians)
gen	genitive
Gn	*Liber Genesis* (Genesis)
Heb	*Epistola ad Hebraeos* (Hebrews)
Iac	*Epistola Iacobi* (James)

ICEL	International Commission on English in the Liturgy
ie	that is
Ier	*Prophetia Ieremiae* (Jeremiah)
imp	imperative
ind	indicative
inf	infinitive
Io	*Evangelium secundum Ioannem* (John)
Iob	*Liber Iob* (Job)
Iol	*Prophetia Ioël* (Joel)
irreg	irregular
Is	*Prophetia Isaiae* (Isaiah)
JB	*Jerusalem Bible*
KJV	*King James Version Bible*
Knox	*Knox Bible*
Lc	*Evangelium secundum Lucam* (Luke)
LG	*Lumen Gentium*
Lv	*Liber Leviticus* (Leviticus)
lit	literally
m	masculine
Mal	*Prophetia Malachiae* (Malachi)
Mc	*Evangelium secundum Marcum* (Mark)
MP	*Monastic Psalter*
Mt	*Evangelium secundum Matthaeum* (Matthew)
n	neuter
nd	no dates
NIV	*New International Version Bible*
nom	nominative
part	participle
pass	passive
perf	perfect
pers	person
Phil	*Epistola ad Philippenses* (Philippians)

pl	plural
PL	*Patrologia Latina*
pp	pages
PP	*Pius X Psalter* (1911-1971)
plu	pluperfect
poss	possessive
prep	preposition
pres	present
pron	pronoun
Prv	*Liber Proverbiorum* (Proverbs)
Ps	*Liber Psalmorum* (Psalms)
℟	*Responsum* (response)
Rev	Reverend
Rom	*Epistola ad Romanos* (Romans)
Rt	*Liber Ruth* (Ruth)
sg	singular
St/s	Saint/s
sub	subject
subj	subjunctive
sup	superlative
Tit	*Epistola ad Titum* (Titus)
trad	traditional
trs	translated
℣	*versiculum* (versicle)
Vat	Vatican
Vatican II	The Second Ecumenical Council of the Vatican
vol/s	volume/s
Vulgate	*Biblia Sacra Vulgata*
Wyc	Wycliffe

CITATIONS

Ælfric of Enysham (955-1010)
Albert Einstein (1879-1955)
Aldous Huxley (1894-1963)
Allen H Simon (1959-)
Aristotle (384-322 BC)
Bishop Fulbert of Chartres (952-1028)
Bishop John AT Robinson (1919-1983)
Bishop Richard Challoner (1691-1781)
Bishop William Placid Morris (1794-1872)
Blessed Alain de la Roche OP (Alanus de Rupe, 1428-1475)
Blessed Alcuin of York (735-804)
Blessed Pope Pius IX (1792-1878)
Cædmon (657-680)
Cardinal Nicholas Wiseman (1802-1865)
Christina Rossetti (1830-1894)
Cynewulf (late 8thC)
Dame Julian of Norwich (1342/3-1416)
Dr Peter Kwasniewski (1971-)
Duns Scotus (John Duns, 1265-1308)
Emmanuel Kant (1724-1804)
Eric Gill (1882-1940)
Erich Auerbach (1892-1957)
Eugene Grimm (1835-1891)
Evelyn Waugh (1903-1966)
Fr Augustine (Austin) Baker OSB (1575-1641)
Fr Edward Caswall CO (1814-1878)

Fr Erich Przywara SJ (1889-1972)
Fr Ethelred Taunton (1857-1907)
Fr Frederick Faber CO (1814-1863)
Fr Frederick Oakeley (1802-1880)
Fr Gerard Manley Hopkins SJ (1844-1889)
FR Leavis (1895-1978)
Fr Matthew Britt OSB (nd)
Fr Scott Randall Paine (1952-)
Fr Simon Mary of the Cross MCarm (1984-)
Fr Thomas Corbishley SJ (1903-1976)
Fr Thomas Keating OCSO (1923-2018)
Fr Vittorio Genovesi SJ (1887-1967)
Fr Walter Ong SJ (1912-2003)
Fr William J Maher SJ (1823-1877)
Francis Thompson (1859-1907)
François Villon (1431-1463)
Friedrich Nietzsche (1844-1900)
Geoffrey Chaucer (c1340 -1400)
Georg Hegel (1770-1831)
George Bernanos (1888-1948)
George Herbert Palmer (1842-1933)
George Ratcliffe Woodward (1848-1934)
George Steiner (1929-2020)
GK Chesterton (1874-1936)
Guigo II (1140-1193)
Henry of Ghent (1217-1293)
Hilaire Belloc (1870-1953)
IA Richards (1893-1979)
Iris Murdoch, Dame (1919-1999)
Jacques Maritain (1882-1893)
James L Stevens (nd)
Jean Jacques Merleau Ponty (1908-1961)
JJ Altizer (1927-2018)
John Gower (1330-1408)

John Keble (1792-1866)
John Laurie Athelstan Riley (1858-1945)
John Lydgate (1370-1451
John the Solitary (John of Apamea, d 394)
John Wycliffe (1328-1384)
JRR Tolkien (1892-1973)
Kabir Das (1398/1440-1448/1518)
King Alfred (the Great) of Wessex (848-899)
King Henry VIII (1491-1547)
Maimonides [Rabbi Moshe ben Maimon] (1135-1204)
Marcus Tullius Cicero (106-43 BC)
Marshall McLuhan (1911-1980)
Martin Buber (1878-1965)
Martin Luther (1483-1546)
Max Picard (1888-1965)
Michael J Oakley (nd)
Monsignor Ronald Knox (1888-1957)
Most Reverend Annibale Bugnini CM (1912-1982)
Most Reverend Archbishop William B Ullathorne OSB (1806-1899)
Myles Coverdale (1488-1569)
Origen of Alexandria (184-253)
Père Jacques Paul Migne (1800-1875)
Père Jean Pierre de Caussade SJ (1675-1751)
Père Pierre Teilhard de Chardin SJ (1881-1955)
Plato (428-347 BC)
Plotinus (204/5-270)
Plutarch (46-120)
Pope Benedict XV (1854-1922)
Pope Benedict XVI (1927-)
Pope Blessed Pius IX (Pio Nono, 1792-1878)
Pope Clement VIII (1536-1605)
Pope Clement XI (1649-1721)
Pope Clement XII (1652-1740)
Pope Damasus I (305-384)

Pope Francis (1936-)
Pope Gregory IX (c1170-1241)
Pope Innocent I (d 417)
Pope Innocent III (1160-1216)
Pope Innocent XI (1611-1689)
Pope John XXII (1244-1334)
Pope John Paul I (1912-1978)
Pope Leo IV (790-855)
Pope Leo X (1475-1521)
Pope Leo XIII (1810-1903)
Pope Pius XI (1857-1939)
Pope Sixtus V (1521-1590)
Pope St Gregory I (Gregory the Great, 540-604)
Pope St John Paul II (1920-2005)
Pope St John XXIII (1881-1963)
Pope St Paul VI (1897-1978)
Pope St Pius V (1504-1572)
Pope St Pius X (1835-1914)
Pope Urban IV (1195-1264)
Pope Urban VIII (1568-1644)
QD (Queenie) Leavis (1906-1981)
Quintus Septimius Florens Tertullianus (Tertullian, 155-220)
Rabbi Moshe ben Maimon (1135-1204)
Raïssa Maritain (1882-1960)
Rev Henry Preston Vaughan Nunn (1876-1962)
Richard Misyn (d 1462)
Richard Rolle of Hampole (1300-1349)
Roger Bacon (c1214-1292)
Rudolf Bultmann (1884-1976)
Rudolf Otto (1869-1937)
Seamus Heaney (1939-2013)
Servant of God Pope Pius VII (1742-1823)
Servant of God Romano Guardini (1885-1963)
Simone Weil (1909-1943)

Sir Francis Bacon (1561-1626)
St Aloysius Gonzaga (1568-1591)
St Alphonsus Maria de Liguori (1696-1787)
St Ambrose of Milan (339-397)
St Anselm, Archbishop of Canterbury (1033-1109)
St Anthony of Padua (1195-1232)
St Athanasius I of Alexandria (296-373)
St Attracta (6^{th}C)
St Augustine of Hippo (354-430)
St Benedict Labre (1748-1783)
St Benedict of Nursia OSB (480-547)
St Bernard of Clairvaux (1090-1153)
St Bernadette of Soubirous (1844-1879)
St Bernardine of Siena (1380-1444)
St Bonaventure (1221-1274)
St Brendan (484-577)
St Catherine of Sienna (1347-1380)
St Charles de Foucauld (Brother Charles of Jesus, 1858-1916)
St Columbanus (540-615)
St Cyprian of Carthage (210-258)
St Cyril of Jerusalem (313-386)
St Denis (Dionysius) the Carthusian (1402-1472)
St Dominic OP (1170-1221)
St Ephraim the Syrian (306-373)
St Faustus of Riez (405-495)
St Francis de Sales (1567-1622)
St Francis of Assisi (1181-1226)
St Gregory of Nyssa (335-395)
St Hilary of Poitiers (310-367)
St Hildegard of Bingen (1098-1179)
St Ignatius of Antioch [d c108/140?)
St Ignatius of Loyola (1491-1556)
St Irenaeus of Lyons (130-202)
St James the Apostle (Jacobus Maior, d 44)

St Jerome of Stridon (342-420)
St John Baptist de la Salle (1651-1719)
St John Cassian (360-435)
St John Chrysostom (347-407)
St John Damascene (675-749)
St John Henry Cardinal Newman (1801-1890)
St John Leonardi (1541-1609)
St John of the Cross (1542-1591)
St John the Apostle (c6-100)
St John Vianney (Curé d'Ars, 1786-1859)
St Justin (100-165)
St Louis Marie Grignion de Montfort (1673-1716)
St Luke the Evangelist (early 1stC)
St María Rafael Arnáiz Báron (1911-1938)
St Mark the Evangelist (12-68)
St Matthew the Apostle (d 74)
St Nicholas of Myra/Bari (270-343)
St Paul the Apostle (5-67)
St Peter the Apostle (c1-64/68)
St Philip Neri (1515-1595)
St Philip the Apostle (3-80)
St Pius of Pietrelcina OFM Cap (Padre Pio, 1887-1968)
St Robert Cardinal Bellarmine (1542-1621)
St Teresa of Calcutta (1910-1997)
St Theresa of Avila (1515-1582)
St Thérèse of the Child Jesus and the Holy Face (1873-1897)
St Thomas Aquinas (1225-1274)
St Thomas More (1478-1535)
St Thomas the Apostle (d 72)
St Timothy of Ephesus (d 97)
St Vincent of Lérins (d 445)
Stephen Hawking (1942-2018)
Søren Kierkegaard (1813-1855)
Thomas à Kempis (1380-1471)

Thomas Merton (Fr Mary Louis OCSO, 1915-1968)
TS Eliot (1888-1965)
Venerable Bede (673-735)
Venerable Pope Pius XII (1876-1958)
Walter Haddon (1515-1572)
Wili Appel (1893-1988)
William Empson (1906-1984)
William Ewart Gladstone (1809-1898)
William Langland (1332 -1386)
William Tyndale (1494-1536)
William Wordsworth (1770-1850)

ACKNOWLEDGEMENTS

Fac me, Pater, quǽrere te, víndica me ab erróre; quaerénti te mihi nihil áliud pro te occúrrat.
(Make me, Father, to seek you, free me from error; seeking nothing else from you that may occur to me. St Augustine *Soliloquia* 1:6)

    I wish to acknowledge the inestimable help of John Paul Bielecki for his encouragement and enthusiasm as this book has developed, and most especially for his astute micro-editing and proofreading of the entire manuscript in many drafts. His linguistic skills, and sharp eyes, have proven invaluable.

    Most especially too, I acknowledge Khairi bin Razaai who has so generously, and patiently, understood the often difficult, and seemingly incomprehensible, at times, over many years of close friendship. Heartfelt thanks too, for his expert eye in advising on this book design.

    Also my thanks must go to Dr Puva Arumugam for her many years of friendship, first as student, then as colleague, and now as valued friend, for her expert advice in initially guiding me in preparing the manuscript for publication.

    My thanks too to Anthony Bidgood, who, ordained with me as *Ostiarii* (Porters) serving the *usus antiquior Roman Rite* as (now retired) Sacristans, has shared with me many years of stimulating conversations: Catholic and otherwise.

    My particular thanks too to Dr Anna Silvas of the University of New England; Michael Sternbeck of the Benedictine inspired St Bede Studio, Wallsend, NSW and Dr David Daintree of the Christopher

Dawson Centre, Hobart, Tasmania, for their most generous comments and support on earlier drafts.

I should also record my thanks to the Mannix Library, Melbourne for its resources in the final stages of compiling the Bibliographies for this book, and to all those, like one-time colleague Dr Elizabeth Braithwaite, who have continued to keep me in their prayers, regardless of our not seeing each other since my retirement into a much more eremitical life.

I also acknowledge:

- Michael Martin's *Thesaurus Precum Latinarum* (Treasury of Latin Prayers 1998 *et seq*): https://www.preces-latinae.org/index.htm
- *Novus Motus Liturgicus* (New Liturgical Movement) founded online in 2005 and dedicated to 'Sacred Liturgy and Liturgical Arts': https://www.newliturgicalmovement.org/
- *Rorate Caeli. International Traditional Catholic Web Log*: https://rorate-caeli.blogspot.com/
- Katrina Edwards' *Saints Will Arise* blogspot focusing on the traditional Benedictine Office in accordance with the 1963 Benedictine calendar and rubrics, including the Farnborough edition of the Monastic Diurnal: https://saintsshallarise.blogspot.com/
- Yale University for use of the image from the *Psalterium cum hymnis secundum usum et consuetudinem Sarum et Eboracensis anno virginei part[ibus] Mccccc.xxii. Die vero. vii. mensis Iunii. Impressum Parisius Expe[n]sis & sumptibus honesti mercatoris Francisci Byrckman*) once owned by St Thomas More and now held in the Beinecke Rare Book and Manuscript Library: https://collections.library.yale.edu/catalog/16662955

- Plainchant images from *Graduale Sacrosanctae Romanae Ecclesiae de Tempore et de Sanctis SS. D. N. PII X. Pontificis Maximi Iussu Restitutum et Editum ad Exemplar Editionis Typicae Concinnatum et Rhythmicis Signis a Solesmensibus Monachis, Desclée & Socii: S. Sedis Apostolicae et Sacrorum Rituum Congregationis Typographi, Parisiis, Tornaci, Romae, Neo Eboraci* (1961): https://archive.ccwatershed.org/media/pdfs/13/08/14/13-43-42_0.pdf
- Simon Knott (Ipswich, UK) for the cover photograph of the *Scutum Fidei* stained glass window from an East Anglian church (UK): http://www.simonknott.co.uk
- The Metropolitan Museum of Art for the 15th C woodcut image *The Crucifixion* (Schr.486). The Elisha Whittelsey Collection, 1956, Accession Number 56.581.10: https://www.metmuseum.org/art/collection/search/382416
- The State Library of Victoria for Raïssa Maritain, *Patriarch tree : thirty poems.* (1965) Translated into English by a Benedictine of Stanbrook; with a preface by Robert Speaight. Stanbrook Abbey Press: Worcester

non nobis, Dómine, non nobis, sed nómini tuo da glóriam.
(not to us, O Lord, not to us, but to your name give the glory.
Ps 113:9)

De VI Die Infra Octavam Paschae
(Easter Friday) 2022
Drouin 3818
david.birch63@gmail.com

INTRODUCTION

Veni, Sancte Spíritus
(Come! O Holy Spirit)

Origins

Latin Prayer. Aspects of Language and Catholic Spirituality was written eleven years after my retirement from a University career in Linguistics (initially Medieval) Stylistics and Communication Studies, and as a book only came into being when the bulk of the religious and Latin part of my academic library became part of a new monastic library in Colebrook, Tasmania, at the end of 2020. Of the books I retained, one I had read in my first undergraduate year (first reading Biblical Studies and then English Language and Linguistics) was Erich Auerbach's *Mimesis. The Representation of Reality in Western Literature*, originally written in German in Istanbul between the war years of 1942 and 1945 and published in 1946. At the end of the book Auerbach (1892-1957) talks about writing it during a war which gave him little or no access to libraries, scholarly resources or international contacts; the absence of which, in fact, enabled him to write it more freely than perhaps he would have done. Although *Latin Prayer* was not written in war, and with libraries available (but usually closed because of Covid-19) it is a book initially written with no public library resources and which, therefore, cites internet references far more often than I once might have done.

It is, first and foremost, a book about Catholic prayer and Catholic spirituality; about Catholic identity; about Catholic patrimony and Catholic Tradition, and about the related importance of the Latin language and its grammar to all of these. It is primarily a spiritual book, through a linguist's eyes, using the vocabulary of grammar, as seen through a variety of Latin prayers and scripture, to express that spirituality. There are many different ways of expressing spirituality. This book concentrates on one of them at the very heart of 2,000 years of Catholic history: Latin prayer. In doing so, I describe, and present, a way of Latin prayer framed as a 'grammar of prayer'.

Contrary to what that might seem to suggest, this book is about enlarging borders, not narrowing them into a fast disappearing Latin Catholic Church. It is about enlarging borders, both linguistically and spiritually, in an increasingly secularised world, where the once unchanging certainties of Latin Catholicism have been dramatically marginalised and de-stabilised both outside of, and also within, Catholicism itself. To enlarge our borders beyond those that are tangibly enlarged for us within secularised globalisation, we have to go into ourselves, as well as out, towards other, intangible, things. Borders are both inside and outside of us. It is, therefore, a book that is uncompromisingly about a life beyond ourselves; about other-worldliness; about the supernatural within a Latin Catholic context. It is a book about a form (and language) of prayer since the Latin beginnings of the ***Ecclesia Catholica*** (καθολικὴ ἐκκλησία - *he katholike ekklesia* - the Universal Church - named as such by St Ignatius of Antioch [d c108/140]).

To enlarge our borders through prayer and seek God's presence, the object of prayer, we need to give our sentient consent, as Trappist monk and Abbot, Fr Thomas Keating OCSO (1923-2018) pointed out in his 1994 book, *Intimacy with God*. We need, therefore, to talk to God, sometimes in words, sometimes in silences, and in doing so, we need to look ahead, and also back, to enable the *spiritual continuity* which joins us to all the prayer and talking to God that has gone before us, and to all the prayer and talking to God that will come after us, in order for us to keep moving; to stay spiritually active; to keep listening to God. As St James the Apostle (d 44 AD) warns:

> ***non habetis, propter quod non postulatis.***
> (You have not, because you ask not. *Ia* 4:2)

If we have an empty spiritual life, it is simply because we are not actively asking for it to be filled. We have to consent in order to ask. Père Jean-Pierre de Caussade SJ (1675-1751) once wrote:

> 'Jesus Christ is the sovereign organ of that action. He was yesterday, he is still today, continuing his life, not beginning it over again.'

We may share in that divine life - as do the Saints of all time - and we may do so through a language of prayer that, for the better part of two millennia, those Saints used themselves - Latin. My focus here is not on the now often politicised 'universality of Latin', enabling the Church to be expressed ***una voce*** (with one voice) but on its hieratic (sacral) qualities as a language enabling personal spiritual development within the sacramental context of a now predominantly vernacular Church. It does so because Latin, like Church Slavonic, Classical Arabic in Islam; Rabbinic Hebrew in Orthodox Judaism, or Sanskrit in Hinduism and Pali in Buddhism, *mystifies*. That 'mystification' is never very far away in any aspect of this book. Catholic 'mysticism', and its long history of devotional practices and mystical theology, lies at the very heart of the Latin Catholic spirituality developed here.

At the heart of this book, then, is a road map, if you like, of how to enlarge our borders. A road map drawn substantially from the public Latin prayers, scripture, and other related texts, as they appear in the officially approved liturgical books of the Latin Catholic church (*Roman Rite*) prior to, but not excluding, the reforms that were made (initially in Latin) from 1969 onwards and approved for public use by Pope St. Paul VI in 1970. These public Latin prayers, amongst others approved only for private prayer, unavailable as most of them now are in Catholic public worship, are not a *panacea* - a magical formula or spell - for personal salvation, or for 'returning' the Catholic Church to its 'right' track post *Vatican II*. They are simply a means to a continuing personal journey: a means to an end for enlarging borders beyond ourselves, and our increasingly secularised/vernacularised world and Church, so that we can enlarge those borders within ourselves.

The distinction between *public* prayer and *private* prayer is an important one. Public (Liturgical) prayer is the prayer composed and designated only by the Church, and formalised in its various books like *Missals* and *Breviaries*, for use in public worship but which may also be prayed privately. Private prayer may not be used for public prayer unless specifically approved. Approved public prayer in Latin Catholicism does not include the unofficial services now often 'created' in the vernacular by enthusiastic and well-meaning liturgists. The officially approved liturgical prayers cannot be added to, deleted or changed in any way except by a formal process within the Church. Private prayer is not bound by these rules. As such, this book gained its initial motivation from the *Ancrene Wisse* written in an early 13thC Middle English dialect, where the writer instructs three sisters who wish to live the solitary and enclosed life of anchoresses (bricked into a small cell, often at the side of a church) on how to pray and to regulate their lives in a life of Latin prayer. That life for them is now dominated by the discipline and necessities of private prayer, given their inability to physically participate in public worship (often only partially glimpsed by the anchorites through a tiny 'squint' in the wall of their cell). The English word 'anchorite' derives from Latin **anachoreta**, itself derived from the Greek ἀναχωρητής - *anachoretes*) originally meaning 'someone who withdraws', and *wisse* from the Anglo Saxon *wisian* 'to guide/instruct'.

The discipline of private Latin prayer, for those of us seeking similar guidance, though not necessarily 'withdrawal', may seem very distant from modern day Catholic realities, but it drives this book. It does so, not to call for a return to bricking up anchorites to the accompaniment of a *Requiem Mass,* as was once done, but as recognition of an almost 2,000 year history of a way of Latin prayer which tends to be, following various interpretations of the documents of *The Second Ecumenical Council of the Vatican* (1962-1965) amongst others, increasingly unavailable to the majority of Catholics now unable, more often than not, to publicly pray in the Latin ways, rites and texts of the hitherto unbroken history of two millennia.

Despite the growing interest in recent years (post *Vatican II*) of these Latin ways, rites and texts, often referred to popularly as 'the old Latin Mass', the churches offering such Latin liturgies are few and far between, and seem set to become even scarcer following the 16 July 2021 Apostolic Letter issued **motu proprio** (by his own initiative) of Pope Francis (1936-) entitled ***Traditionis custodes*** (guardians of the Tradition) sub-titled *On the Use of the Roman Liturgy Prior to the Reform of 1970* which seeks to significantly restrict where such Latin liturgies may be celebrated. That said, Latin prayer, as understood in this book, is not presented as a relic or a fossilised museum piece, but with the recognition of its continuing value as a form of, and way of praying in, Latin which now has to increasingly turn inwards, mostly as private prayer, in much the same way as the anchorites had to.

It is a book designed to explore, shape and more fully understand *anagogically* a way of prayer mediated in Latin. It will also be, I hope, an introduction to the treasure house of Latin prayers to those encountering them for the first time, or to those re-engaging with them, simultaneously using, as a unique language and grammar of spirituality, the terminology of Latin grammar. This is motivated not by linguistics *per se* but by a wish to revitalise now sometimes marginalised or even lost Catholic sensibilities, towards what the anonymous author of the mystical 14[th]C *Cloude of Unknowyng* referred to as 'goostlynesse'.

'Goostlynesse' as a deep spiritual Catholic awareness is no longer used in this way in contemporary English. Neither is the word 'anagogically' an easy one to the modern ear. It derives from the Latin loan word *anagoge* (ἀναγωγή - anagoge - 'elevation') and came to mean in Medieval Latin a 'going beyond' the surface or literal meaning of a word or a text, to a higher order spiritual meaning. It is to this anagogical/spiritual purpose that this book is written.

Readers who know no Latin will, I hope, be persuaded by the beauty of the patrimony of Latin Tradition in the Catholic Church, and the spiritual rewards this book may alert them to, to learn Latin. Those who know Latin will, I hope, make a journey with me in this book through the grammar and linguistics of a language already learnt, though probably in quite different ways to some of those suggested here, and perhaps, through texts already well known, come to what St Thomas Aquinas (1225-1274) referred to, speaking of Paradise, as a *locus spiritualis* (spiritual place) as against the everyday *locus corporeus* (corporeal place) within which we live our daily lives.

Praying Latin

GK Chesterton (1874-1936) famously said in 1929 that every language is a dying language, but for it to become immortal it has to die completely. Some think of Latin as that dead immortal language and see its 'unchanging' nature, as a result of that 'death', as a perfect vehicle for expressing the unchanging truths and liturgy of the Catholic Church. But that is not my position here. Latin is not more suitable for prayer and liturgy because of its 'deadness'. As Chesterton recognised, pagan Latin may have died, but Christian Latin only died to the world. It found a new, and continuing, life in the Church. The continuing suitability of Latin as a hieratic language rests on the long history of its use and status as a sacral language in the Tradition of the Church. It has become such by its being disciplined by the liturgy, prayer (public and private) and patrimony it functions within. Fr Scott Randall Paine (1952-) emphasised this point when he wrote in 2018 that:

> 'The whole glory of Christian Latin is that it abides in the greatest present tense of all: the "now" of eternity. Never needing to be up-to-date, it stands free of the danger of ever getting out-of-date. And we who spend hours speaking interminably about things that pass, must be able to turn in theological reflection to God's unchanging mysteries, and in a language still inspired by a Breath from the land of the living.'

Catholic writer and composer Dr Peter Kwasniewski (1971-) has called this process 'the law of liturgical entropy', demonstrating that without the ordered guidance of Tradition:

> 'willed by the Holy Spirit and the example of many Saints who have shown us how to walk the often gruelling uphill path of fidelity, fallen man will make liturgy conform to his own whims and wants, his own programs and purposes - something easier and more damaging.'

The discipline of Latin has been an essential part of that 'ordered guidance of Tradition'. In his 1962 ***Veterum sapientia*** (Wisdom of the ancients) on the promotion of the study of Latin, Pope St John XXIII (1881-1963) quoted Pope Pius XI (1857-1939) who said in his ***Litterae Apostolicae*** (Apostolic Letter) ***Officiorum Omnium*** (Of all Duties) in 1922 that:

> *Etenim Ecclesia, ut quae et nationes omnes complexu suo contineat, et usque ad consummationem saeculorum sit permansura, et prorsus a sui gubernatione vulgus arceat, sermonem suapte natura requirit universalem, immutabilem, non vulgarem.*

> (For the Church, since it contains all nations in its embrace, since it is going to endure until the consummation of the ages, and since it utterly excludes the common people from its governance, requires by its own nature a universal language, unchangeable, not that of the common people. *trs* prayinglatin.com)

Often quoted, but almost always now missing out the section about 'common people' and 'governance', much has been written for and against this view before, during and since *Vatican II*. Those arguments are not revisited in this book. The power of praying in Latin, or a vernacular, does not imbue those prayers with any extra religious authenticity, but as Venerable Pope Pius XII (1876-1958) anxious to defend the Church against Modernism, taught in his 1947 Encyclical *Mediator Dei* (Mediator of God):

> *Latinae linguae usus, ut apud magnam Ecclesiae partem viget, perspicuum est venustumque unitatis signum, ac remedium efficax adversus quaslibet germanae doctrinae corruptelas.*
> (The use of the Latin language, customary in a considerable portion of the Church, is a manifest and beautiful sign of unity, as well as an effective antidote for any corruption of doctrinal truth. *Vat*)
> *In non paucis tamen ritibus vulgati sermonis usurpatio valde utilis apud populum exsistere potest;*
> (In spite of this, the use of the mother tongue in connection with several of the rites may be of much advantage to the people; *Vat*)
> *nihilominus unius Apostolicae Sedis est id concedere.*
> (nevertheless the Apostolic See alone is empowered to grant this permission. *Vat*)

The decline of Latin in the Church needs perhaps to be understood, then, not in the context of its linguistic incomprehensibility for Latin by people in the pews, but as more of a power play, by some very senior clerics within the Church itself, for control of that Church. Shifting the political dynamic from a generally unquestioned, and unchanging, Latin culture, to one which vernacularised that culture, gave some a power not previously able to be exercised, especially by some put in charge of revising the Liturgy, like the Most Reverend Annibale Bugnini CM (1912-1982). The exercise of that power continues today, and has led to increased secularisation and ecumenical protestantisation within the Catholic Church, which, paradoxically, might appear to be about shifting the focus of power to 'the common people'/'the people of God', but which, in reality, has been much more about a handful of senior clergy taking ideological control in order to change the Church to better suit their own more liberal agendas.

That said, those political issues are important and are still being played out, often with significant consequences for us all, and upon Christ's Church on earth. But they are not the main concerns motivating this book. What are, are the linguistic and spiritual ways in which praying in Latin positions the pray-er within a very specific, but disappearing, Latin Catholic context, namely the patrimony and Tradition of the praying of those prayers continually for almost two millennia in what the 1994 *Catechismus* refers to as ***Oratio tamquam Foedus*** (Prayer as covenant *Cat* §2562) which is a ***relatio Foederis inter Deum et hominem in Christo*** (a covenant relationship between God and man in Christ *Cat* §2564):

> ***Dei et hominis est actio; a Spiritu Sancto et a nobis oritur, prorsus ad Patrem directa, in unione cum voluntate humana Filii Dei hominis facti.***
>
> (It is the action of God and of man, springing forth from both the Holy Spirit and ourselves, wholly directed to the Father, in union with the human will of the Son of God made man. *Cat* §2564)

In this book, understanding prayer as covenant effectively involves looking at Latin and its grammar, not simply as the means to a linguistic end, but to a spiritual one through anagogical journeys. It basically means thinking about Latin grammar not as a linguistic hurdle to be overcome in order to enable a text to be *read*, but as a spiritual text to be *prayed*, bringing with it the Catholic sensibilities of the patrimony of which it is an indissoluble part. That then said, this book is not a call to arms for Catholic Latin isolationists; nor does it, in any way, reject the authority of the contemporary Church, its Councils and **Magisterium** (teaching) or the validity and licitness of post *Vatican II* Liturgies celebrated according to the official books of the Catholic Church, in Latin or various vernaculars. But it does recognise the significant loss to this Catholic Church if this patrimony and Latin Tradition is marginalised, or expunged altogether.

I also recognise my own limitations in writing this book, and I am very conscious of the many, far greater experts in Latin and the ***usus antiquior*** (more ancient usage) Liturgy, than me, many of whom contribute to very significant online sites like *New Liturgical Movement* (https://www.newliturgicalmovement.org/); **Rorate Caeli** (https://rorate-caeli.blogspot.com/); the *International* **Una Voce** *Federation* (http://www.fiuv.org/); *The Latin Mass Society of England and Wales* (https://lms.org.uk/); **Ecclesia Dei** (http://www.ecclesiadei.org/) and numerous other sites and blogs that I have had, and continue to have, recourse to. I acknowledge their greater expertise in many of the issues I raise in this book, and I wish to record my debt to them over the years since their sites and blogs began to appear.

Latin Catholicism

All the Latin used in this book is highlighted in bold italics, and all translations are my own unless specifically referenced otherwise, or are given as 'approved' English texts on Vatican websites (*Vat*) or are considered 'traditional' (*trad*). Many of the prayers and texts included here from the Latin liturgy (***liturgia Latina***) have been with us, some first in Greek, and then in Latin, since the early development of the Western Catholic Church. They come with a history, not just linguistic or archaeological. They come with a much more glorious spiritual history from the many millions who have prayed them for millennia. That is a priceless patrimony, and actively creates a priceless spiritual fellowship through that history. It is Tradition worth preserving, not by putting these texts into a glass case in a museum, like old vestments in cathedral crypts, nor just by praying them to keep them alive, but through that praying, by continuing to seek our own sanctification (*sanctificatio*) through them. As we pray with St Paul in the *Epistle* of the *usus antiquior* Mass for the 7th Sunday after Pentecost:

Nunc vero liberáti a peccáto, servi autem facti Deo, habétis fructum vestrum in sanctificatiónem, finem vero vitam aetérnam.
(Now truly freed from sin, and thus made servants to God, you have your fruit unto sanctification, truly the end, eternal life. Rom 6:22)

The **Breviarium Romanum** (*Roman Breviary*) revised in 1911 by Pope St Pius X (1835-1914) divides each day into a *cursus* (course) of eight Offices (**Matutinae** (Matins) **Laudes** (Lauds) **Hora Prima** (Prime) **Hora Tertia** (Terce) **Hora Sexta** (Sext) **Hora Nona** (None) **Vesperae Primae/Secundae** (First/Second Vespers) and **Completorium** (Compline) with their specific *Psalms*, scripture, other readings, hymns, canticles and Collects varying, like the *Missa* (Mass) of the day according to the type of Feast being celebrated for any given day. Prayer in this way takes its motivation from the penultimate *Psalm* of the *usus antiquior* Sunday *Vespers*, when we pray:

A solis ortu usque ad occásum laudábile nomen Dómini.
(From the rising of the sun unto the going down of the same, the name of the Lord is worthy of praise. DR Ps 112:3)

We journey in this prayer from sunrise to sunset each day in what might best be described as 'a journey towards the heart', not, as might popularly be thought 'a journey *of* the heart', but 'towards' it and thus 'towards God'. The ultimate form of this journey of prayer for a Catholic is the Mass which is designated for each day in the **Missale Romanum** (*Roman Missal*) with its differing prayers and readings in the **Proprium Missae** - Proper of the Mass) for each day and its unchanging texts (**Ordinarium Missae** - Ordinary of the Mass) as well as the various votive options subject to varying **kalendaria** (calendars) and **ordines** (daily arrangements of the liturgy). Taken together, in the *Missal* and the *Breviary*, there is a wealth of Latin prayer, in just these books alone. St Benedict of Nursia OSB (480-547) refers, understandably, to the glories of this complete *Divine Office* of the Church as **Opus Dei** (the work of God).

Revisions to the Latin liturgical books have occurred a number of times most particularly by Pope Clement VIII (1536-1605) and Pope Urban VIII (1568-1644) and more recently in 1911 by Pope St Pius X, whose revised texts were used in public worship from 1913 until some minor revisions were made by Pope Benedict XV (1854 -1922) and Venerable Pope Pius XII. Pope St John XXIII made further revisions in 1960 (resulting in what tend now to be called the 1962 liturgical books) and major changes to the content (and often theology) of the books and individual texts were further made, in Latin, prior to various vernaculars, by Pope St Paul VI (1897-1978) in 1969-70 following *Vatican II*.

When I refer to *Psalms* in the *Breviary*, I use the Pope St Pius X *Psalter* schema (1911-1971 abbreviated as *PP*) throughout, and where I quote from the Proper or Common (Ordinary) of the Mass I do so from the 1962 **usus antiquior** books. When the *Psalter* schema differs between the **usus antiquior** Roman Rite and the Monastic Rite, I refer (if necessary) to the *Monastic Psalter* schema initially developed c540 and abbreviated here as *MP*.

Rather than choose between often politically loaded terms like 'Tridentine Mass', 'old Latin Mass', 'Extraordinary/Ordinary' forms of the Mass'; **vetus ordo** (old order) as a generic term for the pre and 1962 books compared with the ***novus ordo*** (new order) books (Latin and vernacular post *Vatican II*) I use the term ***usus antiquior*** (more ancient usage) to signal that these texts have an ancient, but continuingly valuable, life and relevance, and I use the term ***usus recentior*** (more recent usage) when referring to post *Vatican II* Latin and vernacular rites. I also use the term 'Latin Catholicism' to distinguish what, in many ways, may well have become a quite distinct Catholic sensibility using the ***usus antiquior*** books from the one most dominant now in post *Vatican II* vernacular Catholicism. But I do so acknowledging that this phrase is of my own making and has no official status.

The normative Mass in Latin Catholicism is a ***Missa cantata*** (sung Mass) and not the spoken 'Low Mass' which originally was usually limited in Religious Houses for the celebration of a ***Missa privata*** ('private' Mass) where ***privata*** refers not to something that happens in private, but comes from the verb ***privare*** 'to strip down', and so signifies a Mass stripped down of some of the forms and rituals that occur in the normative sung Mass. Probably the most 'stripped down' of all Masses was the ***Missa sicca*** (dry Mass) celebrated by Medieval Carthusian monks after *Matins* in the privacy of their cell at the *prie-dieu* (prayer stool) where everything but the Canon and Consecration were prayed. This was effectively a private devotion before the conventual Mass and private Masses were celebrated in full later in the morning. That said, Latin liturgical texts reflect the primacy of the ***Missa cantata*** in many ways, not least of which is the system of accenting the text. The Church's definitive guide to the pronunciation of Liturgical Latin as recommended by Pope St Pius X is to be found in the 1961 Latin ***Liber Usualis*** (pp xxxvi-xxxix). The ***Liber Usualis*** (Book of Common Use) is a book containing the approved Gregorian chants and texts used throughout the liturgical year since the 11[th]C, but sung in various earlier forms since the 6[th]C and probably before. It is most often referred to simply as the ***Liber***.

Rhythm and stress matter in a sung Mass, and Liturgical Latin is marked for this with accents, whereas the Latin used for all other purposes in the Church is not. A Latin encyclical issued by a Pope is not designed to be sung in church, and so, therefore, does not require accenting. Nor do the Latin instructions in a *Missal* or *Breviary*, usually marked in red and known as rubrics (***rubrica*** - red ochre/ink) as these rubrics are not sung in public worship. A Latin *Bible* is not normally accented, but selected texts taken from it (περικοπή - *pericope* - 'cutting-out') and put into *Missals* and *Breviaries*, and used in public worship, are. The titles of those missals and breviaries, **Missale Romanum** and **Breviarium Romanum** are not accented, because these titles are not used in public worship, but the contents of those books, when they are prayers and not simply instructions, are. Latin is accented in this book only when presented as a prayer to be prayed, either publicly or privately. (For full details see Appendix: Accenting and Pronunciation).

The Latin prayer of the ***usus antiquior*** *Divine Office* is assumed here to be either spoken/sung aloud publicly, or privately *sotto voce* (with a soft voice) or if not that, silently, but with the lips moving, following the example of Anna (Hannah) who is recorded as being unable to have a child, but who prayed fervently for one. We are told:

> ***Porro Anna loquebatur in corde suo, tantumque labia illius movebantur, et vox penitus non audiebatur.***
> (Then Anna spoke in her heart, and only her lips moved, and her inner voice was not heard. *1 Reg* 1:13)

The High Priest Heli (Eli) thought her to be drunk, but she replied to him that she was not drunk but so unhappy that: ***effudi animam meam in conspectu Domini*** (I have poured out my soul in the sight of the Lord. *1 Reg* 1:15). As she did so, she moved her lips in silent prayer, just as the Priest does in the powerfully silent recitation of the Canon of the ***usus antiquior*** Mass, and as many older Catholics, like myself, were taught to do in private prayer.

Scripture: Latin and English

The original scriptures were composed in Hebrew, Aramaic and Greek, not Latin. The emphasis in this book on Latin scriptures (and their direct English translation in specific versions from the *Vulgate*) is not because the **Biblia Sacra Vulgata** (late 4thC revised as the **Vulgata Clementina** in 1592) is better than the original languages, but because the Latin translation of scripture, formally approved by the Council of Trent (1545-1563) lies at the heart of the *usus antiquior* texts.

The English versions translated directly from the *Vulgate* used in this book are: *Douay-Rheims* (*DR*) (original 1582-1609 revised in 1749-1752 by Bishop Richard Challoner [1691-1781]) and used in many *Missals* and *Prayer Books*, and the *Ronald Knox* version (*Knox*) 1945-1950 translated directly from the *Vulgate* but with original source languages consulted where greater clarity in the Latin was needed, and often found in modern parallel Latin/English *Missals*. Other approved Catholic *Bible* versions (amongst growing numbers now) translated from original Biblical sources include:

- *Revised Standard Version Catholic Edition* (1965-6)
- *The Jerusalem Bible* (1966)
- *New American Bible* (1970)
- *The New Jerusalem Bible* (1985)
- *New American Bible Revised Edition* (1986 & 2011)
- *New Revised Standard Version Catholic Edition* (1991 following the ecumenical 1989 *NRSV*) and approved in 2007 for public use in the light of the Congregation for Divine Worship and the Discipline of the Sacrament's **Liturgiam Authenticam.** *On the Use of Vernacular Languages in the Publication of the Books of the Roman Liturgy* (2001)
- *Good News Translation Catholic Edition* (1993)
- *Holy Bible. Contemporary English Version* (1995) Catholic additions 1997

- *New Catholic Bible* (2007) Catholic Truth Society: London (*Jerusalem Bible* and *Grail Psalter* texts authorised for public liturgical use)
- *English Standard Version Catholic Edition* (2017 following the 2001 *ESV*)
- *Revised New Jerusalem Bible* (2019)

The *Psalms* in the ***usus antiquior*** books follow the Greek *Septuagint* numbering in the *Vulgate*. This varies in places from the original Hebrew which was re-adopted in Protestant Bibles, and is a system of numbering increasingly used in ***usus recentior*** liturgical texts and approved Catholic Bibles like *The Jerusalem Bible*:

usus antiquior *Psalms*	***usus recentior*** *Psalms*
1-8	1-8
9	9-10
10-112	11-113
113	114-115
114-115	116
116-145	117-146
146-147	147
148-150	148-150

In a talk he gave on translating the *Vulgate* and published in 1949, Monsignor Ronald Knox (1888-1957) quotes Catholic writer Hilaire Belloc (1870-1953) who suggested that, 'the business of a translator [into English] is not to ask, "How shall I make this foreigner talk English?" but "What would an Englishman have said to express this?"' This is sound advice, but it does mean that very often the translation is not likely to be an effective guide to the grammar of the language being translated. As Knox himself was to say, the translator must never be afraid of paraphrase. But paraphrase can be very misleading for sorting out, for example, the sometimes complex Latin grammar involved, so the message in this book is to be aware, especially in the parallel Latin/English missals, breviaries and prayer books, of the way the actual Latin works linguistically. All Latin scripture used in this book is taken from the ***Vulgata Clementina*** (http://www.catholicbible.online/) and abbreviations for all scripture used here are to the *Vulgate* books.

Whenever I offer my own translation I do so by seeking to ensure that the grammar of the English translation reflects (sometimes literally) the grammar of the Latin, even when inelegance may result. I do that, not simply to aid an accurate cross-reference between the Latin and English, but to foreground the language differences between praying in Latin and praying in English. The focus in this book is always on the linguistic distinctiveness of Latin, and not in treating it simply as a conduit through which to pray in English in our heads, even though we may be praying in Latin words.

Franciscan philosopher and grammarian Roger Bacon (c1214-c1292) popularly heralded as **Doctor Mirabilis** (Wonderful Teacher) though never officially proclaimed a Doctor of the Church, accepted that translation from one language to another is a necessary, but very imperfect art; one that could never fully capture what he called the ***potestas*** (power/potency) of the original language. It is that very difficult-to-capture spiritual 'potency' of prayer, in what St Thérèse of Lisieux (1873-1897) described as an ***impetus cordis*** (a surge of the heart) which lies at the very centre of this book. It is offered here in that same spirit of prayer, and in the face of tumultuous times in the world and in the Catholic Church itself, with which French poet François Villon (1431-1463) wrote from his prison cell, as the certainties of Catholicism were coming under the uncertain clouds of Reformation Europe, saying:

> 'Mais priez Dieu que tous nous veuille absoudre!'
> (But pray God that he wills to absolve us all!)

In these simple words we see the vicissitudes of politics (then, and now, within, and external to, the ***Ecclesia Catholica*** fade into insignificance compared to the challenges of ensuring personal salvation through that Church.

A Grammar of Prayer

My aim in this book is to present a spiritual grammar of Latin Prayer using selected Latin prayers and scripture which have been prayed, and continue to be prayed, to *address* God, with the *focus* and *force* of the long and rich patrimony of Latin Catholic liturgical and meditative practice and prayer that anagogically opens up a way for spiritual *affect*. 'Prayer' (***oratio***) 'text' (***textus***) 'context' (***contextus***) 'form' (***forma***) 'function' (***officium***) 'address' (***appellatio***) 'focus' (***attentio***) 'force' (***fortitudo***) and 'affect' (***affectus***) are key terms used in this book, and in many ways, form the architecture of the chapters as they develop more and more depth in the grammar of prayer outlined here. They are terms which will not be found used like this in Latin grammar books, even those designed specifically to teach the Latin of the *Missal* and the *Breviary* (see Bibliography : Liturgical Latin).

To that end too, key grammatical terms like 'nominative', 'vocative', 'genitive', 'attributive', 'imperative', 'accusative', 'transitive', 'dative', 'purposive', 'ablative', 'instrumental', 'sociative', 'indicative', 'subjunctive', 'dispositional', and 'experiential', amongst others, are here directed to building up that spiritual grammar of Latin prayer in order to offer a powerful linguistic means to an even more powerful spiritual end; the ultimate goal of which is, for Christians, sanctification. In that respect, Latin is not presented here as a means of mystifying religion itself, as many might say it does, arguing against its use. Latin Catholicism is not a mystery religion hiding its secrets and rituals behind a veil of Latin for only the elite. The use of Latin forms (***formae***) and functions (***officia***) in the address (***appellatio***) and context (***contextus***) of prayer (***oratio*** puts a focus (***attentio***) upon, and adds force (***fortitudo***) to, by reverencing, the mystery (***mysterium***) of an inexpressible God, consequently resulting in a potentially very powerful affect (*affectus*) on those worshipping him.

We understand this as Catholics in two main ways: through the prayer of public liturgy in the Church and through our own prayer; our 'interior life' nourished by that liturgy. Increasingly, within Catholicism, especially in the immediate years leading up to, and particularly, in the years after *Vatican II*, the mystical theology once at the beating heart of Catholicism, has greatly diminished as a dominant Catholic sensibility. However, it is that undiminished mystical sensibility, which, in many ways, drives this book. And it does so, unapologetically, and most especially, by my often referring to the mysticism driving medieval Catholicism, and by my often quoting medieval writers, mystics and theologians. That this book does this, not only reflects my own background as a linguist initially trained in medieval languages, but also as a reflection of those times, now long gone, when to be Christian in Western Europe in particular, was to be Catholic only. There was no other way. It is the revitalising of the mystical theology at the core of that once unquestioned Western Latin Catholicism, which, in many ways, lies at the centre of this book. Again, it does so by understanding the word 'mystic' (μυστικός - *mustikós* - 'secret') as developed through an interior (mystic) way of prayer, which does not seek to fetishize Latin, but which celebrates Latin as a hieratic means of approaching the mystical/spiritual union with God, through an interior life focussed upon Christ, through his Mother and the Saints and Angels, and always with the guidance of the Holy Spirit.

That 'interior life' involves prayer, first and foremost at the public liturgical level, but also prayer at the private level. It involves language, and it involves the spiritual. It may involve praying out loud and it involves, to use a word no longer fashionable because of its past infelicities, a more 'quietist', meditative contemplation of the mysteries that are God. Fr Augustine (Austin) Baker OSB (1575-1641) mystic and founding member of the restored English Benedictine Congregation in the still dangerous (for Catholics) penal times in 17thC England, is often quoted today as saying:

> 'Prayer is the most perfect and most divine action that a rational soul is capable of. It is of all actions and duties the most indispensably necessary.'

We all pray privately in our different ways, something Dom Austin recognised when he goes on to say in his posthumously composed book ***Sophia Sancta*** (Holy Wisdom):

> 'This, I say, is the duty and indispensable obligation of all Christians, of what condition soever, not only seriously to aspire to the divine love, but also to the perfection thereof suitably to their several states and vocations, for it is morally impossible for a soul to love God, as He ought to be loved (that is, as the only object of our love, and as the only universal end of our being and life, for the procuring of an inseparable union with whom and for no other reason the use and comfort of creatures was permitted and given to us) I say, it is morally impossible for such a soul so loving God deliberately and habitually to yield to the love of anything but God only, or to stop in any inferior degree of love to Him.' (Sweeney (1876) I:XI)

That requires discipline. But above all it requires Divine Grace, especially in our active lives today. To do this, again in the words of Dom Austin, we:

> 'are to betake [ourselves], and always to continue in such internal exercises as are suitable to their natural propensions, to wit, the quiet, solitary, spiritual exercises of a *contemplative life*.'

The key phrases here are 'suitable to their natural propensions' and 'spiritual exercises'. We, all of us, have different 'natural propensions', and will all of us exercise our spiritual and interior lives in different, perhaps even, contemplative, ways. The Latin word ***contemplatio*** is derived from the word ***tempus*** (time) developing into ***templum*** which became synonymous with a sacred space within which one would gaze at divinity. I can think of no better way of thinking, as Christians, about space, time and Divinity. Nor could St Augustine of Hippo (354-430). In his ***De civitate Dei contra paganos*** (On the City of God against the pagans [426AD]) for example, he refers to both the ***exercitatio animi*** (exercise of the soul/spirit) and the ***exercitatio mentis*** (exercise of the mind/disposition) not as might be thought nowadays, perhaps, as mutually exclusive activities, but as completely complementary, like time and space; the one dependent upon the other. I offer this book in the spirit of St Augustine's understanding of how we exercise our spirit and mind in complementary, and contemplative, ways in order to, following Dom Austin in the words of Doctor of the Church (***Doctor Mellifluus***) St Bernard of Clairvaux (1090-1153) and founder of the reformed Benedictine Cistercian Order, who instructed his monks:

> *Aliorum est Deo servire; vestrum adhaerere. Aliorum est Deo credere, scire, amare, revereri; vestrum est sapere, intelligere, cognoscere, frui.*
> (It is [the duty] of others to serve [to]God; yours to adhere. It is [the duty] of others to believe, to know, to love, to reverence [to]God; it is yours to taste, to understand, to comprehend, to enjoy.)

And to do that requires both spirit and mind. Whatever state we find ourselves in our active life, we, all of us who pray, might usefully aspire to this advice in our lives, and most especially to pray through the intercessions of the Blessed Virgin Mary, who is described, in the words of ***Doctor Ecstaticus*** (Ecstatic Teacher) St Denis (Dionysius) the Carthusian (1402-1472) as ***Summa Contemplatrix*** (Greatest Contemplative) who the *Compendium of the Catholic Church* (2006) and Pope Francis' 2016 Apostolic Constitution ***Vultum Dei quaerere*** (to seek [the] Face of God) recognise, with St Denis, as 'the perfect pray-er'. In this book, imperfect though this will always be in comparison to the perfect prayer of Our Lady as **Summa Contemplatrix**, a way of prayer is suggested, through the exercise and discipline (and consequent shift in our dispositions by doing so) of continuing to pray in the same Latin that has been prayed for almost 2,000 years; a disposition enhanced by a language which Pope St John XXIII beautifully describes in his 1962 Apostolic Constitution **Veterum Sapientia** (Wisdom of the Ancients) when he teaches that:

> *sapientiae ipsius auream quasi vestem*
> (wisdom itself is dressed as gold)

That 'gold' is the Latin and Greek languages. He goes on to say, most importantly, that Latin: ***invidiam non commoveat*** (may excite no envy). Prayer that 'excites no envy' is surely gold indeed. It is, Pope St John says, quoting Venerable Pope Pius XII:

> *thesaurus incomparandae praestantiae*
> (a treasure of incomparable worth):

and Pope St John then continues:

> *et vinculum denique peridoneum, quo praesens Ecclesiae aetas cum superioribus cumque futuris mirifice continetur.*
> (and is also a most effective bond, binding the Church of today with that of the past and of the future in wonderful continuity.)

It is that treasure and bond which drives this book. I have compiled a Bibliography of Liturgical Latin resources, and in the absence of footnotes or endnotes, I have provided a detailed Bibliography:References section which contains further bibliographic information for references to people or texts made in the book itself. I have also, at times, given online references to available texts. This book is offered:

Ut in ómnibus glorificétur Deus per Iesum Christum et per Beátam ac semper Vírginem Maríam, Christi Matrem sanctíssimam, Matrem Ecclésiae Matrémque Fídei nostrae. Amen.

(So that in all things God may be glorified through Jesus Christ and through the Blessed and ever Virgin Mary, the most Holy Mother of Christ, Mother of the Church and Mother of our Faith. Amen.)

DAVID BIRCH

NOMINATIVE PRAYER

Ego Dominus, hoc est nomen meum
(I [am the] Lord, this is my name *Is* 42:8)

Naming

At the very beginning of the *Bible* God's own identity is revealed. He names himself to Abraham by saying ***Ego protector tuus sum*** (I am your protector *Gn* 15:1). Further on when Moses at the burning bush asks God his name, God says to Moses ***Ego sum qui sum*** (I am who I am). God names himself as 'I am' (***Ego sum*** *Ex* 3:14). He declares himself to be, in effect, the cause of all and everything. As the Dominican theologian St Thomas Aquinas was later to describe it in his now famous five proofs of God (***Quinque viae*** - Five Ways) God was the first (and only) mover in the cause and creation of the universe. Those five proofs of God's existence are: motion (***momentum***) cause (***causa***) perfection (***perfectio***) design (***intentio***) and necessity (***necessitas***).

Christ names himself by saying 'Before Abraham was, I am' (*ego sum Io* 8:58) and at the very end of the *Bible* Christ names himself again by saying ***Ego Iesus... ego sum*** (I Jesus... I am) ***radix, et genus David*** (the root, and stock of David) ***stella splendida et matutina*** (the bright and morning star *Apc* 22:16). These are names, unlike those we hear every day around us, which demand attention from the very moment of hearing them. They are not everyday names. They are not everyday identities. We pray in Thursday *Vespers*:

> *Confitébor tibi, Dómine, in toto corde meo, quóniam audísti verba oris mei. In conspéctu angelórum psallam tibi; adorábo ad templum sanctum tuum, et confitébor nómini tuo: super misericórdia tua et veritáte tua; quóniam magnificásti super omne, nomen sanctum tuum. In quacúmque die invocávero te, exáudi me; multiplicábis in ánima mea virtútem. Confiteántur tibi, Dómine, omnes reges terræ, quia audiérunt ómnia verba oris tui. Et cantent in viis Dómini, quóniam magna est glória Dómini;*

> (I will praise thee, O Lord, with my whole heart: for thou hast heard the words of my mouth I will sing praise to thee in the sight of the angels: I will worship towards thy holy temple, and I will give glory to thy name. For thy mercy, and for thy truth: for thou hast magnified thy holy name above all. In what day soever I shall call upon thee, hear me: thou shalt multiply strength in my soul. May all the kings of the earth give glory to thee: for they have heard all the words of thy mouth. And let them sing in the ways of the Lord: for great is the glory of the Lord. *DR Ps* 137:1-5)

Naming is clearly important in prayer. There are many hundreds of times throughout the *Bible* where its importance shines out. In Judaism, then, and now, a name is considered to capture the very essence of the one being named; their very identity. We see this right at the beginning of the *Bible* when we pray in the 1st lesson of the long ***usus antiquior*** Easter Vigil that:

> *Appellavítque lucem Diem, et ténebras Noctem... firmaméntum, Caelum... áridam Terram, congregationésque aquárum appellávit María.*

(He called the light Day, and the darkness Night... the firmament, Heaven... and the dry land, Earth, and the gathering together of the waters, he called Seas. *DR Gn* 1:5-10)

And in the 1st Nocturn of Tuesday *Matins* of Septuagesimatide we pray:

Formátis ígitur Dóminus Deus de humo cunctis animántibus terrae, et univérsis volatílibus caeli, addúxit ea ad Adam, ut vidéret quid vocáret ea: omne enim quod vocávit Adam ánimae vivéntis, ipsum est nomen eius.

(And the Lord God having formed out of the ground all the beasts of the earth, and all the fowls of the air, brought them to Adam to see what he would call them: for whatsoever Adam called any living creature the same is its name.' *DR Gn* 2:19)

God gave an incredible power to Adam: the power to name. Several chapters later we read that when the Prophet Abram was 99 years old God appeared to him and said:

Dixitque ei Deus: Ego sum, et pactum meum tecum, erisque pater multarum gentium. Nec ultra vocabitur nomen tuum Abram, sed appellaberis Abraham: quia patrem multarum gentium constitui te.

(And God said to him: I AM, and my covenant is with thee, and thou shalt be a father of many nations. Neither shall thy name be called any more Abram: but thou shalt be called Abraham: because I have made thee a father of many nations. *DR Gn* 17:4-5)

Similarly several chapters on we read that Jacob (the brother of Esau) rose early one day: 'took his two wives, and his two handmaids, with his eleven sons', and crossing the ford of Jabok 'remained alone: and behold a man wrestled with him till morning' after which the man said:

> *Quod nomen est tibi? Respondit: Iacob.*
>
> (What is thy name? He answered: Jacob.)
>
> *At ille: Nequaquam, inquit, Iacob appellabitur nomen tuum, sed Israël: quoniam si contra Deum fortis fuisti, quanto magis contra homines praevalebis?*
>
> (The man replied: Thy name shall not be called Jacob, but Israel: for if thou hast been strong against God, how much more shalt thou prevail against men?)
>
> *Interrogavit eum Iacob: Dic mihi, quo appellaris nomine? Respondit: Cur quaeris nomen meum? Et benedixit ei in eodem loco.*
>
> (And Jacob asked him, tell me by what name art thou called? He answered: Why dost thou ask my name? And he blessed him in the same place.)
>
> *Vocavitque Iacob nomen loci illius Phanuel, dicens: Vidi Deum facie ad faciem, et salva facta est anima mea.*
>
> (And Jacob called the name of the place Phanuel, saying: I have seen God face to face, and my soul has been saved.' *DR Gn* 32:27-30)

We pray in the *Gospel* of the Christmas Eve Mass when an Angel of the Lord appeared to Joseph saying:

> *Ioseph, fili David, noli timére accípere Maríam cóniugem tuam: quod enim in ea natum est, de Spíritu Sancto est. Páriet autem fílium: et vocábis nomen eius Iesum: ipse enim salvum fáciet pópulum suum a peccátis eórum.*
>
> (Joseph, son of David, fear not to take unto thee Mary thy wife, for that which is conceived in her, is of the Holy Ghost. And she shall bring forth a son: and thou shalt call his name JESUS. For he shall save his people from their sins. *DR Mt* 1:20-21)

St Matthew the Apostle (d 74 AD) then comments on this by saying:

> *Hoc autem totum factum est, ut adimpleretur quod dictum est a Domino per prophetam dicentem: Ecce virgo in utero habebit, et pariet filium: et vocabunt nomen eius Emmanuel, quod est interpretatum nobiscum Deus.*
>
> (Now all this was done that it might be fulfilled which the Lord spoke by the prophet, saying: Behold a virgin shall be with child, and bring forth a son, and they shall call his name Emmanuel, which being interpreted is, God with us. *DR Mt* 1:22-23)

Names and naming (even re-naming) are clearly very important. Simon is renamed Peter by Jesus. Saul is renamed Paul. Popes generally take on a new name. Those entered into the religious life traditionally take a new name. At Baptism we are named, and at Confirmation we are re-named with a Saint's name. As Adam was given the power to name the animals and the world they inhabited, so the names we all have not only identify us individually, they fix us into time and history. We address not only each other by our names but we can address the world, its past, present, and future, in which we live. Children learn this before they learn almost anything else. They learn to name their parents and siblings and those around them. Christian children learn to name the Son of God as Jesus, his mother as Mary, her spouse as Joseph. They learn that when they pray they are naming, and when they name these specific names they are praying. And in that naming and praying, they are recognising and even more importantly, 'acknowledging'. And in doing that, they are determining their identities and through those identities are forming relationships. It is that relationship-building which is at the heart of all prayer, and we pray not just *with* names (God, Jesus, Mary, Joseph) but *by* names. For example when we say of ourselves 'I am David' or 'I am Janet' the words identify who we are, but behind those words there is a deeper relationship between the 'I am' of self, and the 'I am' that is God, who created us. It is this recognition of the deeper relationship between those words and the grammar of those words that *anagogically* shifts us in prayer from the world around us to the world beyond us.

Naming God is to address God. If done reverently it becomes prayer, and one word or phrase in the nominative form in Latin may have as much force and be as powerful and as meaningful as the most beautifully composed prayer that has ever been written. For example, if we pray:

Deus, Deus, Deus. Iesus, Iesus, Iesus.

Iesus Christus Redémptor, Iesus Christus Redémptor, Iesus Christus Redémptor.

This is a form of prayer known as 'cataphatic' prayer (κατάφασις - cataphasis - 'affirmation') as it signals a forceful action affirming through naming (**nominans**) and address (**appellatio**) in this case the Latin noun **Deus**, or **Iesus**, or the noun phrase **Iesus Christus Redemptor**. We learn as children not by reading, but by listening, and as such this process probably mirrors exactly how prayer developed in the Church. *Litanies*, the *Divine Office*, the *Psalter*, the Mass, the Rosary and Stations of the Cross, all involve repetition; speaking and listening over and over again, initially to learn, and then to communicate to God, through iterative (repetitive) prayer. *Psalm* 135 prayed at Thursday *Vespers* repeats the simple phrase **quóniam in aetérnum misericórdia eius** (for his mercy endureth for ever *trad*) at the end of every one of its 27 verses, and may well be the model for all the *litanies* that were later developed. Indeed, the 150 *Psalms* of the *Psalter*, as a whole, might be seen, like this repetition, as an extended litany, and in that respect, also the **cursus** of the *Divine Office* which seeks to pray every one of those 150 *Psalms* as a litany in action over a week of prayer, and then even further, the repetition of the entire liturgical year, year after year, and so on.

Even if we were stranded on a desert island and we only had the nominative form of nouns available to us for some reason, we could still pray effectively and purposefully, not just by praying powerful nominatives like, **Deus, Dóminus, Iesus, María** and so on, but by praying what is probably the oldest form of prayer ever used by anyone: repetition. By repetition in this way we not only *address* God but we can create considerable *focus*, in prayer, and with it a considerable *force* and subsequent *affect*, as indeed the very early Christians in Apostolic times must have prayed, just through simple repetition.

We may name and address God as **redemptor** or **protector**, for example, or his son as **Iesus,** or as **radix, et genus David** (the root and stock of David) or **stella splendida et matutina** (the bright and morning star) and, in doing so, that naming in prayer is not just our way of addressing God, but through that address we enter into a relationship with God: the very motivation of all prayer. The Latin verb 'to name' is **nominare** and has a range of meanings including 'to call by name', 'to give a name to', 'to mention out of respect', 'to make famous', 'to bring renown', 'to celebrate', 'to report', 'to designate', 'to talk of', 'to call attention to', 'to urge' and 'to nominate', amongst others. There is a lot happening with this one simple word. When we address someone by name, all of these possible meanings, and others, are all wrapped up and 'layered' in what we are saying and who we are addressing. But we are not just naming people. We are *nominating* them to be in a relationship with us. We address them *nominatively*, which is a central feature of the text-context dynamic involved in what we do when we pray.

The Text-Context Dynamic

In Latin grammar when the nominative form of a noun like **Deus** (God) specifically refers to the subject of an action as in **Deus** (subject) *est* (verb) - 'God is' - it is said to be functioning grammatically in a very specific way. That way is when a noun in the nominative form performs a grammatical function beyond that of being a word in a list or dictionary, but now functions as the 'subject' of a verb. When it does that, the noun, in Latin, is said to 'take' or 'be in' the nominative case (*casus nominativus*). The nominative form of the noun remains the same, but the function of that noun in a text, changes. **Deus** (God) as a word by itself is in the nominative form. But by itself it is not functioning as the subject of any verb. **Deus** in **Deus est** (God is) is still in the nominative form but now it is functioning grammatically as the subject of the verb *est* (is).

Latin dictionaries list their entries in the nominative form but language is not just a list of words. Every word is part of a 'text-context dynamic'. Consider, for example, the following list of Latin words all in the nominative form which, amongst many others, are all central to the practice and understanding of Latin prayer. Each and every one of these words, as texts, only makes Catholic sense when seen, and used, in a Catholic context, and in other contexts may well produce very different meanings for the same nominative form of the word. It is useful to think of this, within Latin Catholic prayer, as its 'Catholic sensibility'. So for example, behind every one of these words in:

> *Septem Dona Spiritus Sancti: Sapientia, Intellectus, Consilium, Fortitudo, Scientia, Pietas, Timor Domini*
> (The Seven Gifts of the Holy Spirit: Wisdom, Understanding, Counsel, Fortitude, Knowledge, Piety, Fear of the Lord

there is a very complex theology, and while they may all signify in some way a particular aspect of Catholic doctrine, practice and belief, to understand their role, through the lens of Catholic sensibility, we absolutely need to understand the text-context dynamic involved. Venerable Pope Venerable Pius XII (1876-1958) in his encyclical ***Mystici Corporis Christi*** ([The] Mystical Body of Christ, 1943) made it clear, for example, that the Holy Spirit in the Mystical Body of Christ (ie the Church) 'is the principle of every vital and truly salvific action in each of the Body's various members', a point reiterated by Pope St John Paul II (1920-2005) in addressing a general audience in July 1998 when he talked of the Holy Spirit enlivening and animating the mystery of

Christ's body which is the Church. The relationship of the Holy Spirit to the Church is, therefore, an integral one, ensuring that the Church is not simply seen as a human institution. For example, the *Vatican II Dogmatic Constitution on the Church*, **Lumen Gentium** (Light of Nations, 1964) sees the Church's mystical unity as 'one complex reality which comes together from a human and divine element.' Later, Pope St John Paul II taught in his July 1998 General Audiences: 'We can think of the Holy Spirit as the soul of our soul, and thus the secret of our sanctification', imploring us 'to dwell in his powerful and discrete, intimate and transforming, presence.'

This understanding of the Holy Spirit is a central Catholic sensibility, and sensibilities like this, are an important means by which we understand, and respond to, tangible circumstances and influences that affect us. But how much more important might such sensibilities be when we need to appreciate and respond to intangible (spiritual) circumstances and influence? Whenever we see a word in a Latin text (*textus*) especially in prayer (*oratio*) we should, therefore, always think about its text, form, function and context and what sensibilities (Catholic or otherwise) we might need in order to be able to pray that text in its immediate context, but also in the larger realm of where it sits in the broader context of, say, Latin Catholicism overall. Consider, then, these same words in the nominative form as words for *praying* and not just saying:

> *Septem Dona Spíritus Sancti*:
> *Sapiéntia, Intelléctus, Consílium, Fortitúdo, Sciéntia, Píetas, Timor Dómini*

St Thomas Aquinas did exactly this prior to writing about them in his 1485 **Summa Theologiae** (Summary of Theology) and reflected that the gift of wisdom prayerfully corresponds to the virtue of charity/love (*caritas*) understanding and knowledge to the virtue of faith (*fides*) counsel to prudence (*prudentia*) fortitude to courage (*virtus*) piety to justice (*iustitia*) and fear of the Lord to hope (*spes*). By praying each gift he was able to discern a Catholic sensibility to each one drawing upon the four cardinal virtues of 'prudence', 'justice', 'temperance', and 'fortitude', and the three theological virtues of 'faith', 'hope' and 'charity'. And while most of us may never have the theological capacity of St Thomas Aquinas, we all of us have the capacity to pray such Catholic sensibilities and teachings. For example:

> *Sapiéntia cáritas est* (wisdom is love)
> *Intelléctus et sciéntia fides sunt* (intelligence and knowledge are faiths)
> *Consílium prudéntia est* (counsel is prudence)
> *Fortitúdo virtus est* (strength is courage)
> *Píetas iustítia est* (piety is justice)
> *Timor Dómini spes est* (fear of the Lord is hope)

Both language and spirituality, when we pray these words, are clearly important. Linguistically, the position of the verb *est* (is) is important because where it sits at the end of the sentence (as here) it carries an emphatic meaning. In saying these Latin words, for example, even more so in praying them, we have to work our way through each of the nominatives before we get to the final position where the verb *est* sits, and only then is the relationship between the nominatives made fully clear. That little journey through the nouns to get to the verb is a spiritual journey as well; a prayer in itself. And it is so, because in praying in Latin as native English speakers for example, our disposition towards the Latin has to change. We have to be more aware; we have to be ready to make meanings which are not immediately clear from the first word. For example, we can re-translate the following as:

> *Sapientia caritas est* (love is wisdom)
> *Intellectus et scientia fides sunt* (faiths are intelligence and knowledge)

Consilium prudentia est (counsel is purpose)
Fortitudo virtus est (courage is strength)
Pietas iustitia est (justice is piety)
Timor Domini spes est (hope is fear of the Lord)

because the Latin grammar of the nominatives here gives us such translation options. The choices we make in that translation might appear to be 'either/or', but within the text-context dynamic of these texts as Latin prayer, they are perhaps best seen as a 'both/and'. Praying in Latin is, more often than not, not just about the linguistic 'either/or', but about the spiritual 'both/and'. The Church understands these gifts of the Holy Spirit as 'charismata/charisms' including (among the 27 referred to in various places in Scripture) the gifts of 'prophecy', 'miracles', 'discerning spirits', 'speaking in tongues', 'administration', 'voluntary poverty' and 'hospitality'. Very early Christian liturgies, in fact, after the Eucharist, would celebrate a 'liturgy' of the Holy Spirit, where prophecies, speaking in tongues, interpreting and supernatural healings might take place. They survived liturgically only into the 2^{nd}C, but we are now seeing a revival of this very early 'extra-liturgy' in the contemporary post *Vatican II* Catholic Charismatic Renewal movement. The Church also recognises twelve fruits of the Holy Spirit: 'charity', 'joy', 'peace', 'patience', 'benignity', 'goodness', 'longanimity', 'mildness', 'faith', 'modesty', 'continency' and 'chastity', and six main sins against the Holy Spirit: 'despair', 'presumption', 'impenitence', 'a fixed determination not to repent', 'obstinacy', 'resisting the known truth' and 'envy of another's spiritual welfare.' In sum, in the words of St. Paul:

nemo potest dicere: "Dominus Iesus", nisi in Spiritu Sancto.
(No one is able to say "Jesus [is] Lord", except within the Holy Spirit.
(*1 Cor* 12:3)

Prayer is not simply saying words, then, it is praying meanings and sensibilities; theologies and beliefs; it is praying senses and experiences;

it is praying doctrine, and, as such, prayer might be best understood as experiential theology in action, where we are not just communicating with God, for example, but are seeking to experience God initially by *addressing* him.

Nominative Address

Jewish philosopher Martin Buber (1878-1965) in his 1923 book *I and Thou* suggests that relationships exist between us because we are able to call someone else 'thou/you'; to recognise them; to name them. He argues that we enter into dialogic relationships by being able to address (***appellare***) each other. He further argues that we do this with each other in what he calls 'ordinary' language, but which, I would argue here, ceases to be 'ordinary' when in church and in prayer. Especially so, when that language is hieratic like Latin. No language can ever actually express (let alone explain) God, the object of our prayer, only address him. As Christians we recognise this very early on; we recognise the power of the name of God as a Trinity of Father (***Pater***) Son (***Filius***) and Holy Spirit (***Sanctus Spiritus***) and know that this is not 'ordinary'. The very fact that when we, as Christians, seek to understand God through the seeming impenetrability of a concept like the Trinity, whatever language we use is never going to 'explain' God as a Trinity.

When we pray to the Trinity in a language like Latin, that language doesn't help us explain God any better than, say English, but what it does is to reinforce the extraordinariness of God in the Trinity by it being prayed in a language extraordinary to our daily lives. Latin prayer, therefore, reinforces how distanced we are from God, because it reinforces how distanced Latin is from the language of our everydayness. This tends not to be a popular view within the Catholicism that has developed post *Vatican II*, which seems to think that we can somehow get closer to, or better understand God, if we use our ordinary language. This very popular view expressed in the Reformation and now post *Vatican II*, would seem to suggest that the more ordinary our language is in addressing God, the closer we can come to him. That would further seem to suggest that the spiritual impenetrability that we are engaged in when in prayer, is more easily penetrated with the vernacular. But more than that, it would also seem to suggest that the 'spiritual impenetrability' of God might somehow be reduced. But this has surely to be, what could only be considered as, the mother and father of all linguistic (and theological) fallacies. No matter what language we use, closeness to God is not, nor can ever be, a linguistic relationship. Whether we use the vernacular 'ordinary', or the Latin 'extraordinary', or both, God is not affected either way. But we are. When the language we use is not ordinary, it reinforces the extraordinariness of what it is we do when we pray. It further reinforces the utter extraordinariness of God. God is totally 'other'; an understanding of which is at the very heart of St Augustine of Hippo's formidable statement in his ***Sermo*** 117: ***si enim comprehendis, non est Deus*** (for if you understand, it is not God).

It is, of course, counter-cultural for us to use Latin in prayer; a language no longer spoken in the street. But to pray is the epitome of what it is to be counter-cultural. Its prime purpose is exactly that: to be counter to the culture of this world. St John Henry Cardinal Newman (1801-1890) recognised this and referred to God's 'incommunicable perfection' in 'Meditation 21' in his *Meditations and Devotions* (published in 1893 three years after his death) and he further recognised that praying in Latin forces us to slow down by our using a quite different language to our 'mother tongue'. Like slow breathing is now a popular form of meditation, for example, it forces us to reflect; to step away from the everyday; to be other-worldly; in effect, to be counter-cultural.

Unlike our ordinary day-to-day recognising, acknowledging and naming, this counter-cultural linguistic process acknowledging the extraordinariness of God is, from its very beginnings, when carried out with reverence, always and ever, an act of prayer, whether it is just one word, or one thousand, but it will always, and only ever will be, an unequal act of address. Praying in Latin, and not in our ordinary language, foregrounds this inequality. Unpopular a view though this may be to many contemporary Catholics and non-Catholic Christians alike, who now seem intent on seeking to reduce this inequality in popular language and popularising liturgy, by seeking to no longer see (or name and address) God as 'other'. But an unequal relationship is surely the whole point of religion. It is certainly a central Latin Catholic sensibility made manifest to us in the very Transfiguration, when Jesus was revealed to us as the Son of God. Just think about that. It was, and still is, totally extraordinary. But this is an extraordinary 'otherness' which seems now to make so many Christians, and now increasingly so many Catholics, uncomfortable. But every name we pray for God in the Trinity is an *other* name. For example:

Abba (Father)
Adiútor (Helper)
Adónai (Lord)
Agnus (Lamb
Alpha et Omega (the Beginning and the End)
Bónitas (Goodness)
Cáritas (Love)
Christus (Christ)
Condítor (Creator)
Defénsor (Defender)
Déitas (Deity)
Deus (God)
Dominátor (Ruler)
Dóminus (Lord)
Emmánuel (the Foretold [Lord])
Felícitas (Felicity)
Fílius (Son)
Homo (Man)
Iesse vírgula (Rod of Jesse)
Iesus (Jesus)
Iudex (Judge)

Lux (Light)
Oriens (the Dawn)
Panis (Bread
Paraclítus (Comforter)
Pastor (Shepherd)
Pater (Father)
Pelicánus (Pelican)
Protéctor (Protector)
Rector (Ruler)
Redémptor (Redeemer)
Rex (King)
Salvátor (Saviour)
Sanctificátor (Sanctifier)
Sapiéntia (Wisdom)
Scrutátor (Examiner)
Spes (Hope)
Spíritus (Spirit)
Trínitas (Trinity)
Triumphátor (Conqueror)
Unítas (Oneness/Unity)
Verbum (Word)
Véritas (Truth)

Most of these nominative words or phrases are ordinary in many contexts, but, when prayed, transform to the extraordinary. We understand *verbum* to be 'word', but to call God 'Word'? Extraordinary. We understand *pelicanus* to be a kind of bird, but to name God ***Pelicanus***? Extraordinary. In English these are linguistically ordinary words made spiritually extraordinary requiring often very complex theological and anagogical explanations (like the pelican feeding its young with its own blood). We have to think about them, but when they are linguistically formed in a language like Latin, for which there are no longer any native speakers, we have to think just that little bit harder. To name

God as 'Bread', as say in 'the Bread of Life' requires a lot of thought, but when that is expressed as **_Panis Vitae_** in Latin it takes just that little bit more thought. There is nothing textual/linguistic in the Latin word **_Dominus_**, for example, that makes 'Lord' a more efficacious word to use in prayer, but the discipline and dynamic required in using it with a Latin text-in-Catholic context does. We have to think more; we have to slow down. For example, if we combine some of these Latin words in their nominative form as given above and seek to pray them with reverence as in:

> **_Deus, Pater, Rex Protéctor_** (God, Father, King Protector)
> **_Iesus Christus, Salvátor Redémptor_** (Jesus Christ, Saviour Redeemer)
> **_Trínitas Deus Unitas_** (Unity God Trinity)
> **_Tu Trínitas Unitas_** (You Trinity Unity)
> **_Christus, Spíritus, Déitas_** (Christ, Spirit, Deity)
> **_Christus homo_** (Christ man)
> **_Deus Adiútor_** (God Helper)

then we have created a private prayer of _nominative address_ which requires us to think harder as we pray the words in Latin especially if we are to reflect anagogically, as we pray, initially on their linguistic meaning and then on their spiritual sensibilities. This is not to suggest that the more complex the Latin is, the more extraordinary God becomes, but, the more we have to think about how we are naming and addressing God linguistically, means that we are having to work harder at thinking _about God_. And thinking about God is prayer. God is not affected by any of this, but we are.

What we pray as Latin Catholics is not serendipitous. It recognises that in just one word, naming Mary as 'Queen', for example, long thought and reflection has gone into this naming, often taking centuries to formalise. There are almost 250 _litanies_ that are currently listed for private prayer in the Catholic Church, but only 6 have actually been formally approved for public liturgical worship. These are:

- *The Litanies of Saints* approved in 590 by Pope St Gregory I (540-604)
- *The Litanies of the Blessed Virgin Mary* (*Litanies of Loreto*) approved in 1587 by Pope Sixtus V (1521-1590)
- *The Litanies of the Holy Name of Jesus* approved by Pope Sixtus V for private prayer in 1585, and then by Pope Leo XIII (1810-1903) for public prayer in 1886
- *The Litanies of the Sacred Heart of Jesus* approved by Pope Leo XIII in 1899
- *The Litanies of Saint Joseph* approved by Pope St Pius X in 1909
- *The Litanies of the Most Precious Blood of Jesus* approved in 1960 by Pope St John XXIII

Why so few from the 250? Because naming and addressing God in the Trinity, directly, or through his Mother, Saints and Angels, is not something to be taken lightly. Every item in these *litanies* expresses the extraordinary, and that has to be thought through very carefully. In the **Litaniae ad Beatam Mariam Virginem [Litaniae Lauretanae]** (*Litanies of Loreto*) for example, thought to have been composed in Paris in the 12thC, we ask the Blessed Virgin Mary to intercede for us with God. As an extended prayer of address it allows us to name and acknowledge her simply as **Maria**, for example, but what do names like **Arca** (Ark) and **Speculum** (Mirror) signify? The 'text' of the *Litanies* lists many such extraordinary names, enabling us to reflect more deeply on the contextual mysteries behind these names, and therefore, on the Blessed Virgin Mary, and through her, on Christ her son, and in turn, upon him as Son of God, and thus upon God as Trinity. So when we pray these names, they are not just flights of fancy dreamt up by medieval monks with nothing better to do, in the way that they often filled up blank spaces in medieval manuscripts of holy texts with cartoons and pictures, they reflect a Church that has a theological responsibility to teach us both 'revealed truths' and 'developed truths' from Scripture and Catholic Tradition. Every name and prayer in these *litanies* moves us linguistically and spiritually into a quite 'other' world:

> *María* (Mary)
> *Arca* (Ark)
> *Auxílium* (Help)
> *Causa* (Cause/Means)
> *Consolátrix* (Consoler)
> *Domus* (House)
> *Génitrix* (Mother)
> *Iánua* (Gate)
> *Mater* (Mother)
> *Refúgium* (Refuge)
> *Regína* (Queen)
> *Rosa* (Rose)
> *Salus* (Health)
> *Sedes* (Seat)
> *Solátium* (Solace)
> *Spéculum* (Mirror)
> *Stella* (Star)
> *Turris* (Tower)
> *Vas* (Vessel)
> *Virgo* (Virgin)

Probably, with the exception perhaps of *Mater* and *Regína*, these are names which might not immediately strike us as obvious to give to anyone. But in naming the Blessed Virgin Mary in this way we are seeing a very prominent side of the language of Latin prayer which seeks to make the ordinary *extraordinary*. But it is not just a linguistic game to see how many synonyms for Mary might be invented. These are all part of the long centuries of deep reflection upon a Mariology (theology of

Mary) which of itself only makes sense when understood in the context of other '-ologies': like theology (dogmatic, moral, systematic) and Christology, ecclesiology, eschatology and so on, which have shaped the teaching of the Church to better enable the teaching of revealed and developed truths to be made. Referring to the Mother of God as a *vas* (vessel/vase) *ianua* (gate) or *domus* (house) for example, is actually about those ordinary words lifting us beyond the normal, and enabling us to focus on the *anagogical*. So, when we pray privately to Mary as ***Portus naufragántium*** (Port of the shipwrecked) ***Sedátio procellárum*** (Calmer of storms) or ***Debellátrix incredulórum*** (Defeater of unbelievers) as we do in the ***Litaniae Dominae nostrae Dolorum*** (*Litanies* of our Lady of Sorrows) written by an imprisoned Servant of God Pope Pius VII in 1809 (under Napoleon) then we are making the ordinary extraordinary, because she is recognised to be extraordinary, and can lead us to the even more extraordinary. When we pray these names as prayers in Latin, we genuinely have to think just that little bit harder in order to consider the spiritual focus and force beyond the linguistic and grammatical surface. There is a deeper structure involved than just the language.

Nominative Focus and Force

If we reverently say the following ***Quattuor Novissima*** (Four Last Things) all written in the nominative form, by placing ourselves at the foot of the cross before we fall asleep, as we might traditionally be taught to do as Catholics:

> ***Mors*** (Death) ***Iudícium*** (Judgement) ***Inférnus*** (Hell) ***Paradísus*** (Heaven)

we are praying. If we reverently say ***Virtutes Cardinales*** ([the]Cardinal Virtues) as soon as we wake up, as a reminder of what Catholic sensibilities should guide our practices in the coming day:

>   *Prudéntia* (Prudence) *Iustítia* (Justice) *Fortitúdo* (Strength) *Temperántia* (Temperance)

then we are praying. If we combine some of the words from the list of names for God given earlier like:

>   *Dóminus Deus; Dóminus Deus Pater; Dóminus Deus Adiútor; Dóminus Deus Rex*

then we are praying. We are both linguistically addressing, and spiritually focussing on, these names for God. If we reverently say the following at the elevation of the consecrated Host at Mass:

>   *Dóminus Iesus Christus, Salvátor, Sanctificátor, Redémptor*

or we reverently say:

>   *Pater Protéctor, Christus Redémptor, Spíritus Salvátor, Trínitas Unitas Déitas*

we are addressing God prayerfully. The focus (***attentio***) when we do so, shifts from us as 'sayer' to us as 'pray-er', and thus, we hope, to God himself. This is the whole point and purpose of nominative prayer. It enables, even with just these few linguistic forms of address, to shift spiritual *focus*. Our point of view shifts; perspectives alter, and so too will the *force* and *affect* upon us of our prayer.

One very specific means of establishing such focus is in the use of certain 'perspective' words, especially pronouns, which often replace nouns in a text. So, for example, in the epigraph from *Isaias* at the beginning of this chapter, ***Ego Dominus, hoc est nomen meum*** (I [am] [the] Lord, this is my name) the pronoun ***hoc*** (this) stands in place of ***nomen***, otherwise it might read as ***Ego Dominus, nomen est nomen meum***. Both ***Dominus*** and ***hoc*** are the nominative subjects of the same verb *est* (is) and the pronoun *ego* (I) is the subject of an unnamed verb *sum* (am). Grammatically they are in agreement; there is *concord* between them. A pronoun like *hoc*, therefore, acts as a point of reference. Pronouns orient the language user (the addresser) and the language receiver (the addressee) to particular points of view. This orientation, technically known as 'deixis' (δεῖξις - *deixis* - 'reference') signifies the way we position ourselves, and are positioned, especially in prayer, and affects, not only how we pray, but on how, and upon what/who we focus ourselves on in prayer. There are many different types of pronouns in Latin, each functioning in specific ways. They are gendered in Latin (masculine/feminine/neuter and so *hoc* here is neuter standing in for the neuter noun *nomen*) and, like nouns and adjectives, change according to person, number and case (if standing in for the masculine noun *Dominus* for example the pronoun would be *hic*) all of which reflects a reference point or 'orientation' specific to that pronoun. Personal deixis indicates the perspective (the focus) of the persons involved, for example:

1st person singular point of view - I perspective (*ego*)
2nd person singular point of view - you (sg) perspective (*tu*)
3rd person singular point of view - he/she/it perspective (*is/ea/id*)
1st person plural point of view - we perspective (*nos*)
2nd person plural point of view - you (pl) perspective (*vos*)
3rd person plural point of view - they perspective (*ei/eae/ea*)

So, in prayer from a 1st person point of view (the 'I/We perspective') the 1st person is fully involved in the prayer in an active participation in the relationship that prayer aims to build with God. The *I/We* is specifically signalled as being an engaged participant. In literary terms *I/We* would be considered the protagonist(s) a term developed from early Greek drama (πρωταγωνιστής - *protagonistes*) as the character in the drama who has the first part hence, the first person. We tend not to think of ourselves as the protagonists when we pray, but in 1st person prayer we are, what in literary terms would be considered, a focal character. We are told so often that we should not let the ego/self get in the way of prayer. That we should sublimate the *ego* and 'lay ourselves bare' before God. But prayer is not, nor should it be, as one commentator once suggested that it should be, an 'ego-less state'. Private prayer, as understood in this book at any rate, is about a dialogic relationship with a 1st person focus between the ***ego sum*** of 'I' and the ***sum*** (I am) of God. God is the 'ego-less' state, not prayer, or us its pray-ers. St John the Apostle (c6AD-c100AD) records the Son of Man saying:

> *Ego quos amo, arguo, et castigo; aemulare ergo, et poenitentiam age.*
> (Whom I love, I rebuke, and chastise; excel therefore, and do penance. *Apc* 3:19)

The pronoun *ego* is not needed with the verb *amo* (I love) but providing it in this way creates considerably more emphatic force, focussing very firmly upon the 'I perspective', which is then repeated with the use of ***arguo*** (1st person singular present active indicative - *arguere* - to rebuke/correct - I rebuke) and ***castigo*** (1st person singular present active indicative - *castigare* - to chastise - I chastise).

If the 1st person perspective (*I/We*) creates a protagonist, the 2nd person point of view, in literary terms, creates an audience; the 'you perspective' where a 2nd person (you) becomes the focal point (referent) of the action. So, on May 31st at the Mass of Our Lady, Mediatrix of All Graces, we pray in the *Epistle*:

> *Omnes sitiéntes, veníte ad aquas, et qui non habétis argéntum, properáte, émite, et comédite: veníte, émite absque argénto et absque ulla commutatióne vinum et lac.*
> (All thirsting, come to the waters, and who have no money, make haste, buy, and eat: come, buy without money, and without any exchange, wine and milk. *Is* 55:1)

And in the *Epistle* for the Mass of the Feast of St Bernadette of Soubirous (1844-1879, 18 February) we pray:

> *Et réquiem tibi dabit Dóminus semper, et implébit splendóribus ánimam tuam, et ossa tua liberábit; et eris quasi hortus irrigúus, et sicut fons aquárum cuius non defíciet aquae.*
> (And the Lord will give rest to you continually, and he will fill your soul with brilliance, and he will liberate your bones; and you will be as a watered garden, and as a fountain of water whose waters do not run out. *Is* 58:11)

The 2nd person perspective, either given implicitly in the verbs (*habetis/eris*) or through the pronouns/adjectives (*qui/tibi/tuam/tua*) bring deictic clarity, but often their own very nuanced meaning as well. Pronouns create and re-create quite different identities at times, and understanding these subtleties and shifts in Latin prayer can be very important in the way we pray a prayer.

The identity, for example, that is established in a 3rd person perspective (like the accusative masculine plural *quos* (whom) of *qui* (who) in the example above) is distanced from both 1st and 2nd person protagonists or beneficiaries. Identity is referenced through third party personification. In literary terms that third party person is often an anonymous narrator, but Latin prayer wants to know who the third party is. We want to know who is telling the story. Is it Jesus himself? Is it the gospel writer or St Paul the Apostle (5AD-67AD)? For example the 3rd person point of view in St Luke the Evangelist's (early 1stC) telling of Christ's Transfiguration where the following words were heard:

> **Hic est Filius meus dilectus, ipsum audite.**
> (This is my beloved Son, hear! him[self] *Lc* 9:35)

is established by the pronoun *hic* (this) referring to Christ and is followed up with the intensive 3rd person pronoun 'himself' (*ipsum*). The

3rd person pronoun *hic* establishes an identity from a distance, just as the Transfiguration itself was seen by Sts Peter the Apostle (c1AD-c64/68AD) James the Greater (d 44AD) and John the Apostle/Evangelist from a distance. But it is far from being anonymous. It is God saying these words, and in prayer we want to know that. So, for example when we pray the following:

> *ego protéctor tuus sum* (I am your protector *Gn* 15:1)
> *Tu es fílius meus* (you are my son *Gn* 27:24)
> *id est* (it is - generally translated as 'that is')
> *nos pauci sumus* (we are few *Gn* 34:30)
> *Testes vos... estis hódie* (you are witnesses today *Rt* 4:9)
> *et aures ei sunt* (and ears they are/[have] *Is* 43:8)

not only the pronouns in Latin hold within them, so to speak, the person perspective/deixis, but so too do the verbs. Hence *sum* by itself means 'I am' and *sunt* by itself means 'they are', without needing to include the pronoun as English does. But there is often a more forceful and often emphatic meaning involved when the personal pronoun is included, as in *ego sum* and *ea sunt*, and in prayer that can be very forceful indeed, because focus is drawn to the additional pronoun, and anagogically we might therefore usefully ask why. One of the thieves crucified along with Jesus turned to him and said:

> **Si tu es Christus salvum fac temetípsum et nos.**
> (If you are [the] Christ save yourself and us. *Lc* 23:39)

which we pray in the *Gospel* of the Mass on Wednesday of Holy Week. The 2nd person pronoun *tu* forcefully focuses the attention totally upon Jesus in contrast with the 1st person plural *nos*. On Christ's own cross were written the words **Hic est Rex Iudaeorum** (This is the King of the Jews) where the 3rd person pronoun *hic* focuses all attention like a flashing neon sign in the form of an arrow pointed directly at Christ.

We pray the textual word *hic*, but we also pray its contextual nominative *focus*. We pray not just the words, but the grammar; we pray the text-context dynamic. This then has *force*. It *affects* us. We cannot escape it. It has its own deep structural spiritual meaning.

On the surface, perspective like this might seem a little thing perhaps, something not to be really thought about as the words tumble out of us in prayer, but anagogically it is just such a little thing that can change the entire focus, force and affect of our prayer. For example in the seemingly simple statement ***Ego sum qui sum*** (I am who am *Ex* 3:14) when prayed with the realisation that this is God speaking directly to Moses; that it is God who is the nominative *ego* ('I') and nominative *qui* ('who') then there is enough nominative force in the focus of those two small pronouns to enable us to pray for a lifetime. It is God (***Deus/Ego***) speaking! Two tiny words with immeasurable nominative force in this context. This is not ordinary. Nothing we do in prayer is ordinary. If we pray, for example, from ***Litaniae Sancti Ioseph*** (Litanies of St Joseph) we can see that St Joseph is named (in the edited selections below in the nominative form) as:

Proles (Offspring)
Lumen (Light)
Sponsus (Spouse)
Custos (Guardian/Protector)
Nutrítius (Foster-father)
Defénsor (Defender)
Praeses (Head)
Spéculum (Mirror)
Amátor (Lover)
Exémplar (Model)
Domésticus (Servant)
Cólumen (Pillar)
Solácium (Solace)
Spes (Hope)

> *Patrónus* (Patron)
> *Terror* (Terror)

These are not ordinary ways of naming someone: for example ***Terror*** or ***Solacium***. They add a powerful nominative force to the name of St Joseph, and therefore to devotion to him, and through him to God. But each of these names emerges often from many centuries of devotion. Centuries of praying these names, and not just saying them, brings into our own times their very powerful nominative force.

When we pray, for example: ***Iustus et Salvátor*** ([the] Righteous and Saviour) we name Christ as ***Salvator*** (Saviour). This is not something we have invented; nor have we invented the notion that he is *iustus*, a righteous man. They are both theological determinations about the person of Christ as God which have been shaped in Christianity since Apostolic times; through both Scripture and Tradition. In Latin Catholicism we can't just apply any name or category to Joseph, Mary or Christ, as increasingly might happen today from some well meaning Parish liturgists anxious to create contemporary variety. It has to be determined, and approved, by the Church within its ***Magisterium*** (teaching authority) as does any new teaching within Catholicism.

That is no easy matter, and would normally be done at an official Council of the Church. Referring to the Virgin Mary as 'Co-Redemptrix', for example, was raised by some at *Vatican II* in the 1960s as worthy of becoming the fifth Marian dogma, but was never formally discussed or taken any further. Venerable Pope Pius XII in the early 1940s had in fact rejected a similar proposal put to him, as did Pope St John Paul II in the early 1990s and as did Pope Benedict XVI (1927-) towards the end of his active Pontificate. Pope Francis (1936-) when it was put to him, actually referred to it very dismissively as 'foolishness'. That said, it is a term used by some very reverently in Catholicism, but, because it has never been promulgated as an approved Marian dogma within the Church, the use of the name 'Co-Redemptrix' must formally remain a name for Our Lady as a doctrinal proposal only, despite its occurring in private prayer. The four Marian dogmas which have been approved are:

- *Divine Motherhood*, proclaimed at the Council of Ephesus in 431, naming Mary as **Mater Dei** (the Mother of God).
- *Perpetual Virginity,* raised at the Second Council of Constantinople in 553 and formally promulgated at the Fourth Lateran Council in 1215 naming Mary as **Virgo Maria** (Virgin Mary).
- The *Immaculate Conception* promulgated as a dogma by Pope Blessed Pius IX (1792-1878 - *Pio Nono*) in 1854, declaring Mary as conceived without original sin.
- The *Assumption* promulgated by Pope Venerable Pius XII on November 1, 1950 proclaiming a very long held belief that Mary was assumed body and soul into heaven.

They each of them took considerable time to develop and be promulgated. As did the feast of 'Our Lord Jesus Christ the King' generally shortened as **Christus Rex** (Christ the King) which was only established as a universal feast in the Church by Pope Pius XI (1857-1939) in the Holy Year of 1925, with a special Mass written for it by Fr Vittorio Genovesi SJ (1887-1967) but that Mass which is celebrated today on the last Sunday of October in the **usus antiquior** calendar, is composed in a liturgical Latin that not only predates the formal declaration of the Feast by almost two millennia of living, active, worship in Latin, but which had long recognised the Kingship of Christ. To know, for example, that worshippers from the 3rdC onwards were using the same Latin words in prayer as we are using now, is a very powerful thing to have before us. To know that many, if not all of our favourite saints were praying in Latin and using the same words that we can use today, is a very powerful thing to know, and by knowing it, and acting upon it, we are able to exercise a function of prayer which goes way beyond words. It enables a focussed and forceful prayer that is drenched in the history of its use. That force *affects* us not just because of its textual form, but because often its contextual use goes back through almost 2,000 years of worship and prayer.

Nominative Affect

The Feast of All Saints (**Omnium Sanctorum**) celebrated with the **Missa Gaudeamus** from the *Introit* which we pray:

> *Gaudeámus omnes in Dómino, diem festum celebrántes sub honóre Sanctórum ómnium: de quorum solemnitáte gaudent Angeli, et colláudant Fílium Dei. 'Exsultáte iusti in Dómino: rectos decet collaudátio'.*
>
> (Let us all rejoice in the Lord, celebrating a festival day in honour of all the Saints: at whose solemnity the Angels rejoice, and give praise to the Son of God. 'Rejoice in the Lord, ye just: praise becometh the upright'. *trad Ps* 32:1)

is one of the oldest we celebrate, with recorded references to it dating back to at least the time of St Ephraim the Syrian (306-373) and which, given all the early martyrs, must have been celebrated long before his time. Today we pray this Collect at *Vespers* (in this edited selection):

> *Angeli, Archángeli, Throni, et Dominatiónes, Principátus, Potestátes, Virtútes, Chérubim atque Séraphim, Patriárchae et Prophétae, Doctóres, Apóstoli, omnes Mártyres, Confessóres, Vírgines, Anachorítae, Sanctíque* [*omnes intercédite pro nobis*]
>
> (Angels, Archangels, Thrones and Dominations, Principalities, Powers, Virtues, Cherubim and Seraphim; Patriarchs and Prophets, Doctors, Apostles, all Martyrs, Confessors, Virgins, Anchorites and Saints [all intercede for us])

The prayer uses the names of various classes of Angels and Saints (here all in the nominative form) asking them to intercede for us with

God, but in doing so, assumes so much that is not at all ordinary. It assumes that we believe in God; that we believe in an after-life; that God is present in that after-life; that there are non-human beings we call Angels in God's presence; that some human beings are recognised by the Church as Saints who are guaranteed, by the holy life they have lived, to be in God's presence in that after-life; that the Church actually has the power to be able to recognise and determine them to be Saints; and that in that after-life those Saints can intercede for us with God; that they share that place before God within a hierarchy of Angels, and so we could continue. But these are no ordinary things to believe. They are extraordinary. God is extraordinary. St Thomas More (1478-1535) once commented that were we to stand before a King we would not shuffle about, or idle about aimlessly, or drop off to sleep. How much more then, he says, should we be completely attentive in our worship of God? St Benedict made the same point many centuries earlier in **Caput XX, De reverentia orationis** (Chapter 20 concerning reverence of prayer) of his **Regula** (Rule) saying:

> *Si, cum hominibus potentibus volumus aliqua suggerere, non praesumimus nisi cum humilitate et reverentia, quanto magis Domino Deo universorum cum omni humilitate et puritatis devotione supplicandum est.*
>
> (If, we want to achieve something with powerful men, we do not presume [to] unless with humility and reverence, how much more is to be prayed to the Lord God of everything with all humility and devotion of purity.)

Worship is extraordinary, and, to say yet again, doing it in Latin accentuates that extraordinariness. But to name and address God is beyond extraordinary. It is only possible as a gift given to us when Christ taught us how to pray; to name God, as 'our Father' (**Pater noster**) or as *Abba, Pater* (*Gal* 4:6). There is nothing more intimate than naming God as *Abba,* **Pater**. *Abba* is a Syriac word used only three times in the *New*

Testament (and never used in the *Old Testament*) and always followed in the *Vulgate* with the word **Pater**. It signifies a caring, intimate fatherly role (developing into the word 'Abbot' as someone caring paternally for his community of monks) except perhaps to make it even more personal and intimate by naming him as '*our* Father' (**noster Pater**). This naming has considerable nominative force. It epitomises the power of all worship and prayer captured in just two simple Latin words **Pater noster**, which is probably the most forceful and focussed prayer of nominative affect we could ever wish for. We are affected because Christianity positions us with the potential for intimate relations with God, as between a father and his children. This did not just happen. It was not something the early Christians just made up. It was certainly not understood in this way prior to Christianity. It is Christ himself who revealed this truth to us; who gave us this incredible gift of seeing and understanding God as Father. Similarly, one of the most famous things Jesus ever said is:

> *Ego sum via, et veritas, et vita.*
> (I am [the] way, and [the] truth, and [the] life. *Io* 14:6)

St Paul refers to him as **Dominus Iesus Christus** ([the] Lord Jesus Christ *Phil* 2:11) who, as we pray in *Matins* for the 3rd Sunday after Easter, is recorded as saying:

> *Ego sum Alpha et Omega, principium et finis... qui est...*
> (I am Alpha and Omega, [the] beginning and [the] end... who is...
>   *Apc* 1:8)

Taking these together we might therefore privately pray:

> *Ego sum via, et véritas, et vita. Ego sum Alpha et Omega, princípium et finis... qui est Dóminus Iesus Christus.*
> (I am the way, and the truth, and the life. I am Alpha and Omega, the beginning and the end... who is the Lord Jesus Christ.)

Edited like this, these few words are affirmations of Christ's name; of who he is; of his identity. As humans we live subjective lives. We are subjective beings. We are formed as subjects by others, and we form others as subjects (interpellation). In effect this formation of subjectivity and identity is the *nominative affect* writ large in life. But everything about the nominatives in this short prayer point to the exact opposite for Christ. He is not a subjective being, despite everything seeming to point to that subjectivity through the grammar. He is not formed as a subject; the subjectivity is all ours. We are affected beings. Christ is not. Everything *we* do is mediated through language. Language determines who we are, but the nominative language of this prayer does not affect Christ; it is not designed to affect Christ. Christ is not determined by language like us, but we are only able to express Christ through language. The nominative affect of that language in this prayer is, therefore, not simply to determine who Christ is for us, but to also enable us to realise that he is 'totally other'.

We may linguistically resolve a phrase like **qui est** with the nominative **Dominus Iesus Christus**, but theologically how can we possibly know what that really means? We have a sense of our own subjective realities through the language we use. But to even glimpse that for Christ requires a quite different set of realities. Prayer may open the door slightly for us to those realities, but if this short private prayer of nominative affect might teach us anything at all, it is for us to be humbled by the fact that we can never fully enter into the 1st person point of view in this short text. The nominative affect upon us here may enable us to recognise, and reflect upon, the absolutely extraordinary concept that while we are, and always will be, subjective beings, our subjectivity only means anything when understood as part of an infinite creation. We only have a subjective identity because of God's identity. Our 'I' has meaning only relative to God's **Ego sum**.

The nominative like this is not taught in grammar books. It becomes apparent only when we parse the grammar, not just to understand and say the words, or even to pray the words, but in order to pray the grammar. And that is powerful indeed in Latin prayer, and the very point and purpose of this book: to present 'a way of Latin prayer' through 'a way of praying Latin grammar'. Understood like this, words and the 'bits of grammar' have *situated* meanings. They are situated within 2,000 years or more of history, theology, philosophy, doctrine, dogma and liturgy. Their *affect* is situated in that history. But more than that, they are *motivated* meanings; motivated by (and situated within) a very specific set of ideas, beliefs and practices, in order to enable a very specific affect. This is not, to use a word much favoured by post-modernist discourse, a 'disinterested' affect. Far from it. It is *interested*, *motivated* and *situated* by, with, from and through, in this case, Latin Catholicism. It is not 'contingent' upon a relativistic view that basically says 'anything goes'. 'Anything' in Latin Catholicism 'does not go.' As [now Emeritus] Pope Benedict XVI said in 2005:

> 'It is the truth revealed through Scripture and Tradition and articulated by the Church's ***Magisterium*** that sets us free.'

We pray, then, not for effect (***effectus***) but to be affected (***affici***). We are, in praying like this, not just naming, recognising or acknowledging God, his Son, Mother, Saints and Angels using the nominative form, as we have done in this first chapter, but we turn to them and call out to them. And for that 'turning to' and 'calling out to', in Latin, there is sometimes a different form of the word, and a different grammatical function along with that form, and it is to that we now turn in *Chapter III: Vocative Prayer.*

III

VOCATIVE PRAYER

Domine Deus, tu es Deus
(O Lord God, you are God *2 Reg* 7:28)

Calling

'The word of the Lord came to the prophet Nathan... Go, and say to my servant David: "Thus saith the Lord: Shalt thou build me a house to dwell in?" And according to all these words and according to all this vision, so did Nathan speak to David. And David sat before the Lord, and said... O Lord of hosts, God of Israel, I will build thee a house: and he prayed a prayer to God saying... And now, ***Domine Deus, tu es Deus*** (O Lord God, thou art God) and thy words shall be true: for thou hast spoken to thy servant these good things.' (edited from *DR 2 Reg* 7:4-28)

We can name God when we pray, as David does after speaking with Nathan, but the aim in prayer is to form a relationship with God and to more fully do that we need to turn to him, and call to him, as David and countless others have done before. This is more than words. It is ***actio*** (action) a 'doing'; a 'performing'; a 'behaviour' and a 'process'. Prayer requires a *habitus* (disposition) which the *Catechismus* refers to as:

> *habitualiter esse in Dei ter Sancti praesentia et in communione cum Eodem*
> 'the habit of being in the presence of the thrice-holy God and in communion with Him' (*Cat* §2565)

As a 'habit of being' it is dispositional because it is about 'character'. This *habitus* requires our consent, but above all, in prayer, it requires submission and a willingness to change, because though we may call to God, it is really, always, God who calls to us. St John Henry Cardinal Newman was acutely aware of this 'habit of being' as a disposition and characteristic that prompts us to turn and call upon God, not just for our sakes in this world, but even more so for our sakes in the world to come, when as an Anglican minister in his very early 30s he ended his 1833 poem *The Elements* (published as 'poem 71' in *Lyra Apostolica*) with:

> 'To Him in wisdom turn,
> Who holds for us the keys of either home,
> Earth and the world to come.'

Twelve years later on October 9, 1845 he turned to God very formally (and for that time in England very dramatically) by changing his Anglican *habitus* by being accepted into the Roman Catholic Church, giving up all his not inconsiderable preferments and privileges as an Anglican minister in a society that still prevented Roman Catholics from going to university, and, indeed, still shut them out from many career (and other) opportunities.

We say he was 'converted' to Catholicism. The English verb 'to convert' comes from the Latin verb *convertere* (to turn upside down/ to turn around/to reverse/to redirect). It is a verb which in Latin is made up of two parts *con* (which marks emphasis) plus the verb *vertere* (to turn/revolve). When Newman converted from Anglicanism to Roman Catholicism he therefore turned around and redirected himself, completely (as the Latin *con* would signify). There was no turning back (*revertens*) for him. He was later to call this God's *mirabilis via* (wondrous way) and in his epitaph, which he composed himself, he referred to his life as a journey *Ex umbris et imaginibus in veritatem* ('Out of shadows and semblances into truth'; the 'truth' being Roman Catholicism. Newman summed it up very simply in his poem 'Some Definite Service' in his *Meditations and Devotions* (1848):

'God knows me and calls me by my name.'

David, in the passage above, also calls God by saying his name 'O Lord God' (*Domine Deus*) several times. He names God: *tu es Deus* (you are God) using the nominative *Deus*. But he also turns towards the Lord and calls to him with the vocative *Domine* (O Lord). The Latin verb for 'to call upon' is *vocare* (as in English 'vocation' - a calling) and the change from *Dominus* to *Domine* is a move from naming to calling. God is named *Dominus* in the *Vulgate* almost 3,500 times and called upon using *Domine* almost 700 times. In the *Psalms* alone we call to the Lord (*Domine*) 237 times. And so we have a simple, but very powerful, two word Latin prayer: *Dómine Deus* which can be said at any time, and anywhere, and many times over in a day. We pray the words, but we are also praying the grammar in the form of a simple vocative-nominative dynamic.

The Vocative-Nominative Dynamic

It took Newman many years to make his decision, saying that 'Catholicism is a deep matter... you cannot take it up in a teacup.' He was not the first to need time to recognise God's call. Samuel, who was called several times in the night, thinking it was his teacher Eli calling him when in fact it was God, finally recognised this after God called out to him 'Samuel, Samuel. And Samuel said: Speak, Lord, for thy servant heareth.' (*DR 1 Reg* 3:10). The *Vulgate* records this as **Samuel, Samuel. Et ait Samuel: Loquere, Domine, quia audit servus tuus.** There are three uses of the Latin noun **Samuel** here, each with exactly the same form, but the first two of them function as vocatives, ([O] Samuel, [O] Samuel) and the third 'Samuel (subject) said (verb)' as a nominative. The textual form here doesn't distinguish the different function, but the context does (unlike **Dominus/Domine**).

There is very often little inflectional distinction made between the nominative and the vocative form in Latin, apart from in a very limited way with some masculine nouns like **Franciscus** (Francis) **Dominicus** (Dominic) **Benedictus** (Benedict) **Antonius** (Anthony) becoming **Francisce** (O Francis) **Dominice** (O Dominic) **Benedicte** (O Benedict) **Antoni** (O Anthony) **filius** becoming **fili** (O son) and rarer occurrences of other forms like **Thomas/Thoma**; **Lucas/Luca**; **Barnabas/Barnaba**. Similarly, the vocative form of all the pronouns is the same as the nominative except that the nom/voc possessive determiner **meus** may be written as **mi**. What this effectively means is that in Latin prayer the majority of the nouns and pronouns may be 'both/and' nominative/vocative, and only in much more restricted situations, 'either/or' nominative/vocative. Either separately, as a distinctive nominative or vocative form, or taken together as a 'both/and' nominative/vocative, the force in prayer is always essentially a vocative one: addressing God by calling to him. So, in this edited and shortened version of **Litaniae ad Deum Patrem** (Litanies to God the Father) we may pray both the nominative and vocative forms of address:

> **Nominative**
> *Pater Sanctus* (Holy Father)
> *Pater Iustus* (Righteous Father)
> *Pater Deus* (Father God)
> *Redémptor Deus* (Redeemer God)

Spíritus Sanctus Deus (Holy Spirit God)
Sancta Trínitas Unus Deus (Holy Trinity One God)
Pater noster (our Father)
Pater miséricors (merciful Father)
Pater Deus benedíctus (Father blessed God)
Pater adorándus (Father to be adored)
Pater gloriósus (glorious Father)
Pater luminósus (radiant Father)
Pater vivíficans (living Father)
Pater videns (seeing Father)
Pater benígnus (benign Father)
Pater pátiens (patient Father)

Vocative
Pater Sancte (O Holy Father)
Pater Iuste (O Righteous Father)
Pater Deus ([O] Father God)
Redémptor Deus ([O] Redeemer God)
Spíritus Sancte Deus (O Holy Spirit God)
Sancta Trínitas Unus Deus ([O] Holy Trinity One God)
Pater noster ([O] our Father)
Pater miséricors ([O] merciful Father)
Pater Deus benedícte (O blessed Father God)
Pater adoránde (O Father to be adored)
Pater glorióse (O glorious Father)
Pater lumíne (O radiant Father)
Pater vivíficante (O living Father)
Pater videns ([O] seeing Father)
Pater benígne (O benign Father)
Pater pátiens ([O] patient Father)

Pater can be both nominative and vocative in form and it is only the adjective modifying **Pater** which signals clearly whether it is to be read specifically as a nominative or a vocative form: ***benígnus*** (nom)/***benígne*** (voc). So, in ***Litaniae de Sacratissimo Corde Iesu*** (Litanies concerning the most Sacred Heart of Jesus) the Latin word ***cor*** (heart) may function as both nominative and vocative without changing inflectional form and be prayed as:

> ***Cor Iesu*** ([The/O] heart of Jesus)
> ***Cor Iesu maiestátis infinítae*** ([The/O] heart of Jesus of infinite majesty)
> ***Cor Iesu vírtutum ómnium abýssus*** ([The/O] heart of Jesus the bottomless pit of all virtues)
> ***Cor Iesu víctima peccatórum*** ([The/O] heart of Jesus the victim of sins)
> ***Cor Iesu rex et centrum ómnium córdium*** ([The/O] heart of Jesus [the/O] king and [the/O] centre of all hearts)

The vocative-nominative dynamic here, however, does more than just signal grammatical options, it also signals spiritual relationships. It offers alternative ways of reading, and therefore alternative ways of praying. So ***desiderium*** (desire) may function as nominative, vocative or accusative and not change in form, and ***Cor Iesu desiderium collium aeternorum*** may be alternatively understood as:

> The heart of Jesus; the desire of eternal hills (nom + nom)
> The heart of Jesus, O desire of eternal hills (nom + voc)
> The heart of Jesus: the desire of eternal hills (nom + acc)
> O heart of Jesus, the desire of eternal hills (voc + nom)
> O heart of Jesus; O desire of eternal hills (voc + voc)
> O heart of Jesus: the desire of eternal hills (voc + acc)

But this does not have to be 'either/or'. These six options for meaning are all 'both/and' in the Latin, and as such the Latin prayer might then become even richer in its spiritual possibilities, because these multiple options for translation taken all together as above, may offer multiple *layered* meanings. This layering of meaning is a crucial aspect of the way we might pray in Latin, and is not something talked about at all in grammar books.

Praying Layered Meanings

In the opening of a hymn thought to have been composed by St Anselm the Benedictine Archbishop of Canterbury (1033-1109) we pray:

> *Ave, crux sancta, virtus nostra.*
> *Ave, crux adoránda, laus et glória nostra.*
> *Ave, crux, auxílium et refúgium nostrum.*

> (Hail, [O] holy Cross, our strength.
> Hail, [O] Cross to be adored, our praise and glory.
> Hail, [O] Cross, our help and refuge.)

> *Salve, crux, victória et spes nostra.*
> *Salve, crux, defénsio et vita nostra.*
> *Salve, crux, redémptio et liberátio nostra.*

> (Hail, [O] Cross, our victory and hope.
> Hail, [O] Cross, our defence and life.
> Hail, [O] Cross, our redemption and liberation.)

There is a powerful vocative force in the forms of address *Ave* and *Salve* but *crux sancta, virtus nostra* may be both nominative and vocative, enabling us to pray in a more layered way:

> Hail, the holy Cross, our strength (nom + nom)
> Hail, the holy Cross, O our strength (nom + voc)

> Hail O holy Cross, our strength (voc + nom)
> Hail, O holy Cross, O our strength (voc + voc)

Such layered meanings are generally suppressed because in translation we generally choose to prioritise one particular layer over another, even though the grammar does not necessarily determine this. But when we pray in Latin all these layers sit there in the background and offer us the possibilities of much greater spiritual depth in what it is we are doing in this prayer. But to reap the benefits of such layered meanings we have to give ourselves up, as it were, to the Latin text, and not simply use this text as a way of our actually praying in English but with Latin words. When we consider layered meanings in this way, the power of Latin prayer, then, goes far beyond just the lexical meaning of the words themselves. We might privately pray:

> ***Dóminus Rex noster*** (Our Lord King) - nom
> ***Dómine Rex noster*** (O our Lord King) - voc
> ***Dóminus noster Christus Rex*** (Christ our Lord King) - nom
> ***Dómine noster Christe Rex*** (O Christ O our Lord King) - voc
> ***Dóminus Iesus Christus*** (Lord Jesus Christ) - nom
> ***Dómine Iesu Christe*** (O Lord Jesus Christ) - voc
> ***Dóminus Iudex noster*** (Our Lord Judge) - nom
> ***Dómine Iudex noster*** (O Our Lord Judge) - voc
> ***Dóminus Rex Magnus*** (Great Lord King) - nom
> ***Dómine Rex Magne*** (O Lord Great King) - voc
> ***Dóminus Altíssimus*** (Lord Most High) - nom
> ***Dómine Altíssime*** (O Lord Most High) - voc
> ***Rex Altíssimus*** (King Most High) - nom
> ***Rex Altíssime*** (O King Most High) - voc

where, even though there is a clear distinction between the lexical form of nominative (***Dominus*** + adj) and vocative (***Domine*** + adj) when we pray beyond the words, the nominative is always implicit (and therefore layered) in the vocative. In other words, when we see the vocative *Rex Altíssime* we don't suddenly forget that we also know the nominative option *Rex Altíssimus*. In our native language we tend not to think about the grammar involved, and perhaps in a learnt language the more fluent we become, the less we also think about the grammar, but we actually learn the grammar in that learnt language in a way that we never do with our native language, and praying in a learnt language like Latin can have a distinct advantage, not just in enabling us to read and understand a text, but to pray its grammar too, as a means of going beyond the words to the deeper structure, and more spiritual purpose, of the text. So when we pray:

Iesu (O Jesus)
Dómine (O Lord)
Dómine Deus (O Lord God)
Deus ([O] God)
Beáte Ioseph (O Blessed Joseph)
O custos (O guardian)
Dómine Deus noster (O Lord our God)
Dómine Iesu Christe (O Lord Jesus Christ)
Pie pellicáne, Iesu Dómine (O pious pelican, O Lord Jesus,)
Dómine Sancte Spíritus (O Lord O Holy Spirit)
Beáta spes ([O] blessed hope)
Aetérna lux, Divínitas ([O] Eternal light, [O]Divinity)
O verítas, O carítas (O truth, O love)
O Finis et Felícitas! (O Purpose and [O] Happiness!)
Tu Christe (You O Christ)
Tu lux (You [O] light)
Princeps gloriosíssime (O most glorious Prince)
Dux invictíssime (O most invincible Leader)
Deus et Pater ([O] God and Father)
O Sancte Angele (O Holy Angel)
Alma Mater ([O] Kind Mother)

Angele (O Angel)
Ave María (Hail ([O] Mary)
Virgo María ([O] Virgin Mary)
O Dómina María (O Lady Mary)
Ave Regína (Hail [O] Queen)
O bone Iesu (O good Jesus)
Benígne Cónditor (O Merciful Creator)
Beáta Trínitas ([O] Blessed Trinity)
Simplex Unítas ([O] Single Unity)
Rex Christe clementíssime (O most merciful Christ [the] King)
Ave augustíssima Regína (Hail [O] most august Queen)
O piíssima Virgo María (O most pious Virgin Mary)
O clemens, O pia, O dulcis Virgo María (O clement, O pious, O sweet Virgin Mary)
Sancta María ([O] Holy Mary)
Ave Mater dolorósa (Hail [O] sorrowful Mother)
O María (O Mary)
Ave Dómina (Hail [O] Lady)
Virgo gloriósa ([O] glorious Virgin)
O valde decóra (O exceeding graces)
Miséricors Deus ([O] Merciful God)
Ave verum Corpus natum (Hail [O] true Body born)
O Iesu dulcis (O sweet Jesus)
O Iesu pie (O pious Jesus)

not only are there distinct 'either/or' nom/voc options, but layers of 'both/and' meanings. **Domina María** - [O] Lady Mary, for example, is both/and nom/voc, and even when it is preceded with the vocative particle 'O' more strongly signalling a vocative function, we can't simply ignore the fact that **Domina** is both/and nom/voc. We may not consciously bring these layers to mind in order to read the text, but how much more depth might we gain when we do bring them to mind when we pray, if only, as in these examples, to add emphasis and force to the mystery of who we are praying to? Similarly in a phrase like *O Iesu pie*, where both *Iesu* and *pie* are inflected as vocatives, the vocative particle is usually considered as 'simply' adding emphasis, as it is already implicit in the inflection, but consider praying an English version which says: 'O, O Jesus, O blessed', all of which is already there in the Latin, and more than just linguistic emphasis is given. Our calling out to Jesus is repeated three times. That repetition layers the meanings of the grammar of these words and turns a Latin text into a more layered prayer. This process of going beyond the words themselves in this way might strike some as stretching the language too far, but that is exactly what we do when we pray. We stretch the language beyond the ordinary within every aspect of the text-context dynamic.

Each one of these forms of address in the examples above may be prayed as a separate prayer, or combined together in various ways. The grammatical form of address, whether distinctively nominative or vocative in form, or 'both/and' nom/voc, reinforces the distance that exists between pray-er and prayed-to. We are often taught that prayer should be about lessening the distance between us and God, but being increasingly conscious of that distance, and foregrounding it within our prayer, rather than hoping our prayer decreases it, must surely heighten our awareness of the awe and majesty that is God. It may be considered generally easier to simply pray such forms as vocatives, and this is usually how they are translated, especially in the *litanies*, but having before us this idea of layering in grammar in this way, potentially lifts the language of prayer into a quite different arena.

But more than just nom/voc layering, as we have seen here, there is a structure in most of these phrases which is based on a noun + adjective (and variations) where the adjective (adj) describes the noun by giving more information about it and its attributes, thereby providing increased focus upon that noun. In Latin, the adjective must agree not only with its noun in case and gender (m/f/n) but also in number (sg/pl). For example a single male/female saint is described with a singular masculine/feminine adjective (nom: *sanctus/sancta*; voc: *sancte/*

sancta) and a plural masculine/feminine adjective (nom: *sancti/sanctae*; voc: *sancti/sanctae*) as in ***Omnes sancti Monachi et Eremitae*** (m pl [O] All holy Monks and Hermits) and ***Omnes sanctae Virgines et Viduae*** (f pl [O] All holy Virgins and Widows) with the adjectives agreeing with the nouns in grammatical gender (m/f/n) and in grammatical case (nom or voc). So, in this heavily edited selection from the ***Litaniae Sanctorum*** (Litanies of Saints):

> ***Omnes sancti Angeli et Archángeli*** (nom/voc) [O] All holy Angels and Archangels
> ***Omnes sancti Apóstoli et Evangelístae*** (nom/voc) [O] All holy Apostles and Evangelists
> ***Omnes sancti Discípuli*** (nom/voc) [O] All holy Disciples
> ***Omnes sancti Innocéntes*** (nom/voc) [O] All holy Innocents
> ***Sancti Fabiánus et Sebastiánus/Sancti Fabiáne et Sebastiáne*** (nom/voc) [O]/O Sts Fabian and Sebastian
> ***Sancti Ioánnes et Paulus/Sancti Ioánnes et Paule*** (nom/voc) [O]/O Sts John and Paul
> ***Sancti Cosmas et Damiánus/Sancti Cosma et Damiáne*** (nom/voc) [O]/O Sts Cosmas and Damian
> ***Sancti Gervásius et Protásius /Sancti Gervási et Protási*** (nom/voc) [O]/O Sts Gervase and Protase
> ***Omnes sancti Mártyres*** (nom/voc) [O] All holy Martyrs
> ***Omnes sancti Pontífices et Confessóres*** (nom/voc) [O] All holy Popes and Confessors
> ***Omnes sancti Doctóres*** (nom/voc) [O] All holy Doctors
> ***Omnes sancti Sacerdótes et Levítae*** (nom/voc) [O] All holy Priests and Levites
> ***Omnes sancti Mónachi et Eremítae*** (nom/voc) [O] All holy Monks and Hermits
> ***Omnes sanctae Vírgines et Víduae*** (nom/voc) [O] All holy Virgins and Widows

we can clearly see that the agreement (concord) involved between the nouns and adjectives not only adds another layer of linguistic meaning to the texts, so that, for example, the adjectives *omnes* and *sancti* agree in case, number and gender with the nouns *Angeli et Archangeli*, but, as prayers, such concord functions at another, more spiritual, layer. When we pray *omnes Angeli et Archangeli* we have to think about everything we might know about angels and what *omnes* might actually signify. When we pray *Omnes sancti Angeli et Archangeli* we have to think about everything that *sancti* might signify. We inevitably have to consider the text-context dynamic in prayer, even the seemingly most simple, like these entries in the *litanies*. In ordinary language we might not think too much about such things, but the more we think about them in prayer, the more meditative that prayer is likely to be. This observation is simply, though very importantly, recognising that prayer is not ordinary. Learning the Latin of Latin prayer is not, then, the same as learning the Latin of Caesar's *Gallic Wars*, even though they are written in basically the same language. Discursively they are radically different.

New and Old Information

The Knights Templar, much popularised in fiction and film, and not always favourably, were officially dissolved in the 14[th]C as a military Order seeking the return of the Holy Land to the Catholic Church through various crusades. When imprisoned a Knight would begin a long prayer with:

> *Dómine, Iesu Christe, sancte Pater, aetérne Deus, omnípotens, sápiens creátor, largítor, administrátor benígnus, et caríssimus amátor, pius et húmilis redémptor, clemens, miséricors salvátor, Dómine...*

(O Lord, Jesus Christ, O Holy Father, O eternal God, [O] omnipotent, wise creator, imparter, kind ruler and most tender lover, pious and humble redeemer; gentle, merciful saviour, O Lord...)

We see in phrases like **sancte Pater, aeterne Deus, sapiens creator, administrator benignus, carissimus amator, pius redemptor,** and **misericors salvator,** that the adjective attributes new information about Jesus, Father and God. In the beautifully simple prayer: **Virgo gloriósa** we see that the adjective **gloriosa** modifying **Virgo** brings that noun into much greater focus by attributing new information about the 'Virgin' being 'glorious'. But more than that, the relational dynamic between the same nominative and vocative forms **Virgo** and **gloriosa** offers a more emphatic means of praying this as simultaneously both '[the] glorious Virgin' and '[O] glorious Virgin'. So too in:

O clemens, O pia, O dulcis Virgo María, Sancta María

where the nom/voc nouns **Virgo** and **Maria** are made to function very specifically as forms of vocative address with the addition of the vocative particle 'O', and are attributed new information, and therefore vocative focus, by the nom/voc/f adjectives **clemens** (clement) *pia* (pious) **dulcis** (sweet) and **Sancta** (Holy). In Latin each adjective describing/modifying a noun must also reflect its gender, but the adjective itself is not gendered. It agrees with its noun. For example in **Pater aeternus** (eternal Father) the adjective **aeternus** actually signals the masculine singular noun **Pater** as nominative. But in **Pater aeterne** (O eternal Father) the adjective **aeterne** signals **Pater** as vocative. This may seem overly elementary to anyone who has learnt any Latin, but what we don't tend to learn, when learning Latin grammar like this, is to consider the impact of the 'both/and' dynamic, rather than just seeing it as an 'either/or'. So in **Deus Pater aeterne** the adjective **aeterne** agrees with the noun **Pater** as vocative, but while there is no ambiguity as to whether ***Pater*** is functioning in a vocative way, there is ambiguity about whether it is modifying ***Deus*** or ***Pater*** or both. Is it 'O eternal Father'; 'O eternal God' or 'O eternal [O] Father [O] God'? Or is it all of them at the same time? A 'both/and' nom/voc? Seen in this way, this offers a much more layered depth of meaning, which, given the whole point and purpose of prayer, focussed as it is on God who is all layers in one at all times, then this approach would seem a valuable one. For example, in ***Virgo gloriosa benedicta*** the adjectives ***gloriosa*** and ***benedicta*** agree with the nom/voc feminine, singular noun ***Virgo*** as 'both/and' nom/voc, so offering more layered meanings:

The blessed, glorious Virgin
O blessed, glorious Virgin
O Virgin, the blessed [and] glorious
O Virgin, O blessed [and] O glorious

The grammar may be prayed with all of these potential layered meanings combined, and that, in prayer, adds considerable focus to what appears to be just a few simple words and bits of grammar. But there are no 'just simple words and bits of grammar' in Latin prayer, when that prayer is specifically designed for, and aimed at, achieving spiritual *affect*. When St Augustine asks in Book 1, Chapter 4 of his ***Confessiones*** (Confessions) written in Latin between 397 and 400 and probably one of the most influential texts of Catholic spirituality ever produced:

Quid es ergo Deus meus? (What therefore are [you] [O] my God?)

the ***Deus meus*** may be read as 'both/and' nom/voc calling out to God as vocative address but at the same time functioning as a *declaration* of God in nominative address. The thrust of the prayer is not 'either/or' but 'both/and'. We name/declare and call out to God simultaneously. St Augustine then goes on to describe God as:

> *summe, optime, potentissime, omnipotentissime,*
> *misericordissime et iustissime, secretissime et praesentissime,*
> *pulcherrime et fortissime*
>
> (O most high, O most supreme, O most powerful, O most omnipotent; O most merciful and O most just; O most secret and O most present; O most beautiful and O most strong)

where every one of these adjectives adds new information about the nom/voc **Deus meus**; that God is powerful, beautiful and strong, and so on. But more than that, they all function specifically as vocatives of address, all of them invoking God, while at the same time focussing on some of the qualities and attributes of God. But even more than that, St Augustine uses a superlative form of each adjective, repeating the form in a seemingly relentless show of vocative force which emphasises just how reliant we are upon God being anything but 'ordinary'. There are layers of meanings involved. In Sunday *Matins* we pray:

> *Tu autem, Dómine, suscéptor meus es, glória mea, et exáltans caput meum.*
>
> (But you, O Lord, are my protector, my glory, and elevating my head. *Ps* 3:4)

where we acknowledge God with a vocative **Domine** and reinforce it with the simple nominative phrases **susceptor meus** and **gloria mea**. We continue:

> *Voce mea ad Dóminum clamávi: et exaudívit me de monte sancto suo.*
>
> (With my voice I called to [the] Lord: and he heeded me from his holy mountain. *Ps* 3:5)

We can easily recognise the different grammatical functions (voc **Domine** for example) once we have learnt how to do this in Latin, but the nominatives *susceptor meus*, *gloria mea*, and the ablative *de monte sancto suo*, require a lot more work to understand anagogically. So too verbs like *exaltans* and *exaudivit*. On the linguistic surface we might consider *clamavi* a straightforward verb 'I called', but to call to God? That takes a lot more thinking about. Similarly with *exaudivit.* It is linguistically straightforward but what is actually involved anagogically in a phrase like God 'heeded' me'? In prayer, we have no choice but to go beyond the grammar and words, because the grammar and words do not hold within them all of the meanings about God, for example, that we seek and need. Such things are beyond surface understanding. When we read in Caesar's *Gallic Wars*:

> *Gallia est omnis divisa in partes tres* (All Gaul is divided into three parts)

probably one of the very first sentences a student of Classical Latin might read, we need to go beyond the surface and engage with its text-context to know what Gaul is, and then why Caesar is talking about it, and where it is, what the three parts are and where they might be relative to each other and so on. But in a prayer where we describe God as three in one, things are not quite so straightforward:

> *quia tres sunt qui testimónium dant in caelo, Pater et Verbum et Spíritus Sanctus, et hi tres unum sunt.*
> (for [there] are three who give witness in heaven, Father and Word and Holy Spirit, and these three are one.)

This powerful and influential assertion of God as Trinity, given as a means of countering heresy in Canon 2 ***De Errore Abbatis Ioachim*** (Concerning the Error of Abbot Joachim) in the Fourth Ecumenical (Lateran) Council (1215) called by Pope Innocent III (1160-1216) is linguistically much the same as Caesar's description of Gaul, but theologically (and therefore doctrinally and prayerfully) dramatically more complicated. Over many centuries before this Council, and many centuries since, the Catholic Church has affirmed this understanding of what the simple word *tres* means in this context. That process of consideration, reflection, affirmation and acceptance is part of the Tradition of the Church. Such an affirmation is informed by, and of itself informs, and forms, Tradition, and this must always be part of the process of praying the text of Latin prayer in a Latin Catholic context: going far beyond just words on a page.

Patrimony and Tradition

Consider the following prayers from the ***Litaniae Sancti Ioseph*** (Litanies of St Joseph):

> *Sancte Ioseph* (O St Joseph)
> *Ioseph iustíssime* (O Joseph most just)
> *Ioseph castíssime* (O Joseph most chaste)
> *Ioseph prudentíssime* (O Joseph most prudent)
> *Ioseph fortíssime* (O Joseph most strong)
> *Ioseph oboedientíssime* (O Joseph most obedient)
> *Ioseph fidelíssime* (O Joseph most faithful)

These are strong signals of vocative address where the noun by itself is not. But they do not explain why St Joseph is attributed with the new information of being *iustissimus* or *oboedientissimus*, for example. This is information developed out of Tradition. Similarly, in various parts of the liturgy (as follows) for the Feast of Christ the King (***Christus Rex***) we pray:

> ***Christus Rex*** (Christ [the] King)
> ***Doctor, Sacérdos, Légifer*** (Doctor, Priest, Lawgiver)
> ***Omnípotens sempitérne Deus*** (O Almighty everlasting God)
> ***Aetérna Imágo*** (Eternal Image)

Lumen Deus (God [the] Light)
Pater Suprémus (Supreme Father)
Rex altíssimus (Most high King)
Omnípotens et Miséricors Dóminus (Almighty and Merciful Lord)

The adjectives assign various attributes and characteristics to their nouns. ***Rex*** (King) for example is ***altissimus*** (a most high) King. But there is more to these phrases than just acknowledgement, recognition, naming or calling. The adjectives connect us into the whole history of the Church and its worship, liturgical practices, dogma, doctrine, theology, philosophy and Tradition, which adds yet another anagogical layer of *focus* and *force* to the way these phrases mean, thereby increasing their layered spiritual *affect*. Tradition, as it is understood in Latin Catholicism (and always capitalised) is not simply a clinging onto old ways, or a set of ideas, rituals and beliefs, the vibrancy of which might seem irrelevant to developing new ways, but is best understood in the way that St Paul instructed the Thessalonians:

itaque fratres state et tenete traditiones quas didicistis sive per sermonem sive per epistulam nostram
(and so brothers stand! and hold! the traditions which you learnt either through discussion or through our letter *2 Thess* 2:15)

where the Latin word ***traditio*** signifies 'teaching'; 'instruction'; 'saying'; 'record' or 'account'. The word itself comes from the verb ***tradere*** - 'to hand down'; 'deliver'; 'transmit'; 'impart'; 'entrust'; 'confide'; 'leave behind'; 'teach'; 'propound'; 'narrate' and 'recount'. 'Tradition' understood in these very layered senses of all these definitions rolled into one within Latin Catholicism begins, then, with the very first teachings of Christ himself, and then with the teachings of those he entrusts the keys of the Church to, beginning with St Peter. So, when St Augustine at the end of Book 1, Chapter 4 of his *Confessions* states, very simply, but quite beautifully:

DAVID BIRCH

Deus meus, vita mea, dulcedo mea sancta.

we might ask how might this mean *in English*, and probably answer with a translation like:

My God, my life, my holy sweetness.

But in Latin prayer this is not the question we should be asking. We should ask how might this mean *in Latin*? And the options are for several layered meanings all wrapped up together in 7 Latin words:

O my God, O my life, O my holy sweetness
My God, O my life, O my holy sweetness
My God, my life, O my holy sweetness
My God, my life, my holy sweetness
O my God, my life, my holy sweetness
O my God, my life, O my holy sweetness

where each layer is focussing on God as the means of identifying the 'me' in the prayer as meaning nothing, unless understood in terms of the 'life', 'holiness' and 'sweetness' that only God can provide. But we really can only reach this conclusion about our relationship with God, when seen in this way, by going beyond the text itself into the context from which this text emerged. The simple linguistic option would be to provide an 'either/or' translation here, but all of these multiple options of meaning are all there simultaneously ('both/and') as we pray the Latin. They are embedded and layered into the Latin text in a way that they are not in an English translation, and that is a very powerful spiritual dynamic. If we have to translate the Latin for a formal reason, then inevitably we need to decide on one single translation, but we don't need to do this when we pray. We can hold all of these multiple layers together as one, just as we hold together, in a layered way, both

Scripture and Tradition as part of the overall Catholic dynamic of what it means to be a Christian.

Much of the dynamism of Latin prayer is simply an extension of this idea of layered meanings. The six approved litanies for public worship, for example, are a good example of the way layer upon layer of meaning builds our sense of the spiritual and Divine. In the ***Litaniae ad Deum Patrem*** (Litanies to God the Father) for example, ***Pater Deus*** is not simply named in the *Litanies* as 'God [the]Father'. There is a very developed theology which positions (and layers) God in numerous ways: as ***Pater luminum*** ([O]Father of lights) ***Pater vivificans*** ([O] life-giving Father) ***Pater videns in abscondito*** ([O] Father seeing within darkness) ***Pater orphanorum et iudex viduarum*** ([O] Father of orphans and justice of widows) ***Pater benigne, patiens, et multae misericordiae*** (O Kind Father, patient, and of much mercy) and ***Agricola usque modo operans*** ([O]Farmer working until now) to name just a few, each assigning to God the Father, through these adjectives, many different functions and layers of attributes. Each of these functions and attributes has been carefully thought through in the theology and doctrine that is at the heart of Scripture, but which has also developed in Latin Catholicism since (and during) Apostolic times: its Tradition. Each name, as set out in these *litanies*, signifies a theology from which these various attributes for God the Father emerge. The theology here is unseen, as it were. It sits in the background, just as layered grammatical meanings may do. But it is as much a part of the vocative-nominative dynamic and meaning of the prayer as the words themselves. Theology (once known as 'The Queen of Sciences') is written into every single Latin word of Latin prayer. Similarly, in the following extract from the ***Litaniae Dominae Nostrae Dolorum*** (Litanies of Our Lady of Sorrows) approved for private prayer only, we pray:

Sancta Maria ([O] Holy Mary)
Mater crucifixa ([O] Mother crucified)

Mater dolorósa ([O] Mother sorrowful)
Mater lacrimósa ([O] Mother tearful)
Mater afflícta ([O] Mother afflicted)
Mater derelícta ([O] Mother forsaken)
Mater desoláta ([O] Mother desolate)
Mater orbáta ([O] Mother bereft)
Mater transverberáta ([O] Mother pierced
Mater confécta ([O] Mother consumed [with grief])
Mater repléta ([O] Mother filled [with anguish])
Mater affíxa ([O] Mother attached [to the cross])
Mater maestíssima ([O] Mother most sad)

All of the adjectives modify **Mater** and build layers of meaning about how we understand **Mater**. This is not pointless repetition, as some in the Church might now suggest, where the praying of *litanies* is now almost non-existent in many **usus recentior** parishes, but nuanced layering. Each adjective is not just making interesting meanings, but *interested* meanings; 'interested' in the sense that they are part of Catholic Tradition and the developed understanding of Our Lady and her role in our redemption and our sought-for salvation, and all the Catholic sensibilities that go with that.

Consider then how this 'interestedness' signifies and reflects (and indeed may add to) the *magisterial force* that lies behind the composition of the following prayers, made up of phrases which occur across a wide range of Latin prayer and scriptural texts. Think also about how *motivated* and *situated* these texts are as prayers within the Catholic context in which they now occur, and have occurred throughout the often very long time of their development into Tradition, and the many centuries in which these words have been prayed, and by the millions of people, some of whom are now declared Saints, who have prayed them. There are distinct options of linguistic meaning, but richer than that could ever be, there is an unplumbable depth of anagogical possibilities in the layered spaces and processes we go through when transforming them from *reading* to *praying* in Latin. Consider the various English translations possible, only one of which is given below, but go further than that, and consider the multiple layered meanings that may be possible when these texts are prayed in Latin. Pray more than the words. Pray the Latin grammar. And pray the patrimony and Tradition of their Catholic contexts.

Anima mea (my Soul)
Ave María (Hail Mary)
Beáta María (Blessed Mary)
Beáta Mater (Blessed Mother)
Beáta Mater et intácta Virgo (Blessed Mother and chaste Virgin)
Beáta Regína (Blessed Queen)
Beáta Trínitas (Blessed Trinity)
Beáta Virgo (Blessed Virgin)
Beáta Virgo María (Blessed Virgin Mary)
Bona Mater (Good Mother)
Bónitas infiníta (infinite Goodness)
Cáritas infiníta (infinite Love)
Clemens, pia, dulcis Virgo María (Gentle, pious, sweet Virgin Mary)
Defénsor noster (our Defender)
Deus meus (my God)
Deus meus et omnía (my God and all)
Deus Pater omnípotens (God almighty Father)
Deus unus (one God)
Dómina Regína (Lady Queen)
Dulcis parens (Sweet parent [in reference to Our Lady])
Gloriósa Regína (Glorious Queen)
Latens Déitas (Invisible/hidden Deity)
Liberátor meus (my Liberator)
Lux beáta (blessed Light)
María Mater (Mother Mary)

María virgo (virgin Mary)
María sanctíssima (Mary most holy)
María, virgo et Mater sanctíssima (Mary, most holy virgin and Mother)
Mater María (Mother Mary)
Mater mea, María sanctíssima (my Mother, most holy Mary)
Mater beatíssima Virgo María (most blessed Mother Virgin Mary)
Omnes Sancti (All Saints)
Pater aetérnus (eternal Father)
Pater Deus (God [the]Father)
Pater noster (our Father)
Pia Deítas, treménda maiéstas (Gracious Deity, awe-inspiring majesty)
Protéctor meus Deus (my Protector God)
Prudéntes vírgines (wise virgins)
Rector potens (mighty Ruler)
Rector potens, verax Deus (mighty Ruler, true God)
Redémptor amábilis (loveable Redeemer)
Redémptor et Deus (Redeemer and God)
Sacrum convívium (Sacred banquet)
Sancta María (Holy Mary)
Sancta Mater María (Holy Mother Mary)
Sancta Trínitas (Holy Trinity)
Sancta Trínitas, Pater et Filius et Spíritus Sanctus (Holy Trinity, Father and Son and Holy Ghost)
Sancti Patriárchae et Prophétae (Holy Patriarchs and Prophets)
Spíritus semper (Spirit forever)
Summa Déitas (Supreme Deity)
Suscéptor meus (my Protector)
Trina Déitas (Triune Deity)
Una Trínitas (One Trinity)

Verax Deus (True God)
Virgo gloriósa (glorious Virgin)
Virgo gloriósa et benedícta (glorious and blessed Virgin)
Virgo perpétua (perpetual Virgin)
Virgo sacráta (sanctified Virgin)
*Virgo sanctíssima, spes mea, María (*most holy Virgin, my hope, Mary)

These are not complex and difficult texts. They are linguistically simple; easy to learn and easy to say. But they are incredibly complex, both theologically and doctrinally, and though the Latin is simple and may be dismissed by some as too simple to be worth much attention, they are extraordinarily complex to pray, especially in a layered way. But, if there is any ambiguity about meaning, we need to include that ambiguity in our prayer. Ambiguity is not something to be wary of, especially in prayer, so long as it does not change or challenge the revealed truths that are at the heart of Catholicism. Ambiguity often contributes to the ever-changing spiritual demands that in prayer we must always be searching for; always focussing upon the multiple (layered) meanings both in and beyond the words themselves, in order to determine the one infinitely layered meaning of God himself. Multiple, layered, meanings require a changed mindset; a re-oriented *habitus*; a dispositional change, perhaps, in the way we pray. And it is not just in words and grammar we find these layered meanings. In the simple phrases **Sancta Attracta** (6[th]C) and **Sancte Brendane** (484-577) for example, we might categorise such multiple (layered) meanings as follows:

- *textual/lexical meaning*: 'Attracta' the woman; 'Brendan' the man
- *grammatical meaning*: nominative or vocative or 'both/and' when we pray [O] *Attrácta*; O *Brendáne*
- *attributive meaning*: adding new information with an adjective when we pray: **Sancta Attrácta; Sancte Brendáne**

- *syntactic meaning*: where the order of the words may shift the focus of meaning. Is the position of the adjective initial (beginning) medial (middle) or final (end)? If this position is changed, for example when we pray: **Sancta Attrácta** to **Attrácta Sancta** or **Deus unus** to **unus Deus** or **Virgo sacráta** to *sacráta Virgo*, while it means the same grammatically, is there any other way the meaning may have changed because the word order has changed?
- *iterative meaning*: where words or phrases are repeated, thereby creating an additional force of meaning, as in the repetition of Saint after Saint in the *litanies*, and also in the repetition of the same grammatical pattern. Such repetition, as a way of making meaning, is central to all Latin prayer.
- *contextual meaning*: listing St Attracta and St Brendan amongst the Saints of Ireland for example.
- *spiritual meaning*: positioning St Attracta and St Brendan as Saints in heaven who by their prayers can intercede for us.

The force of all of these multiple meanings, amongst others, are vested here in just two simple Latin phrases: **Sancta Attracta** and **Sancte Brendane** coming together as single prayers: **Sancta Attrácta** and **Sancte Brendáne**, for the ultimate purpose of praising God through his Saints. Latin prayer, though always layered in multiple meanings, does not need to be complicated and linguistically difficult to be effective and to *affect*. Christ himself taught us this. When one of the disciples asked him:

Domine, doce nos orare, sicut docuit et Ioannes discipulos suos.
(O Lord, teach! us to pray, just as John taught his disciples *Lc* 11:1)

Jesus replies saying:

> *Cum oratis, dicite: Pater, sanctificetur nomen tuum.*
> (When you pray, say!: Father, hallowed be your name. *Lc* 11:2)

Nothing could be simpler, and yet so theologically complex. *Psalm* 2, prayed at Sunday (and Feast day) *Matins,* has at its heart the relationship between Father and Son. The Son repeats what the Father has told him, saying:

> *Dóminus dixit ad me: Fílius meus es tu; ego hódie génui te.*
> ([The] Lord said to me: you are my Son; today I begot you. *Ps* 2:7)

The nominative-vocative force here lies not just in the words themselves, but in the fact that they were words initially uttered by God the Father and now repeated by God the Son. That takes some thinking about. Linguistically it all looks so simple, so much so that we could just skim over the words without a passing thought. But what they actually signify is God the Father talking to the Son of God, and then the Son of God talking to us. That is not something we should be skimming over by any stretch of the imagination. These are words designed to spiritually *affect*. We then continue to pray:

> *Póstula a me, et dabo tibi gentes haereditátem tuam, et possessiónem tuam términos terrae.*
> (Ask from me, and I will give to you the nations [for] your inheritance, and the ends of the earth [for] your possession. *Ps* 2:8)

The Father is saying to the Son something like 'ask of me that which I want to give you'. This is the theology of prayer in a nutshell. These are not just words to be repeated unthinkingly; the theology has impact; it has *affect*.

DAVID BIRCH

Vocative Affect

Prayer is meant to affect *us* the pray-er. It will not, nor could ever, affect the one to whom we pray. Consider, then, the potential spiritual affect of the following selection from a wide range of Latin prayers. There may be shared affect amongst groups of people, of course, but even when in public worship, we bring to bear upon the meanings we make from the language and contexts before us, our own **habitus** and awareness, even though that may be shaped in large degree by others, and in this context, by Tradition and the shared teachings and truths of the Church. But, at the end of the day, and chief amongst Catholic sensibilities, as St John Henry Newman so powerfully recognised and wrote about in his 1864 ***Apologia pro Vita Sua*** (Defence for his Life) is the indisputable maxim that nothing should be allowed to come between the soul and its creator God. He writes:

> 'It is face to face, ***solus cum solo***, in all matters between man and his God, He alone creates; He alone has redeemed; before His awful eyes we go in death; in the vision of Him is our eternal beatitude.'

Solus cum solo ('alone with alone', ie the soul 'all alone') signifying not desolation of the individual person, but the fact that our soul is always alone before what St John Henry calls 'the incommunicable glory of the Eternal'. Our soul is laid bare and alone before God. How much more comfort, then, does the embrace of the Catholic Church and its treasure house of prayer bring to us standing alone, housing within it the boundless patrimony of Latin prayer? We will all of us pray these prayers in some similar and some different ways. For those who might consider this too simple a Latin to spend so much time on, I would say: think beyond the language and take on board the anagogical:

> ***Ah! Dómine mi*** (Oh! my Lord)
> ***Amantíssime Iesu, Redémptor et Deus*** (O most loving Jesus, Redeemer and God)

LATIN PRAYER

Amantíssime Pater (O most loving Father)
O caelístis médice et comes fidelíssime Sancte Ráphael
(O heavenly doctor and most faithful companion Holy Raphael)
Amor mi (O my love)
Benígne Cónditor (O Merciful Creator)
Bone pastor, panis vere (O good shepherd, O true bread)
Christe Deus noster (O Christ our God)
Christe, Redémptor (O Christ, [O] Redeemer)
Clementíssime Deus (O most merciful God)
Clementíssime Dominátor, Redémptor noster
(O most merciful Lord, [O] our Redeemer)
Clementíssime Pater (O most merciful Father)
Custos et pater, Sancte Ioseph ([O] guardian and father, O Saint Joseph)
Dómine (O Lord)
Dómine Deus (O Lord [O] God)
Dómine Deus Omnípotens (O Lord God Almighty)
Dómine Deus Rex Salvátor (O Lord God Saviour King)
Dómine Iesu (O Lord Jesus)
Dómine Iesu Christe (O Lord Jesus Christ)
Dómine, Iesu Christe, Rex aetérne, Deus et homo
(O Lord, Jesus Christ, eternal King, God and man)
Dómine, sancte Pater, omnípotens aetérne Deus
(O Lord, holy Father almighty eternal God)
Dulcíssime Dómine Iesu (O most sweet Lord Jesus)
Dulcíssime Dómine Iesu Christe (O most sweet Lord Jesus Christ)
Magne sancte Pater Deus (O great holy God [the] Father)
Mitíssime Deus (O most tender God)
Nunc Sancte Spíritus (Now O Holy Spirit)
O bone et dulcíssime Iesu (O good and most sweet Jesus)
O bone Iesu (O good Jesus)
O felix vir, beáte Ioseph (O happy man, O blessed Joseph)

O Iesu (O Jesus)
O lux beáta (O blessed light)
O pia Déitas, O treménda máiestas (O gracious Deity, O awe-inspiring majesty)
O Rex divine, O Iesu dulcíssime (O divine King, O sweetest Jesus)
O vere beáta nox (O truly blessed night)
Omnípotens Deus sempitérne (O everlasting almighty God)
Omnípotens sempitérne Deus (O almighty everlasting God)
Panis candidíssime (O purest Bread)
Panis dulcíssime (O sweetest Bread)
Panis sancte, Panis vive, Panis munde (O holy Bread, O living Bread, O pure Bread)
Pater caeléstis, clementíssime Pater (O heavenly Father, most merciful Father)
Pater piíssime (O most gracious Father)
Pater sancte (O holy Father)
Piíssime Dómine (O most gracious Lord)
Salvátor Iesu bone (O good Jesus Saviour)
Sancte Benedícte (O Saint Benedict)
Sancte Dómine Deus (O holy Lord God)
Sancte Dómine Iesu (O holy Lord Jesus)
Sancte Dómine Iesu Christe (O holy Lord Jesus Christ)
Sancte Ioseph (O Saint Joseph)
Sancte Micháel Archángeli (O Saint Michael the Archangel)
Sancte Pater Deus (O holy God [the] Father)
Sancte Spíritus (O Holy Spirit)
Sancti Patriárchae et Prophétae (Holy Patriarchs and Prophets)
Summe Sacérdos et vere Póntifex, Iesu Christ (O High Priest and true Pontiff, Jesus Christ)
Tu, Dómine omnípotens (You, O Lord almighty)

These phrases are not simply addressing/calling out to the Lord invoking him through their adjectives as ***dulcissime*** (most sweet) or ***omnipotens*** (almighty). They also signify that these attributes and characteristics are drawn from a theological/Christological world well beyond any that we are a part of in our normal daily lives. Each one of these simple prayers could take a lifetime of reflection and never be fully grasped. Each one of these simple prayers could provide enough material for a life time of spiritual retreats. There is a force of scripture, history and Catholic Tradition which demonstrates, through the adjectives alone in these prayers, that they do far more than describe something linguistically, they can *affect* us spiritually. For example, a woman of Canaan who sought help for her daughter called out to Jesus:

> *Miserere mei, Domine fili David: filia mea male a daemonio vexatur.*
> (Be merciful! to me, O Lord son of David: my daughter is badly disturbed by a demon. *Mt* 15:22)

But she received no answer, and so a little later on she cries out to him:

> *Domine, adiuva me*
> (O Lord, help me. *Mt* 15:25)

This time Jesus responds to her and says:

> *O mulier, magna est fides tua: fiat tibi sicut vis. Et sanata est filia eius ex illa hora.*
> (O woman, great is your faith: be it done to you as you wish. And her daughter was cured from that hour.' (*Mt* 15:28)

The text of the noun ***Domine*** tells us it is a form of vocative address and ***mulier*** tells us the same, not because the noun changes its form but because it is preceded in the Latin version with the vocative particle

'O'. But Jesus is not simply calling out to the woman to gain her attention, as if she were far away. In Latin this form of vocative address with a particle more often than not signals intimacy. Jesus is expressing emotion towards the woman who, being from Canaan, would normally not be paid attention to at all in Jesus' day by the more culturally dominant Jews. What then appears to be a very simple, and even unnecessary emphatic addition 'O' to the form of vocative address here, has an added extra layer of very subtle, but powerful, intimate meaning. Jesus focuses on this woman by his form of vocative address preceded by 'O' which, with its highly significant cultural force, will, therefore, (and does) greatly affect the woman. Similarly, in a different context, St James calls out:

> ***Vis autem scire, O homo inanis, quoniam fides sine operibus mortua est?***
> (But wish you to know, O vain man, that faith without works is dead? *Iac* 2:20)

The context would normally tell us that the noun ***homo*** (man) is a form of vocative address, but the inclusion of the 'O' makes it much more personal, as if St James has personal knowledge of this man, and so is deliberately making his words more forceful and resonant for the affect they might have on him. Likewise, when St Paul is on board a ship en route to Rome and addresses the men on board frightened by the storm and raging seas, he says:

> ***O viri, audito me, non tollere a Creta, lucrique facere iniuriam hanc et iacturam.***
> (O men, having heard me, not to depart from Crete, and [now] to gain this injury and hurt. *Ac* 27:21)

using the vocative form ***viri*** which is much more personal with the particle 'O' than when he addressed them earlier by more simply saying:

> *Viri, video quoniam cum iniuria et multo damno non solum oneris, et navis, sed etiam animarum nostrarum incipit esse navigatio.*
>
> ([O] Men, for I see the voyage begins to be with injury and much damage not only of the load, and of the ship, but also of our souls. *Ac* 27:10)

When he uses the 'O', St Paul is not simply emphasising the growing danger of their situation, but is seeking to be emotionally supportive; to intimately *affect* the men, just as when Jesus says **O mulier** or St James says **O homo inanis**. This appears to be a very simple bit of grammar, and easily glossed over, but it is one which perhaps suggests we need to be able to read (and pray) the text-context dynamic, and not just the words, and then to reflect on the affect that they might have upon us.

Understood in this way, then, prayer is more than just saying the words, it is praying the spaces in between those words, and those spaces may be filled with multiple meanings from the patrimony and Tradition of the Church. We need to pray the Latin words, but we also need to pray beyond these words and their grammatical forms and functions. We need to be able to read between the lines. We need to be able to pray between the lines. We need to pray anagogically (as well as linguistically) the multiple (layered) meanings these texts are capable of making through the grace of the Holy Spirit who is the One who calls us to the very act of prayer in the first place. We need to competently read the linguistic surface, but to use that competence to lead us towards praying the deep structure. So, for example, when, on the Feast (December 21) of St Thomas the Apostle (d 72AD) St Thomas is finally convinced that Jesus really has risen from the dead, we pray with him:

> *Dóminus meus et Deus meus.*
>
> (My Lord and my God. *Io* 20:28)

We might expect the vocative form of address to be used here: **_Domine mi_** (O my Lord) to attract Jesus' attention, but the nominative form **_Dominus meus_** is used. The context of the situation, where St Thomas has expressed serious doubts about Jesus rising from the dead, would suggest that this is not simply St Thomas calling out to Jesus, but in addressing him in this way with the nominative form we, as readers of the *Vulgate*, are being encouraged to see St Thomas as actually acknowledging him; recognising him at last, and nominatively *declaring* him as *the* risen Lord; as 'my Lord and my God'. St Thomas subsequently ceases to doubt Christ's resurrection from the dead, as he does here, and he does so with a tiny bit of grammar. The nominative **_Dominus_** in the *Vulgate* version of this event *both* becomes a statement of recognition, acceptance and submission *and* a form of address as well.

This is made even more powerful by the fact that in the various Greek versions of the *New Testament* which Doctor of the Church St Jerome (of Stridon 342-420) had before him as he translated the *Vulgate*, this is the only time that the equivalent nominative form κύριος (Lord) is used. Every other time Jesus is addressed in this way the Greek text uses the vocative form κύριε (still used in *Litanies* and the Mass as *Kyrie eleison* [O Lord have mercy]). The Latin nominative form may appear to be innocent in the text, but the context suggests otherwise. Its affect is to declare Christ as Lord in a way that St Thomas had been reluctant to do before. It is a *motivated* moment because its utterance by St Thomas suddenly turns a reunion into the realisation of redemption. It is *momentous*, as a moment now *situated* in what the *Catechism* calls **_Oeconomia salutis_** (the economy of salvation). Redemption (**_redemptio_**) and salvation (**_salvatio_**) form part of the revealed doctrine of the Church; revealed not as many commentators like to concentrate on with St Thomas putting his finger in Christ's wounds, but in him using a tiny bit of grammar to both declare and address Christ as Lord in a very distinctive, but often unnoticed way.

Our prayers, we are told by St John are held like incense in **_phialas aureas plenas_** (filled golden vessels *Apc* 5:8) and like the thurible used in church we send those precious prayers (worthy of being stored in golden vessels) rising up towards God. Of the countless prayers in those golden vessels are innumerable repetitions of the prayer Christ taught us himself the **Pater Noster** (Our Father) where the very name of God is far more theologically complex than those two simple words could ever articulate. We might pray **Pater noster** as a form of vocative address at the start of this prayer millions of times in a lifetime, but often without thinking through what is happening *attributively* to that word **Pater**, with the addition of the determiner **noster**, and all that means for a theology of a prayer worthy to be repeatedly placed in the golden vessels described by St John and offered up as incense to God. It is to those issues that we now turn in *Chapter IV: Attributive Prayer*.

IV

ATTRIBUTIVE PRAYER

Ausculta haec: sta, et considera mirabilia Dei
(These [things] hear: stand, and consider the wonders of God
Iob 37:14)

Attribution

St Pius of Pietrelcina OFM Cap (Padre Pio 1887-1968) was a Capuchin Franciscan canonised in 2002 by Pope St John Paul II. He famously said that 'Prayer is the oxygen of the soul', and that while 'in books we seek God' it is 'in prayer we find him.' He bore the *stigmata* (the five wounds of Christ) like his spiritual Father in religion St Francis of Assisi (1181-1226) who is described as ***O divi amoris victima*** (O victim of divine love) in a hymn of the same name found in the *Raccolta* (1910):

O Divi Amóris víctima,
Quino cruénta vúlnere,
Francísce, qui vivam Crucis
Christi refers imáginem.

(O victim dear of heavenly love,
 impurpled by thy fivefold sign,
 Saint Francis, father of the poor,
 of Jesus' Cross a living shrine. *trs* CE Spence)

Often prayed in novenas to St Francis, for such a holy man to be attributed the status of 'victim' might strike many, more used to the restrained language of much post-Reformation Christianity, as unusual. But Latin Catholicism has never shied away from attributing characteristics in this way. In these *litanies*, **victima** is actually used in the Classical Latin sense of 'a beast set aside for sacrifice to the gods'. St Francis would have considered such a role for himself, in the name of Christ who is the ultimate **hostia** (victim) to be a very humbling, but enormously, privileged one, despite all the pain and discomforts the **stigmata** would have brought him. The Son of God sacrificed himself through a most gruesome form of execution: crucifixion. He became the ultimate **victima/hostia**, which is why we refer to the communion bread/wafer at Mass, once consecrated, as **Sacra Hostia** (Sacred Victim). We pray privately in thanksgiving after Mass in the words of a hymn composed by St Thomas Aquinas for the Feast of **Corpus Christi** in 1264:

Adóro te, O panis cælice,
O Dómine, O Deus máxime.
Sanctus, sanctus, sanctus, sine fine sanctus.
Semper tibi glória sacra sit sub hóstia.
(I adore you, O heavenly bread,
O Lord, O most great God.
Holy, holy, holy, holy without end.
To you within the sacred host may always be glory)

Adóro te devóte, látens Déitas,
Quae sub his figúris, vere látitas:
tibi se cor meum totum súbiicit, quia,
te contémplans, totum déficit.
(I adore you devoutly, O Deity concealing,
Who under these appearances, you truly lie mysteriously:
To you my whole heart itself submits, because,
contemplating you, everything [else] falls short.)

We pray to Christ as **panis caelice, Domine, Deus maxime**, and **latens Deitas**. We are assigning very specific attributes to God **sub hostia** who is **sanctus sine fine**. In more of St Thomas' words, at the most beautiful of para-liturgical services, *Exposition and Benediction*, we pray:

O salutáris Hóstia, quae caeli pandis óstium:
Bella premunt hostília, da robur, fer auxílium.
(O saving Victim, who opens up the mouth of heaven,
Hostile armies bear down, give strength, bring help.)

Christ is the Victim who saves and we continue to pray at the exposition of the real and physical presence of the **salutáris Hóstia**:

Adorémus in aetérnum Sanctíssimum Sacraméntum.
(Let us adore for ever the Most Holy Sacrament)
Laudáte Dóminum, omnes gentes; Laudáte eum omnes pópuli.
Quóniam confirmáta est super nos misericórdia eius;
et véritas Dómini manet in aetérnum.
(Praise the Lord, all nations; Praise him, all people.
For his mercy is confirmed upon us; and the truth of the Lord remains for ever. *Ps* 116)
Glória Patri et Fílio, et Spíritui Sancto. Sicut erat in princípio,
et nunc, et semper, et in sécula saeculórum. Amen.
(Glory be to the Father and to the Son, and to the Holy Spirit.

As it was in the beginning, and now, and ever, and in the ages of ages. Amen)
Adorémus in aetérnum sanctíssimum Sacraméntum.

We literally bow down in adoration before the most Holy Sacrament praying:

Tantum ergo Sacraméntum, venerémur cérnui
(Let us therefore much bowed down venerate the Sacrament)

But we are not just 'falling down in adoration' for the sake of a beautiful ritual. We are bowed down before the real physical presence of Christ. We genuflect with one knee every time we enter a church that reserves the Blessed Sacrament. We genuflect on both knees whenever that real presence is openly exposed to us. We do so, not just out of respect, but in adoration and worship. We recognise in doing so, that Christ as Victim has literally changed the world for ever and pray to this effect in St Thomas' words:

et antíquum documéntum novo cedat rítui
(so may the old instruction give way to the new custom)

In other words, 'May the old law give way to the new'. The gift that Christ gave us, and which is embodied in the real presence of Christ transubstantiated from the bread and wine of the Mass in the **Sanctissimum Sacramentum**, and embodied in the very core of our Latin Catholic sensibilities, is food for the soul, because it has brought us out of the old law into the new. It is life-changing because Christ changed everything. St Thomas Aquinas really understood this and in his glorious Sequence for the Feast of **Corpus Christi** we pray:

Ecce Panis Angelórum, factus cibus viatórum:
vere panis filiórum, non mitténdus cánibus.

> (Behold the Bread of Angels, made food of pilgrims:
> truly bread of children, not thrown to dogs.)

The Latin is very powerful. The image of not throwing ***panis filiorum*** to the dogs is one we encounter perhaps with a shock to our modern sensibilities. But this contrast between the ***Panis Angelorum*** and hungry dogs is made more powerful still when in the next verse we pray:

> *Bone pastor, panis vere, Iesu, nostri misérere:*
> *tu nos pasce, nos tuére, tu nos bona fac vidére in terra vivéntium.*
>
> (O good shepherd, true bread, O Jesus, be merciful to us: feed and care for us yourself, make us yourself to see good [things] in the land of the living.)

We pray to Christ as a supportive shepherd caring for his flock, and attributed with one of the most evocative names we have for him in Christianity **Bone Pastor**. Attributing the characteristics of a shepherd tending his sheep is central to the way we have come to think of Christ. It is sutured into our Christian DNA so to speak. It is at the heart of our motivation as Catholics to seek him as **Sacra Hostia**, because the contrast between shepherd and victim stands large in our Catholic psyche about how we live in a world that often knows no bounds. The Blessed Sacrament holds both these attributes 'shepherd' and 'victim' in an indissoluble way that brings assurance in the uncertainties of our daily lives. Anyone who has entered a Catholic Church with the Blessed Sacrament reserved, and a Church without it, knows all too well the emptiness that the church without it holds. The Catholic Anglo Saxon scholar (later novelist) JRR Tolkien (1892-1973) knew this so well, and wrote movingly to his son Michael in 1941:

> 'Out of the darkness of my life, so much frustrated, I put before you the one great thing to love on earth: the Blessed Sacrament. There

you will find romance, glory, honour, fidelity, and the true way of all your loves upon earth, and more than that: death: by the divine paradox, that which ends life, and demands the surrender of all, and yet by the taste (or foretaste) of which alone can what you seek in your earthly relationships (love, faithfulness, joy) be maintained, or take on that complexion of reality, of eternal endurance, which every man's heart desires.'

He talks of Christ, as Anglo Saxon texts do, as *hælend* (healer) an attribute for Christ which the Church has recognised from its very beginnings, and most especially in the greatest healing miracle of all, the **Sanctissimum Sacramentum**. Tolkien talks of other attributes: romance, glory, honour, fidelity, love, desire and truth. They, and many others like them, form the backbone of what it is to be Catholic, and through the *usus antiquior* Mass, *Breviary* and services like *Exposition and Benediction*, what it is to be Latin Catholic. And Latin Catholicism is not afraid of using words which may challenge. In the prayer that is recited privately when the daily *Divine Office* is completed (and based on *Lc* 11:27) we pray:

> *Sacrosánctae et indivíduae Trinitáti, crucifíxi Dómini nostri Iesu Christi humanitáti, beatíssimae et gloriosíssimae sempérque Vírginis Maríae foecúndae integritáti, et ómnium Sanctórum universitáti sit sempitérna laus, honor, virtus et glória ab omni creatúra, nobísque remíssio ómnium peccatórum, per infiníta sǽcula saeculórum. Amen. Beáta víscera Maríae Vírginis quae portavérunt aetérni Patris Fílium. Et beáta úbera, quae lactavérunt Christum Dóminum. Pater noster. Ave María.*

(To the most holy and undivided Trinity, to the humanity of our Lord Jesus Christ crucified, to the fruitful virginity of the most blessed and most glorious Mary ever Virgin, and to the whole company of Saints be ascribed everlasting praise, honour, strength and glory by every creature, and to us be granted the forgiveness of all our sins, world without end. Amen. And blessed be the womb of the Virgin Mary, which bore the Son of the eternal Father. And blessed the breasts, which suckled [the] Christ Lord. Our Father. Hail Mary.)

Et beata ubera, quae lactaverunt Christum Dominum can be found translated as 'blessed be the paps which gave suck to Christ our Lord' which might seem to some Christians quite shocking, and even irreverent, attributing, as it does, physical qualities (and words) to the Blessed Virgin Mary which are not usually talked about 'in polite society'. Christ, most certainly in his life and ministry on earth, was never shy of taking that polite society to task and continually shocking it. Nor has been the Catholic Church. When Pope Leo XIII wrote his 1891 encyclical **Rerum Novarum** (of New Things) for example, he asked of that 'polite society': 'How must one's possessions be used?' and he answered that:

> *Ecclesia quidem sine ulla dubitatione respondet: quantum ad hoc, non debet homo habere res exteriores ut proprias, sed ut communes, ut scilicet de facili aliquis eas communicet in necessitate aliorum.*
>
> (The Church replies without hesitation in the words of the same holy Doctor: "Man should not consider his material possessions as his own, but as common to all, so as to share them without hesitation when others are in need. *Vat*)

It was a shocking Encyclical to many with wealth and power, but presented a thoroughly Catholic understanding of 'ownership', which is actually a mirror reflection (*simulacrum*) of God's ownership of all that we possess. Consequently, as stewards of those possessions, we need to treat them accordingly. 'Distributism' like this, as promulgated by Pope Leo, and championed by people like GK Chesterton, was considered by many in power to be an extraordinary thing to teach, let alone do. Just as referring, in a very Catholic way, to 'the paps that give suck', Pope Leo teaches in uncompromising language that there is a marked attributive relationship between man and God, making it very clear that while man *actionum suarum sit ipse dominus* (may be the master himself of his own acts) he is so *sub lege aeterna, sub potestate omnia providentissime gubernantis Dei* (under the eternal law, under the providential power of the governing of God). In other words, any attributes we may have, we have only because of God.

Eliu (Elihu) one of the 4 comforters of the long suffering Job, knew this well, referring, as his *exhortatio* (encouragement) for Job quoted in the epigraph to this Chapter shows, and indeed for all of us, that we must be prepared to recognise and, attend to, the attributes of God himself: his *mirabilia* (wonders). As we saw in the last chapter, St Joseph is assigned a range of different attributes in *Litaniae Sancti Ioseph* (Litanies of Saint Joseph) approved for public use by Pope St Pius X in 1909. These are St Joseph's 'attributive names', in the same way as Jesus is named attributively as 'victim', 'kind' and 'gentle'; as 'Shepherd' and as 'food of Angels', as we will see in some detail below. Following the release of Pope Francis' *Epistula Apostolica Patris Corde* (Apostolic Letter with a Father's Heart) on the 150th anniversary of the proclamation of St Joseph as patron of the universal church (8 December 2020) the *Congregatio de Cultu Divino et Disciplina Sacramentorum* (Vatican Congregation for Divine Worship and the Discipline of the Sacraments) proposed seven new attributive names for St Joseph, which Pope Francis approved for us to pray publicly in the *litanies*:

Custos Redemptóris (Guardian of the Redeemer)
Serve Christi (Servant of Christ)
Miníster salútis (Minister of salvation)
Fulcímen in difficultátibus (Support in difficulties)
Patróne éxsulum (Patron of exiles)
Patróne afflictórum (Patron of the afflicted)

LATIN PRAYER

Patróne páuperum (Patron of the poor)

Pope Francis ended the *Apostolic Letter* with the following prayer:

Salve, Redemptóris custos et sponsus Maríae Vírginis.
Tibi Deus suum Fílium commísit;
in te María fidúciam suam repósuit; tecum Christus vir factus est.
O beáte Ioseph, etiam nobis monstra te esse patrem,
atque duc nos in vitae itínere.
Impetra nobis grátiam, misericórdiam et ánimum,
et tuére nos ab omni malo. Amen.

(Hail, Guardian of the Redeemer, Spouse of the Blessed Virgin Mary.
To you God entrusted his only Son;
in you Mary placed her trust; with you Christ became man.
Blessed Joseph, to us too, show yourself a father
and guide us in the path of life.
Obtain for us grace, mercy and courage,
and defend us from every evil. Amen. *Vat*)

St Joseph is 'Guardian', 'Spouse', 'Father'. He is 'trusted' as a 'guide', an 'obtainer of grace' and 'a defender'. Attributive naming like this is important in Catholicism, as it is in many other religions, because by praying, repeating and meditating upon these names and attributes, we are able to build our relationship, with God, with Jesus, the Holy Spirit, Our Lady and the Saints and Angels. Every different name and attribute is like food for our soul, nourishing our awareness and consciousness to become as much like those names and attributes as possible. They are not simply ways of adding interest and variety to the same name, they serve both a didactic and a spiritual purpose. Devotion to St Joseph does not appear to have such a long history as that to the Blessed Virgin Mary, but records dating back to the 4thC indicate that this devotion was to grow. It did so throughout the centuries, most especially with the support of saints like Thomas Aquinas and the Franciscan Bernardine of Siena (1380-1444) and known as the 'Apostle of the Laity', with prayers to St Joseph which often mirror those to Our Lady:

> *Meménto nostri, beáte Ioseph, et tuae oratiónis suffrágio apud tuum putatívum Fílium intercéde; sed et beatíssimam Vírginem Sponsam tuam nobis propítiam redde, quae mater est eius, qui cum Patre et Spíritu Sancto vivit et regnat per infiníta sǽcula saeculórum. Amen.*
>
> (Remember us, O blessed Joseph, and intercede with your foster-son by the suffrage of your prayer; and implore the most blessed Virgin Mary your spouse for us, for she is the mother of him, who with the Father and the Holy Spirit lives and reigns through the infinite ages of ages. Amen.)

Pope Blessed Pius IX in his 1870 Decree **Quemadmodum Deus** (Just as God) declared St Joseph patron of the universal Catholic church, and not long afterwards Pope Leo XIII in his 1889 encyclical **Quamquam pluries** (Although many times) developed St Joseph's role in the 'economy of salvation' teaching that:

> *Beatissimus Patriarcha commendatam sibi peculiari quadam ratione sentiat multitudinem christianorum, ex quibus constat Ecclesia, scilicet innumerabilis isthaec perque omnes terras fusa familia, in quam, quia vir Mariae et pater est Iesu Christi, paterna propemodum auctoritate pollet. Est igitur consentaneum, et beato Iosepho apprime dignum, ut sicut ille olim Nazarethanam familiam, quibuscumque rebus usuvenit, sanctissime tueri consuevit, ita nunc patrocinio caelesti Ecclesiam Christi tegat ac defendat.*

(The Blessed Patriarch looks upon the multitude of Christians who make up the Church as confided specially to his trust - this limitless family spread over the earth, over which, because he is the spouse of Mary and the Father of Jesus Christ he holds, as it were, a paternal authority. It is, then, natural and worthy that as the Blessed Joseph ministered to all the needs of the family at Nazareth and girt it about with his protection, he should now cover with the cloak of his heavenly patronage and defend the Church of Jesus Christ. *Vat*)

Pope St John Paul II in his Apostolic Exhortation **Redemptoris Custos** (Guardian of the Redeemer) on August 15 1989 taught that:

Praeter certam ideo eius tutelam confidit item Ecclesia perinsigni Iosephi exemplo, quod nempe singulos excedit vitae status omnique proponitur christianae communitati, quaecumque in illa condicio est et quaecunque Christifidelis cuiusque sunt munera.

(Besides trusting in Joseph's sure protection, the Church also trusts in his noble example, which transcends all individual states of life and serves as a model for the entire Christian community, whatever the condition and duties of each of its members may be. *Vat*)

and so it seems more than fitting that we should pray in the words of Pope Leo XIII:

Ad te beáte Ioseph, in tribulatióne nostra confúgimus, atque, imploráto Sponsæ tuae sanctíssimae auxílio, patrocínium quoque tuum fidénter expóscimus. Per eam, quǽsumus quae te cum immaculáta Vírgine Dei Genetríce coniúnxit, caritátem, perque patérnum, quo Púerum Iesum ampléxus es, amórem, súpplices deprecámur, ut ad hereditátem, quam Iesus Christus acquisívit Sánguine suo, benígnus respícias, ac necessitátibus nostris tua virtúte et ope succúrras.

(To thee, O blessed Joseph, do we come in our tribulation, and having implored the help of your most holy Spouse, we confidently invoke your patronage also. Through that charity which bound you to the immaculate Virgin Mother of God and through the paternal love with which you embraced the child Jesus, we humbly beg you to graciously regard the inheritance which Jesus Christ has purchased by his blood, and with your power and strength to aid us in our necessities. *Vat*)

There are clearly various ways of naming attributively, but all of them have one aim in mind: to attribute new information. In **Litaniae de Sancto Spiritu** (Litanies concerning the Holy Spirit) for example, the Holy Spirit is named ***Spiritus Domini Deus Israel*** (Spirit of the Lord, God of Israel) and ***Dominator hominum, replens orbem terrarum*** (Master of men, filling the whole earth). He is further attributively named as we pray these *litanies*:

> *Spíritus sancte a Patre Filióque procédens*
> (Holy Spirit proceeding from the Father and the Son)
> *Habens omnem virtútem*
> (Having every virtue)
> *Omnia bona óperans, et ómnia prospíciens*
> (Working all good, and watching over all)
> *Ornans caelos, stábilis, et secúrus*
> (Adorning [the] heavens, stable, and secure)
> *Spíritus veritátis ómnia súggerens, et distríbuens*
> (Spirit of truth, supplying and distributing all)
> *Spíritus sapiéntiae et intelléctus*
> (Spirit of wisdom and understanding)
> *Spíritus consílii, fortitúdinis, sciéntiae, et pietátis*
> (Spirit of counsel, fortitude, knowledge, and piety)

Spíritus timóris Dómini et prudéntiae
(Spirit of fear of [the] Lord and prudence)
Spíritus, quo inspiránte, locúti sunt sancti Dei hómines
(Spirit, who by inspiring, [the] holy men of God spoke)
Donum et promíssio Patris
(Gift and promise of [the] Father)
Spíritus sancte Paraclíte árguens mundum
(Holy Spirit, [the] Paraclete, denouncing [the] world)
Spíritus, in quo daemónia eiiciúntur
(Spirit, by whom demons are expelled)
Spíritus, ex quo renáscimur
(Spirit, from whom we are reborn)
Spíritus, per quem cáritas Dei diffúsa est in córdibus nostris
(Spirit, through whom [the] love of God is diffused within our hearts)
Spíritus adoptiónis filiórum Dei
(Spirit of adoption of [the] sons of God)
Spíritus grátiae et misericórdiae
(Spirit of grace and mercy)
Spíritus ádiuvans infirmitátem nostram et reddens testimónium spirítui nostro, quod simus fílii Dei
(Spirit helping our weakness and restoring our spiritual witness, that we may be sons of God)
Spíritus suávis, benígne, super mel dulcis
(Spirit of sweetness, kindness, above sweet honey)
Spíritus pignus hereditátis nostrae, dedúcens nos in terram rectam
(Spirit, pledge of our inheritance, leading us into right lands)
Spíritus principális, vivíficans et confórtans
(Spirit of principal, life-giving and strengthening)
Spíritus salútis, iudícii et gáudii
(Spirit of salvation, judgement, and joy)
Spíritus fídei, pacis, et ardóris
(Spirit of faith, peace, and passion)

Spíritus humilitátis, caritátis, et castitátis
(Spirit of humility, charity, and chastity)
Spíritus benignitátis, bonitátis, longanimitátis, ac mansuetúdinis
(Spirit of kindness, goodness, patience, and gentleness)
Spíritus lenitátis, veritátis, unitátis ac consolatiónis
(Spirit of mildness, truth, unity, and consolation)
Spíritus compunctiónis, promissiónis, renovatiónis, ac sanctificatiónis
(Spirit of remorse, promise, renewal, and sanctification)
Spíritus vitae, patiéntiae, continéntiæ, ac modéstiae
(Spirit of life, patience, continence, and modesty)
Spíritus ómnium gratiárum
(Spirit of every grace)

Each attributive name here (and there are many more) adds new information to what we know already of the Holy Spirit. Each one becomes an intercessory prayer by repeating **miserere nobis** (be merciful to us) asking the Holy Spirit as God in the Trinity to hear us as we pray, and watch over us as we live our lives: **omnia bona operans, et omnia prospiciens** (working all good, and watching over all) with many of them, as here, using the present participle to signal that the work of the Holy Spirit is ongoing and continuous. Just one of them, like **donum et promissio Patris** (gift and promise of the Father) would provide enough resources for a full week's retreat; combined, we would not have enough time in a whole life to exhaust their meditative potential.

The Genitive Dynamic

The word **Patris** in **donum et promissio Patris** (gift and promise of the Father) is written as a genitive masculine singular inflection of the nominative *pater*, just as **rerum novarum** in Pope Leo's *Encyclical* referred to above is the plural genitive form of the nominative feminine noun phrase *res novae* (new things) which in Latin, since the time of Marcus Tullius Cicero (106-43 BC) idiomatically came to mean 'revolutionary change'. The Vatican English translation for the opening line (and title) of this *Encyclical* mirrors this with its 'Of revolutionary change'. The title itself, therefore, suggests something (revolution) not usually associated with the pre *Vatican II* Catholic Church, but it also signals grammatical possession, and more than that it signals, through its descriptive use of **novarum**, the *genitive dynamic* of attribution. In the **Commemoratio Beatae Virginis Mariae** (Commemoration of the Blessed Virgin Mary) with its opening prayer composed by Bishop Fulbert of Chartres (952-1028) we pray to Our Lady:

Ora pro pópulo, intérveni pro clero, intércede pro devóto foemínio sexu
(Pray for the people, plead for the clergy, intercede for all the devoted feminine sex)
Quia ex te ortus est Sol iustítiae
(Because from you is risen the Sun of justice)

Prayed on some Marian feasts and in the **Officium Parvum Beatae Mariae Virginis** (Little Office of the Blessed Virgin Mary) the three words **Beatae Virginis Mariae** are each written in the genitive signalling that this is a **commemoratio** and an **officium parvum** 'of the Blessed [of] the Virgin [of] Mary', where **Beata** and **Virgo** both agree, as genitive adjectives, with **Mariae** in case, number and gender. The commemoration prayed in this particular form in the **usus antiquior** calendar from the 3rd Sunday after the Epiphany through to the Purification, ends by asking God who 'has given to mankind the rewards' (**humano generi praemia praestitisti**) of eternal salvation 'by the virginity of the fruitful Blessed Mary' (gen sg f: **beatae Mariae virginitate fecundae**, to 'grant, we beseech you, that we may know that she intercedes for us, through whom we have been made worthy to receive the author *of life* (gen sg) (**auctorem vitae**) our Lord Jesus Christ, your

Son. Amen.' Christ is gloriously given the attributive name ***Sol iustitiae*** (Sun of justice) demonstrating the attributive power of the genitive dynamic at work here. While the nominative nouns ***commemoratio*** and ***officium*** could stand by themselves in Latin, ***Beatae Mariae*** (of [the] blessed Mary) and ***Virginis*** (of [the] virgin) could not. Nor could the genitive singular ***iustitiae***. The genitive forms are signalling more than possession then. They are dynamically attributing new information (and offering a new *focus* here) to the nominatives ***commemoratio***, ***officium*** and ***sol***.

Hence, in a phrase like ***Agnus Dei*** (Lamb of God) new information about ***agnus*** enables us to focus not just on the noun (lamb) but on the attribute of that noun: that it is ***Dei*** (of God). In this sense, ***agnus*** is 'given/old' linguistic information, but when combined with a genitive attribute like ***Dei*** we are provided with attributive information which is 'new.' There is, therefore, a grammatical dynamic between cases which, in turn, creates a semantic dynamic between old and new linguistic information. This, in turn, attributes a linguistic vibrancy that makes the words and 'bits of grammar' of Latin prayer like this, even in the shortest of phrases, live anew every time they are prayed. For example, in the hymn ***Iesu Rex admirabilis*** (O Jesus King most admirable) part of a much larger hymn ***Iesu, Dulcis Memoria*** (O Jesus, sweet memory) composed by St Bernard of Clairvaux which is prayed at *Matins* on the Feast of the Holy Name of Jesus, we pray various parts of the larger hymn in various *Offices*, including:

> ***Iesu, Rex admirábilis et triumphátor nobílis,***
> ***Dulcédo ineffábilis, totus desiderábilis.***
> (O Jesus, wondrous king and noble conqueror,
> ineffable sweetness, wholly desirable.)

where new information is given about Jesus. He is 'King' and 'conqueror'. He is 'wondrous', 'ineffable sweetness' and is 'wholly desirable'. These attributes are all about developing the complexities of Jesus, and grammatically in this verse are achieved by the concord of nom noun + nom adjective agreeing in case, number and gender. But in the third verse, for example:

Iesu, dulcédo córdium, fons vivus, lumen mentíum,
excédens omne gáudium et omne desidérium.
(O Jesus, sweetness of hearts, living fountain,
light of minds, surpassing all joy and all desire.)

we see that while there is a similar noun + adjective (*fons vivus*) means of attributing this development of new information, in the phrases *dulcedo cordium* and *lumen mentium* the English translation 'sweetness of hearts' and 'light of minds' requires the inclusion of an 'of' to *cordium* and *mentium* to signal genitive possession. Effectively what this means is that by using the genitive form of a noun, that noun then functions attributively like the adjective in a phrase like *fons vivus*, and in that sense, like in all grammar, the way meanings are made becomes about the different relationships that are created in a text, affecting then, as here, the way we may attributively address God in prayer. At the heart of this hymn is the submission of the individual to Jesus, who over its course, is described with a fountain (*fons*) of new attributes. Similarly we read:

Lingua sapientium ornat scientiam; os fatuorum ebullit stultitiam.
(The tongue of the wise embellishes knowledge; the mouth of fools
spouts out stupidity.)
In omni loco, oculi Domini contemplantur bonos et malos.
(In every place, the eyes of the Lord in every place consider [the] good
and [the] bad. *Prov* 15:1-2)

where the nouns *lingua, os* and *oculi* are all attributed new information by the genitives *sapientium, fatuorum* and *Domini*, (just as the noun *liber* is provided with new information by the gen pl ***proverbiorum***). The 'tongue' is now understood to be the 'tongue *of the wise*'; the 'mouth' to be the 'mouth *of fools*' and the 'eyes' now 'the eyes *of the Lord*'. So, in the following selected prayers from **Litaniae Sancti Ioseph** (*Litanies* of Saint Joseph) for example, we pray the genitive dynamic:

> *Spéculum patiéntiae* (O Mirror of patience)
> *Amátor paupertátis* (O Lover of poverty)
> *Exémplar opíficum* (O Model of artisans)
> *Domésticae vitae decus* (O Glory of domestic life)
> *Custos vírginum* (O Guardian of virgins)
> *Familiárum cólumen* (O Pillar of families)
> *Solátium miserórum* (O Solace of [the] wretched)
> *Spes aegrotántium* (O Hope of [the] sick)
> *Patróne moriéntium* (O Patron of [the] dying)
> *Terror dǽmonum* (O Terror of demons)
> *Protéctor sanctae Ecclésiae* (O Protector of holy Church)

not as genitives of possession but as genitives of attribution. Furthermore, each intercessory prayer is followed by the exhortation ***Ora pro nobis*** (Pray for us) making the *litanies* increasingly more dynamic as we pray to God through them:

> ***Proles David ínclyta*** (nom/voc sg f *proles* + gen sg m *David* + nom/voc sg f *inclytus*) - [O] renowned offspring of David
> ***Lumen Patriarchárum*** (nom/voc sg n *lumen* + gen pl m *patriarcha*) - [O] light of Patriarchs
> ***Dei Genitrícis sponse*** (gen sg m *Deus* + gen sg f *genitrix* + voc sg m *sponsus*) - O spouse of [the] Mother of God
> ***Custos pudíce Vírginis*** (voc sg m *custos* + voc sg adj m *pudicus* + gen sg f *virgo*) - O chaste guardian of [the] Virgin

Christi defénsor sédule (gen sg m *Christus* + voc sg m *defensor* + voc sg adj m *sedulus*) - O attentive defender of Christ

Almae Famíliae praeses (gen sg adj f *almus* + gen sg f *familia* + nom/voc sg m *praeses*) - [O] Protector of [the] Holy Family

Spéculum patiéntiae (nom/voc sg n *speculum* + gen sg f *patientia*) - [O] mirror of patience

Amátor paupertátis (nom/voc sg m *amator* + gen sg f *paupertas*) - [O] lover of poverty

Exémplar opíficum (nom/voc sg m *exemplar* + gen pl m *opifex*) - [O] model of craftsmen

Doméstica vitae decus (gen sg adj f *domesticus* + gen sg f *vita* + nom/voc sg n *decus*) - [O] pride of domestic life

Custos vírginum (nom/voc sg m *custos* + gen pl f *virgo*) - [O] guardian of virgins

Familiárum cólumen (gen pl f *familia* + nom/voc sg n *columen*) - [O] pillar of families

Solátium miserórum (nom/voc sg n *solatium* + gen pl m *miser*) - [O] solace of [the] miserable

Spes aegrotántium (nom/voc sg m *spes* + gen pl m *aegrotans* - [O] hope of [the] sick

We cannot escape the underlying grammar in every single phrase we pray in Latin, even when not written out as here. Fluency in reading Latin may well mean that we no longer need to think about that underlying grammar, but fluency in praying Latin requires the opposite, because prayer necessarily involves our praying, as here, the attributive theology as it is played out in the grammar, with, through, and beyond the words of the text.

The simplicity of the Latin, especially in *litanies* seen so far in this book, may frustrate some wishing to see that language used more expressively, and in greater complexity, but the simplicity has a purpose. We may read Latin fluently but this does not mean we pray fluently, because prayer is always much more than its language. What might appear to be simple descriptions, say, of St Joseph, as here, are in prayer, much more complex attributive ways of seeking God. When we pray we are not passive consumers of the words on a page. We actively participate, because of those words in many cases, in a quite different reality; inevitably so, because we are drawn (whether we are conscious of it or not) to that prayer by the Holy Spirit; himself indicative of a quite different reality altogether. What this effectively means is that while grammatically we may be able to make distinctions between objective and subjective structures of grammar, in prayer we can never be objectively distanced from the new spiritual reality we are subjectively seeking.

The attributes assigned to St Joseph, therefore, in these *litanies* over the years, and more recently by Pope Francis, are more than just linguistic descriptors of his character or life, they are attributes which effectively light our way to God. By doing so, this begins to shift the focus of our address to God through St Joseph in these *litanies*, for example, to being a much more subjective and participatory dynamic, because St Joseph, although seemingly the sole subject of these attributes of 'protector', 'guardian', 'hope' and 'pillar', for example, is only able to be attributed with these characteristics because of his participation in God's own character, so to speak. In other words, if St Joseph is described as 'just', it is only because subjectively he is participating in God's own 'justness'. If he is described as a 'mirror' or 'light', then it is only because God is the ultimate expression of what it is to be a 'mirror' or 'light'. In other words we can only understand our subjectivity and the attributes that go with that, through God's own attributes, and that is not a popular view today, given how much we now celebrate the predominance of 'self'.

The attributive genitive seen in many of the simple forms of *litanies*, by focussing on a range of attributes, add both textual and contextual force to our awareness of (and for some, devotion to) some of the world's most favourite Saints, who we ask, in these *litanies*, to intercede for us to God. One such Saint, St Francis of Assisi canonised by Pope Gregory IX (c1170-1241) on 16 July 1228, just two years after Francis died close to the Chapel of the Portiuncula in Assisi where the Franciscan order he founded was initially based. His ministry began at Rivo Torto in a dilapidated and abandoned hut where, after he had walked away from the riches of his family in 1208, which St Francis described as being done *summa humilitate* (with the highest humility) he lived with his first companions for 2 years drawing up his *Rule*.

If we think of St Francis, we may think of him, especially in popular culture, as a saint in ragged habit who loved animals, gave away his riches and inheritance, seeking poverty, and, like his son in religion, Padre Pio, received the *stigmata*. In many ways by thinking of him in this way we are defining and identifying him through popular culture, but when we are given attributes like 'seraphic', 'conqueror' and 'athlete' (as below) these attributes are not just aimed at letting us know more about St Francis himself, they are attributive names for him which are designed to help us walk with St Francis towards God. The focus of these attributes, therefore, like the hut with no roof at Rivo Torto did for St Francis, lifts our perceptions beyond the worldly.

Many of these attributes are drawn from the early 14thC ***Actus Beati Francisci et Sociorum eius*** (Acts of Blessed Francis and his Companions) later resulting in the now famous *Fioretti di San Francesco* (Little Flowers of St Francis) and from centuries of prayer, devotion to, and careful consideration of him through texts like these. This is what the **Litaniae de Sancto Patre Nostro Francisco** (Litanies concerning Our Holy Father Francis) approved for private prayer, capture: a *textual* attributive focus on character and identity made even more powerful by the *contextual* focus on the iterative, mantra-like, quality of these individual intercessory attributive prayers and exhortations which pile up one after the other. The edited selection of prayers below is just part of the full *Litanies*:

Sancte Francísce Seraphíce
(O seraphic St Francis)
Sancte Francísce Patriárcha páuperum
(O St Francis patriarch of the poor)

Sancte Francísce imitátor Salvatóris
(O St Francis imitator of the Saviour)
Sancte Francísce norma castitátis
(O St Francis standard of purity)
Sancte Francísce forma humilitátis
(O St Francis model of humility)
Sancte Francísce via erràntium
(O St Francis the way of [those] erring/going astray)
Sancte Francísce medéla infirmórum
(O St Francis remedy of the sick)
Sancte Francísce colúmna Ecclésiae
(O St Francis pillar of the Church)
Sancte Francísce fídei defénsor
(O St Francis defender of faith)
Sancte Francísce athléta Christi
(O St Francis athlete of Christ
Sancte Francísce propugnáculum militántium
(O St Francis bulwark of soldiers)
Sancte Francísce scutum inexpugnábile
(O St Francis invincible shield)
Sancte Francísce málleus haereticórum
(O St Francis hammer of heretics)
Sancte Francísce convérsio paganórum
(O St Francis conversion of pagans)
Sancte Francísce exstirpátor vitiórum
(O St Francis destroyer of vices)

I have focussed a lot in this book so far on *Litanies* like this one as a way of showing just how powerful they can be in Latin prayer. They have been increasingly marginalised as prayer in contemporary Catholicism, and many Catholics would now live out their entire lives without ever praying a *Litany* publicly in Church, or privately. They are generally simple in linguistic form, and iteratively, I believe, return us to the basic linguistic pulse and spiritual heartbeat of who we actually are as humans. For example, in such words and phrases as we see below in the centuries old ***Litaniae de Sanctissimo Sacramento*** (Litanies concerning the Most Blessed Sacrament) that heartbeat consists of some attributes which appear to be relatively plain like ***mensa purissima*** (most pure meal) but others like ***Vinum germinans virgines*** (vine budding out virgins) or ***Divinae affluentia largitatis*** (affluence of divine largesse) seem to focus much more on the extraordinary, with phrases like ***Deus absconditus*** (hidden God) so theologically complex that a full explanation is really impossible. Whether textually plain, picturesque or complex, they all of them, when prayed, lift us out of the ordinary into the extraordinary, by reflecting a very careful and well thought out doctrine and theology of the Most Blessed Sacrament, itself extraordinary beyond measure:

Fili Redémptor mundi Deus
O God [the] Son Redeemer of the world
Deus abscónditus et Salvátor
[O] hidden God and Saviour
Fruméntum electórum
[O] grain of [the] elect
Vinum gérminans vírgines
[O] vine budding out virgins
Panis pinguis et delíciae regum
[O] full-bodied bread and delicacy of kings
Iuge sacrifícium
O abiding sacrifice
Mensa puríssima
 [O] most pure meal
Angelórum esca
 [O] food of angels
Memória mirabílium Dei
 [O] memory of [the] wonders of God

Calix benedictiónis
[O] chalice of blessing
Mystérium fídei
[O] mystery of faith
Sacrifícium ómnium sanctíssimum
[O] most holy sacrifice of all
Sacratíssima Domínicae Passiónis commemorátio
[O] most sacred commemoration of Lordly Passion
Memoriále praecípuum divíni amóris
[O] principal memorial of divine love
Divínae affluéntia largitátis
[O] affluence of divine largesse
Phármacum immortalitátis
[O] medicine of immortality
Panis omnipoténtia Verbi
[O] omnipotence of [the] bread of [the] Word
Sacraméntum pietátis
[O] sacrament of piety
Vínculum caritátis
[O] bond of love
Pignus futúrae glóriae
[O] pledge of future glory
Reféctio animárum sanctárum
[O] refreshment of holy souls

Attributive naming, like **Vinculum caritatis,** may be metaphoric. But it may also be more linguistically simple like **Sacramentum pietatis**, though theologically both are very challenging. It may seem to be florid in appearance, but in reality is spiritually very deep, like **Panis pinguis et deliciae regum**. But whatever they are, in all their various forms, they are often a dominant feature in many Latin prayers. And as such, to repeat the mantra at the heart of this book, Latin prayer is not about the ordinary, it is about the extraordinary. It is designed, like the entries in these *litanies*, to *address*, to give *focus* and *force* to the counter-cultural; in short to *affect*. Above all, to lead to **divina natura** (the divine nature) and **divinitas** (divinity). To lead to what I call in this book, the *numinous*.

The Numinous Function

Origen of Alexandria (184-253) one of the Church's very first theologians, referred to the anagogical approach to reading and praying a text (though not in these words) almost 2,000 years ago at the dawn of Christianity, in what he described as θεοειδής (*theoeidés*) the God-like meaning hidden behind words. It is a dimension to grammar and textual analysis in prayer that I call in this book the *numinous function* of language, which is not a term that will be found in grammar books or in the discipline of linguistics. In pre-Christian Classical Latin a term often used was **numen** meaning 'divine presence' hence in English 'numinous'. In contemporary western society this is a word that has been appropriated by some, who wish either to restrict this word to pagan belief, and by others, who have replaced acceptance of a Divine Presence with belief in magic and wizardry, or self-reliance, or simply upon love of self or for each other or just 'nature'. It is, however, a word worth reclaiming here because with it, as an attribute of Latin prayer, the 'natural' is not a replacement for, but opens up, the 'supernatural'; where ordinary humans may participate in extraordinary Divinity.

The Greek term for that participation in divinity is θέωσις (*theosis*) which celebrates human participation in divinity, as impossible though that may seem. Our aim in life, the Church teaches, is salvation (*salvatio*) and true salvation according to the *Catechism* means becoming as like God as possible. We learn therefore that to act as Christians we do so in order to be sanctified, and as Latin Catholics we believe that we cannot be sanctified without the sanctifying actions of the Church; its practices, sacraments, liturgies, doctrines, texts and teachings through both Scripture and Tradition. The Church mediates the relationship of the individual with God through its performative sacramental economy (***oeconomia sacramentalis***) which is seen by Latin Catholics as the only true and perfect vehicle for salvation. There is no other way. In that sense, the Church, contrary to much contemporary Catholic thinking, is *exclusive*. Because to be Catholic, and therefore to be a part of the economy of salvation, requires exclusive demands to be met by those of us who are members of the Catholic Church. And that is not considered to be a politically correct point of view these days.

To share in the Divine Nature seems such an impossibility. We most certainly can't achieve this alone. Christ's very Incarnation is witness to this. The ultimate prayer for Catholics, Latin or otherwise, is the Sacrifice of the Mass. Nothing else we do, liturgically or privately in prayer, outweighs this. But everything else that we do supports that Sacrifice. Prayer, therefore, through its language, patrimony and Tradition within the Church, is performative: it is a sanctifying, numinous, act. What we are attempting to pray in the *litanies* (and other such supportive prayers) as part of that overall performative act of prayer within the Church, is a form of *mimesis* (μίμησις) an ***imitatio*** (representation) in words that seeks to imitate the numinous realities of a particular world by repeating (and then imitating *mimetically*) those attributes in our own spiritual lives.

The Jesuit Priest Fr Gerard Manley Hopkins SJ (1844-1889) referred to this numinous reality (though not in these words) in poetry as 'inscape'; an empathy (*Einfühlung*) capturing the linguistic and emotive core of a meaning both within and beyond the text itself. 'Inscape' when used in describing prayer, as I suggest we do here as 'the numinous function', takes on a focus clearly designed to achieve a particular force, which in turn is designed to affect us spiritually. Through it, every prayer, every time it is prayed, is made into a new prayer. This is a form of *poesis* (ποησις - to make) through *mimesis* (imitation) which gives new life to every text through every repetition of that text. The attributive forms and functions, discussed in this Chapter, therefore, have a purpose in Latin prayer far more than just linguistic and grammatical, emotive or experiential. They enable greater focus to be made on the numinous road map to *theosis*.

St Thomas Aquinas writes in his highly influential **Summa Theologiae** that participation in divinity (deification) is 'man's true blessing and the destiny of human life'. He picks up on the Aristotelian (384-322 BC) maxim developed by Cicero of **summum bonum** (the highest good) which for Aquinas is a life lived in communion with God. That takes some thinking about, because if that communion with God (deification of ourselves so to speak; to become Godlike: *theosis*) is the ultimate aim of prayer, then it can only be possible because God became man: the Incarnate Jesus, who, St Peter tells us (*2 Pe* 1:4) came on earth to transform us to be able to do this. Christ as man becomes the model for us to become as much like him, as much like God, as possible, and we are able to do so in prayer through processes involving *mimesis*, *poesis* and *theosis*.

Prayer is not an innocent activity. It is forceful, focussed, interested, motivated and situated, not just in its linguistic texts, but in its spiritual contexts. Attributive language and prayer can enable relationships between words to be made which offer a new focus and force by changing textual information to a new spiritual meaning that not only recognises, for example, Jesus as 'the father of poor people', but also calls upon **pater pauperum** (father of the poor) not to give us money to relieve our poverty, but to be merciful to us (*miserere nobis*) and thereby *affect* us. So, for example, in these edited selections from **Litaniae Pretiosissimi Sanguinis Domini Nostri Iesu Christi** (Litanies of the Most Precious Blood of Our Lord Jesus Christ) approved in its current form by Pope St John XXIII in 1960, but which existed for several centuries in various forms, we see an emphasis upon the Blood of Christ designed to lead very definitely to the *numinous*:

Sanguis Christi, Unigéniti Patris aetérni, salva nos
  [O] Blood of Christ, only-begotten Son of [the] eternal Father, save us

Sanguis Christi, Verbi Dei incarnáti
   [O] Blood of Christ, of [the] incarnate Word of God
Sanguis Christi, Novi et Aetérni Testaménti
   [O] Blood of Christ, of [the] New and Eternal Testament
Sanguis Christi, prétium nostrae salútis
   [O] Blood of Christ, price of our salvation
Sanguis Christi, flumen misericórdiae
   [O] Blood of Christ, stream of mercy
Sanguis Christi, victor dǽmonum
   [O] Blood of Christ, conqueror of demons
Sanguis Christi, fortitúdo Mártyrum
   [O] Blood of Christ, strength of Martyrs
Sanguis Christi, virtus Confessórum
   [O] Blood of Christ, fortitude of Confessors
Sanguis Christi, robur periclitántium
   [O] Blood of Christ, help of [those in] perils
Sanguis Christi, levámen laborántium
   [O] Blood of Christ, relief of [the] labouring
Sanguis Christi, spes poeniténtium
   [O] Blood of Christ, hope of penitents
Sanguis Christi, solámen moriéntium
   [O] Blood of Christ, comfort of [the] dying
Sanguis Christi, pignus vitae aetérnae
   [O] Blood of Christ, pledge of eternal life

A noun like ***sanguis*** (blood) can change dramatically by the addition of an adjective like ***pretiossimus*** (most precious) as its attribute, and even more with the addition of a genitive acting like an adjective (***Christi*** - of Christ). In short, this attributive function enlarges the noun with qualities and characteristics that not only add linguistic information but which also adds significant numinous force in prayer. Reflection upon them as ways of defining the Divine, and those aspects of Jesus himself, like his name, precious blood, sacred heart, or his real presence in the Eucharist, enable us not just to have more information about the person or attribute itself, but to consider how we might numinously apply the force of that attribute to ourselves, as part of our way of seeking the Divine. The attribute defines, identifies and expands the person, place or thing it is modifying, and as such can open up a whole new world to us. Attributive prayer, therefore, expands information and textual knowledge about a thing or person, but it also creates spiritual force; it mystifies; it affects; it enables the numinous.

There is also a contextual force of devotion (*cultus*) involved in the spiritual journey, which, for example, often precedes the canonisation of an individual as a Saint (a process only formalised as late as 1642 by Pope Urban VIII [1568-1644]). As a consequence, particularly during the Middle Ages, a great deal of imaginative elaboration in the lives (*vitae*) of many Saints took place. In the Middle Ages the *hagia grapha* ('hagiography' from ἅγιος - *hagios* - holy) were in fact the *Holy Scriptures*, not the lives of Saints, which were usually referred to as ***Vitae*** (Lives). But regardless of some of the imaginative leaps that may have taken place in an individual ***Vita*** (as seen very clearly in many of the readings for the ***usus antiquior*** Matins, many of which were expunged in the shift from *Matins* to *The Office of Readings* in the ***usus recentior Liturgia Horarum*** [more recent usage Liturgy of Hours] often, it must be said, very beneficially, given the much wider range of readings) the point of all that devotional force was (and is) to put the focus on the extraordinary and its spiritual affect upon us.

We tend to think of some of the more wildly imaginative 'hagiography' as a somewhat spurious practice now long gone, but the force of devotion is a powerful one, and, more than anything, the composers of 'fanciful' and 'flowery' ***Vitae*** and ***Orationes*** recognised, perhaps more than we do now, the powerful force of the extraordinary. They may have attributed some very questionable activities and characteristics to many of the Saints, but they did so to lift the supplicant from the ordinary world around us to the extraordinary world of the Saints and God himself, in just the same way as the extraordinary was built into the magnificent edifices of medieval cathedrals and the stained glass and carvings and statuary within them, seen nowhere else then in the ordinary world of everyday life. In the following selections from the ***Litaniae Sanctorum*** (Litanies of [the] Saints) we see this seemingly 'ordinary' in attributive prayer very clearly when we pray very linguistically simple attributive names like:

> *Fili, Redémptor mundi, Deus*
> O God [the] Son, Redeemer of the world
> *Sancta Dei Génitrix*
> [O] Holy Mother of God
> *Sancta Virgo vírginum*
> [O] Holy Virgin of virgins
> *Omnes sancti beatórum Spiríutuum órdines*
> [O] All holy orders of blessed Spirits
> *Omnes Sancti et Sanctae Dei*
> [O] All (male) Saints and (female) Saints of God
> *Fili Dei*
> O Son of God
> *Agnus Dei*
> [The] Lamb of God
> *Iesu coróna Sanctórum ómnium,*
> (O Jesus crown of all [the] Saints)

but which in numinous terms are all extremely complex: theologically and otherwise. These few entries from the *Litanies* use the genitive form to give new information about whoever is being addressed. The **Redemptor** is the *Redemptor **mundi*** (of the world) the **Sancta Genitrix** is the *Sancta Genitrix **Dei*** (of God) the **Sancta Virgo** is the *Sancta Virgo **virginum*** (of virgins) the **Omnes sancti ordines** are *Omnes sancti ordines **beatorum Spirituum*** (of blessed Spirits) **Omnes Sancti et Sanctae** (male Saints and female Saints) are *Sancti et Sanctae Dei* (of God) **Fili** (O Son) is *Fili Dei* (of God) **Agnus** (the Lamb) is

Agnus Dei (the Lamb of God). When we invoke Christ with words and phrases from the *Litanies* like **Iesu corona Sanctorum omnium** (O Jesus crown of all the Saints) for example, we are not simply declaring our own personal belief, but the belief the Church has expressed through its **Magisterium** which has attributed to Christ the personification of being the crown of all the Saints. There is a powerful intangible attributive focus here on Christ. That focus is not just linguistic. It is doctrinal. It is poetic. It is representational (mimetic) and it is theological and Christological. In effect, the grammatical medium also becomes an integral part of the message, and so, anagogically, may enable the unseen (the *numinous*) to come to the surface.

Attributive Affect

When the disciples asked Jesus how to pray he didn't just give them a few words, but a radically new form of prayer; a new theology; a new Law; a new Covenant, but above all, a new numinous relationship, where God, as Jesus taught them, is 'Father', which, as we saw earlier, is a quite dramatically different way of understanding (and focussing on) God attributively than their Jewish culture had taught them. Praying to God is not simply referring to him in prayer, but directly (and intimately) addressing him in prayer as St Matthew records Jesus as saying:

> **Sic ergo vos orabitis: Pater noster...**
> (So, therefore you will pray: Our Father... *Mt 6:9*)

There is a theological emphasis in the *Gospels* of both St Matthew and St Luke on attributing a numinous focus to God as 'Father'; something that is actually not found in the other books of the *New Testament*, with the notable exception of the *Gospel* and *First Letter of St John*. Compared to the 25 times or so that St Luke uses the term **Pater** in this way, St John uses the term about 250 times; the difference seeming to point to a theological emphasis by St John on the relationship between Father and Son, and, as a consequence, its numinous function and consequent affect upon us in this new theology. As the Son lives in the Father, so we must live in the Son. This was a radical new way of thinking numinously about God, and our relationship with him. In 1971 Pope St Paul VI delivered his ***Constitutio Apostolica de Sacramento Confirmationis Divinae Consortium Naturae*** (Apostolic Constitution concerning the Sacrament of Confirmation Sharing in Divine Nature) which opens with the words:

> *Divinae consortium naturae, quo homines per Christi gratiam donantur, similitudinem quandam prae se fert ortus vitae naturalis, eius incrementi et alimonii.*
> (The sharing in the divine nature given to individuals through the grace of Christ bears a certain likeness to the origin, development, and nourishing of natural life. *ICEL*)

That takes some thinking about, as indeed it should, given that to seek to share in the Divine Nature seems to be outrageously presumptuous. But this is the numinous function of prayer and the Christian way of life writ large. St Paul makes it clear that God's attributes, the *mirabilia* in the Divine Nature which we are seeking to share, have never changed for:

> *Invisibilia enim ipsius, a creatura mundi, per ea quae facta sunt, intellecta, conspiciuntur: sempiterna quoque eius virtus, et divinitas: ita ut sint inexcusabiles.*
> (From the foundations of the world men have caught sight of his invisible nature, his eternal power and his divineness, as they are known through his creatures. Thus there is no excuse for them. *Knox Rom* 1:20)

But our thinking about him has changed, since the birth, life, death and resurrection of Christ, as we see in all of the many different forms of address in the *litanies* and prayers of the Church, and most especially in the now little known **Litaniae Vitae et Passionis Domini Nostri Iesu Christi** (Litanies of the Life and Passion of Our Lord Jesus Christ) developed over many centuries and particularly popularised by the Benedictine Servant of God Pope Pius VII. When we pray these *litanies* we are praying the attributive names of Jesus, and all the history, tradition, theology, Christology and doctrine they encapsulate. These are *litanies* worth exploring, praying and meditating upon in full, and I make no apologies for what appears to be a very long selection below, but which, in fact, is only a part of the full *litanies*:

Iesu, verbum Patris. Miserére nobis
O Jesus, Word of [the] Father. Be merciful to us
Iesu, splendor patérnae glóriae
O Jesus, splendour of paternal glory
Iesu, figúra substántiae Patris
O Jesus, figure of [the] substance of [the] Father
Iesu, sapiéntia aetérna
O Jesus, eternal wisdom
Iesu, candor lucis aetérnae
O Jesus, radiance of eternal light
Iesu, spéculum sine mácula
O Jesus, mirror without blemish
Iesu, per quem facta sunt ómnia
O Jesus, through whom everything was made
Iesu, verbo virtútis tuae ómnia portans
O Jesus, by [the] word of your power carrying everything
Iesu, magni consílii Angele
O Jesus, Angel of great council
Iesu, princeps pacis
O Jesus, prince of peace
Iesu, sanctis Pátribus promísse
O Jesus, promised to [the] holy Patriarchs

Iesu, cunctis géntibus desideráte
O Jesus, desired by all people
Iesu, in mundum a Patre misse
O Jesus, sent into the world by [the] Father
Iesu, de Spíritu Sancto concépte
O Jesus, conceived by [the] Holy Spirit
Iesu, Verbum caro factum
O Jesus, Word made flesh
Iesu, nobíscum Deus
O Jesus, God with us
Iesu, in formam servi facte
O Jesus, made in [the] form of [a]slave
Iesu, de vírgine María nate
O Jesus, born of [the] Virgin Mary
Iesu, a tua Genitríce adoráte
O Jesus, adored by your Mother
Iesu, pannis involúte
O Jesus, wrapped in rags
Iesu, in praesépio reclináte
O Jesus, laid in [a] manger
Iesu, úbere Virgíneo lactáte
O Jesus, suckled by[the] Virginal breast
Iesu, a pastóribus in praesépio cógnite
O Jesus, acknowledged by shepherds in [the] manger
Iesu, per circumcisiónem sub lege facte
O Jesus, subjected to [the] law through circumcision
Iesu, a Magis adórate
O Jesus, adored by [the] Magi
Iesu, in templo praesentáte
O Jesus, presented in [the] temple
Iesu, in ulnis iusti Simeónis excépte
O Jesus, received into [the] arms of righteous Simeon

Iesu, in Aegýptum deláte
O Jesus, carried into Egypt
Iesu, ab Heróde ad necem quaesíte
O Jesus, sought by Herod to [the] slaughter
Iesu, in Názareth nutríte
O Jesus, nurtured in Nazareth
Iesu, in templo invénte
O Jesus, found in [the] temple
Iesu, paréntibus súbdite
O Jesus, subjected [to] parents
Iesu, a Ioánne baptizáte
O Jesus, baptised by John
Iesu, in desérto tentáte
O Jesus, tempted in [the] desert
Iesu, cum homínibus conversáte
O Jesus, [who] conversed [with] men
Iesu, paupéribus discípulis sociáte
O Jesus, [who] united poor disciples
Iesu, lux mundi
O Jesus, light of [the] world
Iesu, via, véritas, et vita
O Jesus, [the] way, [the] truth, and [the] life
Iesu, exémplar virtútum ómnium
O Jesus, model of all virtues
Iesu, ómnibus languéntibus misericórditer opituláte
O Jesus, [who] mercifully helped all languishers
Iesu, gratis ódio hábite
O Jesus, freely held [with] hate
Iesu, contuméliis vexáte
O Jesus, troubled [with] insults
Iesu, lapídibus impetíte
O Jesus, pelted [with] stones

Iesu, in monte coram pátribus transfiguráte
O Jesus, transfigured on [the]mountain before [the] patriarchs
Iesu, rex mitis Hierosólymam ingrésse
O Jesus, [who] entered Jerusalem [as] a calm king
Iesu, prae compassióne lacrimáte
O Jesus, [who] cried through compassion
Iesu, trigínta argénteis appretiáte
O Jesus, valued [for] thirty pieces of silver
Iesu, ad Discipulórum pedes inclináte
O Jesus, bowed down at [the]feet of [the] Disciples
Iesu, panis vivus nos confírmans
O Jesus, living bread strengthening us
Iesu, potus verus nos laetíficans
O Jesus, true drink delighting us
Iesu, in oratióne prostráte
O Jesus, prostrated in prayer
Iesu, in agónia sanguíneo sudóre perfúse
O Jesus, in agony bathed by bloody sweat
Iesu, ab Angelo confortáte
O Jesus, comforted by [an] Angel
Iesu, ósculo a Iuda trádite
O Jesus, handed over by Judas [with a] kiss
Iesu, a minístris ligáte
O Jesus, tied up by attendants
Iesu, a Discípulis derelícte
O Jesus, deserted by Disciples
Iesu, Annae et Caíphae praesentáte
O Jesus, presented to Annas and Caiphas
Iesu, a falsis téstibus accusáte
O Jesus, accused by false witnesses
Iesu, reus mortis iudicáte
O Jesus, judged guilty of death

Iesu, in fáciem conspúte
O Jesus, spat on [the] face
Iesu, óculis veláte
O Jesus, [with] eyes veiled
Iesu, cólaphis caese
O Jesus, struck [with] blows
Iesu, cuius corpus percutiéntibus, et genae velléntibus, dedísti
O Jesus, whose body and cheeks you gave for persecutions and piercings
Iesu, a Petro negáte
O Jesus, denied by Peter
Iesu, vinctus Piláto trádite
O Jesus, bound and handed over to Pilate
Iesu, ab Heróde et eius exércitu sprete et illúse
O Jesus, by Herod and his army despised and ridiculed
Iesu, veste alba indúte
O Jesus, dressed [in a] white robe
Iesu, Barábbae postpósite
O Jesus, disregarded [for] Barabbas
Iesu, flagéllis caese
O Jesus, struck [with] scourges
Iesu, propter scélera nostra attríte
O Jesus, scourged because of our sins
Iesu, quasi leprósus reputáte
O Jesus, considered as if [a] leper
Iesu, veste purpúrea indúte
O Jesus, clothed [with a] purple robe
Iesu, spinis coronáte
O Jesus, crowned with thorns
Iesu, arúndine percússe
O Jesus, struck with a cane
Iesu, a Iudéis ad crucem postuláte
O Jesus, by [the] Jews prosecuted to [the] cross

Iesu, morte turpíssima condemnáte
O Jesus, condemned to [the] filthiest death
Iesu, voluntáti Iudaeórum trádite
O Jesus, passed on to [the] will of [the] Jews
Iesu, Crucis póndere graváte
O Jesus, weighed down by [the] weight of [the] Cross
Iesu, tamquam ovis ad occisiónem ducte
O Jesus, led like [a] sheep to murder
Iesu, véstibus exúte
O Jesus, stripped [from] robes
Iesu, clavis in cruce confíxe
O Jesus, secured [with] nails onto [the] Cross
Iesu, propter iniquitátes nostras vulneráte
O Jesus, wounded through our iniquities
Iesu, pro inimícis Patrem deprecáte
O Jesus, prayed to [the] Father for enemies
Iesu, cum iníquis reputáte
O Jesus, reflected with [the] wicked
Iesu, oppróbrium hóminum facte
O Jesus, made [the] censure of men
Iesu, in crucis blasphemáte
O Jesus, blasphemed on [the] Cross
Iesu, a Iudáeis derise
O Jesus, derided by [the] Jews
Iesu, a milítibus in crucis illúse
O Jesus, ridiculed on [the] Cross by soldiers
Iesu, a latróne convítiis lacéssite
O Jesus, provoked by [the] thief with scorn
Iesu, oppróbriis saturáte
O Jesus, drenched with insults
Iesu, latróni paeniténti Paradísum pollícite
O Jesus, [who] promised Paradise to [the] penitent thief

LATIN PRAYER

Iesu qui Ioánnem Matri tuae in fílium tradidísti
O Jesus, who passed John to your Mother as son
Iesu te a Patre derelíctum attestáte
O Jesus, [having] declared yourself derelict by [the] Father
Iesu felle et acéto in siti potáte
O Jesus, gall and vinegar drank in thirst
Iesu consummáta ómnia de te scripta testáte
O Jesus, everything accomplished from testified scripts
Iesu cuius spíritus in manus Patris commendáte
O Jesus, your spirit commended into [the] hands of [the] Father
Iesu a Patre pro tua reveréntia semper exaudíte
O Jesus, always heeded by your Father for your reverence
Iesu usque ad mortem Crucis obœdiens facte
O Jesus, made obedient in accordance with death on the Cross
Iesu láncea transfíxe
O Jesus, pierced by [a] lance
Iesu de cuius latére exívit sanguis et aqua
O Jesus, from whose side poured out blood and water
Iesu cuius livóre sanáti sumus
O Jesus, by whose bruises we are healed
Iesu propitiátio nobis facte
O Jesus, atonement made for us
Iesu de Cruce depósite
O Jesus, taken down from [the] Cross
Iesu in sindóne munda involúte
O Jesus, wrapped in [a] pure shroud
Iesu in monuménto novo tumuláte
O Jesus, buried in [a] new tomb
Iesu vinctos tuos de lacu inférni prǽdate
O Jesus, your bonds robbed from [the] depths of hell
Iesu ab ínferis victor revérse
O Jesus, [the] victor returned from hell

Iesu post resurrectiónem cum homínibus conversáte
O Jesus, after [the] resurrection conversed with men
Iesu in Caelum eleváte
O Jesus, ascended into Heaven
Iesu in Patris déxtera collocáte
O Jesus, positioned at [the] right hand of [the] Father
Iesu glória et honóre coronáte
O Jesus, crowned with glory and honour
Iesu Rex regum et Dóminus dominántium
O Jesus, King of kings and Lord of dominions
Iesu Spíritum Paraclítum discípulis elárgite
O Jesus, bestowed [the] Spirit, [the] Paraclete upon [the] disciples
Iesu Matrem tuam super choros Angelórum exáltans
O Jesus, exalting your Mother above [the] choirs of Angels
Iesu vivos et mórtuos iudicatúre
O Jesus, about to judge [the] living and [the] dead
Iesu réprobos in ignem aetérnum missúre
O Jesus, about to send [the] rejected into [the] eternal fire
Iesu parátum eléctis regnum collatúre
O Jesus, having prepared [the] kingdom about to gather [the] elect
Iesu ubertáte Domus tuae Sanctos omnes inébrians
O Jesus, intoxicating all [the] Saints of your House with riches
Iesu pater futúri sǽculi
O Jesus, father of [the] age to come
Iesu iúbilus Angelórum
O Jesus, joy of Angels
Iesu Rex Patriarchárum
O Jesus, King of [the] Patriarchs
Iesu inspirátor Prophetárum
O Jesus, inspirer of [the] Prophets
Iesu magíster Apostolórum
O Jesus, master of [the] Apostles

Iesu doctor Evangelistárum
O Jesus, teacher of [the] Evangelists
Iesu fortitúdo Mártyrum
O Jesus, strength of Martyrs
Iesu lumen Confessórum
O Jesus, light of Confessors
Iesu púritas Vírginum
O Jesus, purity of Virgins
Iesu coróna Sanctórum ómnium
O Jesus, crown of all Saints

This selection is given at length here to demonstrate how powerful the narrative of the life and passion of Jesus can be when expressed through the attributive prayer of naming, especially when each entry also prays *miserere nobis* (be merciful to us). Attribute after attribute of Christ's character builds one upon the other, most using past participles to show events long gone, and others using present participles to show the continuing action involved. Prayed iteratively in this form, every one of these individual intercessory prayers demands our fullest attention, but is evidence too of the myriad of numinous ways, through these attributes of Christ, that the Church offers for us to help seek, in some way, the Divine Nature. Every one of them demands reflection upon what particular attribute of Jesus might be signalled by a specific event. But importantly, we are confidently assured by both Scripture and Tradition, that behind every one of these attributes, is Jesus the man of prayer, because every event described, and every attributive name in these *litanies*, was/is an event of prayer. We know this because we pray with Jesus himself at the 2nd Mass of All Souls (November 2) who St John records as saying:

Quia descéndi de caelo, non ut fáciam voluntátem meam, sed voluntátem eius qui misit me.

> (Because I came down from heaven, not to do my own will, but the will of him who sent me. *Io* 6:38)

There would not have been a single moment in his life when he was not doing 'the will of him who sent me.' At every moment of his life on earth Jesus was/is in the presence of God. Every moment, therefore, was/is a moment of prayer. Prayer for us seeks the presence of God, not just as a reflection of what Jesus practiced every second of every day, but as a means of becoming like Jesus. This is surely why St Paul tells the Thessalonians:

> ***Semper gaudete. Sine intermissione orate.***
> (Always rejoice! Pray! without ceasing. *1 Thess* 5:16-17)

because this is exactly what Jesus did. As St James tells us:

> ***Subditi ergo estote Deo***
> (Be! subject therefore to God. *Iac* 4:7)
> ***Appropinquate Deo, et appropinquabit vobis.***
> (Come near! to God, and he will come near to you. *Iac* 4:8)

Within Latin Catholicism we do that, not just in the isolation of our own homes, but with the sanctifying grace offered with the sacraments of the one, true, Church. We pray in the *Epistle* on the 3rd Sunday of Advent with St Paul's advice to the Philippians:

> ***Nihil sollíciti sitis: sed in omni oratióne, et obsecratióne, cum gratiárum actióne petitiónes vestrae innotéscant apud Deum.***
> (May you be disturbed about nothing: but in everything by prayer, and by supplication, with [the] actions of thanks, let your petitions be made known before God. *Phil* 4:6)

This is not simply the current preoccupation with self-reliance repeating the mantra 'stay calm' and we will be fine by ourselves. It is recognising that to have the confidence to 'be disturbed about nothing' we need a support system in place, and Christ founded the Catholic Church to be that very support system. St Peter, upon whom Christ founded that very Church, puts it this way:

> *Quomodo omnia nobis divinae virtutis suae, quae ad vitam et pietatem donata sunt, per cognitionem eius, qui vocavit nos propria gloria, et virtute, per quem maxima, et pretiosa nobis promissa donavit: ut per haec efficiamini divinae consortes naturae: fugientes eius, quae in mundo est, concupiscentiae corruptionem.*

(See how all the gifts that make for life and holiness in us belong to his divine power; come to us through fuller knowledge of him, whose own glory and sovereignty have drawn us to himself! Through him God has bestowed on us high and treasured promises; you are to share the divine nature, with the world's corruption, the world's passions, left behind. *Knox 2 Pe* 2-3)

The Church teaches that it is by sanctifying grace that we receive this ***divinae consortes naturae*** (sharing in the Divine Nature). For example, the Council of Trent under the guidance of Pope St Pius V (1504-1572) asserted in the *Roman Catechism* (composed for Parish Priests to educate their congregations in the face of the Reformation) that the Church is unlike all other societies, for:

> *Nec vero levia mysteria in hoc vocabulo [Ecclesia] continentur*
> (In this word [Church] are contained truly not light mysteries.)

'Other bodies', the *Catechism* continues, 'rest on human reason and prudence' (***humana ratione et prudentia nituntur***) but the Church is constituted on the wisdom and counsels of God (***Dei sapientia et consilio constituta est***) who has called us inwardly (***intimo***) by the inspiration of the Holy Ghost, and who opens the hearts of men (***qui corda hominum aperit***) outwardly (***extrinsecus***) through the labour and ministry of pastors and preachers (***pastorum et praedicatorum opera ac ministerio***. §1091). The Church, therefore, is like no other human institution, and so requires a quite different disposition towards it, but most importantly, the Council of Trent went on to say that:

> 'This Church, built upon the foundation of the apostles and prophets, belongs to all the faithful (***omnes fideles***) who have existed from Adam to the present day, or who shall exist, in the profession of the true faith (***veram fidem profitentes***) to the end of time; all of whom are founded and raised upon the one corner-stone, Christ, who made both one, and announced peace to them that are near and to them that are far.' (*Vat* §1092)

Those two words *intimo* and *extrinsecus* say everything we need to know about the way we might pray: 'inward' in our hearts and minds, and 'outward' in the liturgy and actions of the Church and its ministers, in order for us to move some way to achieving ***Divinae Consortium Naturae*** (a sharing in Divine Nature). We pray at Saturday *Vespers*:

> *Prope est Dóminus ómnibus invocántibus eum, ómnibus invocántibus eum in veritáte.*
> (The Lord is near to all calling upon him, to all calling upon him in truth. *Ps* 144:18)

The Hebrew word, for which ***veritas*** (truth) is a translation, is אמת (*emet*) and, according to the Kabbalists, signifies the unique linguistic relationship humans have with God, as it is composed of the first, middle, and the last characters of the Hebrew alphabet, signifying that truth continues from the beginning (א) through the middle (מ)

to the end (ת). While philosophically the Latin Catholic understanding of 'truth' differs from the Jewish (and from the pagan Greek and Roman) interpretations, importantly the phrase *in veritate* with its little preposition *in* suggests that 'truth' is not simply laid upon us, as God marked Adam's forehead, or as the ashes from Palm Sunday are inscribed on our heads on Ash Wednesday, but, has to be earned, in order for those standing in God's presence to have **nomen eius, et nomen Patris eius scriptum in frontibus suis** (his name [Jesus], and the name of his Father, written on their foreheads *Apc* 14:1). Earning a place in that Divine Presence is not an easy task, nor, for Latin Catholics, is it assumed that simply accepting (*intimo* - inward) Christ as our personal Saviour (being 'born again in Christ') is sufficient. There are outward (*extrinsecus*) responsibilities and requirements too.

One of the most familiar prayers within Latin Catholicism, which has as its heart the relationship between *intimo* and *extrinsecus*, is the **Anima Christi** (Soul of Christ). St Ignatius of Loyola (1491-1556) co-founder of the Society of Jesus (**Societas Iesu**) included it in the beginning of his highly influential 1520s *Ejercicios Espirituales* (*Spiritual Exercises*) which were later translated from the original Spanish into Latin by Andreas Frusos in 1547 as **Exercitia Spiritualia** and known to Jesuits as the **Vulgata**. This prayer is thought to date back to at least the 1300s if not before. It is still a favourite prayer of many in both Latin and English, and can be found in most missals and prayer books. It became a popular hymn in English Catholic churches as 'Soul of my Saviour' with a melody composed by Jesuit Priest William J Maher SJ (1823-1877) and with words by Fr Edward Caswall CO (1814-1878) whose translations of the hymns in the **Breviarium Romanum** are still widely used today. The opening line is **Anima Christi sanctifica me** (Soul of Christ sanctify me) and includes a grammatical feature absolutely central to Latin prayer: the 'imperative mood' (*sanctifica* imperative singular of *sanctificare*). St Paul, using this same grammatical feature (as translated in the *Vulgate*) tells the Romans in the *Epistle* we pray on the 1st Sunday after the Epiphany:

nolíte conformári huic sǽculo;
(be not conformed to this age)
sed reformámini in novitáte sensus vestri
(but be reformed in [the] newness of your mind)
ut probétis quae sit volúntas Dei bona, et benéplacens, et perfécta.
(that you may demonstrate what may be [the] good, and [the] pleasing,
and perfect will of God. *Rom* 12:2)

In other words: act on the imperatives. Don't just *be* (indicative) Christian; *do!* (imperative) Christian. This is a crucial feature of Latin prayer to which we now turn in *Chapter V: Imperative Prayer.*

V

IMPERATIVE PRAYER

O bone Iesu exáudi me
(O good Jesus heed me)

Directives

Learning to read Latin, essential though that is, is not enough in Latin prayer. Fr Simon Mary of the Cross MCarm (1984-) says of prayer in general (2021): 'As a most intimate spiritual reality, prayer, and even more so, contemplation, evades finite expressions of speech and the rules of grammar.' There is a spiritual dynamic which is completely dependent upon the Christian *kerygma* (κήρυγμα - *kérugma* - proclamation). That proclamation declares what it is to *be* Christian (indicative) but, as we pray in the *Epistle* for the 14th Sunday after Pentecost:

> **Spíritu ambuláte, et desidéria carnis non perficiétis.**
> (Walk! with the Spirit, and you will not perform the desires of the flesh. *Gal* 5:16)

St Paul does more than proclaim what it is to *be* a Christian to the Galatians, he directs them through his teaching (διδαχή - *didache* - teaching): *do!* Christian. The spiritual *kerygma-didache* dynamic here rests on a grammatical 'indicative-imperative' dynamic. The Galatians are directed by St Paul in an imperative like **ambulate** so that **non** *perficietis* (you will not perform [indicative]) 'the desires of the flesh'. We are similarly directed as we pray the Mass and *Office*:

> *accípite* - imp pl of *accipere* - to accept - [you pl] accept!
> *admítte* - imp sg of *admittere* - to admit - [you sg] admit!
> *aufer* - imp sg of *auferre* (irreg) - to take away - [you sg] take away!
> *bénedic* - irreg imp sg of *benedicere* - to bless - [you sg] bless!
> *bíbite* - imp pl of *bibere* - to drink - [you pl] drink!
> *convérte* - imp sg of *convertere* - to turn - [you sg] turn!
> *da* - imp sg of *dare* - to give - [you sg] give!
> *defénde* - imp sg of *defendere* - to defend - [you sg] defend!
> *detrúde* - imp sg of *detrudere* - to drive away - [you sg] drive away!
> *dimítte* - imp sg of *dimittere* - to dismiss - [you sg] - dismiss!
> *discérne* - imp sg of *discernere* - to discern - [you sg] discern!
> *dona* - imp sg of *donare* - to give - [you sg] give!
> *emítte* - imp sg of *emittere* - to send out - [you sg] send out!
> *erípe* - imp sg of *eripere* - to deliver - [you sg] deliver!
> *érue* - imp sg of *eruere* - to cast out - [you sg] cast out!
> *esto* - fut imp sg of *esse* - to be - [you sg] be!
> *exáudi* - imp sg of *exaudire* - to heed - [you sg] heed!
> *fac* – irreg imp sg of *facere* - to do/make - [you sg] do/make!
> *ite* - imp pl of *ire* - to go - [you pl] go!
> *iúdica* - imp sg of *iudicare* - to judge - [you sg] judge!
> *líbera* - imp sg of *liberare* - to free - [you sg] free!
> *manducáte* - imp pl of *manducare* - to eat - [you pl] eat!
> *meménto* - fut imp sg of *meminisse* - to remember - [you sg] remember!
> *munda* - imp sg of *mundare* - to wash - [you sg] wash!
> *ora* - imp sg of *orare* - to pray - [you sg] pray!
> *oráte* - imp pl of *orare* - to pray - [you pl] pray!
> *osténde* - imp sg of *ostendere* - to show - [you sg] show!
> *percúte* - imp sg of *percutere* - to strike - [you sg] strike!

pone - imp sg of *ponere* - to place - [you sg] place!
praesta - imp sg of *praestare* - to present - [you sg] present!
rédime - imp sg of *redimere* - to redeem - [you sg] redeem!
réspice - imp sg of *respicere* - to look upon - [you sg] look upon!
spera - imp sg of *sperare* - to hope - [you sg] hope!
súscipe - imp sg of *suscipere* - to receive - [you sg] receive!
veni - imp sg of *venire* - to come - [you sg] come!

As a list highlighting the specific grammatical feature of active voice singular and plural imperative forms of some selected verbs, it is useful linguistically, but is much more powerful spiritually when viewed as a 'to do list' of actions for Catholics. In the *Gospel* for this same 14th Sunday after Pentecost Jesus directs his disciples:

Nolíte thesaurizáre vobis thesáuros in terra.
(Do not! [to] treasure up treasures for yourselves on earth.)
Thesaurizáte autem vobis thesáuros in caelo.
(But treasure up! treasures for yourselves in heaven.)

The plural imperatives **nolite** and **thesaurizate** are given in the active voice. We know who the agents are in those directions; they are the [you pl] implicit in the imperative. But for those imperatives to have any significant meaning the agents [Galatians] also need indicatives, either explicitly, as in the actions involved in the infinitive *thesaurizare* (to treasure up) or implicitly as in the actions involved in the imperative *thesaurizate* (treasure up!). Even then, such actions only have significant (contextual) meaning for Christians when it is understood that each of these directives, and the real agency involved, have their source in Christ's own actions and agency as the Incarnate Son of God.

In Chapters 5 to 7 of *The Gospel According to Matthew* we are given three chapters in which Jesus, going up to a high mountain, teaches us not only how to pray using the **Pater Noster** (Our Father) but delivers the eight *Beatitudes* (**Octo Beatitudines**) and a whole series of other teachings which form the central core of Christianity. At the heart of this teaching, initially from the *Book of Leviticus*, is what in Judaism became known as *Lev ha-Torah* (the heart of the Jewish Scriptures) summed up with this single maxim:

> ***Diliges amicum tuum sicut teipsum.***
> (You will love your neighbour as yourself. *Lv* 19:18)

The *Talmud* (Jewish religious law) says:

> 'What is hateful to you, do not do to your fellow man. This is the law: all the rest is commentary.'

St James refers to this as the 'royal law' saying:

> ***Si tamen legem perficitis regalem secundum Scripturas: Diliges proximum tuum sicut teipsum: bene facitis:***
> (If then you fulfil the royal law according to the Scriptures: 'Thou shalt love thy neighbour as thyself': you do well.' (*DR Ia* 2:8)

This **lex regalis** later became well known in Protestant Christianity after the Reformation as 'the Golden Rule', and was formalised as such in Catholicism only when this phrase first appeared as **Regula aurea** in the 1994 **Catechismus**:

> ***In omnibus casibus quaedam applicantur regulae:***
> ***- Nunquam licet malum facere ut ex eo bonum proveniat.***
> ***- "Regula aurea" : "Omnia [...], quaecumque vultis ut faciant vobis homines, ita et vos facite eis."*** (*Mt* 7:12)
> (Some rules apply in every case:- One may never do evil so that good may result from it;- the Golden Rule: "Whatever you wish that men would do to you, do so to them." *Vat* §1789)

Recorded, then, in these three chapters, Jesus is giving the new law of the *Gospels* compared to the old law of the *Talmud*. That new law Jesus delivers not in 'Thou shalts' and 'Thou shalt nots', but 'opening his mouth, he taught them, saying' first the Beatitudes (*Mt* 5:3-11) and then in the very next verse (which we pray in the *Gospel* for the Feast of All Saints [November 1]) announcing:

gaudéte, et exsultáte, quóniam merces vestra copiósa est in caelis.
(be glad!, and **rejoice!**, for your reward is very great in heaven. *Mt* 5:12)

Jesus directs the crowds gathered there:

Nolite putare quoniam veni solvere legem aut prophetas: non veni solvere, sed adimplere.
(Think not! that I come to destroy the law or the prophets: I come not to destroy, but to fulfil. *Mt* 5:17)

He talks of the need to keep the commandments so that:

qui autem fecerit et docuerit, hic magnus vocabitur in regno caelorum.
(thus [he] who will have done and will have taught, he will be called great in the kingdom of heaven. *Mt* 5:19)
vade prius reconciliari fratri tuo:
(go! first to be reconciled to your brother *Mt* 5:24)
Esto consentiens adversario tuo cito dum es in via cum eo:
(Be! soon harmonious with your adversary while you are on the road with him: *Mt* 5:25)
Quod si oculus tuus dexter scandalizat te, erue eum, et proiice abs te:
(For if your right eye shocks you, tear! it out, and throw! [it] away from you. *Mt* 5:29)

> *Et si dextra manus tua scandalizat te, abscide eam, et proiice abs te:*
>
> (And if your right hand shocks you, cut! it off, and throw! [it] away from you: *Mt* 5:30)

Jesus continues:

> *Audistis quia dictum est: Diliges proximum tuum, et odio habebis inimicum tuum.*
>
> (You heard that it has been said: you will love your neighbour, and you will hate your enemy.)
>
> *Ego autem dico vobis: diligite inimicos vestros, benefacite his qui oderunt vos, et orate pro persequentibus et calumniantibus vos:*
>
> (But I say to you: love! your enemies, do! good to those who hate you, and pray! for those persecuting and falsely accusing you: *Mt* 5:43-44)

And why?

> *ut sitis filii Patris vestri, qui in caelis est: qui solem suum oriri facit super bonos et malos: et pluit super iustos et iniustos.*
>
> (that you may be the children of your Father, who is in heaven: who makes his sun to rise upon the good and the bad: and rains upon the just and the unjust. *Mt* 5:45)
>
> *Estote ergo vos perfecti, sicut et Pater vester caelestis perfectus est.*
>
> (Be! you therefore perfect, as so your heavenly Father is perfect. *Mt* 5:48)
>
> *Attendite ne iustitiam vestram faciatis coram hominibus ut videamini ab eis:*
>
> (Pay attention! lest you do your justice before men, that you may be seen by them.' *Mt* 6:1)

And the imperatives and prohibitives flow on:

noli tuba canere ante te
(sound not! a trumpet before you *Mt* 6:2)
ora Patrem tuum in abscondito
(pray! to your Father in secret *Mt* 6:6)
nolite multum loqui, sicut ethnici
(speak not! much, as the heathens *Mt* 6:7)
Nolite ergo assimilari eis
(Do not! [to] be similar to them *Mt* 6:8)

We are then taught how to pray the **Pater Noster** (*Mt* 6:9-13) calling on God:

Panem nostrum supersubstantialem da nobis hodie
(Give! to us today our life-supporting bread)
et dimitte nobis debita nostra
(and discharge! from us our dues)
Et ne nos inducas in tentationem, sed libera nos a malo. Amen.
(And may you not lead us intowards temptation, but free! us from
  evil. Amen. *Mt* 6:11-13)

Further on in his teaching we are directed that when we fast 'be not! (***nolite fieri***) as the hypocrites, sad' (*Mt* 6:16) but 'when you fast, anoint! (***unge***) your head, and wash! (***lava***) your face' (*Mt* 6:17). 'Behold! (***respicite***) the birds of the air' (*Mt* 6:26) and 'consider! (***considerate***) the lilies of the field' (*Mt* 6:28). 'Seek! (***quaerite***) first the kingdom of God' (*Mt* 6:33) and 'judge not! (***nolite iudicare***) that you may not be judged.' (*Mt* 7:1). 'Cast out! (***eiice***) the wood from your eye' (*Mt* 7:5). 'Give not! (***Nolite dare***) the holy to dogs' (Mt 7:6). 'Ask! (***petite***) and it will be given you: seek! (***quaerite***) and you will find: knock! (***pulsate***) and it will be opened to you.' (*Mt* 7:7). 'All things therefore whatsoever you would that men should do to you, do! (***facite***) also to them.' *Mt* 7:12). 'Enter! (***intrate***) at the narrow gate' (*Mt* 7:13). 'Beware! (***attendite***) of false prophets' (*Mt* 7:15):

> *Et tunc confitebor illis: Quia numquam novi vos: discedite a me, qui operamini iniquitatem.*
> (And then I will reveal to them: for I never knew you: depart! from me, who work iniquity. *Mt* 7:23)

And the section ends:

> ***Erat enim docens eos sicut potestatem habens, et non sicut scribae eorum, et pharisaei.***
> (For he was teaching them as one having power, and not as the scribes and pharisees.' DR *Mt* 7:29)

'As one having power' or, as Knox translates it, 'like one who had authority'. As one, therefore, who exercises that power by commanding with an authority with directives expressed grammatically in Latin as imperatives and prohibitives, that come directly from the Divine, and thus investing the words with the power of Divine authority. That authority Christ makes very clear is one which is marked by a shift from the old law to the new law. In the Gospel for the Friday after Ash Wednesday we pray in Christ's own words:

> *Díliges próximum tuum, et ódio habébis inimícum tuum*
> (You will love your neighbour, and you will hate your enemy.)
> ***Ego autem dico vobis: dilígite inimícos vestros, benefácite his qui odérunt vos, et oráte pro persequéntibus et calumniántibus vos:***
> (But I say to you: love! your enemies: do well! to those who hate you, and pray! for those persecuting and hating you. *Mt* 5:43-44)

The singular future indicatives (*indicare* - to state) **diliges** and **habebis** now become the plural imperatives (*imperare* - to command): **diligite!**, **benefacite!** and **orate!** This is not just a shift from individual to collective responsibility. It is an ideological shift from the old to the new law. And it is marked by a grammatical shift in mood where 'you will' functions as a declaration/statement and 'love!' functions as a directive in the imperative mood. The term 'mood' in grammar does not mean the way someone or something may feel, as it tends to do in many other circumstances, it comes from the Latin word ***modus*** which means 'manner/method'. What we see here, then, is that the *manner* of speaking has changed from stating something as if it is a fact (indicative) to directing something to be done (imperative). The Lord spoke to the people of Israel through Moses saying:

Sanctificamini et estote sancti, quia ego sum Dominus Deus vester.
(Be sanctified!, and be! holy, because I am the Lord your God. *Lv* 20:7)

Both *sanctificamini* and *estote* are plural imperatives but with a different grammatical voice: *estote* is the 2nd person plural future active imperative of *esse* (to be) and *sanctificamini* is the 2nd person plural present passive imperative of *sanctificare* (to sanctify/to set apart). Both are directing something to be done, but with the passive voice we are not told who the agent of the action is, so we might ask the question here: 'be sanctified by whom?' But in the active imperative 'be' (holy) the agent is implicit as the 'you pl'. The imperative mood is not simply about ordering someone to do or not to do something. It is about changing, and affirming, realities and hence identities. In prayer, that is powerful indeed, because the dynamic of indicative-imperative-subjunctive moods, for example, involves a change from everyday reality to a supernatural reality. It involves a change of reality from the ordinary to the extraordinary; a change from the everyday to the numinous.

The Imperative-Indicative Dynamic

The ***Anima Christi*** prayer which we saw at the end of the last chapter, and which is quoted in the epigraph to this chapter, is a good example of that change of mood, changed reality and hence, changed identity. We pray the imperatives:

Anima Christi sanctífica me.
(Soul of Christ sanctify me!)
Corpus Christi salva me.
(Body of Christ save me!)
Sanguis Christi inébria me.
(Blood of Christ drench me!)
Aqua láteris Christi lava me.
(Water from the side of Christ wash me!)
Péssio Christi confórta me.
(Passion of Christ strengthen me!)
O bone Iesu exáudi me.
(O good Jesus heed me!)

Each of the first five lines here from this beautiful prayer is in two parts: (1) nom/voc noun (*anima*) + gen sg noun (*Christi*) + imperative singular verb (*sanctifica*) + pronoun *me*. In effect the prayer directs (imperative) the first part of the line to do something: sanctify (*sanctifica*) save (*salva*) drench (*inebria*) wash (*lava*) and strengthen (*conforta*). They are essentially commands to do something. They are not statements indicative of something being done, for example, 'The soul of Christ sanctified me' or 'the Body of Christ saved me', but imperatives directing something to be done, as in the last line of this prayer with its vocative phrase **O bone Iesu** (O good Jesus) *exaudi me* (heed me!). The form, force and function of these actions in these forms of imperative address (as verbs) is to achieve something, not from our own doing, but from God's actions (his affect) upon us.

One of the first things we encounter as Catholics, when we learn to pray, is to recognise that however we might pray, it is always directed towards God. It always addresses God. Prayer, even if it is mediated through the Blessed Virgin Mary and/or the Saints and Angels, is always an ***actus fidei*** (act of faith) in the very existence of God. That phrase 'an act of faith' is far more important than many might realise. Not simply because of the importance of faith which, more often than not is what people concentrate on, and so make the most significant part of this phrase, but because of the word 'act'. Central to language, Latin or any other, is the way in which we make the words, phrases, clauses and sentences of those languages 'act' discursively. An act of faith does not simply 'signify' a belief; it 'performs' that belief. That action can then transform the believers themselves, not through their own actions and volition (as the Scribes and Pharisees thought) but as St Paul tells the Philippians:

> *Deus est enim, qui operatur in vobis et velle, et perficere pro bona voluntate.*
> (For it is God, who works in you both to will, and to perfect according to his good will. *Phil* 2:13)

God is doing the action in the infinitives **velle** and **perficere**, not St Paul and not us. When we address God, therefore, we are not simply calling out to him. We are asking him to affect us. The motto of the Dominicans is **Laudare, Benedicere, Praedicare,** all active infinitives, which, may be translated into English as 'to Praise, to Bless, to Preach' or as passive imperatives, 'Be praised!, Be blessed!, Be made known! Every time an imperative is used in Latin prayer a choice has been made to determine what it is we must do for God. As St Paul makes clear to the Colossians, and which we pray in the *Epistle* for the Mass of the Easter Vigil on Holy Saturday, picking up on both St Matthew and St Luke:

> *si consurrexístis cum Christo: quae sursum sunt quaérite, ubi Christus est in déxtera Dei sedens:*
> (if you have arisen with Christ: seek! [those things] that are above, where Christ is sitting at the right hand of God. *Col* 3:1-2)

This imperative dynamic, however, is only fully understandable as non-negotiable actions that we must perform if, as St Paul says, and only if, 'you are arisen with Christ' (*Col* 3:1). In other words our realities change, not because we are ordered to in a grammatical imperative, 'do this!' but because the focus of that imperative - its power and authority - is totally dependent upon our accepting an indicative statement of fact: 'Christ is risen and sits at the right hand of God'. Without our accepting that indicative fact, the imperative not only has no force or power, it actually makes no sense at all. In other words, accepting the indicative fact creates the imperative dynamic; a dynamic at the very heart of prayer itself. In Biblical studies and some theology, this is often described as the 'imperative-indicative dynamic', meaning simply that if we are told to do something as Christians: 'pray!', for example, the imperative 'pray!' has no point at all unless there is an underlying indicative: 'God is'. Imperative address (directive) relies on an underlying indicative (declaration): the imperative-indicative dynamic.

When St Peter writes to 'the elect [who are] strangers dispersed through Pontus, Galatia, Cappadocia, Asia, and Bithynia' (***electis advenis dispersionis Ponti, Galatiae, Cappadociae, Asiae, et Bithyniae***) (*1 Pe* 1:1) we pray in the *Epistle* of the 3rd Sunday after Easter, where he exhorts them:

> ***Omnes honoráte: fraternitátem dilígite: Deum timéte: regem honorificáte.***
> (Honour! all men: Love! the brotherhood: Fear! God: Honour! the king. *1 Pe* 2:17)

The subjects of the imperative verbs [implicit you pl] are being asked to perform an action upon someone or something else. They are being urged to be active. And they are being urged to do this in present time. This is not something that was done in the past, or to be put off until some time into the future; but to be done now. And it involves the subjects doing something actively to others. St Peter then goes on to name these subjects (***Servi***). He tells them:

Servi, súbditi estóte in omni timóre dóminis, non tantum bonis et modéstis, sed étiam dýscolis.
(O servants, be! subjects at all times to your masters, not only to the good and gentle, but also to the peevish. *1 Pe* 2:18)

The *domini* are now the ones who are effectively performing an action on the *servi* by imposing their superiority upon them, and thereby requiring suitable actions from the *servi* which recognises this master-servant relationship. The *servi* did nothing to actively bring about this relationship, they are in fact passive recipients of it, not the agents of the action, although they must then act upon it accordingly as expressed by the active future imperative phrase *subditi estote* (*estote* fut imp pl of *esse* - 'to be') regardless of the characters of the 'masters'. We pray at Saturday *Matins*:

Meménto nostri, Dómine, in beneplácito pópuli tui; vísita nos in salutári tuo
(Remember! us, O Lord, with kindness of your people; visit! us with your salvation *Ps* 105:4)

where *memento* is the 2nd pers sg fut act imp of *meminisse* and *visita* is the 2nd pers sg pres act imp of *visitare*. In practice, the distinction between future and present imperative is not one that is marked strongly in Latin prayer. When the Priest at a *usus antiquior* Mass prays:

Meménto, Dómine, famulórum, famularúmque tuárum N et N et ómnium circumstántium
(Be mindful! O Lord, of your men servants, and women servants N and N and of all here present standing round)

he is using a future imperative, but, like the *memento* in *Psalm* 105, it has considerable force in the present. When St Luke records the good thief saying to Jesus from the cross, which we pray in the *Passion* on [Spy] Wednesday in Holy Week:

> *Dómine, meménto mei cum véneris in regnum tuum.*
> (O Lord, be mindful! of me when you will have come into your kingdom. *Lc* 23:42)

Jesus replies:

> *Amen dico tibi: hódie mecum eris in paradíso.*
> (Amen I say to you: today you will be with me in paradise. *Lc* 23: 43)

where future and present are linked by the force of the imperatives, while the sense of past time is never far away. We are in a particular state of being at any given time (indicative) and through prayer we are seeking a new state of being: a 'what needs to be' state which the imperative directs us to strive for. Being a Christian requires actions that bring about change (imperatives) not simply contentment with the *status quo* (indicatives). The Christian proclamation (κήρυγμα) of this new law involves being told *do!* (imperative) something new, not *rest* (indicative) on what is already. This is the distinction that lies at the very heart of the grammatical uses of both the indicative and imperative moods in Latin prayer, where the grammar of the 'imperative-indicative dynamic' has a life beyond just its linguistic form and function. It has a numinous life, and often in the most unexpected way. For example a prayer, attributed to the Franciscan St Anthony of Padua (1195-1232) was carved into the base of the Egyptian obelisk in St Peter's Square in Rome by order of the Franciscan Pope Sixtus V:

> *Ecce Crucem Domini!* (Behold [the] Cross of [the] Lord!)
> *Fugite partes adversae!* (Go adverse parts!)
> *Vicit Leo de tribu Iuda,* (The Lion from [the] tribe of Judah has conquered)

Radix David! Alleluia! ([The] Root of David! Alleluia!)

There are no pronouns, but the 2nd person [you pl] is implicit in the interjection *ecce* ([you] behold!) and in the active imperative *fugite* [you pl]. The point of view throughout is a 2nd person perspective, and in the context of the obelisk in St Peter's Square, that 2nd person - the [you pl] - are all those walking by and being addressed by that implicit 'you'. We are given an identity as we walk by, as if the obelisk itself is calling out to us, addressing us, directing us and reshaping our realities as a result.

Our identity is always shaped by the world we live in, even by obelisks. We live in a contemporary world where 'self' and the natural world, are promulgated as prime, through the pages and screens of the world we live in; privileging this world as being the only worthwhile referent. Individual personality - the 'ego perspective' - now dominates. Materiality dominates. Prayer, if it is considered at all, is seen by so many now, as inconsequential and peripheral to the 'real' business of being human, just as the obelisk is not actually seen as a source of prayer by the millions who walk by it and never read the inscription. But like the imperative *fugite* carved into its stone, the imperative focus of the towering monument itself stands testimony to the force of its prayer.

Imperative Identity

St Benedict created a rule of life which has at its heart a constantly repeating rhythm of prayer and work. The Prologue of **Regula Sanctissimi Patris Nostri Benedicti** (The Rule of Our Most Holy Father Benedict) opens with:

> *Obsculta, O fili, praecepta magistri, et inclina aurem cordis tui et admonitionem pii patris libenter excipe et efficaciter comple, ut ad eum per oboedientiae laborem redeas, a quo per inoboedientiae desidiam recesseras.*

(Listen! O son, to [the] precepts of [the] master, and bend! [the] ear of your heart and freely receive! and effectively complete! [the] correction of [the] holy father, that through [the] labour of obedience you may return to him, from whom through [the] sloth of disobedience you had recoiled.)

The imperative: **Obsculta** [also written *Ausculta*] + voc *O fili* (Listen! O son) is followed by another imperative *inclina aurem cordis tui* (bend! the ear of your heart) directing an action that makes it clear that what is to follow is not just a set of practices for everyday living in the monastery, but also how to live interiorly towards the numinous. The Rule itself is for those who would listen and re-focus their lives with the imperatives ***ora, labora, lege*** (pray! work! read!). Similarly, when St Paul writes from Corinth in response to St Timothy of Ephesus (d 97AD) both directing and encouraging the Thessalonians:

> ***Propter quod consolamini invicem, et aedificate alterutrum, sicut et facitis.***
> (For which comfort! the enemy, and edify! one another, as you also do. *1Thess* 5:11)

And continues by saying:

> 'we beseech you, brethren to know them who labour among you and are over you in the Lord, and admonish you that you esteem them more abundantly in charity for their work's sake. Have! (***habete***) peace with them. And we beseech you brethren rebuke! (***corripite***) the unquiet, comfort! (***consolamini***) the feeble minded, support! (***suscipite***) the weak, be! (***estote***) patient towards all men. See! (***videte***) that none render evil for evil to any man; but ever follow! (***sectamini***) that which is good towards each other, and towards all men. Always rejoice! (***gaudete***). Pray! (***orate***) without ceasing. In all things give! (***agite***) thanks; for this is the will of God in Christ Jesus concerning

you all. Extinguish not! (***nolite extinguere***) the spirit. Despise not! (***nolite spernere***) prophecies. But prove! (***probate***) all things; hold fast! (***tenete***) that which is good. From all appearance of evil refrain! (***abstinete***) yourselves. And may the God of peace himself sanctify you in all things; that your whole spirit and soul and body may be preserved blameless in the coming of our Lord Jesus Christ. He is faithful who hath called you, who also will do it. Brethren, pray! (***orate***) for us. Salute! (***salutate***) all the brethren with a holy kiss. I charge you by the Lord, that this epistle be read to all the holy brethren. The grace of our Lord Jesus Christ be with you. Amen.' (*DR 1 Thess* 5:11-28)

But these are not simply directives; they are exhortations for realities and identities to change; to 'see' and 'live' in new ways, in just the same way as St Benedict's *Rule* sought, and still seeks, to do in a never-ending round of prayer, work and reading, for example:

> *Duodecimus humilitatis gradus est, si non solum corde monachus, sed etiam ipso corpore humilitatem videntibus se semper indicet, id est Opere Dei, in oratorio, in monasterio, in horto, in via, in agro vel ubicumque sedens, ambulans vel stans, inclinato sit semper capite, defixis in terram aspectibus, reum se omni hora de peccatis suis aestimans iam se tremendo iudicio repraesentari aestimet, dicens sibi in corde semper illud, quod publicanus ille evangelicus fixis in terram oculis dixit: Domine, non sum dignus, ego peccator, levare oculos meos ad caelos. Et item cum Propheta: incurvatus sum et humiliatus sum usquequaque.* (**Caput VII: De humilitate**)

([The] twelfth step in humility is, if a monk not only by heart, but also always in his very body shows humility to those seeing him, that is, by [the] Work of God, in [the] oratory, in [the] monastery, in [the] garden, on [the] road, in [the] field or elsewhere, sitting, walking, or standing, he, with head always bowed, may be focussed on aspects on

[the] ground, counting himself at all times as guilty concerning his sins soon to be shown up by fearful judgement, saying always in his heart to himself what [the] publican in [the] Gospel with eyes fixed on [the] ground said: O Lord, I a sinner am not worthy, to lift up my eyes to heaven. And again with [the] Prophet: I am bowed inwards and am humbled at all times. Chapter 7: *Concerning humility*)

This is the imperative ***inclina aurem cordis tui*** personified in the monk by his seeking (and showing himself) to be transformed by the imperative into the 'new indicative' by way of him seeking the numinous, through 'the labour of obedience'. St Mark the Evangelist (12-68 AD) records Jesus saying to his disciples on the Mount of Olives:

videte, vigilate, et orate (look!, watch! and pray!, *Mc* 13:33)

These are the same kind of imperatives St Benedict uses and which St Augustine heard one day in the year 386 inspiring him to lift up the *Bible* and read, thus beginning his final conversion to Catholicism:

Tolle lege! Tolle lege! (Lift up! read! Lift up! read!)

But of course, imperatives like this don't exist in isolation. We don't simply say 'Praise!' by itself (though some evangelical Christians do as part of their worship). They come, in Latin prayer, as part of a pattern which involves functions other than the directive of the imperative. They form relationships with other parts of speech; other grammatical functions; other dynamic relationships and have other spiritual and numinous purposes. We pray *Psalm* 25 in Wednesday *Prime* with the words:

Iúdica me, Dómine
(Judge! me, O Lord)

Proba me, Dómine, et tenta me
(Test! me, O Lord, and try! me)

These are imprecatory imperatives addressing God for an affect to be made on the person praying. They are petitionary prayers, but more than that, they are simultaneously declarations of faith. Addressing God with a petition like this assumes, indicatively, that we actually believe in God. It assumes, indicatively, that we have faith. It is, therefore, an assertion (*assertio*) of belief, but also a supplication (*supplicatio*) and indicates in the very word itself that the person praying assumes a more suppliant role than the one being prayed to. *Supplicatio* comes from the Latin verb *supplicare* which is made up of the preposition *sub* (under/below) and the verb *plicare* (to bend). This combination of words immediately indicates that the person addressing God with the prayer of petition is not on an equal footing with God, and the verb *supplicare* (to bend low) implies that when we do so we are not just asking for something, we are imploring/entreating/beseeching, from an inferior position. The **Catechismus** explains this by saying that:

> *Per petitionis orationem conscientiam patefacimus nostrae relationis cum Deo: ut creaturae, nostra non sumus origo, neque adversitatum domini, neque noster ultimus finis, sed etiam ut peccatores, scimus, utpote christiani, nos a Patre nostro averti. Petitio est iam quidam ad Eum reditus.*
>
> (By prayer of petition we express awareness of our relationship with God. We are creatures who are not our own beginning, not the masters of adversity, not our own last end. We are sinners who as Christians know that we have turned away from our Father. Our petition is already a turning back to him. *Cat* §2629)

St Mark records that Jesus tells Peter:

> ***omnia quaecumque orantes petitis, credite quia accipietis, et evenient vobis***
> (all things, whatsoever you seek praying, believe! that you will receive; and they will come to you. *Mc* 11:24)

A ***petitio/supplicatio*** requires ***fides*** (faith). This is more than an ***opinio*** (opinion/belief) about something: as St Paul says to the Hebrews:

> ***Est fides autem sperandarum substantia rerum, argumentum non apparentium.***
> (For faith is the substance of the things hoped for, the proof of the [things] not apparent. *Heb* 11:1)

This might take a little thinking about. In earlier forms of English there was a distinction made between 'belief' (Anglo Saxon *geleafa*) which always meant 'trust in God', and 'faith' (*feith/fei* by way of Old French *feid/fay* through Latin *fides*) which generally meant 'loyalty to a person or superior'. While there is no apparent semantic distinction made between 'faith' and 'belief' in the *Bible*, the original Greek verb πιστεύω (*pisteuo* and its variants) tends to be translated in the *Vulgate* with the Latin verb and its variants ***credere*** (to believe) while the original Greek noun πίστις (*pistis* and its variants) tends to be translated with the Latin noun ***fides*** and its variants. There are over 400 uses of the verb ***credere*** and its variants in the *Vulgate*, and over 450 entries of the noun ***fides*** and its variants, and while the distinction between the use of the verb and the noun (***credere*** and ***fides***) tends also to be mirrored by the English translations 'belief' and 'faith', in the original Greek they come from the same root word.

In English and Latin, then, we have different words for saying 'we believe' and 'we have faith', but the act of prayer involved, which, as Catholicism teaches us, is 'the raising of one's mind and heart to God', remains the same. It is not 'either/or' 'belief' and 'faith' but 'both/and' 'belief' and 'faith', and according to the *Catechism* involves 'adoration', 'contrition', 'thanksgiving' and 'supplication'. The grammatical mood may change from one stating/declaring that one believes (indicative) to one that entreats/petitions (imperative) for belief, and vice versa, but both can only be done in faith. What we believe does not just completely determine who we are as Christians, but also what we do. That is the force that makes the 'imperative-indicative relationship' so dynamic in theology and, even more so when see through a numinous lens.

The English word 'dynamic', which I have used as a core word in describing the grammar of Latin prayer in this book, comes from the Greek δυναμικός (*dynamikos* - forceful/powerful) and is derived from the verb δύναμαι (*dynamai* - I am able). 'To be able' means to have force of some description, and so, an indicative declaration that states that 'Christ is risen' as a dynamic part of our belief as Christians, is not just a statement, it is a show of force. The *Apostles' Creed* prayed at the beginning of *Matins* and *Prime*, in *Compline* and as part of the *Rosary*; or the *Nicene Creed* prayed at Mass on Sundays and Feast Days, is a show of force. How we respond to that show of force determines who we are as Christians. Why would we 'seek' or 'mind' ('see' and 'live') the things that are above, and not the things of the earth, if there were no indication that Christ had risen, ascended to Heaven and was sitting at the right hand of God? Why would we accept the imperatives, if there were no underlying indicatives? Why would we accept the *didache* (teaching) of Christianity if there were no initial *kerygma* (proclamation) from Christ himself?

Declaring indicatively that we are saved because we believe and have accepted Christ as our personal Saviour is considered by many non-Catholic Christians to be a sufficient assurance of salvation, but this is not the Catholic way. An indicative theology of salvation (what is stated) needs also its counterpart dynamic: an imperative theology of action (what needs to be done). This is the Catholic way. So when we pray:

Ave María
(imp sg *avere* + nom/voc sg f *María*)
Hail [O] Mary

Ave Mater dolórosa
(imp sg *avere* + nom/voc sg f *Mater* + nom/voc sg f adj *dolorosus*)
Hail [O] sorrowful Mother

Oráte fratres
(imp pl *orare* + nom/voc pl m *frater*)
Pray [O] brethren

Meménto, Dómine
(fut imp sg dep *meminisse* + voc sg m *Dominus*)
Remember, O Lord

Exáudi Dómine sancte, Pater omnípotens, aetérne Deus
(imp sg *exaudire* + voc sg m *Dominus* + voc sg m adj *sanctus* + nom/voc sg m *pater* + nom/voc sg m adj *omnipotens* + voc sg m adj *aeternus* + voc sg m *Deus*)
Heed O holy Lord, [O] Father almighty, O eternal God

Memoráre, O puríssime Sponse Vírginis Maríae,
O dulcis Protéctor mi, sancte Ioseph
(imp sg *memorari* + voc sg m *purissimus* + voc sg m *sponsus* + gen sg f *virgo* + gen sg f *Maria* + voc sg m adj *dulcis* + voc sg m *protector* + voc sg m det *meus* + voc sg adj m *sanctus* + voc sg m *Ioseph*)
Remember, O most pure Spouse of the Virgin Mary, O my sweet Protector Saint Joseph

O Ioseph, virgo pater Iesu,
puríssime Sponse Vírginis Maríae, quotídie deprecáre

(voc sg m *Ioseph* + nom/voc sg m *virgo* + nom/voc sg m *pater* + gen sg m *Iesus* + voc sg m *purissimus* + voc sg m *sponsus* + gen sg f *Virgo* + gen sg f *Maria* + adverb + imp sg of dep *deprecari*)

O Joseph, virgin father of Jesus, O most pure Spouse of the Virgin Mary, pray daily

Princeps gloriosíssime, Ráphael Archángele, esto memor nostri
(voc sg m *princeps* + voc sg m *gloriosissimus* + voc sg m *Raphael* + voc sg m *Archangelus* + fut imp sg *esse* + nom/voc sg m *memor* + gen pl *ego*)

[O] most glorious Prince, O Archangel Raphael, be mindful of us.

Recordáre, Virgo Mater Dei
(Remember, (imp sg of dep *recordari* + nom/voc sg f *Virgo* + nom/voc sg f *Mater* + gen sg m *Deus*) [O] Virgin Mother of God

Sancti Angeli, custódes nostri, deféndite nos
(nom/voc adj m pl *sanctus* + nom/voc adj m pl *angelus* + nom/voc pl m *custos* + nom/voc adj pl m *noster* + imp pl *defendere* + acc pl m/f *ego*)

[O] Holy Angels, our guardians, defend us

Suscípe, sancte Pater omnipótens, aetérne Deus
(imp sg *suscipere* + voc sg adj m *sanctus* + voc sg m *pater* + voc sg adj m *omnipotens* + voc sg adj m *aeternus* + voc sg m *Deus*)

Receive, O holy Father almighty, eternal God

Tuére, O Custos providentíssime divínae Famíliae
(imp sg *tueri* + voc sg m *custos* + voc sg m *providentissimus* + gen sg adj f *divina* + gen sg f *familia*)

Watch over, O most providential Guardian of the Holy Family.

the language and grammar of these texts is relatvely easy to parse, but in praying these texts the Latin becomes far more than just grammatical description. It is not language in isolation. These texts as prayers are about imperative action resulting from indicative assertions, leading to numinous/mystical *affect*.

Numinous Affect

The opening verses of a prayer we saw earlier, which was included amongst the writings of St Anselm, begins with an imperative *Ave* (imp sg *avere*):

Ave crux sancta virtus nostra
(Hail [O] holy cross our Strength)

This *Ave* (Hail) is a powerful means of communication in any circumstance, but addressing the Cross itself, an inanimate object, creates a quite different reality, and with it, requires a quite different dynamic; one where we necessarily have to suspend our earthly reasoning. We do so again in the 16[th]C *Litaniae de Sancta Cruce* (Litanies of the Holy Cross) originally designed for praying in Lent, where we pray, for example:

Crux spécula Patriarchárum et Prophetárum
[O] Cross watchtower of Patriarchs and Prophets
Praecónium Apostolórum
Proclamation of [the] Apostles
Coróna Mártyrum
Crown of Martyrs
Gáudium Sacerdótum
Joy of Priests
Gloriátio Vírginum
[The] glorying of Virgins

Crux poténtia Regum
[O] Cross power of Kings
Ornaméntum Ecclésiae
Jewel of [the] Church
Spes Christianórum
Hope of Christians
Glória ómnium Orthodoxórum
Glory of all [the] Orthodox
Crux coróna nostra
[O] Cross our crown
Pacis firmaméntum
Support of peace
Reserátrix Paradísi
Opener of Paradise
Virga mirabílium Dei
Rod of [the] wonders of God
Propugnáculum fídei
Bulwark of faith
Crux vita Iustórum
[O] Cross life of the Just
Resurréctio mortuórum
Resurrection of [the] dead
Clavis regni caelórum
Key of the kingom of the heavens
Procurátrix páuperum
Agent of [the] poor
Portus periclitántium
Port of those in danger
Crux signáculum castitátis
[O] Cross sign of purity
Sanctimóniae documéntum
Lesson of sanctity

Administrátrix castitátis
Administrator of chastity
Palma immortalitátis
Palm of immortality
Thesáurus ómnium bonórum
Treasure of all good [things]
Crux consolátrix afflictórum
[O] Cross consoler of [the] afflicted
Servátrix desperatórum
Servant of the despairing
Profligátrix haerésium
Destroyer of heresies
Fuga tentatiónum
Flight of temptations
Expugnátrix hóstium
Conqueror of enemies
Crux salus fidélium
[O] Cross salvation of [the] faithful
Signum Fílii Dei vivíficum
Life-giving sign of the Son of God
Crux datrix sanitátis
[O] Cross giver of health
Contráctus libertátis
Contract of freedom
Caeli altitúdo
Height of Heaven
Terrae profúnditas
Depth of the earth
Latitúdo orbis terrárum
Breadth of the world
Crux triumphátrix dǽmonum
[O] Cross victory [over] demons

Extínctio peccáti
Extinction of sin
Victória mundi
Victory of the world
Victrix mortis
Conqueror of death

The word 'cross', in English, referring to the cross on which Christ was crucified, is a term which only became common from the 12th C onwards. The original word used (from Anglo Saxon) was 'rod' (rood) and is still used in this way to refer to a cross often placed high in the chancel of a church and often part of a 'rood screen' separating the Choir and Sanctuary (Chancel) from the main part of the church (Nave). Devotion to the Holy Cross is a very well established tradition in Catholicism, but one which tended to disappear in the reformed Protestant churches, where many of the original medieval rood screens in English churches were destroyed as part of the anti-Catholic iconoclastic destruction of statues, sculptures, architectural features and so on; many of those things that signalled 'the extraordinary' to ordinary people.

Part of that destruction included the 8th C Ruthwell Cross which was destroyed by Scottish Presbyterians in 1642. On that cross (restored after all its parts were put back together in 1823) is considered to be what may be the oldest existing fragment of English literature, the Anglo Saxon *Dream of the Rood*, variously attributed to poets like Cædmon (657-680) and Cynewulf (late 8thC?) with the earliest written copy extant in a 10th C manuscript known as the *Vercelli Book*, held in Vercelli, Italy. It is a very beautiful and extraordinary poem describing Christ's passion and death from the point of view of the Cross itself. It begins with a call to attention:

Hwæt! Ic swefna cyst secgan wylle,
hæt me gemætte to midre nihte,
syðþan reordberend reste wunedon.
þuhte me þæt ic gesawe syllicre treow
on lyft lædan, leohte bewunden,
beama beorhtost.

(Listen! I will talk of the choicest of dreams,
what came to me in the middle of the night,
when speech-bearers stayed at rest.
Thought me that I saw a wondrous tree
lifted in the air, bewound with light,
the brightest of beams.)

My translation here retains the Old English kenning (a metaphor replacing a noun) *reord-berend* (speech-bearers) rather than translating it as 'men' or 'human beings', as there are wonderfully evocative echoes here of ourselves as **homo loquens.** This is poetry which contrasts these *reordberend* with the Cross itself which says: *Rod wæs ic aræred* (I was reared a cross) and tells us *þurh drifan hi me mid deorcan næglum* (they pierced me with dark nails) and:

> 'on me are the wounds visible, the open wounds of malice; I did not dare to injure any of them. They mocked us both together. I was all drenched with blood poured out from that man's side after he had sent forth his spirit.'

The Cross (*wuldres treow wædum geweorðod wynnum scinan, gegyred mid golde* (the tree of glory beautifully vested with honour and shining with joy, adorned with gold) itself is communicating, and Christianity, like the Rood itself, is, at its very core, like the obelisk in St Peter's Square, a communicating religion. Russian born French Catholic poet and mystic, Raïssa Maritain (1882-1960) knew this very well. In her hauntingly evocative poem *Ô Croix* (O Cross) she writes:

> Ô Croix qui divises le cœur
> Ô Croix qui partages le monde
> Ô Croix divine bois amer
> Prix sanglant des Béatitudes
> Royale Croix Signe impérieux
> Croix ténébreuse gibet de Dieu
> Étoile des Mystères
> Clé de la certitude.
>
> (O Cross you divide the heart,
> O Cross you split the world,
> Cross divine and wood of bitterness,
> Bloodstained price of the Beatitudes,
> Royal rood, imperious impress,
> Most sombre Cross, gibbet of God,
> Star of Mysteries,
> Key to certitude.
> *trs*: a Benedictine of Stanbrook Abbey)

where the attributive names she creates for the Cross from 'Royale Croix' and 'Étoile des Mystères' to 'Prix sanglant des Béatitudes' and 'gibet de Dieu' seem to numinously come together in that one powerful final phrase, 'Clé de la certitude'. She forcefully recognises, like the *Dream of the Rood* poet, that the Cross itself communicates, and through it (and her poetry) God communicates.

At the heart of Catholicism, then, is the central maxim that God is a communicating God and continues to communicate with us, most especially in the ultimate way through the person, life, work, teachings and continuing sacramental presence of his Son, and the wisdom of the Holy Spirit in his Church. The entire *New Testament* is just that:

a testament to new forms of communicating a new law; a new way. Monsignor Ronald Knox was very aware of this in his approach to translating the *Vulgate*. For example, we pray in the *Gospel* for the Votive Mass for the Propagation of the Faith:

Vulgate: **Rogáte ergo Dóminum messis, ut mittat operários in messem suam**

Douay-Rheims: Pray ye therefore the Lord of the harvest, that he send forth labourers into his harvest.

Knox: You must ask the Lord to whom the harvest belongs to send labourers out for the harvesting. *Mt* 9:38

The *DR* captures the grammar of the imperative **rogate** (*rogare* - to ask) but Knox, while he captures the modality of the imperative, with its obligation to do something, uses a quite different form of grammar to do so. It is effective, but not as a guide to the grammar of the Latin imperative **rogate**. Knox's intention, of course, is not to provide such a guide, but to capture the communicative dynamism of the *New Testament*. We see that communicative dynamism everywhere in Latin prayer. For example, one of the most famous Marian prayers begins **Salve Regina**. **Salve** is the singular imperative of the infinitive *salvere* (to be well). So it effectively means '[You sg] be well O Queen' and as such developed as the greeting which it has come to mean today 'Hail'. But notice how we pray it a second time at the end of the full Latin line:

Salve Regína Mater misericórdiae;
vita dulcédo et spes nostra salve
(Hail! O Queen O Mother of mercy;
O [our] life O [our] sweetness and O our hope hail!)

The beginning (initial position) and end (final position) of a Latin sentence are very prominent points. When a word is used in these positions in Latin it is not simply because the meaning of the word is located in its inflected ending, and so can be positioned anywhere. Its positioning is often an important stylistic decision which, by repeating this same word in these two prominent positions (as here) emphasises the imperative wish 'be well!' ('Hail!'). It is given positional force. Add then to this opening sentence of the prayer, the closing sentence:

O clemens O pia O dulcis Virgo María
(O clement O pious O sweet Virgin Mary)

where the opening sequence of vocatives is repeated in this final sequence, and a prayer is created which is framed by these two strings of vocatives. 'Framing' in this way has its own Latin term in formal rhetoric and poetics: *inclusio* (enclosure) and we see its use many times, particularly in the *Psalms* (reflecting a dominant feature of Hebrew poetry) which form such a crucially important part of Latin daily prayer. It is a stylistic feature which serves the very forceful dynamic of drawing a person's attention to a particular theme, idea or set of words. It is not accidental. Nor is it just literary artistry or being clever with words. It functions as an important linguistic/stylistic structure that enables the words enclosing (and being enclosed) to operate at a level far beyond just their dictionary meanings. Consider, for example, perhaps one of the most magnificent examples of *inclusio* in all of Latin prayer: the great 'O Antiphons' of Advent. In the last seven days of Advent, at *Vespers*, before and after the praying of the great hymn of Our Lady, the *Magnificat*, we pray seven different antiphons, each beginning with a simple, but totally memorable, vocative particle:

O Sapiéntia
(O Wisdom)
O Adonái et Dux domus Israël
(O Lord and Leader of the house of Israel)

O Radix Iesse
(O Root of Jesse)
O Clavis David et sceptrum domus Israël
(O Key of David and sceptre of the house of Israel)
O Oriens splendor lucis aetérnae, et sol iustítiae
(O Dayspring/Dawn, splendour of the light eternal, and the sun of justice)
O Rex Géntium et desiderátus eárum, lapísque anguláris
(O King of the peoples/Gentiles and their desired, and cornerstone)
O Emmánuel Rex et légifer noster
(O the Foretold [Lord] King and our lawgiver)

Known as 'The Greater Antiphons' (***Antiphonae Maiores***) they have been included in the last seven days of Advent *Vespers* since at least the 6[th]C and each of the vocatives used here is another way of attributively naming Jesus the Messiah as foretold by Isaias. The force of this ***inclusio*** is not for rhetorical effect, but numinous *affect*. It is designed to achieve something; to affect us in prayer. Each of these great antiphons (as indeed do all antiphons when recited in full) wrap around the *Canticle*, enclosing it with the magnificent attributes of Christ; for example at *Vespers* December 17 we pray:

O Sapiéntia, quae ex ore Altíssimi prodiísti, attíngens a fine usque ad finem, fórtiter suavitérque dispónens ómnia: veni ad docéndum nos viam prudéntiae.

Magníficat ✠ ánima mea Dóminum.
Et exultávit spíritus meus: in Deo salutári meo.
Quia respéxit humilitátem ancíllae suae:
Ecce enim ex hoc beátam me dicent omnes generatiónes.
Quia fecit mihi magna qui potens est: et sanctum nomen eius.
Et misericórdia eius a progénie in progénies timéntibus eum.
Fecit poténtiam in bráchio suo: dispérsit supérbos mente cordis sui.

Depósuit poténtes de sede: et exaltávit húmiles.
Esuriéntes implévit bonis: et dívites dimísit inánes.
Suscépit Israel púerum suum: recordátus misericórdiae suae.
Sicut locútus est ad patres nostros: Abraham, et sémini eius in sǽcula.
Glória Patri, et Fílio, et Spirítui Sancto,
Sicut erat in princípio, et nunc, et semper, et in sǽcula saeculórum. Amen.

O Sapiéntia, quae ex ore Altíssimi prodiísti, attíngens a fine usque ad finem, fórtiter suavitérque dispónens ómnia: veni ad docéndum nos viam prudéntiae.

(O Wisdom, who proceeded out of the mouth of the Most High, reaching from end to end, and ordering everything powerfully and sweetly: come [*for the purpose of*] teaching us the way of prudence.)

(My soul ✠ doth magnify the Lord, and my spirit hath rejoiced in God my Saviour. Because he hath regarded the humility of his handmaid: for behold from henceforth all generations shall call me blessed. Because he that is mighty hath done great things to me, and holy is his name. And his mercy is from generation unto generations to them that fear him. He hath shewed might in his arm: He hath scattered the proud in the conceit of their heart. He hath put down the mighty from their seat, and hath exalted the humble. He hath filled the hungry with good things, and the rich he hath sent empty away. He hath received Israel his servant, being mindful of his mercy. As he spoke to our fathers; to Abraham and his seed forever. Glory be to the Father, and to the Son, and to the Holy Ghost. As it was in the beginning is now, and ever shall be, world without end. Amen. *trad*)

(O Wisdom, who proceeded out of the mouth of the Most High, reaching from end to end, and ordering everything powerfully and sweetly: come [*for the purpose of*] teaching us the way of prudence.)

Each *Psalm* and *Canticle* recited in the major hours (*Matins, Lauds, Vespers*) of the *Breviarium Romanum* and minor hours, *Prime, Terce, Sext, None* and *Compline* (with some exceptions in these minor hours on certain days) is framed in this way by an antiphon. Prior to the changes made in 1960, where, depending on the importance of the day the whole of the antiphon would be recited both before and after the *Psalm* marking what is known as a Double Feast (***Festum Duplex***) the whole antiphon is doubled. A Semi Double (***Festum semi-Duplex***) is where the first part of the antiphon is recited before the *Psalm* followed at the end of the *Psalm* with the full antiphon; similarly a simple Feast (***Festum Simplex***). The 1960 changes removed these distinctions for feasts based on the antiphons, and determined that all antiphons would be recited in full both before and after the *Psalms* and *Canticles*. Those still praying the *Office* from earlier books, however, particularly the 1910 *Office*, maintain this distinction. But however the antiphons are prayed, they remain a force of powerful communication, at the heart of this form of prayer, and such communication needs to be, invariably is in Latin prayer, dynamic and forceful, as it is here, otherwise it ceases to have any point or purpose.

Influential literary critics like IA Richards (1893-1979) FR Leavis (1895-1978) and his wife QD (Queenie) Leavis (1906-1981) and also William Empson (1906-1984) teaching at the University of Cambridge from the 1930s, argued that literature, and in particular, specific forms of poetry, is/are the supreme form of human communication, and in many ways, for them, had replaced religion in what they considered to be a post Christian culture following the ravages of the First World War. They were not Catholic, and in some cases even anti-Christian. But to an Anglican literary critic and poet, like TS Eliot (1888-1965) or to Catholics, perhaps like Jacques Maritain (1882-1973) Josephite husband of Raïssa Maritain, there is no doubt that it was/is prayer that must take that highest of accolades. As literary critic, and later communication specialist, the Canadian Catholic convert Marshall McLuhan (1911-1980) recognised, prayer is necessarily dynamic. It is about focus and force. It is not, he was to say, a monologue, but ideally consists of 'a constant, nonstop dialogue with the Creator'. Life without it, he maintained, is not life at all. Our prayer, then, is always in imitation of Christ's own life of prayer:

> *Filius Dei, Filius Virginis effectus, secundum Suum hominis cor, orare etiam didicit.*
> (The Son of God who became Son of the Virgin also learned to pray according to his human heart. *Cat* §2599)

It is always, therefore numinous; always mystical; as the *Catechism* tells us:

> *Spiritualis progressus ad semper arctiorem cum Christo tendit unionem. Haec unio appellatur "mystica" quia... Deus nos omnes ad hanc intimam cum Eo vocat unionem, etiamsi gratiae speciales vel signa extraordinaria huius vitae mysticae solum quibusdam concedantur ad donum gratuitum omnibus factum manifestandum.*
>
> (Spiritual progress tends toward ever more intimate union with Christ. This union is called "mystical" because... God calls us all to this intimate union with him, even if the special graces or extraordinary signs of this mystical life are granted only to some for the sake of manifesting the gratuitous gift given to all. *Cat* §2014)

The *Anima Christi*, for example, which we have seen in part already, is thought to have been composed by the second Avignon Pope, Pope John XXII (1244-1334). It is a very beautiful prayer and while the Latin has been unchanged for many centuries, there are many translated variations, for example:

Anima Christi, sanctífica me.
Corpus Christi, salva me.
Sanguis Christi, inébria me.
Aqua láteris Christi, lava me.
Pássio Christi, confórta me.
O bone Iesu, exáudi me.
Intra tua vúlnera abscónde me.
Ne permíttas me separári a te.
Ab hoste malígno defénde me.
In hora mortis meae voca me.
Et iube me veníre ad te,
Ut cum Sanctis tuis laudem te,
In sǽcula saeculórum. Amen.

St John Henry Cardinal Newman CO

Soul of Christ, be my sanctification;
Body of Christ, be my salvation;
Blood of Christ, fill all my veins;
Water of Christ's side, wash out my stains;
Passion of Christ, my comfort be;
O good Jesus, listen to me;
In Thy wounds I fain would hide;
Ne'er to be parted from Thy side;
Guard me, should the foe assail me;
Call me when my life shall fail me;
Bid me come to Thee above,
With Thy saints to sing Thy love,
World without end.
Amen.

Fr Edward Caswall CO

    Soul of my Saviour, sanctify my breast,
body of Christ, be thou my saving guest,
blood of my Saviour, bathe me in thy tide,
wash me with water flowing from thy side.
    Strength and protection may thy Passion be,
O blessèd Jesu, hear and answer me;
deep in thy wounds, Lord, hide and shelter me,
so shall I never, never part from thee.
    Guard and defend me from the foe malign,
in death's dread moments make me only thine;
call me and bid me come to thee on high
where I may praise thee with thy saints for ay.

Catholic Online

Soul of Christ, make me holy.
Body of Christ, save me.
Blood of Christ, fill me with love.
Water from Christ's side, wash me.
Passion of Christ, strengthen me.
Good Jesus, hear me.
Within your wounds, hide me.
Never let me be parted from you.
From the evil enemy, protect me.
At the hour of my death, call me.
And tell me to come to you.
That with your saints I may praise you. Through all eternity. Amen.

Beneath these diverse English translations is an unchanging force of Latin grammar: the structure of which is of a noun phrase made up of a nom/voc sg noun + gen sg m noun + imp sg + pron *me* (me). That pronoun answers a question after the imperative verb: ***sanctifica*** who? ***salva*** who? ***inebria*** who? ***lava*** who? ***conforta*** who? and ***exaudi*** who? The answer to those questions ***me***, which is expressed in the accusative case (***casus accusativus***) not derived from the Latin verb ***accusare*** (to accuse) but based on a loan from *Greek* (αἰτιατικός - *aitiatikos)* indicating 'something caused or affected by the verb'. The ***me*** here is affected by the verbs, ***salva***, ***lava***, ***conforta***, ***exaudi*** and so on, and as such, the action of these verbs is *carried over* into the pronoun. This 'carrying over' is a grammatical process known as 'transitivity', and it is also, crucially, a central, and sometimes, defining, process in Latin prayer to which we now turn in *Chapter VI: Transitive Prayer.*

VI

TRANSITIVE PRAYER

ad destinatum persequor, ad bravium supernae vocationis Dei in Christo Iesu (*Phil* 3:14)

Transitivity

St Paul tells the Philippians that ***ad destinatum persequor*** (I press towards the mark) ***ad bravium supernae vocationis Dei in Christo Iesu*** (to the prize of the celestial vocation of God in Christ Jesus *Phil* 3:14). He has a purpose; his life is motivated; he has a 'mark' (***destinatum***) to reach; a prize (***bravium***) to win; that prize is celestial. The allusion made here by St Jerome in the *Vulgate* is from archery where ***destinatus*** in Classical Latin is the point/destination (mark) being aimed at. It is purposive, not just as an idea, but as a physical action of doing something. A goal in archery is tangible, it can be seen - it has a bulls-eye - literally. Prayer is the same. It has purpose, but with the ultimate intangible 'bulls-eye'/goal being salvation. St Paul tells the Romans that:

> ***Spe enim salvi facti sumus. Spes autem, quae videtur, non est spes: nam quod videt quis, quid sperat?***
>
> (It must be so, since our salvation is founded upon the hope of something. Hope would not be hope at all if its object were in view; how could a man still hope for something which he sees? *Knox Rom* 8:24)

That 'something' Knox refers to here is goal-oriented. Salvation is purposive. But we are not left alone to do this. St Paul also tells the Romans:

> *Similiter autem et Spiritus adiuvat infirmitatem nostram: nam quid oremus, sicut oportet, nescimus: sed ipse Spiritus postulat pro nobis gemitibus inenarrabilibus.*
>
> (Only, as before, the Spirit comes to the aid of our weakness; when we do not know what prayer to offer, to pray as we ought, the Spirit himself intercedes for us, with groans beyond all utterance *Knox Rom* 8:26)

The Latin verb used (where Knox uses 'intercedes') is **postulare** - 'to demand/call for/request'. The *DR* follows the *Vulgate* where Ronald Knox prefers the original Greek verb ὑπερεντυγχάνω (*hyperentygchano* - to intercede) *hyperentygchano* is made up of two words *hyper* (for/on behalf of/over) and *entygchano* (come upon/meet/entreat) and is a *hapax legomenon,* that is, it is used only once in the *Bible*; *entygchano* is also made up of two words: *en* (in) an intensifier and *tygchano* (to hit the mark). In other words, to hit the bulls-eye; to be spot-on. Its opposite in Greek is ἁμαρτάνω (*hamartano*) 'to miss the mark' which has come to mean 'to sin'. The goal of the Holy Spirit, then, (to use Knox's translation of **destinatum** - goal) as St Paul clearly understands it, is not just to ask for things on our behalf, but to line us up to the mark, to the bulls-eye; to the will of God. Purposive goals in prayer are therefore about alignment; to line up our wills to God's will.

St Paul also writes of this goal when we pray in the *Epistle* of the Mass of **Septuagesima** as we prepare for the long penitential fast of Lent, when St Paul talks of the Christian needing to be like an athlete: disciplined and in control, chastising one's body and bringing it into line:

Ego ígitur sic curro, non quasi in incértum: sic pugno, non quasi áerem vérberans: sed castígo corpus meum, et in servitútem rédigo: ne forte cum áliis praedicáverim, ipse réprobus effíciar. (1 Cor 9:26-27)

The Christian, as athlete, must fight in order to win the ultimate prize. Ronald Knox translates the Latin of the *Vulgate* here quite freely, but effectively, by saying:

'So I do not run my course like a man in doubt of his goal; I do not fight my battle like a man who wastes his blows on the air. I buffet my own body, and make it my slave; or I, who have preached to others, may myself be rejected as worthless.' (*Knox 1 Cor 9:26-27*)

In order for him to receive the prize: the ***incorruptam coronam*** (the incorruptible crown *1 Cor* 9:25) St Paul says: ***currite*** (run! 'for victory!' *Knox 1 Cor 9:24*). Knox's translation is a contemporary way of saying what St Peter talks of as 'hope' (***spes***) when he writes to the Christians of Pontus, Galatia, Cappadocia, Asia, and Bithynia, part of which we pray at the end of the *Epistle* of the 5th Sunday after Pentecost:

Dóminum autem Christum sanctificáte in córdibus vestris, [paráti semper ad satisfactiónem omni poscénti vos ratiónem de ea, quae in vobis est, spe.]

(Therefore sanctify the Lord Christ in your hearts, [prepared always to the satisfaction for/[of] every one requesting you for a reason, by that hope, which is in you.] *1Pe 3:15*)

Grammatically that 'hope'/'goal', is expressed in the Latin of the *Vulgate* here by way of an imperative plural ***sanctificate*** (*sanctificare* - to sanctify) which is an action that has as its purposive goal: ***Dominum Christum*** (the Lord Christ). Ask the question: sanctify (who?) and if you have an answer, as here, 'the Lord Christ', then that answer is the grammatical goal/direct object of the verb, and in Latin is expressed (as here) in the accusative case. When the Priest, before a **usus antiquior** Mass (with or without a server) stops before reaching the altar and prays *Psalm 42* beginning:

> **Iúdica me, Deus et discérne causam meam**
> (Judge me, [O] God and discern my cause)

he is calling upon **Deus** as the grammatical subject of the singular imperative verbs *iudica* and *discerne*. **Deus** is also the real life 'subject/agent' who will judge who? answer: *me* and what? answer: *causam meam* (my cause). The answers to the questions 'who?' or 'what?' as direct objects of God's action are also participants in this process. This process is known in grammar as 'transitivity', where the action of a verb, like 'judging' or 'discerning', as here, may be transferred onto a dependent object, like 'me' or 'my cause', in very much the same way as God as 'subject/agent' acts upon a dependent 'object' the pray-er. The Latin verb *transferre*, with its multiple meanings of: 'to carry across'; 'to bring over'; 'to transfer'; 'to process'; 'to change'; 'to transform'; 'to apply'; 'to make use of' and even 'to translate'; 'to communicate' and 'to interpret' is useful here. As a single word it holds within it all these layered possibilities, positioning what might seem to be a simple accusative form, like *me* and *causam meam* as part of a much more potentially complicated accusative dynamic of goals.

The Accusative Dynamic

Probably one of the most famous Christmas carols in western Christianity is 'O Come, All Ye Faithful'. Originally composed in Latin centuries ago, its now famous English version was translated by Catholic Priest Fr Frederick Oakeley (1802-1880) in 1841. We sing/pray the opening verse of the original Latin hymn as:

Adéste fidéles laeti triumphántes
Veníte, veníte in Béthlehem.
Natum vidéte
Regem angelórum:
Veníte adorémus (3×)
Dóminum.

There are seven imperative verbs in this one verse: *adeste, venite* x 5 and *videte*, all directing us to do something: *adeste* (imp pl *adesse*) 'be present!', *venite* (imp pl *venire*) 'come!', *videte* (imp pl *videre*) 'see!'. The hymn is calling out to 'the faithful' (*fideles* nom/voc pl m) 'the joyful' (*laeti* nom pl m adj) and 'the triumphant' (*triumphantes* nom/voc pl m adj): 'the faithful joyful triumphant: 'be present!' 'Make yourselves available and come! come!' (*venite venite*) 'to Bethlehem and see!' (*videte*). See what? See 'the birth' (*natum*). The 'faithful joyful triumphant' are the subjects of the actions required from the imperative verbs *adeste, venite* and *videte* but *natum* (the birth) is the goal or direct object of that action. The goal/object *natum* and its verb *videte* are in a transitive relationship (*transitivus - transire* - to go across). Transitivity *causes* something to happen; it describes the action of a verb transiting - crossing over - to an object (goal) and affecting that object (goal). It *causes* the nominative to change to the accusative. For example, when, in one form of grace before meals (*Benedictio ante mensam*) known since at least the 8th century, we pray:

Bénedic, Dómine, nos et haec tua dona
quae de tua largitáte sumus sumptúri.
Per Christum Dóminum nostrum. Amen.
    (Bless! O Lord, us and these your gifts
which from your abundance we are about to take.
    Through Christ our Lord. Amen.)

the imperative ***benedic*** (bless) is calling on the subject of the action of blessing ***Domine*** (O Lord) to do what? 'To bless'. To bless who? ***nos*** (us) ***et*** (and) what? ***haec*** (these) ***tua*** (your) ***dona*** (gifts) ***nos*** and ***haec tua dona***, are all objects of the action of blessing; they are the objects to be blessed by the subject ***Domine***, and as such in Latin all function transitively. Similarly in Tuesday *None* we pray:

> *Exsúrge, Dómine, adiúva nos, et rédime nos propter nomen tuum.*
> (Arise!, O Lord, help! us, and redeem! us according to your name. *Ps* 43:28)

The 1st pers pl acc pron ***nos*** references 'us' as participants in a dependency relationship; our identity is not as the protagonists of an action, but as the recipients and beneficiaries of that action ('help' and 'redemption'). The focal point of view that is established is not *from* us but *towards* us, and that dependency relationship is further emphasised by the repetition of ***nos***. The pronoun may grammatically replace the noun that is 'the pray-ers', but it becomes 'us' metonymically, that is, the pronoun doesn't just stand in for the pray-ers but *becomes* the pray-ers. Pronouns do more than just 'stand-in' for nouns; they create identities. The author of the 14thC mystical work *The Cloud of Unknowing* says that, whatever we do and whatever we think, there will always be a cloud of unknowing 'bitwix' us and God; in the *Cloud*'s words:

> *Byneþe þi God þou arte* (beneath thy God thou art)

There is, therefore, always an unremitting dependency relationship, because we can never fully know God. We are always in a subservient role (***subservire*** - to serve under/to be subject to). But that dependency is crucial to understand in any transitive relationship, whether that relationship is in grammar, or in a spiritual cloud of unknowing between us and God. One of the most frequent prayers in Latin Catholicism opens every hour of the *Divine Office*:

℣. *Deus,* ✠ *in adiutórium meum inténde.*
(O God, ✠ make speed to save me. *trad*)
℟. *Dómine, ad adiuvándum me festína.*
(O Lord, make haste to help me. *trad*)

What is happening grammatically in a phrase like ***in adiutorium meum*** is an accusative form (***adiutorium meum***) following a preposition (***in***) and similarly in ***ad adiuvandum me***, both of which signal an accusative dynamic signifying movement (***in adiutorium meum***) and purpose (***adiuvandum me***). We might better reflect this by translating them as

℣. *Deus,* ✠ *in adiutórium meum inténde.*
([O] God, ✠ intowards my help turn!)
℟. *Dómine, ad adiuvándum me festína.*
(O Lord, ontowards my help hurry!)

We don't have words like 'intowards' and 'ontowards' in English (any more) but simply because we do not have these words does not mean that the intent of such words is not there in the Latin. Translated this way, these phrases, prayed so many times each day in the full *Divine Office*, retain their Latin dynamism; they are dramatic, and that drama is not something to shy away from in prayer. Prayed at the opening of each individual hour of the *Office*, seen in this way, we are shouting out our intentions; we are calling out loud to God, the object goal of all our prayers this day; we are purposively announcing ourselves, not shyly slipping into the back pew hoping not to be noticed. Instead we are actively *moving purposively towards* God, and the Latin grammar announces us as doing exactly that. The linguistic structure of prep + acc like this is at the core of the spiritual aim, not just of our opening prayers like this, but of many of the Latin prayers we pray throughout the *Office* and Mass. It is an absolutely central form of transitive address in Latin prayer generally. So when we pray:

> *súscipe deprecatiónem nostram Dómine*
> (receive! our prayer O Lord)

we actually have a very familiar pattern imp + acc + voc in liturgical prayer which recurs over and over again in various permutations with the noun phrase **deprecationem nostram** written in the accusative form, the dynamism of the phrase as a transitive prayer in itself is located not just in this specific noun phrase, but in the relationship of the imperative verb **suscipe** to the accusative **deprecationem nostram**. The prayer is saying 'You, O Lord receive (what?) answer: our prayer'. The action of receiving is not completed, it is in transit, until it is completed in the direct object (**deprecationem nostram**) and consequently, in Latin, the inflection changes, because the grammatical function of the word has changed. The spiritual focus is not on the individual verb, or the individual direct object, or indeed the individual vocative **Domine**, it is on the *process* of transit; upon its 'transitive relations'.

Transitive Relations

Transitive prayer is not simply about which words go into the accusative form in a Latin text, it is much more about the dynamic relationships between those words, and their texts in their contexts as well. So for example in the prayer prayed every night at *Compline*:

> **Salva nos, Dómine, vigilántes, custódi nos dormiéntes**
> (Save! us, O Lord, waking, guard! us sleeping)

There is a transitive relationship between words in the text, but also a transitive relationship between the text itself and us the pray-ers.

But there is also a dependent relationship as part of, and within, the *Divine Office* of *Compline*. This prayer relates to all the other prayers in *Compline*. It does not sit in isolation. It is part of the narrative of prayer that is itself a dialogue, not just between us and God, but between the prayers themselves and the pray-ers in *Compline*. And not just those present, but all those who have every prayed this prayer. So, for example, when we pray:

> *Absólve, Dómine, ánimas ómnium fidélium defunctórum*
> (*absolvere* imp sg + voc sg m ***Dominus*** + acc pl f ***anima*** + gen pl m/f
> adj ***omnis*** + gen pl m/f ***fidelis*** + gen pl m/f ***defunctus***)
> Deliver! O Lord, the souls of all the departed faithful

there are transitive relationships between the parts of speech, but also between the whole text of this prayer and the larger contexts in which it appears, for example, as part of the *Tract* in a Requiem Mass. That *Tract*, as a whole, is then also in a transitive relationship with the Requiem Mass overall, and that Mass is in a transitive relationship with the liturgy overall. Transitivity in prayer is not, therefore, just about the *text*, but also about the *context*. The words and text of a Latin prayer are always connected to contexts; they are never sufficient unto themselves; they are always part of a larger text-context dynamic, liturgical or otherwise. Consider, then, the grammar of transitive address (imp + nom + voc + acc in various permutations) which is central to each of the following drawn from a wide range of Latin prayer, and consider how that transitive address might be further understood in the larger (more discursive) contexts of prayer, both liturgical and private:

> *auférte gentem pérfidam*
> (*auferre* irreg imp pl + acc sg f ***gens*** + acc sg f adj ***perfidus***)
> remove! the faithless people

adiúva me Dómine Deus meus
(*adiuvare* imp sg + acc sg m *ego* + voc sg m *Dominus*
+ nom/voc sg m *Deus* + nom/voc sg m adj *meus*)
help! me O Lord my God

apéri, Dómine, os meum ad benedicéndum nomen sanctum tuum
(*aperire* imp sg + voc sg m *Dominus* + acc sg n *os* + acc sg n adj
  meus + prep + acc sg n part/adj *benedicendus* (*benedicere*) + acc
  sg n *nomen* + acc sg n *sanctus* + acc sg n *tuus*)
open! O Lord, my mouth for the [*purpose of*] blessing your holy name

avérte fáciem tuam
(*avertere* imp sg + acc sg f *facies* + acc sg f adj *tuus*) turn away!
  your face

benedícite Dóminum omnes elécti eius
(*benedicere* imp pl + acc sg m *Dominus* + voc pl m *omnis* + voc pl m
  electus + gen sg m det *is*) Bless! the Lord O all his chosen ones

concéde nos fámulos tuos
(*concedere* imp sg + acc pl m *ego* + acc pl m *famulus* + acc pl m *tuus*)
  grant! us your servants

convérte nos Deus salutáris noster et avérte iram tuam
(*convertere* imp sg + acc pl m/f *nos* + voc sg m *Deus* + voc sg m adj
  salutaris + voc sg m *noster* + prep + *avertere* imp sg + acc sg f
  ira + acc sg f det *tuus*)
change! us O our saving God and turn away! your anger

da pacem Dómine (*dare* imp sg + acc sg f *pax* + voc sg m *Dominus*)
  give! peace O Lord

Dómine exáudi oratiónem meam
(voc sg m *Dominus* + *exaudire* imp sg + acc sg f *oratio* + acc sg f det *meus*) O Lord heed! my prayer

Dómine inclína caelos tuos et descénde
(voc sg m *Dominus* + *inclinare* imp sg + acc pl n *caelus* (m alt form of n *caelum*) + acc pl n *tuus* + conj *et* + *descendere* imp sg) O Lord lay low! your heavens and come down!

Dómine líbera ánimam meam
(voc sg m *Dominus* + *liberare* imp sg + acc sg f *anima* + acc sg f det *meus*) O Lord free! my soul

exsúrge Christe adiúva nos
(*exsurgere* imp sg + voc sg m *Christus* + *adiuvare* imp sg + acc pl m/f *ego*) rise up! O Christ help! us

inclína cor meum Deus (*inclinare* imp sg + acc sg n *cor* + acc sg n adj *meus* + nom/voc sg m *Deus*) bend! my heart [O] God

inténde ad deprecatiónem meam
(*intendere* imp sg + prep *ad* + acc sg f *deprecatio* + acc sg f det *meus*) listen! untowards my prayer

iúdica me Deus et discérne causam meam
(*iudicare* imp sg + acc sg m/f *ego* + nom/voc sg m *Deus* conj *et* + *discernere* imp sg
+ acc sg f *causa* + acc sg f *meus*) judge! me [O] God and determine! my cause

lauda Hierúsalem Dóminum
(*laudare* imp sg + voc sg n *Hierusalem* + acc sg m *Dominus*) praise! the Lord Jerusalem

laudáte Dóminum omnes gentes
(*laudare* imp pl + acc sg m *Dominus* + voc pl f adj *omnis* + voc pl f *gens*) praise! the Lord all peoples

líbera nos Dómine
(*liberare* imp sg + acc pl m/f *ego* + voc sg m *Dominus*) free! us O Lord

meménto Dómine David
(*meminisse* imp sg + voc sg m *Dominus* + acc sg m *David*) Remember! O Lord David

munda cor meum
(*mundare* imp sg + acc sg n *cor* + acc sg n *meus*) cleanse! my heart

O Dómine salvum me fac
(voc sg m *Dominus* + acc sg m adj *salvus* + acc sg m/f *ego* + *facere* irreg imp sg) O Lord make! me safe

osténde magnitúdinem tuam magnificéntiam
(*ostendere* imp sg + acc sg f *magnitudo* + acc sg f det *tuus* + acc sg f *magnificentia*)
show! your magnificence [and] greatness

paráte viam Dómini rectas fácite sémitas eius
(*parare* imp pl + acc sg f *via* + gen sg m *Dominus* + acc pl f adj *rectus* + acc pl f *semita* + gen sg m *is*)
prepare! the way of [the] Lord make! straight his paths

pláudite vestras manus
(*plaudere* imp sg + acc f pl *vestra* + acc pl f *manus*) clap! your hands

súscipe confessiónem meam piíssime ac clementíssime Dómine Iesu Christe
(*suscipere* imp sg + acc sg f *confessio* + acc sg f *meus* + voc sg m sup *pius* + conj *ac* + voc sg m sup *clemens* + voc sg m *Dominus* + voc sg m *Iesus* + voc sg m *Christus*)
receive! my prayer O most pious and most clement Lord Jesus Christ

timéte Dóminum omnes Sancti
(*timere* imp pl + acc sg m *Dominus* + voc pl adj m *omnis* + voc pl adj m *sanctus*) fear! the Lord O all Saints

verba mea pércipe Dómine; intéllige clamórem meum
(acc pl n *verbum* + acc pl n det *meus* + *percipere* imp sg + voc sg m *Dominus* + *intelligere* imp sg + acc sg m *clamor* + acc sg m det *meus*)
my words receive! O Lord; understand! my cry

Transitive address like this repeatedly occurs in Latin prayer, and while it may seem unnecessary to see each word parsed in this way, this tends to be the way we learn Latin, and it also tends to be what we have in our heads when we are working out what a particular Latin text might mean, at least until we attain a certain fluency in the language. But that fluency might also lead us to think we no longer need to parse the grammar, and, for Latin prayer, that brings dangers. Not dangers that we will incorrectly translate the Latin, but dangers that we will ignore the numinous force of actually praying the grammar as well as the words. The exclamation mark used in my translations above might also seem unnecessary, even very odd, but I do so here simply to make the point that these imperatives are not so benign in Latin as they might appear to be in an English translation. The grammar of the imperative often *means*, in and of itself, more powerfully than the actual word.

Transitive Focus

The English version of the 1994 *Catechismus* quotes St John Damascene (675-749) saying that prayer is 'the raising of the mind and heart to God' (§2559). The words of Latin prayer most certainly enable a focus to be made on the first part: 'raising the mind' to God. The much harder part, of course, is 'raising the heart' to God. The Latin verb used in the Latin text of the *Catechismus* is *ascendere* (to ascend/raise up) but this normative text only says of prayer:

> *Oratio est ascensus mentis in Deum.* (§2559)
> (Prayer is [the] raising up of the mind intowards God.)

It is only the Vatican approved English translation of the *Catechismus* which extends *mentis* (of the mind) to 'of the mind and heart'. The original French text, promulgated by Pope St John Paul II on the 30th anniversary of *Vatican II* in 1992, says: 'La prière est l'élévation de l'âme vers Dieu' ('Prayer is the raising of the soul to God'). The Italian says the same, 'La preghiera è l'elevazione dell'anima a Dio' as does the German 'Das Gebet ist die Erhebung der Seele zu Gott'. So where does 'the heart' come from in the English version? Latin writers have used the word *mens* in various ways over its many centuries of use, including for 'mind', 'disposition', 'reason', 'understanding', 'will', 'conscience', 'plan', 'purpose', 'intention', 'heart', 'soul' and many others. In English, 'mind' does not capture the layered sense it may have in Latin beyond reason and intellect, in the way that the use of the word 'soul' does in other translations, so the addition of 'heart' would seem to help, because whoever translated the English version recognised that *mentis* (of the mind) involved more than calling on God by raising one's mind upwards to him, it required *focus* from the heart. And that is considerably more challenging in the world of transitive prayer, where our dependency is not just a matter of mind, but very much a matter of the heart and soul. So, for example, the Canticle sung at Sunday and festal *Lauds* begins:

> *Benedícite ómnia ópera Dómini, laudáte et superexaltáte eum in sǽcula.*
> (Bless! all works of the Lord, praise! and highly exalt! him intowards [the] ages.)

Address like this has always been a central part of prayer, and so too the subjects and goals of this transitive address. This particular Canticle is not just throwing the verbs 'bless', 'praise' and 'exalt' into the air and leaving them to hang there by themselves, they are also saying, as a transitive prayer, *who* to bless, praise and exalt: *eum* - 'him' is who we are to praise. The focus here is upon the accusative form, just as it is when in the *Divine Office* prayed privately (or when publicly there is no Priest or Deacon) we pray instead of **Dóminus vobíscum** ([The] Lord [be] with you):

> *Dómine exáudi oratiónem meam.*
> (O Lord heed! my prayer.)

Transitive focus is given to **orationem meam** showing the transition from the vocative subject **Domine** through the imp verb *exaudi*. That focus is not completed until it transits into the accusative **orationem meam**. Transiting the action like this from subject through the verb to the dependent direct object is a crucially important part of the dynamic force of the transitive focus involved in Latin prayerful address, as we can see in the dawn *Office* of *Lauds* which, as its Latin name indicates, is about praise (*laus*). St Benedict recognised the importance of beginning the day at dawn to the praise of God after the long night vigils (*Matins*) by including instructions (in Chapters 12-13 of the **Regula Sancti Benedicti** for how *Lauds* should be recited in monasteries beginning with *Psalm* 66 (without an antiphon followed by the penitential *Psalm* 50 with an antiphon (which would vary according to the Feast) then two *Psalms* which would change according to the day of the week, followed by a Canticle then followed by what is described as the *laudates* (praises) these being *Psalms* 148, 149 and 150. *Psalm* 148 begins:

> *Laudáte Dóminum laudáte eum*
> (Praise! [the] Lord praise! him)

So, praying *Psalm* 148 as night turns to dawn, begins to take on a new prayerful light itself, when the transitivity of its verbs, together with the grammatical form of its nouns/pronouns, creates a dynamic transitive focus through the repetition of the transitive address of imp + acc. We pray:

> *Laudáte Dóminum... laudáte eum...*
> (Praise! [the] Lord... praise! him..)
> *Laudáte eum omnes Angeli eius: laudáte eum omnes virtútes eius.*
> (Praise! him all his Angels: praise! him all his hosts.)
> *Laudáte eum sol et luna: laudáte eum omnes stellae et lumen.*
> (Praise! him sun and moon: praise! him all stars and light.
> *Laudáte eum caeli caelórum...*
> (Praise! him heaven of heavens...)

Similarly in the third of the **Laudates**, *Psalm* 150 we pray:

> *Laudáte Dóminum... laudáte eum...*
> (Praise! [the] Lord... praise! him...)
> *Laudáte eum... laudáte eum secúndum multitúdinem magnitúdinis eius.*
> (Praise! him... praise! him according to [the] greatness

of his excellence.)
Laudáte eum... laudáte eum...
(Praise! him... praise! him...)
Laudáte eum... laudáte eum...
(Praise! him... praise! him...)
Laudáte eum... laudáte eum...
(Praise! him... praise! him...)

The transitive focus in *Psalms* like this lies in the repetition of the relationship between the imperative verb (***laudate***) and the accusative form that follows (***Dominum*** or ***eum***). The focus is created, not in the words themselves, as such, but on the repetition of the dependency of the accusative form upon the preceding verb. So it is in prayer generally. The focus of prayer is not necessarily determined by what we pray (the words themselves) but on the dependency relationship we have with the one we are praying to. Prayer is itself in a transitive relationship between pray-er and God, and as such brings with it its own transitive focus and force.

Transitivity then is about dependency, whether we are talking about nouns or pronouns, and the action of the verb passing across (transiting) to those nouns and pronouns, or, understood anagogically, through the underlying grammar enabling our own dependency relationship to transit *towards* God. This is the heart of prayer. And grammar books, which are not about prayer, do not explain the accusative in Latin in this way. Many Latin verbs can function both 'transitively' (taking a direct object) and 'intransitively' (not taking a direct object) and verbs may express transitive or/and intransitive relations, but in the grammar of Latin prayer, all affects of prayer are transitive. Every person praying is a 'goal/object' directly affected by the 'subject' (God) and his actions, whether or not that person recognises, acknowledges, or even wants to know that. The grammar of the words we pray may change, but the transitive focus involved between pray-er and prayed-to does not. Whatever the options of meanings available to us in the language and grammar of Latin prayer, and the often many different relationships involved in these options, the transitive focus and force of praying to God remains a constant. For example, when we pray a grammatically simple imperative prayer like:

intérroga me et cognósce sémitas meas
(question! me and know! my ways)

The imp + acc dynamic (*interroga me*) may raise questions about volition, ie the power of determining or choosing (***velle*** - to will, wish, choose). To then say *interroga me* with a conjunction like *et* linking this dynamic with a similar one like imp + acc **cognosce semitas meas** may well be to place yourself in a position of vulnerability. In effect, in praying it, we have not only wished the other person (in this instance God) to know things about us others may not know, but we have also positioned ourselves - willed ourselves - into a subordinate/dependent role. Volition is therefore about intentions. Do you intend to submit yourself to questioning, and hence to realising, through that questioning, that God already knows what we question ourselves to discover? The transitive relationship of imp + acc gives a very clear signal that whatever the questions, we will be *affected* as a result, because while the imperative *interroga* (question!) has a certain force by itself, with the accusative personal pronoun *me* it takes on quite a different transitive force. The accusative pronoun *me* is not simply a useful grammatical tool standing in for something else. It is providing a perspective by which to contextualise the way in which the imperative might mean beyond just what the dictionary says it can mean: *interroga me* (question [who?] 'me') suggests all sorts of new connections; all sorts of new goals; all sorts of new transitive relations between the subject (in this case 'God') and the object/goal (in this case 'me'). When we pray in Thursday *Compline*:

líbera me, et éripe me: inclína ad me aurem tuam, et salva me.
(deliver! me, and rescue! me: incline! your ear ontowards me, and save! me. *Ps* 70:2)

we are praying to be affected; to be changed; to be transformed. But more than that: we are praying for the transitive affect of the imperative verbs ***libera, eripe, inclina*** and ***salva*** to confirm and increase our dependency on God as iteratively signalled by the repetition of the accusative ***me***. The message, I would wish to suggest in all of this, even at the expense of seeming to unnecessarily go over very basic grammatical ground, is that in prayer, the slightest, smallest, most innocuously seeming bit of grammar, may well change the entire direction of the prayer, and put the pray-er onto quite new and different spiritual/numinous tangents of that prayer. For example, the longest *Psalm* in the *Psalter*, *Psalm* 118 (176 verses) prayed in 13 parts across *Prime*, *Terce*, *Sext* and *None* in the *MP* and 11 parts in the *PP* across the same *Offices*, we pray:

Deduc me in sémitam mandatórum tuórum
(Lead! me intowards [the] way of your commands)

The *JB* translates this as: 'Guide me in the path of your commandments', whereas the *DR* translates it as: 'Lead me into the path of thy commandments'. The *JB*, closer to the original Greek, assumes the movement is inevitable if walking with God, but the *DR* specifies this as being led 'into the path' by God; a more specifically stated physical activity. Both translations are clearly designed to inspire spiritual affect but the *JB* loses some sense of the physicality of the movement insisted upon by the Latin preposition ***in*** + acc. Knox translates it as: 'Eagerly I long to be guided in the way of thy obedience'. The difference between 'in', 'into' and 'intowards', as translated here then, becomes very significant indeed. Little prepositions like this can enable grammatical relationships which then may have greater subtleties of meaning and affect than, perhaps, might first appear, especially in English translations. But little things matter in Latin prayer. When St Paul opens his ***Epistola B Pauli Apostoli ad Romanos*** (and notice how this is written in Latin as ***ad Romanos*** [*ad* + acc] mirroring the movement actually involved in sending a letter) as we saw earlier from the *Epistle* of the Christmas Eve Mass, he writes:

> ***Paulus, servus Iesu Christi, vocátus Apóstolus, segregátus in Evangélium Dei***
> (Paul, a servant of Jesus Christ, called to be an Apostle, separated unto the Gospel of God. *DR Rom* 1:1)

The *DR* 'separated *unto* the gospel of God' (*segregatus in Evangelium Dei*) probably means very little to a modern ear. Knox translates it as 'set apart to preach the gospel of God', which probably makes more modern sense, but if we read the verb *segregare* ('to separate') as Knox does as 'to set apart'/'to remove oneself', then a translation of 'removed "into" or "intowards" the Gospel of God' implies that St Paul has actively moved from one life *outside* of the gospel of God (the old law) to a new one which has moved *intowards* the Gospel of Christ (the new law). The transitive affect is quite startling when seen in this way. In effect, his life story as one who persecuted the early Christians, saw the light, and became a Christian, is all captured in the transitive movement signalled by one little preposition *in* + acc (into/intowards).

The grammar of transitivity then, is not just a grammar of movement, it is an ontological 'grammar of being'. Read anagogically in prayer, the syntax of transitivity is the 'syntax of spirituality'. Like St Paul, for an active Catholic, the interactions and relationships of language and spirituality accompany everything we do and think in life. The words and grammar of our prayer verbalise our spiritual life. The grammar of that prayer may seem to suggest an underlying simple model of verbal communication, but it is really one seeking ever more complicated spiritual affects and outcomes.

Heavenly Incognita

English poet William Wordsworth (1770-1850) whose contact with praying in Latin may only have been saying Latin grace before and after meals as a student at St John's College, Cambridge, much as it is still prayed there now, and at formal dinners in some Universities around the world. Before the meal (*ante cibum/ante prandium/ante mensam*) is prayed:

> *Benedíctus, benedícat, per Iesum Christum Dóminum nostrum. Amen.*
>
> ([The] blessed, may he bless [this meal], through Jesus Christ our Lord. Amen.)

sometimes shortened to just: *Benedictus benedicat. Amen.* And after the meal (*post cibum/post prandium/post mensam*):

> *Benedícto, benedicátur, per Iesum Christum Dóminum nostrum. Amen.*
>
> (By [the] blessed [one] may [the meal] be blessed, through Jesus Christ our Lord. Amen.)

sometimes shortened to: *Benedicto benedicatur. Amen.* The full Latin grace before the meal, which Wordsworth would have known, and which is still prayed, at St John's College, Cambridge, a part of which we saw earlier, is:

> *Oculi ómnium in te sperant, Dómine, et tu das illis cibum in témpore, áperis manum tuam, et imples omne ánimal benedictióne. Bénedic, Dómine, nos et dona tua, quae de tua largitáte sumus sumptúri, et concéde ut illis salúbriter nutríti, tibi débitum obséquium praestáre valeámus, per Iesum Christum Dóminum nostrum.*

(The eyes of all wait upon thee, O Lord: and thou givest them their meat in due season. Thou openest thine hand: and fillest all things living with plenteousness. Bless us, O Lord, and these thy gifts which out of thine abundance we are about to receive, and grant that by their saving nourishment we may have power to fulfill the obedience due to thee, through Jesus Christ our Lord. *trad*)

And after the meal in the version still prayed today:

Infúnde, quǽsumus, Dómine Deus, grátiam tuam in mentes nostras, ut his donis datis a Margareta Fundatríce nostra aliísque Benefactóribus ad tuam glóriam utámur; et cum ómnibus qui in fide Christi decessérunt ad caeléstem vitam resurgámus, per Iesum Christum Dóminum nostrum. Deus pro sua infiníta cleméntia Ecclésiae suae pacem et unitátem concédat, augustíssimam Regínam nostram Elizabetham consérvet, et pacem univérso Regno et ómnibus Christiánis largiátur.

(Pour forth, we beseech thee, Lord God, thy grace into our minds, that we may use these gifts, given by Margaret our Foundress and other Benefactors, to thy glory, and together with all who have died in the faith of Christ rise again to life in heaven, through Jesus Christ our Lord. May God, of his infinite mercy, grant his Church unity and peace, preserve our most august queen, Queen Elizabeth, and grant peace to the whole Realm and to all Christians. *trad*)

These were originally Catholic prayers, and while Wordsworth remained religiously conservative within the Church of England all his life, it is perhaps not widely known, that there was, and still is, a Latin version of the Anglican *Book of Common Prayer*, including, for example, the full text of the *Athanasian Creed*, and there has been since the very beginnings of Anglicanism. The first Latin translation was made of the 1549 Prayer Book in 1551, just two years after the death of King Henry

VIII (1491-1547) and then from the revised 1559 edition by the highly acclaimed Latinist Walter Haddon (1515-1572) in 1560 as: ***Librum Latinum Publicarum Precum, ad usum "Collegiorum Cantabrigiae, Oxoniae, Wintoniae, et Etoniae"***, and was particularly aimed at the two Universities and principal schools, where Latin was still very dominant as the language of education. Wordsworth certainly understood Latin, but more than that, he understood spiritual affects and outcomes, which he talked of as 'the sublime', though probably more so through the lens of the 'natural world', rather than through the supernatural. In his beautifully lyrical 'Lines Written a Few Miles above Tintern Abbey' (1798) writing of nature he says:

'And I have felt
A presence that disturbs me with the joy
Of elevated thoughts; a sense sublime
Of something far more deeply interfused,
Whose dwelling is the light of setting suns,
And the round ocean, and the living air,
And the blue sky, and in the mind of man,
A motion and a spirit, that impels
All thinking things, all objects of all thought,
And rolls through all things.'

Imagine, then, that sublime 'motion' and 'spirit' of which he talks so beautifully through the lens of the natural world, now being seen in prayer through a supernatural lens, and what that might then do to what he calls:

'the language of the sense,
The anchor of my purest thoughts, the nurse,
The guide, the guardian of my heart, and soul
Of all my moral being.'

His 'language of the sense' is often understood, sometimes disparagingly, in terms of 'romantic idealism'; but idealism is a road that must be travelled in prayer, and nor is 'romanticism' in prayer something to avoid. Wordsworth saw the sublime through nature. Some, like Plato (42-348 BC) Plutarch (46-120 AD) Plotinus (204/5-270 AD) Aristotle and Cicero, saw it, variously, through the *summum bonum* (the highest good) in order to live the best possible life, as indeed do many contemporary thinkers and writers now, but Catholicism, particularly as interpreted by St Thomas Aquinas, understands it, not as the concept of 'goodness' in and of itself, but as the seeking of the best possible life lived in communion with God, through the sanctifying grace of the Catholic Church. To understand the 'sublime', therefore, as Catholics, we need to understand it, not as Wordsworth did through nature, or as Emmanuel Kant (1724-1804) was later to do in determining that the 'highest' good' was the supreme fulfillment of human rational will, and which has come to dominate contemporary secular thinking and values, but through one way; one ethics only: the sublime good that is God.

For Catholics who still hold to the revealed truth that faith, works and prayer within the embrace of Christ's Church on earth is a more secure (if not, in fact, the only sure) way of approaching salvation, these truths, as indicative statements therefore, are totally transformative. As one of the very earliest Church Fathers, St Irenaeus of Lyons (130-202) wrote in Ἔλεγχος καὶ ἀνατροπὴ τῆς ψευδωνύμου γνώσεως (*Elenchos kai anatrope tes pseudonymou gnoseos* - On the detection and overthrow of the so-called Gnosis) translated into Latin and known as ***Adversus Haereses*** (*Against Heresies*):

> *qui in Christum credunt, sine charta vel atramento scriptam habentes per Spiritum in cordibus suis salutem, et veterem traditionem diligenter custodientes, in unum Deum credentes fabricatorem caeli et terrae, et omnium quae in eis sunt, per Christum Iesum Dei Filium. Qui propter eminentissimam erga figmentum*

suum dilectionem, eam quae esset ex Virgine generationem sustinuit, ipse per se hominem adunans Deo...

[those] who believe intowards Christ, without paper or ink, having salvation written in their hearts through [the] Spirit, and diligently guarding ancient tradition, believing in one God maker of heaven and earth, and of all things which are in them, through Christ Jesus Son of God. Who because of his most eminent formation from love, deigned that he may be begotten from the Virgin, uniting man through himself to God...)

The key clause here is ***ipse per se hominem adunans Deo***: that through his Incarnation, Jesus unites humanity to God. Christ became man that we might become as sons of God through him. That is *theosis* in a nutshell, and is numinously jaw-dropping. We only need to turn to the account of St Philip's encounter with the powerful Ethiopian eunuch reading the *Book of Isaias* and wondering who the prophet was referring to, to see the affect. St Philip the Apostle (3-80 AD) tells him it is Jesus and we pray with him in the *Epistle* of the Mass of Easter Thursday, when he tells the eunuch, who now seeks to be baptised:

Si credis ex toto corde, licet. Et respóndens ait: credo Fílium Dei esse Iesum Christum.

(If you believe with your whole heart, it is permitted. And answering he said: I believe Jesus Christ to be [the] Son of God. *Ac* 8:37)

The eunuch was baptised and:

Cum autem ascendíssent de aqua, Spíritus Dómini rápuit Philíppum, et ámplius non vidit eum eunúchus. Ibat autem per viam suam gaudens.

(When then they had emerged out from the water, [the] Spirit of the Lord carried off Philip, and [the] eunuch saw him no more. Thus he went on his way rejoicing. (*Ac* 8:39)

Jaw-dropping perhaps, but as St Luke tells us:

> ***Quae impossibilia sunt apud homines, possibilia sunt apud Deum.***
> (Which [things] are impossible among men, are possible with God. (*Lc* 18:27)

Many of the early Church Fathers said the same thing. The 2,000 year old doctrine of *theosis* is, therefore, still totally relevant. As the *Catechism* makes clear, quoting St Peter, there are a number of reasons why God became man (**secundum hominem**) but principal among them is that:

> ***Verbum caro factum est ut nos efficeret "divinae consortes naturae"*** (*2 Pe* 1:4)
> (The Word became flesh to make us "partakers of the divine nature" *Cat* §460)

The enormity of that statement would suggest that prayer should not be taken lightly, and the language we use in which to pray should be very special indeed. The Catholic poet Francis Thompson (1859-1907) famed for his long poem 'The Hound of Heaven' captures this perfectly in his 'To a Poet Breaking Silence' when he writes:

> The loom which mortal verse affords,
> Out of weak and mortal words...
> Vain are all disguises! Ah,
> Heavenly incognita!

In this 'Heavenly incognita' as St Paul tells us (though not using this phrase):

'we look not at the things which are seen, but at the things which are not seen; for the things which are seen are temporal, but the things which are not seen are eternal.' (*DR 2 Cor* 4:18).

They are *numinous*. We seek this 'Heavenly incognita' through the discipline (and layering) of Latin prayer. Underneath the words of that prayer, and below its external surface, so to speak, lie other messages; other histories; other 'inscapes': a spiritual palimpsest. There is, therefore, always a numinous function underlying the language of prayer; a function designed to *affect* (to bring about) *theosis*. This is not a linguistic grammatical function, but a spiritual function; one made possible through the grammar of the language in which we pray. It is not a function restricted only to Latin, but the act of praying in a hieratic language like Latin helps considerably in its affect upon us through its not being ordinary.

The language of prayer is not, therefore, simply a vehicle or medium using words to carry a message made up of those words. The medium of language functions as the message as well, as has famously been said in the past about language and communication by the Catholic academic Marshall McLuhan we saw earlier and who was received into the Catholic Church in 1937 just a few years years after GK Chesterton, by whom he was heavily influenced. Probably unbeknown to many of the thousands of students who still read McLuhan he was also influenced especially by the theology and thinking of St Thomas Aquinas, mostly through his reading of Jacques Maritain. McLuhan argued very persuasively that the medium of a text: print, voice, visual and so on, is often more effective in making meaning than the message the medium carries. As we have seen already in this book, this is not a case of 'either/or', but 'both/and', and we see what McLuhan called the 'mosaic' effect of this 'both/and', time and time again in the layering of Latin prayer, where what might appear to be just 'a bit of grammar' to be learnt, actually has a power in prayer in and of itself, well beyond the 'bit' of grammar's structural or functional role in the language. It is a mosaic that creates, through *mimesis*, a *poesis* of new meanings leading towards *theosis*; a numinously beautiful equation (though McLuhan did not use these terms in this way). In another of his poems, 'Her Portrait' published in 1893, Francis Thompson declares that:

> '... if that language yet with us abode. Which Adam in the garden talked with God!'

we would still have a language with which to speak to God directly. We would, in effect be standing outside of our human selves to do this, because what in Greek is known as ἔκστασις, and was directly borrowed into Latin as **ecstasis** (ecstasy) means that we would have no other focus than God himself. It is just such an ecstasy that the mystics of the Church, through many centuries, have sought to achieve. We have watered down its meaning through the ever-increasing secularised world we live in, where advertisements for chocolate or mattresses talk of 'ecstasy', but it is always useful - in fact essential - to return to its original religious/spiritual (numinous) sense, and to keep it always in mind as we pray.

The ***Litaniae vitae et passionis Domini nostri Iesu Christi*** (Litanies of the life and passion of our Lord Jesus Christ) which we saw at some length in the last chapter was composed several centuries ago, when the articulation of a specific world-view of Catholicism became necessary in ways the Church had not needed before the Reformation. Many of the Latin phrases and attributes included within these *litanies* would have been very familiar for many centuries before it was composed, and remain just as relevant today. There are some very familiar scriptural allusions; some more complex theological concepts; and some doctrinal truths, all forming together what we might term a **norma colloquens** (a conversing way [of speaking]) a *conversational disposition* through litanies, so to speak, about the life, death and passion of Christ, each entry providing new information about Jesus Christ. We pray, as these *litanies* open, with a quotation from St Paul:

> *Humiliávit semetípsum factus obédiens usque ad mortem, mortem autem crucis.*
> (He humbled himself made obedient untowards death, even [the] death of [the] cross.)
> *Propter quod et Deus exaltávit illum, et donávit illi nomen, quod est super omne nomen:*
> (And for which God has exalted him, and has given to him a name, which is above every name:)
> *ut in nómine Iesu omne genu flectátur caeléstium, terréstrium et infernórum,*
> (that in [the] name of Jesus every knee should bend of [the] heavens, of [the] lands, and of [the] depths:)
> *et omnis lingua confiteátur, quia Dóminus Iesus Christus in glória est Dei Patris*
> (and every tongue should confess, because [the] Lord Jesus Christ is in [the] glory of God [the] Father. *Phil* 2:8-11)

and after a litany of almost 400 prayers (including individual petitions and repeated invocations) we end by praying:

> ℣. *Adorámus te, Christe, et benedícimus tibi*
> (We adore you, O Christ, and we give praise to you)
> ℟. *Quia per sanctam crucem tuam redemísti mundum.*
> (For through your holy cross you redeemed [the] world.)

where we clearly demonstrate our obeisance to Christ, as we do when we pray this prayer genuflecting before each one of the 14 **Stationes Crucis** (Stations of the Cross) in the **Via Crucis** (Way of the Cross). 'Obeisance' is a word which has become extremely unfashionable in these 'politically correct' times now, but which powerfully (and perfectly) demonstrates just exactly where we stand in this relationship. Much contemporary Christianity, and increasingly much contemporary Catholicism, assumes a more equal relationship than has ever been the case in Latin Catholicism. This inequality (again a now very unfashionable word) becomes even clearer in the prayer we pray at the end of these *litanies*:

> *Dómine Iesu Christe, Fili Dei vivi, pone passiónem, crucem et mortem tuam inter iudícium tuum et ánimam meam, nunc et in hora mortis meae: et mihi largíri dignéris grátiam et misericórdiam, vivis et defúnctis réquiem et véniam, ecclésiae tuae pacem et concórdiam et nobis peccatóribus vitam et glóriam sempitérnam. Qui vivis et regnas in sǽcula saeculórum. Amen.*

(O Lord Jesus Christ, O Son of [the] living God, place! your passion, cross, and death between your judgement and my soul, now and in [the] hour of my death: and may you deem [it] worthy to grant me grace and mercy, for [the] living and for [the] dead, rest and pardon, to your church peace and concord and to us sinners life and everlasting glory. Who lives and reigns in the ages of ages. Amen.)

One very small Latin preposition *inter* announces the huge difference between *iudícium tuum* as metonymic of Christ and *animam meam* as representative of us. This is recognition of the distance between us and Christ, but by these prayers we seek to lessen this distance. This creates a potentially sublime vision of the *heavenly incognita* that we seek through our prayer where, after every individual prayer of nominative-vocative address in *litanies* like this, we pray repeatedly an imperative prayer like *miserere nobis* (be merciful! to us). Taken all together, *litanies* like this create a transitive *norma collequens* between the pray-er, and the narrative history of Christ, and the way this has been understood over many centuries and developed into specific teachings, doctrines, dogmas, rituals and liturgies down the ages. When at Thursday *Terce* we pray:

et ego ad níhilum redáctus sum, et nescívi:
ut iuméntum factus sum apud te, et ego semper tecum.
Tenuísti manum déxteram meam, et in voluntáte tua deduxísti me, et cum glória suscepísti me.
Quid enim mihi est in caelo? et a te quid vólui super terram?
Defécit caro mea et cor meum; Deus cordis mei, et pars mea, Deus in aetérnum...
Mihi autem adhaerére Deo bonum est; pónere in Dómino Deo spem meam: ut annúntiem omnes praedicatiónes tuas in portis fíliae Sion.

(and I was all dumbness, I was all ignorance standing there like a brute beast in thy presence. Yet ever thou art at my side, ever holdest me by my right hand. Thine to guide me with thy counsel, thine to welcome me into glory at last. What else does heaven hold for me, but thyself? What charm for me has earth, here at thy side? What though flesh of mine, heart of mine, should waste away? Still God will be my heart's stronghold, eternally my inheritance. I know no other content but clinging to God, putting my trust in the Lord, my Master; within the gates of royal Sion I will be the herald of thy praise. *Knox Ps 72: 22-28*)

we are praying with the knowledge that we are not alone in this journey. It is not an easy journey to make, but with the Psalmist we can have the confidence to pray, very simply, but forthrightly, that **adhaerére Deo bonum est** (to adhere to God is good). As St Louis Marie Grignion de Montfort (1673-1716) recognised so clearly, as the author of what must be the best book ever written on devotion and consecration to Our Lady, *Traité de la vraie dévotion à la Sainte Vierge* (Treatise on the True Devotion to the Blessed Virgin) where he recognised that our Catholic journey to the sublime highest good; to the *heavenly incognita*, is best made possible through the Blessed Virgin Mary. Pope St John Paul II travelled a similar journey, taking as his own motto *Totus Tuus* (All Yours) in 1958 when first appointed as a Bishop, and inspired by St Louis' own prayer:

> *Totus tuus ego sum, et ómnia mea tua sunt. Accípio te in mea ómnia. Praebe mihi cor tuum, María.*
> (All yours I am, and my everythings are yours. I accept you for my all. Give! to me your heart, [O] Mary.)

St Louis founded the order of the 'Missionaries of the Company of Mary' in 1705, more popularly known as the Montfort Missionaries (***Societas Mariae Monfortana***) or the 'De Montfort Fathers', whose motto is **ad Iesum per Mariam** and usually translated as 'To Jesus through Mary'. This translation though, as we have seen similarly throughout this chapter, tends to lose the force of the transitive dynamic involved in the prep (*ad*) + acc (*Iesum*) and the prep (*per*) + acc (*Mariam*). There is powerful transitive movement involved in this affect, metonymic of the movement to the sublime in God, and perhaps may be better translated as 'ontowards Jesus onthrough Mary'. When we pray in Sunday *Terce*, an *Office* which traditionally precedes Sunday Mass in many communities.

> *deduc me in sémitam mandatórum tuórum*
> (lead! me intowards [the] path of your commands)
> *Inclína cor meum in testimónia tua, et non in avarítiam.*
> (Incline! my heart intowards your testimonies and not intowards avarice.)
> *Avérte óculos meos, ne vídeant vanitátem; in via tua*
> *vivífica me.*
> (Turn away! my eyes, that they may not see vanity; on your way enliven! me. *Ps* 118:35-37)

we are not just praying hopeful words that may lead to change. We are praying as part of a physical movement towards the Mass that is to come; the sacrifice that we are to be a part of. The movement involved in what we are doing is palpably purposive, and not at all accidental. The 'movement towards' of a phrase like *ad/per* + acc is always described, sometimes in detail, in Latin grammar books, but never with reference to the dynamic and purposive movement intowards/ontowards the numinous in prayer, and the transitive relationship that movement is a part of. It is to this 'dynamic of purpose' in Latin prayer we now turn in *Chapter VII: Purposive Prayer*.

DAVID BIRCH

VII

PURPOSIVE PRAYER

in fidem
(intowards faith)

Purpose

In one of his notebooks GK Chesterton famously wrote that:

> 'You say grace before meals. All right. But I say grace before the concert and the opera, and grace before the play and pantomime, and grace before I open a book, and grace before sketching, painting, swimming, fencing, boxing, walking, playing, dancing and grace before I dip the pen in the ink.'

Grace is about seeking a blessing on everything we do, and returning that blessing by offering our activity, whatever it is, to God, as beautifully captured in the phrase we pray that ends many prayers, including grace before and after meals:

> ***Per Dóminum nostrum Iesum Christum***
> (Through our Lord Jesus Christ)

To end a prayer in this way is not simply a dedication of the prayer to Christ. In Latin, as we have seen already, certain prepositions (*praepositiones - praeponere -* to put before) like *per* (through) are followed by the accusative, as here. The preposition *per* is actually signalling a purposive effect. It is *per Iesum* (on through Jesus) that the prayer of blessing is caused and transited on, through Jesus. 'Onthrough' as a devised English word captures the fact that the action of blessing has a purpose beyond just a formulaic way of closing a prayer with a dedication. Its purpose is to cause something to happen. In the simple epigraph to this chapter, *in fidem*, for example, it is tempting to translate this into English as simply 'in faith'. But to do so would be to lessen the purposive intent of the prayer. As we saw in the last Chapter, the Latin preposition *in* followed by the accusative *fidem* shows purpose towards 'faith', and to show that purpose of movement in English we would have to write something like 'intowards faith'. So, for example, before praying the *Canonical Office* every day (usually before *Matins* even if the specific Feast begins with *Vesperae Primae* [First Vespers] the evening before) a short prayer is traditionally prayed kneeling and privately, even if the *Office* is then prayed publicly in choir. Making the sign of the cross on the lips, it begins:

> *Aperi,* ✠ *Dómine, os meum ad benedicéndum nomen sanctum tuum*
>
> (Open! ✠ O Lord, my mouth ontowards the [*purpose of*] blessing your holy name)

The imp + voc + acc dynamic here calls upon the Lord to prepare us for praying the *Divine Office*, not just accurately, but with a purpose *in order* to bless his holy name. This purposive modality is strongly indicated by the preposition *ad* followed by the accusative of the participial form of the verb ***benedicere*** (to bless) acting like an adjective. This preliminary prayer before *Office* continues:

munda quoque cor meum ab ómnibus vanis, pervérsis et aliénis cogitatiónibus; intelléctum illúmina, afféctum inflámma, ut digne, atténte ac devóte hoc Offícium recitáre váleam, et exaudíri mérear ante conspéctum divínae Maiestátis tuae. Per Christum Dóminum nostrum. Amen.

(cleanse! also my heart from all vain, perverse, and corrupt thoughts; enlighten! [my] intellect, inflame! [my] affect, that I may be worthy to pray attentively, and devoutly this Office, and so may be deserving to be heeded before [the] presence of your divine Majesty. Onthrough Christ our Lord. Amen)

My translation is not an elegant one, but it seeks to capture the underlying purposive grammar of the Latin. And remember, we are praying Latin, not an English version of that Latin. This usually short period of private prayer then ends with:

Dómine, in unióne illíus divínae intentiónis, qua ipse in terris laudes Deo persolvísti, has tibi Horas (*vel hanc tibi Horam*) *persólvo.*

(O Lord, in [the] unity of that divine intention by which yourself here on earth submitted praises [to/for] God, these Hours to/for you [*or this Hour to/for you*] I submit.)

irrespective of whether one or more hours of the *Office* is then to be prayed, there is purposive intent here, located within the purposive dynamic of prep + acc but also in the verb itself: *per* (through) + *solvere* (acquit/release) and so meaning 'to pay up'; 'to discharge'; 'to render'; 'to perform'; 'to accomplish', 'to fulfil' or, as here, 'to submit'. The connotation from its use in Classical Latin is of 'discharging a debt' or 'fulfilling a duty', and given that for those ordained in Major Holy Orders and/or Professed in Religion, it is mandatory to pray the full *Divine Office* every day, the purposive modality of a verb like ***persolvere*** is a powerful reminder of this obligation. Similarly powerful purposive modalities may be found in the prayer prayed every day in each of the 8 daily *Offices*, including making the sign of the cross in the normal way:

Deus ✠ *in adiutórium meum inténde*
(O God, ✠ intowards my help be attentive!
[O God ✠ come to my help *trad*])

Dómine, ad adiuvándum me festína
(O Lord, ontowards my assistance hurry!
[O Lord make haste to help me *trad*])

There is clearly a forceful relationship here between the prepositions and the accusatives that follow them. The preposition does not decline, but it has a powerful effect upon what follows it. The vast majority of Latin prepositions change the grammatical case of the part of speech that follows them by acting upon them in the same way as a verb used transitively. The movement involved signals that there is purpose; the prayer is designed to cause something to happen through its grammar. This is not just a grammatical quirk, but one which signals very specific causative relationships about purpose: direction/movement ('in', 'into', 'unto', 'to', 'towards') location/space ('behind', 'by', 'besides', 'above', 'below', 'under') time ('after', 'before', 'during', 'within', 'at') space manner/cause and effect ('according to') and so on. It is grammar designed to address; it is grammar with focus and force. It is grammar dynamically designed for purpose.

The Purposive Dynamic

In one of the oldest extant manuscripts of an English *Psalter*, the *Midland Prose Psalter* (c1350) there is a translation of *Psalm 42:5* which reads:

'Ha God, my God, y shal schryue me to þe in þe in-mast of myn hert; ha þou my soule, whi ertou sori, and why trublestou me?'

This is translated from the *Psalm* prayed before the **usus antiquior** Mass:

Confitébor tibi in cíthara, Deus, Deus meus. Quare tristis es, ánima mea? et quare contúrbas me?
(I will give praise to you upon the harp [O] God, my God. Why are you sad, [O] my soul? and why [do you]confound me? *Ps* 42:4-5)

The Middle English is certainly a very free translation from the *Vulgate*. But importantly, in its use of the preposition 'to' in 'y shal schryue me to þe in þe in-mast of myn hert' (I will confess myself to you in the inmost of my heart) the prepositions 'to', 'in' and the 'in' of 'in-mast', are all very suggestive of the purposive 'movement towards' in the original Latin. Similarly, the very frequently occurring phrase *in aeternum* is usually translated as 'for ever', but actually implies considerable movement towards the everlasting, and so may more accurately be translated as 'ontowards/intowards/untowards eternity'. Likewise *in saeculum* is usually translated as 'for ever' and *in saeculum saeculi* as 'for ever and ever' when, to capture the movement involved, they might be better translated as 'intowards time/age' (*saeculum*) and 'intowards the time/age of time/age'. Similarly *in salutem* has considerably more force when translated with movement 'intowards/untowards/ontowards salvation', than just 'in salvation', or more often than not, just as 'salvation'. In Latin constructions like *in/ad* + acc there is, then, a purposive dynamic involved which indicates that some action is happening; some intent is involved or some movement required. There is a marked difference, for example, in translating *in verbum tuum* as 'in your word' than 'into/intowards your word'. The focus dramatically shifts onto the action and movement involved in the whole purpose and intent of the prepositional phrase. In *Psalm* 129 prayed in Wednesday *Vespers*, the Psalmist pleads to God in the second verse:

> **Dómine, exáudi vocem meam.**
> (O Lord heed my prayer.)

and then asks God:

> ***Fiant aures tuae intendéntes in vocem deprecatiónis meae.***
> (Let thy ears be attentive to the voice of my supplication. DR *Ps* 129:2)

Knox translates this as 'let but thy ears be attentive to the voice that calls on thee for pardon', and the *JB* as 'Listen compassionately to my pleading!'. But look what happens if it is translated as 'listen into/intowards my voice of prayer'. A more intimate, dynamic, relationship between God and the supplicant, or if not that, the possibility of establishing one, is immediately implied. This is a pattern of grammar repeated often in purposive prayer, and while I may appear to be labouring a simple grammatical point, I do so because of its frequency in Latin prayer and its consequent importance in the way both linguistic and numinous relationships are established in the Latin text, but often missed or glossed over in English translations. For example, when we pray the following in most traditional English translations we tend to lose the purposive intent of the Latin:

> *ad Deum* (prep + acc sg m *Deus*) to God

> *ad déxteram Patris*
> (prep + acc sg f *dexter* + gen sg m *pater*) to the right hand of [the] Father

> *ad Dóminum* (prep + acc sg m *Dominus*) to the Lord

ad excusándas excusationes
(prep + acc pl fut part/adj f *excusandus* + acc pl f *excusatio*) to excusing excuses

ad honórem (prep + acc sg m *honor*) to the honour

ad laudem et glóriam nóminis sui, ad utilitátem quoque nostram, totiúsque Ecclésiae suae sanctae
(prep + acc sg f *laus* + conj + prep + acc sg f *gloria* + gen sg n *nomen* + gen sg n adj *suus* + prep + acc sg f *utilitas* + adv + prep + acc sg f adj *noster* + gen sg m adj *totus* + conj + gen sg f *ecclesia* + gen sg f adj *suus* + gen sg f adj *sanctus*)
to the praise and glory of his name, also to our benefit and of all his holy Church

ad medélam percipiéndam
(prep + acc sg f *medela* + acc sg part/adj f *percipiendus*) to the perceived cure

ad perditiónem animárum
(prep + acc sg f *perditio* + gen pl f *anima*) to the perdition of souls

ad salútem (prep + acc sg f *salus*) to salvation

ad salútem in vitam aetérnam
(prep + acc sg f *salus* + prep + acc sg f *vita* + acc sg f adj *aeternus*) to salvation in eternal life

ad sancta sanctórum
(prep + acc pl n *sanctus* + gen pl n *sanctus*) to the holies of holies

ad te (prep + acc sg m *tu*) to you

ad te clamantem
(prep + acc sg m *tu* + acc sg part/adj m *clamans*) to you crying

ad te Deum Patrem suum omnipoténtem
(prep + acc sg m *tu* + acc sg m *Deus* +
acc sg m *pater* + acc sg m *suus* + acc sg m *omnipotens*)
to you God his almighty Father

ad tutaméntum mentis et córporis
(prep + acc sg n *tutamentum* + gen sg f *mens* + conj + gen sg n *corpus*) to the defence of body and mind

apud Deum
(prep + acc sg m *Deus*) with God

apud Deum Patrem omnipoténtem
(prep + acc sg m *Deus* + acc sg m *pater* + acc sg m adj *omnipotens*)
with God the almighty Father

contra nequítiam et insídias diáboli
(prep + acc sg f *nequitia* + conj + acc pl f *insidia* + gen sg m *diabolus*) against the wickedness and snares of the devil

et in honórem beátae Maríae semper Vírginis, et beáti Ioánnis Baptístae, et sanctórum Apostolórum Petri et Pauli, et istórum, et ómnium Sanctórum.
(conj + prep + acc sg f *honor* + gen sg f adj *beatus* + gen sg f *Maria* + adv + gen sg f *virgo* + conj + gen sg m adj *beatus* + prep + gen pl m adj *sanctus* +gen sg m *Ioannes* + gen sg m *Baptista* + conj + gen pl m *Apostolus* + gen sg m *Petrus* + conj + gen sg m *Paulus* + conj + gen pl m *iste* + conj + gen pl m *omnis* + gen pl m *sanctus*)

and in honour of the blessed Mary ever Virgin, and blessed John the Baptist, and of the holy Apostles Peter and Paul, and of these, and of all saints.

et unam, sanctam, cathólicam et apostólicam Ecclésiam
(conj + acc sg adj f *unus* + acc sg f adj *sanctus* + acc sg f adj *catholicus* + conj + acc sg f adj *apostolicus* + acc sg f *ecclesia*)
and one, holy, catholic and apostolic Church

in caelos (prep + acc pl m *caelus*) in the heavens

in diem ad caeléstis vitae... actiónem
(prep + acc sg m/f *dies* + prep + gen sg adj f *caelestis* + gen sg f *vita* + acc sg f *actio*) in the day (daily) action of heavenly life

in hunc mundum
(prep + acc sg m det *hic* + acc sg m *mundus*) in this world

in inférnum (prep + acc sg n *infernum*) in hell

in iudícium et condemnatiónem
(prep + acc sg n *iudicium* + conj + acc sg f *condemnatio*)
in judgement and condemnation

in unum Deum. Patrem omnipoténtem, factórem caeli et terrae, visibílium ómnium, et invisibílium. Et in unum Dóminum Iesum, Christum Fílium Dei unigénitum.

(prep + acc sg m adj *unus* + acc sg m *Deus* + acc sg m *pater* + acc sg m adj *omnipotens* + acc sg m *factor* + gen sg n *caelum* + conj + gen sg f *terra* + gen pl n adj *visibilis* + gen pl n *omnis* + conj + gen pl adj n *invisibilis* + conj + prep + acc sg m adj *unus* + acc sg m *Dominus* + acc sg m *Iesus* + acc sg m *Christus* + acc sg m *filius* + gen sg m *Deus* + acc sg m adj *unigenitus*) in one God. Almighty Father, maker of heaven and earth, of all visible and invisible. And in one Lord Jesus, Christ only begotten Son of God.

in mei memóriam
(prep + gen sg m *ego* + acc sg f *memoria*) in memory of me

in montem sanctum tuum
(prep + acc sg m *mons* + acc sg m adj *sanctus* + acc sg m adj *tuus*) on your holy mountain

in odórem suavitátis
(prep + acc sg m *odor* + acc sg f *suavitas*) in [the] smell of sweetness

in sanctas ac venerábiles manus suas
(prep + acc pl f adj *sanctus* + conj + acc pl f adj *venerabilis* + acc pl f *manus* + acc pl f adj *suus*) in his holy and venerable hands

in Spíritum Sanctum, Dóminum et vivificántem
(prep + acc sg m *spiritus* + acc sg adj m *sanctus* + acc sg m *Dominus* + conj + acc sg m *vivificans*) in [the] Holy Spirit, Lord and life-giving

in verba malítiae
(prep + acc pl n *verbum* + gen sg f *malitia*) in words of malice

in vitam aetérnam
(prep + acc sg f *vita* + acc sg f adj *aeternus*) in life eternal

inter innocéntes
(prep + acc pl m/f *innocens*) amongst [the] innocents

ob memóriam passiónis, resurrectiónis, et ascensiónis Iesu Christi Dómini nostri (prep + acc sg f *memoria* + gen sg f *passio* + gen sg f *resurrectio* + conj + gen sg f *ascensio* + gen sg m *Iesus* + gen sg m *Christus* + gen sg m *Dominus* + gen sg m adj *noster*) to [the] memory of the passion, resurrection and ascension of Jesus Christ our Lord

per Christum Dóminum nostrum
(prep + acc sg m *Christus* + acc sg m *Dominus* + acc sg m adj *noster*)
through Christ our Lord

per Dóminum nostrum Iesum Christum Fílium tuum
(prep + acc sg m *Dominus* + acc sg m adj *noster* + acc sg m *Iesus* + acc sg m *Christus* + acc sg m *Filius* + acc sg m adj *tuus*)
through our Lord Jesus Christ your Son

per eúmdem Christum Dóminum nostrum
(prep + acc sg m det *idem* + acc sg m *Christus* + acc sg m *Dominus* + acc sg m adj *noster*) through the same Christ our Lord

per hoc sacrosánctum Corpus et Sánguinem tuam
(prep + acc sg n adj *hic* + acc sg n adj *sacrosanctus* + acc sg n *corpus* + conj + acc sg f *sanguis* + acc sg f adj *tuus*)
through this your most holy Body and Blood

per huius aquae et vini mystérium
(prep + gen sg f det *hic* + gen sg f *aqua* + conj + gen sg n *vinum* + acc sg n *mysterium*)
through [the] mystery of this water and wine

per illum (prep + acc sg m *ille*) through him

per ipsum (prep + acc sg m *ipse*) through himself

per intercessiónem beáti Michaélis Archángeli
(prep + acc sg f *intercessio* + gen sg m adj *beatus* + gen sg m *Michael* + gen sg m *archangelus*)
through the intercession of blessed Michael [the] Archangel

per manus sancti Angeli tui
(prep + acc pl f *manus* + gen sg m adj *sanctus* + gen sg m *angelus* + gen sg m adj *tuus*)
through the hands of your holy Angel

per mérita Sanctórum tuórum
(prep + acc pl n *meritum* + gen pl m a*sanctus* + gen pl m adj *tuus*)
through the merits of your Saints

per mortem tuam
(prep + acc sg f *mors* + acc sg f adj *tuus*) through your death

per ómnia sécula saeculórum
(prep + acc pl n adj *omnis* + acc pl n *saeculum* + gen pl n *saeculum*)
through all ages of ages

per quem (prep + acc sg m *quis*) through whom

propter magnam glóriam tuam
(prep + acc sg f adj *magnus* + acc sg f *gloria* + acc sg f adj *tuus*)
according to your great glory

propter nos hómines et propter nostram salútem
(prep + acc pl m *ego* + acc pl m *homo* + conj + prep + acc sg f adj *noster* + acc sg f *salus*) for us men and for our salvation

secúndum magnam misericórdiam tuam
(prep + acc sg adj f *magnus* + acc sg f *misericordia* + acc sg f adj *tuus*) according to your great mercy

secúndum Scriptúras
(prep + acc pl f *scriptura*) according to [the] Scriptures

sub tectum meum
(prep + acc sg n *tectum* + acc sg n adj *meus*) under my roof

unum baptísma in remissiónem peccatórum
(acc sg n adj *unus* + acc sg n *baptisma* + prep + acc sg f *remissio* + gen pl n *peccatum*) one baptism in remission of sins

These forms of purposive address are all translated here as they tend to be in the parallel Latin/English missals and prayer books. But if we go back through them all and translate each one more dynamically ('into' instead of 'in' or 'intowards' instead of 'into' and so on) then the prayers of the Mass, for example, using such forms of address, more forcefully signal the active participatory movement involved in why we go to Mass in the first place: to move closer intowards/uptowards/ontowards God. When we do the same with 'through' by translating *per* as 'inthrough' or 'onthrough' we see a similar forceful, and participatory, movement. Praying a *usus antiquior* Mass, even if in the very back pew, is a highly participative and purposive activity. And not just physically. It requires considerable mental activity, as St John Vianney (1786-1859 and popularly known as the Curé d'Ars) famously said:

'If we really understood the Mass, we would die of joy.'

The fact that we can never really understand the numinousness of the Mass requires that we continually have to participate in trying to. That requires the purposive dynamism which is encoded into the very linguistic architecture of the Latin prayers, but often lost completely in translation. But it is never lost in the Latin itself. I may have laboured this point, but do so to emphasise the relationship values which may be lost between pray-er and prayed-to when (or if) we pray Latin as if it is English. Consider, for example, the difference between saying:

Credo in Deum (I believe in God)

and

Credo in Deum (I believe into/unto/intowards/untowards God)

The movement and purpose of the Latin prep + acc dynamic is maintained with 'into'/'intowards', and more than that, signals strongly that belief itself is actually an intentional movement; a journey towards God, not a passive activity. We have to make an effort. The Latin purposive dynamic shouts that out. In a very beautiful arrangement of the famous 19[th]C English hymn 'Nearer, my God, to thee, nearer to thee!' based on Jacob's dream of the ladder with Angels going up to, and down from, heaven, James L Stevens (nd) includes an additional Latin text (with phrases used often in a range of Latin prayers) as a way of framing, almost antiphonally, the English hymn itself, while also acting as a commentary upon it in the background:

In artículo mortis
Cælitus mihi vires
Deo adiuvánte non timéndum
In perpétuum
Dírige nos Dómine
Ad augústa per angústa
Sic itur ad astra
Excélsior.

(At the moment of death
My strength is from heaven
God helping, nothing should be feared
For ever
Direct us, O Lord
To high places by narrow roads
Such is the path to the stars
Ever upward. *trad*)

But this traditional translation tends to lose the purposive force of the Latin prayer and might more literally be:

Within the moment of death
Strengths to me from heaven
With God helping, nothing to be feared
Into perpetuity
Direct us O Lord
Ontowards glory onthrough narrow [ways]
So therefore ontowards the stars
More high.

We are not just praying in the Latin text for something to be given to us; we are praying the purposive dynamic that we might actually change the direction of our lives. When Job calls out:

Quis mihi tribuat ut cognoscam et inveniam illum, et veniam usque ad solium eius?
(Who may grant to me that I may know and find him, and come unto his throne? *Iob* 23:3)

the ***usque ad solium eius*** (prep + acc) does more than acknowledge the throne of God, it signals real movement towards it. When he says:

> *Proponat aequitatem contra me, et perveniat ad victoriam iudicium meum.*
>
> (May he propose equity against me, and let my judgement come through towards victory *Iob* 23:7)

the *perveniat* (*per* + *venire*) is not simply stating a possibility, it is affirming with **ad victoriam iudicium meum** (prep + acc) that real movement is involved if Job is to 'come through to victory'. When he goes on to say:

> *Si ad orientem iero, non apparet; si ad occidentem, non intelligam eum.*
>
> (If I will have moved forward ontowards the east, he appears not; if ontowards the west, I will not comprehend him *Iob* 23:8)

the Latin verb *iero* from the infinitive *ire* is an incredibly powerful verb of movement. There is power in this movement, just as there is power in the grammar of movement. In the graffiti daubed on the wall in the Monty Python movie *Life of Brian*, for example, and corrected by the Roman centurion from the grammatically incorrect **Romanes eunt domus** ('Romane go the house') daubed everywhere in protest against Roman rule in Jerusalem (when the protestors meant to say 'Romans go home!') the accusative motion towards was needed, as in the grammatically correct **Romani ite domum!** ('Romans, go! [towards] home') which then, in the very haughty manner of an English school teacher, the centurion makes Brian correct and re-graffiti 100 times, in the manner of the written lines once handed out as punishment to school children. This was a film that upset many Christians, for all sorts of reasons, but this scene makes a valuable (and very funny) point: movement towards/forward as in 'to go [home]'; 'to proceed'; 'to go forth'; 'to move on'; 'to move along'; 'to keep going'; 'to set off', not only signals movement, as such, but intent and purpose. The unwitting Brian gets his purposive intent grammatically off kilter, much as we might do if we pray Latin as if it means the same as the English we sometimes want to make it mean.

Job, for example, in the Latin St Jerome gives him, purposively indicates what he wants (and needs) to do in order to really move closer to God. In the Latin prayer sung as part of the hymn 'Nearer my God' the repetition of the purposive dynamic emphasises the physical activity needed in pursuing the numinous. In the Latin of these texts we see that purpose is more than just a hope or wishful thinking. For Job there is real purposive movement involved in the prep + acc phrases **ad orientem** and **ad occidentem**; movement Job reaffirms when he continues:

> *Si ad sinistram, quid agam? non apprehendam eum; si me vertam ad dexteram, non videbo illum.*
> (If ontowards the left, what will I do? I will not embrace him; if I turn myself ontowards the right, I will not see him. *Iob* 23:9)

Job has moved around in circles doing whatever he can to find God: east, west, north and south, anxiously never staying still. But in so doing he comes to the conclusion that:

> *Ipse vero scit viam meam, et probavit me quasi aurum quod per ignem transit.*
> (But he truly knows my way, and has tested me as gold which passes through fire. *Iob* 23:10)

Job did not know the way, but God always does. This is Job's insight, and it is made the more more forceful by the grammar of purposive intent in the Latin *Vulgate*.

The very first English commentary (that we know of) on any book of the Old Testament (an account of **Liber Iob**) is one of forty sermons in Ælfric of Eynsham's (955-1010) **Sermones Catholici** (Catholic Homilies) written with very strong influences from Pope St Gregory I's

Moralia in Iob (Morals on Job) parts of whose sermons are still closely read today in *Matins*. Ælfric was an Anglo-Saxon Benedictine Abbot, scholar and grammarian, praised for his Latin homilies which he made more widely available as teaching and learning aids by translating them into the English language (Anglo Saxon) of his day. The story of Job's troubles, and his consequent value to Christian living, Ælfric simply sums up by saying:

> Ne geðafode God þis to forwyrde þam eadigan were, ac þæt he wære to bysne eallum geleaffullum mannum and wurde swiðor gemærsod þurh his miccle geðyld and earfoðnyssum.
>
> (God did not allow this fortunate man to be destroyed, and after[wards] he was a model to all faithful men and was roundly celebrated for his considerable restraint and hardships.)

Without a doubt, there is something very special in quoting a Benedictine Abbot who was writing almost 1,200 years ago on Job, in Anglo Saxon, a language which now has to be learnt as a distinct language, just as Latin does. But to Ælfric, and the even earlier Benedictine, the Venerable Bede (673-735) and other such Anglo Saxon writers of the time, it was as vibrant and contemporary a language to them as the Catholic life they and every other 'Western' Christian at that time, embraced as the only form of 'Western' Christianity that existed. The language they spoke and taught in has changed dramatically, but the language they prayed in, Latin, has not. We pray exactly the same words today from **Liber Job** as Ælfric did. But the one very big difference now is that for Ælfric, Christianity *was* Catholicism. There was no other form; no concept of 'alternative' Christianities. Our Catholic patrimony today, therefore, extends far beyond just the tangible treasures we hold in museums; it includes the history of people like Ælfric who, in prayer, sought the same purposive intents and dynamic movements, through the same language and grammar St Jerome gave to Job in the *Vulgate*. That is a priceless treasure indeed.

Purposive Movement

In *Psalm* 114, prayed in Monday *Vespers*, the Psalmist opens the first verse with:

> *Diléxi, quóniam exáudiet Dóminus vocem oratiónis meae.*
> *Quia inclinávit aurem suam mihi, et in diébus meis invocábo.*
> (I have loved, because [the] Lord will hear [the] voice of my prayer. Because he inclined his ear to me, so I will invoke [him] in my days/[everyday] *Ps* 114:1-2)

Like Job, the Psalmist is calling upon God because he has met with great sorrow and trouble in the past, but in verse 4 we pray in his voice:

> *O Dómine, líbera ánimam meam.*
> (O Lord, free my soul. *Ps* 114:4)

Again like Job's own prayer:

> *Libera me, Domine, et pone me iuxta te, et cuiusvis manus pugnet contra me.*
> (Deliver me, O Lord, and place me next to you, and let anyone's hand fight against me. *Iob* 17:3)

These are cries from the heart for a move from the troubles and sorrows to something better, where Job is protected by being at the side of God. This change requires movement from one state of being to another. It requires focus. It has to be dynamic, otherwise it is no change at all. Both Job and the Psalmist recognise that to be at God's side, and so therefore, protected, does not just happen. We pray this recognition with them at *Vespers*:

> *et nomen Dómini invocávi: O Dómine, líbera ánimam meam.*
> (so I called upon [the] name of [the] Lord: O Lord, deliver! my soul. *Ps* 114:4)

and again:

> *Convértere, ánima mea, in réquiem tuam.*
> (Be turned! [O] my soul, intowards your rest. *Ps* 114:7)

Addressing your own soul in this way involves action; it involves, as shown here by the grammar of imp + voc + prep + acc, a moving forward from a state of unrest to a hoped-for state of rest. At Monday *Vespers*, then, we are praying the words, but like Job and the Psalmist, how much more powerful it is to pray the grammar of purpose too. Crying out to God, like this, is not simply asking for the help to change the sorrow and troubles into something else - a happier life perhaps - but with the preposition *in* followed by the accusative **requiem tuam**, is a call for turning one's life inside out; a call for the help which requires actively and dynamically moving into/intowards God's rest. It is a call involving purposive focus. And so, the seemingly simple imperative followed by a nom/voc phrase **anima mea** followed by a preposition *in* followed by the accusative **requiem tuam**, is not, therefore, simple at all. It is all about purposive movement towards an actual life change; a new life force; a new reality and a new identity. This is what we are praying for here. But consider these:

> *Douay-Rheims* (1609-10): 'Turn, O my soul, into thy rest'
> *King James Version* (1611 renumbered as *Psalm* 116): 'Return unto thy rest, O my soul'
> *American Standard Version* (1901): Return unto thy rest, O my soul'
> *Knox* (1949): 'Return, my soul, where thy peace lies'

Revised Standard Version (1952 renumbered as *Psalm* 116): 'Return, O my soul, to your rest'

Jerusalem Bible (1966 renumbered as *Psalm* 116): 'Return to your resting place, my soul';

New International Version (1973): 'Return to your rest, my soul'

Good News Bible (1976): 'Be confident, my heart'

New King James Version JV (1982): 'Return unto thy rest, O my soul'

New Jerusalem Bible (1985): 'My heart, be at peace once again'

English Standard Version (2001): 'Return O my soul to your rest'

some of which are based on the *Vulgate* and others directly on the original Hebrew, but all of them, with the exception of the *DR*, including all the recent Catholic approved versions, lose the urgency, movement and dynamism St Jerome injected into his Latin translation. God tells Job:

Circumda tibi decorem, et in sublime erigere, et esto gloriosus, et speciosis induere vestibus.

(Wrap around! beauty to yourself, and be encouraged! in greatness, and be! glorious, and be clothed! with splendid garments *Iob* 40:5)

The *DR* translates this as:

'Clothe thyself with beauty, and set thyself up on high, and be glorious, and put on goodly garments.'

and Knox as:

'Come, deck thyself with glory, up with thee to the heights; shew all thy splendours, robe thyself in dazzling array!'

There are 4 imperatives in the *Vulgate,* two are active (***circumda/esto***) and two are passive (***erigere/induere***). Both the *DR* and *Knox* translate the passive imperatives as active verbs, and so the agency of ***erigere*** (be encouraged) and ***induere*** (be clothed) is shifted in a more active way to Job himself, especially in the Knox version, whereas the Latin passive imperatives are much more like the future active imperative ***esto*** (be!) where we are much more uncertain about who the agent is for enabling Job to 'be encouraged in greatness' and 'be clothed with splendid garments'. Is Job himself responsible for these actions, as the *DR* and *Knox* seem to suggest, or is it someone else? Is the actual agent of the change in Job's life hidden from view in the grammar here? Job later asks the rhetorical question of God:

> ***Quis est iste qui celat consilium absque scientia?***
> (Who is this who hides counsel without knowledge? *Iob* 42:3)

knowing that it is Job himself, out of his own ignorance (***absque scientia***) who has done this. He continues:

> ***ideo insipienter locutus sum, et quae ultra modum excederent scientiam meam.***
> (thus [for that reason] I have spoken foolishly, and those [things] above measure may have exceeded my knowledge. *Iob* 42:3)

He acknowledges that while he is the agent of his own foolishness, he (like the passive imperatives) is not the agent of the changes he will need to make:

> ***Scio quia omnia potes, et nulla te latet cogitatio.***
> (Because I know you can do all, and no thought hides from you. *Iob* 42:2)

God is the agent. God, as Job recognises, is the cause of everything, but, like the agents hidden in the passives, is not easily known. Hard work is needed. The purposive movement which is expressed in various grammatical ways here needs also to be transformed in life. Job's agency - any personal agency - is only possible because of God's ultimate, numinous, agency, gifted by God to us. That simple little phrase 'to us' is key in all of this. When, for example, we pray the following from *Psalm* 104, in Saturday *Matins*:

Confitémini Dómino, et invocáte nomen eius: annuntiáte inter gentes ópera eius. Cantáte ei et psállite ei: narráte ómnia mirabília eius.

(Give thanks! to [the] Lord, and invoke! his name; announce! his works among [the] people. Sing! to him and pray *Psalms!* to him: narrate! all his wonders. *Ps* 104:1-2)

the imperative plural ***confitemini*** (confess/give thanks!) might be expected to be translated as a passive imperative 'be confessed!', but it is not because the verb ***confiteri*** is a deponent verb, which is passive in form but always active in meaning. The imperative is not followed by an accusative form ***Dominum*** (confess the Lord) as might be expected but by ***Domino***. We know the nominative form is ***Dominus***, the vocative is ***Domine***, the genitive ***Domini*** and the accusative ***Dominum*** but this inflectional change is signalling that ***Domino*** is actually the recipient of the confession/thanks: 'confess **to** the Lord' or 'give thanks **to** the Lord', and in grammatical terms the recipient of an action like this is known as the 'indirect object' of the verb (just as ***Dominum*** would be the 'direct object' of the verb). Something is being given **to** the Lord with purposive force (***dativus*** - 'giving' from ***dare*** - to give). There is a new dynamic involved in the prayer here.

The Dative Dynamic

The opening line of the **Canticum trium puerorum** (Canticle of three children) prayed at *Lauds* on Sundays and feast days is:

> *Benedícite ómnia ópera Dómini Dómino laudáte et superexaltáte eum*
> (Bless! all works of [the] Lord to the Lord praise! and magnify! him)

The dative in English is generally considered as something being done 'to' something or someone, but in Latin there is in the dative function a much more forceful sense of purpose, as here with **Domino**. We can translate **Domino** as 'to the Lord', but in the Latin text there is a much more forceful sense that the blessings involved are for the Lord, and so an English translation of 'All the works of the Lord give blessings for the Lord' might better reflect the dynamic involved. That dynamic. though, is perhaps better understood, like much of what we have seen in Latin prayer already, not as an 'either/or' but as a 'both/and', signalling a whole new relationship difference; a whole new modality of agency and with that a new way of thinking linguistically (and then anagogically) about the theology of purpose. We can see this very clearly, for example, when after the recitation of every *Psalm* Pope Damasus I (305-384) at the very beginnings of the transition from using Greek in the Western Catholic Liturgy to Latin, introduced the practice of saying the **Gloria Patri** (Glory [be] to the Father...) one of the earliest prayers (in existence long before Pope Damasus I) and known as the **doxologia minor** (δοξολογία - *doxologia* - praise):

> *Glória Patri, et Fílio, et Spirítui Sancto, sicut erat in princípio, et nunc, et semper, et in sǽcula saeculórum. Amen*
> (Glory to [the] Father, and to [the] Son, and to [the] Holy Spirit, as it was in [the] beginning, and now, and ever, and in [the] ages of ages. Amen)

The *gloria* (glory/praise) to be given is 'to/for' the Father (***Patri***) 'to/for' the Son (***Filio***) and 'to/for' the Holy Spirit (***Spiritui Sancto***). In the antiphon below for the *Magnificat* prayed at *Vespers* on Trinity Sunday (***Dominica Sanctissimae Trinitatis***):

> *Te Deum Patrem ingénitum, te Fílium unigénitum, te Spíritum Sanctum Paráclitum, sanctam et indivíduam Trinitátem, toto corde et ore confitémur, laudámus, atque benedícimus: tibi glória in sǽcula.*
>
> (You God [the] unbegotten Father, you [the] only begotten Son, you [the] Holy Spirit [the] Comforter, [the] holy and undivided Trinity, with our whole heart and voice we confess, praise, and bless: to/for you glory for ever.)

Deum, ***Filium*** and ***Spiritum*** are expressed in the accusative as direct objects of the verbs ***confitemur***, ***laudamus***, and ***benedicimus*** but at the end of this antiphon, we pray *tibi glória in sǽcula* (glory 'to/for' you for ever) where the pronoun changes from nom *tu* (acc *te*) to dative *tibi*. The grammatical form is different because the agency is different, and the agency is different because the point of view (***punctum visus***) is different. In the antiphon, the point of view is a direct one from the verbs 'confess', 'praise' and 'bless' towards the direct objects: ***Deum Patrem***, ***Filium*** and ***Spiritum Sanctum***, and so put into the accusative form. In the *Gloria Patri* the point of view is indirect from the unspoken verb 'be' (Glory [be] to...) to the indirect objects ***Patri***, ***Filio*** and ***Spiritui Sancto***, and so put into the dative form. The dative case in grammar, then, expresses an indirect relationship from a subject to a direct object and then onto an indirect object. In Latin prayer this distinction can be very significant. At Christmas, for example, we give each other gifts. We do so because at this time God gave to us the greatest of all gifts, himself, through his Son:

> *Non enim misit Deus Filium suum in mundum, ut iudicet mundum, sed ut salvetur mundus per ipsum.*
>
> (God sent not his Son into [the] world, in order to judge [the] world, but so that [the] world may be saved through himself. *Io* 3:17)

This is the dative case/form personified - literally. God (subject) gave (who?) his son (direct object) ('to/for' whom?) 'to/for' us (indirect object). We reflect this *dative personification* (referred to by some theologians as 'the dative self') in a great deal of Latin prayer, as we pray in Sunday *Vespers*:

> *Non nobis, Dómine, non nobis, sed nómini tuo da glóriam*
>
> (Not unto us [indirect object - dat pl ***nos***], O Lord, not unto us [indirect object - dat pl ***nos***], but to your name [indirect object dat sg n ***nomen***] give [the] glory [direct object acc sg f ***gloria***] *Ps* 113:9)

In the prayer prayed at the foot of the altar before the Mass begins, prayed first by the Priest and then by the server(s) and in some forms of this Mass, by the server(s) again before their own and the peoples' communion, which in its earliest forms dates back to at least the 8[th]C, the **Confíteor** appears to be a prayer simply about confessing one's sins, but might be better seen as actually a prayer giving glory 'to/for' God given his gift of grace to us enabling us to confess those personal sins. The Priest prays:

> ***Confíteor Deo omnipoténti, beátae Maríae semper Vírgini, beáto Michaéli Archángelo, beáto Ioánni Baptístae, sanctis Apóstolis Petro et Paulo, ómnibus Sanctis, et vobis, fratres, quia peccávi nimis cogitatióne, verbo et ópere*** (*percutit sibi pectus ter, dicens:*) ***mea culpa, mea culpa, mea máxima culpa. Ideo precor beátam Máriam semper Vírginem, beátum Michaélem Archángelum, beátum Ioánnem Baptístam, sanctos Apóstolos Petrum et***

Paulum, omnes Sanctos, et vos, fratres, oráre pro me ad Dóminum Deum nostrum.

(I confess to God almighty, to [the] Blessed Mary ever Virgin, to [the] blessed Michael Archangel, to [the]blessed John Baptist, to [the] holy Apostles Peter and Paul, to all [the] Saints, and to you, brethren, because I have sinned excessively in thought, word, and deed (*he strikes his breast three times, saying*:) [by] my fault, [with] my own fault, [through] my greatest fault. Therefore I beseech [the] blessed Mary ever Virgin, [the] blessed Michael the Archangel, [the] blessed John the Baptist, [the] holy Apostles Peter and Paul, all [the] Saints, and you, brethren, to pray for me to [the] Lord our God.)

and the server/s pray the same but replace *et vobis, fratres/et vos, fratres* with *ettibi, Pater/et te, Pater*. After the opening verb *confiteor* we pray 7 times with 7 dative phrases before we reach the next verb where we declare *peccavi nimis*. Confession might always appear to be about us, because our sins are so personal to us, but in Latin Catholicism it is not; it is always about confessing (giving praise to) God. The whole point of Confession is not primarily to chastise ourselves, but to praise and give glory 'to/for' God for the very act of our confessing. We confess God (acc). We don't just confess *to* God (dat). We confess Christ (acc). We don't just confess *to* Christ (dat) through the person of the Priest at sacramental confession. But we do confess *for* God and *for* Christ. The dative dynamic in this prayer, then, is really about giving purposive thanks and praise both *to* and *for* God for what he has given to us through his Son (the ultimate dative gift of self) Our Lady and the Saints.

We tend to think when we pray: 'I confess to God'; that somehow God stands apart from us. We are actively taught as Catholics, and rightly so, that sin separates us from God, but consider how much more forceful it is to pray the dative **Deo** as 'I confess *for* God'. In other words 'I am making a confession *for* God' and 'I am giving praise *for* God' *through* that confession. But more than that. How much more forceful is this purposive prayer when prayed not as an 'either/or': 'to' or 'for', but as a 'both/and': 'to' and 'for'; a 'both/and' already implicit in the grammar of the Latin dative. Seen in this way, then, confession is not just about beating ourselves up over sin, though it certainly requires forceful soul-searching and penitence, especially in the Sacrament of Confession before a Priest *in loco Christi*, but about forcefully 'acknowledging' (**con** +**fateri** - to speak with force) our sin *before* God, with the multiple layered meanings implicit within the Latin infinitive **confiteri** (to confess) also meaning 'to admit', 'to own up', 'to avow', 'to acknowledge', 'to agree', 'to reveal', 'to show', 'to praise' and 'to give thanks': all contributing to the purposive force of the dative dynamic. In one of the seminal books of Latin Catholic devotion, **De Imitatione Christi** (*On the Imitation of Christ*) we pray with Thomas à Kempis (1380-1471):

> *Concéde mihi, benigníssime Iesu, grátiam tuam... Da mihi hoc semper desideráre et velle... quod tibi accéptum est cárius...*

Michael J Oakley (nd) who completed Ronald Knox's unfinished translation of **De Imitatione Christi** (which he only completed as far as Book II chapter 4 before his death in 1957) translates this in the 1963 edition (with the help of Catholic convert and novelist Evelyn Waugh [1903-1966]) as:

> 'O most kind Jesus, give me your grace... Grant that I may always will and desire what is more acceptable to you...' (III:3)

where, while he shifts the purposive responsibility more fully onto the individual praying the prayer by changing the Latin infinitives **desideráre** and **velle** into English subjunctives ('that I may will and desire') he translates the datives **mihi** and **tibi** (the dative forms of the pronoun **ego** (I) and **tu** [you sg]) as 'to me' and 'to you' signalling that they are functioning as indirect objects in this prayer. But look what happens when it is prayed in English as:

> (Most merciful Jesus vouchsafe your grace for me... give this always for me to desire and to wish... that which is more dear [and] acceptable for you...)

We tend to assume that the dative in Latin needs always to be translated by the English 'to', and we usually find that it is, but in Latin both 'to' and 'for' rather than either 'to' or 'for' are implicit in the dative form. In earlier stages of English this 'both/and' was often achieved in many forms of the language by the combining of two words into a single blended word (sometimes referred to as a 'portmanteau') and was much more common than it is in contemporary English (and is still common in modern German) and so creating a 'both/and' word rather than two 'either/or' words. Blend words of 'to-for', and 'for-to' as we pray these Latin dative dynamics forms might more usefully be uppermost in our minds, then, as readers/pray-ers of Latin. But, however we think of it in English, à Kempis' beautiful prayer in Latin demonstrates the theology of the accusative-dative dynamic: ***concede mihi*** 'grant to-for' (dat) what? ***gratiam tuam*** 'your grace' (acc). Affecting someone or something directly (accusative) and/or indirectly (dative) is not just about grammar, then. When understood anagogically it is a reflection of God's numinous gifts to us. It is everywhere in Latin prayer. For example, in the ***usus antiquior*** Mass we have already seen the direct object role of the accusative pronoun in phrases like:

> *ad **te*** (prep + acc sg m ***tu*** - unto/towards you)
> *exaudi **nos*** (imp sg ***exaudire*** + acc pl ***ego*** - heed us!)

but in phrases like:

> ***Glória tibi, Dómine*** (Glory 'to/for' you, O Lord)

prayed before the *Gospel* at Mass and

Laus tibi, Christe (Praise 'to/for' you, O Christ)

prayed after the *Gospel,* or the **Laus tibi, Dómine** prayed in Lent to replace the *Alleluia* in the *Divine Office,* the indirect object does not mean that God is being addressed indirectly, and possibly indifferently, it signals a much more complex relationship of *giving* from the pray-er to and for God, which can only be fully understood within the context of God's gift to us in the form of the Incarnation. Every time we use a dative pronoun like **tibi** in this way in prayer, despite our thinking it is probably 'just a pronoun' it is a seriously significant reflection of this gift; of the Incarnation, of the ultimate theology of the giving dative self. There is a purposive (numinous) affect involved.

Purposive Affect

Latin Catholicism celebrates the birth of Christ in three Christmas Masses: the first at midnight, the second at dawn and the third later on Christmas morning. At these, and most other **usus antiquior** Masses throughout the year (except during Advent, Lent, Vigils and Requiems) the Priest prays the words of the Angel on that first Christmas night:

Glória in excélsis Deo et in terra pax homínibus bonae voluntátis

(Glory to-for God on high and on earth peace to-for men of good will)

addressing God with the dative **Deo.** These words are repeated in the *Epistle* (*Tit* 2:11-15) of the first *Mass* of Christmas (midnight) which begins with the vocative acclamation:

Caríssime (O most beloved)

and then announces that:

Appáruit grátia Dei Salvatóris nostri ómnibus homínibus
([The] grace of our Saviour God has appeared to-for all men
Tit 2:11)

At the end of the *Epistle* the server responds:

Deo grátias
(Thanks to-for God)

In the *Gospel* for this Mass (*Lc* 2:1-14) the Angel is recorded as saying: *Nolíte timére* (Fear not!) *ecce enim* (for behold) I bring *vobis gáudium magnum* (to-for you a great joy) which will be *omni pópulo* (to-for all people) *quia vobis hódie* (because this day to-for you) is born, *Salvátor Christus Dóminus* (the Saviour Christ the Lord). *Et hoc vobis signum* (and this a sign to-for you)... *Glória Deo* (Glory to-for God) in the highest and on earth *pax homínibus bonae voluntátis* (peace to-for men of good will). The 'to-for' translation offered here, clumsy though it is, foregrounds the dependency relationship at the heart of all prayer. We have seen many times already that the pray-er can never be equal with God; we cannot do things *to* God, but we can offer things *for* him. For example, at the end of the first Mass of Christmas *Lauds* is traditionally prayed including the glorious *Psalm* 99 which opens:

Iubiláte Deo, omnis terra: servíte Dómino

and is often translated as:

'Give joy to God, all the earth. Give service to the Lord'

but how much more powerful to translate this in English as:

'Give joy *for* God, all the earth. Give service *for* the Lord.'

knowing that the Latin datives **Deo** and **Domino** implicitly hold a 'to-for' meaning, whatever vernacular they are translated in, and so:

'Give joy *to* and *for* God, all the earth. Give service *to* and *for* the Lord.'

The gift of Jesus through the Incarnation that has been given to us all at Christmas, is now to be reciprocated by us, and is the ultimate expression of a reciprocal gift for the Incarnation (**Gloria Deo** - Glory to-for God). It is the *summa* - the main principle (the summation of all that is Christian) - to give glory to/for God. And we repeat it after every *Psalm* in the *Office* during all of the liturgical year (with one or two exceptions) and at various other times throughout Latin prayer by saying:

Glória Patri, et Fílio, et Spirítui Sancto

which is traditionally translated as 'Glory [be] to the Father and to the Son and to the Holy Ghost', but when it is prayed in English as 'Glory *for* the Father, and *for* the Son and *for* the Holy Ghost' better reflects the implicit dative dynamic in Latin. When we pray:

confitémini Dómino, et invocáte nomen eius
(imp pl dep **confiteri** + dat sg m **Dominus** + conj + imp pl *invocare* + acc sg n **nomen** + gen sg m pron *is*)

it is usually translated as:

'Give praise to the Lord, and call upon his name' (*DR 1 Par* 16:8)

but pray this beautifully simple prayer as:

> 'Give praise *to* and *for* the Lord, and call upon his name'

and consider the quite different purposive affect it makes. Furthermore, at the beginning of *Matins,* we pray the invitatory *Psalm 94*:

> **Veníte, exultémus Dómino, iubilémus Deo salutári nostro**

which is traditionally translated as:

> 'Come let us praise the Lord with joy: let us joyfully sing to God our saviour' (*DR Ps* 94:1)

and certainly in this way invites us to come into God's presence, a wonderful thing to do, but pray it as:

> 'Come! let us give praise *to* and *for* the Lord with joy: let us joyfully sing *to* and *for* God our saviour.'

and reflect on what a significant difference this might make to the way we approach the praying of the *Divine Office* for the rest of that day, not as an 'either/or' but as a 'both/and': ' to and for' the Lord God our Saviour. Similarly at Monday *Matins* we pray:

> **Psállite Dómino, sancti eius: et confitémini memóriae sanctitátis eius.**
> (Sing to the Lord, O ye his saints: and give praise to the memory of his holiness. *DR Ps* 29:5)

and at Monday *Lauds* we pray:

> **Afférte Dómino, fílii Dei, afférte Dómino fílios aríetum. Afférte Dómino glóriam et honórem; afférte Dómino glóriam nómini eius. Adoráte Dóminum in átrio sancto eius.**

(Bring to the Lord, O ye children of God: bring to the Lord the offspring of rams. Bring to the Lord glory and honour: bring to the Lord glory to his name: adore ye the Lord in his holy court. *DR Ps* 28:1-2)

and then in Tuesday *Matins*:

Revéla Dómino viam tuam
(Commit to the Lord your way *DR Ps* 36:5)

and also:

Vovéte et reddíte Dómino Deo vestro
(Vow ye, and pay to the Lord your God *DR Ps* 75:12)

but combine these as a private prayer as follows:

Afférte Dómino, fílii Dei, afférte Dómino fílios aríetum. Afférte Dómino glóriam et honórem; afférte Dómino glóriam nómini eius. Psállite Dómino, sancti eius; et confitémini memóriae sanctitátis eius. Revéla Dómino viam tuam. Vovéte et réddite Dómino Deo vestro.

we might then pray this in English as:

Bring to and for the Lord, O sons of God, bring to and for the Lord the offspring of rams. Bring to and for the Lord glory and honour; bring to and for the Lord the glory of his name. Sing a *Psalm* to and for the Lord, O his saints: and give praise to and for the memory of his holiness. Commit to and for the Lord your way. Vow and restore to and for the Lord your God.

and consider the difference the translation can make. This, of course, is not an officially approved prayer, and in English may appear clumsy. But in Latin the clumsiness of repeating 'to and for' in the *Psalms* like this is not there because the dative dynamic holds this 'to and for' implicitly layered within its grammar. If we pray that dynamic of layered grammar in these *Psalms*, we also pray the numinous dynamic it holds within it. Doctor of the Church St Hilary of Poitiers (310-367) in his 365 AD ***Tractatus super Psalmos*** (Commentary on the *Psalms*) insightfully recognised that all of the Psalms are:

> 'A texture woven of allegorical and typical meanings, whereby are spread before our view all the mysteries of the only-begotten Son of God, who was to be born in the body, to suffer, to die, to rise again, to reign forever with those who share His glory because they believed on Him, to be the Judge of the rest of mankind.'

This powerful exposition of the role of the *Psalms* through a Latin Catholic lens is probably even better expressed when St Hilary writes that:

> 'There is no doubt that the language of the *Psalms* must be interpreted by the light of the teaching of the *Gospel*.'

and goes on to make the point that the whole purpose of the Psalmist's words :

> 'is our instruction concerning the glory and power of the coming, the Incarnation, the Passion, the kingdom of our Lord Jesus Christ, and of our resurrection.'

The Jesuit Doctor of the Church St Robert Cardinal Bellarmine (1542-1621) in his 1611 ***In omnes Psalmos dilucida expositio*** (A clear exposition on all the *Psalms*) similarly reads the *Psalms* through the same lens, with almost every one of the 150 *Psalms* he comments upon referring to Christ, in both the title of his individual commentary, and in his often extensive commentary itself. Likewise, St Ambrose of Milan (339-397) in his exposition of *Psalm* 118 talks of the *Psalms*, like all Scripture, as 'breathing God's grace upon us' saying that the **Liber Psalmorum**:

> 'is medicine for our spiritual health. Whoever reads it will find in it a medicine to cure the wounds caused by his own particular passions. Whoever studies it deeply will find it a kind of gymnasium open for all souls to use, where the different *Psalms* are like different exercises set out before him. In that gymnasium, in that stadium of virtue, he can choose the exercises that will train him best to win the victor's crown.'

Citing St Ambrose, the *Catechism* says that the prayer of the *Psalms*:

> 'recalls the saving events of the past, yet extends into the future, even to the end of history; it commemorates the promises God has already kept, and awaits the Messiah who will fulfill them definitively. Prayed by Christ and fulfilled in him, the *Psalms* remain essential to the prayer of the Church.' *Cat* §2586

and continues:

> 'The prayer of the *Psalms* is always sustained by praise; that is why the title of this collection as handed down to us [ie *The Psalter*] is so fitting: "The Praises." Collected for the assembly's worship, the *Psalter* both sounds the call to prayer and sings the response to that call: *Hallelu Yah!* ("Alleluia") "Praise the Lord!"' *Cat* §2589

The purposive affect, then, of praying the *Psalms* lies in the continuing repetition of praise given to and for God in and through these

Psalms and in all Latin prayer, and we might usefully ask, in the words of linguist and critic George Steiner (1929-2020) from a very different context:

> 'Are there, in the common locution, felt realities, "too deep for words"?'

and in what ways might this 'too deep for words' be reflected in different grammatical, and hence anagogical, ways. When, for example, the Priest prays:

> **Dóminus vobíscum**
> ([The] Lord [be] with you)

it is usually translated not with a dative *vobis* ('to-for') but following the preposition *cum*, with the ablative *vobis* (with you). The response is:

> **Et cum spíritu tuo**
> (And with your spirit)

where, again following the preposition *cum*, the ablative *spiritu tuo* is given. The function has changed from a dative 'to-for' dynamic to a 'by/with/from' instrumental one, and it is to this, and its consequences for our beginning to engage with Steiner's question: 'is it too deep for words?' that we now turn in *Chapter VIII: Instrumental Prayer*.

DAVID BIRCH

VIII

INSTRUMENTAL PRAYER

Glory to God in the Lowest (GK Chesterton)

Instrumentality

In his poem, 'Gloria in Profundis', GK Chesterton shapes an understanding of the mysteries of the Incarnation in a way that might shock us into re-assessing our often comfortable reflections on this mystery when we read a phrase like 'Glory to God in the lowest'. He writes:

> There has fallen on earth for a token
> A god too great for the sky.
> He has burst out of all things and broken
> The bounds of eternity:
> Into time and the terminal land...
> Glory to God in the Lowest...
> In the cavern of Bethlehem.

This is not what one might expect. In two simple phrases Chesterton captures the enormity of God ('Glory to God') becoming man ('in the lowest'). But more than that. He paints a picture in this poem of a very tangible and physical presence of God coming 'into time and the terminal land' and taking on the glory that in all other circumstances is expressed instrumentally as *in excelsis* (in the highest) but here has taken on human/corporeal nature and is expressed instrumentally in the phrase *in profundis* (in the lowest) to reflect that human state. That human state of God, the Incarnation, is central to Catholicism where it is instrumental in changing lives; a fact that is signalled every time the very first prayer Catholics learn, the Sign of the Cross (***Signum Crucis***) is both prayed and physically enacted on the body:

> ☩ *In nómine Patris, et Fílii, et Spíritus Sancti. Amen*
> (☩ In the name of [the] Father, and of [the] Son and of [the] Holy Spirit. *trad*)

After the symbol of the fish, where each letter of the Greek word ἰχθύς - *ichthys* - fish - stands for Ἰησοῦς Χριστός Θεοῦ Υἱός Σωτήρ (*Iesous Christos Theou Uios Soter* - Jesus Christ of God Son Saviour) and the *chi-rho* ☧ which uses the first two capital letters of ΧΡΙΣΤΟΣ (*Christos*) making the sign of the cross is probably one of the most ancient symbols and acts of devotion within the Catholic Church. Marking oneself with the sign of the cross was well established by the 2nd C and for many years was principally made on the forehead. It was also carved on stones, put into manuscripts and marked places of worship. By the 4th C it had become common as a gesture over the whole body (from head to feet) and by the 9th C, during the pontificate of Pope Leo IV (790-855) the current western practice of signing the cross, using the words ***In nomine Patris, et Filii, et Spiritus Sancti. Amen***, from forehead to breast and from the left side (***sinister***) of the shoulder to the right side (***dexter***) became a tradition for Latin Catholics as the first act upon waking and the last act upon going to sleep. Only the right hand is used, representative of Christ sitting at the right hand of the Father. The forehead symbolises God the Father, and the movement from forehead to the lower part of the body represents Christ's Incarnation because, as Pope Innocent III wrote in ***De Sacro Altaris Mysterio*** (*On the Sacred Mystery of the Altar*) before he was elected Pope in 1198, 'Christ descended from heaven to earth and passed over from the Jews to the

Gentiles'. Others, he continued, 'make the sign of the cross from the left to the right, because from misery (left) we must cross over to glory (right) just as Christ crossed over from death to life, and from Hades to Paradise.' Each movement signifies the instrumentality of Christ's life, passion, death and resurrection. Christ is the instrument of everything. During the ***usus antiquior*** Mass the congregant will make the ***signum crucis*** numerous times, sometimes in threes, as on the forehead, lips and heart at the *Gospel* and *Last Gospel*, but the Priest will make the ***signum crucis*** over 40 times, each of which is made whenever the sacrifice Christ made is mentioned or referred to in any way. Every time the Priest repeats the ***signum crucis*** he is reinforcing the agency and instrumentality of Christ through the Trinity. Whenever we ourselves pray this prayer we are, to rephrase what Chesterton said, signifying both the *in excelsis* (the numinousness of God) and the *in profundis* (the humanness of ourselves through Christ's Incarnation). This 'numinousness' was often expressed by the medieval mystics in a single phrase:

> ***Deus incognito***
> (God unknown)

signifying with the ablative masculine adjective ***incognito*** that the masculine nominative ***Deus*** can never be fully known and as such, signalling that the unknowability of God's instrumentality in all things was to be expressed, not by what God is, but by what God is not - the apophatic *via negativa* (negative way). The seemingly discordant use of the ablative adjective (***incognito***) with the nominative noun (***Deus***) signals that a quite different theology is involved than would be if the phrase were expressed as the nominative ***Deus incognitus***. The striking grammar tells us to pay attention to the theology. An alternative view to this is to see God as Isaiah saw him saying:

> ***Vere tu es Deus absconditus, Deus Israël, salvator.***
> (Truly you are a hidden {nom} God {nom} [the] God {nom} of Israel, [the] saviour {nom}. *Is* 45:15)

as Augustinian Martin Luther (1483-1546) was later to do. The theological difference between the Latin adjectives *incognito* (abl) and *absconditus* (nom) is very marked. The assumption made by Luther, and later, others, was that understanding God as the **Deus incognito** was part of a system (Catholicism) that effectively involved people actively searching *for* (abl) an unknowable God, and so the emphasis shifts away from God himself to the people who are searching, and so was not fully upon God, as they thought it should be. Whereas understanding God as the **Deus absconditus** (nom) involved, for Luther and others, a greater focus on God and not on the people searching for him. In that sense Luther considered God as *absconditus* (nom) to be more actively engaged with us than he might be more passively perceived to be as *incognito* (abl).

To the modern eye this might seem to be just playing about with words, but it is an important example of the way in which, as the medieval mystics and early theologians recognised before Luther, whatever language we use to try to understand God is never going to be sufficient, and how that insufficiency might then affect the theology we develop. Grammar is used in striking ways to foreground that theology, as it is here in these two quite distinct phrases: **Deus incognito** (nom/abl) and **Deus absconditus** (nom/nom). The Catholic medieval mystic searched for the unknowable (ablative) God in a journey into an 'unknowing' (apophatic prayer) whereas Luther, casting this apophatic theology aside, assumed God to be already found (nom) and so developed a cataphatic theology and way of prayer. This resulted in forms of service across all forms of Protestantism which concentrated much more on the word of Scripture, on congregational hymn singing, and on the idea of 'fellowship' at the heart of worship rather than 'sacrifice'. Accepting this 'already found God' then came to be considered sufficient for salvation in Protestantism, and what has become known as 'born-again Christianity', whereas the Latin Catholic way maintains the need for a continuing search for the unknowable to be for ever undertaken.

Prayer, like these theological arguments, involves grammatical instrumentality in language where, we give glory 'to/for' God (***Gloria Deo*** [dat]) 'with/by/from' the highest (*in excelsis*) and 'with/by/from' the lowest *in profundis* (abl) and we make the sign of the cross 'by/with/from' the name of the Father (*in nomine Patris*...). We are so used to saying the Latin *in* in the English translations of these phrases as just 'in' that it appears to be an innocent, and relatively meaningless, word. But in Latin, as we have seen in detail already, it may signify movement with *in* + acc phrases (***requiescat in pacem*** - may he/she rest at/into-wards peace) or instrumentality in various ways with *in* + abl phrases (***requiescat in pace*** - may he/she rest at/within peace).

The Ablative Dynamic

Latin reflects the relations of instrumental meaning, time, space, cause, agency and manner, by the way in which a noun, pronoun, or adjective shows 'by/from/with' whom (instrument) what (agent) or 'how/where' (manner/place) something happens or is. In English these relations are now generally shown with prepositions mostly 'by', 'with', 'from', and 'in'. Where these prepositions are used in Latin (and much more often in Medieval/Liturgical Latin than in Classical) as we saw with ***in excelsis, in profundis, in pace*** and ***in nomine***, and in many other circumstances too, the ablative inflectional form usually follows ('ablative' originally signalled movement 'away/from', hence its name ***ab-latus*** - taken from/away). Understanding this instrumentality, especially with regard to prayer, is an extension of a theology of instrumentality which, for example, would argue that the *Bible* has two authors: God and man. The source of the *Bible* is God but the story is told by the human writer. The writer becomes the instrument of God (as the Priest is the instrument of Christ at Mass, or at Confession) just as the pray-er of a prayer is the instrument of the Holy Spirit who inspires the pray-er to pray in the first place.

The fact that we pray in different ways, and with different effect and affect, simply underlines the human-ness of our instrumentality in the action of prayer, and God's omniscience in all his. Our minds wander off into all sorts of tangents when we pray; we show our human-ness in a hundred different ways. But whatever may reveal our human-ness in prayer, we are always instruments of the Divine; our prayer, no matter how poorly delivered, does not lose any of its authority. That authority comes from the instrument of God's will through the Holy Spirit, not from us. St Luke tells us before he relates Jesus' parable of the reluctant and impatient Judge finally giving way to the persistence of the Widow:

> *oportet semper orare et non deficere*
> (it is necessary to always pray and not to give up *Lc* 18:1)

and St Paul tells the Colossians:

> *Orationi instate, vigilantes in ea in gratiarum actione.*
> (Persevere! [to/for] prayer, watching within it in an action of thanks. *Col* 4:2)

There are two ablative phrases here: *in ea* and *in actione*, each signalling that even though prayer may become, what many of the Saints referred to as 'dry', and seemingly barren and directionless; a 'spiritual desert', it is always alive and worthwhile; always functioning 'in' and 'with' some form of instrumentality, because, that 'spiritual desert' holds within it, always and never failing, the Holy Spirit, even when seeming to have abandoned us. St Augustine in his **Ennaratio in Psalmum LXVII** (Exposition on *Psalm* 67) has a wonderful image of Job, and all like him, drawn from both *Old Testament* and Classical Latin imagery, as the ant who, in arid times in winter, when food is scarce, must fall back on what it has stored up over summer, if it has been diligent. As *formicae Dei* (ants of God) we too should store things up ready for the arid times, because aridity in prayer (***ariditas***) may strike us, at any time, with a feeling of abandonment, where prayer brings no apparent sensory feelings or consolations, especially when we might hope for some spiritual gratification of our actions and intentions. St Philip Neri (1515-1595) founder of the Oratorians talked about the narrative of prayer as one beginning with sweetness and often journeying through bitterness. But the continuing lesson of those, like him and so many others, who have given over their entire lives to prayer, is that God's presence is to be found in persistent, and repeated, prayer, irrespective of whether we 'feel' that presence; whether the experience is bitter or sweet; a barren desert or a verdant oasis. Saints like St John of the Cross (1542-1591) and much later St Thérèse of the Child Jesus and the Holy Face (1873-1897) for example, interpreted spiritual aridity as a sign from God for us to continue to pray, but perhaps more simply (and, therefore, perhaps paradoxically, more profoundly, as a means to greater contemplation). St Theresa of Avila (1515-1582) in her 1577 *El Castillo Interior* (*The Interior Castle*) talks of us as sometimes 'walking through a mist', where:

> 'Those who do not receive these consolations may feel a despondency that is uncalled for, since perfection does not consist in consolation but in greater love; our reward will be in proportion to this, and to the justice and sincerity of our actions.' (Stanbrook: II:15)

But all prayer is about seeking the presence of God already present. Spiritual aridity does not mean God is not present. There are always joys, because God is always present. As St Catherine of Sienna (1347-1380) tells us in her *Libro della divina dottrina* (*Dialogue of Divine Providence*): 'Let us endure, let us endure', because:

'no suffering will be so richly rewarded as weariness of heart and spiritual pain. These are the greatest sufferings there are, and so they are deserving of greater fruit.' (§4)

St Teresa of Avila understood this, saying:

'When these joys are from God they come laden with love and strength, which aid the soul on its way and increase its good works and virtues. Do not imagine that it is unimportant whether you try to obtain these graces or no; if you are not to blame, the Lord is just: what He refuses in one way, His Majesty will give you in another, as He knows how; His secret ways are very mysterious, and doubtless He will do what is best for you.' (Stanbrook: II:17)

But, as we learn very early on as Catholics, persistence and perseverance in prayer does not mean that eventually God will hear us by answering our prayer in the way we want, but **Deo Volente** (God willing) we will hear God, whatever his answer may be. As St Teresa of Calcutta (1910-1997) wrote:

'God speaks in the silence of the heart, and we listen.
And then we speak to God from the fullness of our heart.
First we listen, and God speaks. And then we speak, and God listens.
And that connection is prayer, is oneness with God.'

Theologically we may think that the instrumentality of prayer understood in this way only applies to those 'greats' of Christian history: the *Bible* Prophets; the Psalmists; the *Gospel* writers; the Apostles and the distinguished theologians, leaders and mystics of the Church, because they have an authority given to them as instruments of God's word. But all prayer, even the most flawed in delivery, has that authority when framed within the agency and instrumentality of the Holy Spirit working through the Church. This is an authority which, at the same time, acknowledges the instrumental causality of Christ's humanity, and which is an absolutely central feature of the Catholic theology of the Incarnation; the hypostatic union of Christ as God and Man. As such, Christ's *theandric* (θεανδρικός - God-human) union when reflected upon in prayer, enables us to consider the multiple ways in which Christ used, and uses, his human-ness as an instrument of his Divinity as a means of salvation and redemption ***pro nobis*** - for us.

It is no accident that the phrase ***pro nobis*** (for us) is so absolutely central in Latin prayer and, therefore, for understanding the instrumentality of that prayer in various ways. As a phrase it is grammatically instrumental; something is being done *for* someone. In so many of the *Litanies*, for example, we implore the Blessed Virgin Mary: 'pray! for us' (***ora pro nobis*** - imp sg *orare* + prep + abl pl of ***nos***) and we similarly implore all the Saints: 'pray! for us' (***orate pro nobis*** - imp pl *orare* + prep + abl pl of ***nos***). We pray in all the *litanies* with:

℣. *Kýrie eléison.* (Lord, have mercy)
℟. *Christe eléison.* (Christ, have mercy)
℣. *Kýrie eléison.* (Lord, have mercy)

which is generally thought how the first form of the Mass began, prayed in Greek for the first two or three hundred years, with a litany, which, more often than not in Latin prayer, begins, even today, with a repetition of the Greek dynamic of instrumental address Κύριε ἐλέησον/ Χριστέ ἐλέησον (*Kýrie eléison/Christe eléison*). We pray at the 3rd Mass on Christmas Day when St Paul tells the Hebrews:

proptérea unxit te Deus, Deus tuus, óleo exultatiónis prae participibus tuis.
(therefore God, your God, anointed you, [with the] oil of gladness before your companions. *Heb* 1:9)

where the 'oil (ἔλαιον- *élaion*)/*oleum*) of gladness' is specifically the olive oil that nourishes, soothes and anoints. The active indicative *unxit* followed by the ablative *oleo* plus prep + abl dynamic *prae participibus* directly signals that the nominative ***Deus*** is the grammatical agent of the anointing of those who have loved *iustitiam* (justice) and hated *iniquitatem* (evil). This is mirrored in the anointing with the sacramental *sacrum chrisma* (sacred chrism) in the Sacrament of Confirmation, when inscribed in the form of a cross on the forehead with the ancient formula explained in Pope St Paul VI's 1971 ***Constitutio Apostolica de Sacramento Confirmationis Divinae Consortium Naturae*** (Apostolic Constitution concerning [the] Sacrament of Confirmation Sharing [in the] Divine Nature) promulgating the ***usus recentior*** rite of Confirmation, where the Bishop prays:

> *Accipe signáculum doni Spíritus Sancti*
> (Receive! [the] sign of [the] gift of [the] Holy Spirit)

The official English translation of this formula which is mandated to be used in the ***usus recentior*** rite (a variation of the words based on *2 Cor* 1:21-22) is: 'Be sealed with the Gift of the Holy Spirit.' (*Cat* §1300). The Bishop, ***manus impositione*** ([the] hand [by] laying on) is the instrument of Christ himself who imparts the Sacrament. The imposition of the ***signum crucis*** with this chrism on the forehead by the Bishop is an outward sign of the interior action of Christ through the Holy Spirit as the ***signum spirituale indelebile*** ([a] mark [with] indelible spirituality) on the soul:

> ***qui significat Iesum Christum sigillo sui Spiritus christianum signavisse, eum virtute superinduens ex alto ut ipse eius sit testis.***

(which is the sign that Jesus Christ has marked a Christian with the seal of his Spirit by clothing him with power from on high so that he may be his witness. *Cat* §1304)

Agency in prayer, then, as here, starts to become very important in its various layers of meaning: grammatical and numinous. When we address the Blessed Virgin Mary in the short prayer **Ave Maria** we do so in a text that became firmly established in the 16thC and was included in Pope St Pius V's *Breviary* of 1568 which instructed it to be recited at the beginning of each of the canonical *offices* together with the **Pater Noster** (Our Father) and which together is known as the 'Dual Prayer'. The Apostles' Creed is also recited at *Matins* and *Prime* and which together with the dual prayer is known as the 'Triple Prayer'.

Ave, María, grátia plena, Dóminus tecum.
Benedícta tu in muliéribus,
et benedíctus fructus ventris tui, Iesus.
Sancta María, Mater Dei, ora pro nobis peccatóribus,
nunc et in hora mortis nostrae. Amen.

The first part, ***Ave, Maria, gratia plena, Dominus tecum; benedicta tu in mulieribus***, is taken from the Archangel Gabriel's words in greeting the Blessed Virgin, as recorded by St Luke (*Lc* 1:28). Similarly, the second part, ***et benedictus fructus ventris tui*** is taken from the greeting of St Elizabeth also recorded by St Luke (*Lc* 1:42). However, the third and final part, ***Sancta Maria, Mater Dei, ora pro nobis peccatoribus, nunc et in hora mortis nostrae. Amen.*** is generally thought to have been added prior to, but confirmed at, the Council of Trent in 1564, although its first recorded use appears in the ancient liturgy of Jerusalem attributed to St James, brother of Jesus, but more likely composed by St Cyril of Jerusalem (313-386). This part of the ***Ave Maria*** was introduced as the *Offertory Antiphon* for the 4th Sunday of Advent in the *Antiphonal* of Pope St Gregory I, but was probably well known long before then in the Roman liturgy.

The traditional English translation of this prayer would suggest that the Latin **gratia plena** is a genitive ('full *of* grace') but it is really an ablative of sympathetic possession and better translated, perhaps, as 'filled *with* grace' to show this. Unlike the genitive of possession, the ablative draws our attention to Our Lady who is instrumentally filled with grace by the agency of God. She does not just 'possess' or 'own' this grace, but as the Latin ablative shows, is an instrument for it. Furthermore, she is greeted with the Latin equivalent of a very restricted greeting **Ave**, given only to royal personages and this, together with so much else in this prayer, especially the ablatives, **nobis, peccatoribus** and **hora**, signal just how distinct she is and how separated we are from God's presence in comparison to her. These ablatives of separation thus demonstrate how much we need her help. St Elizabeth, who is pregnant with St John the Baptist recognises this and announces Mary as **Benedicta in mulieribus** expressed in Latin in the prayer with the prep + abl dynamic. We address Our Lady as the **Sancta Mater Dei** (Holy Mother of God). But there is no human language that could even begin to describe what being the Mother of God is, and her consequent role in salvation (soteriology). It is no small wonder that we pray in the *Introit* of the Mass of the Assumption of Our Lady (August 15) with the words St Jerome gives to St John as a series of ablatives in the *Vulgate*:

> *múlier amícta sole, et luna sub pédibus eius, et in cápite eius coróna stellárum duódecim*
> ([a] woman clothed [with the] sun, and [the] moon under her feet, and on her head [a] crown of twelve stars *Apc* 12:1)

We pray in the first recorded prayer in honour of the Blessed Virgin Mary as Θεοτόκος - *Theotokos* - 'bearer of God' (**Dei Genitrix/Deipara**) dating back to well before the 3rd C:

Sub tuum praesídium confúgimus, Sancta Dei Génitrix.
Nostras deprecatiónes ne despícias in necessitátibus [nostris],
sed a perículis cunctis líbera nos semper,
Virgo gloriósa et benedícta.
(Under your protection we take refuge, O Holy Mother of God.
Our prayers despise not in [our] necessities,
but from all dangers deliver us always, [O] glorious and blessed Virgin.)

The ablatives following the prepositions *in* and *a* add considerable focus to our understanding of the agency involved in both the ***necessitatibus* [*nostris*]** and the ***periculis cunctis***. But instrumentality is not just something that involves people doing things to other people, it also applies to things or qualities (as here distresses and dangers) when these 'things' perform actions like people do. They are, so to speak, expressed in Latin prayer as focussed (and forceful) ablatives of agency/personification following prepositions. Both *necessitas* and *periculum* are personified here (*necessitatibus* and *periculis*). This is a common occurrence in Latin prayer, and occurs where ablatives also follow other prepositions. It is important to stress that it is not the preposition that is doing the main work involved in creating the focus of instrumental meaning here, but the ablative dynamic. In the ***usus antiquior*** minor *Hours* a short prayer (***Responsorium*** - response) is prayed, as in the example below, with prepositions (*de* and *a*) followed by the ablative. These ***responsoria*** vary according to the feast and season. The one for Passion Sunday (***Dominica Passionis***) from *Psalm* 21:21 is prayed as follows:

℞. *Erue a frámea Deus ánimam meam*
(Deliver my soul [O] God from [the] sword (prep + abl sg f *framea*)
℞. *Erue a frámea Deus ánimam meam*
℣. *Et de manu canis únicam meam.*

| 277 |

> (And from [the] hand/paw (prep + abl sg f *manus*) of [the] dog my only one [soul])
>
> ℞. *Deus ánimam meam.*
>
> ([O] God my soul)
>
> ℞. *Erue a frámea Deus ánimam meam.*
>
> ℣. *De ore leónis líbera me Dómine.*
>
> (From [the] mouth of [the] lion free me O Lord)
>
> ℞. *Et a córnibus unicórnium humilitátem meam.*
>
> (And from [the] horns (prep + abl pl n *cornu*) of [the] unicorns my humility/lowness)

Both separately, and/or with a preceding preposition, the ablative in Latin prayer carries with it, in these patterns, an instrumental force in the Latin not always carried through in the various English translations. For example one *Breviary* translates it as:

> ℣. Deliver my soul, O God, from the sword.
>
> ℞. Deliver my soul, O God, from the sword.
>
> ℣. My darling from the power of the dog.
>
> ℞. O God, from the sword.
>
> ℞. Deliver my soul, O God, from the sword.

The *Knox* translation in the original *Psalm* has:

> 'Only life is left me; save that from the sword, from the power of these dogs.'

The *JB* (numbering the *Psalm* as 22:20) has:

> 'Rescue my soul from the sword, my dear life from the paw of the dog, save me from the lion's mouth, my poor soul from the wild bulls' horns!'

The *DR* tends to be the closest to the Latin of the *Vulgate* with:

'Deliver, O God, my soul from the sword: my only one from the hand of the dog.'

But none of them truly capture the narrative journey of the Latin prepositions *de* and *a* instrumentally cascading down through the response. The ablative dynamic is forceful, then, not simply because of its textual grammar, but also because of its stylistic context, like this narrative flow. Consider, for example, this passage from St Paul which at first may seem a little daunting: the ablatives are marked in bold type:

Repletos **omni iniquitate, malitia, fornicatione, avaritia, nequitia,** *plenos* **invidia,**
homicidio, contentione, dolo, malignitate: *susurrones, detractores, Deo odibiles,*
contumeliosos, superbos, elatos, inventores malorum, parentibus non obedientes, insipientes,
incompositos, **sine affectione, absque foedere, sine misericordia.**

(Replenished **with all iniquity, malice, fornication, avarice, wickedness,** filled **with**
envy, murder, contention, deceit, malignity: whisperers, detractors, hateful to God,
contumelious, proud, haughty, inventors of evils, not obedient to parents, foolish,
disorganised, **without affection,** and **without fidelity, without mercy.** *Rom* 1:29-31)

The two main ways of using the ablative are demonstrated in this text:

(1) inflectional change only: ***omni, iniquitate, malitia, fornicatione, avaritia, nequitia, invidia, homicidio, contentione, dolo, malignitate***

(2) prep + abl: ***sine affectione, absque foedere, sine misericordia***

Both ways involve a dynamic of meaning which, more often than not, goes well beyond the lexical meaning of the word. For example, in the Mass when the Priest prays:

> *una cum fámulo tuo Papa nostro N et Antístite nostro N et ómnibus orthodóxis atque cathólicae et apostólicae fidei cultóribus*
> (one with your servant our Pope N and our Bishop N and with all true worshippers of [the] catholic and apostolic faith)

whether the instrumentality is expressed like ***cum famulo tuo*** or as ***omnibus orthodoxis cultoribus***, the ablative dynamic signals that meanings are involved which have nothing to do with the lexical meaning of the word. Like the meaning of 'manner', 'movement', 'reason', 'place', 'agency', 'cause', 'comparison' and 'time', amongst others, all of which bring with them a force of layered meaning beyond the words themselves. This force of meaning cannot be set aside when we pray, but, considered anagogically, adds so much more force to both our understanding of, and our praying Latin prayer.

Too Deep For Words

One of the most frequently prayed prayers in Latin Catholicism, which we saw earlier is prayed in full as:

> *Glória Patri et Fílio et Spirítui Sancto.*
> *Sicut erat in princípio et nunc et semper et in sǽcula saeculórum.*
> *Amen.*
> (Glory [to/for the] Father and [to/for the] Son, and [to/for the] Holy Spirit. As [it] was in [the] beginning and now and always and intowards [the] ages of ages. Amen.)

There is a timelessness in the words of the **Gloria Patri** giving focus to, through the dative 'to/for', the glory through all time, past, present and future, to be given to the Trinity and reinforced with the dynamic between *nunc* (now) and *semper* (always). That focus on timelessness is further reinforced with the use of the ablative following the preposition *in* signalling the manner of the glory vested *within* the Trinity; its timelessness. *et nunc*, for example is traditionally translated as 'is now', but I use *et* (and) here because it reinforces the force of the three repetitions of *et* in the second half of the prayer, which the traditional translation loses as:

> 'Glory be to the Father, and to the Son and to the Holy Ghost/Spirit; as it was in the beginning, is now, and ever shall be world without end. Amen. *trad*'

A closer translation of the Latin would be:

> 'Glory to/for [the] Father, and to/for [the] Son, and to/for [the] Holy Ghost; as was being from the beginning, and now, and always and intowards [the] ages of ages. Amen.'

We generally translate the Latin verb *erat* simply as 'was' in English, as if it is just signalling past time (an action that once happened but is now over). But this is not what the Latin *erat* is actually saying. In grammar this form of the infinitive *esse* (to be) is known as the 'imperfect tense' and signals that while something did happen in the past, it is/

was an ongoing action. In other words there is also a timelessness about the verb used in this prayer; 'as it was in the beginning' is not something that took place once and was then over (grammatically 'perfect' time) it continues (imperfect time) and so might better be translated in English as:

> 'was being from the beginning, and now, and always and intowards the ages of ages. Amen.'

In English we can express this sense of an ongoing action in the past compared to an action that was completed by saying something like 'I prayed' to show completion and 'I was praying' to show the action is not completed. This sense of completion, duration, or repetition in time, is known in grammar as 'aspect'. We can show the Latin aspect with most verbs in English but there is no similar equivalent when we translate the Latin verb *esse* (to be) as in the 1st person imperfect *eram*. The nearest we could say would be something like 'I was being'. But the clumsiness of this translation, apart from raising some interesting linguistic issues about why this is so clumsy in English, perhaps more strikingly, raises issues about the very concept of 'time' itself. To what extent, we might ask, does 'time' exist outside of the grammar in which it is couched in language? Do we understand 'time' simply because of the grammar we use? Certainly, when it comes to language in prayer we bring the impact of time with us every time we pray, because we never leave behind us all that we have ever read, said, thought or prayed about (in and through) the past, present and future. We appear to read time through the grammar of the language we are using, and different languages have different grammars of time. The Hebrew writers of the *Old Testament* never thought of actions as 'past', 'present' or 'future', but simply as 'completed' (perfect) or 'uncompleted' (imperfect). Time in this sense was not expressed verbally by these Hebrew writers, but thinking about a Latin imperfect verb like *erat* in English, we lose the focus of the 'imperfect 'ongoingness' of time' when we translate the verb simply as 'was'. In Latin this different view of time remains because of the ongoing (imperfect) aspect of the verb, which we apply to what we understand the tense of the word *erat* to be. It becomes especially important when accompanied by the prep + abl dynamic structure of *in principio* (in [the] beginning). Similarly in the **doxologia maior** (major doxology):

> *Glória in excélsis Deo et in terra pax homínibus bonae voluntátis.*
> *Laudámus te, benedícimus te, adorámus te, glorificámus te,*
> *grátias ágimus tibi propter magnam glóriam tuam, Dómine Deus, Rex caeléstis,*
> *Deus Pater omnípotens. Dómine Fili unigénite, Iesu Christe,*
> *Dómine Deus, Agnus Dei, Fílius Patris, qui tollis peccáta mundi, miserére nobis;*
> *qui tollis peccáta mundi, súscipe deprecatiónem nostram.*
> *Qui sedes ad déxteram Patris, miserére nobis.*
> *Quóniam tu solus Sanctus, tu solus Dóminus, tu solus Altíssimus, Iesu Christe, cum Sancto Spíritu ✠ in glória Dei Patris. Amen.*

(Glory to-for God in [the] highest, and on earth peace to-for people
 of good will.
We praise you, we bless you, we adore you, we glorify you,
we give thanks to you for your great glory, O Lord God, [O]
heavenly King, God almighty Father. O Lord only begotten Son, O
 Jesus Christ,
O Lord God, Lamb of God, Son of [the] Father, who destroys [the]
sins of the world, be merciful to us; who takes away [the] sins of [the]
world, receive our prayer;
Who sits at [the] right hand of [the] Father, be merciful to us.
For you alone are Holy, you alone are Lord, you alone are [the] Most
High, O Jesus Christ, with [the] Holy Spirit, ✠ within [the] glory of
God [the] Father. Amen.)

Every verb here in the ***doxologia maior*** is in the present tense. The active present indicatives *laudamus; benedicimus; adoramus; glorificamus; gratias agimus; tollis* x 2, *sedes* and the two passive imperatives *miserere* separated by the active imperative *suscipe*, sing out the 'here and nowness' of the prayer, just as, perhaps paradoxically, the 3rd person imperfect indicative *erat* of the ***doxologia minor*** picks up, in its progressive aspect, on the implicit present tense *est* and, in effect, glorifies it, just as it glorifies the Holy Trinity. The lexical meaning is powerful in words like 'we praise'; 'we glorify' and 'we adore', but the meaning within the grammar, beyond these particular words, foregrounds a theology of time, which has no ontological limits, unlike those constraints of time we feel will limit us when we consider ourselves, as this secular world currently does more and more, sufficient unto ourselves. In this prayer, we go beyond these constraints as we recognise that God alone in a most marked *inclusio* in Latin prayer, enclosing all of the numinous theology of God alone in our own here-and-now time *in terra* (abl) with the opening ***Gloria in excelsis*** (abl) and the closing ***in gloria Dei Patris*** (abl). These are not just words being prayed. It is a dynamic use of grammar and rhetoric; it is time and tense; it is the theology of God's instrumentality ***qui tollis peccata mundi***; and ***qui sedes ad dexteram Patris*** and the Christology of ***Altissimus Iesus Christus*** who is ***solus Sanctus, solus Dominus***, and ***solus altissimus cum Sancto Spiritu in gloria Dei Patris***. No wonder we say ***Amen*** to this prayerful, transcendent and numinous celebration of the Holy Trinity, in which we are made to realise that our own sense of time has meaning only because of the timelessness of God. No wonder the Church calls this a ***doxologia maior***. St Paul says (translated in the *Vulgate* with a prep + abl dynamic):

> *in omni oratione et obsecratione*
> (in everything by prayer and supplication *Phil* 4:6)

But how many ways might we translate *in* here? What different affect might be made in prayer by using English 'by', 'with', 'within', 'from', 'through', 'for' and so on, instead of just 'in' to better reflect the ablative dynamic involved in the original Latin? When we pray the hymn **Ave Maris Stella** (Hail Star of the Sea) which we do often at *Vespers* on Marian feasts, and which is thought to have been composed by St Bernard of Clairvaux, but probably dates back to at least the 8thC, and using an attributive name for Mary, **Stella Maris**, first used by St Jerome, we have many options of meaning open to us reflected in the various ways the hymn has been translated over the years. My literal translation given immediately after the Latin text below, demonstrates how 'economical' the Latin text may be, with relatively few words, and with often even less explanatory linking grammar and syntax to provide the sort of cohesive narrative flow we might be more accustomed to in 'story-telling'. With often enticing brevity, much may appear to be left unsaid, and often the translations that were made over the years, tended to provide what might be considered in English as 'missing', but which stylistically, in this often highly compressed form, is actually part of the attraction and force of the Latin hymn. In the days when medieval hymns generally had to be memorised, brevity of line was often invaluable. An inflected language like Latin lends itself to unelaborated precision at times, so that often to pray less, is to pray more. As the French Catholic writer George Bernanos (1888-1948) wrote in his insightful (and often disturbing) *Journal d'un Curé de Campagne* (The Diary of a Country Priest):

'Le désir de prier est une prière en soi-même.' (The desire to pray is a prayer in itself.)

And so:

Ave maris stella,
Dei Mater alma,
atque semper Virgo,
felix caeli porta.

Hail! star of [the] sea, nourishing Mother of God, and also ever [a] Virgin, happy gate of heaven. (*literal*)

Hail, O Star of the ocean, God's own Mother blest, ever sinless Virgin, gate of heav'nly rest. (*trad*)

Ave, Star of Ocean, Child Divine who barest, Mother, Ever-Virgin, Heaven's Portal fairest. (*John Laurie Athelstan Riley* [1858-1945] 1891)

Hail, Star of the sea! Blessed Mother of God, yet ever a virgin! O happy gate of heaven! (*Anon*)

Hail, Sea-Star we name thee, Ever-Maid acclaim thee, God His Mother, Portal To the life immortal. (*George Ratcliffe Woodward* [1848-1934] 1922)

Hail, star of the sea, loving Mother of God, and also always a virgin, Happy gate of heaven. (*Allen H Simon* 1959 -)

Hail, star of the sea, Nurturing Mother of God, And ever Virgin, Happy gate of Heaven. (**usus recentior** *Liturgy of the Hours* 1970)

Sumens illud Ave
Gabriélis ore,
funda nos in pace,
mutans Hevae nomen.

Claiming that Ave from Gabriel's mouth, establish! us in peace, changing [the] name of Eve. (*lit*)

Taking that sweet Ave, which from Gabriel came, peace confirm within us, changing Eve's name. (*trad*)

Taking that sweet Ave, Erst by Gabriel spoken, Eva's name reversing, Be of peace the token. (*Riley*)

Thou that didst receive the Ave from Gabriel's lips, confirm us in peace, and so let Eva be changed into an Ave of blessing for us. (*Anon*)

Ave was the token By the Angel spoken: Peace on earth it telleth, Eva's name re-spelleth. (*Woodward*)

Receiving that Ave from Gabriel's mouth confirm us in peace, Reversing Eva's name. (*Simon*)

Receiving that "Ave" From the mouth of Gabriel, Establish us in peace, Transforming the name of "Eva" (***usus recentior***)

Solve víncula reis,
profer lumen caecis
mala nostra pelle,
bona cuncta posce.

Free! [the] offender's chains, offer! light for [the] blind, banish! our evils, request! all good. (*lit*)

Break the sinners' fetters, make our blindness day, Chase all evils from us, for all blessings pray. (*trad*)

Break the sinners' fetters, Light to blind restoring, All our ills dispelling, Every boon imploring. (*Riley*)

Loose the sinner's chains, bring light to the blind, drive from us our evils, and ask all good things for us. (*Anon*)

Free the worldly-minded, Luminate the blinded. Every ill repressing, Win us every blessing. (*Woodward*)

Break the chains of sinners, Bring light to the blind, Drive away our evils, Ask for all good. (*Simon*)

Loosen the chains of the guilty, Send forth light to the blind, Our evil do thou dispel, Entreat (for us) all good things. (***usus recentior***)

Monstra te esse matrem:
sumat per te preces,
qui pro nobis natus,
tulit esse tuus.

Show! yourself to be [a] mother: prayers through you may you beg, who born for us, declared to be yours. (*lit*)

Show thyself a Mother, may the Word divine born for us thine Infant hear our prayers through thine. (*trad*)

Show thyself a Mother In thy supplication; He will hear who chose thee, At His Incarnation. (*Riley*)

Show thyself a mother, and offer our prayers to him, who would be born of thee, when born for us. (*Anon*)

Plead, and play the Mother! He will, and none other, Born for our salvation, Hear thy supplication. (*Woodward*)

Show yourself to be a mother, May he accept prayers through you, he who, born for us, Chose to be yours. (*Simon*)

Show thyself to be a Mother: Through thee may he receive prayer Who, being born for us, Undertook to be thine own. (*usus recentior*)

Virgo singuláris,
inter omnes mites,
nos culpis solútos,
mitis fac et castos.

Singular Virgin, meek amongst all, released [from] faults, make! us mild and pure. (*lit*)

Virgin all excelling, mildest of the mild, free from guilt preserve us meek and undefiled. (*trad*)

Maid all maids excelling, Passing meek and lowly, Win for sinners pardon, Make us chaste and holy. (*Riley*)

O incomparable Virgin, and meekest of the meek, obtain us the forgiveness of our sins, and make us meek and chaste. (*Anon*)

Maiden meek and lowly, Singularly holy, Loose the sins that chain us; Sanctify, sustain us. (*Woodward*)

O unique virgin, Meek above all, Make us, absolved from sin, Gentle and chaste. (*Simon*)

O unique Virgin, Meek above all others, Make us, set free from (our) sins, Meek and chaste. (***usus recentior***)

Vitam praesta puram,
iter para tutum:
ut vidéntes Iesum
semper collaetémur.

Bestow! [a] pure life, provide! [a] safe path: that seeing Jesus we may rejoice always. (*lit*)

Keep our life all spotless, make our way secure till we find in Jesus, joy for evermore. (*trad*)

As we onward journey Aid our weak endeavour, Till we gaze on Jesus And rejoice forever. (*Riley*)

Obtain us purity of life, and a safe pilgrimage; that we may be united with thee in the blissful vision of Jesus. (*Anon*)

Help us live in pureness, Smooth our way with sureness, Till we also eye Thee, Jesu, ever nigh Thee. (*Woodward*)

Keep life pure, Make the journey safe, So that, seeing Jesus, We may always rejoice together. (*Simon*)

Bestow a pure life, Prepare a safe way: That seeing Jesus, We may ever rejoice. (***usus recentior***)

Sit laus Deo Patri,
summo Christo decus,
Spirítui Sancto,
tribus honor unus. Amen.

Let praise be to Father God, glory to Christ on high, honour to [the] Holy Spirit, one in three Amen. (*lit*)

Praise to God the Father, honour to the Son, in the Holy Spirit, be the glory one. Amen. (*trad*)

Father, Son, and Spirit, Three in One confessing, Give we equal glory Equal praise and blessing. (*Riley*)

Praise be to God the Father and to the Lord Jesus, and to the Holy Ghost: to the Three one self-same praise. Amen. (*Anon*)

Father, Son, we bless Thee, Likewise do confess Thee, Holy Spirit, Trinal, Onely, first and final. (*Woodward*)

Let there be praise to God the Father, Glory to Christ in the highest, To the Holy Spirit, One honour to all three. Amen. (*Simon*)

Praise be to God the Father, To the Most High Christ (be) glory, To the Holy Spirit (Be) honour, to the Three equally. Amen. (***usus recentior***)

The 1922 *The Hymns of the Breviary and Missal* by Fr Matthew Britt OSB (nd) records at least 19 translations of this hymn, and more have been made since. Clearly different translations will reflect the times in which they are made; the reasons they are made and different constraints of rhythm and scansion, and so on, involved in creating new translated texts. Each of these translations is perfectly valid within the context of these constraints, but if we simply isolate one part:

Sumens illud Ave Gabrielis ore

Claiming that Ave of Gabriel's mouth (*lit*)

Taking that sweet Ave, which from Gabriel came, peace confirm within us, changing Eve's name. (*trad*)

Taking that sweet Ave Erst by Gabriel spoken, Eva's name reversing, Be of peace the token. (*Riley*)

Thou that didst receive the Ave from Gabriel's lips, confirm us in peace, and so let Eva be changed into an Ave of blessing for us. (*Anon*)

Ave was the token By the Angel spoken: Peace on earth it telleth, Eva's name re-spelleth.(*Woodward*)

Receiving that Ave from Gabriel's mouth confirm us in peace, Reversing Eva's name. (*Simon*)

Receiving that "Ave" From the mouth of Gabriel, Establish us in peace, Transforming the name of "Eva" (***usus recentior***)

we see that the genitive ***Gabrielis*** (of Gabriel) is variously translated as if ablative by using the English prepositions 'from' or 'by'. Central to each of these translations is the function and force of the ablative of personal agency so that regardless of how it might be translated in English, the agent is always Gabriel. The primary meaning of 'personal agency' becomes of particular importance; that it is Gabriel, as the *Gospel* records, who is personally responsible for greeting Mary with an 'Ave'. In the second verse the prep + abl phrase *in pace*, translations vary, with only 4 of the 7 translations here actually translating the 2nd pers pres act imp sg ***funda*** - ***fundare*** - to 'establish', 'confirm', 'found' and 'to lay a foundation' as an imperative. 3 translate *in pace* as 'in peace', 1 as a genitive 'of peace', 2 as a nominative and 1 as an accusative noun, transposing the ablative *in pace* into a number of different meanings. The closest of the translations above might perhaps be 'within peace', but consider translating *in* as 'amongst' for example and the 'manner' of the peace involved begins to change, situating it as part of a much larger, collective, context of the existence of peace, raising questions then about whose 'peace' is being talked about.

The very frequent prep + abl dynamic phrase ***pro nobis*** (for us) receives quite radically different treatment here in places, especially where the translation of the participle ***natus*** of the deponent verb ***nasci*** (to be born) is made as either the noun 'incarnation' or 'salvation' or the participial 'incarnate'. Generally the preposition ***pro*** is translated as 'for', or 'from' (for example when implied in ***culpis*** (abl pl f ***culpa*** - from sins) but again consider what a phrase like ***pro nobis*** might mean when prayed as 'before us', 'like us', 'in front of us', 'on account of us' or 'for the sake of us'. The instrumental force of the ablative phrase begins to change, and as a consequence, the affect upon us also changes.

When, for example, we pray ***Audi nos***; ***Exáudi nos*** or ***Líbera nos***, they are all calls 'hear us', 'heed us' and 'free us'. But when we pray ***Ora pro nobis***; ***Oráte pro nobis***; ***Intercédite pro nobis***; ***Parce nobis Dómine***, in the *litanies* for example, which are all forms of address asking for the intercessory help of the saints 'pray for us' and to God, 'forbear for us' (usually translated as 'spare us') we are seeking the help of the Saints on our behalf. The Latin preposition *pro* in itself generally means 'for' but followed by the ablative (***nobis*** here) it may carry the stronger force of 'before us', even, indeed of 'instead of us'. We are, therefore, calling upon the Saints, for example, to pray not just 'for us', but, 'before us' and 'in [the] stead of us', in the sense that we do not stand before God's presence as they do. We are asking them to pray 'in our stead', 'on our behalf'. The use of the ablative form here in Latin reinforces this 'in stead of' and signals the instrumental force of the place and manner of that 'in stead of' prayer, and, therefore indeed our own separation from God. This is not something we might immediately think of when praying ***pro nobis*** repeatedly in the *litanies*, but the affect of seeing 'in our stead' instead of 'for us' is quite dramatic, and reinforces the fact that the Saints stand directly before God and we don't.

One of the prayers most often prayed privately (and now less frequently paraliturgically) by Catholics is a compelling recognition of the place where Our Lady stands 'in our stead' interceding on our behalf in Heaven: the *Rosary* (***Rosarium*** - a rose garden) which is a meditation, through the repetition of prayers to Our Lady, on the main events in the life and death of Christ, and may be prayed in various ways. A dominant one is a schema of the five Joyful Mysteries (***Mysteria Gaudiosa***) the five Sorrowful Mysteries (***Mysteria Dolorosa***) and the five Glorious Mysteries (***Mysteria Gloriosa***) more fully developed by

St Louis Marie Grignion de Montfort, and made up of a total of 150 *Ave*s to match the 150 *Psalms* in the *Psalter*, long thought to have been revealed by Our Lady to St Dominic OP (1170-1221) in 1214. Pope St John Paul II introduced an additional five Luminous mysteries (*Mysteria Luminosa*) in his Apostolic Letter **Rosarium Virginis Mariae** (The Rosary of the Virgin Mary) in 2002. Dominican Pope St Pius V on 17 September 1569, confirming the indulgences associated with the praying of the *Rosary*, in **Consueverunt Romani Pontifices** (The Roman Pontiffs were accustomed) outlined the view of St Dominic's role in more detail, referring to the *Rosary* as the *Psalter of the Blessed Virgin*, promoted in particular by the Dominican, Blessed Alain de la Roche (Alanus de Rupe 1428-1475). The *Rosary*, therefore, became a significant means for the illiterate people at the time (including lay brothers and sisters in Religious Houses) to mirror the *Divine Office* in some form, and while it is sometimes seen today as a personal devotion only, its place in Tradition and connections to the para-liturgical life of the Church, through its powerful instrumental address to Our Lady, is a deep one. It is rare now, to see a Priest, as I remember the Priest from whom I took my own confirmation name (Lawrence) publicly reciting the Rosary in Church every day at exactly the same time, come rain or shine, feast or feria, regardless of whether anyone joined him or not.

Pope St Pius V also established the 'Feast of the Holy Rosary' for the 1st Sunday of October in 1571. This Feast was originally restricted to churches which had a side Altar dedicated to the Holy Rosary, but over the years was gradually extended to the whole Church and was confirmed by Pope Clement XI (1649-1721) in 1716. Pope Leo XIII, who had a great devotion to the *Rosary* (he wrote 13 encyclicals on this topic alone and is often referred to as 'The Pope of the Rosary') and who added the words 'Queen of the Most Holy Rosary' to the *Litanies of Loreto*, increased the importance of this feast by granting a plenary indulgence to those who visit a side altar dedicated to the *Rosary*. It is for this reason that many chapels dedicated to Our Lady (but not specifically to the *Rosary*) often (or at least used to) have a set of Rosary beads placed on the Lady statue in order to 'qualify' the chapel/altar as devoted to the *Rosary*, and thus enabling the plenary indulgence subject to the necessary conditions. In more recent times, Pope St John Paul II declared 2002 as the Year of the *Rosary*, and in his Apostolic Letter **Rosarium Virginis Mariae**, issued in October 2002, he talked of the *Rosary* as:

> 'A prayer so easy and yet so rich truly deserves to be rediscovered by the Christian community.'

Saying at the beginning of this Letter that:

> 'It blends easily into the spiritual journey of the Christian life which, after two thousand years, has lost none of the freshness of its beginnings and feels drawn by the Spirit of God to "set out into the deep (***duc in altum!***)" in order once more to proclaim, and even cry out, before the world that Jesus Christ is Lord and Saviour'. (*Vat*)

Mary is the instrument through whom we may hear those words of Christ to St Peter upon the waters: ***duc in altum*** (pull out! intowards the deep *Lc* 5:4) which we pray in the *Gospel* for the 4th Sunday after Pentecost. St Peter responded:

> ***Praecéptor, per totam noctem laborántes nihil cépimus: in verbo autem tuo laxábo rete.***
> (Teacher, through the whole night labouring we have taken in nothing: but by your word I will release the net. *Lc* 5:5)

The accusative ***in altum*** from Christ to Peter now becomes the ablative ***in verbo*** from Peter to Christ. The instrumentality of Christ's word was enough:

Et cum hoc fecíssent, conclusérunt píscium multitúdinem copiósam: rumpebátur autem rete eórum.
(And when they had done this, they caught an abundant multitude of fish: and their net was bursting. *Lc* 5:6)

A powerful instrumental affect indeed.

Instrumental Affect

When Pope Urban IV (1195-1264) requested St Thomas Aquinas and St Bonaventure (1221-1274) to compose a feast in honour of Christ in the Blessed Sacrament (what we now know as the feast of **Corpus Christi**) St Thomas' version was chosen, and within it he refers to the *panis angelicus* (angelic bread) made into the *panis hominum* (the bread of men) as the *panis caelicus* (heavenly bread) a *res mirabilis* (wondrous thing) which is reserved *solis presbyteris* (for Priests alone) transforming the bread and wine into the real, substantial, Body and Blood of Christ (*transubstantiatio* - transubstantiation). It is no accident that *solis presbyteris* is expressed here as an ablative because the Priest is the instrument of Christ himself who creates with his own hands (abl pl f *manibus*) this transubstantiated change in the sacrifice (*sacrificium*) which he, Christ, offers through the human agency of the priest. This sacred banquet (*sacrum convivium*) to continue using St Thomas' words, which *sub sacramento mirabili* (prep + abl sg n *sacramentum* + abl sg n adj *mirabilis* - under a wonderful sacrament) creates the *sacra mysteria Corporis et Sanguinis tui* (the sacred mysteries of your Body and Blood). The Priest is not doing this. Christ is. The Priest in Catholic Tradition is understood as being *in loco Christi* (in the place of Christ - prep + abl sg m *locus* + gen sg m *Christus*).

When Martin Luther announced his many objections to the excesses and corruptions within the Church, much of his concern about some of the materiality of the Church at that time was probably well founded. But he went well beyond those issues, to those which impacted upon the theological, doctrinal and liturgical revealed truths and Tradition of the Church, by extending his (and some earlier) calls for reform on all fronts of the Church. Chief amongst these was his formulation that *sola scriptura* (abl sg f 'by/from Scripture alone') should determine the practices of the Church, and as such, led to his conclusion that salvation can be achieved *sola scriptura*. This marked a major rejection of the concept that Tradition in the Church, and not just Scripture, could (together with Scripture) determine the development of doctrine, theology and other aspects of Christianity, and so, because transubstantiation, and indeed devotion to Our Lady and the Angels and Saints, and much else, was not specifically named in Scripture, those following on from Luther mostly excised them from their now Protestant (protesting against Catholicism) worship.

Scripture itself, the argument then developed, when accepted *sola fide* (abl sg f 'by/from faith alone') through *sola gratia* (abl sg f 'by/from grace alone') and as reflected by the grammatical use of the ablative in these phrases, is the sole means - the sole instrument of God and his Son with the Holy Spirit - through which salvation will be achieved. The grammatical ablatives of instrument and agency are, therefore, utilised within the armoury of theological and doctrinal reform, which has a central message: that the Catholic Church is not the chief instrument of God, but Scripture alone (*sola scriptura*). This new protestant meaning was made linguistically possible by the grammar of the ablative: *sola scriptura/sola fide/sola gratia*. Put simply, and perhaps startlingly, a changed, Protestant world-view, across the entire globe eventually (and increasingly so in some parts of the Catholic Church today) was enabled by the force of one little bit of Latin grammar. The instrumental affect of the ablative in this instance has been enormous; as has its continuing spiritual, social and political [dis]affect. This affect is not something grammar books talk about. But grammar has consequences; sometimes world-changing.

This is not the inevitable change (*tempora mutantur*) over which we have no control but the changes (*mutantur mundi*) over which we do. World-changing views are clearly developed in many different ways, and for many different purposes, often creating confusion and ambiguity along their way, but central to the history and traditions of Latin Catholicism has been (and still is, despite the vagaries that have emerged in Catholicism in recent decades) an imperative to maintain the unchanging nature and centrality of revealed truth, *semper et pro semper* (always and for ever) given to the Church *semel et pro semper* (once and for all) so that it may be *semper eadem* (always the same). The Church is *unam sanctam catholicam et apostolicam Ecclesiam* (one, holy, catholic, and apostolic Church). As long ago as 140 AD we read in the Latin translation of the *Didache* (a summary of the teaching of the Apostles):

> *Recordare, Domine, Ecclesiae tuae... et collige eam a quattuor ventis sanctificatam in regnum tuum, quod ei parasti, quoniam tua est virtus et gloria in saecula.*
> (Remember! O Lord, your Church... and gather! her from [the] four winds sanctified intowards your kingdom, which you have prepared for it, because your glory and power is intowards [the] ages [for ever].)

The Latin verb *colligere* has a range of meanings, including 'to gather', 'to collect together into a whole', 'to draw/bring together', 'to collect', 'to concentrate', 'to think upon', 'to weigh', and 'to consider'. Whoever translated this text from the original Greek (which used the word τελειῶσαι [*teleiosai* - 'to complete', 'to perfect', 'to fulfil']) had a very strong sense of the social power of the Church as one which would be united, and not broken up into separate parts, *in saecula* (for ever). We pray in and from the corporeal, but with the aim of moving beyond that, to the spiritual: to the numinous; to what St Thomas Aquinas refers as *immutatio* (changelessness). The *Didache* tells us that the Church is sanctified into a kingdom *quod parasti* (which you [*Domine*] have prepared). This is a seriously significant declaration about the relations between us as pray-ers and God to whom we pray. *in saecula* also means that Christ has never left his Church, and that Church, at its Catholic core, despite all the variations now in existence, remains as Christ established it, unrecognised though that might now be by many Latin Catholics.

In what must still be considered one of, if not the, best **vade mecum** (travel with me) pocket size books ever written on the grammar of Ecclesiastical Latin (published in 1921) the Anglican minister Rev Henry Preston Vaughan Nunn (1876-1962) of St John's College Cambridge, makes the important point that the term 'ablative' (taking away) for example, is actually potentially misleading, because the word 'ablative' only describes a very small part (*ab-latus* - separation or place from) of the functions of this form. As almost an aside (and something not generally referred to outside of the grammar of some languages like Greek or Hungarian) in distinguishing between the ablative of separation and the instrumental ablative, he uses the term 'sociative' (*socius* - company) to denote 'the instrument by means of which anything is done'. It is a term that could be used to signal that prayer is not something that happens in isolation. Prayer is always *sociative* because it is always about 'being together', not 'with each other' (social) but 'together with God' (sociative). It is always, in the words of the scholastic philosopher and **Doctor Solemnis** Henry of Ghent (1217-1293) about **pertinens ad Deum** (reaching out towards God) by *sociatively* seeking 'togetherness' with God in, by, with, through and for him, most notably for Catholics, instrumentally through the ultimate sacrifice of the Mass. Prayer is never an isolated act, even if we are alone on a desert island praying. It is always a sociative action, because it is always done in the company of God, whether we are conscious of that or not. This does not mean, as has resulted in some of the interpretations of the *Vatican II* documents (especially the 1963 **Constitutio de Sacra Liturgia. Sacrosanctum Concilium** (Constitution on the Sacred Liturgy. [This] Sacred Council) that prayer and liturgy are now 'better' understood, and practised, as *social events*. This is not the Latin Catholic way, for no matter where, when or how we might pray, in a Pontifical *Missa Solemnis* or a whispered *Ave* on the way to work, prayer is not always social, but it is always *sociative,* and it is to this we now turn in *Chapter IX: Sociative Prayer.*

DAVID BIRCH

IX

SOCIATIVE PRAYER

Non dabitur aurum obrizum pro ea, nec appendetur argentum in commutatione eius.
(The finest gold shall not purchase it, neither shall silver be weighed in exchange for it. DR *Iob* 28:15)

Exchange

Language is inseparable from action and thought; from its contexts and from the values and ideas developed, promulgated and exchanged within and beyond those contexts. As native speakers of a language we tend to take it for granted. We use language instinctively, mostly not having to plan ahead what we are about to say. Our ability to communicate in this way is a most remarkable thing, and without a doubt has resulted in our classification as **homo loquens** (talking man). We have uncanny facilities with grammar and syntax, even though we may not be aware of it, or be able to describe the way these function. Language is primarily about exchange, not simply as the exchange of ideas, relations, values and emotions between people communicating with each other through language (socially) but the *sociative* exchange (the 'togetherness') that takes place within the words and structures of language itself;

the lexical, grammatical, syntactic, stylistic and discursive relations that necessarily occur to make language work.

The English word 'sociative' derives from ***socius -a -um*** a Latin adjective signifying 'sharing in', 'joining in', 'associating with', 'participating in', 'partaking in' and perhaps more importantly in the context of language and prayer, 'exchanging' and 'being together'. It is not a word we tend to use in contemporary English. But to use it in the context of language and prayer, as here, and probably for the first time in this way, is to draw attention to the way in which all prayer, and all language in prayer, functions as a form of exchange in sociative ways, between the pray-er and God, expressing the way in which all the words and linguistic structures of prayer, and ourselves as the pray-ers of prayer, participate in the actions and reactions of what the *Catechism* refers to as **Revelationis Oeconomia** (the 'Economy of Revelation' *Cat* §1103). This 'economy' might best be understood as the sociative exchange involved between God and humanity and which finds its ultimate expression, for Catholics, in the relationship between our words and our actions through **Oeconomia Sacramentalis** (the 'Sacramental Economy' *Cat* §1076). Further understood within the overall context of **Oeconomia Salutis** (the 'Economy of Salvation' *LG* II 55) made possible by the exchange of grace in **Oeconomia Verbi Incarnati** (the 'Economy of the Word Incarnate' *Cat* §1066) and ourselves.

The Church uses the word ***oeconomia*** (οἰκονομία - oikonomía - household management) many times in its teaching, and as used within the Church has almost as long a history as Christianity itself, and is thought to have been first used in this way by Origen. At its heart is not only the very central sense of 'management' and 'administration', but also the way it signifies 'parts/divisions', 'order' and 'arrangements', in a play or speech for example. It has increasingly become understood, especially in contemporary financial terms, as signifying a system of 'exchange'. More often than not, that understanding of 'exchange' is all about 'transactional exchange', but the Church has always taught, and which is especially foregrounded post *Vatican II* in **Lumen Gentium**, that:

> *Propter ipsam oeconomiam salutis, fideles discant sedulo distinguere inter iura et officia quae eis incumbunt, quatenus Ecclesiae aggregantur, et ea quae eis competunt, ut sunt humanae societatis membra. Utraque inter se harmonice consociare satagent, memores se, in quavis re temporali, christiana conscientia duci debere, cum nulla humana activitas, ne in rebus temporalibus quidem, Dei imperio subtrahi possit.*
>
> (Because of the very economy of salvation the faithful should learn how to distinguish carefully between those rights and duties which are theirs as members of the Church, and those which they have as members of human society. Let them strive to reconcile the two, remembering that in every temporal affair they must be guided by a Christian conscience, since even in secular business there is no human activity which can be withdrawn from God's dominion. *LG* 36)
>
> *Sicut enim agnoscendum est terrenam civitatem, saecularibus curis iure addictam propriis regi principiis, ita infausta doctrina, quae societatem, nulla habita religionis ratione, exstruere contendit et libertatem religiosam civium impugnat et eruit, merito reiicitur.*
>
> (For it must be admitted that the temporal sphere is governed by its own principles, since it is rightly concerned with the interests of this world. But that ominous doctrine which attempts to build a society with no regard whatever for religion, and which attacks and destroys the religious liberty of its citizens, is rightly to be rejected. *LG* 36)

The way we understand the economy of exchange in our everyday activities and within the economy of salvation might, therefore, be very different. There is very restricted room, if any, for the world of transactive relations in the **Oeconomia salutis.** The world of that economy, and its prayer, is, first and foremost, a world (though this phrase is not used by the Church) of 'sociative' not 'transactive' relations. St Paul, as the *Catechism* points out, uses the phrase ***dispensatio [oeconomia] mysterii*** (the plan [economy] of the mystery *Eph* 3:9) which is, St Paul says, ***dispositionem sapienter ordinatam*** (a wisely ordered plan). If we understand the word 'economy' through a spiritual understanding of the word 'plan', then we will perhaps better understand, and be part of the numinous sociative exchange involved in God's 'wisely ordered plan'; what the *Catechism* calls his ***beneplacitum*** (good pleasure) ***super totam creationem*** (for all creation).

Job, learned this the hard way. ***Erat vir ille simplex, et rectus*** (He was a simple man, and upright) ***timens Deum, et recedens a malo*** (fearing God, and recoiling from evil *Iob* 1:1) and talking of wisdom (*sapientia*) and ***locus intelligentiae*** (the place of intelligence) was warned, as the epigraph of this chapter records, that gold cannot buy wisdom and silver cannot be exchanged for intelligence. The Latin word used in the *Vulgate* is ***commutatio*** which signifies more than just a commercial exchange (***excambio***) but also an 'alteration', a 'change', a 'conversation' and 'interchange', and perhaps more importantly an 'upheaval'. In that respect the economy of salvation involves Christ taking on the sins of us all (*2 Cor* 5:21) and offering himself to us in exchange for our sins, as foretold by the Psalmist who sings of ***commutatio[nem] christi tui*** (the exchange of your Christ) bearing all the reproaches and assaults of the world upon him (*Ps* 88:52). Translated variously in many English versions as 'the footsteps of thine anointed' (*KJV*) and 'every step of your anointed one' (*NIV*) 'the sense of 'upheaval', 'alteration', 'interchange' and 'exchange' in the Latin word ***commutatio*** (as for example when Christ changed the water into wine at the Marriage of Cana) is lost. The *DR* retains the Latin sense here translating it as 'the change of thy anointed' as does the *CPDV* as 'the commutation of your Christ'.

St Anselm in his ***Cur Deus Homo*** (Why God Man) teaches that as mere humans we are unable to fully (and personally) atone for our sin ourselves. Only Christ's ***commutatio*** on the Cross is sufficient to atone for all of humanity's sin, not just past, present and future, but also, as

St Thomas Aquinas teaches, in every possible world and universe. This understanding of Christ's atoning exchange of his life, as sinless God and Man, for our sins governs what it is to be Catholic through every doctrine, sacrament and sensibility. It is for this reason that images of Christ crucified are everywhere in traditional Catholic life and Catholic churches. They are not crosses without a corpus, but crucifixes, paintings and ***Stationes Crucis*** (Stations of the Cross) often very vividly portraying Christ's passion, agony and death. St Anselm understands Christ as ***peccatorum reconciliator*[em]** (reconciler of sinners II:26) a powerful expression for understanding the atoning role of Christ, through his death for us, as reconciling a separated humanity with God his Father. Sydney Norton in his 1903 translation of ***Cur Deus Homo*** uses the term 'restorer of sinners'. By Christ's death we are restored. We now share in his ***commutatio***, for, as St Anselm tells us:

> ***Nulla tamen anima ante mortem Christi paradisum coelestem ingredi potuit.***
> (Nevertheless no soul before [the] death of Christ has been able to enter heavenly paradise. II:16)

The Catholic understanding of this, is that Christ's atoning act is a continuing one, and so our part of this exchange requires a similar continuing effort from us in order to continue to avoid sin, the very reason for the Atonement in the first place. We need the grace of God in our lives to be able to do this, and prayer is central to that. It is not easy; it is not a one-off transaction; it is always a sociative exchange. St Anselm talks of our God-given ***potestatem discernendi*** (power of discernment II:1) which means that we can choose not to participate in this exchange, as indeed so many people increasingly have chosen not to do, including Catholics, but St Anselm's clarion warning remains firm: salvation ***necesse est fieri per Christum*** (must be achieved through Christ. I:25).

At the layered heart of ***commutatio*** is the Latin verb ***commutare***: to 'change', 'alter', 'modify', 'correct', 'reform', 'transform', 'exchange', 'interchange', 'replace', 'substitute', 'converse', 'discourse' and 'communicate'. When we pray we don't just say the words, we need to participate interactively with those words; what they mean; what they involve and suggest, and even more than that, to seek an upheaval (***commutatio***) and transformation (***transformatio***) through that prayer. The only way we can do that, is to accept the sociative exchange of grace offered to us by God to whom we are praying; an exchange which only has any meaning when understood in terms of the greatest exchange Christ made for us: the Atonement. We, therefore, 'partake in/participate in' prayer. And that is a sociative act. It involves exchange. It may be 'social', but not necessarily so. It involves almost every sense of the word ***commutatio*** including one we perhaps would not want to think about: 'decay' (used when talking of fruit and food). Prayer is not always alive and vibrant for us. There are often many dark nights of the soul. Our prayer life may seem at times to be in decay as we saw in the last chapter. But Christ taught his disciples:

> ***oportet semper orare et non deficere***
> (it is necessary to always pray and not to be discouraged *Lc* 18:1)

Our motivation may wane at times, but the language always remains, and what is true of all language is that every bit of it is *situated* within a context and is *motivated* by the values and ideas determining, and associated with, those contexts, including the Latin Catholicism of Latin prayer. The way we make meanings, in large part by language, though by no means the only part, is, more often than not, from language in use. Understanding the meaning of a word, or bit of grammar or the way syntax works, is not just because of dictionary definitions (denotation) but knowing how to use the word, grammar or syntax, in a variety of contexts (connotation). Language is *performative*, it does something; it is instrumental in many of its causative actions and it is *relational* both to the words and grammatical structures around it that form the text itself, and beyond the text to the wider *sociative* context in which the text performs and functions. Linguists call this the 'perlocutionary function' of language; people affecting themselves and others through - *per* - speech (*loquens*). What in prayer we might think of as 'the sociative dynamic'.

The Sociative Dynamic

When we pray this first verse of the hymn at a ferial Friday *Matins*:

> *Tu, Trinitátis Unitas,*
> *orbem poténter qui regis,*
> *atténde laudis cánticum*
> *quod excubántes psállimus.*
> (You, [O] Oneness of [the] Trinity,
> who powerfully rules [the] world,
> hear [the] song of praise
> which we watchers sing [in psalms].)

thought to have been composed by Pope St Gregory I we pray it conscious of the fact that the opening line **Tu, Trinitatis Unitas** (You, Trinity, Oneness) is not simply making a statement about God, but is a declaration of an act of faith. That declaration, and who it signifies, is unchanging. It is a declaration that not only *says* what it signifies, but we *pray* that declaration, and we do so together with all who pray and have prayed it for almost two millennia. In that sense, then, every act of praying is *sociative*, even in the most isolated and eremitical corners of our lives. It is a speech act which connects us to all those people, and all those times this prayer has been prayed before. It may be social, if some of those people physically pray this prayer with us, but is always sociative, connecting us to God through every occasion it has ever been prayed. Our praying this hymn, therefore, goes beyond these three words of the opening line, by performing something beyond the dictionary meanings of these words. It is 'performing' a sociative act of faith; an act that millions before us have made.

When we pray the imperative ***attende laudis canticum*** (hear! [the] song of praise) we are using words to call upon God to do something - hear! - but more than that we are performing an act of submission. We are placing ourselves before God as worshippers. We are using language to go beyond language. In effect, in prayer, we are performing an *exchange* of 'togetherness', not in the 'touchy-feely' way so popular in some contemporary Catholic liturgies, nor only with the *texts* of words, but with all the *contexts* of those words throughout their history in this prayer, and ultimately then, through that text-context dynamic, we seek a numinous exchange - a sociative dynamic - with God. This is a state St Anselm gloriously describes (though not in these words) at the beginning of Book II of his ***Cur Deus Homo*** by saying that our:

> *rationalem naturam a Deo factam esse iustam, ut illo fruendo beata esset*
> (rational nature was made righteous by God, in order to be happy in enjoying him)

where our 'enjoying of God' is only made possible through the Atonement. When we use language to talk about language, as in this book, we are conjuring up spectres of semantic inexactness and uncertainties. Using language to talk about language invariably results in what George Steiner referred to as a 'dynamics of instability'. There is no stepping outside of language to talk about language; there is no 'extraterritorial immunity', to use Steiner's phrase; no neutral zone. Language always 'gets in the way' when talking about language. And yet, in the way of Latin prayer, it might seem that we are actually seeking to do exactly that. We might seem to be seeking to step outside of the-language-of-our-everyday in order to use a-language-not-of-our-everyday in which to pray. In some of the writings of Père Jean-Pierre de Caussade SJ published posthumously in 1861 as *Abandon à la Providence Divine* and translated into English under the title of *Abandonment to Divine Providence*, but may also be found as *The Sacrament of the Present Moment* (trs Kitty Muggeridge) he writes:

> 'Faith is our light in this life. By it we possess the truth without seeing it; we touch what we cannot feel, and see what is not evident to the senses. By it we view the world as though it did not exist. It is the key of the treasure house, the key of the abyss of the science of God. It is faith that teaches us the hollowness of created things; By it God reveals and manifests Himself in all things. By faith the veil is torn aside to reveal the eternal truth. All that we see is nothing but vanity and deceit; truth can be found only in God. What a difference between the thoughts of God and the illusions of man! How is it that although continually warned that everything that happens in the world is but a shadow, a figure, a mystery of faith, we look at the outside only and do not perceive the enigma they contain? We fall into this trap like men without sense instead of raising our eyes to the principle, source and origin of all things, in which they all have their right name and just proportions, in which everything is supernatural, divine, and sanctifying; in which all is part of the plenitude of Jesus Christ, and each circumstance is as a stone towards the construction of the heavenly Jerusalem, and all helps to build a dwelling for us in that marvellous city. We live according to what we see and feel and wander like madmen in a labyrinth of darkness and illusion for want of the light of faith which would guide us safely through it. By means of faith we should be able to aspire after God and to live for Him alone, forsaking and going beyond mere figures.'

This is powerful teaching, and meat and drink to many Latin Catholics who grew up with this seemingly uncompromising position about the 'shadow of the world', its enigmas, vanities, deceits, traps and dangers. Perhaps 'as madmen in a labyrinth of darkness and illusion' we need this absolutist 'shock of the real', and as people seeking a way of prayer, while living in this world, it certainly presents its challenges. But perhaps, as St Augustine recognised, removing the evils of the world does not necessarily make for a better world, for, in St Augustine's view, a better one is actually enabled if those evils help develop the growth of virtues. It is not an 'either/or' situation, and as such de Caussade's position is best seen as an ideal to be sought; the goal of the ordinary 'you and me' who are not mystics, nor may never be so, but who, following Père de Caussade's contrast between 'faith' and the 'world', seek not to abandon the world (an impossibility) but to use, as he says, 'the light of faith' to 'guide us safely through it'. And to do that we have no choice but to use language. Again, as George Steiner puts it, using similar metaphors as Père de Caussade, though talking about linguists and not pray-ers, in reality we: 'no more step out of the mobile fabric of actual language... than does a man out of the reach of his own shadow.' Steiner cites French philosopher Maurice Jean-Jacques Merleau Ponty (1908-1961) who refers to the impossibility of this 'stepping outside' of language in the hope of more effectively being able to talk about language, and instead argues for 'stepping inside' (not Steiner's or Merleau Ponty's phrase) the *hasards du langage* (chances of language) in order to use those *hasards*, rather than to pretend they are just simply innocent instruments designed to help us speak, communicate, read or pray.

Language creates relations in words and grammatical structures. But language functions beyond those words and structures, and in prayer it functions *numinously*, not something discussed or described in language books or by linguists. 'Modality' enables words and bits of language and grammar to mean beyond themselves; to enable action; to determine results; to cause things to happen; to reflect attitudes and moods; to relate and to create associations. The modality of language variously shows language at work: performing things; doing things; questioning things; achieving things; addressing things; interacting with things; determining things; relating to things; focussing on things and affecting things. These modalities are generally classified in traditional approaches to understanding grammar as the 'interrogative' (questioning) 'imperative' (commanding) and 'indicative' (declaring) moods. With these different modalities, language performs many acts creating an *illocutionary* force beyond the words themselves, in other words, an affect which is produced by a language user, and not necessarily by the words the user says (ie: 'not [*ill-*] the locution'). We might promise, or apologise; we might be kind or angry; we might offer something or take something away. There are multiple acts that language performs in our daily lives, many of which are not reliant at all upon the actual words we are using, but they may create considerable *illocutionary* force, and result in considerable *perlocutionary* affect. St Paul recognised this and warned the Ephesians not to be deceived/seduced by **inanibus verbis** (abl pl n - empty words - *Eph* 5:6). He understood, though not in these terms, that the act of using language (illocutionary force) can, more often than not, mean with far more perlocutionary force than the words (locutionary force) themselves. As we pray at Tuesday *None*:

> *Tu es ipse rex meus et Deus meus.*
> (You are yourself my king and my God. *Ps* 43:5)

God is expressed grammatically here with the Latin 2nd person active indicative present tense form of the verb *esse* - 'to be' - *es* ('you sg' are). The grammatical relation between the *tu* and the *es* is clear, but the relationship between the *tu* and the *es* is far beyond the words themselves, as indeed is the *ipse*. We could never explain what *tu es ipse* (you are yourself) actually means in relation to God, or what, in effect, the act of saying it, let alone, indeed, the act of praying it, actually involves and means. Philosophers since the dawn of time have tried and will keep on trying. We pray at Friday *Compline*:

> *Tu es Deus qui facis mirabilia*
> (You are God who does wonders. *Ps* 76:15)

and that will always remain relationally awesome and spiritually impossible to explain, in every sense. The sociative functions of the verb *esse* between its specific grammatical forms like 'I' and 'am' (*sum*) 'you' (sg) and 'are' (*es*) 'he/she/it' and 'is' (*est*) 'we' and 'are' (*sumus*) 'you' (pl) and 'are' (*estis*) and 'they' and 'are' (*sunt*) are basically straightforward and indicative of the relations between subjects and verbs, but the spiritually sociative functions beyond that grammar are unfathomable. Their unexplainable depths lie at the heart of all Latin prayer as performative and numinous; they signify modalities mirroring the even more unfathomable sociative relations between God and humanity. Without the Incarnation and Christ's becoming human; without his Atonement, that unfathomability would be even more unapproachable and unknowable. That is one of the great gifts of the Incarnation: awareness beyond the human.

Sociative Modality

We learn in **Liber Genesis** that God called Jacob to him (renaming him 'Israel') with a simple indicative form of the verb saying:

> *Ego sum fortissimus Deus patris tui: noli timere, descende in Aegyptum, quia in gentem magnam faciam te ibi.*
> (I am [the] most mighty God of your father: be not! fearful, go down! into Egypt, because I will make you into [a] great nation there. *Gn* 46:3)

The grammar and syntax of **Ego sum fortissimus Deus** is repeated in this form many times throughout the *Bible*: a dynamic of pronoun + indicative verb 'to be' + attributive + noun, (where the attributive may be an adjective, determiner, pronoun or even another noun) modifying the noun it is describing by attributing further qualities and properties, and thereby, making additional meanings. So, for example, we pray at various times:

Ego sum Dóminus Deus vester
(I am [the] Lord your God. *Dt* 29:6)

Deus, Deus tuus ego sum
(I am God, your God. *Ps* 49:7)

Ego sum, ego sum Dóminus, et non est absque me salvátor
(I am, I am [the] Lord: and there is no saviour besides me. *Is* 43:11)

Ego sum Deus, et non est ultra deus
(I am [the] God, and there is no god higher. *Is* 46:9)

Ego sum pastor bonus
(I am [the] good shepherd. *Io* 10:11)

Ego sum panis vitae
(I am [the] bread of life. *Io* 6:48)

Ego sum resurréctio et vita
(I am [the] resurrection and [the] life. *Io* 11:25)

Ego sum primus, et novíssimus, et vivus
(I am [the] first, and [the] last, and [the] living. *Apc* 1:17-18)

Ego sum radix, et genus David, stella spléndida et matutína
(I am [the] root, and [the] stock of David, [the] bright and morning star. *Apc* 22:16)

In all of these texts the pronoun *ego* makes a simple indicative statement *sum* (am) and is modified with additional information, through other pronouns, adjectives and nouns. 'I am': what/who? – 'God', 'the Lord, your God', 'the good shepherd', 'the bread of life', 'the resurrection and life', 'the first, last and living' and 'the root and stock', all of them attributing qualities and properties to ***Ego*** and linked to it by the indicative verb ***sum***. But more than that: the dynamic structure of pronoun + indicative verb 'to be' + attributive + noun (and locutionary variations) has an additional illocutionary way of meaning beyond the lexical meanings of the words. While there is attributive meaning given by the words (***Ego sum pastor bonus*** - 'I am [the] good shepherd') there is also a relational/sociative meaning given by the grammar of those words. ***Ego*** is the grammatical subject of the verb ***sum*** and ***pastor*** *bonus* is that part of the sentence which attributes information about the subject, and in grammar is known as the 'predicate'. In the examples above, following the verb *esse* (to be) this predicate is said to *complement* the subject. The English word 'predicate' derives from the Latin neuter noun ***praedicatum*** (a thing said of a subject) from the verb ***praedicare***: to 'proclaim', 'declare', 'announce', 'make known', 'praise', 'preach', and so on. The grammatical 'predicate', especially in the context of Latin prayer, is suggestive of many interpretations and might have many layered connotations. So, for example, in a short prayer/acclamation like ***Tu es Deus***, the subject ***Tu*** is followed by the predicate *es Deus*, where the verb *esse* (to be) is linking the predicate to the subject in a complementary way; they cannot really stand alone, and so in grammar this relationship is known as a copular (usually written as 'copula') association. The grammatical function then, of subject + predicate, goes beyond what the actual words may mean lexically, linking the predicate to the subject of the verb, and so forming a sociative (indicative) relationship. This, in turn, attributes a further way of making meaning: an illocutionary modality, beyond the words themselves. So, for example, ***Tu es*** signals the locutionary force of 2nd pers sg 'you are' but that indicative declaration might say considerably more than that, for example when we pray in the long *Epistle* for the 3rd Saturday in Lent:

> ***Tu es fílius meus Esau?***
> (Are you my son Esau? *Gn* 27:24)

or in the *Epistle* for the Masses of St Josaphat (Bishop and Martyr, 1580-1623, November 12) and St Thomas (29 December):

> ***Tu es sacérdos in aetérnum, secúndum órdinem Melchísedech.***
> (You are [a] priest for ever, according to [the] order of Melchisedech. *Heb* 5:6)

or in declaring:

> *Nunc ergo Dómine Deus, tu es Deus*
> (Now, therefore, O Lord God, you are God. *2 Reg* 7:28)

Tu es Deus may well be the only prayer we ever really need to privately pray, because the illocutionary force of this one simple clause is potentially beyond anything else we could ever say, except, perhaps, when we repeat it as:

> *Tu enim, Dómine Deus meus... Nunc ergo, Dómine, tu es Deus*
> (You indeed, O Lord my God... Now therefore, O Lord, you are God. *2 Par* 17:25-26)

Said reverentially, and bringing to it all the intertextual history of our awareness of God, *Tu es* holds the key to a lifetime of prayer: not in just two simple words, but in the sociative relationship of subject and predicate, both linguistically and spiritually. Similarly:

> *Unus est bonus, Deus*
> (One is good, [O] God *Mt* 19:17)

where the *est* signals the locutionary force of 3rd person singularity. But when St John tells us:

> *quoniam Deus lux est, et tenebrae in eo non sunt ullae*
> (because God is light, and in him there are not any darknesses *1 Io* 1:5)

Deus (God) is attributed with the property of *lux* (light) through the act of declaring *est* and a further attribution that there are not (3rd pers pl *sunt*) *ullae tenebrae* (any darknesses) in him. The adjective *ulla* (any) like all adjectives needs to agree with its noun in case, gender and number (in this case nom f pl to agree with the pl (never sg) f nom noun *tenebrae*). The attributive relationship is about the actual properties of God. The predicative relationship is about the grammatical relations (locutionary force) between **Deus** (subject) *lux* and ***non ullae tenebrae*** (complements) linked by the two copulas (*est* sg and *sunt* pl) and resulting in an illocutionary act of God's attributes, but a further, perlocutionary, sociative relationship, results because of that, and is about the affect of God's attributes upon the pray-er.

This might all seem academically obtuse but the locutionary relationship between a predicate and its subject is crucial in understanding the way the language of address works to bring about illocutionary *effect* and perlocutionary *affect*. We have seen this with the verb *esse* and its use as a copula: *tu* (nominative subject) *es* (2nd pers sg copula) *sacerdos* (nominative complement) forms of which we see frequently in prayer. The powerful message for prayer, I would suggest, is that we pray the better not by leaping **out** of language but by leaping **into** it. We might see this as a 'sociative leap', not out of the world, as many writers have advocated for centuries, and sometimes, most uncompromisingly, but as Doctor of the Church and patron Saint of writers, St Francis de Sales (1567-1622, whose 1606 *Introduction à la Vie Dévote* [Introduction to a Devout Life] must surely be required reading for any Latin Catholic seeking a way of prayer) writes in his *Lettres de S François de Sales à des Gens du Monde* (letters from St Francis de Sales to people in the world) published after his death:

> 'Perfection does not lie in avoiding the world, but in not clinging to it.'

For a way of prayer which (as seen and understood through my linguist's eyes, but also my Latin Catholic heart) this book seeks to do by wrestling with Latin and its translation as a way of sociatively wrangling the grammatical together with the spiritual as a 'both/and' and not as an 'either/or', this is sound advice from St Francis de Sales. When we variously pray in the *Divine Office*:

Præsta, Pater piíssime, Patríque compar Unice,
cum Spíritu Paráclito, regnans per omne sǽculum.
(Bestow, O most holy Father, and O only Son equal to [the] Father with [the] Spirit [the] Paraclete reigning through all [the] age.)

the sociative dynamic, and the speech acts made, in this this one verse of this one hymn are numerous, and do not require us to be physically (socially) in the same space or time. But while we may have a collective understanding of the force involved, sung as this hymn is in a Catholic liturgical context governed by the **Magisterium**, we each of us will individually pray this prayer differently. Our different backgrounds; our different associations; our different experiences and our different hopes and dreams, and our different understanding and interpretation of the same language, are all multi-faceted, and layered 'intertextual' histories which we inescapably bring to our prayer. What doesn't change (and shouldn't change) are the revealed truths situated in both Tradition and Scripture which motivate this prayer.

Modality, and the sociative relationships it enables, then, positions our humanity as always being secondary to the God we worship, adore and give glory to in prayer. The very acts of prayer, regardless of the words used, determine a specific mode of address for human beings; require a certain attitude that functions for purposes beyond the everyday; establish particular ways of focussing away from the material and onto the immaterial and involve a perlocutionary force beyond ourselves which embodies that immaterial and supernatural, affecting us, often in relational and sociative ways we can never adequately describe. Our linguistic behaviour matters in prayer, but much more than that, our extra-linguistic (outside of language) associations and dispositions matter even more, and a hieratic language like Latin can help discipline those dispositions. At the heart of sociative modality in prayer, then, of God as 'being', whether that prayer is public or private, whether liturgical or paraliturgical, whether in Latin or any of the thousands of vernacular languages that exist in the world, is 'revelation', and understanding that begins with Scripture, though not for Catholics, exclusively. Both Scripture and Tradition lie at the heart of all Catholic prayer, and at the heart of Scripture is the revelation of 'being of the Divine' as St Paul wrote to St Timothy in his second letter to him which we pray very appropriately in the *Epistle* for the Mass of the great St Irenaeus (June 28) who was instrumental in developing so much Christian theology, when he said:

> *Omnis Scriptúra divínitus inspiráta útilis est ad docéndum, ad arguéndum, ad corripiéndum, ad erudiéndum in iustítia.*
> (All Scripture is divinely inspired [and] is profitable to [*the purpose of*] teaching, to [*the purpose of*] reproving, to [*the purpose of*] correcting and to [*the purpose of*] instructing [us] in justice. *2 Tim* 3:16)

The Latin verb ***inspirata*** is the past (perfect) participle (acting as an adjective) from the infinitive verb ***inspirare*** - 'to breathe upon'; 'to inspire'; 'to excite'. God breathes upon all Scripture, and so, when we engage with that Scripture; when it becomes the heart of whatever it is we make as our prayer, we are engaging with the sociative modality of the performative action of God's breathing upon those words, 'so that', as the *Epistle* continues:

> *ut perféctus sit homo Dei, ad omne opus bonum instrúctus.*
> (so that [the] man of God may be perfect, prepared ontowards every good work. *2 Tim* 3:17)

through the sociative exchange of God's breath. The Latin words ***Sanctus Spiritus*** (Holy Spirit) derive from the verb ***spirare*** 'to breathe', and we need always to keep that in mind as we pray. 'To breathe' is 'to live', so if we are said in English to be 'spirited' it means we are '*live*-ly'. Life as we know it comes from God. God's breath (his spirit) gives us life, both physical and spiritual. We are affected by God's breath. St Paul captures this perfectly when he tells the Christians in Rome:

> *ut iustificatio legis impleretur in nobis, qui non secundum carnem ambulamus, sed secundum spiritum.*
>
> (so that [the] justification of [the] law might be fulfilled in us, who walk not according to flesh, but according to [the] spirit. *Rom* 8:4)
>
> *Nam prudentia carnis, mors est: prudentia autem spiritus, vita et pax*
>
> (For knowledge of [the] flesh, is death: but prudence of [the] spirit, [is] life and peace. *Rom* 8:6)

Walking in the way of the Spirit lies at the heart of being Catholic and engaging in Catholic worship and Catholic sensibilities. St Luke reports Christ's opening actions of his ministry when, following the temptations in the desert, which we pray in the *Gospel* of the 1st Sunday of Lent. Jesus entered into Galilee and:

> *ipse docebat in synagogis eorum, et magnificabatur ab omnibus.*
>
> (he himself was teaching in their synagogues, and was magnified by all. *Lc* 4:15)

and entering the synagogue in Nazareth on the Sabbath he opened the book at *Isaias* and read aloud:

> *Spiritus Domini super me*
>
> ([The] Spirit of the Lord [is] upon me *Lc* 4:18)

and thus began his ministry with probably the most powerful indicative statement ever made, and in the Latin *Vulgate*, without the need for a verb at all.

Sociative Spirituality

In this popular prayer dating back to at least the 4ᵗʰC and prayed separately, or as one of the antiphons for *Vespers* on the Feast of the Immaculate Conception:

℣. *Tota pulchra es, María.*
℟. *Tota pulchra es, María.*

℣. *Et mácula originális non est in te.*
℟. *Et mácula originális non est in te.*

℣. *Tu glória Ierúsalem.*
℟. *Tu laetítia Israël.*

℣. *Tu honorificéntia pópuli nostri.*
℟. *Tu advocáta peccatórum.*

℣. *O María.*
℟. *O María.*

℣. *Virgo prudentíssima.*
℟. *Mater clementíssima.*

℣. *Ora pro nobis.*
℟. *Intercéde pro nobis ad Dóminum Iesum Christum.*

(You are all beauty, O Mary.
You are all beauty, O Mary.

And [the] original stain is not in you.
And [the] original stain is not in you.

You [are the] glory of Jerusalem.
You [are the] joy of Israel.

You [are the] honouring of our people.
You [are the] advocate of sinners.

O Mary. O Mary.

[O] Virgin most prudent.
[O] Mother most tender. Pray for us.

Intercede for us towards our Lord Jesus Christ.)

we see that the simple copula relationship between subject and predicate *tu es* or *macula originalis non est* does not need to even be specified in *Tu gloria Ierusalem*; *Tu laetitia Israël*; *Tu honorificentia populi nostri* or *Tu advocata peccatorum*. There is no verb, and yet the locutionary force of the verb is there, as is the illocutionary force of the act of calling upon Mary for help, as well as the perlocutionary force of the affect upon us as we pray: seeking assistance in a situation where we have no real material influence. When prayed separately, the prayer ends with a Collect:

> *Sancta María, regína caelórum, mater Dómini nostri Iesu Christi, et mundi dómina, quae nullum derélinquis, et nullum déspicis: réspice me, dómina, cleménter oculo pietátis, et impétra mihi apud tuum diléctum Fílium cunctórum veníam peccatórum: ut qui nunc tuam sanctam et immaculátam conceptiónem devóto afféctu recólo, aetérnae in futúrum beatitúdinis, bravíum capíam, ipso, quem virgo pepéristi, dónante Dómino nostro Iesu Christo: qui cum Patre et Sancto Spíritu vivit et regnat, in Trinitáte perfécta, Deus, in sǽcula saeculórum. Amen.*

([O] Holy Mary, queen of [the] heavens, mother of our Lord Jesus Christ, and mistress of [the] world, who forsakes no one, and despises no one: look kindly upon me, [O] lady with [an] eye of pity, and implore for me from your beloved Son pardon of all sins; that, as I now recall, with devout affection, your holy and immaculate conception, I may in [the] future receive [the] prize of eternal blessedness, given from our Lord Jesus Christ himself who you, as virgin, gave birth to: who with [the] Father and [the] Holy Spirit, lives and reigns, in perfect Trinity, God, into [the] ages of ages. Amen)

One very noticeable verb in this Collect is ***donante***. It is the present participle (***donans***) of the verb ***donare*** (to give) and as a participle acts very much like an adjective agreeing with its noun, in this case the abl m sg phrase ***donante Domino nostro Iesu Christo*** (given [from] our Lord Jesus Christ). A participle, like ***donante*** has a little more work to do than an adjective, as it also continues to work as the verb from which it is formed, signifying (and focussing upon) the type of sociative relationship that exists between the subject and the verb. In particular, that relationship can be about time (past, present and future) or voice (active or passive). For example, when we pray in Nocturn III of *Matins* on the 1st Sunday in Advent:

Terra vestra desérta; civitátes vestrae succénsae igni
(Your land [is] desolate, your cities [are] burnt with fire *Is* 1:7)

the sense of present time, in particular, is reinforced by the participles of verbs that are used as adjectives. Here, ***deserta***, doing the work of an adjective, is also doing the work of the verb from which it is formed and which I translate, not as it is in the *DR*, as 'your desert land' but as 'your land [is] desolate' emphasising not just the land itself but the action that has created the desolation, hence expressing past time and passive voice, all emphasising more powerfully the idea of past time, than a simple adjective could. Similarly, in ***civitates vestrae succensae igni*** (your cities [are] burnt with fire) by using the passive voice for the past (perfect) participle ***succensae***, acting as an adjective, past time is signalled without including a separate verb as required in English (are burnt). Time is expressed in these examples then, through the participles of the verbs, and in this case are all past (perfect) passive participles. Present and future time are expressed in these examples by the active imperatives, but can also be expressed by participles as well. So, for example, when St Mark opens his *Gospel* in the third verse by referring to the prophecy recorded in *Isaias*:

> **Vox clamantis in deserto: Parate viam Domini, rectas facite semitas eius.**
> ([The] voice of crying in [the] desert: Prepare [the] way of [the] Lord, make straight his paths. *Mc* 1:3)

clamantis is the present active participle of the verb ***clamare*** (to cry out) written in the genitive masculine singular and functioning as a verbal adjective expressing present time, effectively meaning 'of one person crying', referring ahead cataphorically (καταφορά - 'downwards') in the text to St John the Baptist. Throughout St Mark's *Gospel* (and especially in St John's *Gospel*) and in other descriptive narratives throughout the *Vulgate* especially in the *New Testament*, the present active participle is used much more frequently than it is generally found in Classical Latin, influenced by translating the *Vulgate* into Latin from the original Greek. In the verse immediately following **Vox clamantis in deserto**, St Mark records that John (***Ioannes***) was:

> ***in deserto baptizans, et praedicans baptismum poenitentiae in remissionem peccatorum***
> (in [the] desert baptising, and preaching [the] baptism of penance, ontowards [the] remission of sins. *Mc* 1:4)

where the present active participles ***baptizans*** (***baptizare***) and ***praedicans*** (***praedicare***) are both declined as nominative masculine singular verbal adjectives describing St John's actions as the subject of the actions involved in baptising and preaching. Probably one of the most frequently occurring present active participles in the *Vulgate* narratives is *dicens* (*dicere* - to say) with over 200 occurrences in the *New Testament* books (with almost 850 in the whole of the *Vulgate*). In a prayer to St Joseph recommended for saying before Mass (**Preces Ad Sanctum Ioseph Ante Missam**) we pray:

> *O felícem virum, beátum Ioseph, cui datum est Deum, quem multi reges voluérunt vidére et non vidérunt, audíre et non audiérunt, non solum vidére et audíre, sed portáre, deosculári, vestíre et custodíre!*
> (O happy man, blessed Joseph, to whom was given God, not only to see and hear, but to carry, to embrace, to clothe and to watch over, whom many kings wished to see, and saw not, to hear, and heard not!)

The verbs are all active in voice except for ***datum est*** while ***deosculari*** is a deponent verb (passive in form but active in meaning) and together with all the verbs clearly signal who the agents of the verbs are: Joseph or the kings. The passive ***datum est*** does not, and we need to work out that the agent of the verb ***dare*** is God giving Jesus (as God) to Joseph, to see, hear, embrace, carry, clothe and protect. As a passive form ***datum est*** functions to distance the agent of the action; in this context, to make that agent more mysterious. Mystery should not be avoided in prayer, as seems to be a popular mantra in much contemporary Catholicism, but embraced head-on. It comes in many forms, including linguistic. St Matthew, for example, describes the moment after the Magi deliver their gifts when, as we pray in the *Gospel* for the Feast of the Holy Innocents (28 December) the Angel of the Lord (***Angelus Domini***) appeared to Joseph ***dicens*** (saying):

> *Surge, et áccipe púerum, et matrem eius, et fuge in Aegýptum*
> (Arise, and take [the] child and his mother, and flee into Egypt.
>   *Mt* 2:13)

LATIN PRAYER

> *Qui consúrgens accépit púerum et matrem eius nocte, et secéssit in Aegýptum:*
> (Who rising up took [the] child and his mother by night, and retired into Egypt: *Mt* 2:14)

where the present active participle of ***consurgere*** is written as a nom m sg to signal St Joseph as subject (***qui***) and which functions, like so many present active participles in descriptive narrative, not just as an attributive adjective, but by signalling time (present tense) and voice (active) and continuing (progressive) aspect, as a means of keeping the story or the action moving forward with verbal/narrative force. The *DR* actually misses this aspect by translating it as 'Who arose' and similarly Knox who translates it as 'He rose up'. But signalling this continuous aspect can be important in prayer (and in the praying of Scripture like this). This may be very clearly seen with the ***Praefatio Missae*** (Preface of the Mass) which changes according to seasons and some feast days, but which generally ends in similar ways prior to the singing of the ***Sanctus***, with the Priest praying:

> *Et ídeo cum Angelis et Archángelis, cum Thronis et Dominatiónibus, cumque omni milítia caeléstis exércitus, hymnum glóriae tuae cánimus, sine fine dicéntes: Sanctus, Sanctus, Sanctus...*
> (And therefore with [the] Angels and Archangels, with [the] Thrones and Dominations, and with all [the] company of [the] heavenly army, we sing [a] hymn to your glory without end saying: Holy, Holy, Holy...)

The present active participle ***dicentes*** here moves the action forward through the ***Sanctus*** to the next stage of the Mass. It is not simply descriptive of something that occurred in the past. Like the regular use of ***In illo tempore*** (At that time) prayed by the Priest or Deacon at the beginning of most *Gospel pericopes*, but not actually recorded in the *Gospel* itself, it is a stylistic device to move the narrative forward.

When understood in these terms, then, prayer is not just about the words being prayed (locutionary force) and it is not just about the acts being performed (illocutionary force) but also about the perlocutionary force, often indescribable in words, but as here, enabling the movement of the prayer of the Mass to continue in its momentum. More likely than not, if the word *dicentes* is heard by those at a *Roman Rite* **usus antiquior** Mass, it might simultaneously function as a signal to kneel for the **Sanctus** and for the server to ring the bell and, if included, to light the **sanctus** candle (an additional single candle placed on the *Epistle* side of the *gradine* (**gradus**- ledge) at the back of a High Altar [*Altare summum*]) which stays lit until after the Priest's Communion and signals Christ's real presence. This single candle replaces those used at this time (in a High Mass) if there are upwards of six (and a minimum of two) torch bearers (***ceroferarii***) available to process into the Sanctuary (led by the thurifer) with a lit processional candle each and (if room) generally kneel opposite each other before the altar and remain there until after the people's communion and the **Sanctissimum** has been placed back into the Tabernacle. Whatever may happen at this point in the Mass, the praying of this one word ***dicentes*** generally involves some considerable movement, from both server(s) and people, whether narratively in the Mass moving forward, or physically in the Sanctuary. There is a lot more happening in context than the word itself would suggest just lexically.

Narrative Prayer

The narrative of the Bible - the story it tells - permeates everything we pray in prayer, both privately and liturgically. From its opening verse in **Liber Genesis** to its closing verse in **Apocalypsis B Ioannis Apostoli**, the narrative is of God who creates and who deserves our worship and praise. God gave us laws to live by, and his Son who died to save us. Through his Son, God gave us the means to become Christians and to look to what we do, not only in this world, but towards eternal salvation in the next. Throughout that narrative, which stretches over many thousands of years in real time, we are called upon to pray, and, through that prayer, to acknowledge and worship God. Narratives (*narrare* - 'to tell'; 'to make known'; 'to describe'; 'to relate'; 'to report' and 'to recount'; 'to explain' and 'to set out') require a form in order for them to function. They describe, but they also expose. They communicate in words and images, but they also communicate actions, ideas, philosophies, histories, values, identities and theologies. Narratives require a narrator and what we might call a narratee - someone who tells the story and someone who receives the story. Narratives make meanings beyond the words of those narratives. When we pray narratives we not only pray those meanings, but we create new narratives; new meanings and new modalities usually with the same narrative forms.

Narrative does not just describe fiction; it creates realities. It offers the spaces in which to make meanings. Scriptural, theological, doctrinal and *Magisterial* narrative frames everything we do as Latin Catholics and everything we pray. Narrative creates perspective, and shapes our point of view. Narrative gives *focus* and *force* to the texts and contexts it enables. Just as narrative is not text-free (there is always some textual vehicle, words, actions or images, through which narrative flows) narrative is not context-free. We have seen the importance of the dynamic between text and context throughout this book in various ways. We have seen that narrative has *affect*. Narrative helps us make sense. We don't just read or see narrative; we experience it.

As we pray, often using words narrated liturgically by someone else, we become narrators ourselves. The narrative voice is shared; it is sociative, and liturgical prayer, especially, becomes a narrative dialogue, not just with someone else's words, but with those words prayed anew, by us, or on our behalf, as when the Priest strikes his breast and prays with slightly raised voice (from within the silent Canon of the *usus antiquior* Mass) ***Nobis quoque peccatoribus*** (also to us sinners). The ***narratio*** (narrative) of prayer is not just a way of repeating old stories or old words; the ***narratio*** of prayer is a channel and conduit to God. The narrative theology involved in the narrative of the liturgy is the authorising force which turns stories and words into prayer; what turns ideas and propositions into religious truths. It is the force which corporatises religious practice as an activity of community to become the ***Mystici Corporis Christi*** (Mystical Body of Christ, a phrase which Venerable Pope Pius XII used as synonymous with the Roman Catholic Church) as well as a personal expression. Scripture, liturgy and prayer are 'storied'. The Christian ***narratio*** is of redemption and salvation. It is both confession and creed. The Catholic ***narratio*** is all of this but with a narrative memory of over two thousand years: Tradition. Latin prayer within that Catholic ***narratio*** not only keeps that narrative memory alive, it recognises that memory is simply not recall of something that belongs in and to the past, but that it actively, and dynamically, 'stories' our consciousness of who we are in an unbroken 'economy of salvation'. The Catholic ***narratio*** is not a claim for an authentic Christianity only to be found in the pages of the *New Testament*, but an uninterrupted, expanding, narrative, where the lives of Saints, and Martyrs, and the development of doctrine are not found in the *Bible*; where rituals and practices develop over time; but where what it is to be a Latin Catholic is shaped (theologised) not simply by a historical narrative, but by the dynamism of time, Tradition and the formative power of the ongoing ***narratio*** of prayer.

The Council of Trent, as indeed all Councils of the Church, both reinforce existing narratives, especially in the light of new ones being created outside the Church, as for example, at the Reformation. So, contrary to the Lutheran assumption of justification by faith alone, Trent determined that 'a sorrow of soul and a hatred of sin committed, with a firm purpose of not sinning in the future' are the absolute essential requirements of confession, penance and contrition. To pray an Act of Contrition (***Actus Contritionis***) is the first step to reconciliation. The word ***contritus*** comes from the compounding of the preposition ***con/cum*** (with) and the verb ***terere*** (to rub/break/crush/grind). After the preposition ***con/cum*** Latin generally takes the ablative case to indicate manner, amongst other things, and so here we have an example of the ablative manner of being contrite: rubbing/grinding our sins away. This is far more than a state of mind or an attitude of sorrow. It is, in its roots, actually a very active process. Pope Leo X (1475-1521) made a clear distinction between 'perfect contrition', which emerges from a love of God who has been grievously offended, and 'imperfect contrition', because of an individual's fear, for example, of not going to Heaven or of going to Hell.

Traditionally, for the Catholic Church, contrition should not simply be an external articulation of repentance, but should be sincere and interior, and, therefore, perfect. It is also taught that contrition arises through God's grace and not from personal motives, and, as such, is supernatural. Furthermore, it should be universal in the sense that a very firm resolution is made not to sin in the future and, therefore, relatedly, contrition should always be 'sovereign': recognising sin as the greatest possible evil. While making an act of perfect contrition does obtain the forgiveness even of mortal sin, it does so only if there is an intention to properly receive the sacrament of penance as soon as possible. Making a perfect act of contrition, therefore, does not remove the obligation to go to confession. This confession is not simply about a Christian narrative encoded in the *New Testament*. It reflects the development of the Catholic Christian narrative over the centuries.

The traditional Catholic ***narratio***, which maintains Latin prayer and older rituals and practices, together with values and doctrines often seen as unfashionable and irrelevant in today's modern world, is not about preservation, but about moving the narrative memory ever forward in order to purposively transform. When the Priest prays the words of the consecration at Mass before the major elevation, he recounts the moment at the last supper when Christ:

> ... *accépit panem in sanctas, ac venerábiles manus suas: et elevátis óculis in caelum ad te Deum Patrem suum omnipoténtem, tibi grátias agens, benedíxit, fregit, dedítque discípulis suis, dicens: Accípite, et manducáte ex hoc omnes. Hoc est enim Corpus meum.*
>
> (... took bread into his holy and venerable hands: and with eyes having been lifted uptowards heaven intowards you God his Almighty Father, giving thanks to you, he blessed, broke, and gave [it] to his disciples, saying: Take!, and eat! from this all. For this is my Body.)

The phrase **elevatis oculis** (an 'ablative absolute' [*ablativus absolutus*]) adds further information about the actions accompanying the verb, most often about time and circumstance, and here means 'eyes having been lifted', but is often translated progressively as 'lifting up his eyes'. Ablative absolutes are frequently found in Latin prayer, and generally indicate the time, condition, or circumstance of a preceding action. Participles occur most frequently with the verb *esse* (to be) a grammatical structure known as 'periphrasis', which simply means that a combination of words (Greek περί [*peri* - around] and φράσις [*phrasis* -way of saying]) is being used, rather than a single inflection, to indicate a specific meaning. So, for example, when God is talking to Abraham after Lot was separated from him, God said:

> *Surge, et perambula terram in longitudine et in latitudine sua: quia tibi daturus sum eam.*
> (Arise!, and walk through! [the] land in [its] length and in its breadth: for I will give it to you. *Gn* 13:17)

The act of giving in the near future is expressed by using a future active participle *daturus* (*dare* - to give) together with a form of the verb *esse* (*sum*) so:

> *Dixitque Moyses Hobab filio Raguel Madianitae, cognato suo: Proficiscimur ad locum quem Dominus daturus est nobis: veni nobiscum, ut benefaciamus tibi, quia Dominus bona promisit Israëli.*
>
> (And Moses said to Hobab son of Raguel [the] Madianite, his kinsman: We are going towards [the] place which [the] Lord will give to us: come with us, so that we may do good for you, because [the] Lord promised good to Israel. *Nm* 10:29)

The future active participle *daturus* (*dare*) is similarly used to signify the act of giving in the near future, together with another form of the verb *esse* (*est*). At *Lauds* every day the *Canticle of Zachary* from St Luke's *Gospel* is prayed (the *Benedictus*) which records Zachary's words after he had declared his son would be named John (the future St John the Baptist) and that John would go:

> *ante fáciem Dómini paráre vias eius*
> (before [the] face of God to prepare his ways)
> *ad dandam sciéntiam salútis plebi eius in remissiónem peccatórum eórum*
> ([*for the purpose*] to be given knowledge of salvation to his people, toward the remission of their sins)
> *ad dirigéndos pedes nostros in viam pacis*
> ([*for the purpose of*] our feet to be directed intowards the way of peace. *Lc* 1:76-77)

dandam (to be given) is the future passive participle of *dare* (to give) and is expressed as an acc sg f of the participle *dandus* to agree with *scientiam* and *dirigendos* (to be directed) is the fut pass participle of *dirigere* and is expressed as an acc pl m of the participle *dirigendus* to agree with *pedes nostros*. Future passive participles (gerundives) like this, following the preposition *ad*, powerfully signal the purposive force of obligation and necessity in a Latin prayer, and while there is no past active participle in Latin, the Latin deponent verb tends to fill this function. For example, one of the most frequent constructions in the *Vulgate* involves the past participle of the deponent verb **locutus** (***loqui*** - to speak) occurring well over 500 times. So, when in Tuesday *Matins* the Psalmist struggles with the sins of his tongue and stays silent as long as he can, but then breaks his silence, we pray with him:

> *Locútus sum in lingua mea: notum fac mihi, Dómine, finem meum*
> (I spoke with my tongue: make! known to me, O Lord, my end. *Ps* 38:5)

where **locutus sum** is the perfect active participle of **loqui** (to speak) and formed with **sum** (I am) (***esse***) and would suggest a passive voice translation of 'I am have been spoken', but deponent verbs like **loqui** are only translated in Latin as if they are active voice, so here better translated as 'I spoke'. Similarly, in many places in the narratives of the *Gospels* Jesus is recorded as speaking to a crowd, or others, with a passive form but with an active meaning (a very frequent occurrence) for example:

> *et locutus est eis multa in parabolis, dicens...*
> (and he spoke to them many things in parables, saying... *Mt* 13:3)

Time and voice are very clearly significantly important concepts (and grammatical structures) in Scripture and prayer. Not perhaps as we might think of time in terms of ticking clocks, for example, but as the means (the agency) by (and through) which God reveals his divine plan: past, present, future. Every time we use a Latin verb in Latin prayer, we also engage with its sociative and spiritual modality. Every time we use a verb of 'being' (***esse*** - to be) we engage with the relational modality of those verbs. And there is always an *affect*.

Sociative Affect

In *Matins* of the 2nd Sunday in Lent we pray in the first Nocturn about the time when Isaac grew old and wished to pass on his inheritance with a blessing to his eldest son Esau, his mother Rebecca plotted to ensure that her youngest son Jacob would receive the blessing instead. Jacob was dressed to look (and feel) like Esau, and was taken to the now blind Isaac who said to him:

> *Quis es tu, fili mi?* (Who are you, O my son?)

and Jacob replied:

> *Ego sum primogénitus tuus Esáu* (I am Esau your firstborn (*Gn* 27:18-19)

Isaac then asked Jacob to come closer so he could feel whether he was Esau, and worried, said:

> **Vox quidem, vox Iacob est: sed manus, manus sunt Esáu.**
> ([The] voice indeed is [the] voice of Jacob; but [the] hands are [the] hands of Esau. *Gn* 27:22)

Unsure, he asked again:

> *Tu es fílius meus Esáu?* (Are you my son Esau?)

and Jacob replied:

> *Ego sum.* (I am. *Gn* 27:24)

So, thinking him to be Esau, he blessed him, but as soon as Jacob had left, Esau came in to receive his rightful blessing as the real firstborn son. Isaac said:

Quis enim es tu? (So, who are you?)

And Esau replied:

Ego sum fílius tuus primogénitus Esáu.
(I am your firstborn son Esau. *Gn* 27:32)

Isaac then realised what had happened, but the blessing could not be undone. Outraged that his younger brother had stolen his blessing, Esau pledged to kill him, and so Isaac sent Jacob away. Importantly, then, when Isaac asks *Quis es tu, fili mi?* (who are you O my son?) where the noun *filius* is in the vocative (*fili*) as a sign that Isaac is addressing his son, and the pronoun *meus* follows suit (vocative *mi*) in order to agree with its noun as masculine, vocative and singular, additional information is given about the nature of *filius*, that he belongs to Isaac. This is done by the use of the adjective *meus* which effectively acts grammatically as an attribute of possession. We have seen how adjectives attribute qualities and properties to their nouns, adding more information, and placing additional focus on them as they do here. Jacob responds by saying *Ego sum primogenitus tuus Esau* (I am Esau your firstborn) where the noun *primogenitus* is also given an attribute of possession by the adjective *tuus*, thus determining that the firstborn is 'your' firstborn and is not someone else (though as readers of this story we actually know differently). In a situation like this, where deceit and stolen identity is key to what is happening, this attribute of possession and the way it is signalled becomes very important, as linguistically it supports the deceit in the dressing up by Jacob as Esau. As adjectives, *meus* and *tuus* modify their nouns *filius* and *primogenitus*, changing the information we have about them, and therefore, changing their meaning. The attribute of possession is not something that can be seen, like the words themselves, and is therefore a perfect vehicle, in this context, for linguistically supporting the deceit. Effectively this is an additional (contextual) way of making meaning in the underlying structure and style of the language used here, and not just in the lexical content of the words.

We don't tend to learn about these contextual ways of meaning in traditional grammar books, but they can have considerable importance in Latin Scripture and prayer. Neither do we learn them formally when we are learning a language naturally as children. The understanding of these contextual subtleties comes from familiarity which, in turn, enables linguistic competency and (increasingly over the centuries) literacy. For example included in the *Raccolta* (collection) a book of devotions first published in Italian in 1807 and later in 1929 in Latin as **Collectio precum piorumque operum quibus Romani Pontifices in favorem omnium Christifidelium aut quorumdam coetuum personarum indulgentias adnexuerunt ab anno 1899 ad 1928** (Collection of prayers and pious works for which the Roman Pontiffs, for the sake of all the Christian faithful or certain groups of persons, have added indulgences, from the Year 1899 to 1928) in a prayer to Our Lady we pray:

> *O excellentíssima, gloriosíssima atque sanctíssima semper intemeráta Virgo María, Mater Dómini nostri Iesu Christi, Regína mundi et totíus creatúrae Dómina...*
>
> (O most excellent, most glorious, and most holy ever inviolate Virgin Mary, Mother of our Lord Jesus Christ, Queen of [the] world and Mistress of every creature...)

and bring to this prayer not only a recognition of the words, grammar and syntax being used, but also the entire history of our using similar words, grammar and syntax in similar prayers and similar contexts. We don't leave this sociative history behind when we start to pray a new prayer, nor do we leave behind the history of our praying other prayers, or reading about them, or hearing them prayed by others. We bring the whole of this intertextual history to bear, often unconsciously, but sometimes with greater awareness, when we pray. We can't forget that we have prayed like this before, even if there are new words. We are, therefore, praying the contexts as well as the texts. We are praying our knowledge, awareness and sense of Our Lady, and all of the attributes given to her in the beautiful opening of this prayer, not just in words, but in memories. We are praying new ways of making meaning. We pray at the end of this prayer:

> *In extrémis meis esto mihi pia auxiliátrix, et ánimam meam ac ánimas ómnium paréntum meórum, fratrum, sorórum et amicórum consanguineórum et benefactórum meórum omniúmque fidélium vivórum et defunctórum ab aetérna calígine et ab omni malo líbera, illo auxiliánte quem in tuo sanctíssimo útero novem ménsibus portásti et in praesépe tuis sanctis mánibus reclinásti, Dóminum nostrum Iesum Christum Fílium tuum, qui est benedíctus in sǽcula saeculórum. Amen.*

(In my last moments be to me [a] holy helper, and my soul and all [the] souls of my parents, brothers, sisters and friends, relatives and of my benefactors, and of all [the] faithful living and dead deliver from eternal darkness and from all evil, by him helping whom you carried in your most holy womb for nine months and laid in [the] manger with your holy hands, our Lord Jesus Christ your Son, who is blessed unto [the] ages of ages. Amen.)

We have clearly never experienced our last moment, but we bring to our understanding of it, all that we have heard, read, thought and prayed about. We were not at the manger, nor do we know what 'eternal darkness' really is, but our facility with language, even in one we have learnt or are still learning like Latin, enables us to follow the narrative journey of how the words, grammar and syntax all relate together. In our native language we do this instinctively, but in a learnt language like Latin we have to think about it. It is that 'thinking about it' which, as St John Henry Newman said, and who was fluent in learnt Latin, and was writing plays and poetry in it, at the age of 11, enables us to focus more, and concentrate more deeply, on the prayer. And when we do, we bring everything else we have ever prayed with us, consciously or not.

A phrase used by St Augustine, in a quite different context, encapsulates all of this in just 3 words: ***praesens de praeteritis*** (the present from [things] past) and generally understood as 'the past is ever present'. And so it is with prayer. Influential German Lutheran theologian and *Bible* exegete, Rudolf Bultmann (1884-1976) used a similar phrase when talking about our readings of Scripture, arguing that there are no 'presuppositionless readings' of the past. We do not read (or pray) without holding positions: some may be presuppositions; others may be firmly embedded realities. But they are all sociative in one way or another; they are none of them just 'of themselves'. The key, as Latin Catholics, is to ensure that the suppositions and presuppositions we bring to the reading of these texts is in accordance with the ***Magisterium*** of the Church, and not simply flights of our own fancy, or as St John Henry Newman talked of so often, our own 'private judgement'.

Henry of Ghent, who we briefly saw earlier, talked about our being (***esse essentiae*** ['being of essence']) as having ***aliquitas*** ('somethingness') and Franciscan scholastic philosopher and theologian and ***Doctor subtilis*** (subtle Doctor) Duns Scotus (John Duns 1265-1308) talked about ***haecceitas*** (*haecceity* ['thisness']) and ***Doctor Angelicus***, St Thomas Aquinas, talked of ***quidditas*** (*quiddity* ['whatness']) of 'being'. We no longer have such wonderful words like 'somethingness', 'thisness' and 'whatness' to describe the qualities and attributes of the ways in which 'being' and 'essence', and indeed, everything else, are not simply 'of themselves', because there is a God-given 'somethingness', 'thisness' and 'whatness' about everything. Gerard Manley Hopkins, whose Priestly 'career' was permanently restricted by his Jesuit superiors for his preference for Duns Scotus (as against St Thomas Aquinas) refers to this essence (especially *haeccity*) as 'inscape', and it is what allowed him to stare for hours at a single leaf, or stone on the ground, in awe at 'God's grandeur', making connections between the leaf, for example, and God himself, a process of making connections for which he used the term 'instress'. We are as we are, because God is as he is. In all things. In other words, we can understand our attributes, say of 'goodness', because we are able to share in God's attributes of 'goodness'. There is then, to use the word at the heart of this Chapter, a *sociative* relationship between 'inscape' and 'instress'; with the way we make meanings *because of* the way God makes meanings. In prayer that therefore means that we need to make anagogical meanings if we are to understand how our linguistic meanings mean relative to the way God means. And to do that we must learn how to read sociative contexts as well as linguistic texts. As a small child we may not recognise the word a parent uses to scold us, but we most certainly understand the tone, and its relational and sociative affect, regardless of the words used. We need to do that in prayer too. When, for example, Isaac says:

> **Vox quidem, vox Iacob est: sed manus, manus sunt Esau.**
> ([The] voice indeed, is [the] voice of Jacob; but [the] hands are [the] hands of Esau. *Gn* 27:22)

as readers we already know that a deceit is under way, but Isaac doesn't. He doesn't say 'Hmmm... something fishy here' (or at least its Hebrew equivalent) he repeats (in the *Vulgate* version) ***manus, manus...*** ([the] hands, [the] hands...) where the repetition itself signals hesitancy and thereby adds to the 'fishiness' of the situation. There is no lexical evidence in the word ***manus*** itself that signals that fishiness of any description, but the context is able to create an affect that means uncertainty, even though that meaning is not actually contained in the word ***manus***. A theatre director would take this moment, for example, and give both Isaac and Jacob other, non-linguistic, ways of making meaning here; other relational, and sociative, 'inscape signals' which an audience would pick up (instress) irrespective of the words being spoken. When Esau does come in to receive his rightful blessing in response to Isaac asking him who he is, he replies:

Ego sum filius tuus primogenitus Esau.
(I am your firstborn son Esau. *Gn* 27:32)

where Esau affirms that he is the *filius primogenitus*, as if to say, linguistically (just using the indicative *sum*) that there can be no room for mistaking who it is. But this simple indicative *sum*, to those of us witness to all that has gone on before, now means so much more.

The term 'indicative', when used like this in grammar generally has a very specific, denotative, meaning, usually referring to the grammatical mood of a verb which expresses, as here, a statement, declaration or a matter of fact, and assumes that what this mood is signifying grammatically is generally accepted to be true. This understanding of the indicative mood generally results in most of the verbs we use and encounter in Latin texts. But while in Latin prayer this denotative, 'dictionary-entry', understanding of the term 'indicative' in grammar, is a very common grammatical mood, there is a much wider range of connotative understandings for it. We can understand it to mean, amongst other things: 'apocalyptic', 'characteristic', 'comparative', 'corroborative', 'declarative', 'demonstrative', 'descriptive', 'designative', 'emblematic', 'evincive', 'evocative', 'exhibitive', 'explanatory', 'expositive', 'expressive', 'factual', 'illustrative', 'implicative', 'indicatory', 'inferential', 'interpretive', 'meaningful', 'pointed', 'predictive', 'referential', 'representative', 'revelatory', 'sensitive', 'significative', 'symbolic', 'testatory' and 'typical'. It is to the exploring of just some of this much broader indicative and layered range of meanings, and their spiritual/numinous connotations, in the *address, focus, force* and *affect* of (and in) Latin prayer that we now turn in *Chapter X: Indicative Prayer*.

X

INDICATIVE PRAYER

Cor hominis disponit viam suam, sed Domini est dirigere gressus eius.
(The heart of man orders his way, but the Lord is to direct his steps. *Prv* 16:9)

Time and Being

St Augustine argued in four simple Latin words a most complex philosophical position, that before God: ***non enim erat tunc*** (for there was not [being a] then) usually translated as 'There was no time before God'. God's time is an eternal present. But our own human experience is understood only in a time that we perceive as having a past, present and future. We understand the histories of ourselves, and others, through a narrative of time which we conceptualise through grammatical 'tense': mostly past, present and future. God is timeless but we are not. St Paul confirms in the *Epistle* prayed at the Mass (9th October) of St John Leonardi (1541-1609) who sought to instil greater discipline into the Church by implementing the teachings of the Council of Trent that we should refocus:

> *non contemplántibus nobis quae vidéntur, sed quae non vidéntur. Quae enim vidéntur, temporália sunt: quae autem non vidéntur, aetérna sunt.*
>
> (by not observing which [things] are seen to us, but those which are not seen. For [the] things which are seen, are temporal: but [the] things which are not seen, are eternal. *2 Cor* 4:18)

Ronald Knox translates this more freely, but very effectively, as:

> 'if only we will fix our eyes on what is unseen, not on what we can see. What we can see, lasts but for a moment; what is unseen is eternal.'

There is, then, a dynamic relationship between a temporal past, present and future time. But the place of 'time' in our prayer, as the things that are not seen, is 'eternal'. One is about the here and now; the other is about the numinous. Prayer seeks the eternal, but can actually only be prayed in the temporal, unless, of course we are granted the gift of seeing it mystically, like some of the Saints. We are, most of us, journeying in prayer between the beginning, which we can see (temporal) and the end (eternal) which we can't. Our relationship with God in prayer, then, is about our temporal relationship with the eternal; as St Augustine put it, time only exists because we were created to exist in time. Creation **ex nihilo** (out of nothing) makes no sense for St Augustine because for him there was never a 'time' when 'nothing' existed out of which creation was made: **non enim erat tunc** (for there was no then).

This understanding of time presents challenges for the pray-er. We think and pray in a language which is temporal; its grammar shapes our understanding of time; it shapes our relationships, because in our everyday world it is both a shared sociative and social, exchange. We function as human beings in this dynamic; in turn we are shaped by it; we identify who we are as individuals and as social groups, through it; we have no individual private language (idiolect) if we did we would have no one to talk to. But the initial way, at least, that we have as ordinary human beings, and not as those especially rare and gifted in non-linguistic mysticism, of talking to God, is through this same language. In effect, we assume, in prayer, a privacy in the language between us (pray-er and God) which is, in practice, an impossibility. There is no such thing as a 'private meaning' in language; it is **de facto** always a shared, sociative, meaning. Every meaning, and every understanding of that meaning, is an interpretation. We trust that the understanding we share in language with another person will be interpreted in the same way. And it is that trust that we must bring with us to our prayer. There is no other relational dynamic we can invoke. We are able to pray in temporal language because we are able to trust God to understand us. If trust is the absolute key to using language in our every-day situation, when the participants of that every-day are on equal terms with respect to the language in use, how much more, then, must that trust be fuller, and more complete, when that language is being used in our stunningly unequal journey to the numinous with God in prayer? If the language is incrementally heightened in prayer, as it is in hieratic Latin, so too must the trust be exponentially heightened. A hieratic language, like Latin, unlike a native mother tongue still spoken by us, and between us, in our everyday, reduces the temporality and contemporaneity of the language we are using in prayer, effectively reducing the 'noise' of the everyday that shapes everything we do in ordinary language. That does not mean that Latin is a better language than our ordinary vernacular; but it certainly makes the language of prayer less ordinary; less everyday. As we pray in Tuesday *Vespers*:

> *Qui confídunt in Dómino, sicut mons Sion: non commovébitur in aetérnum, qui hábitat in Ierúsalem.*
> (Who[ever] trusts in [the] Lord, [is] as mount Sion: [he/she] will not for ever be moved, who lives in Jerusalem. *Ps* 124:1-2)

In other words, we will be as unmoveable as Mount Zion if we believe. The Church metaphorically captures this journey to Mount Zion perfectly by structuring each year into liturgical seasons as the chronology of the year moves forward. The Liturgical Year has a quite different form of time to the chronological year; it is determined by events both in the Scriptural life of Christ and in the Tradition of the Church that, historically, are in the past, but which theologically are also in the present and in the future. The 'economy of liturgical time' in Latin prayer is not about when something happened, or the 'amount' of time spent in prayer, but the 'qualitative' use of that time across its seasons and feasts. It is perhaps best thought of as 'the economy of opportunity' so that the way we engage with the seasons and feasts of the year, and the teachings, scriptures, prayers and readings that underpin them, are opportunities for salvation.

If, every evening, we pray *Compline* (**Completorium**) the *Office* composed by St Benedict himself to 'complete' the day, and designed, in part, to enable us individually to focus upon our faults, we begin by seeking a blessing and a reminder for us all to be sober and watchful in the face of the cause of these faults. We examine our conscience and pray the **Confiteor** (I confess). The growing darkness (actual or metaphorical) in which we pray this *Office* here and now is the same darkness that enveloped Christ himself in the Garden of Gethsemane. That darkness is timeless, but *Compline* might take us, at the very most, just 30 minutes to pray. It completes the day, hence its name, but also takes us into 'sempiternal' time, reinforcing the simple fact that the *chronos* part of that time (χρόνος - *chronos* - sequential time) spent in *Compline* is not at all that relevant; what is, is the *kairos* (καιρός - *kairos* - season/moment) part. We might think of it as 'sempiternal' (forever) time and therefore demanding *sempiternal* prayer. We have one eye on the here and now, and the other eye on the future when **tempus non erit amplius** (time will be no longer *Apc* 10:6).

What does that mean, then, for praying in a language like Latin that has such distinct, and varied, grammatical forms for the past, present and future? Chronologically, in Latin prayer and Scripture, it means we are able to trace God's specific actions as actions in history, but it also means we are able to use those 'sempiternal moments' in time (past, present and future) to understand history as a redemptive history: as God's plan for redeeming the world which is ongoing and timeless. There are three great evangelical Canticles which are repeated every day in the Roman Rite liturgy: the **Benedictus** (*Lauds*) the **Magnificat** (*Vespers*) and the **Nunc Dimittis** (*Compline* but not in the *Benedictine Rite*) all of which speak volumes about those sempiternal moments. Prayed since at least the early 4th C *Compline* is a most beautiful way of ending the day. It begins by seeking a blessing **Iube, Dóm[i]ne, benedícere** (Bid, O Lord to bless) and is followed with a simple, but inspiring, subjunctive prayer:

> *Noctem quiétam et finem perféctum concédat nobis Dóminus omnípotens. Amen.*
> (May [the] Lord almighty grant to us [a] quiet night and [a] perfect end. Amen.)

This is immediately followed by the **Lectio Brevis** (short lesson):

> *Fratres: sóbrii estóte, et vigiláte: quia adversárius vester diábolus tamquam leo rúgiens círcuit, quaerens quem dévoret: cui resístite fortes in fide. Tu autem, Dómine, miserére nobis.* ℟. *Deo grátias.*
> (Brethren: be! sober, and keep watch!: because your adversary [the] devil circles about like [a]roaring lion, seeking whom he may devour: to whom resist! strong in faith. You, then, O Lord, be merciful to us. *1 Pet* 5:8 ℟. Thanks to/for God.)

After various *Psalms* (varying in the *PP* but unvarying [*Psalms* 4, 90 and 133] in the *MP*) and a hymn with a final Collect, *Compline* begins to draw to a close, as indeed the evening may do at this time, and we pray the beautifully evocative **Responsorium**:

℣. *In manus tuas, Dómine, comméndo spíritum meum.*
℟. *In manus tuas, Dómine, comméndo spíritum meum.*
℣. *Redemísti nos, Dómine, Deus veritátis.*
℟. *Comméndo spíritum meum.*
℣. *Glória Patri, et Fílio, et Spirítui Sancto.*
℟. *In manus tuas, Dómine, comméndo spíritum meum.*
℣. *Custódi nos, Dómine, ut pupíllam óculi.*
℟. *Sub umbra alárum tuárum prótege nos*

(℣. Intowards your hands, O Lord, I commend my spirit.

℟. Intowards your hands, O Lord, I commend my spirit.

℣. You have redeemed us, O Lord, God of truth.

℟. I commend my spirit.

℣. Glory to/for [the] Father, and to/for [the] Son, and to/for [the] Holy Spirit.

℟. Intowards your hands, O Lord, I commend my spirit.

℣. Keep us, O Lord, as the pupil of [an] eye.

℟. Under [the] shadow of your wings protect us.)

After which, in the *Roman Rite*, we pray the **Nunc Dimittis** with its varying antiphons according to the Feast (with the traditional English translation given here):

Nunc dimíttis ✠ *servum tuum, Dómine, secúndum verbum tuum in pace.*

(Lord, ✠ now lettest thou thy servant depart in peace, according to thy word.)

Quia vidérunt óculi mei salutáre tuum,

(For mine eyes have seen thy salvation)

Quod parásti ante fáciem ómnium populórum,

(Which thou hast prepared before the face of all people;)

Lumen ad revelatiónem Géntium, et glóriam plebis tuae Israël.

(To be a light to lighten the Gentiles, and to be the glory of thy people Israel.

Lc 2:29- 32)

Glória Patri, et Fílio, et Spirítui Sancto.

(Glory be to the Father, and to the Son, and to the Holy Ghost.)

Sicut erat in princípio, et nunc, et semper, et in sǽcula saeculórum. Amen.

(As it was in the beginning, is now and ever shall be, world without end. Amen *trad*)

Following which is the final, very beautiful, and unchanging, Collect (*Oratio*):

Orémus.
Vísita, quǽsumus, Dómine, habitatiónem istam, et omnes insídias inimíci ab ea longe repélle: Angeli tui sancti hábitent in ea, qui nos in pace custódiant; et benedíctio tua sit super nos semper. Per Dóminum nostrum Iesum Christum Fílium tuum, qui tecum vivit et regnat in unitáte Spíritus Sancti, Deus, per ómnia sǽcula saeculórum. Amen.

(Let us pray.
Visit, we beseech thee, O Lord, this habitation, and drive far from it all the snares of the enemy: let thy holy Angels dwell herein, to preserve us in peace; and may thy blessing be upon us evermore. Through Jesus Christ, thy Son our Lord. Who liveth and reigneth with thee, in the unity of the Holy Ghost, ever one God, world without end. Amen. *trad*)

We are affected by prayer. That is the point. It has sensuality. It is experiential. And as such we seek to be affected. We perhaps also seek consolations through prayer. But the more we pray, the more we may realise that it is not consolations that are best sought in prayer, but the God of consolations himself. This is not always an easy realisation to reach, and is a grace only given to us by God. This is sociative prayer writ large both spiritually and sometimes physically too.

Perhaps, of all the *Offices* we pray, *Compline* may well put us in mind of monasteries and convents as places of prayer, but also, perhaps, as places of intense silence, away from the noise of life. Indeed, they may be, but, for the most part, they existed, certainly as we now know of them from medieval records, especially during the day, and even when out of choir and reading/praying alone or while working, not quite as silent as perhaps we might now understand that word, or expect it to be in modern enclosed communities. The sound of reading and praying *sotto voce*; learning everything by rote by it being said out loud and repeated back, time and time again; memorising everything by repeating it out loud many times over; like *Compline* made the most easiest of all to memorise fully; practising the chants by having a teacher before you sing them, and then singing these back until they were memorised; ***lectio divina*** (spiritual reading) which would have begun by reading (or saying from memory) a text out loud several times and any number of other countless activities. These would all have created a constant buzz echoing throughout the medieval buildings. An almost ceaseless 'murmuration'. Silent, or otherwise, we most of us may not be able to pray as monks and nuns do, nor to be able to experience the joy of that constant communal prayer in a community dedicated to unceasing prayer, but we can pray privately at the beginning and end of our every day:

> *Actiónes nostras, quǽsumus, Dómine, aspirándo prǽveni et adiuvándo proséquere: ut cuncta nostra orátio et operátio a te semper incípiat, et per te coepta finiátur. Per Christum Dóminum nostrum. Amen.*

(Precede and accompany our actions, we beseech you, O Lord, with inspiration and help: so that our every prayer and activity may always begin from you, and through you may come to completion. Through Christ our Lord. Amen.)

Catholic Sensibilities

To help us come to that 'completion', the great Latinist Pope Clement XI, chiefly responsible for building up the superb resources of the Vatican library, composed *A Universal Prayer for All Things Necessary to Salvation*. It is one of the most comprehensive of Catholic prayers. It is not included in the liturgy, but is nevertheless a very succinct synthesis of Catholic doctrine and prayer:

Oratio Universalis
Credo, Dómine, sed credam fírmius;
spero, sed sperem secúrius;
amo, sed amem ardéntius;
dóleo, sed dóleam veheméntius.
(O Lord, I believe, but may I believe more firmly;
I hope, but may I hope more securely;
I love, but may I love more ardently;
I sorrow, but may I sorrow more passionately.)

Adóro te ut primum princípium;
desídero ut finem últimum;
laudo ut benefactórem perpétuum;
ínvoco ut defensórem propítium.
(I adore you as [the] first belief;
I desire [you] as [the] last aim;
I praise [you] as perpetual benefactor;
I invoke [you] as benevolent defender.)

The prayer opens with 8 simple indicatives which are absolutely central in expressing Catholic sensibility in prayer: *credo*; *spero*; *amo*; *doleo*; *adoro*; *desidero*; *laudo* and *invoco*, and recur time and time again throughout all Latin prayer. They effectively epitomise all that we would want to state as a matter of fact about ourselves and our desire to transform that indicative statement with a change of grammatical mood 'I believe' (indicative) to 'may I believe' (subjunctive): *credo/credam*; *spero/sperem*; *amo/amem* and *doleo/doleam* and the repetition throughout these two verses of the purposive adverb *ut* through to an even stronger one to be expressed indicatively before God. There is a journey involved in the opening of this prayer; and one expressed very poetically. The mood then shifts again in the third verse to the imperative:

> *Tua me sapiéntia dírige,*
> *iustítia cóntine,*
> *cleméntia soláre,*
> *poténtia prótege.*
> (Direct! me by your wisdom;
> enclose! [me] with [your] justice,
> comfort! [me] with [your] mercy,
> protect! [me] with [your] power.)

and we then use one very powerful indicative offering of self:

> *Offero tibi, Dómine, cogitánda, ut sint ad te;*
> *dicénda, ut sint de te;*
> *faciénda, ut sint secúndum te;*
> *ferénda, ut sint propter te.*
> (I offer to you, O Lord, [my] thoughts, that they may be towards you;
> [my] words, that they may be from you;
> [my] actions, that they may be according to you;
> [my] sufferings, that they may be through you.)

and then seek to make our indicative, God's indicative:

Volo quidquid vis,
volo quia vis,
volo quómodo vis,
volo quámdiu vis.
(I wish whatever you wish,
I wish because you wish,
I wish in [the] way you wish,
I wish for as long as you wish.)

Oro, Dómine: intelléctum illúmines,
voluntátem inflámmes,
cor emúndes,
ánimam sanctífices.
(I pray, O Lord: [that] you may illumine [my] understanding,
[that] you may inflame [my] will,
[that] you may cleanse [my] heart,
[that] you may sanctify [my] soul.)

Défleam praetéritas iniquitátes,
repéllam futúras tentatiónes,
córrigam vitiósas propensiónes,
éxcolam idóneas virtútes.
(May I weep for past iniquities,
may I repel future temptations,
may I correct sinful tendencies,
may I improve proper virtues.)

Tríbue mihi, bone Deus, amórem tui,
ódium mei,
zelum próximi,
contémptum mundi.

(Grant to me, O good God, [the] love of you,
hatred of me,
zeal for neighbour,
contempt of [the] world.)

Stúdeam superióribus oboedíre,
inferióribus subveníre,
amícis consúlere,
inimícis párcere.
(May I strive to obey superiors,
to support inferiors,
to have regard for friends,
to spare enemies.)

Vincam voluptátem austeritáte
avarítiam largitáte,
iracúndiam lenitáte,
tepiditátem fervóre.
(May I conquer passion [with] austerity,
greed [with] generosity,
anger [with] gentleness,
apathy [with] fervour.)

Redde me prudéntem in consíliis,
constántem in perículis,
patiéntem in advérsis,
húmilem in prósperis.
(Render! me prudent in counsels,
steadfast in dangers,
patient in adversities,
humble in prosperities.)

Fac, Dómine, ut sim in oratióne atténtus,
in épulis sóbrius,
in múnere sédulus,
in propósito firmus.
(Make! [it], O Lord, that I may be attentive in prayer,
temperate in feasting,
diligent in service,
firm in purpose.)

Curem habére innocéntiam interiórem,
modéstiam exteriórem,
conversatiónem examplárem,
vitam regulárem.
(May I make sure to have [an] innocent interior,
[a] modest exterior,
exemplary speech,
[a] regular life.)

Assídue invígilem natúrae domándae,
grátiae fovéndae,
legi servándae,
salúti promeréndae.
(May I be watchful in overcoming [the] weakness of nature,
cherishing grace,
observing [the] law,
working up to salvation.

Discam a te quam ténue quod terrénum,
quam grande quod divínum,
quam breve quod temporáneum,
quam durábile quod aetérnum.
May I learn from you how flimsy [is] this earth,
how grand that divine,

how fleeting this opportunity,
how durable that eternity.)

Da, ut mortem praevéniam,
iudícium pertímeam,
inférnum effúgiam,
paradísum obtíneam.
(Grant!, that I may anticipate death,
may greatly fear judgement,
may flee from Hell,
may obtain Paradise.)

Per Christum Dóminum nostrum. Amen.
(Though Christ our Lord. Amen.)

Grammatically this may appear to be very simple, but the sweep of grammar, from indicatives to subjunctives through imperatives and future tense commitments; from the accusative movement forward to ablatives of instrument and manner, suggests a majesty in the sense that the 'indicative personal *ego*' seeks in every line of this prayer to transform into the 'indicative Divine *ego*'. The grammar, however, is a much easier prospect than the numinous quest. It is a very demanding prayer; there is much here that, for many in this heavily secularised world, including Catholics, is no longer considered palatable; no longer 'acceptable', no longer thought appropriate or teachable. But Pope Clement XI knew that only too well in his own time composing this prayer in the face of the Jansenism then sweeping across France and southern Europe. His 1713 Apostolic Constitution **Unigenitus Dei Filius** (Only Begotten Son of God) issued against the skewed theology of Jansenism which, for example, denied the role of free will in our accepting God's grace, but which with 'perfect contrition' God would grant, whether or not we chose to accept it. This inevitably led to a concentration on sin and how to be 'perfectly' contrite. ***Unigenitus*** condemned in comprehensive detail 101 of Jansenism's claims and closed with:

> '*Declared and condemned* as false, captious, evil-sounding, offensive to pious ears, scandalous, pernicious, rash, injurious to the Church and her practice, insulting not only to the Church but also the secular powers, seditious, impious, blasphemous, suspected of heresy, and smacking of heresy itself, and, besides, favouring heretics and heresies, and also schisms, erroneous, close to heresy, many times condemned, and finally heretical, clearly renewing many heresies respectively and most especially those which are contained in the infamous propositions of Jansen, and indeed accepted in that sense in which these have been condemned.' *Vat*)

It is hard to imagine language like this now being used. But I include it here to demonstrate that being Catholic was never considered, as it seems to be increasingly viewed now by so many, as an easy option. It is not. But the Church recognises that as Catholics we can't do this alone. St Thomas Aquinas so brilliantly showed us in this following prayer that we always have the Blessed Virgin Mary to help us to properly dispose ourselves intowards God at any time:

> *O beatíssima et dulcíssima Virgo María, Mater Dei, omni pietáte pleníssima, summi regis fília, Dómina Angelórum, mater ómnium credéntium: in sinum pietátis tuae comméndo hódie et ómnibus diébus vitae meae corpus meum et ánimam meam, omnésque actus meos, cogitatiónes, voluntátes, desidéria, locutiónes, operatiónes, omnémque vitam, finémque meum: ut per tua suffrágia dispónantur in bonum, secúndum voluntátem dilécti Fílii tui Dómini nostri Iesu Christi: ut sis mihi, O Dómina mea sanctíssima, adiútrix et consolátrix contra insídias et láqueos hostis antíqui, et ómnium inimicórum meórum.*

(O most blessed and most sweet Virgin Mary, Mother of God, most full [with] all piety, daughter of [the] most high King, Lady of [the] Angels, mother of all believers: into [the] bosom of your piety I commend today and through all [the] days of my life, my body and my soul, and all my acts, thoughts, wishes, desires, conversations, activities and all [my] life and my final end: that through your prayers [these] may be disposed intowards good, according to [the] will of your beloved Son, our Lord Jesus Christ: that you may be to me, O my most holy Lady, helper and consoler against [the] evils and snares of [the] ancient enemy and against all of my enemies.)

This prayer echoes the very forceful indicative ***commendo*** of Pope Clement's Universal Prayer, and the transformation of our commending of all those things necessary from us to submit ourselves to God through the passive subjunctive ***disponantur***, recognising that all of what we need to do as Catholics is much better done through the prayers of the Blessed Virgin Mary who we pray may be our helper. This is a powerful way of indicatively asserting a central Catholic sensibility, that, contrary to Jansenist theology, we choose freely to commend ourselves to God, and we need help along this journey to do that. St Faustus of Riez (405-495) though sometimes controversial in his views, as a strong proponent for the role of our own free will in contrast to uncompromising ideas about predestination, knew this over 1,500 years ago, when he wrote that:

'To believe in God is to seek him in faith, to hope piously in him, and to pass into him by a movement of choice.'

'To pass *into* him' says it all. For example, early catechumens at the end of their long formation to be Christians were simply asked:

Credis in Deum?
(Do you believe intowards God?)

Their answer was indicatively simple, yet, like the question they were answering, theologically enormously complex:

Credo.
(I believe.)

This is not passive belief. It is active and we, pray privately as Catholics four absolutely central prayers which [Emeritus] Pope Benedict XVI included amongst over 20 other 'basic' prayers, in the Appendix of the *Compendium of the Catholic Church* (2005) recommending them to be learnt off by heart in both Latin and the vernacular, by all Catholics:

Actus Fidei
Dómine Deus, firma fide credo et confíteor ómnia et síngula quae sancta Ecclésia Cathólica propónit, quia tu, Deus, ea ómnia revelásti, qui es aetérna véritas et sapiéntia quae nec fallére nec falli potest. In hac fide vívere et mori státuo. Amen.

(Act of Faith. Oh Lord my God, with a firm faith I believe and confess each and every thing that the Holy Catholic Church teaches, because Thou, my God, has revealed all these things, who is eternal truth and wisdom, who can neither deceive nor be deceived. In this faith, I resolve to live and to die. Amen. *trad)*

Actus Spei
Dómine Deus, spero per grátiam tuam remissiónem ómnium peccatórum, et post hanc vitam aetérnam felicitátem me esse consecutúrum: quia tu promisísti, qui es infiníte potens, fidélis, benígnus, et miséricors. In hac spe vivére et mori státuo. Amen.

(Act of Hope. Oh Lord my God, I hope through Thy grace to obtain the forgiveness of all my sins and after this life eternal happiness, because Thou hast promised, who is infinitely powerful, faithful, kind, and merciful. In this hope, I resolve to live and to die. Amen. *trad)*

Actus Caritatis

Dómine Deus, amo te super ómnia próximum meum propter te, quia tu es summum, infinítum, et perfectíssimum bonum, omni dilectióne dignum. In hac caritáte vivére et mori státuo. Amen.

(Act of Love. Oh Lord my God, I love Thee above all things and love my neighbour because of Thee, because Thou art the greatest, infinite, and most-perfect Good, worthy of all my love. In this charity, I resolve to live and to die. Amen. *trad*)

Actus Contritionis

Deus meus, ex toto corde pǽnitet me ómnium meórum peccatórum, eáque detéstor, quia peccándo, non solum pœnas a te iuste statútas proméritus sum, sed praesértim quia offéndi te, summum bonum, ac dignum qui super ómnia diligáris. Ideo fírmiter propóno, adiuvánte grátia tua, de cétero me non peccatúrum peccandíque occasiónes próximas fugitúrum. Amen.

(Act of Contrition. Oh, my God, I am heartily sorry for having offended thee, and I detest all my sins, because I dread the loss of heaven, and the pains of Hell; but most of all because they offend thee, my God, who are all good and deserving of all my love. I firmly resolve, with the help of thy grace, to confess my sins, to do penance, and to amend my life. Amen. *trad*)

These are not liturgical prayers, but they hold within them the central indicative sensibilities of what it is to be active Catholics: ***credo*, *spero*, *amo*** and ***paeniteo***. Each of these indicative statements require action. They are not just descriptive maxims. As Catholics we 'do' 'believing', 'hoping', 'loving' and 'repenting', just as we 'do' the liturgy (***liturgiam facere***). We don't just simply, as a Priest, 'say' the liturgy, or as layperson just 'hear Mass'. We participate in it, as part of our journey to the numinous, as we do in these four indicative declarations of who we are, and what we do, as Catholics. St Anselm in his *Proslogion* (**Proslogium** - prayer/meditation/address) asks:

> *An invenisti, anima mea, quod quaerebas? Quaerebas Deum et invenisti eum esse quiddam summum omnium, quo nihil melius cogitari potest; et hoc esse ipsam vitam, lucem, sapientiam, bonitatem, aeternam beatitudinem et beatam aeternitatem; et hoc esse ubique et semper.*
>
> (Can it be that you found, my soul, what you were seeking? You were seeking God and you found him to be that certain highest of all, for whom nothing better is able to be thought; and he to be life itself, light, wisdom, goodness, eternal blessedness and blessed eternity; and he to be everywhere and always.)

We cannot begin to understand this wonderful declarative/indicative statement of who God is except in numinous/mystical terms. Those terms are perfectly captured when we pray in Wednesday *Matins*:

> *Vacáte, et vidéte quóniam ego sum Deus; exaltábor in géntibus, et exaltábor in terra.*
>
> (Be still!, and see! that I am God; I will be exalted among [the] nations, and I will be exalted within [the] earth. *Ps* 45:11)

which in a single, most beautifully expressed indicative statement (*ego sum Deus*) encapsulates the very core (and also unimaginability) of who it is we seek, when we meditate and pray. Pope St John XXIII well understood the difficulties involved in this when he recorded in his *Journal of a Soul*:

> 'I profess to aim at perfection but in practice I like the way of perfection to be mapped out by me and not by God.'

Indeed. Living God's ways is not always easy. And Latin Catholic ways are not as easy as the world's ways, or indeed now of much of contemporary Catholicism's ways. We cannot begin to understand, for example, the indicative nature of the Holy Trinity, except in numinous/mysticalterms, lifting the seemingly simple linguistic (and explainable) indicative declaration that 'God is Three in One', into the realm of the complex numinous (and spiritually unexplainable) declaration. As Catholics we pray:

credo Ecclésiam (I believe the Church)

not:

credo in Ecclésiam (I believe in/into the Church)

but we do pray:

credo in Deum (I believe in/intowards God)

which, for this indicative phrase to make any sense at all, requires it to be prayed through a a numinous lens. As St Faustus said: we 'pass into God by a movement of choice'. But wherever, and however, we pray, prayer is about God's time, not ours, and 'time' we are told in **Liber Genesis** (and asserted as we saw earlier by St Augustine) it had its beginnings with creation. God is the God of life, space and time. As humans we are limited by that life, space and time. God is not limited, as we pray in Thursday *Lauds*:

quóniam mille anni ante óculos tuos tamquam dies hestérna
(because a thousand years before your eyes [are] like yesterday *Ps* 89:4)

But in prayer we can seek to share in that sense of limitless time in God's time; in Christ as the *Alpha* and *Omega* of all time. Père Pierre Teilhard de Chardin (1881-1955) a Jesuit priest who devoted his whole life to trying to understand Christ as simultaneously the beginning and the end, whilst often leading the way as a world-renowned palaeontologist, talked and wrote often about our need to understand 'the slow work of God'. We were created by the God of time, he argued, as spiritual beings. Deep within us, both as individuals and collectively as the human race, there is a spiritual (cosmic) power which, if harnessed, can change us and the world. The way to that spiritual power is through prayer.

Albert Einstein (1879-1955) whose life span ran almost simultaneously with Teilhard's, changed the entire scientific world by arguing that time is relative: its beginning is its end and its end its beginning. He accepted God as a force in the Universe who reveals himself in the 'orderly harmony' of the Cosmos. But Teilhard de Chardin went much further, and centred his whole life upon the Mass, **Officium Divinum** and prayer in general, even when travelling in the middle of nowhere, as a means of harnessing the spiritual power placed within him by God, and at the heart of all humanity, in the Universe/Cosmos. Church authorities struggled with some of his teachings, and to this day there is a ***monitum*** (warning) about using some of his writings for teaching, particularly those on the way in which he viewed humanity evolving as a spiritual being, and of our being collaborators in creation. But he accepted Christ as the Lord of all time, which we pray in the *Epistle* in the Mass (6 December) of St Nicholas of Myra/Bari (270-343) one of the Bishops who approved the first part of the *Nicene Creed* in the First Council of Nicaea (325 AD) as:

Iesus Christus heri, et hódie: ipse et in sǽcula.
(Jesus Christ yesterday, and today: and himself [the] same for ever. *Heb* 13:8)

In his commentary on *1 John, Tract 2*, St Augustine engages with this relationship of past, present and future time with respect to God, and writes:

> ***Deus autem esse tantum novit, fuisse et futurus esse non novit.***
> (For God knows only to be, and does not know to have been and to be about to be.)

God is, therefore, always dynamically indicative, irrespective of time.

The Indicative Dynamic

This timelessness of God, St Augustine expresses by the active infinitive *esse* (to be) and argues that the past (expressed by the passive infinitive *fuisse* - 'to have been') and the future (expressed by the active future participle + active infinitive *futurus esse* [to be about to be]) are not useful descriptors of God who is 'time' itself; is 'being' itself. He went on to talk of this timeless essence of God (***Qui est***: 'Who is' [*Ex* 3:14]) as ***actus essendi***, 'an act of being', expressed here by Aquinas with a distinctive future participle *essendus* for the verb *esse*. Henry of Ghent talked about the *esse essentia* (the being of essence) using an infinitive, and Duns Scotus (though not always agreeing with Aquinas or Henry of Ghent) similarly used the infinitive *esse* to indicate 'the act of being'. They did so because there is no present participle of *esse* in Classical Latin, but a new form (*ens*) was developed in Medieval Latin, especially as used by Aquinas in his discussions on the metaphysics of 'being', with phrases like ***ens commune*** ('being in common') in arguments differentiating essence and existence. Like all participles, *ens* declines like an adjective, so ***de ente*** is the ablative singular form of the present participle *esse* 'on being', part of the title of Aquinas' book ***De Ente et Essentia*** (On Being and Essence) where he talks of God as 'First Being/Cause', writing:

> *Patet ergo quod intelligentia est forma et esse et quod esse habet a primo ente, quod est esse tantum. Et hoc est causa prima, quae Deus est.*
>
> (It is clear therefore that intelligence is form both to be [*existence*] and that it has to be [*existence*] from the first being, that is to be [*existence*] alone. And this is [the] first cause, which is God. §80)

Aquinas tends to use ***ens*** when referring to the idea of 'being' in the abstract form, or as applied to us (***ens ipsum*** - being itself) but uses the present infinitive *esse* (***esse ipsum*** - being himself) as a way of expressing the being (timeless existence) of God. God understood as 'existence' tends to give way to understanding God as 'essence' so that ***ipsum esse subsistens*** (subsisting existence itself) using the present participle of *subsistere* - to stand still/remain) begins to be expressed as ***ipsa essentia subsistens*** (subsisting essence itself). This is not the place to enter into these scholastic debates which went on for years, suffice it to say that these debates were not pointless (as some may say, with them ending up arguing about how many Angels could fit on the head of a pin) but were all genuine attempts to find a way of thinking linguistically about the numinously impossible task of understanding what really is involved in a seemingly simple indicative like ***Deus est*** or ***Ego sum***. This was a medieval scholastic search for a vocabulary in which to talk about God, using language, all of which is incapable of properly expressing God, let alone explaining him.

The *Athanasian Creed* (***Quicumque vult*** - Whoever wishes) was composed in the 6thC to confirm the teachings of Nicene theology in the face of Arianism (which denied the Divinity of Christ) and though named after St Athanasius I of Alexandria (296-373) was not actually written by him. It is no longer prayed publicly in the ***usus recentior*** liturgy, and now only on Trinity Sunday in the ***usus antiquior*** *Office of Prime*. But within it, we see the force of this search for a vocabulary (using *esse*) in action. Inadequate language is being used to express the inexpressible theology of God as 'being'; as 'essence'; as Trinity.

This Creed is often summarised diagrammatically by the ***Scutum Fidei Christianae/Scutum Sanctae Trinitatis*** (Shield of Christian Faith/Shield of [the] Holy Trinity) known to us in this form since at least the early 12thC, and pictured (from a stained glass window in an East Anglian church, UK) on the covers of this book:

Scutum Fidei Christianae

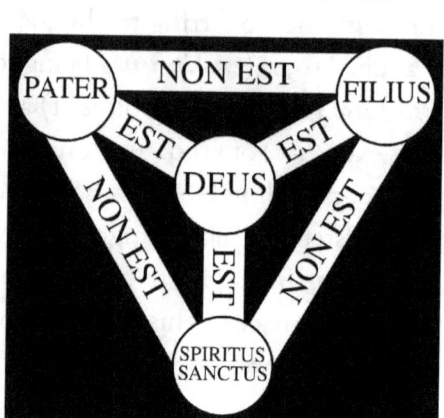

This shows clearly not only the three Persons of the Trinity, but their indicative relationships with each other, linked by the copula verb *esse*. Each of the Persons is named in the nominative form and the relationships between ***Pater*** and ***Deus***; ***Filius*** and ***Deus*** and ***Spiritus Sanctus*** and ***Deus*** are diagrammatically clear, but theologically extremely complex, and often formed the central subjects of debates sometimes lasting centuries.

- ***Pater est Deus*** ([The] Father is God)
- ***Filius est Deus*** ([The] Son is God)
- ***Spiritus Sanctus est Deus*** ([The] Holy Spirit is God)
- ***Deus est Pater*** ([The] Father is God)
- ***Deus est Filius*** ([The] Son is God)
- ***Deus est Spiritus Sanctus*** ([The] Holy Spirit is God)

- *Pater non est Filius* ([The] Father is not [the] Son)
- *Pater non est Spiritus Sanctus* ([The] Father is not [the] Holy Spirit)
- *Filius non est Pater* ([The] Son is not [the]Father)
- *Filius non est Sanctus Spiritus* ([The]Son is not [the] Holy Spirit)
- *Sanctus Spiritus non est Pater* ([The] Holy Spirit is not [the] Father)
- *Sanctus Spiritus non est Filius* ([The] Holy Spirit is not [the] Son)

Each of these propositions is intransitive, that is, the relationship between the nouns **Deus, Pater, Filius** and **Spiritus Sanctus** and the verb *est* is not one of dependency (as it would be in a transitive relationship) but a complementary relationship. **Filius** is complementary to **Deus**, not dependent upon it. In other words, the nouns in this proposition (and in the other eleven) are in an indicative relationship of equivalence. Understanding that the sociative relations between the persons of God are intransitive (equivalent) and that between pray-er and these persons of the Trinity are transitive (non-equivalent) is an absolutely key element at the heart of all prayer. Transitive and intransitive relations are central to the way meanings might be made, and especially in prayer, where those meanings are more often than not about the incomprehensibility and mystery of God, seen, most effectively here, in the metaphysical contrast between **Deus est** and **Deus non est**. This *est/non est* relationship is not, as some might think, a dispiriting negative apophatic theology, but an opportunity to understand and to grasp, even very partially, some of the cataphatic indicative mystery involved in why (and what it is we do when) we pray. It is this opportunity that lies at the heart of prayer. Inevitably this means, as I have returned to in each chapter of this book so far, that we are involved in yet another form of movement in prayer: from the dynamic exchange of our every-day language, where meanings only mean because we share interpretations, to the numinous dynamic where meanings mean, not because of anything we do, except to accept with the Psalmist when we pray at Monday *Sext* that:

> *in mánibus tuis sortes meae*
> (my parts [fate] [are/is] in your hands, *Ps* 30:15)

And again, as we pray at Friday *Vespers*:

> ***Ecce, Dómine, tu cognovísti ómnia, novíssima et antíqua. Tu formásti me, et posuísti super me manum tuam.***
> (Behold, O Lord, you have known everything, [the] newest and [the] oldest. You have formed me, and laid your hand upon me. *Ps* 138:5)

There are three verbs in this short verse: ***cognovisti***, ***formasti*** and ***posuisti***. They are all expressing the same thing about 'time'. That it is 2nd pers sg perf tense act ind of the three infinitives: ***cognoscere*** - to know; ***formare*** - to form/shape and ***ponere*** - to place/lay hands on/ordain. The form may change (*cognovisti* compared to *formasti* and *posuisti*) but exactly the same function of time is being expressed. Time is relative in prayer: but to God's time (*kairos*) not ours (*chronos*). As the writer of **Liber Ecclesiastes** says:

> ***Omnia tempus habent, et suis spatiis transeunt universa sub caelo.***
> (All things have [their] time, and [in] their spaces [times] all things pass under heaven. *Eccle* 3:1)

The Latin words ***tempus*** and ***spatium*** can mean both 'time' and 'space' simultaneously, something that would not have escaped Teilhard's attention when all around him fellow scientists like Einstein were finding new, and very radical, ways of understanding the space-time continuum. As Teilhard knew, and which Einstein and later Stephen Hawking

(1942-2018) also knew, but perhaps in not quite the same way as Teilhard, God had got there first. God always gets there first. Teilhard de Chardin recognised this so vividly with St Paul, and would have prayed this many times in his life in the *Epistle* for the 1st Sunday in Lent:

> *Témpore accépto exaudívi te, et in die salútis adiúvi te. Ecce nunc tempus acceptábile, ecce nunc dies salútis.*
>
> (In [a] welcome time I heeded you, and in [the] day of salvation I helped you. Behold, now is [the] acceptable time, behold, now is [the] day of salvation. *2 Cor* 6:2)

Even though grammatically there is a distinction being made between past time (***exaudivi**; **adiuvi***) and present time (***nunc** [**est**]*) the whole point of St Paul's teaching here, about Christ's own teaching, is that what might appear to be past is present, and what might appear to be present, is past. There is a dynamic relationship (what Einstein referred to as 'relativity' in a different context) in God's time which, though expressed in these Latin words in human time, leads us to better understand what Teilhard referred to when he thought of us not as 'physical beings having a spiritual experience' but as 'spiritual beings having a physical experience'.

Language does not get in the way of this spiritual experience; it enables it in a way that stands counter to much contemporary belief in today's Church and liturgy, that somehow language, especially so-called difficult language like Latin, or 16thC English translations of that Latin, distance us from God; that we will be 'nearer to God' if we use more contemporary language. Such views, common as they are post Reformation (and post *Vatican II* in contemporary Catholic circles) fundamentally misunderstand 'time' and 'language' and our role in them with respect to prayer, and most certainly with respect to God. Latin gets us no closer to God than any other language, but what it can do is to distinguish the extraordinary from the ordinary and the sacral from the everyday in a way that using the language of the street does not.

Spiritualised Metaphor

In a short prayer which has, at its heart, the indicative essence of all Latin prayer, we pray:

In te credo, in te spero, te amo, te adóro, beáta Trínitas unus Deus, miserére mei nunc et in hora mortis meae et salva me. Amen.

(I believe in you, I hope in you, I love you, I adore you, blessed Trinity, one God; be merciful! to me now and at [the] hour of my death and save! me. Amen.)

The present active indicative here indicates that the action has not been completed; it is not over. The statements that are made declare the subject of the verb 'I' to be the agent of the action. It is 'I' who believes, who hopes, who loves and who adores. These forms of the indicative address the action in the present time, but there is a very forceful sense that this is not a one-off action in present time, but is a continuing action. This is further emphasised by the present active imperative verbs, *miserere* and *salva* which both suggest a continuing force at work. This is just one of the major ways of illustrating the often complex spiritual and theological aspects of the indicative narrative of salvation as it is laid out in various ways in both the *Bible* and through Tradition, and by various people, including Jesus himself, often with figurative metaphor. Effectively we have little choice but to use metaphor when the often unexplainable is attempted at being explained using language. For example, St John records Jesus saying, and which is prayed in the *Alleluia* of the Common of One Martyr outside of Eastertide:

Ego sum lux mundi: qui séquitur me, non ámbulat in ténebris, sed habébit lumen vitae.

(I am [the] light of [the] world: who follows me, walks not in darkness, but will have [the] light of life. *Io* 8:12) and:

> *quamdiu sum in mundo, lux sum mundi*
> (while I am in [the] world, I am [the] light of [the] world *Io* 9:5)

There is no other way of getting this message across linguistically except by metaphor (in this case 'light') because how else, except through metaphor, might Christ explain who he is to people who have no other means of meaning available to them other than language? We are helped to understand this metaphor by recognising the force of the indicative modality of the iterative *sum*; we recognise the ablative force of *in mundo* and the genitive focus provided by the attributive *mundi*, and this grammatical literacy (even if we don't know the technical terms) provides a framework for our instinctive understanding of what is effectively not readily understandable in ordinary language: the power and force of the glorified Incarnate Son of God. But we can only get a little closer to that understanding, in any language, by the metaphor provided by Christ himself, using an image we do understand: *lux*. Just as we do in the glorious procession into a church at the opening of the magnificent *usus antiquior* Easter Vigil, when the coals have been ignited with a flint, and the Paschal Candle ignited and carried into the completely dark church to the sound of **Lumen Christi** ([the] Light of Christ) sung three times on ever higher tones. This single flame, as a sacramental, if looked after properly, and kept burning permanently from Sanctuary lamp to Sanctuary lamp, for example, should then ideally be the source of light for every candle and thurible ever lit in this church from this moment on until the next Easter Vigil creates a new one. To do so successfully, as a Sacristan, for example, is a source of unparalleled satisfaction. But a remarkably rare (and increasingly difficult) occurrence these days, but one still worth attempting, particularly within an enclosed Religious Community that might still have, or can still create, the required discipline, to do this. The luminous metaphor is a powerful one, as is all numinous metaphor. When St John records Jesus saying to St Martha:

> *Ego sum resurrectio et vita: qui credit in me, etiam si mortuus fuerit, vivet*
> (I am [the] resurrection and [the] life: who believes in me, even if [he/she] will have died, will live *Io* 11:25)

The force of the indicative **sum** almost demands an answer to the questions 'I am what?; I am whom?'. The answer, while a declaration of what might be a simple fact for Angels and Saints in Heaven to understand, may only be expressed metaphorically in our human world, as St John himself records in the preceding chapter, **autem non cognoverunt** (for they understand not *Io* 10:6). How could we understand when it all seems so not of our own world? But we are helped, by Jesus himself (as recorded in the *Vulgate*) to make this interpretive leap, by his using the active indicatives **credit** and **vivet**. The force of the change in tense from the indicative active present (**credit**) to the future active indicative **vivet** through the future perfect active indicative **fuerit**, doesn't explain the difficult metaphor of 'dying in order to live', but it gives us familiar ground as people used to using language as a principal means of understanding things. That was true for those Jesus was speaking to 'then' is as true for us 'now'. This use of metaphor is at the heart of Scripture and prayer, as we variously prayer in the Mass and *Office*:

> *Numquid non ipse est pater tuus, qui possédit te, et fecit, et creávit te?*
> (Is he himself not your father, who possessed you, and made, and created you? *Dt* 32:6)

> *Et nunc, Dómine, pater noster es tu, nos vero lutum; et fictor noster tu, et ópera mánuum tuárum omnes nos.*

(And now, O Lord, you are our father, we are truly clay; and you are our sculptor, and we [are] all [the] works of your hands. *Is* 64:8)

Numquid non pater unus ómnium nostrum? Numquid non Deus unus creávit nos? Quare ergo déspicit unusquísque nostrum fratrem suum, víolans pactum patrum nostrórum?
(Is there not one father for us all? Has not one God created us? Why then does every one of us despise his brother, violating [the] covenant of our fathers? *Mal* 2:10)

Unus Deus et Pater ómnium, qui est super omnes, et per ómnia, et in ómnibus nobis.
(One God and Father of all, who is above all, and through all, and in us all. *Eph* 4:6)

Qui regis Israël, inténde; qui dedúcis velut ovem Ioseph. Qui sedes super chérubim, manifestáre.
(Listen! [you] who rules Israel; [you] who leads Joseph like [a] sheep. [You] who sits above [the] cherubim, to make manifest. *Ps* 79:2)

Quia haec dicit Dóminus Deus: Ecce ego ipse requíram oves meas, et visitábo eas..
(For this says [the] Lord God: Behold I myself will seek my sheep, and I will visit them...)
Sicut vísitat pastor gregem suum, in die quando fúerit in médio óvium suárum dissipatárum, sic visitábo oves meas, et liberábo eas de ómnibus locis in quibus dispérsae fúerant in die nubis et calíginis.
(As [the] shepherd visits his flock, in [the] day when he will have been in [the] midst of his dispersed sheep, so I will visit my sheep, and I will deliver them out of all [the] places in which they had wandered in [the] day of cloud and mist.)

Et edúcam eas de pópulis, et congregábo eas de terris, et indúcam eas in terram suam, et pascam eas in móntibus Israël, in rivis, et in cunctis sédibus terrae.

(And I will lead them from [the] peoples, and I will gather them from [the] lands, and I will lead them into their own land, and I will feed them on [the] mountains of Israel, by [the] rivers, and in all [the] settlements of [the] land.)

In páscuis ubérrimis pascam eas, et in móntibus excélsis Israël erunt páscua eárum: ibi requiéscent in herbis viréntibus, et in páscuis pínguibus pascéntur super montes Israël.

(In [the] most fertile pastures I will feed them, and on [the] highest mountains of Israel will be their pastures: where they will rest in verdant grass, and in rich pastures they will be nourished above [the] mountains of Israel.)

Ego pascam oves meas, et ego eas accubáre fáciam, dicit Dóminus Deus.

(I will feed my sheep, and I will make them to lie down, says [the] Lord God.)

Quod períerat requíram, et quod abiéctum erat redúcam, et quod confráctum fúerat alligábo, et quod infírmum fúerat consolidábo, et quod pingue et forte custódiam: et pascam illas in iudício.

(What had wandered I will seek, and what was lost I will bring back, and what had broken, I will mend: and what had been sick I will restore, and what was fat and strong I will preserve: and I will feed them in judgement. *Ez* 34:11-16)

Ego sum pastor bonus. Bonus pastor ánimam suam dat pro óvibus suis.

(I am [the] good shepherd. [The] good shepherd gives his soul for his sheep. *Io* 10:11)

Et ait: Dóminus petra mea, et robur meum, et salvátor meus.
(And he said: [the] Lord [is] my rock, and my strength, and my saviour. *2 Reg* 22:2)

Dixit autem eis Iesus: Ego sum panis vitae: qui venit ad me, non esúriet, et qui credit in me, non sítiet umquam
(Jesus thus said to them: I am [the] bread of life: who comes to me, will not hunger, and who believes in me, will never thirst. *Io* 6:35)

Et ego Ioánnes vidi sanctam civitátem Ierúsalem novam descendéntem de caelo a Deo, parátam sicut sponsam ornátam viro suo.
(And I John saw [the] holy city [the] new Jerusalem coming down from heaven from God, prepared as [a] bride adorned for her husband. *Apc* 21:2)

Et dixit mihi: factum est: ego sum Alpha et Omega, inítium et finis. Ego sitiénti dabo de fonte aquae vitae, gratis.
(And [he] said to me: it is done: I am Alpha and Omega, [the] beginning and [the] end. For [those] thirsting I will give from the fountain of the water of life, freely. *Apc* 21:6)

Ego sum vitis, vos pálmites: qui manet in me, et ego in eo, hic fert fructum multum, quia sine me nihil potéstis fácere.
(I am [the] vine; you [are the] branches: who remains in me, and I in him, this brings much fruit, for without me you are able to do nothing. *Io* 15:5)

Díligam te, Dómine, fortitúdo mea. Dóminus firmaméntum meum, et refúgium meum, et liberátor meus. Deus meus adiútor meus, et sperábo in eum; protéctor meus, et cornu salútis meae, et suscéptor meus.

(I will love you, O Lord, my strength. [The] Lord [is] my firmament, and my refuge, and my deliverer. My God [is] my helper, and I will hope in him; my protector, and [the] horn of my salvation, and my support. *Ps* 17:2-3)

Dicit ei Iesus: Ego sum via, et véritas, et vita. Nemo venit ad Patrem, nisi per me.

(Jesus says to him: I am [the] way, and [the] truth, and [the] life. No one comes towards [the] Father, unless through me. *Io* 14:6)

Vos estis sal terrae. Quod si sal evanúerit, in quo saliétur? ad níhilum valet ultra, nisi ut mittátur foras, et conculcétur ab homínibus.

(You are [the] salt of [the] earth. What if [the] salt will have faded, in what will [it] be salted? [it] is worth nothing more, unless that [it] may be thrown out, and be trampled on by men. *Mt* 5:13)

Simile and metaphor like this address other realities; attribute other names and identities and focus the narrative onto other worlds, other possibilities and new horizons. They seek to provide a vocabulary for expressing, and to some extent, explaining, what language is not really able to do. They do so in many different ways, and in Scripture, prayer and liturgy, many times. At the blessing of the ashes before the **usus antiquior** Ash Wednesday Mass (Feria IV **Cinerum**) the Priest prays:

Omnípotens sempitérne Deus, parce pœniténtibus, propitiáre supplicántibus, et míttere dignéris sanctum Angelum tuum de caelis, qui benedícat, et sanctíficet hos cíneres, ut sint remédium salúbre ómnibus nomen sanctum tuum humíliter implorántibus...

(Almighty and everlasting God, spare those who are penitent, be merciful to those who implore Thee; and vouchsafe to send Thy holy Angel from heaven, to bless and sanctify these ashes, that they may be a wholesome remedy to all who humbly implore Thy holy Name... *Trad*) as he blesses the ashes in the first of four Collects. This is not ordinary language at all. The metaphor of *cineres* (ashes) being *remedium salubre* (a wholesome remedy) is likely to seriously disrupt our sensibilities of what we consider normal. But this powerful metaphor works, because we see the actual ashes being blessed, crushed from the burnt palms of last year's Palm Sunday, and we know that we are soon to be signed with the *signum crucis* on our foreheads with them. We understand the physical nature of the ashes, but ashes as the 'wholesome remedy', and how that works, will always be a mystery. But the metaphor works because it enables us to pray with the Priest and meditate upon the messages within the Collect. In the English *usus recentior* rite at the similar moment the Priest prays:

> 'Dear brethren [*or brothers and sisters*],
> let us humbly ask God our Father
> that he be pleased to bless with the
> abundance of his grace these ashes, which
> we will put on our heads in penitence.'

which, with respect to the *usus recentior* liturgy, is certainly lacking in *gravitas*. Simile and metaphor in prayer, no matter how extraordinary they may seem to our everydayness, lift us from the crass and banal of that everyday, to the mysteries that are God, including by simile and metaphor, which, more often than not, bring the dynamic of prayer to life in a way we might better understand, but which in so doing, can also disrupt our ordinary sensibilities. At the *usus antiquior* Epistle of the same Mass we pray as the Priest (or Sub-Deacon or Lector) prays from the *Prophecy of Joel*:

> *Nunc ergo, dicit Dóminus, convertímini ad me in toto corde vestro, in ieiúnio, et in fletu, et in planctu.*
> (Now therefore, says [the] Lord, be converted! intowards me within your whole heart, within fasting, and within weeping, and

within mourning. *Iol* 2:12)

> *Et scíndite corda vestra, et non vestiménta vestra; et convertímini ad Dóminum Deum vestrum, quia benígnus et miséricors est, pátiens et multae misericórdiae, et praestábilis super malítia.*
>
> (And rend! your hearts, and not your garments; and be converted! intowards [the] Lord your God, for [he] is benign and merciful, patient and of much mercy, and exalted above evil. *Iol* 2:13)

We may not practice the Jewish tradition of 'rending/tearing' our garments in grief and mourning, but we recognise what it means in ordinary terms. But **scindite corda**? How do we do this except metaphorically? In the *Gospel* for this same Mass we pray with the Priest or Deacon:

> *Nolíte thesaurizáre vobis thesáuros in terra: ubi aerúgo, et tínea demolítur: et ubi fures effódiunt, et furántur. Thesaurizáte autem vobis thesáuros in caelo, ubi neque aerúgo, neque tínea demolítur, et ubi fures non effódiunt, nec furántur. Ubi enim est thesáurus tuus, ibi est et cor tuum.*
>
> (Lay not up! to you treasures on earth: where [the] rust, and moth demolish: and where thieves break in, and steal. But lay up! to you treasures in heaven, where neither rust, nor moth demolishes, and where thieves [do] not break in, nor steal. For where your treasure is, there is your heart also. *Mt* 6:19-21)

We would have no problems understanding the rusting of treasure and the damage of moths to our clothes, but **Thesaurizáte autem vobis thesáuros in caelo**? That takes some thinking about. As indeed does **Ubi enim est thesáurus tuus, ibi est et cor tuum.** The passage quoted here ends the *Gospel* for Ash Wednesday, but not included in the Liturgy are the next two verses:

Lucerna corporis tui est oculus tuus. Si oculus tuus fuerit simplex, totum corpus tuum lucidum erit. Si autem oculus tuus fuerit nequam, totum corpus tuum tenebrosum erit. Si ergo lumen, quod in te est, tenebrae sunt: ipsae tenebrae quantae erunt?

([The] light of your body is your eye. If your eye will have been pure, your whole body will be full of light. But however if your eye will have been wretched, your whole body will be dark. If therefore [the] light, that is in you is [the] darkness: how great will be [the] darkness itself? *Mt* 6:22-23)

What we might ask is *lucerna corporis*? And if, as here, it is *oculus tuus*, how does that work? Also, how can an eye be *simplex* and how then does that enable the *totum corpus tuum* to be *lucidum*? Similarly with *nequam* and *tenebrosum*. There is no singular form when the Latin noun *tenebra* is used for 'darkness', hence the plural verbs in the Latin text, but that does not help explain how light within us can be darkness[es]. The metaphors are powerful ones, and we can only begin to understand them when we go beyond the language they are expressed in. We have to go beyond the linguistic indicative dynamic to begin to grasp the indicative affect involved.

Indicative Affect

St Catherine of Siena stigmatist and Doctor of the Church (one of only four female Doctors [of the 36 in the Church] and all declared post *Vatican II*) and great mystic, dictated her *Il Dialogo* or *Trattato della divina provvidenza* (*Dialogue on Divine Providence*) in the Tuscan dialect in 1370 (and usually just referred to as *Il Libro*). She did so when in a state of ecstasy and, like the numerous examples above, it is full of spiritualised metaphor, often one piling upon another, to a point where one translator of her work has suggested she introduces a metaphor, forgets she has done so, and introduces another, often in rapid succession. The following selection from her *Gratiarum actio ad Trinitatem* (Act of thanksgiving towards the Trinity) appears in the *usus recentior Officium Lectionis* (Office of Readings) of the *Liturgia Horarum* (Liturgy of Hours) on her feast day April 29 (in the *usus antiquior* books her feast is April 30):

> *O Déitas aetérna, O aetérna Trínitas, quae per uniónem divínae natúrae fecísti tantum valére prétium sánguinis unigéniti Fílii tui! Tu, Trínitas aetérna, es quoddam mare profúndum, in quo quanto plus quaero, plus invénio; et quanto plus invénio, plus quaero te. Tu quodámmodo instabíliter ánimam sátias; quóniam in abýsso tua ita sátias ánimam, quod semper remáneat esúriens atque famélica, te, Trínitas aetérna, peroptans desideránsque te vidére lumen in lúmine tuo.*

(Eternal God, eternal Trinity, you have made the blood of Christ so precious through his sharing in your divine nature. You are a mystery as deep as the sea; the more I search, the more I find, and the more I find the more I search for you. But I can never be satisfied; what I receive will ever leave me desiring more. When you fill my soul I have an even greater hunger, and I grow more famished for your light. I desire above all to see you, the true light, as you really are.)

> *Gustávi et vidi cum lúmine intelléctus, in lúmine tuo abýssum tuam, aetérna Trínitas, atque pulchritúdinem creatúrae tuae: propter quod intuéndo meipsam in te, vidi me fore tuam imáginem: donánte vidélicet mihi te, Pater aetérne, de poténtia tua et de sapiéntia tua, quae sapiéntia Unigénito tuo est appropriáta. Spíritus vero Sanctus, qui procédit a te Patre et Fílio tuo, dedit mihi voluntátem, per quam me facit aptam ad amándum.*

(I have tasted and seen the depth of your mystery and the beauty of your creation with the light of my understanding. I have clothed myself with your likeness and have seen what I shall be. Eternal Father, you have given me a share in your power and the wisdom that Christ claims as his own, and your Holy Spirit has given me the desire to love you.)

Nam tu, Trínitas aetérna, factor es, et ego factúra: unde cognóvi, te illuminánte, in recreatióne quam me fecísti per sánguinem unigéniti Fílii tui, quod amóre captus es de pulchritúdine factúrae tuae.

(You are my Creator, eternal Trinity, and I am your creature. You have made of me a new creation in the blood of your Son, and I know that you are moved with love at the beauty of your creation, for you have enlightened me.)

O abýssus, O Trínitas aetérna, O Déitas, O mare profúndum: et quid máius mihi dare póteras quam teipsum? Tu es ignis qui semper ardes et non consúmeris tu es qui consúmis calóre tuo quemcúmque próprium amórem ánimae. Tu es íterum ignis qui tollis omnem frigiditátem, et illúminas mentes lúmine tuo, quo lúmine fecísti me cognóscere veritátem tuam.

(Eternal Trinity, Godhead, mystery deep as the sea, you could give me no greater gift than the gift of yourself. For you are a fire ever burning and never consumed, which itself consumes all the selfish love that fills my being. Yes, you are a fire that takes away the coldness, illuminates the mind with its light and causes me to know your truth.)

In huius lúminis spéculo cognósco te summum bonum, bonum super omne bonum, bonum felix, bonum incomprehensíbile, bonum inaestimábile, pulchritúdinem super omnem pulchritúdinem, sapiéntiam super omnem sapiéntiam: quia tu es ipsa sapiéntia, tu cibus angelórum qui igne caritátis te dedísti homínibus.

(By this light, reflected as it were in a mirror, I recognise that you are the highest good, one we can neither comprehend nor fathom. And I know that you are beauty and wisdom itself. The food of angels, you gave yourself to man in the fire of your love.)

Tu vestiméntum coopériens nuditátem meam, pascis nos famélicos tua dulcédine, qua dulcis es absque ulla amaritúdine. O Trínitas aetérna.

(You are the garment which covers our nakedness, and in our hunger you are a satisfying food, for you are sweetness and in you there is no taste of bitterness, O triune God! *usus recentior*)

The metaphors in her writings (and there are many in this prayer) are not just figments of a 'spiritualised imagination', as one commentator once said of her, but are a means by which she seeks to find a vocabulary to explain what is happening to her in prayer. Metaphor is the linguistic means by which she tries to express the affect of the unexplainable force of God's mystical actions upon her.

Prayer for her, and for us, is not simply about linguistic form but about our putting aside 'our time' and entering into God's time, not for us to use more words, but to listen to God's voice. 'God's slow work' is not affected by metaphor, but expressing that 'slow work' perhaps is. How else might we get even part way to expressing what God has done for us *indicatively* through the Incarnation; through Christ. This is the very heart of understanding 'indicative theology'; the indicative actions God has taken on our behalf; the declaration, expression and statement of love he has made for us. The Incarnation is the ultimate indicative affirmation of God's love for us, the truth of which is indicative of God himself. It is a statement of what 'is', and we seek that indicative 'is' through what we hope, subjunctively 'might be'. We express this in Latin prayer in many ways. For example, a most theologically telling moment is expressed when, in the Wednesday *Matins* of the 3rd week of the Epiphany we pray with St Paul:

cum audissétis verbum veritátis, Evangélium salútis vestrae, in quo et credéntes signáti estis Spíritu promissiónis Sancto.
(when you had heard [the] word of truth, [the] Gospel of your salvation, also in which believing, you have been signed [with the] promise of [the] Holy Spirit. *Eph* 1:13)

signati estis is a 2^(nd) pers pl nom m pass perf ind verb from the infinitive *signare* - 'to sign', 'to mark' and 'to seal'. But more than that we might better translate this in English as 'to set a mark upon'; 'to mark out'; 'to set a seal upon'; 'to designate'; 'to license'. In effect: 'to affect'. That signing (just as the Bishop signs the **confirmandi** at the Sacrament of Confirmation with the *sacrum chrisma* (holy chrism [oil]) enabling the indicative affect necessary to make the individual part of the Christian community, is made upon their foreheads (like the holy water and chrism at Baptism) *confirming* them as Catholic Christians (**confirmati**). St Paul is telling the Ephesians that after hearing the *Gospel* of Christ, they have now been designated as Christians; they have had Christ's seal set upon them; they have been indicatively 'licensed' as Christians, because in hearing that *Gospel* they did so ***Spiritu promissionis Sancto*** ([by the] promise of the Holy Spirit). They are *indicatively affected* as Christians.

Earlier in verse 11 St Paul says **vocati sumus** ([we] have been called) with the *Vulgate* using another passive perfect verb form from **vocare** - to call. It is a verb that is used in Latin to express many things: 'to call upon'; 'to invoke'; 'to invite'; 'to urge'; to summon', and perhaps more tellingly in English, 'to challenge'. St Paul is saying simultaneously that the Ephesians - all of us - have been called, but more than that: we have been challenged as a group to be indicatively declared as Christians. And the agent of that challenge? It is:

> ***Deus, Dómini nostri Iesu Christi Pater glóriae.***
> ([the] God, of our Lord Jesus Christ [the] Father of glory. *Eph* 1:17)

God, as the force behind calling us together as Christians, indicatively shifts our disposition as individuals; as people. The indicative force of **vocati sumus** challenges us to actually live that call; to live the indicative theology at the heart of that call which we might pray, for example, in these selections from the *Athanasian Creed*:

Fides autem cathólica haec est...
(Thus [the] catholic faith is this...)
ália est enim persóna Patris, ália Fílii, ália Spíritus Sancti:
(for there is one person of [the] Father; one of [the] Son; and one of [the] Holy Spirit)
Sed Patris, et Fílii, et Spíritus Sancti una est divínitas, aequális glória, coaetérna maiéstas...
(But [the] divinity of [the] Father, and of [the] Son, and of [the] Holy Spirit, is one, [the] glory equal, [the] majesty coeternal...)
Qualis Pater, talis Fílius, talis Spíritus Sanctus.
(What kind [the] Father [is]; such [is the] Son; such [is the] Holy Spirit.)
Increátus Pater, increátus Fílius, increátus Spíritus Sanctus.
([The] Father uncreated, [the] Son uncreated, [the] Holy Spirit uncreated.)
Imménsus Pater, imménsus Fílius, imménsus Spíritus Sanctus.
([The] Father infinite, [the] Son infinite, [the] Holy Spirit infinite.)
Aetérnus Pater, aetérnus Fílius, aetérnus Spíritus Sanctus.
([The] Father eternal, [the] Son eternal, [the] Holy Spirit eternal.)
Et tamen non tres aetérni, sed unus aetérnus.
(And yet [there are] not three eternals, but one eternal.)
Sicut non tres increáti, nec tres imménsi, sed unus increátus, et unus imménsus.
(As [there are] not three uncreated, nor three infinites, but one uncreated, and [so too] one infinite.)
Simíliter omnípotens Pater, omnípotens Fílius, omnípotens Spíritus Sanctus. (Likewise [the] Father [is] almighty, [the] Son [is] almighty; and [the] Holy Spirit [is] almighty.)
Et tamen non tres omnipoténtes, sed unus omnípotens.
(And yet [there are] not three almighties, but one almighty.)
Ita Deus Pater, Deus Fílius, Deus Spíritus Sanctus.
(So [the] Father [is] God, [the] Son [is] God, [the] Holy Spirit [is] God.)

Et tamen non tres dii, sed unus est Deus.

(And yet [there are] not three gods, but God is one.)

Ita Dóminus est Pater, Dóminus est Fílius, Dóminus est Spíritus Sanctus.

(So [the] Father is Lord, [the] Son is Lord, [the] Holy Spirit is Lord.)

Et tamen non tres dómini, sed unus Dóminus...

(And yet [there are] not three lords, but one Lord...)

Pater a nullo est factus: nec creátus, nec génitus.

([The] Father is/was made from nothing: neither created, nor begotten.)

Fílius a Patre solo est: non factus, nec creátus, sed génitus.

([The] Son is from [the] Father alone: not made, nor created, but begotten.)

Spíritus Sanctus a Patre et Fílio: non factus, nec creátus, nec génitus, sed procédens.

([The] Holy Spirit [is] from [the] Father and [the] Son: not made, neither created, nor begotten; but proceeding.)

Unus ergo Pater, non tres Patres: unus Fílius, non tres Fílii: unus Spíritus Sanctus, non tres Spíritus Sancti.

(Therefore [there is] one Father, not three Fathers: one Son, not three Sons: one Holy Spirit, not three Holy Spirits.)

Et in hac Trinitáte nihil prius aut postérius, nihil maius aut minus:

(And in this Trinity nothing [is] before or after [another], nothing [is] greater or lesser:)

Sed totae tres persónae coaetérnae sibi sunt et coaequále...

(But [the] whole three persons themselves are coeternal and co-equal...)

This is just an edited part of the full Creed, but notice how in even this long section from the first part of the Creed, there is only one verb used, *esse*, and then only in two forms: 3rd person singular present *est* (used and also assumed many times) and 3rd person plural present *sunt* (used only once but assumed many times) but with participles from other verbs used as adjectives (eg *factus* (*facere*) *creatus* (*creare*) *procedens* (*procedere*) *subsistens* (*subsistere*). Without a doubt, this is a very forceful declaration of Catholic belief in the Trinity, expressed through the indicative force of just one verb *esse*, with additional attributive focus provided by a few participles used adjectivally. The affect of this sort of emphatic indicative theology is unescapable, and is declared in a Creed that well deserves reviving beyond just the **usus antiquior** *Office* of *Prime* on Trinity Sunday. Doctor of the Church and Benedictine mystic St Hildegard of Bingen (1098-1179) in her own **Explanatio Symboli Sancti Athanasii** (An Explanation of the Athanasian Symbol [Creed]) engages with this powerful indicative theology, well beyond its language, as its being *theophanic* (θεοφάνεια - *theophaneia* - divine manifestation) that is, as indicative of God's revelation of his Divinity to humanity through the Incarnation, and its consequences for our role in salvation history. She writes:

> **Unde et caritas in Sapientia dicit**
> (From where [whence] love speaks in Wisdom)

but this is not ordinary love: it is Divine Love, and she continues:

> **Ego ab antiquo ordinata sum**
> (I [Wisdom] was ordained from old)

personifying Wisdom as a declaration of the timelessness of God which is so often repeated in this Creed, with its continual indicative force declaring the indivisible unity of triune Divinity. This declaration and expression of the Trinity is absolutely central to the indicative theology at the heart of Christian belief, and St Hildegard looks to the way the metaphor of a word may work to understand it. A word has sound (***sonus***) she says. It has a force of meaning (***virtus***) and it has 'soul', which combined, she calls, the 'breath of life' (*flatus*) a powerfully expressed metaphor for the unexplainable Trinity. She writes:

> *quia etiam homo creaturas per animam cognoscit, ipsas in iucunditate et gaudio habet. Sic namque homo in carne et anima velut de misericordia et caritate amabilis est, quemadmodum sapientia et caritas unum sunt.*
>
> (for because [a] man knows creatures through [their] spirit, he holds them in joy and gladness. So since [a] man is lovely in body and spirit, even as mercy and charity is lovely, in like manner wisdom and love are one.)

To know this is to be deeply affected by the unexplainable. We only have words to describe it, but in prayer we seek to go beyond those words and, as the Benedictine mystic St Hildegard did herself, to subjunctively seek to experience it. Every Sunday at *Prime*, *Terce*, *Sext* and *None*, and on Mondays at *Terce*, *Sext* and *None* in the **Breviarium Monasticum**, St Hildegard would have prayed the wonderfully comprehensive *Psalm 118* exactly as it is still prayed 1,000 years later in the **usus antiquior** *MP* (and in the Minor Hours on Sundays and Feast days in the *PP*. She would have prayed:

> *Bonitátem, et disciplínam, et sciéntiam doce me, quia mandátis tuis crédidi.*
>
> (Teach! me goodness, and discipline, and knowledge, for I have believed your commandments. *Ps* 118:66)

as we still do. The disposition of the Psalmist changes from using the imperative *doce* to *credidi*, the 1st pers sg perf act ind form of *credere* (I have believed). The imperative exhortation of *doce* becomes the indicative declaration of *credidi*. This imperative-indicative dynamic is powerful in prayer. A few verses later we pray:

> *Fiat misericórdia tua ut consolétur me, secúndum elóquium tuum servo tuo.*
>
> (Let your mercy be done that [it] may comfort me, according to your declaration to your servant. *Ps* 118:76)

The mood shifts again with the verb *fiat:* the 3rd pers sg pres pass/act subjunctives of the verbs *facere/fieri* (to happen/to be done) and with this linguistic shift comes a significant dispositional spiritual/numinous shift. We see this often in Latin prayer. For example, in a prayer offered to the Ephesians by St Paul :

> *Flecto genua mea ad Patrem Domini nostri Iesu Christi, ex quo omnis paternitas in caelis et in terra nominatur ut det vobis secundum divitias gloriae suae, virtute corroborari per Spiritum eius in interiorem hominem, Christum habitare per fidem in cordibus vestris: in caritate radicati, et fundati, ut possitis comprehendere cum omnibus sanctis, quæ sit latitudo, et longitudo, et sublimitas, et profundum: scire etiam supereminentem scientiae caritatem Christi, ut impleamini in omnem plenitudinem Dei. Ei autem, qui potens est omnia facere superabundanter quam petimus aut intelligimus, secundum virtutem, quae operatur in nobis: ipsi gloria in Ecclesia, et in Christo Iesu, in omnes generationes saeculi saeculorum. Amen.* (*Eph* 3:14-21)

This, like so many scriptural prayers, is rarely, if ever, prayed as a separate prayer, in any language, but which contains within it the Catholic narrative in a nutshell. The two versions given below, the first from the unauthorised 2015 *Catholic Public Domain Version* and the second from the now authorised 1945 *Knox* version, both translated directly from the Latin *Vulgate*, demonstrate the beauty of this prayer:

> 'I bend my knees to the Father of our Lord Jesus Christ, from whom all paternity in heaven and on earth takes its name. And I ask

him to grant to you to be strengthened in virtue by his Spirit, in accord with the wealth of his glory, in the inner man, so that Christ may live in your hearts through a faith rooted in, and founded on, charity. So may you be able to embrace, with all the saints, what is the width and length and height and depth of the charity of Christ, and even be able to know that which surpasses all knowledge, so that you may be filled with all the fullness of God. Now to him who is able to do all things, more abundantly than we could ever ask or understand, by means of the virtue which is at work in us: to him be glory, in the Church and in Christ Jesus, throughout every generation, forever and ever. Amen.' (*CPDV Eph* 3:14-21)

'I fall on my knees to the father of our Lord Jesus Christ, that father from whom all fatherhood in heaven and on earth takes its title. May Christ find a dwelling-place, through faith, in your hearts; may your lives be rooted in love, founded on love. May you and all the saints be enabled to measure, in all its breadth and length and height and depth, the love of Christ, to know what passes knowledge. May you be filled with all the completion God has to give. He whose power is at work in us is powerful enough, and more than powerful enough, to carry out his purpose beyond all our hopes and dreams; may he be glorified in the Church, and in Christ Jesus, to the last generation of eternity. Amen.' (*Knox Eph* 3:14-21)

In both versions it reads most elegantly and hauntingly as a very beautiful blessing of faith, hope and love, encapsulating the very essence of Christian faith in one simple phrase: ***ut impleamini in omnem plenitudinem Dei***, translated by the *CPDV* as 'so that you may be filled with all the fullness of God' and by Ronald Knox as 'may you be filled with all the completion God has to give'. Both very elegant. The Latin verb form ***ut impleamini***, as several verbs are in this passage, and which we have seen briefly in some other prayers in this chapter, and as many other verbs in many Latin prayers are, is in the subjunctive mood, and it is to this we now turn in *Chapter XI: Subjunctive Prayer*.

XI

SUBJUNCTIVE PRAYER

Tristatur aliquis vestrum? Oret. Aequo animo est? Psallat.
(Is any of you sad? Let him pray. Is he cheerful in mind? Let him sing. DR Iac 5:13)

Subjunctivity

St John the Evangelist records the moment when:

'Jesus passing by, saw a man, who was blind from his birth. And his disciples asked him: Rabbi, who hath sinned, this man, or his parents, that he should be born blind? Jesus answered: Neither hath this man sinned, nor his parents; but that the works of God should be made manifest (*manifestentur*) in him.' (*DR Io* 9:1-3).

For something 'to be made manifest' might strike us as a very old-fashioned way of talking in this day and age. Ronald Knox probably thought so, even in the 1940s, and translated this sentence as 'Jesus answered; it was so that God's action might declare itself in him.' He modernised the word to 'declare' but in doing so lost the sense of awe and mystery that the word 'manifest' might have. The Latin word *manifestus* comes from two words - *manus* (hand) + *festus* (infinitive *fendere* - to strike/hit). *Manifestare* (to manifest) is therefore 'to strike by the hand'. There is a force to this action, especially when it is God 'making manifest', that the word 'declare' in English just doesn't have. God's making manifest his works on the blind man clearly struck him like a blow on the head especially when Jesus later put clay on his eyes and his sight was restored (*Io* 9:6-7).

The *DR* translates **manifestentur** as 'should be made manifest', where the grammatical mood is neither indicative (statement) nor imperative (command) but an expression of possibility and so subjunctive. It is also a passive form of the verb (3rd pers pl pres pass subj of **manifestare**). We are not told who the agent of this verb is, although, as the story unfolds, we know it to be God the Father working through Christ. Our understanding of the force of this simple verb 'manifest' is contingent, then, upon our understanding both the grammar of the word as a text; and upon the context of its 'subjunctivity'. St Thomas Aquinas explored these issues in considerable depth arguing that: **contingens est quod potest esse et non esse** (contingency is what is able to be and not to be). In other words, unlike the truths of God, which are necessary and unchanging, things which are contingent upon other things hold within them an inherent uncertainty, maybe even fragility. St Anselm writing about the attributes of God, understood that in this uncertainty of our reasoning and intellect there is something: **quo nihil maius cogitari potest** (for which nothing greater is able to be imagined). That 'something' is the certainty of God: **et intellectu, et in re** (both in the intellect, and in reality).

Subjunctivity (**subiungere** - to subjoin - under [**sub**] connect [**iungere**]) describes the way one dependent state of being connects/subjoins to another more independent one; the way it connects/subjoins one uncertainty to a more certain one; one reality to another. In other words, subjunctivity signals an uncertain attitude and disposition and is expressed in English with words like 'might', 'may', 'would', 'should', 'could', 'lest', for example. Wishes, desires, concessions, hopes, exhortations, questions, doubts, concerns, possibilities, opinions, hypotheses, uncertainties, obligations, judgements, purpose, suggestion, result, time, condition, potential and emotions, in the here and now or in some potential future, may all be addressed, and often in very layered ways, in Latin, using the subjunctive mood.

Subjunctivity, then, in grammar, is about contingency. It is about disposition, and the way we understand the world and dispose its realities in specific ways. As we have seen, prayer is always dispositional. It is always about the way we dispose ourselves; about the attitudes we adopt and the mindset we have. Disposition describes character, and it describes **habitus**; a way of understanding the tendencies people have to act in particular ways. That has led some philosophers to argue for a worldview that argues that everything is contingent; that there are multiple realities and none of them should hold a privileged position; that all meanings are relative, contingent and should be considered equal. That, in turn, has led some theologians and philosophers, including some contemporary Catholics, to establish what is now being called 'subjunctive theology', saying that even God is contingent. It is a theology which seeks to create an understanding of God to accord to a secular worldview that says man's reality, and not God's, is (and should be) the primary one.

This view is not new. The announcement that God is considered to be 'dead' was initially made by the philosophers Georg Hegel (1770-1831) and Friedrich Nietszche (1844-1900) reworking Martin Luther's wife Kate's own phrase 'Gott ist tot' - God is dead - which she solemnly announced to bring Luther out of his depression. It worked. God was not dead for Luther, though much in Catholicism for him was. As indeed for Hegel and Nietszche for whom much in Christianity overall was dead. In their view, the Enlightenment had done away with the need for us to persist with the idea of the existence of a transcendent God; a view picked up rather more stridently in the 1960s with the American protestant theologian Thomas JJ Altizer (1927-2018) and filtering into contemporary revisionist Christianity, including the influential Anglican Bishop of Woolwich John AT Robinson (1919-1983) who wrote several very popular books which argued that God was better understood as either a fiction invented by (contingent upon) man's need for the spiritual, or simply as just 'love', and so popularising the view that 'God', as we have traditionally understood him to be, 'is dead'. That is not, of course, the position in Latin Catholicism or in this book, so shades of it were (and still are) current in some contemporary Catholic circles, including from some of the 86 *periti* (experts) advising the Fathers of *Vatican II* over its four sessions.

But the reality of God is not contingent upon anything. Though the reality of humanity is. That reality and its very humanity is contingent upon God. Prayer is the vehicle by which the uncertain contingencies (subjunctivities) we have as humans may focus on the certainties of God. The subjunctive world of that prayer is the subjunctive world we actually live in. We make no sense as humans if we stand alone; if our focus is on us alone. We only make sense as uncertain/fragile humans when connected/subjoined to a certainty, and the only certainty is God.

The Subjunctive Dynamic

Benedictine St Anselm of Canterbury often thought of as the father of Scholasticism, was instrumental in shaping rational arguments for the existence of God, and other such things, which greatly influenced Aquinas and other scholastics. He knew all about subjunctivity, as we can see in the beautiful prayer below which is attributed to him. In it he seeks to recognise his own uncertain weaknesses, and to put aside his own will as much as he could, in order to replace it with a surrender of uncertain self in service to the certain God; to be personally contingent upon God:

Ad Deum

Omnípotens Deus, et miséricors Pater, et bone Dómine, miserére mihi peccatóri.

([O] Almighty God, and merciful Father, and O good Lord, be merciful! to me [a] sinner)

LATIN PRAYER

Da mihi véniam peccatórum meórum,
(Grant! to me pardon of my sins,)
cavére et vincére omnes insídias, et tentatiónes et delectatiónes nóxias,
(to guard against and to conquer all snares, and temptations and harmful delights,)
perfécte mente et actu vitáre, quae próhibes,
(perfectly [in] mind and deed to avoid, what you forbid,)
fácere et serváre quae iubes,
(to do and watch over what you command,)
credére, speráre, amáre,
(to believe, to hope, to love,)
velle quod et quantum et tu scis et vis,
(to wish both what and how much you know and will,)
compunctiónem humilitátis et pietátis, discrétam abstinéntiam et carnis mortificatiónem,
([the] remorse of humility and of piety, prudent abstinence and mortification of [the] flesh,)
ad te amándum, orándum, laudándum, meditándum,
(for [the] loving, praying, praising, meditating towards you,)
ad omnem secúndum te actum et cogitátum,
(secondly towards every act and thought for you,)
puram, sóbriam, devótam mentem,
([a] pure, sober, devoted mind,)
verácem et efficácem mandatórum tuórum notítiam, dilectiónem, facilitátem et efféctum,
([a] truthful and efficacious knowledge of your mandates, love, willingness, and accomplishment,)
semper, Domíne ad melióra cum humilitáte profícere et nunquam defícere.
(always, O Lord towards better [ways] to go forward with humility and to never fail.)

> *Ne COMMITTAS me, Dómine, voluntáti meae, nec humánae ignorántiae, aut infirmitáti, neque meis méritis, nec ulli álii quam tuae piae dispositióni.*
>
> (May you not commit me, O Lord, to my will, nor to human ignorance, or infirmity, nor to my merits, nor to anything than to your holy disposition.)
>
> *Sed tu ipse cleménter dispóne me et omnes cogitátus et actus meos in beneplácito tuo, ut FIAT a me, et in me et de me, tua semper sola volúntas.*
>
> (But mercifully guide! me yourself and all my thoughts and actions in your pleasure, that by me, and in me and from me, your will alone may always be.)
>
> *Líbera me ab omni malo, et perduc me in vitam aetérnam. Amen.*
>
> (Deliver! me from all evil, and lead! me intowards life eternal. Amen.)

There are 22 verbs in this prayer, and 4 participles acting as verbal nouns (gerunds) (***amandum, orandum, laudandum, meditandum***: 'the loving', 'the praying', 'the praising' and 'the meditating') with most of the adjectives formed from other participles of verbs. It is a prayer packed with imperatives, infinitives and indicative declarations of God's will and capabilities. Yet it is also a prayer packed with the spaces and gaps where verbs would/could be, but in which numerous nouns stand alone, powerful and contingent upon our filling in those gaps with 'understood' verbs. But two verbs stand out from them all and encapsulate within them everything that St Anselm is praying for, and marked above in capital letters: ***committas*** and ***fiat***, mirroring, as this entire prayer does, the ***Pater Noster*** (Our Father) ***ne committas = ne nos inducas*** (may you not lead us) and ***fiat semper sola voluntas = fiat voluntas tua*** (may your will be done) signalling a journey from the uncertain to the certain; the contingent towards the non-contingent.

It becomes clear that the dominant grammatical moods (imperative and indicative) of St Anselm's prayer completely change gear with the dynamic introduction of the subjunctives ***committas*** and ***fiat***. The mood switches, in an instant, to one which is expressing desire and hope; it is expressing a wish and, above all, a new disposition which expresses potential and possibility; a world that might be; a disposition that may become more like God's own disposition. ***Dispositio***, as specifically used by St Anselm in this prayer (and in Latin prayer generally) is formed from the verb ***dis*** + ***ponere*** ('to place in parts') and which formed one of five main ways (canons) in Classical Latin rhetoric as a means of organising and arranging arguments and meanings, a process central to Classical Latin education. The other four canons were ***inventio*** (the initial stage of finding an argument) ***elocutio*** (the style of an argument) ***memoria*** (the recalling of an argument) and ***pronuntiatio*** (the delivery of an argument). 'Disposition', therefore, is about the way we, as Christians, organise and arrange ourselves to develop character and identity, just as it was about organising and arranging arguments in pre-Christian oratory and rhetoric. We see here, then, a dispositional change when the grammatical mood changes to the subjunctive, and it does so in the form of a verb (***fiat***) that is contingent upon a main verb (***dispone***). The 'may/might' element of this subjunctive verb is expressing a potential reality - a 'subjunctivity', but ***tua semper sola voluntas*** (your will alone always) resolves that potential, and creates another, more certain, indicative, reality. As such, the subjunctive in Latin prayer is not about 'imagined worlds', a phrase common to the postmodernist way of thinking that everything is relative and contingent; that every reality is an imagined reality, that subjunctivity is about imagining the possible in human terms only. In prayer it is not about imagining the possible, but about seeking and focussing on the realities of the seemingly impossible. Thomas à Kempis understood this well when he prayed in ***De Imitatione Christi***:

> *Fac mihi possíbile, Dómine, per grátiam, quod mihi impossíbile vidétur per natúram.*

> (Make possible to me, O Lord, through grace, what seems to me impossible through nature.)

The contrast here between grace and nature; between the world here and now and the supernatural; between the possible and impossible; between the contingent and non-contingent; between ourselves and God; indeed the whole of Latin prayer and Catholicism, is summed up in this one single sentence. Similarly, St Thomas Aquinas puts it all so cogently when he writes in his ***Summa Theologiae***:

> *de rebus divinis, de quibus, cum sint supra nos, non debemus iudicare, sed simpliciter ea credere.*
> (of divine things, concerning which, may be beyond us, we ought not to examine, but simply to believe them. II-II, Q60)

In this single sentence, like à Kempis, Aquinas is taking us out of the world of contingent relativities and uses the infinitive *credere* rather than the imperative *credite*, as he does with *iudicare* following the 1st pers pl pres act ind *debemus* from the infinitive *debere* - 'to be bound to/ought'. The force of a command 'believe!' lies in this verb and the two infinitives that follow, but there is an uncertainty in that force, signalled by the preceding subjunctive *sint*. We are told that 'divine things' may be beyond us (subjunctive) but not to examine - *iudicare* (indicative) but to just simply believe - *credere* (indicative). The subjunctive dynamic of uncertainty is therefore replaced by the indicative dynamic of certainty, by disposing ourselves to God's will and not our own. St Thomas talks in this section about *de intentione cordis vel de aliis incertis* (concerning intention of the heart or concerning other uncertain things). These are not matters for concrete proof, but contingent upon faith. The subjunctive uncertainties are designed to lead to indicative certainties. But, as he makes clear, we must do so with care; to avoid *iudicium temerarium* (rash judgement). When that rashness determines that 'private judgement' is privileged over and above the right judgement of the Church, as St John Henry Newman warned so often about as an ominous sign of the times he was living in, then that, as we certainly see now, is the time to worry.

Rash judgement, or indeed private judgement, does not mean no judgement at all though. And there have been times in the history of the Catholic Church when restrictions on debate and enquiry have created intellectual vacuums which then, sadly, seem to be resolved by them going too far in the opposite direction, as we see in much contemporary Catholicism post *Vatican II*. The Jewish tradition of *ma'amat* (debate) about the meanings of Scripture is central to its traditions. Interpretations of even just a single word may be disputed for days, weeks, even centuries, such that Judaism, in its many forms, is noted for famously saying that 'for every question there is a *machloket* (dispute) about it.' In Latin Catholicism we should not be afraid of such debates, as indeed we saw in the deliberations of the Fathers at *Vatican II*. The problems arise when the revealed and determined truths of the Church, and what they say about the truths of God, give way to rash, private, and therefore, uncertain, judgement. The subjunctive mood, above all grammatical forms in Latin, is emblematic of uncertainty, but the Church through its prayer and revealed truths, seeks to resolve that uncertainty. Struggling with an interpretation, and its possibilities of meaning, is not a flaw, but an opportunity to turn that struggle into meditation and prayer in order to better see the truth.

Subjunctive Dissonance

At the end of each hour (except *Prime* and *Compline*) of the **usus antiquior** Roman Rite *Office*, if prayed privately without a Priest or Deacon, we pray:

℣. *Dómine, exáudi oratiónem meam.* ℟. *Et clamor meus ad te véniat.*

(℣. O Lord, hear my prayer. ℟. And let my cry come unto thee. *trad*)

℣. *Benedicámus Dómino.* ℟. *Deo grátias.*
(℣. Bless we the Lord. ℟. Thanks be to God. *trad*)
℣. *Fidélium ánimae* ✠ *per misericórdiam Dei requiéscant in pace. Amen.*
(℣. May the souls ✠ of the faithful departed, through the mercy of God, rest in peace. ℟. Amen. *trad*)

To which, with the exception of *Matins*, we add:

Pater Noster...
℣. *Dóminus* ✠ *det nobis suam pacem.* ℟. *Et vitam aetérnam. Amen.*
(℣. Vouchsafe to us ✠ thy peace, O Lord. ℟. And life everlasting. Amen. *trad*)

With the exception for the end of *Compline* when we pray:

℣. *Dómine, exáudi oratiónem meam.* ℟. *Et clamor meus ad te véniat.*
(℣. O Lord, hear my prayer. ℟. And let my cry come unto thee. *trad*)

Orémus.
Vísita, quǽsumus, Dómine, habitatiónem istam, et omnes insídias inimíci ab ea longe repélle: Angeli tui sancti hábitent in ea, qui nos in pace custódiant; et benedíctio tua sit super nos semper. Per Dóminum nostrum Iesum Christum Fílium tuum, qui tecum vivit et regnat in unitáte Spíritus Sancti, Deus, per ómnia sǽcula saeculórum. ℟. *Amen.*

(Let us pray.
Visit, we beseech thee, O Lord, this habitation, and drive far from it all the snares of the enemy: let thy holy Angels dwell herein, to preserve us in peace; and may thy blessing be upon us evermore. Through

Jesus Christ, thy Son our Lord. Who liveth and reigneth with thee, in the unity of the Holy Ghost, ever one God, world without end. ℟. Amen. *trad*)

℣. *Dómine, exáudi oratiónem meam.* ℟. *Et clamor meus ad te véniat.*

(℣. O Lord, hear my prayer. ℟. And let my cry come unto thee.)

℣. *Benedicámus Dómino.* ℟. *Deo grátias.*

(℣. Bless we the Lord. ℟. Thanks be to God.)

Benedícat et custódiat nos omnípotens et miséricors Dóminus, Pater, ✠ et Fílius, et Spíritus Sanctus. ℟. *Amen*

(May the Lord Almighty and merciful vouchsafe to bless us and keep us, the Father, ✠ the Son, and the Holy Ghost. ℟. Amen. *trad*)

(*Then the Marian Antiphon according to season*)

℣. *Divínum auxílium ✠ máneat semper nobíscum.* ℟. *Amen.*

(℣. May help divine ✠ be with us all, for ever abiding. ℟. Amen. *trad*)

There are a total of 22 verbs: 5 are imperatives (***exaudi*** x 3, ***visita*** and ***repelle***) 3 are indicative (***quaesumus***, ***vivit*** and ***regnat***) and the rest are all subjunctives, ***oremus***, ***veniat*** x 3, ***benedicamus*** x 2, ***requiescant***, ***det***, ***habitent***, ***custodiant***, ***sit***, ***benedicat***, ***custodiat*** and ***maneat***. We pray, for example, ***Benedicámus Dómino*** (Let us give blessings to the Lord) where ***benedicamus*** is a subjunctive of the infinitive ***benedicere*** (to speak well of/to) but by itself, 'Let us speak well to' makes little sense. Let us speak well to what? to whom? where? how? and so on. Its meaning is contingent upon our being told something else. In this case ***Domino***, the dative form of ***Dominus***, 'to/for the Lord', repeated in the response with the dative ***Deo gratias*** (thanks to/for God). Subjunctive forms of address like these in these prayers are grammatically subordinate to other forms of language for them to make their meanings. They position us as contingent upon God. We pray 'may' and 'let', as here, addressing God not as an equal, but from a submissive, uncertain, position. We pray the possibility of something happening to us: 'may help divine be with us'; 'may the Lord bless and keep us'; 'may my cry come to you' and so on. When we are praying with optative subjunctives like this, as with **benedicat et custodiat**, we are expressing a wish (***optare*** - to wish). We are hoping for something; we desire something, but there is no certainty of that desire being fulfilled. When we are praying with jussive subjunctives (***iubere*** - to bid) we are exhorting (*oremus* - let us pray) but not commanding. In the ***usus recentior*** Latin *Mass* the Priest prays:

> *Fratres, agnoscámus peccáta nostra, ut apti simus ad mystéria celebránda.*
> (Brethren/ [*Brothers and Sisters*], let us acknowledge our sins, and so prepare ourselves to celebrate the sacred mysteries. *ICEL*)

The 2 subjunctives prayed by the Priest, ***agnoscamus*** (let us acknowledge) and ***simus*** (let us be) bid the people to do something; they are being invited rather than ordered. Prayers like this have become known as 'bidding prayers' (like those prayed in Latin and at some length in the Good Friday ***usus antiquior Missa praesanctificatorum*** (Mass of the presanctified, revised in the 1955 books) and in the ***usus recentior Solemnis actio liturgica postmeridiana in Passione et Morte Domini*** (Solemn afternoon liturgy of the Passion and Death of the Lord) where this form of petitionary prayer features very distinctively as well as in most ***usus recentior*** Masses. They are generally known as 'Prayers of the Faithful/People' and prayed in the vernacular even if the Mass itself is (very rarely) celebrated in the still normative Latin text of this rite. As intercessory prayers they tend to be petitions, supplications and/or thanksgivings, and as 'General Intercessions' they are positioned to function on behalf of all the people and their needs. Most Latin prayers contain a mixed narrative of moods, like this, as in one of the most frequently prayed prayers in any language, the ***Pater Noster***:

Pater noster, qui es in caelis, sanctificétur nomen tuum. Advéniat regnum tuum. Fiat volúntas tua, sicut in caelo et in terra. Panem nostrum quotidiánum da nobis hódie. Et dimítte nobis débita nostra, sicut et nos dimíttimus debitóribus nostris. Et ne nos indúcas in tentatiónem: sed líbera nos a malo. Amen.

(Our Father, who art in heaven, hallowed be thy name. Thy kingdom come. Thy will be done, on earth as it is in heaven. Give us this day our daily bread. And forgive us our trespasses, as we forgive them that trespass against us. And lead us not into temptation, But deliver us from evil. Amen. *trad*)

We see that of the 9 verbs here 3 are in the imperative mood:

- *da* (2nd pers sg pres act imp of *dare* - to give (give!)
- *dimitte* (2nd pers sg pres act imp of *dimittere* - to dismiss/forgive (dismiss/forgive!)
- *libera* (2nd pers sg pres act imp of *liberare* - to free/deliver - free/deliver!)

2 are in the indicative mood:

- *es* (2nd pers sg pres act ind of *esse* - to be - you are)
- *dimittimus* (1st pers pl pres act ind of *dimittere* - to dismiss/forgive - we dismiss/forgive)

and 4 are in the subjunctive mood:

- *sanctificetur* (3rd pers sg pres pass subj of *sanctificare* - to sanctify - may be sanctified)

- *adveniat* (3rd pers sg pres act subj of *advenire* - to come - may come)

- *fiat* (3rd pers sg pres pass subj of *facere* - to make/do - may do/happen)

- *inducas* (2nd pers sg pres act subj of *inducere* - to lead into - may you lead into)

It is relatively clear how best to translate both the imperative and indicative forms here, but is **sanctificetur nomen tuum** expressing a wish, a command, a hope, a possibility or something else? Is it contingent upon anything? Is it better to translate it as optative: 'may your name be sanctified/hallowed' or jussive: 'let your name be sanctified/hallowed'? Might it perhaps be translated as 'would that your name be sanctified/hallowed' or 'in order for your name to be sanctified/hallowed'? Similarly might **adveniat regnum tuum** be translated as 'may your kingdom come' or 'let your kingdom come', or simply 'your kingdom come'? The subjunctive form of address may be linguistically clear (though not always) but its prayerful function requires thought and reflection.

Overall then, Latin prayer is 'imperative', to the extent that it is about calling upon God; 'indicative', to the extent that it is about declaring things about God and 'subjunctive', to the extent that it is about desire, potential and possibility. We may tend to think about this difference in modality as though the imperative and the indicative were somehow more focussed than the subjunctive, because they are less uncertain. That may be true to a certain extent in some circumstances, but there is a spiritual focus in 'subjunctive uncertainty/dissonance' which may begin in its grammar, and is then often seen in the sometimes complicated syntax of a Latin prayer, and which results in a journey of discovery, linguistic and spiritual, as the prayer develops. The **Canticum Trium Puerorum** (The Song of the Three Holy Children) which we pray at Sunday *Lauds* and on many feast days is prayed as follows:

Benedícite, ómnia ópera Dómini, Dómino: laudáte et superexaltáte eum in sǽcula.
(Bless! [O] all works of the Lord, for the Lord: praise! and magnify! him for ever.)

Benedícite, Angeli Dómini, Dómino: benedícite, caeli, Dómino.
(Bless! [O] Angels of the Lord, for the Lord: bless! [O] heavens, for the Lord.)

Benedícite, aquae omnes, quae super caelos sunt, Dómino: benedícite, omnes virtútes Dómini, Dómino.
(Bless! [O] all waters, which are above the heavens, for the Lord: bless! [O] all powers of the Lord, for the Lord.)

Benedícite, sol et luna, Dómino: benedícite, stellae caeli, Dómino.
(Bless! [O] sun and moon, for the Lord: bless! [O] stars of heaven, for the Lord.)

Benedícite, omnis imber et ros, Dómino: benedícite, omnes spíritus Dei, Dómino.
(Bless! [O] every shower and dew, for the Lord: bless! [O] all spirits of God, for the Lord.)

Benedícite, ignis et aestus, Dómino: benedícite, frigus et aestus, Dómino.
(Bless! [O] fire and heat, for the Lord: bless! [O] winter and summer, for the Lord.)

Benedícite, rores et pruína, Dómino: benedícite, gelu et frigus, Dómino.
(Bless! [O] dews and hoar-frosts, for the Lord: bless! [O] frost and cold, for the Lord.)

Benedícite, glácies et nives, Dómino: benedícite, noctes et dies, Dómino.
(Bless! [O] ice and snows, for the Lord: bless! [O] nights and days, for the Lord.)

Benedícite, lux et ténebrae, Dómino: benedícite, fúlgura et nubes, Dómino.

(Bless! [O] light and darkness, for the Lord: bless! [O] lightnings and clouds, for the Lord.)

BENEDICAT terra *Dóminum:* **LAUDET** et **SUPEREXALTET** *eum in sǽcula.*

(May the earth bless the Lord: may [it] praise him, and may [it] magnify him for ever.)

Benedícite, montes et colles, Dómino: benedícite, univérsa germinántia in terra, Dómino.

(Bless! [O] mountains and hills, for the Lord: bless! [O] all sproutings in the earth, for the Lord.)

Benedícite, fontes, Dómino: benedícite, mária et flúmina, Dómino.

(Bless! [O] wells, for the Lord: bless! [O] seas and floods, for the Lord.)

Benedícite, cete, et ómnia, quae movéntur in aquis, Dómino: benedícite, omnes vólucres caeli, Dómino.

(Bless! [O] whales, and all that are moving in the waters, for the Lord: bless! [O] all birds of the air, for the Lord.)

Benedícite, omnes béstiae et pécora, Dómino: benedícite, fílii hóminum, Dómino.

(Bless! [O] all beasts and cattle, for the Lord: bless! [O] sons of men, for the Lord.)

BENEDICAT *Israël Dóminum:* **LAUDET** et **SUPEREXALTET** *eum in sǽcula.*

(May Israel bless the Lord: may [it] praise and magnify him for ever.)

Benedícite, sacerdótes Dómini, Dómino: benedícite, servi Dómini, Dómino.

(Bless! [O] priests of the Lord, for the Lord: bless! [O] servants of the Lord, for the Lord.)

Benedícite, spíritus, et ánimae iustórum, Dómino: benedícite, sancti et húmiles corde, Dómino.

(Bless! [O] spirits, and souls of the just, for the Lord: bless! [O] holy and humble in heart, for the Lord.)

Benedícite, Ananía, Azaría, Mísaël, Dómino: laudáte et super-exaltáte eum in sǽcula.
(Bless! [O] Ananias, Azarias, Misael, for the Lord: praise! [him] and magnify! him for ever.)
(*Fit reverentia* (reverence is done [*bow*])
BENEDICAMUS *Patrem et Fílium cum Sancto Spíritu:*
LAUDEMUS *et* **SUPEREXALTEMUS** *eum in sǽcula.*
(May we bless the Father and the Son, with the Holy Ghost: may we praise and may we magnify him for ever.)
Benedíctus es, Dómine, in firmaménto caeli: et laudábilis, et gloriósus, et superexaltátus in sǽcula.
(You are blessed, O Lord, in the firmament of heaven: and both praiseworthy and glorious and magnified for ever. *Dn* 3: 57-88 & 56)

There are 19 imperatives piling up one on top of another in this most glorious praise of God's creation, and then the grammatical mood suddenly shifts to *Benedicat terra Dominum: laudet et superexaltet eum in saecula*, where the 3 verbs, rather than commanding praise and blessings for the Lord, are suddenly re-oriented towards wishing and hoping for that praise and blessing to be given:

- *benedicite* (bless!) becomes *benedicat* (may/let bless)

- *laudate* (praise!) becomes *laudet* (may/let praise)

- *superexaltate* (magnify!) becomes *superexaltet* (may/let magnify)

This very focussed shift in mood from imperative to subjunctive happens three times (*benedicat* (sg) x 2 and *benedicamus* (pl) and finally one more time from imperative to passive indicative with:

Benedictus es, Domine, in firmamento caeli: et laudabilis, et gloriosus, et superexaltatus in saecula.

(You are blessed, O Lord in the firmament of heaven: and praiseworthy, glorious and magnified for ever.)

The certainty is less sure when the indicative and imperative moods shift to the subjunctive, while **benedicite** - 'bless!' and **benedictus es** 'you are blessed' don't suggest many options for different meanings from the one form. One of the hymns we pray in *Matins* on most of the Sundays after Pentecost and generally thought to have been composed by Pope St Gregory I is:

> *Nocte surgéntes vigilémus omnes,*
> *Semper in Psalmis meditémur, atque*
> *Voce concórdi Dómino canámus*
> *Dúlciter hymnos.*
>   *Ut pio Regi páriter canéntes,*
> *Cum suis Sanctis*
> *mereámur aulam*
> *Ingredi caeli, simul et perénnem*
> *Dúcere vitam.*
>   *Praestet hoc nobis Déitas beáta*
> *Patris, ac Nati, paritérque Sancti*
> *Spíritus, cuius résonat per omnem*
> *Glória mundum. Amen.*

and is recorded in the 1910 *Catholic Encyclopedia* as having more than 20 English translations. There are probably many more now. Four of the common translations to be found in *Breviaries* and *Hymnals* are as follows:

Fr Edward Caswall

Let us arise and watch ere dawn of light,
  And to the Lord our hearts and voices raise;

And meditate in Psalms, and unite
In holy hymns of praise.
So joining in the strains of Saints on high,
Hereafter, in the courts of Heaven's great King,
May we be meet his praise eternally
With them in bliss to sing.
Father supreme! this grace on us confer,
And Thou, O Son by an eternal birth!
With Thee, coequal Spirit Comforter!
Whose glory fills the earth. Amen.

Traditional

Wake, thou that sleepest! rise and keep thy vigil,
Chanting the holy Psalmody of David;
Hymning sweet praises to the Lord eternal
In a glad chorus.
So may our Monarch pitifully hear us,
That we may merit with his Saints to enter
Mansions eternal, therewithal possessing
Joy beatific.
This, he vouchsafe us, God for ever blessed,
Father eternal, Son, and Holy Spirit,
Whose is the glory which through all creation
Ever resoundeth. Amen.

The English Hymnal

Father, we praise thee, now the night is over,
Active and watchful, stand we all before thee;
Singing we offer prayer and meditation:
Thus we adore thee.
Monarch of all things, fit us for thy mansions;

Banish our weakness, health and wholeness sending;
Bring us to heaven, where thy Saints united
Joy without ending.
All-holy Father, Son and equal Spirit,
Trinity blessèd, send us thy salvation;
Thine is the glory, gleaming and resounding
Through all creation. Amen

George Herbert Palmer

Now from the slumbers of the night arising,
chant we the holy Psalmody of David,
hymns to our Master, with a voice concordant,
sweetly intoning.
So may out Monarch pitifully hear us,
that we may merit with His Saints to enter
mansions eternal, there withal possessing
joy beatific.
This be our portion, God forever blessed,
Father eternal, Son, and Holy Spirit,
Whose is the glory, which through all creation
ever resoundeth. Amen.

These translations vary widely, and often for very good reasons, usually due to the demands of rhyme, scansion, metre, poetic force and so on, but interestingly, in a more or less literal translation of the first verse:

Nocte surgéntes vigilémus omnes,
Semper in Psalmis meditémur, atque
Voce concórdi Dómino canámus
Dúlciter hymnos.

([By] night rising may we keep vigil all,
Always in *Psalms* may we meditate, and so
[with] harmonious voice to/for [the] Lord may we sing hymns sweetly.)

we can see that by keeping closely to the grammar of the original Latin, a very different version of this verse to each of those given above appears. The optative focus of the three subjunctives: ***vigilemus***, ***meditemur*** and ***canamus*** is maintained in the more literal translation, which, in this form, presents a prayerful disposition of submission more forcefully than some of the imperative or indicative choices made in some of the translations above. But, of course, more often than not, choices are made in translating hymns like this to suit a melody line, rather than to necessarily reflect the original meaning of the text. So for example, the 3rd pers sg pres act subj ***praestet*** from ***praestare*** - to 'provide', 'supply', 'offer' or 'bestow' - in the final verse, and literally translated as 'may provide/bestow', is nowhere to be seen in this form in the other translations except perhaps in the Palmer translation where the subjunctive 'This be our portion' might suggest it. The rest of the original subjunctives are translated into the indicative or imperative moods. The point at issue here, is not the accuracy, or otherwise of the translations, but the loss of the subjunctive focus in the original Latin texts. The forcefulness of the prayer through its subjunctive uncertainties (dissonance) and certainties (consonance) may therefore change, and with them, the spiritual/numinous affect.

Subjunctive Consonance

In a ***usus antiquior*** Mass the Priest prays ***Orémus*** (1st pers pl pres act subj of ***orare*** - to pray - 'let us pray') and it is one of the most forceful prayers we hear at Mass, because as a jussive subjunctive it does more than invite us to pray; it is effectively an exclamation, which is how this prayer began (and still acts imperatively in the liturgy of the Greek Orthodox Church with the Deacon intoning Ἐν εἰρήνῃ τοῦ Κυρίου δεηθῶμεν - *En eirene tou Kyriou deithomen* - In peace let us pray to the Lord) eliciting the response Κύριε, ἐλέησον - *Kyrie eleison* - Lord have mercy). In the early liturgies it is thought that **Orémus** was an initial call for silent prayer, with the Deacon intoning **Flectámus génua** (let us kneel) and after a short period of private prayer, intoning the imperative plural **Leváte** (Stand!) after which the Priest would then pray the Collect(s) or whatever was to follow. This continues now in the *usus antiquior* Latin liturgy only on certain occasions like Ember Days and at times during Holy Week, and, in the general Ordinary of the Mass, **Orémus** is followed immediately in most places by a Collect, as in the blessings of the church and people conducted before the principal Mass on a Sunday: most of the year with the antiphon **Asperges me** (You will sprinkle me) and, from Easter Sunday to the Feast of Pentecost, with the antiphon **Vidi Aquam** [I saw water]). So, for example at the conclusion of the *asperges* the Priest prays:

Orémus

Exáudi nos, Dómine sancte, Pater omnípotens, aetérne Deus, et míttere dignéris sanctum Angelum tuum de caelis, ut qui custódiat, fóveat, prótegat, vísitet atque deféndat omnes habitántes in hoc habitáculo. Per Christum Dóminum nostrum. Amen.

(Heed us, O holy Lord, Father almighty, O eternal God, and may you vouchsafe to send your holy Angel from heaven, that he may guard, cherish, protect, visit, and defend all present in this house. Through Christ our Lord. Amen.)

This prayer begins with the 2nd pers sg pres act imp *exaudi*, followed by the 2nd pers sg pres subj of dep verb *dignari* and is preceded by the pres act inf *mittere* and followed by one of the most common Latin constructions, the *ut* + subjunctive dynamic: *ut* + *qui* + 3rd pers sg pres act subj of *custodire* + 3ʳᵈ pers sg pres act subj of *fovere* + 3ʳᵈ pers sg pres act subj of *protegere* + 3ʳᵈ pers sg pres act subj of *defendere*. In one of its most common English translations:

> 'O Lord, holy Father almighty, everlasting God, we beseech thee to hear us: and vouchsafe to send thy holy Angel from heaven, to guard and cherish, protect and visit, and evermore defend all that dwell in this dwelling-place. Through Christ our Lord. Amen.'

The consonant force of the subjunctive dynamic tends to be lost by translating the optative subjunctives as purposive infinitives. Linguistically, subjunctive dissonance does not always need to be resolved into more positive indicatives. But the narrative journey involved in prayer is, in the end, all about that resolution of uncertainty into certainty. We don't always need the language to do the work on our behalf, even before we have prayed the prayer, so to speak. For example, the *Postcommunion Antiphon* prayed at the Mass of Our Lady of Mount Carmel on July 16:

> *Adiuvet nos, quǽsumus, Dómine, gloriósae tuae Genitrícis sempérque Vírginis Maríae intercéssio veneránda: ut quos perpétuis cumulávit benefíciis, a cunctis perículis absolútos, sua fáciat pietáte concórdes: Qui vivis et regnas, cum Deo Patre in unitáte Spíritus Sancti, Deus per ómnia sǽcula saeculórum. Amen.*

might be literally translated:

> (May the intercession to be venerated of your glorious Mother and ever Virgin Mary help us, we beseech, O Lord: that those lavished with perpetual blessings, from all dangers having been absolved, by her piety she may make, like-minded: Who lives and reigns, with God [the] Father in unity of the Holy Spirit, God, though all ages of ages. Amen.)

This is clumsy on the face of it as an English prayer, but it reflects not only the grammar of the Latin original, but also foregrounds the Latin of that original as a very specific language in its own right, and not one that necessarily follows 'English' rules. In other words, praying in Latin is about praying *in Latin*, and not turning that Latin into a version of English in our heads. We all do this, of course, especially when the Latin, as it can, might become very complex at times, especially when highly compressed as in some of the Latin hymns of the *Breviary*. One *Missal* translates this prayer as:

> 'May the august intercession of Mary, Thy glorious Mother, ever a virgin, help us, O Lord, that those whom it hath heaped with benefits it may deliver from all perils, and by her tender kindness, make to be of one mind. Who livest and reignest...'

Another translates it as:

> 'May we be assisted, we beseech Thee, O Lord, by the worshipful intercession of Thy glorious Mother, the ever-Virgin Mary; that we, who have been enriched by her perpetual blessings, may be delivered from all dangers, and through her loving kindness made to be of one heart and mind: Who livest and reignest...'

and another one as:

> 'May the holy intercession of thy glorious Mother Mary, ever virgin, help us, we beseech thee, O lord, that those on whom she has lavished unceasing favours, may be freed from all dangers, and by her loving kindness become of one mind, who livest and reignest...'

There are two subjunctives in the original Latin antiphon: **adiuvet** and **faciat** and both are 3rd pers sg pres act subj of **adiuvare** and **facere**. The issue in translating these subjunctives, then, is what they actually refer to. It is clearly not as one translation puts it, 'May we be assisted'; so who or what is the subject of the verb *adiuvet*? In two of these versions it is assumed rightly to be the nominative singular phrase *intercessio veneranda*, and so the literal translation would be transformed into:

> 'May the venerable intercession of your glorious Mother and ever Virgin Mary help us, we beseech [you] O Lord.'

The subjunctive verb *adiuvet* needs a subject, but we have to go to the end of the sentence to find it. This is quite different to English word order, and as we have seen earlier, in Latin this final position of a subject at the end of a sentence may make it stylistically more prominent than if it was at the beginning (especially given normal Latin word order where the verb generally comes at the end). The subjunctive force of the verb is given greater narrative force by our having to 'search' for its subject in the original Latin. We lose this narrative force in all of the translations, including my own literal version, because Latin works differently from English, and English works differently from Latin. What then of the second subjunctive *faciat*? Who or what is the subject of this verb, and where is it? It is a singular verb and so must have a singular subject, but everything around it is either plural or not in a nominative form. The only singular nominative phrase is *intercessio veneranda* and so, as recognised by one of the versions here, it must be the subject of *faciat*. That translation reads:

> 'May the august intercession of Mary, Thy glorious Mother, ever a virgin, help us, O Lord, that those whom it hath heaped with benefits it may deliver from all perils, and by her tender kindness, make to be of one mind. Who livest and reignest...'

where the subject 'august intercession' becomes the subject 'it' of 'it hath heaped' and the subject 'it' of 'it may deliver' and the unnamed 'it' of the verb 'make'. It is a clumsy translation, but one which recognises the importance of the subject 'intercession'. Recognising that *intercessio* is the subject of *faciat* the earlier literal translation would then become:

> May the venerable intercession of your glorious Mother and ever Virgin Mary, by her piety, we beseech you O Lord, help us, and may [it] make those absolved from all dangers, whom she has lavished with perpetual blessings, like-minded: Who lives and reigns, with God the Father in the unity of the Holy Spirit, God, through all ages of ages. Amen.

The word order of the Latin often requires a quite different mind-set to the one we may be used to in English, and hence, involves some thought. At the core of that thought is a simple principle, which is variously glossed over in some parts of the translations given above, that there is a force of grammatical logic with an inflected language like Latin, which means that phrases in the ablative like ***perpetuis beneficiis*** and ***a cunctis periculis*** will not be the subjects of a singular verb like *faciat*, and nor will plural words like ***absolutos*** and ***concordes***. The key point in all of this, is that we are not simply *reading* Latin text, or parsing its grammar, to better read that text, we are *praying* this text as a prayer, and unlike the grammar books designed to teach Latin, including those specifically designed to teach the Latin of the Mass and *Breviary*, praying Latin prayer requires a completely different mind-set to reading Latin text.

Latin prayers, like this, are not designed to be a test of our linguistic skills, though they might at first appear to be so; they are simply composed in a language that works differently in various ways to the English we use to translate them. The force of the Latin prayer for a native English speaker lies not just in the grammar and syntax of the prayer, but in that grammar and syntax slowing us down to better pray the prayer; and the larger (contextual) subjunctive force often lies in the uncertainty of doing that. Just two little subjunctive verbs like ***adiuvet*** and *faciat* and where they (and their subjects) occur in a text may create that uncertainty. While the English translations that often run side by side of the Latin texts in *Missals, Breviaries* and some prayer books, may appear to be equivalent to the Latin text, as we have seen often here, they may not be.

Probably one of the most forceful (and ancient) Latin prayers is the ***Te Deum laudamus*** (We praise you [the] God) c387AD in its current form, sung and recited at times of great celebration and joy and on most days of the year at the end of *Matins*:

TE DEUM

Te Deum laudámus: te Dóminum confitémur.
(We praise you God: we acknowledge you to be [the] Lord.)
Te aetérnum Patrem omnis terra venerátur.
(All the earth bows before you [the] Father everlasting.)
Tibi omnes Angeli, tibi Caeli, et univérsae Potestátes:
(To you all Angels, to you [the] Heavens, and all [the] Powers:)
Tibi Chérubim et Séraphim incessábili voce proclámant:
(To you Cherubim and Seraphim continually proclaim with voice:)
(*fit reverentia - a bow is made*)
Sanctus, Sanctus, Sanctus Dóminus Deus Sábaoth.
(Holy, Holy, Holy, Lord God of Sabaoth.)
Pleni sunt caeli et terra maiestátis glóriae tuae.
(Heaven and earth are full of [the] majesty of your glory.)
Te gloriósus Apostolórum chorus,
(You [the] glorious company of [the] Apostles,)
Te Prophetárum laudábilis númerus,
(You, [the] praiseworthy number of [the] Prophets,)
Te Mártyrum candidátus laudat exércitus.
(You [the] white-clothed army of Martyrs praise.)
Te per orbem terrárum sancta confitétur Ecclésia,
([The] holy Church through [the] orb of [the] lands praises you,)

Patrem imménsae maiestátis;
([The] Father of [an] infinite majesty;)
Venerándum tuum verum et únicum Fílium
(Your venerable true and only Son)
Sanctum quoque Paráclitum Spíritum.
(Also [the] Holy Spirit [the] Paraclete.)
Tu Rex glóriae, Christe.
(You are [the] King of Glory, O Christ.)
Tu Patris sempitérnus es Fílius.
(You are [the] everlasting Son of [the] Father.)
(*fit reverentia - a bow is made*)
Tu, ad liberándum susceptúrus hóminem: non horruísti Vírginis úterum.
(You, about to undertake to [the] freeing of man: you shrunk not from [the] Virgin's womb.)
Tu, devícto mortis acúleo, aperuísti credéntibus regna caelórum.
(You, [the] sting of death having been overcome, opened [the] kingdom of [the] heavens to all believers.)
Tu ad déxteram Dei sedes, in glória Patris.
(You sit at [the]right hand of God, in [the] glory of [the] Father.)
Iudex créderis esse ventúrus.
([O] Judge you will be believed to be about to come.)
(*hic genuflectitur - here is genuflected*)
Te ergo quǽsumus, tuis fámulis súbveni, quos pretióso sánguine redemísti.
(We therefore beseech you, assist your servants, whom you have redeemed with precious blood.)
Aetérna fac cum Sanctis tuis in glória numerári.
(Make! them to be numbered with your Saints in glory everlasting.)
Salvum fac pópulum tuum, Dómine, et bénedic haereditáti tuae.
(O Lord save! your people, and bless! your inheritance.)
Et rege eos, et extólle illos usque in aetérnum.
(And rule! them, and lift! them up until eternity.)

Per síngulos dies benedícimus te.
(Through every day we bless you.)
(*fit reverentia - a bow is made*)
Et laudámus nomen tuum in sǽculum, et in sǽculum sǽculi.
(And we praise your name in [the]age, and in [the] age of age.)
Dignáre, Dómine, die isto sine peccáto nos custodíre.
(Vouchsafe! O Lord, this day to keep us without sin.)
Miserére nostri, Dómine, miserére nostri.
(Be merciful! of us, O Lord, be merciful! of us.)
Fiat misericórdia tua, Dómine, super nos, quemádmodum sperávimus in te.
(May your mercy, O Lord, be upon us, just as we have hoped in you.)
In te, Dómine, sperávi: non confúndar in aetérnum.
(In you, O Lord, I have hoped: I will not be confounded intowards eternity.)

The 'we' of *laudamus* contrasts forcefully with the 'you' (sg m) in *te*. The 'we' signifies finite humanity and the 'you' the infinite God, and powerfully distinguishes between the material and immaterial; between the subjunctive uncertainty of humanity and the indicative certainty of God. The 'we' further establishes not only a time frame of the 'here and now', but also an aspect of that 'here and now' which clearly acknowledges that the 'we' as subject of the verb 'to praise' is also the agent of that verb: the voice is active and not passive, and is reinforced by the active meaning of the passive form of the deponent verb *confitemur* (1st pers pl pres act ind of the dep verb *confiteri* - 'we praise'). We know deponent verbs are passive in form but active in meaning, and here that active voice signals very clearly that the subject 'we' is responsible for the actions of praising. Praising who? *Deum* and *Dominum* - both accusatives signalling that they are the recipients and beneficiaries of the action of praising. In one short opening sentence *Te Deum laudamus: te Dominum confitemur* this prayer presents the difference between the human 'we' and the eternal 'you', and by praise (*laudamus* and *confitemur*) offers, throughout the narrative journey we make when we pray it, a resolution to the dissonance (uncertainty) of humanity and the consonance (certainty) of God. And we make that journey by means of worship and adoration.

There is a strong narrative in the ***Te Deum*** made up almost entirely of indicative verbs (19) with 2 infinitives, 4 participles acting purposively, and 9 imperatives acting forcefully, and again we see a single subjunctive in the penultimate line - ***fiat*** - shifting the focus from present and past time to the future, culminating in the future certainty (consonance) of the last line of the prayer. The 'we' (that is us) has journeyed from the very first line, through the 'they' praising God and acknowledging through the 'you' of God and now finally comes to rest in the very last line with the 'I' of ***speravi*** (1st pers sg perf act ind) and ***non confundar*** (both 1st pers sg fut pass ind of ***confundere*** - 'I will not be confounded' and 1st pers sg pres pass subj of ***confundere*** - 'I may not be confounded'. The journey of this 'I' 'you' and 'we', together with the changing grammatical moods, throughout this majestic prayer, is a spiritual journey where the narrative actually proclaims the message, at the heart of this book, about letting the grammar open up our spiritual understanding.

The narrative journey in this prayer strikingly demonstrates that grammatical form and function can enable linguistic *address*, *focus* and *force* of grammar, to have a potentially powerful, spiritual/numinous, *affect* beyond the words. Praying Latin prayer is not simply about praying these words; nor simply about praying the ideas, the dogmas, the doctrines, and the truths of faith and Church teaching, which we do, of course, all the time. It is not just about the uncertainties, the hopes and the possibilities; it is not just about asking for things; for change; for resolution; it is not just about the difference between the 'I/we' and 'you/God'. It is about bringing all of these contingent/dissonant/subjunctive forces together in a consonant/certain/indicative way in order to create a 'both/and' not just an 'either/or', and thereby creating a disposition in the praying of a prayer like the ***Te Deum*** - indeed in the praying of all

Latin prayer - which has a textual, structural and grammatical architecture which also contextually and anagogically means beyond its words, syntax and narrative. We may seek to resolve subjunctive dissonance with indicative consonance, as an 'either/or', but in prayer it is always about both subjunctive dissonance *and* consonance. It is both about the world as it is here and now, and the eternal world as it might be. In the here and now it is a 'latreutic' (λατρευτικός - latreutikós - of [divine] service) world of uncertain adoration, emerging falteringly from a 'didactic' (διδακτικός - didaktikós - teaching) world of certain truths and values; it is an actual world of revelation and an anticipated world of hope and salvation for a ***vita beata***.

Subjunctive Affect

A Christian's primary purpose is to be saved; to achieve the ***vita beata***. St Augustine makes the telling point in one of his sermons:

> ***Si enim a vobis quaeram quare in Christum credideritis, quare christiani facti fueritis; veraciter mihi omnis homo respondet propter vitam beatam.***
> (For if I may seek from you why you will have believed in Christ, why you will have become Christians; a man truly responds to me because of [the] blessed life.)

This ***vita beata*** might also be understood as the 'fullness of joy' to come. It is not what we do here and now; not what we feel here and now; not what good we do here and now, that constitutes this joy. It is what is fulfilled in the next world that becomes the 'blessed life'. The Christian's primary purpose is not fellowship with others; not doing good works; not being charitable and kind to others; all these are important but not the primary purpose of being a Christian. As St Augustine says at the very beginning of his Rule:

> *Ante omnia, fratres carissimi, diligatur Deus, deinde et proximus, quia ista sunt praecepta principaliter nobis data.*
>
> (Before everything, dearest brothers, let God be loved, and then [your] neighbour, because these are [the] principal commandments given to us.)

A Priest's primary purpose is not to be a social worker, nor primarily to do earthly good. A Priest's primary purpose is to save souls. Our primary purpose as Christians is the salvation of our soul. The Church offers many opportunities for our being able to do that, but those ways individually are not the end purpose; they are a focussed means to one end: salvation (***vita beata***) through sanctification. For example, we may pray:

> *O Dómina mea! O Mater mea! Tibi me totum óffero, atque, ut me tibi probem devótum, cónsecro tibi óculos meos, aures meas, os meum, cor meum, plane me totum. Quóniam ítaque tuus sum, O bona Mater, serva me, defénde me ut rem ac possessiónem tuam. Amen.*
>
> (O my Lady! O my Mother! To you I offer myself in full, and, so that I may prove to you [the] devoted me, I consecrate to you my eyes, my ears, my mouth, my heart, fully my whole self. And so, since I am yours, O good Mother, keep me, defend me, as your subject and property. Amen.)

And again with St Aloysius Gonzaga (1568-1591):

> *O Dómina mea, sancta María, me in tuam benedíctam fidem ac singulárem custódiam et in sinum misericórdiae tuae, hódie et quotídie et in hora éxitus mei ánimam meam et corpus meum tibi comméndo. Omnem spem et consolatiónem meam, omnes angústias et misérias meas, vitam et finem vitae meae tibi commítto, ut per tuam sanctíssimam intercessiónem et per tua mérita, ómnia*

mea dirigántur et disponántur ópera secúndum tuam tuíque Fílii voluntátem. Amen.

(O my Lady, holy Mary, into your blessed faith and singular custody and into [the] protection of your mercy, this day, and every day of my life and at [the] hour of my death, I commend me to you, my soul and my body. All my hope and consolation, all my trials and miseries, my life and [the] end of my life, I commit to you, that through your most holy intercession and by your merits, all my actions may be ordered and disposed according to your will and of your Son. Amen.)

These prayers are a fully Catholic recognition that we cannot reach salvation alone. They are prayers of submission to the Mother of God, knowing that it is through her that we may come to Jesus, and, through Jesus we may come to the Father, and thus, we hope, to ultimate sanctification and salvation: the *vita beata*. We may also pray:

O intemeráta et in aetérnum benedícta, singuláris atque incomparábilis Virgo Dei Génetrix María, gratíssimum Dei templum, Spíritus Sancti sacrárium, iánua regni caelórum, per quam post Deum totus vivit orbis terrárum. Inclína, Mater misericórdiae, aures tuae pietátis indígnis supplicatiónibus meis, et esto mihi misérrimo peccatóri pia, et propítia in ómnibus auxiliátrix.

(O unviolated and blessed into eternity, singular and incomparable Virgin Mary, Mother of God, most graceful temple of God, sanctuary of [the] Holy Spirit, gate of [the] kingdom of [the] heavens, through whom after God [the] whole world lives. Incline, [O] Mother of Mercy your ears of piety to my unworthy supplications, and be merciful to me [a] most wretched sinner, and [a] kind helper in all things.))

This is complete submission. This is not saying 'help me a little bit'. This is acceptance not only of her unique status, but also of her unique position before her Son and his Father: to stand in our stead, as the Angels and Saints do, to pray for us and to intercede for us. It seems, from a Catholic point of view, unthinkable to not include the Blessed Virgin Mary in our prayers and meditations. Indeed later in the prayer we pray:

> *Credo enim fírmiter et indubitánter fatéor, quia velle vestrum velle Dei est et nolle vestrum nolle Dei est; unde et quicquid ab illo petítis sine mora obtinétis. Per hanc ergo tam potentíssimam vestrae dignitatis virtútem poscíte, quaeso, mihi peccátori, corpóris et ánimae salútem.*
>
> (For I firmly believe and accept without doubt, because to wish yourself of God is to wish [to be] of God, and to not wish yourself is not [to be of God]; and from where you can gain whatever you ask from him without delay. Beg, therefore, for this, [the] most powerful virtue of your dignity: [the] salvation, [for] me a sinner, of my body and soul, I beseech you.)

Sanctification, as prayed for here through Mary, is about *theosis*; seeking to share in the sanctity of God. In the index compiled to the 1886 edition of St Alphonsus de Liguori's *The Way of Salvation and of Perfection, Meditations - Pious Reflections - and Spiritual Treatises* edited by Fr Eugene Grimm CSSR, from the original Italian, under the listing 'Sanctity', we read:

> 'SANCTITY. Sanctity or perfection consists in divine love, p353. To be saintly the soul must give itself to God without reserve, p181. Two great means of sanctity, desire and resolution, p184.'

It might seem unusual to quote from an index to a book, rather than the book itself, but what more powerful a summary of both the Church's teaching, and saintly considerations of 'sanctity' could there be than this short index entry? Fr Grimm's 1926 edition opens with a marvellous 'Notice' declaring: 'This volume contains the quintessence of the science of the saints.' That 'science' is the science of sanctity, but we cannot strive for sanctity alone, and nor did the Saints. St Paul tells the Corinthians, which we pray at the end of the *Epistle* for the Mass of St Justin (100-165) one of the very first martyrs, who we celebrate on the 14th of April that:

> ***Ex ipso autem vos estis in Christo Iesu, qui factus est nobis sapiéntia a Deo, et iustítia, et sanctificátio, et redémptio.***
> (Thus you are in Christ Jesus himself, who wisdom made for us from God, and justification, and sanctification, and redemption. *1 Cor* 1:30)

The spiritual journey is therefore always one which seeks to share in Jesus; in Divinity. Again St Paul writes:

> *sanctificatis in Christo Iesu, vocatis sanctis, cum omnibus qui invocant nomen Domini nostri Iesu Christi, in omni loco ipsorum et nostro.*
> (to [the] sanctified in Christ Jesus, having been called holy, with all who invoke [the] name of our Lord Jesus Christ, in every place of theirs and ours. *1 Cor* 1:2)

The crucial phrase here is the ablative absolute ***vocatis sanctis*** with the perfect passive participle of ***vocare*** - to call - 'having been called' to be holy. St Paul tells the Hebrews:

> ***Pacem sequimini cum omnibus, et sanctimoniam, sine qua nemo videbit Deum:***
> (Follow! peace with all, and [the] sanctity, without which no one will see God. *Heb* 12:14)

Therefore with the *Epistle* for the 7th Sunday after Pentecost we pray with St Paul:

> *exhibéte membra vestra servíre iustítiae in sanctificatiónem*
> (yield! your members to serve justice intowards sanctification. *Rom* 6:19)

The word 'yield' (borrowed here from the *DR*) serves a very Catholic purpose: we give way before God at all times, just as we genuflect before the real presence in church. Before Confession (**Oratio Praeparatoria ad Confessionem**) we are encouraged in **usus antiquior** missals to pray:

> *Cónditor caeli et terrae, Rex regum et Dóminus dominántium, qui me de níhilo fecísti ad imáginem, et similitúdinem tuam et me próprio tuo sánguine redémisti, quem ego peccátor non sum dignus nomináre, nec invocáre, nec corde cogitáre.*
>
> (Creator of heaven and earth, King of kings, and Lord of dominations, who has made me from nothing in your image and likeness, and has redeemed me with your own blood, whom I, a sinner, am neither worthy to name, to call upon, nor to cogitate by heart. [contemplate])

The first verb *fecisti* is a 2nd pers sg perf act ind of the infinitive *facere* (to make). At the very beginning of what is, in fact, a very long prayer, the indicative certainty of God doing something for us (making us) is established. What can be more fundamental than being made, and even more than that, being made in the image and likeness of God? But there is more. The second verb is **redemisti** a 2nd pers sg perf act ind of the infinitive **redimere** (to redeem/atone/rescue) again a powerful indicative statement of what God has done for us. The third verb we see is **sum** where the narrative point of view has shifted from the certainties of God to the uncertainties of who I am: *peccator* (a sinner) who is not worthy, and then come three infinitives, **nominare, invocare, cogitare** (to name, to call upon, and to cogitate *corde* (by heart). The indicative focus of the certainty of God (*fecisti/redemisti*) begins to transform into the uncertainty (***non sum***) of us as humans, and in the next part of the prayer, fully transforms into a forceful imperative call for mercy:

> *Te supplíciter déprecor, et humíliter exóro, ut cleménter respícias me servum tuum nequam. Et miserére mei, qui misértus fuísti muliéri Canáneae, et Maríae Magdalénae: qui pepercísti publicáno, et latróni in cruce pendénti.*
>
> (I humbly beg you, and I earnestly beseech, that you may look mercifully on me your wicked servant. And be merciful! of me, [you] who was merciful to the woman of Canaan, and to Mary Magdalene: [you] who spared the publican, and [the] thief hanging upon [the] cross.)

With the exception of the subjunctive ***respicias***, the indicative verbs of this prayer focus on God as the creator/provider/redeemer paving the way for the single imperative ***miserere*** calling upon him to be merciful. The prayer continues:

> *Tibi confíteor, Pater piíssime, peccáta mea, quae si volo abscóndere, non possum tibi, Dómine. Parce mihi, Christe, quem ego nuper multum offéndi cogitándo, loquéndo, operándo, et in ómnibus modis, in quibus ego frágilis homo et peccátor peccáre pótui, mea culpa, mea culpa, mea maxíma culpa.*
>
> (To you, I confess, O most compassionate Father, my sins, which if I wished to hide from you, I am not able, O Lord. Be sparing! to me, O Christ, whom I recently much offended in thinking, speaking, doing, and in all ways, in which I, [a] weak man and sinner have been able to sin, through my fault, my fault, my most grievous fault.)

As the recognition of sinfulness develops, so the pleading for mercy continues, and does so even more in the next part of the prayer. The imperatives continue, but gain even more force by the incredibly powerful indicative ***tu es***, creating a quite beautiful prayer of human supplication and recognition of the Divine. The prayer continues for many more paragraphs with the imperative-indicative dynamic at its heart, indicative itself of the force of the divine-human dynamic focussed at the centre of all prayer and concludes with:

> *Ideo, Dómine, precor tuam cleméntiam, qui de caelo pro mea salúte descendísti, qui David a peccáti lapsu erexísti, parce mihi, Dómine, parce mihi Christe, qui Petro te negánti pepercísti. Tu es Creátor meus et Redémptor meus, Dóminus meus et Salvátor meus, Rex meus et Deus meus.*

(Therefore, O Lord, I plead your clemency, you who descended from heaven for my salvation, who raised up David from [his] fall by sin, be sparing! to me O Lord, be sparing! to me, O Christ, who spared Peter having denied you. You are my Creator and my Redeemer, my Lord and my Saviour, my King and my God.)

> *Deprécor te, clementíssime Pater, propter misericórdiam tuam, súpplico et exóro, ut perdúcas me ad bonum finem, et ad veram paeniténtiam, puram confessiónem, et dignam satisfactiónem ómnium peccatórum meórum. Amen.*

(I implore you, O most clement Father, according to your mercy, I beseech and I beg, that you may lead me ontowards [a] good end, and ontowards true penance, [a] pure confession, and worthy satisfaction for all my sins. Amen.)

The imperative-indicative dynamic which, repeated as it is throughout, with the exception of the subjunctive ***perducas***, provides a focus to the prayer which reinforces the power of God and the fragility of us, the pray-er, seeking the fortitude and grace to be sufficiently repentant in order to receive forgiveness. We fail as people before God. We experience that failure by confessing our sin. We are affected by sin. St Paul understood this well:

Peccatum enim vobis non dominabitur: non enim sub lege estis, sed sub gratia.

(Sin will not be able to play the master over you any longer; you serve grace now, not the law. *Knox Rom* 6:14)

And he then asks:

Quid ergo? peccabimus, quoniam non sumus sub lege, sed sub gratia? Absit.

(And if it is grace, not the law, we serve, are we therefore to fall into sin? God forbid. *Knox Rom* 6:15)

Serving grace is an ongoing business, and to do so we need to be *servi facti Deo* (made slaves to God) and in doing so ***habetis fructum vestrum in sanctificationem, finem vero vitam aeternam*** (you have your fruit intowards sanctification, the end truly life everlasting. *Rom* 6:22). Petition, confession, contrition and penance are therefore an integral part of the journey to sanctification.

In a prayer referred to in **Liber Secundus Paralipomenon** (The Second Book of Paralipomenon [2 Chronicles] 33:13,18) and presumed to have been written later, and then included at the end of the book, but following the Council of Trent was later considered apocryphal and so was relocated into the Appendix of the *Vulgate* by Pope Clement VIII. It is known as the *Prayer of Manasseh*, a 2[nd]C BC King, sent into exile for his sins, and who eventually sought forgiveness of God. Despite its apocryphal status it holds within it a powerful architecture of 'petition', 'confession', 'contrition' and 'penance' which has been at the very heart of Catholicism since its earliest days. As part of his prayer Manasseh acknowledges God:

Et, tu, igitur, Domine, Deus iustorum, non posuisti paenitentiam iustis Abraham et Isaac et Iacob his qui tibi non peccaverunt, sed posuisti paenitentiam propter me peccatorem.

| 427 |

(Therefore thou, O Lord, God of the righteous, hast not appointed repentance for the righteous, for Abraham and Isaac and Jacob, who did not sin against thee, but thou hast appointed repentance for me, who am a sinner. *RSV*:8)

confesses his sins:

Quoniam peccavi super numerum harenae maris, multiplicatae sunt iniquitates meae, Domine, multiplicatae sunt iniquitates meae! Et non sum dignus intueri et aspicere altitudinem caeli prae multitudine iniquitatum mearum.

(For the sins I have committed are more in number than the sand of the sea; my transgressions are multiplied, O Lord, they are multiplied! I am unworthy to look up and see the height of heaven because of the multitude of my iniquities. *RSV*:9)

is contrite and sorrowful:

Incurvatus sum multo vinculo ferro, ut non possim attollere caput meum et non est respiratio mihi, quia excitavi iracundiam tuam et malum coram te feci statuens abominationes et multiplicans offensiones.

(I am weighted down with many an iron fetter, so that I am rejected because of my sins, and I have no relief; for I have provoked thy wrath and have done what is evil in thy sight, setting up abominations and multiplying offenses. *RSV*:10)

and seeks forgiveness:

Et nunc flecto genua cordis mei, precans ad te bonitatem Domine. Peccavi, Domine, peccavi, et iniquitatem meam agnosco. Quare peto rogans te, Domine, remitte mihi, remitte mihi! Ne simul perdas me cum iniquitatibus meis neque in aeternum iratus reserves mala mihi neque damnes me in infima terrae loca.

(And now I bend the knee of my heart, beseeching thee for thy kindness. I have sinned, O Lord, I have sinned, and I know my transgressions. I earnestly beseech thee, forgive me, O Lord, forgive me! Do not destroy me with my transgressions! Do not be angry with me for ever or lay up evil for me; do not condemn me to the depths of the earth. *RSV*: 11-13)

Quia tu es, Deus, Deus inquam paenitentium, et in me ostendes omnem bonitatem tuam! Quia indignum salvabis me secundum magnam misericordiam tuam, et laudabo te semper omnibus diebus vitae meae. Quoniam te laudat omnis virtus caelorum et tibi est gloria in saecula saeculorum. Amen.

(For thou, O Lord, art the God of those who repent, and in me thou wilt manifest thy goodness; for, unworthy as I am, thou wilt save me in thy great mercy, and I will praise thee continually all the days of my life. For all the host of heaven sings thy praise, and thine is the glory for ever. Amen. *RSV*: 14-15)

This might be summarised in this much shorter prayer:

Líbera me, Dómine, Iesu Christe, ab ómnibus iniquitátibus meis et univérsis malis, fac me tuis semper inhaerére mandátis et a te numquam separári permíttas. Amen.

(Deliver me, Lord Jesus Christ, from all my iniquities and from every evil, make me hold ever fast to Thy commandments and never allow me to be separated from Thee. Amen. *trad*)

As Catholics we are blessed with the sacramental grace of Confession. We cannot escape the sense of shame by that confession, made even more experiential by the physical act of confessing to Christ through a Priest, usually in a physical confessional in church (fewer and fewer of which exist post *Vatican II*). The experiential (sensory) *address, focus, force* and *affect*, both bodily and spiritual, of such confessions, and all other forms of prayer and submission, should never be marginalised, but celebrated, and although we do this as Catholics most effectively through the Liturgy as the very best and ultimate form of Latin prayer, all prayer is about all of these issues, connecting the subjunctive and uncertain frailties of finite humanity, before the indicative and certain face of an infinite, transcendent God. To that end, one of the most significant subjunctive affects of prayer is the 'dissonant-consonant dynamic' which lies at the heart of subjunctive prayer. St Alphonus' very first meditation, originally written in Italian and headed 'On Eternal Salvation' reads:

> 'Our most important affair is that of our eternal salvation; upon it depends our happiness or misery for ever. This affair will come to an end in eternity, and will decide whether we shall be saved or lost for ever; whether we shall have acquired an eternity of delights, or an eternity of torments; whether we shall live for ever happy, or for ever miserable. O God, what will my lot be ? Shall I be saved, or shall I be lost? I may be either. And if I may be lost, why do I not embrace such a life, as may secure for me life eternal? O Jesus, thou didst die to save me; yet have I been lost, as often as I have lost thee my sovereign good: suffer me not to lose thee any more.' (trs Jones [1836])

'Our most important affair' and what this means for our disposition in prayer on the journey to sanctification (the whole point of prayer) is explored in more detail in *Chapter XII: Dispositional Prayer*.

XII

DISPOSITIONAL PRAYER

Bihoueð us to rennen to cristes quike welle... gingen us to godeward & gemen us siðen forðward.
(It is necessary for us to run to Christ's living well... for us to go Godward and forward happily after. c1275 *English Bestiary*)

Godliness

When St Paul wrote his first letter to Timothy he captured a central axiom of the Christian faith which has, in the ensuing two thousand years, proven to be both enduring and life-changing for billions of people. He wrote:

Est autem quaestus magnus píetas cum sufficiéntia.
(For piety with sufficiency is a great advantage. *1 Tim* 6:6)

which we pray in the *Epistle* for the Mass of St Benedict Labre (1748-1783) who lived his life as a holy pilgrim, and is the patron Saint of the homeless. We probably have a good idea of what we think St Paul means here by 'piety', but what exactly is meant by 'sufficiency'? Ronald Knox translates the verse very freely as:

'And indeed, religion is ample provision for life, though no more than a bare sufficiency goes with it.'

which seems at first not to help much at all, unless we go to what we pray in the *Epistle* for the 12th Sunday after Pentecost from St Paul:

> *non quod sufficiéntes simus cogitáre áliquid a nobis, quasi ex nobis: sed sufficiéntia nostra ex Deo est.*
> (not that we may be sufficient to think anything by ourselves, as from ourselves: but our sufficiency is from God. *2 Cor* 3:5)

Sufficiency is not simply about filling a material need. It is not simply about the self. As St Paul says, it describes a disposition gifted to us by God. There is, in fact, no sufficiency except that it is gifted by God. Ronald Knox tries to get this sense of sufficiency into the way he translates the verse:

> 'not that, left to ourselves, we are able to frame any thought as coming from ourselves; all our ability comes from God.' (*2 Cor* 3:5)

In other words we are not sufficient unto ourselves. Any sufficiency we may have is from God. Everything we are as humans and every word we use, only has the fullest of its potential when understood through the lens of this gift of God. Recognising this, the *DR* translates *pietas* (piety) from *Est autem quaestus magnus pietas cum sufficientia*, by going beyond the standard uses of this Latin noun as 'duty', 'conduct', 'affection', 'love', 'piety', 'compassion' and 'devotion' (all of which can be, and indeed are in Latin used without any reference to God) to one which only has any meaning, any sufficiency, when that meaning and sufficiency is seen to come from God. The word the *DR* uses is 'Godliness'. It occurs several times in the *First Letter to Timothy*, though much more infrequently in the rest of the *DR,* but its most prominent use is when we pray the 1st Nocturn of *Matins* on the Thursday of the 5th week after Epiphany when St Paul introduces himself to Titus as:

Paulus servus Dei, Apóstolus autem Iesu Christi secúndum fidem electórum Dei, et agnitiónem veritátis, quae secúndum pietátem est.
(Paul, a servant of God, moreover an apostle of Jesus Christ according to the faith of the elect of God, and the acknowledging of the truth, which is according to godliness. *DR Tit* 1:1)

Truth for St Paul can only be understood through the lens of 'Godliness'. It is a powerful word in English in a way in which the English word 'piety' no longer tends to be. It focusses on God in ways which reflect God's centrality in all things. In this light our sufficiency is simply a fragment of God's, and words like 'Godliness' emerged in the English language at a time when, long before the Reformation, Catholicism was inextricably woven into the very fabric of everyone's life, language and activities. Another such word is 'Godward' which occurs several times in Middle English in phrases like 'His hope is al to gode ward.' and, as in part of the epigraph to this Chapter, 'Gingen us to godeward.' (Let us go towards God) which occurs in the only surviving manuscript of a 13[th]C Middle English *Bestiary* based on the 11[th]C **Physiologus** of Theobaldus, an Italian monk.

The daily round for everyone, before the Reformation opened the flood gates of Christian variations and spiritual indifference, no matter the status, low or high-born, was totally influenced by the Catholic Church. Everything a person thought or did was shaped by Catholicism, even those like John Wycliffe (1320-1384) one of the forerunners of the Protestant Reformation, sought their reforms through the lens of Catholicism. His translation of the *Vulgate* into English, then against the law, was done so in the belief that ordinary people needed to know the words of Scripture in their own language. His views, and those of the Lollards who supported him, were condemned at the time as heretical. English poet John Gower (1330-1408) and contemporary of Wycliffe calls such heretical views (with an English word now sadly no longer used) 'ungoode'. Written in various ways in medieval manuscripts 'ungod/ungode' means exactly what it looks like: *un* + *God* - to be *un* + *good* is to be *unGod* - without God. It is the opposite of 'good', and it is so because 'good' is understand only as something/someone that is made *sufficient* because of God. Something is understood as 'ungood' because it is insufficent, and insufficient is understood as something/someone *without God*. Something that is good is therefore considered to be 'Godly'. In a 12thC poem of Biblical commentaries and homilies written in Middle English by a monk of Bourne Abbey in Lincolnshire named Orm (Ormin) and referred to by the author himself as the *Ormulum* we read:

> 'Þatt mann hemm hallt forr gode menn, Forr rihhtwise & clene,
> & sinndenn þohh biforenn Godd Unngode & unnrihhtwise.'

Where a distinction is made between flawed men (*hallt* - lame or crippled men and *gode* men, whole men - men with God. A contrast is made between *gode* and *unngode*; between the *rihhtwise* (righteous) and *unnrihhtwise* (unrighteous) who, both stand before *Godd* as 'gode' or 'ungode'. The very concepts of 'hallt', 'gode', 'rihtwisse', 'clene', 'unngode' and 'unrihhtwise', indeed man himself, can only be talked about, let alone comprehended, in terms of God himself.

English, as it was emerging as a national language from Anglo-Saxon (5th-10thC) through Middle English (11th-15thC) heavily influenced as it was from Saxon and Viking invasions and settlement, had ways of expressing (like *gode/ungode*) which were often superceded by the much heavier influences of Norman French following the invasion in 1066, and from the all pervasive Latin of the Church throughout the whole period. What we might consider to be 'native' English has a forceful character (*rihhtwisse/unrihhtwisse*) often lost to us now. But including comment on it here is a recognition of the times in which this English developed when God and Catholicism were not just at the heart of the changing nation, but at the very heart of the vernacular they were using. Middle English is replete with the contrasting use of 'gode' and 'ungode'. John Gower writes, for example:

'The vice of hem that ben ungoode is no reproef unto the goode.'

This is not simply a description of good and bad, it is referring to those 'who have God' and those 'who do not have God', a considerably more forceful understanding of what 'good' and 'bad' actually is. Gower (poet and friend of English language pioneering poets Geoffrey Chaucer (c1340-1400) William Langland (1332 -1386) and John Lydgate (1370-1451) wrote in Latin, French and English, when French was the dominant language of the Court and Chancery, and Latin the dominant language of the Church and education. His poetry in English is just one dialect of the various dialects of Middle English that formed the vernacular of the ordinary person. These were the people that he wrote so eloquently about, and against (in Latin) in his poem about the Peasants' Revolt, **Vox Clamantis** (Voice of Crying out). His poem **Confessio Amantis** (Confession of Loving c1386-90) written in an East Anglian Middle English dialect (compared with the London based dialect of Chaucer and the East Midland dialect of Orm) is a confession told through a number of 'tales', and very much like his contemporaries, Chaucer and Langland, they are tales of morality narrated through stories mostly of the immorality of the times. These are the days before the invention of the printing press, and such English vernacular tales, which circulated widely in written manuscripts, and in an age of considerable illiteracy, would have mostly been recited aloud, often from memory, rather than read privately. They were generally composed in (or translated into) various regional dialects of Middle English and words like *Godlinesse* and *Godcundnesse* (Godliness/Godhead) tended to better capture the sense of 'God in everything' than similar words do today. For example, Richard Misyn (d 1462) translated Richard Rolle's **Incendium Amoris** (Fire of Love) into the English used in his area of Yorkshire at that time, for example:

> 'Godis gudelynes... is getyn be meditacion & prayer... ***Bonitatem & disciplinam & scienciam doce me***, þat is to say, guydlynes, disciplyn, and conynge tech me.'
>
> (God's goodliness... is got by meditation and prayer... ***Bonitatem & disciplinam & scienciam doce me*** that is to say, Godliness, discipline and knowledge teach me.)

Few today would immediately associate 'goodness/goodliness' as integrally emerging from God. The separation of 'good' from God, has, in fact, become the watchword of entire philosophical and secular movements that see the concept of the 'good' as defined only in terms of the 'self' and 'society' with no reference whatsoever to God. Dame Iris Murdoch (1919-1999) Oxford philosopher and novelist explored this position of the concept of 'the good' (the *summum bonum* we saw earlier) and the primacy of self in all her work, saying that:

> 'There is no beyond, there is only here, the infinitely small, infinitely great and utterly demanding present.'

For her, and so many like her, 'the good' of the ego is completely self-sufficient. It is the only sufficiency needed: an existential sufficiency of self. God not only has nothing to do with it, he is often completely excised from the scene. This, of course, is a totally untenable position where Latin Catholicism and prayer is concerned, and would have been unimaginable pre-Reformation, even to those seeking reform. So, introducing words like 'Godliness', as here, back onto the agenda of English translations of Latin prayer, re-orients the focus back to a God based world, even if only in just a tiny way. St Paul says:

> ***Sive ergo manducatis, sive bibitis, sive aliud quid facitis: omnia in gloriam Dei facite.***
>
> (Therefore, whether you eat or drink, or whatsoever else you do, do all to the glory of God. *DR 1 Cor* 10:31)

LATIN PRAYER

Wycliffe's 1382 version translates this as:

> 'Therfor whether ye eten, or drynken, or don ony other thing, do ye alle thingis in to the glorie of God.'

It appears to be much the same, but there is a crucial difference between the 'to the glory of God' of the *DR* and the 'in to the glorie of God' in Wycliffe. The Latin ***in gloriam*** is a preposition *in* + *accusative* which indicates movement *towards* God and Wycliffe picks this up. We have seen this often in this book: 'do ye alle thingis in to the glorie of God'. This is not just a straightforward imperative ***facite;*** it is an imperative requiring action of a very specific sort; an action that will move the 'you' of this command from their own realm *into* the realm of God. In other words 'towards God': in Gower's words, 'Gode-ward'. When the Priest stands at the foot of the altar before beginning a ***usus antiquior*** Mass, he prays:

> ***Introíbo ad altáre Dei.***
> (I will go uptowards/ontowards the altar of God.)

and the server responds:

> ***Ad Deum qui laetíficat iuventútem meam.***
> (Uptowards/ontowards God who delights my youth.)

There are various translations in *Missals*, but the Latin is really saying 'I will go Godward', initially uptowards the altar and via that altar and the sacrifice about to be made upon it, towards God himself. Architecturally, in a pre-*Vatican II* church, or one still retaining the architecture of the High Altar for the ***usus antiquior*** rites, this movement is signified by the Priest climbing the physical steps uptowards the altar itself, to where, standing on the top step (***predella***) facing away from the congregation (***ad orientem***) the Priest stands ***in loco Christi*** to offer the sacrifice of the Mass to God. Before he does this, the Priest and server continue by reciting the whole of *Psalm* 42 and pray:

> ***Emítte lucem tuam, et veritátem tuam: ipsa me deduxérunt, et adduxérunt in montem sanctum tuum, et in tabernácula tua.***
> (Send! out your light and your truth: they themselves have brought me, and led me ontowards your holy hill, and intowards your tabernacles.)

Again, there are several translations in various *Missals*, but look at the verbs **deduxerunt** and **adduxerunt**. Both are based on the verb **ducere** - 'to lead', but both are prefixed with a different preposition **de** (from) and **ad** (to). Taken together they linguistically signal an actual journey from (**de**) to (**ad**) and to capture that journey - that movement uptowards - we might translate the text as we have done at other times in this book, 'they have brought me down and led me intowards/ontowards'. This movement 'Godward' is further emphasised in the next part of the *Psalm* with the repetition of:

> ***Et introíbo ad altáre Dei: ad Deum qui laetíficat iuventútem meam.***

This is not just a statement of intent to worship given by the Priest (and server) on behalf of all. It is already Godward worship, made even more forceful by the Priest and server not positioning themselves ***versus populum*** (towards the people) as in the ***usus recentior*** Mass. This is not simply a preliminary call to worship, but as the beginning of the *Mass of Catechumens* (now referred to in the ***usus recentior*** Mass as 'The Liturgy of the Word') which originally focussed on those who had not yet been baptised, and so therefore were not yet prepared for the Sacrifice of the Mass proper that would come later, it is already worship. It already has within it a certain 'sufficiency'. This *Psalm* and the verb ***ducere*** - 'to lead', and its closeness to the verb ***docere*** - 'to teach', which is the focus of this part of the Mass, are a signal to the Catechumens that they are moving towards their own Baptism and therefore 'Godward' to one day fully participating as baptised Catholics, and then able to share in the sacrifice of the Mass itself, from which they were excluded as Catechumens. Baptism brings with it a sufficiency, a Godliness (*pietas*) which shifts the dispositional dynamic of worship 'Godward'.

The Dispositional Dynamic

Latin Prayer is liturgical; it is ritual; it is sacramental; it is physical; it is audible; it is musical; it is ceremonial and, as either private or public prayer, it is ancient and it is living. Of all the many things, that may describe Latin prayer, it is always dispositional. It is always about the way we dispose ourselves; about the attitudes we adopt and the mindset we have. Latin prayer is also, of course, about the Latin language and an important part of that language is the dynamic of grammatical disposition. Formal grammar uses the term *diathesis* (διάθεσις) to understand the *disposition* - the arrangement - of grammatical patterns, which, as we have seen many times in this book so far, are incredibly important in Latin prayer. We do this in language with words and grammar, and we do it in prayer with the way we dispose ourselves and our thoughts by means, initially, of those words and grammar. St Augustine in one of his Homilies (and which we pray in Nocturn III of *Matins* on the Feast of the Invention [Finding] of the Holy Cross - May 3) writes:

> *Si dixérimus catechúmeno: Credis in Christum? respóndet, Credo, et signat se Cruce Christi: portat in fronte, et non erubéscit de Cruce Dómini sui. Ecce credit in nómine eius. Interrogémus eum: Mandúcas carnem Fílii hóminis, et bibis sánguinem Fílii hóminis? nescit quid dícimus, quia Iesus non se crédidit ei.*

(Should you have said to [a] Catechumen: do you believe in Christ? he responds: I believe, and signs himself with [the] Cross of Christ: places [it] on [the] forehead, and he is not ashamed of [the] Cross of his Lord. Behold, he believes in his name. Let us ask him: Do you eat [the] flesh of [the] Son of man, and drink [the] blood of [the] Son of man? and he knows not what we say, for Jesus has not yet entrusted himself to him.)

This passage begins with ***dixerimus***, and the question we need to ask is whether to translate this as a 1st pers pl fut perf act ind of ***dicere***, 'if you will have said' or a 1st pers pl perf act subj of ***dicere***, 'if you might have said'. Both are possible and both make perfect sense in this context. In formal contemporary English we might render this as 'were you to have said', or as I do here, 'should you have said'. The grammar of the subjunctive sets up the question as hypothetical, thereby allowing St Augustine to offer some answers. And the answers that follow are all in the indicative:

- ***credis*** - 'you believe'

- ***respondet*** - 'he/she responds'

- ***credo*** - 'I believe'

- ***signat*** - 'he/she signs'

- ***portat*** - 'he/she places'

- ***erubescit*** - 'he/she is [not] ashamed'

- ***credit*** - 'he/she believes'

- ***manducas*** - 'you eat'

- ***bibis*** - 'you drink'

- ***nescit*** - 'he/she knows not'

- ***dicimus*** - 'we say'

- *credidit* - 'he/she has entrusted'

with the exception of *interrogemus* which is a 1st pers pl pres act subj of *interrogare* - 'may we/let us ask'. These indicatives said by, and about, the Catechumens in the first part of the text, grammatically indicate their assertion of faith. They are prepared by catechesis to become Christians through Baptism. They are being readied for Baptism because they believe, but as the second half of the text says, they have not yet been prepared for them to enter into the full sacramental life of a Catholic. That will take time and the right disposition. St Peter recognises this and greets the various (and much persecuted) Christians of Asia Minor with:

> *Gratia vobis, et pax adimpleatur in cognitione Dei, et Christi Iesu Domini nostri*
> (Grace to you, and may peace be fulfilled in [the] knowledge of God, and of Christ Jesus our Lord)

and continues:

> *Quomodo omnia nobis divinae virtutis suae, quae ad vitam et pietatem donata sunt, per cognitionem eius, qui vocavit nos propria gloria, et virtute, per quem maxima, et pretiosa nobis promissa donavit.*
> (As all things of his divine power, which are towards life and Godliness, through his knowledge are given to us, who has called us by his proper glory and virtue, through which he has given us most great and precious promises. *2 Pe* 1: 2- 3)

Here *pietas* (Godliness) is fully explained. Through God's divine power (*divinae virtutis*) we can move ontowards life (*ad vitam*) and ontowards Godliness (*ad pietatem*). It is only onthrough God's knowledge (*per cognitionem*) given to us from God by his proper glory and virtue (*propria gloria et virtute*) that we may be called to receive that sufficiency of Godliness, through the most great and precious promises (*per maxima et pretiosa promissa*). These don't fall out of the sky. They involve a journey and everything in this text shouts out 'movement towards' with the prepositions + accusatives. St Peter is saying to these Christians persecuted (and often martyred) for their Christian beliefs 'move Godward' because it is:

> *ut per haec efficiamini divinae consortes naturae.*
> (that through these you may become sharers of the divine nature.)

'Godliness', he writes, lies *in patientia* (within patience) and from that Godliness will come love (*caritatem*) (*2 Pe* 1:4-7). And so:

> *abundanter ministrabitur vobis introitus in aeternum regnum Domini nostri et Salvatoris Iesu Christi*
> ([an] entrance will be ministered to you abundantly intowards [the] everlasting kingdom of our Lord and Saviour Jesus Christ 2 *Pe* 1:11)

introitus in aeternum regnum - (an entrance intowards the everlasting kingdom) the dispositional goal of Godwardness.

In the *Catechism* we are urged to 'obey in faith' (*in fide oboedire* §144) in other words 'to submit'. The Latin word *oboedire* is formed from a preposition *ob* + *audire* which literally means 'towards to hear'. To obey is therefore to submit to a journey; a movement towards God; a Godward journey. Submission is therefore a movement towards hearing the word of God; the call of God; the grace of God. It is not simply a passive 'giving-in', but an active dispositional acceptance. We have to arrange ourselves - dispose ourselves - as the *Catechism* affirms:

In fide oboedire est se libere audito submittere verbo, quia eius veritas a Deo, qui ipsa veritas est, praestatur. Abraham huius oboedientiae est exemplar, nobis a sacra Scriptura propositum. Virgo autem Maria eius effectio est perfectissima.

(To obey in faith is to submit freely to the word that has been heard, because its truth is guaranteed by God, who is Truth itself. Abraham is the model of such obedience offered us by Sacred Scripture. The Virgin Mary is its most perfect embodiment. *Cat* §144)

Deus hominem ad Suam creavit imaginem et in amicitia constituit Sua. Homo, creatura spiritualis, in hac amicitia vivere non potest nisi per modum liberae submissionis ad Deum.

(God created man in his image and established him in his friendship. A spiritual creature, man can live this friendship only in free submission to God. *Cat* §396)

liberae submissionis ad Deum (free submission towards God) is expressed with a dispositional dynamic prep + acc (**ad Deum**) 'free submission', therefore, is a dispositional address in/ontowards God - 'Godward'. The *Catechism* (§2516) quotes St Paul, who does not condemn 'self', but is concerned **de operibus vel potius** (with morally good or bad works) that go with that 'self' (*Gal* 5:25). They are **de stabilibus habitibus** (permanent dispositions) **virtutibus et vitiis** (with the virtues and vices) **quoad actionem salvificam Spiritus Sancti** (subject to the saving action of the Holy Spirit). Quoting St Paul:

Si Spiritu vivimus, Spiritu et ambulemus.
(If we live by the Spirit, let us also walk by the Spirit. *Gal* 5:25)

In other words: **ambulemus** (1st pers pl pres act subj **ambulare**) - let us walk - Godward. Being a Catholic means developing a disposition that is prepared to submit to a Christian spirituality which involves submitting to the transforming grace of the Holy Spirit through the institution of the Church. The only contingency here is that true submission is contingent upon God's grace; the only social disposition (*habitus*) here is, as St Augustine says, (quoted in the *Catechism*):

> *Fideles Symboli credere debent articulos, 'ut credendo subiugentur Deo, subiugati recte vivant, recte vivendo cor mundent, corde mundato quod credunt intellegant.*

That 'the faithful must believe the articles of the Creed "so that by [the] believing (*credendo* - abl sg n gerund of *credere*) they may be subjected to (*subiugentur* 3rd pers pl pres pass subj *subiugare*) God, having obeyed (*subiugati* nom pl m perf pass participle of *subiugare*) and may live (*vivant* - 3rd pers pl pres act subj *vivere*) well, by [the] living well (*vivendo* abl sg n gerund of *vivere*) may purify (*mundent* 3rd pers pl pres act subj *mundare*) their heart[s], and with pure heart[s] may understand (*intellegant* 3rd pers pl pres act subj *intellegere*) what they believe." §2518). And so:

> 'The faithful must believe the articles of the Creed "so that by believing they may obey God, by obeying may live well, by living well may purify their hearts, and with pure hearts may understand what they believe."'

This is what *habitus* in prayer is all about. It is about submission, and not about contingent social habits. It is about the fruits of the Holy Spirit, not the fruits of 'self' and it is written very elegantly here in the *Catechismus* where the verbs transform from infinitive (*credere*) to indicative *credunt* through the gerund (*credendo*) and subjunctive (*subiugentur*) to participle (*subiugati*) providing a stylistic cohesion at the same time as suggesting a narrative journey. So, when we address the Holy Spirit:

> *Veni, Sancte Spíritus,*
> *reple tuórum corda fidélium, et tui amóris in eis ignem accénde.*

(Come!, O Holy Spirit, fill! [the] hearts of your faithful, and kindle!
in them [the] fire of your love).

a many centuries-old prayer with its imperatives ***veni, reple*** and ***accende*** commanding action, which is used every day by many in private prayers, and which liturgically is used for the Feast of Pentecost, especially as an antiphon for the ***Magnificat***, we are not seeking help from the social groups of which we are a part; or of the congregation in church. We are asking the Holy Spirit to light a fire within us that will fuel love in our hearts, not for those social groups, nor for short-term fellowship with that congregation, even of like-minded people sharing the same ***habitus***, but what the English 14thC mystic Richard Rolle of Hampole (1300-1349) called ***incendium amoris*** - 'the fire of love'. The opening of the prayer is usually followed by:

> *Emítte Spíritum tuum et creabúntur.*
> *Et renovábis fáciem terrae.*
> (Send forth Thy Spirit, and they shall be created, and Thou shalt renew the face of the earth. *trad*)

Send (*emitte* imp sg *emittere*) forth thy Spirit and they shall be created (*creabuntur* 3rd pers pl fut pass ind *creare*). And thou shalt renew (2nd pers sg fut act ind *renovare*) the face of the earth.) which is emphasising that the fire of love - the Holy Spirit - will create and will renew, not for the purposes of 'self', but to enkindle Godliness. It is then followed by a short Collect which is prayed as:

> *Orémus: Deus, qui corda fidélium Sancti Spíritus illustratióne docuísti, da nobis in eódem Spíritu recta sápere, et de eius semper consolatióne gaudére. Per Christum Dóminum nostrum. Amen.*
> (Let us pray: O God, who taught the hearts of the faithful by the light of the Holy Spirit, grant to us in the same Spirit to relish right

things, and to always rejoice from his consolation. Through Christ our Lord. Amen. *trad*)

where *sapere* is generally translated as 'to be wise'. Our contemporary sense of wisdom is that it is about 'knowledge'. But the Latin verb *sapere* can refer to 'taste' as in 'to have good taste'; 'to savour'; 'to have discernment'; 'to be able'; 'to be sensible' and 'to be skillful'. In effect the prayer is asking the Holy Spirit to fill (arrange/dispose) the hearts of the faithful with good taste and with discernment, to refocus their disposition, not to understand the worldly knowledge of God, or even to inspire good works and charity to others in the hearts of these people (necessary though these are) but to create the means within their hearts for 'Godliness'; to burn away the worldliness in their hearts with an *incendium amoris* which will create and renew the new Christian with the fruits of the Holy Spirit. This act of creation and renewal lies at the very heart of Judaeo-Christian spirituality. As Job was told:

> *Acquiesce igitur ei, et habeto pacem, et per haec habebis fructus optimos.*
> (Submit! therefore to him, and have! peace, and through this you will have [the] best fruits. *Iob* 22:21)

Not easy when Job was put through every hardship and test of faith imaginable. But this is the demanding ***habitus*** of the Holy Spirit, not of comfortable relativised social fictions. Judaism asks/asked a lot of its followers. Latin Catholicism asks it too. It asks that we shift our focus away from ourselves, not, as is the way of the world increasingly to shift that focus firmly onto ourselves, but dispositionally Godwards.

Godwardness

No more focussed a prayer of submission and dispositional Godwardness has ever been prayed, or ever will be, than that by Christ himself when in the Garden of Gethsemane, when he withdrew a little way from his disciples, knelt down and prayed:

verúmtamen non mea volúntas, sed tua fiat
(nevertheless not my will, but may yours be done *Lc* 22:42)

as we do with him when we pray this in the *Epistle* for the Wednesday of Holy Week. It is this total submission of Godliness which marks the Catholic way of Godwardness, and one of the reasons why every day many Latin Catholics, brought up in the rigours and discipline of such submission for Godliness, pray with St Ignatius of Loyola:

Súscipe, Dómine, univérsam meam libertátem. Accipe memóriam, intelléctum, atque voluntátem omnem. Quidquid hábeo vel possídeo mihi largítus es; id tibi totum restítuo, ac tuae prorsus voluntáti trado gubernándum. Amórem tui solum cum grátia tua mihi dones, et dives sum satis, nec áliud quidquam ultra posco. Amen.

(Receive, O Lord, my entire liberty. Accept [my] memory, intellect, and whole will. Whatever I have or possess you gifted to me; I return and surrender it all absolutely to you, to be submitted to your will. May you give to me only love of you with your grace, and I am [then] rich enough, I desire nothing more than this. Amen.)

St Ignatius of Loyola composed his *Spiritual Exercises* in Spanish between 1522 and 1524, as we saw earlier, and they were then translated into Latin and published in 1548 as **Exercitia Spiritualia,** within which he included this prayer. The *Exercises* were designed to take a retreatant through the life, passion and death of Christ over a period of 30 days. Throughout the course of those days the retreatant (now strongly advised to be led by an experienced retreat giver rather than to follow the *Exercises* without guidance) examines and empties themselves of anything and everything that would get in the way of complete submission to the Divine Will - the Divine Majesty. It is not an easy process, or indeed, an easy spirituality. It is demanding, it may be very draining, and requires a discipline of self which has to be trained (much as a soldier is trained) to submit completely to the will of God. It is not an approach to shaping the spiritual self which is suited to everyone. Fr Frederick Faber CO (1814-1863) one time companion of St John Henry Newman, and both founding members of the Oratorians in England, but poles apart in so many other ways, is reported to have once preached on St Ignatius for well over an hour, only to end by saying: 'This then, my dear brothers, is St Ignatius' way to heaven and thank God it is not the only way!' Presumably leaving his congregation somewhat stunned. It is not an easy way, and it is not everyone's way, as the opening makes clear:

> *Sicut enim deambulare, iter facere et currere exercitia sunt corporalia; ita quoque praeparare et disponere animam ad tollendas affectiones omnes male ordinatas, et iis sublatis ad quaerendam ac inveniendam voluntatem Dei circa vitae suae institutionem et salutem animae, exercitia vocantur spiritualia.*
>
> (For as to walk, to make [a] journey and to run are bodily exercises; so also to prepare and to dispose [the] soul ontowards removing all inordinate attachments, and their having been removed, ontowards searching and finding [the] will of God about [the] management of one's life and [the] salvation of [the] soul, [which] are called spiritual exercises.)

This one sentence coming right at the beginning of the *Exercises* is alluring, yet devastatingly difficult to accomplish in practice. It is the perfect definition of submission Godwards. The challenges are huge: to prepare the soul; to focus the soul; to remove inordinate attachments from the soul; to search for the will of God; to find the will of God; to manage one's life; in short, to dispose one's soul in order to practice Godwardness. Trappist Priest, mystic and martyr Saint Charles de

LATIN PRAYER

Foucauld (Brother Charles of Jesus, 1858-1916) knew this only too well. He prayed:

Mon Père,
Je m'abandonne à toi,
fais de moi ce qu'il te plaira.
Quoi que tu fasses de moi,
je te remercie.
Je suis prêt à tout, j'accepte tout.
Pourvu que ta volonté
se fasse en moi, en toutes tes créatures,
je ne désire rien d'autre, mon Dieu.
Je remets mon âme entre tes mains.
Je te la donne, mon Dieu,
avec tout l'amour de mon cœur,
parce que je t'aime,
et que ce m'est un besoin d'amour
de me donner,
de me remettre entre tes mains, sans mesure,
avec une infinie confiance,
car tu es mon Père.

(My Father,
I abandon myself to you;
do with me what it will please you.
Whatever you may do with me, I thank you:
I am ready for all, I accept all.
May your will only be done in me,
and in all your creatures.
I wish nothing more than this, O Lord.
I commend my soul into your hands:
I give it to you, my God, with all the love of my heart,
because I love you, and so must needs give myself,
to surrender into your hands without measure,

and with infinite confidence, for you are my Father.)

Martyred in his Algerian hermitage in 1916 (and canonized May 15 2022) he understood, more than most, that prayer required a disposition 'avec une infinie confiance', as indeed did St Thomas More (1478-1535) awaiting his own martyrdom in the Tower of London for upholding the true Catholic Faith, and refusing to accept King Henry VIII as the self-proclaimed Head of the English Church. More knew all about disposing one's soul with confidence when he composed a very beautiful prayer, made up of quotations from *Psalms* he had prayed (and memorised) all his life:

> *Dómine Deus, doce me fácere voluntátem tuam. Fac me cúrrere in ódere unguentórum tuórum. Apprehénde manum déxteram, et deduc me in via recta propter inimícos meos. Trahe me post te. In clamo et freno maxíllas meas constrínge, quum non approxímo ad te. Amen.*
>
> (O Lord God, teach me to do your will. Make me run in [the] scent of your ointments. Take my right hand, and lead me intowards [the] path of righteousness because of my enemies. Draw me after you. In [a] bit and bridle constrain my jaws, when I come not near you. Amen.)

He is locked in the Tower of London; his fate has been determined, and yet he is still focussed enough, Godward, to pray with imperatives calling on God: ***doce***; ***fac***; ***apprehende***; ***deduc***; ***trahe*** and ***constringe***, not to save him from his death, but to save his soul. He is close to death, yet he continues to pray for submission to God's will. He doesn't condemn his enemies, but effectively thanks them for enabling him to ask God to lead him 'intowards the path of righteousness'. He asks to be restrained, as a horse would be, in order to control him, and point him only in the direction of God. He quotes *Psalm* 142 (one of the 20 imprecatory

Psalms that call for judgement and even curses, upon people) and which we pray at Friday *Lauds* in the *PP* ever since the Pope St Pius V revisions in 1568, and which opens with the very familiar prayer:

> *Dómine, exáudi oratiónem meam; áuribus pércipe obsecratiónem meam in veritáte tua; exáudi me in tua iustítia.*
> (O Lord, heed! my prayer; perceive! [with your] ears my supplication within your truth; heed! me within your justice. *Ps* 142:1)

St Thomas More would have prayed this *Psalm* at Friday *Vespers* from his 1530 Book of Hours.

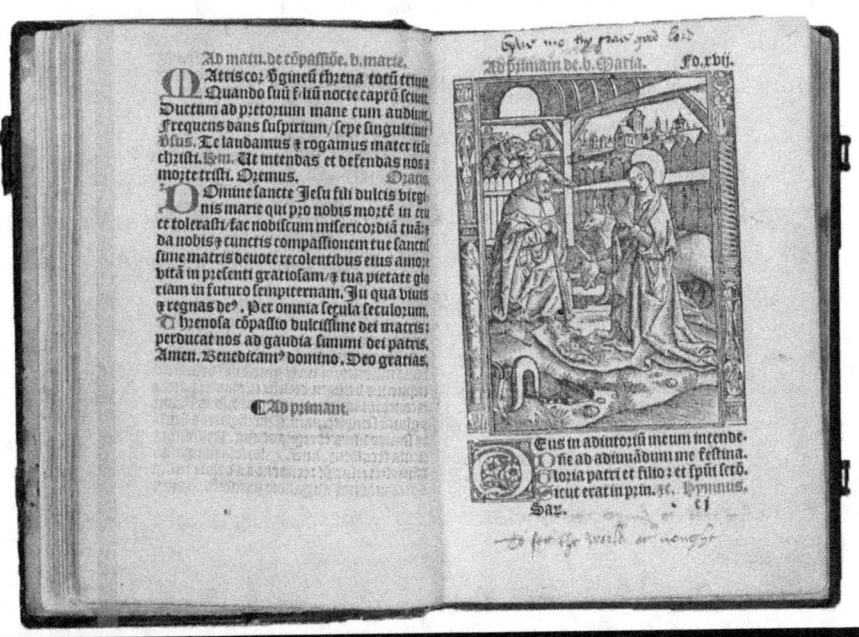

[*Psalterium cum hymnis secundum usum et consuetudinem Sarum et Eboracensis anno virginei part[ibus] Mccccc.xxii. Die vero. vii. mensis Iunii. Impressum Parisius Expe[n]sis & sumptibus honesti mercatoris Francisci Byrckman*]

Folio xvii records in his own handwriting at the top of the page the beginning of an English prayer written by him in the margins of this book while he was awaiting execution in the Tower of London: 'Give me thy grace good Lord', and at the bottom of the page: 'To sett the world at nought'. He carried this prayer book with him into the Tower praying from it to the very end, and, knowing what we do about him, these are very moving words and written in his own hand. They are carefully chosen, like those parts of the *Psalm* he chose to include in his own prayer. He could have included:

> *Eripe me de inimicis meis, Domine: ad te confugi.*
> (Deliver me from my enemies, O Lord: to you I have fled. *Ps* 142:9)

He might also have included:

> *et in misericordia tua disperdes inimicos meos, et perdes omnes qui tribulant animam meam, quoniam ego servus tuus sum.*
> (and in your mercy you will destroy my enemies, and you will cut off all who afflict my soul, because I am your servant. *Ps* 142:12)

But he chose not to. At the heart of his prayer, like St Ignatius just a few years earlier, and St Brother Charles of Jesus many centuries later, was his dispositional focus on submission Godward; not a desire for vengeance. Verse 10 of this *Psalm* with which he begins the prayer:

> *Doce me fácere voluntátem tuam*
> (Teach! me to do your will)

continues:

> *quia Deus meus es tu. Spiritus tuus bonus deducet me in terram rectam.*

(for you are my God. Your good spirit will lead me intowards [the] right land. *Ps* 142:10)

which he does not include. In his circumstances this is clearly implicit in everything he is praying for. He could have included the next verse:

Propter nomen tuum, Domine, vivificabis me: in aequitate tua, educes de tribulatione animam meam.
(According to your name, O Lord, you will enliven me within your justice, you will lead my soul out of trouble. *Ps* 142:11)

But he doesn't. Submission to God to do God's will, regardless of his dire situation and the injustice meted out to him, is his only concern:

Fiat volúntas tua. (May your will be done.)

Thomas à Kempis 100 years earlier had included a similar prayer in his ***De Imitatione Christi***:

Concéde mihi, benigníssime Iesu, grátiam tuam, ut mecum sit et mecum labóret mecúmque in finem usque persevéret. Da mihi hoc semper desideráre et velle, quod tibi magis accéptum est cárius placet. Tua volúntas mea sit, et mea volúntas tuam semper sequátur, et óptime ei concórdet. Sit mihi unum velle et nolle tecum, nec áliud posse velle aut nolle, nisi quod tu vis et nolis. Amen

(Grant to me your grace, O most merciful Jesus, that [it] may be with me and may work with me and may persevere with me even on-towards the end. Grant this to me always to desire and wish for what to you is more acceptable and more dear. May your will be mine, and may my will ever follow yours and agree perfectly with it. May my willing and not-willing be all one with you, nor to be able to will or not will anything else unless what you will or not will. Amen.)

This is a prayer of absolute submission Godwards, but recognising at the same time the challenges involved. No wonder this book was often the one book, other than the *Breviary*, that lay on the bedside tables of so many Popes, and countless other Latin Catholics, for nightly reading/praying, and is said to have been in the hands of Pope John Paul I (1912-1978) when he was found dead in bed. The subjunctives in this prayer hold a challenge within them as uncertain outcomes; hopefulness, as well as willingness to submit, is at the heart of the prayer. Likewise, Franciscan Doctor of the Church St Bonaventure (the 'Seraphic Doctor') lauded with St Thomas Aquinas as being one of just a handful of medieval philosophers and theologians who changed the scholastic directions of the Church, was thought for a long time to have composed the following prayer which also encapsulates this centrality of dispositional submission Godwards; of denial of self to the will of God:

Dómine sancte, Pater omnípotens, aetérne Deus, propter tuam largitátem et Fílii tui, qui pro me sustínuit passiónem et mortem, et Matris eius excellentíssimam sanctitátem, atque ómnium Sanctórum mérita, concéde mihi peccátori, et omni tuo benefício indígno, ut te solum dilígam, tuum amórem semper sitíam, benefícium passiónis contínuo in corde habéam, meam misériam recognóscam, et ab ómnibus conculcári et contémni cupíam; nihil me contrístet nisi culpa. Amen.

(O holy Lord, Father almighty, everlasting God, for [the] sake of your largesse and of your Son, who for me sustained passion and death, and of [the] most excellent holiness of his Mother, and [the] merits of all [the] Saints, grant to me [a] sinner, and unworthy of your every benefit, that I may love you only, may always thirst for your love, may continually have in my heart [the] benefit of passion, may recognise my misery and may desire to be despised and condemned by all; may nothing sadden me except sin. Amen.)

At the heart of all of these prayers are structures of language, form and style which when prayed reverently create a dispositional focus (*devotio*) often more powerful than the words and prayers (*devotiones*) themselves: a dispositional *focus* that can, through the *force* of their *address, affect* our lives - Godwards.

Devotio

Pope St Paul VI in his 1974 *Adhortatio Apostolica Marialis Cultus* (Apostolic Exhortation on Marian Devotion) delivered *Ad Episcopos universos pacem et communionem cum Apostolica Sede habentes* (To all Bishops having peace and communion with the Apostolic See) taught that:

> *Progressus autem, quem exoptamus, devotionis erga Mariam Virginem, insertae... in illum veluti cursum unius cultus, qui iure meritoque christianus appellatur cum a Christo originem et efficaciam trahat, in Christo integram absolutamque exprimendi rationem habeat per Christum ad Patrem ferat in Spiritu.*
>
> (The development, desired by us, of devotion to the Blessed Virgin Mary is an indication of the Church's genuine piety. This devotion fits... into the only worship that is rightly called "Christian," because it takes its origin and effectiveness from Christ, finds its complete expression in Christ, and leads through Christ in the Spirit to the Father. *Vat* §4)

The significant phrase used here is ***devotionis erga Mariam Virginem*** where the preposition ***erga*** is distinctively used in Medieval Latin to signify that a person is applying themselves to someone or something, in this case 'devotion to' the Blessed Virgin Mary. In Latin prayer it is important to distinguish between ***devotio*** as an abstract noun (like ***pietas*** - piety/Godliness) signalling 'a state of being devoted', from ***devotio/devotiones*** as a concrete noun referring to the actual prayer/s and act/s of devotion. As an abstract noun this requires dispositional change from us, and it is the concrete noun that may contribute to that change. Pope St Paul VI is referring here to devotion to Mary as a state of being; a disposition which 'leads to Christ in the Spirit to the Father.' He then refers to this *eadem devotio* (same devotion) as *cultus exhibitione intimo* (a special form of veneration) which, quoting *Lumen Gentium* (1965):

> *ipsa historia devotionis ostendit "varias formas pietatis erga Dei Genetricem, quas Ecclesia intra limites sanae et orthodoxie doctrinae approbavit" effectas esse et viguisse convenenti ratione subiectas cultui, qui Christo praebetur, et ad eum ferri quasi ad centrum, quo suapte natura et necessario referuntur.*
> (the history of piety shows how 'the various forms of devotion towards the Mother of God that the Church has approved within the limits of wholesome and orthodox doctrine' have developed in harmonious subordination to the worship of Christ, and have gravitated towards this worship as to their natural and necessary point of reference. *LG* §4)

That point of reference is the truth of revelation at the heart of Catholicism, and which is why *Marialis Cultus* concludes with the words:

> *Ecclesiae pietas erga Beatam Mariam Virginem pertinet ad naturam ipsum christiani cultus.*
> (The Church's devotion to the Blessed Virgin is an intrinsic element of Christian worship. *Vat* §56)

A significant part of that worship is Marian devotion. In the most glorious prayer prayed by the Blessed Virgin Mary (and prayed every day at *Vespers*) when the Archangel Gabriel appeared to her to announce (*annuntiare*) that Mary would conceive a child, and the child's name would be Jesus, found only in St Luke's *Gospel* (*Lc* 1:46-55) we pray the greatest of all Marian hymns and prayers, the *Magnificat*, which we saw earlier with an antiphon. There is a marvellous story told by Fr Ethelred Taunton (1857-1907) a member of *The Congregation of Oblates of St Charles* founded by Cardinal Nicholas Wiseman (1802-1865) in his magnificent treatise on *The Little Office of Our Lady* (1903) of a group of elderly monks who had sung the *Magnificat* every evening all their lives in their monastery, but with no new monks joining their ranks, and feeling their voices to now be too frail, they hired professional singers to sing this nightly praise to the Blessed Virgin. After some time of this, Our Lady appeared to the Prior and asked why the *Magnificat* was no longer being sung in her honour. Why was everything now silent, she asked? Distraught, the Prior fell to his knees recognising that the quality of the singing could never replace the worthy **dispositio** and **devotio** of the monks, regardless of their faltering singing (**devotiones**). The Prior's eyes were opened, and they dismissed the professional singers and continued to chant their *Office* themselves.

These monks would also have prayed the **Officium Parvum Beatae Mariae Virginis** (Little Office of the Blessed Virgin Mary) which mirrors (though more briefly) each of the *Offices* of the full *Divine Office* and is traditionally prayed by some (not mandated to pray the full *Office*) as an alternative to the full *Breviary*, or by those mandated to pray the full *Breviary*, like Carthusians, as an additional private prayer before each major *Office* is prayed. It is a beautiful discipline to embrace, recognising with Pope Blessed Pius IX (1792-1878) in **Ineffabilis Deus** (God ineffable) when promulgating the Marian dogma of the Immaculate Conception in 1854, and making Mary's position very clear at the beginning of this *Apostolic Constitution* writing:

> *Ab initio et ante saecula unigenito Filio suo Matrem, ex qua caro factus in beata temporum plenitudine nasceretur, elegit atque ordinavit, tantoque prae creaturis universis est prosecutus amore, ut in illa una sibi propensissima voluntate complacuerit.*

(From the very beginning, and before time began, the eternal Father chose and prepared for his only-begotten Son a Mother in whom the Son of God would become incarnate and from whom, in the blessed fullness of time, he would be born into this world. Above all creatures did God so love her that truly in her was the Father well pleased with singular delight. *Vat*)

Quapropter illam longe ante omnes angelicos Spiritus, cunctosque Sanctos coelestium omnium charismatum copia de thesauro divinitatis deprompta ita mirifice cumulavit, ut ipsa ab omni prorsus peccati labe semper libera, ac tota pulchra et perfecta, eam innocentiae et sanctitatis plenitudinem prae se ferret, qua maior sub Deo nullatenus intelligitur, et quam praeter Deum nemo assequi cogitando potest.

(Therefore, far above all the Angels and all the Saints so wondrously did God endow her with the abundance of all heavenly gifts poured from the treasury of his divinity that this Mother, ever absolutely free of all stain of sin, all fair and perfect, would possess that fullness of holy innocence and sanctity than which, under God, one cannot even imagine anything greater, and which, outside of God, no mind can succeed in comprehending fully. *Vat*)

The status of Mary *ab initio* is made especially clear in the 2[nd]C *Protoevangelium of James* which, while probably imaginative in parts, and never accepted as part of the approved Canon of the *New Testament*, nevertheless was highly influential, and bears witness to the fact that the position of Mary in the 'economy of salvation' being articulated and developed within the early Church at that time, was a dominant one. Mary, the Mother of God, was (and is) clearly a crucial part of God's plan to bring humanity to a redeeming sanctification. Pope St Paul VI's *Apostolic Exhortation* **Marialis Cultus** (Marian Devotion) confirmed this view almost 2,000 years later, with his teaching that:

> *sanctificantem actionem Spiritus in Virgine Nazarethana inter actiones eius recenseri in salutis historia.*
> (the sanctifying intervention of the Spirit in the Virgin of Nazareth was a culminating moment of the Spirit's action in the history of salvation. *Vat* §26)

Emeritus Pope Benedict XVI understood Mary's role in this 'economy of salvation' when, ahead of the February 11, 2008 celebrations of the 150th anniversary of the apparitions of Mary at Lourdes, he wrote in his *Message for the Sixteenth World Day of the Sick* (11 January 2008) that:

> 'Mary is a model of total self-abandonment to God's will: she received in her heart the eternal Word and she conceived it in her virginal womb; she trusted in God and, with her soul pierced by a sword (cf *Lc* 2:35) she did not hesitate to share the Passion of her Son, renewing on Calvary at the foot of the Cross her "yes" of the Annunciation. To reflect upon the Immaculate Conception of Mary is thus to allow oneself to be attracted by the "yes" which joined her wonderfully to the mission of Christ, Redeemer of humanity; it is to allow oneself to be taken and led by her hand to pronounce in one's turn *"fiat"* to the will of God, with all one's existence interwoven with joys and sadness, hopes and disappointments, in the awareness that tribulations, pain and suffering make rich the meaning of our pilgrimage on the earth.'
> (*Vat* §1)

Mary's *fiat* to God's call joined her to the redeeming power of Christ, and, by doing that, showed us all the way to say our own *fiat* to the will of God and effecting our own dispositional force for change. Pope Blessed Pius IX ends *Ineffabilis Deus* with a call for recourse to Mary:

Audiant haec nostra verba omnes nobis carissimi Catholicae Ecclesiae filii, et ardentiori usque pietatis, religionis, et amoris studio pergant colere, invocare, exorare beatissimam Dei Genitricem Virginem Mariam sine labe originali conceptam,

(Let all the children of the Catholic Church, who are so very dear to us, hear these words of ours. With a still more ardent zeal for piety, religion and love, let them continue to venerate, invoke and pray to the most Blessed Virgin Mary, Mother of God, conceived without original sin. *Vat*)

atque ad hanc dulcissimam misericordiae et gratiae Matrem in omnibus periculis, angustiis, necessitatibus, rebusque dubiis ac trepidis cum omni fiducia confugiant.

(Let them fly with utter confidence to this most sweet Mother of mercy and grace in all dangers, difficulties, needs, doubts and fears. *Vat*)

Nihil enim timendum nihilque desperandum Ipsa duce, ipsa auspice, ipsa propitia, ipsa protegente, quae maternum sane in nos gerens animum, nostraeque salutis negotia tractans deuniverso humano genere est sollicita,

(Under her guidance, under her patronage, under her kindness and protection, nothing is to be feared; nothing is hopeless. Because, while bearing toward us a truly motherly affection and having in her care the work of our salvation, she is solicitous about the whole human race. *Vat*)

et caeli temeque Regina a Domino constituta, ac super omnes Angelorum choros Sanctorumque ordines exaltata adstans a dextris Unigeniti Filii sui Domini Nostri Iesu Christi maternis suis precibus validissime impetrat, et quodquaerit invenit, ac frustrari non potest.

(and since she has been appointed by God to be the Queen of heaven and earth, and is exalted above all the choirs of Angels and Saints, and even stands at the right hand of her only-begotten Son, Jesus Christ our Lord, she presents our petitions in a most efficacious manner. What she asks, she obtains. Her pleas can never be unheard. *Vat*)

One hundred years later Pope Pius XII in his *Apostolic Constitution **Munificentissimus Deus*** (The most bountiful God) in which the dogma of the Assumption was formally proclaimed (November 1, 1950) recognised that the Blessed Virgin Mary had been considered 'the new Eve' (***novam Hevam***) from the very earliest times. Declared Θεοτόκος (*Theotokos* - Mother of God) devotion to her has grown, not as a sideline to Christian worship, but, as we have seen earlier in this book, as a palpable means of sanctification ***ad Iesum per Mariam.***

Dispositional Affect

There are many prayers and devotions dedicated to the Blessed Virgin Mary, one very popular one, was, for a long time, thought to have been composed by the Founder and Abbot of the Cistercian Abbey of Clairvaux, St Bernard of Clairvaux, but it was probably composed in the early 17thC although in part had been included in several much older prayers. There are several versions of this very venerable prayer, with the following approved by Pope Blessed Pius IX in 1846:

> *Memoráre, O piíssima virgo María, non esse audítum a século, quemquam ad tua curréntem praesídia, tua implorántem auxília, tua peténtem suffrágia, esse derelictum. Ego tali animátus confidéntia, ad te, Virgo Vírginum, Mater, curro, ad te vénio, coram te gemens peccátor assísto. Noli, Mater Verbi, verba mea despícere; sed audi propítia et exáudi. Amen.*

(Remember, O most gracious Virgin Mary, that never was it known in any age that anyone who fled to thy protection, implored thy help, or sought thy intercession was left unaided. Inspired with this confidence, I fly to thee, O Virgin of virgins, my Mother; to thee do I come; before thee I stand, sinful and sorrowful. O Mother of the

Word Incarnate, despise not my petitions, but in thy mercy hear and answer me. Amen. *trad*)

Like this prayer, all Marian devotions are Godward devotions. They have no meaning outside of this Godwardness. They do not exist for the sake of a Marian cult. They, like the Blessed Virgin Mary herself, are gifts ***gratia plena*** (filled with grace) given to us for the express purpose of aiding the dispositional force of the sanctifying affects of our journey Godwards. There is nothing new in this quest for dispositional affect. St Paul writing to the Colossians talks of Epaphras:

> *qui ex vobis est, servus Christi Iesu, semper sollicitus pro vobis in orationibus, ut stetis perfecti, et pleni in omni voluntate Dei*
> (who is one of you, [a] servant of Christ Jesus, always solicitous for you in prayers, that you may stand perfect, and full in all [the] will of God *Col* 4:12)

Standing 'perfect and full in all the will of God' is a prayer that Christians, even in those very early days, could stand in 'the gaze of faith'. It is as true now as it was then. Adoration is the ultimate gaze upon God. Latin prayer always involves that gaze. To begin with it involves learning another language, but learning with numinous purpose. That purpose shapes the rest of the journey; a spiritual journey Godwards. Spirituality is not simply being 'pious', or even rigorously disciplined and devoted in liturgy. Scripture and private prayer, requires what, to use a colloquialism, 'it says on the tin' - the Spirit. Spiritual growth is growth in the Holy Spirit; it is a journey designed to enable the pray-er to not only pray effectively, but to mature and grow in the presence of the Spirit. Such a God-governed process requires great grace to be given to us to recognise, as St Paul does:

> *Quoniam ex ipso, et per ipsum, et in ipso sunt omnia: ipsi gloria in saecula. Amen.*

(For from him[self], and through him[self], and in him[self] are all things: to him[self] glory for ever. Amen. *Rom* 11:36)

This is systematic theology in a nutshell, and which we pray in the *Epistle* of the Mass of Trinity Sunday. It is at the heart of every prayer we pray; every *Bible* reading we pray; every liturgy we celebrate and participate in; every gaze upon God. Its one aim is to enable us to think, submit to, and dispose ourselves to God's will, systematically, so that we may be affected by that disposition. St Vincent of Lérins (d 445) an early defender of the Church and opponent of heresy, though living at a time when some of the doctrines of the Church were still in debate and being formed, put it very simply in his ***Commonitorium*** (Calling to mind) where he attempted to bring together both the laws and the traditions of the Church in the face of many different interpretations at that time, summarising it as:

> *Id teneamus, quod ubique, quod semper, quod ab omnibus creditum est; hoc est etenim vere proprieque Catholicum.*
> (Let us maintain this, what everywhere, what always, what is believed by all; for this is truly and properly Catholic.)

We need to proactively make ourselves receptive to this systematic understanding of God and his works, through his Church. Scripture is the basis of the way of understanding God. It is central, but it is not all. In Catholicism we have both Scripture and Tradition to guide us. We should never forget what Pope Leo XIII taught in his 1893 encyclical on the study of Holy Scripture ***De Studiis Scripturae Sacrae*** (usually referred to as ***Providentissimus Deus***) that:

> *Illud autem maxime optabile est et necessarium, ut eiusdem divinae Scripturae usus in universam theologiae influat disciplinam ei usque prope sit anima*

> (Most desirable is it, and most essential, that the whole teaching of theology should be pervaded and animated by the use of the divine word of God. *Vat* §16)

That 'divine word of God', within Catholicism, was never denied to the laity for private reading, at any time in the Church's history, though for most of that time very few were able to read, but the Church did pass strict judgement on vernacular translations of that divine word at various times in its history. Often very vigorously. Maintaining the Scriptures in Latin was always considered to provide protection to Catholics from errors of teaching that might occur in vernacular versions and St Thomas More, for example, spent many of his final years writing often long, and sometimes very withering, polemical texts, at first in Latin and then in English, against the influx into England of Lutheran ideas and vernacular Scripture translations, which had been growing in number since the much earlier (and illegal) translations directly from the *Vulgate* by Catholic dissident John Wycliffe (1328-1384). Wycliffe argued strongly for the primacy of Scripture in humanity's quest for salvation, and for it to be made more easily available to all in the vernacular. As a consequence (and contrary to Church law) he was the first person to translate the entire Bible into the vernacular Middle English of his day, directly from the Latin *Vulgate*, which he did between 1382 and 1395. This was long before printing, and every manuscript of his entire Bible was handwritten and circulated in their hundreds.

It was also at a time when the writing of English was poised between the orthography of Middle English and the changes that would be made, especially with printing, to Early Modern English. The Anglo Saxon letter ȝ (yogh) moved to 'y' and 'gh'; the ſ to 's'; the þ (thorn) to 'y' and later 'th', as was the Old English ð (ðæt) and manuscripts were heavily abbreviated or with contractions like y ᵉ for 'the' (as in Ye [always pronounced 'the'] Olde Tea Shoppe) some of which in the text below I have used to signal what a manuscript of the Wycliffe Bible looked like. Consistency, especially in orthography, was not something that emerged consistently in written English until the development of printing in the late 15ᵗʰC, when the typefaces, imported mostly from Germany, did not contain these older Anglo Saxon letters in their type sets. Consistency in spelling really only emerged in the 18ᵗʰC. Just four years after St Thomas More's death:

> *The Byble in Englyſhe, that is to ſaye the content of all the holy ſcrypture, bothe of yͤ olde and newe teſtament, truly tranſlated after the veryte of the Hebrue and Greke textes, by yͤ Dylygent ſtudye of dyuerſe excellent learned men, expert in the forſayde tonges*

was authorised in 1539 by King Henry VIII to be read publicly in the Churches of England, which were then still mostly Catholic, and some only slowly adjusting to the new Protestant ways that would later emerge more fully. Known as the *Great Bible* simply because it was printed in such a large format, and chained to lecterns in churches, Myles Coverdale (1488-1569) compiled it using much of William Tyndale's (1494-1536) earlier English translations (from the original Greek and Hebrew and inspired by Wycliffe which were translated and printed overseas and smuggled into England from 1525 onwards.) This was to form the basis of the *King James Version* issued in 1611 and still used widely today. Wycliffe was burned at the stake in 1536 for heresy, just one year after St Thomas More's martyrdom.

The importance of the divine word of God, and its consequent vulnerability to protestantisation of the revealed truths of Catholicism, has been a central theme of Catholic teaching and practice, and resulted in the *Douay-Rheims* translation produced to ensure accurate Catholic teaching and doctrine in the vernacular (English) in 1610. Taking as an example one of the most insightful *Psalms* considered to centrally pre-figure Christianity, *Psalm* 138, prayed in Latin in the Roman Rite **usus antiquior** books, just as St Thomas More prayed it from his own

Sarum Psalter almost 500 years ago, at Friday *Vespers*. The *Vulgate* below is followed by the Wycliffe translation (1328) the Coverdale (1525) and then the *Douay-Rheims* (1610) translations:

Psalmus 138

Dómine, probásti me, et cognovísti me:
Tu cognovísti sessiónem meam, et resurrectiónem meam.

(Lord, þou haſt preued me, and haſt knowē me; þou haſt knowē my ſitting, and my riſing ayen. *Wyc*)

(O Lorde, thou searchest me out, and knowest me. Thou knowest my downe syttinge & my vprisynge, thou vnderstodest my thoughtes a farre of. *Cov*)

(Lord, thou hast proved me, and known me:
Thou hast known my sitting down, and my rising up. *DR*)

Intellexísti cogitatiónes meas de longe: sémitam meam, et funículum meum investigásti.
Et omnes vias meas praevidísti: quia non est sermo in lingua mea.

(Þou haſt vndirsſonde my þouȝtis fro fer; þou haſt enquerid my path and my cordet. And þou haſt bifor ſeien alle my weies; for no word is in my tunge. *Wyc*)

(Thou art aboute my path & aboute my bedd, & spyest out all my wayes. For lo, there is not a worde ī my tōge, but thou (O LORDE) knowest it alltogether. *Cov*)

(Thou hast understood my thoughts afar off: my path and my line thou hast searched out.
And thou hast foreseen all my ways: for there is no speech in my tongue. *DR*)

Ecce, Dómine, tu cognovísti ómnia novíssima, et antíqua: tu formásti me, et posuísti super me manum tuam.
Mirábilis facta est sciéntia tua ex me: confortáta est, et non pótero ad eam.

(Lo! Lord, þu haſt knowē alle thingis, yᵉ laſte thingis and elde; þou haſt formed me, and haſt set þin hond on me. Þi kunnyng is maad wondirful of me; it is coumfortid, and Y ſhal not mowe to it. *Wyc*)

(Thou hast fashioned me behinde & before, & layed thine hode vpon me. Soch knowlege is to wonderfull & excellet for me, I can not atteyne vnto it. *Cov*)

(Behold, O Lord, thou hast known all things, the last and those of old: thou hast formed me, and hast laid thy hand upon me.
Thy knowledge is become wonderful to me: it is high, and I cannot reach to it. *DR*)

Quo ibo a spíritu tuo? et quo a fácie tua fúgiam?
Si ascéndero in caelum, tu illic es: si descéndero in inférnum, ades.

Whidir ſhal Y go fro thi ſpirit; and whider ſchal Y fle fro þi face? If Y ſchal ſtie in to heuene, þou art þere; if Y ſhal go doun to helle, þou art preſent. *Wyc*)

Whither shal I go then from thy sprete? Or, whither shal I fle from thy presence? Yf I clymme vp in to heauen, thou art there: yf I go downe to hell, thou art there also. *Cov*)

(Whither shall I go from thy spirit? or whither shall I flee from thy face?
If I ascend into heaven, thou art there: if I descend into hell, thou art present. *DR*)

Si súmpsero pennas meas dilúculo, et habitávero in extrémis maris.

Etenim illuc manus tua dedúcet me: et tenébit me déxtera tua.

(If Y ſhal take my fetheris ful eerli; and ſhal dwelle in yᵉ laſt partis of yᵉ ſee. And ſoþeli þider þin hond ſhal leede me forth; and þi riȝt hond ſhal holdē me. *Wyc*)

(Yf I take the wynges of the mornynge, & remayne in the vttemoſt parte of the see: Euen there also shal thy honde lede me, and thy right hande shal holde me. *Cov*)

(If I take my wings early in the morning, and dwell in the uttermost parts of the sea:
Even there also shall thy hand lead me: and thy right hand shall hold me. *DR*)

Et dixi: Fórsitan ténebrae conculcábunt me: et nox illuminátio mea in delíciis meis.

Quia ténebrae non obscurabúntur a te, et nox sicut dies illuminábitur: sicut ténebrae eius, ita et lumen eius.

And Y ſeide, In hap derkneſsis ſhulen defoule me; and yᵉ nyȝt is my liȝtnyng in my delicis. For whi derkneſsis hulen not be maad derk fro þee, aud yᵉ niȝt ſhal be liȝtned as yᵉ dai; as yᵉ derkneſsis þerof, so and yᵉ liȝt þerof. *Wyc*)

(Yf I saye: peradueture the darcknesse shal couer me, then shal my night be turned to daye. Yee the darcknesse is no darcknesse with the, but the night is as cleare as the daye, the darcknesse & light are both alike. *Cov*)

(And I said: Perhaps darkness shall cover me: and night shall be my light in my pleasures.

But darkness shall not be dark to thee, and night shall be light as day: the darkness thereof, and the light thereof are alike to thee. *DR*)

Quia tu possedísti renes meos: suscepísti me de útero matris meae. Confitébor tibi quia terribíliter magnificátus es: mirabília ópera tua, et ánima mea cognóscit nimis.

(For þou haddiſt in poſſeſsioun my reines; þou tokiſt me vp fro yᵉ wombe of my modir. I ſhal knouleche to þee, for þou art magnefied dreedfuli; þi werkis ben wondirful, and my ſoule ſhal knouleche ful miche. Mi boon, which þou madiſt in priuete, is not hyd fro þee; *Wyc*)

(For my reynes are thyne, thou hast couered me in my mothers wombe. I wil geue thakes vnto the, for I am woderously made: maruelous are thy workes, and that my soule knoweth right well. *Cov*)

(For thou hast possessed my reins: thou hast protected me from my mother's womb.
I will praise thee, for thou art fearfully magnified: wonderful are thy works, and my soul knoweth right well. *DR*)

Non est occultátum os meum a te, quod fecísti in occúlto: et substántia mea in inferióribus terrae.

(Þine eyes se myne vnparfitneſse, þey ſtonde all writte i þy boke: and my ſubſtaunce in yᵉ lower partis of erþe. *Wyc*)

(My bones are not hyd from the, though I be made secretly, and fashioned beneth in the earth. *Cov*)

(My bone is not hidden from thee, which thou hast made in secret: and my substance in the lower parts of the earth. *DR*)

Imperféctum meum vidérunt óculi tui, et in libro tuo omnes scribéntur: dies formabúntur, et nemo in eis.

(Þin iyen ſien myn vnperfit þing, and alle men ſhulen be writun in þi book; daies ſhulen be formed, and no man is in þo. *Wyc*)

(my dayes were fashioned, when as yet there was not one of them. How deare are yi coucels vnto me O God? O how greate is the summe of them? *Cov*)

(Thy eyes did see my imperfect being, and in thy book all shall be written: days shall be formed, and no one in them. *DR*)

Mihi autem nimis honorificáti sunt amíci tui, Deus: nimis confortátus est principátus eórum.
Dinumerábo eos, et super arénam multiplicabúntur: exsurréxi, et adhuc sum tecum.

(Forſoþe, God, þi frendis ben maad onourable ful myche to me; yᵉ princeheed of hem is coumfortid ful myche. I ſhal noumbre hem, and þei ſhulen be multiplied aboue grauel; Y roos vp, and yit Y am with þee. *Wyc*)

(Yf I tell them, they are mo in nombre then the sonde: when I wake vp, I am present with the. Wilt thou not slaye ye wicked (oh God) that the bloudethyrstie mighte departe fro me? *Cov*)

(But to me thy friends, O God, are made exceedingly honourable: their principality is exceedingly strengthened. I will number them, and they shall be multiplied above the sand: I rose up and am still with thee. *DR*)

Si occíderis, Deus, peccatóres: viri sánguinum, declináte a me.
Quia dícitis in cogitatióne: Accípient in vanitáte civitátes tuas.

(For þou, God, ſhalt flee ſynneris; ye menquelleris, bowe awei fro me. For ye ſeien in þouyt; Take þei her citees in vanite. *Wyc*)

(For they speake vnright of the, thine enemies exalte them selues presumptuously. I hate them O LORDE) that hate the, & I maye not awaye with those that ryse vp agaynst the? *Cov*)

(If thou wilt kill the wicked, O God: ye men of blood, depart from me: Because you say in thought: They shall receive thy cities in vain. *DR*)

Nonne qui odérunt te, Dómine, óderam? et super inimícos tuos tabescébam?
Perfécto ódio óderam illos: et inimíci facti sunt mihi.

(Lord, wheþer Y hatide not hem that hatiden þee; and Y failide on þin enemyes? Bi perfite haterede Y hatide hem; þei weren maad enemyes to me. *Wyc*)

(Yee I hate them right sore, therfore are they myne enemies. Trye me (O God) and seke the grounde of myne hert: proue me, & examen my thoughtes. *Cov*)

(Have I not hated them, O Lord, that hated thee: and pine away because of thy enemies?
I have hated them with a perfect hatred: and they are become enemies to me. *DR*)

Proba me, Deus, et scito cor meum: intérroga me, et cognósce sémitas meas. Et vide, si via iniquitátis in me est: et deduc me in via aetérna.

God, preue þou me, and knowē þou myn herte; axe þou me, and knowē þou my pathis. And se þou, if weie of wickidnesse is in me; and lede þou me forþ in euerlastinge wei. *Wyc*)

(Loke well, yf there be eny waye of wickednesse in me, & lede me in the waye euerlastinge. *Cov*)

(Prove me, O God, and know my heart: examine me, and know my paths.
And see if there be in me the way of iniquity: and lead me in the eternal way. *DR*)

This Latin *Psalm* is prayed at Thursday *Vespers* in the *MP*, but regardless of when it is prayed, in the *Vulgate* it remains unchanged, wherever and whenever and in whatever form of English it might be translated. At its heart is the recognition of God as ever-present and omniscient. It was retranslated in the **Nova Vulgate** (***editio typica*** 1979) as **Psalmus** 139, and may be used as such in the ***usus recentior*** Office:

Domine, scrutatus es et cognovisti me,
 tu cognovisti sessionem meam et resurrectionem meam.
Intellexisti cogitationes meas de longe,
semitam meam et accubitum meum investigasti.
Et omnes vias meas perspexisti,
quia nondum est sermo in lingua mea,
et ecce, Domine, tu novisti omnia.
A tergo et a fronte coartasti me
et posuisti super me manum tuam.
Mirabilis nimis facta est scientia tua super me,
sublimis, et non attingam eam.
Quo ibo a spiritu tuo
et quo a facie tua fugiam?
Si ascendero in caelum, tu illic es;
si descendero in infernum, ades.
Si sumpsero pennas aurorae
et habitavero in extremis maris,
etiam illuc manus tua deducet me,
et tenebit me dextera tua.
Si dixero: "Forsitan tenebrae compriment me,
et nox illuminatio erit circa me",

etiam tenebrae non obscurabuntur a te,
et nox sicut dies illuminabitur
- sicut tenebrae eius ita et lumen eius -.
Quia tu formasti renes meos,
contexuisti me in utero matris meae.
Confitebor tibi, quia mirabiliter plasmatus sum;
mirabilia opera tua,
et anima mea cognoscit nimis.
Non sunt abscondita ossa mea a te,
cum factus sum in occulto,
contextus in inferioribus terrae.
Imperfectum adhuc me viderunt oculi tui,
et in libro tuo scripti erant omnes dies:
ficti erant, et nondum erat unus ex eis.
Mihi autem nimis pretiosae cogitationes tuae, Deus;
nimis gravis summa earum.
Si dinumerabo eas, super arenam multiplicabuntur;
si ad finem pervenerim, adhuc sum tecum.
Utinam occidas, Deus, peccatores;
viri sanguinum, declinate a me.
Qui loquuntur contra te maligne:
exaltantur in vanum contra te.
Nonne, qui oderunt te, Domine, oderam
et insurgentes in te abhorrebam?
Perfecto odio oderam illos,
et inimici facti sunt mihi.
Scrutare me, Deus, et scito cor meum;
proba me et cognosce semitas meas
et vide, si via vanitatis in me est,
et deduc me in via aeterna.

Venerable Pope Pius XII had earlier ordered a new translation of the *Psalms* to be made directly from the Hebrew: ***Versio Piana***,

DAVID BIRCH

Psalterium Vaticanum, or ***Novum Psalterium,*** sometimes referred to as the 'Pian Psalter' (1945). These new translations were included in a revised *Breviary*, but were never popular, not only because of its language and style, but because to adopt it would have involved rewriting all the existing liturgical books and chants. It reads:

Domine, scrutaris me et novisti,
Tu novisti me, cum sedeo et cum surgo.
Intellegis cogitationes meas e longinquo;
Cum ambulo et cum recumbo, tu perspicis,
Et ad omnes vias meas advertis.
Cum verbum nondum est super linguam meam:
Ecce, Domine, iam nosti totum.
A tergo et a fronte complecteris me,
Et ponis super me manum tuam.
Nimis mirabilis est mihi scientia haec,
Sublimis: non capio eam.
Quo abeam procul a spiritu tuo?
Et quo a facie tua fugiam?
Si ascendam in caelum, illic es;
Si apud inferos me sternam, ades.
Si sumam pennas aurorae,
Si habitem in termino maris:
Etiam illic manus tua ducet me,
Et tenebit me dextera tua.
Si dicam: Tenebrae saltem operient me,
Et nox instar lucis circumdabit me:
Ipsae tenebrae non erunt obscurae tibi,
Et nox sicut dies lucebit:
Caligo est tibi sicut lux.
Tu enim formasti renes meos,
Texuisti me in utero matris meae.
Laudo te, quod tam mirifice factus sum,

Quod mirabilia sunt opera tua.
Et animam meam novisti perfecte,
Non latuit te substantia mea,
Quando in occulto formabar,
Quando texebar in profundis terrae.
Actus meos viderunt oculi tui,
Et in libro tuo scripti sunt omnes;
Dies sunt definiti, priusquam esset vel unus ex eis.
Mihi autem quam ardua sunt consilia tua, Deus,
Quam ingens summa eorum!
Si dinumerem ea, plura sunt quam arena;
Si pervenerim ad finem, adhuc sum tecum.
Utinam occidas impium, Deus,
Et viri sanguinum recedant a me!
Nam rebellant contra te dolose,
Perfide se efferunt hostes tui.
Nonne, qui oderunt te, Domine, eos odio habeo,
Qui insurgunt in te, sunt mihi taedio?
Perfecto odio odi eos;
Inimici facti sunt mihi.
Scrutare me, Deus, et cognosce cor meum;
Proba me, et cognosce sensa mea,
Et vide, num via prava incedam,
Et deduc me via antiqua.

It is, however, regardless of which Latin translation might be preferred, perhaps the one *Psalm* that encapsulates within it everything we have been exploring in this book about prayer, **devotio**, and Godwards spirituality. Submission to God's will, even in the darkest and most hidden places, is its primary motivation. God sees everything; there is no escaping God; God is omnipresent; we live in a God-centred world, even if this is neither recognised, or is rejected by many. The wisdom of God, and knowledge of him, drives this *Psalm* as a celebration of submission to him, and central to it, and to all subsequent Catholic teaching, is the plain and simple fact, that not only is God omnipresent, but that God reveals the truth about that omnipresence; about his omniscience, and about our need to submit to this, through our dispositions.

Significantly though, Latin Catholicism, in the sense I am using it in this book, takes responsibility for guiding and teaching us those dispositions. Not the *Psalm* itself. This marks a considerably different approach to how this position on the role of Scripture and the Church was to develop through the translations of Wycliffe, Coverdale and Tyndale. As the *Psalm* suggests, we can imagine what we like; we can create as many fictions as we like; but God's truth will prevail, because it is God's truth not ours. Our personal dispositions and interpretations make no sense (for Latin Catholics) except as reflections of revealed truths, from both Scripture and Tradition. But the only way we can really be confident about understanding God's truth, again as Latin Catholics, is from the teaching of the Church. Doctor of the Church, Cardinal Bishop and Minister General of the Franciscan Friars Minor and noted philosopher and theologian, St Bonaventure knew all about this, and composed a very beautiful prayer which begins with the most forceful imperative:

> *Transfíge, dulcíssime Dómine Iesu, medúllas et víscera ánimae meae suavíssimo ac salubérrimo amóris tui vúlnere, vera serenáque et apostólica sanctíssima caritáte.*
>
> (Pierce through! O most sweet Lord Jesus, [the marrow/s] and innards of my soul with [the] most joyous and health-giving wound of your love, with true and serene, and most holy, apostolic love.)

Most translations of this tend to miss out the **medullas et viscera** (marrow/s and innards) part, and usually translate this more benignly as something like 'my inmost soul'. But the force of this image of 'innards' is not only startling, especially to modern sensibilities, but shocks us into paying attention, then thinking, and then seeking to submit to, God's will, conscious as this phrase makes us of our own frailties. This is the force of spiritual *affective* language. And why would we ask this of God? St Bonaventure answers with 5 of the most illustrative subjunctives:

> *ut lángueat et liquefíat ánima mea solo semper amóre et desidério tui; te concupíscat et defíciat in átria tua, cúpiat dissólvi et esse tecum.*
> (that my soul alone may always languish and melt with love and longing for you; that it may yearn for you and withdraw intowards your courts, and to be dissolved and to be with you.)

'languish', 'melt', 'long', 'yearn' and 'withdraw', are powerful images. But the traditional English translation usually translates *te concupiscat et deficiat in atria tua* as 'may yearn for thee and faint for thy courts' which misses the inner spiritual journey involved in the subjunctive *deficiat in atria tua* (may withdraw intowards your courts). The word *atrium/atria* occurs more than 130 times in various forms in the *Vulgate*, referring mainly to the court/s of the Temple in Jerusalem, and the courts of Heaven. Perhaps the most telling occurs in *Psalm 64* at Wednesday *Lauds*, when we pray:

> *Beátus quem elegísti et assumpsísti: inhabitábit in átriis tuis. Replébimur in bonis domus tuae, sanctum est templum tuum: mirábile in aequitáte.*
> (Blessed [is he] whom you have chosen and received: he will live in your courts. We will be filled with [the] benefits of your house, holy is your temple: wonderful in equity. Ps 64:5-6)

when the Temple on earth becomes the Temple of Heaven. St Bonaventure shows us how to get to this Temple of Heaven: not by an outward journey, but by withdrawing into ourselves, that in so doing we withdraw into the courts of God. It is a very powerful image. St Bonaventure then prays:

> *Da ut ánima mea te esúriat, pánem Angelórum, refectiónem animárum sanctárum; panem nostrum quotidiánum, supersubstantiálem, habéntem omnem dulcédinem et sapórem, et omne delectaméntum suavitátis.*
>
> (Grant! that my soul may hunger for you, [the] bread of Angels, [the] refreshment of holy souls, our daily bread, supersubstantial, having all sweetness and taste and every delight of deliciousness.)

This is love of God personified in the words of someone who not only 'feels' love but can 'taste' it; is physically affected by it, exactly as we physically taste the real presence of Christ in the Eucharist at Mass. St Bonaventure then lifts his ecstasy even higher and prays:

> *Te, in quem desíderant Angeli prospícere, semper esúriat et cómedat cor meum, et dulcédine sapóris tui repleántur víscera ánimae meae; te semper sítiat fontem vitae, fontem sapiéntiae et sciéntiae, fontem aetérni lúminis, torréntem voluptátis, ubertátem domus Dei.*
>
> (You, intowards whom Angels desire to look, let my heart ever hunger and consume, and [the] guts of my soul be filled with [the] sweetness of your taste; may it ever thirst after you, [the] fountain of life, [the] fountain of wisdom and knowledge, [the] fountain of eternal light, [the] torrent of pleasure, [the] richness of [the] house of God.
>
> *Te semper ámbiat, te quaerat, te invéniat, ad te tendat, ad te pervéniat, te meditétur, te loquátur, et ómnia operétur in laudem et glóriam nóminis tui, cum humilitáte et discretióne, cum dilectióne, et delectatióne, cum facilitáte et afféctu, cum perseverántia usque in finem;*

(May [it] ever strive for you, seek you, find you, run to you, reach you, mediate upon you, speak to you, and do all things intowards [the] praise and glory of your name, with humility and discretion, with love and delight, with ease and affection, with perseverance up intowards [the] end;)

After this torrent of subjunctives he concludes by praying, again in a sweep of repetitions:

ut tu sis solus semper spes mea, tota fidúcia mea, divítiae meae, delectátio mea, iucúnditas mea, gáudium meum, quies et transquíllitas mea, pax mea, suávitas mea, odor meus, dulcédo mea, cibus meus, reféctio mea, refúgium meum, auxílium meum, sapiéntia mea, pórtio mea, posséssio mea, thesáurus meus, in quo fixa et firma et immobíliter semper sit radicáta mens mea et cor meum. Amen.

(that you alone may be my hope always, my total assurance, my riches, my delight, my pleasure, my joy, my rest and tranquillity, my peace, my sweetness, my fragrance, my sweet taste, my food, my refreshment, my refuge, my help, my wisdom, my portion, my possession, my treasure, within whom may my mind and my heart be always fixed and firm and rooted immovably. Amen.)

This is at one and the same time poetry and prayer; at one and the same time creating numinous (ecstatic) dispositional affect through subjunctive affect. We will not all reach these dizzy heights of ecstasy through prayer. Most of us simply have to ground ourselves and soldier on in as disciplined and as regular a way as we are able. But we are not alone in doing this. The liturgical year, whichever calendar we may use, is designed to reinvigorate us daily with the truths of revelation. There have been varying calendars in the history of the Catholic Church marking out the specific days of the Liturgical Year; some remaining on the same day, like Christmas, and others, like Easter, changing according to the lunar, rather than the solar calendar. Most Catholic Christians celebrate days of the Liturgical Calendar principally by the Sunday of each week and the major feasts of the year. Most do not celebrate the daily entries of the Calendar, though for some, particularly those in Consecrated and Religious lives, especially if mandated to recite the ***Divinum Officium*** everyday, which is governed by an ***Ordo*** specifiying what and how to celebrate a particular day, there is no 'time-off' from the Calendar. For some, whose every day is structured completely around this Calendar and Ordo, particularly in strict ***usus antiquior*** religious and monastic Orders, there is no 'in-between time'. The Calendar rules every waking moment, whether in Church celebrating *Office*, or elsewhere doing a multitude of other things. These things, like working in the fields, or with a printing press, or cooking meals, or cleaning and sweeping, whatever it may be, these activities are not taking place 'in-between' times of prayer. They are that continuing narrative of prayer. Most of us do not live our lives like this; are unable to live our lives like this, as we do not have vocations to this very special calling from God, and so we assume we have a lot of 'in-between time'. But, whatever our calling, we do not journey through the Liturgical Year by ourselves. St Alphonsus Maria de Liguori (1696-1787) Doctor of the Church and founder of the Congregation of the Most Holy Redeemer (***Congregatio Sanctissimi Redemptoris*** - the Redemptorists) echoing the words of St Augustine, tells us that:

> 'the grace of salvation is not a single grace, but is a chain of graces all united with the grace of final perseverance.'

and to this chain of graces 'there must be a corresponding chain of prayers on our part.' This chain of prayers as 'a gaze of faith' (with which we can redefine our understanding of our 'in-between time') all starts with our being able to pray with the Psalmist as we do at Wednesday *Sext*:

> ***In quacúmque die invocávero te, ecce cognóvi quóniam Deus meus es.***

(On whatever day I will have called upon you, behold I have known because you are my God. *Ps* 55:10)

Citing the Council of Trent, St Alphonsus in his *A Short Treatise on Prayer. Its Efficacy, and the Conditions Requisite for its Due Performance* says that no matter how difficult prayer may seem to be, in the words of the Council:

Deus impossibilia non iubet, sed iubendo monet, et facere quod possis, et petere quod non possis; et adiuvat ut possis.

(God does not order [the] impossible; but, by ordering he admonishes, and to do what you are able, and to pray for that which you are not able; so that he may help you be able.)

He is not just using the words of the *Psalm* to teach him, but is seeking the teaching of the Church through one of its Councils, to help him (and us) on the way. He recognises, with the Council, that this requires special assistance, and furthermore, that God, as we learn from **De Dogmatibus Ecclesiasticis** (*PL* 83) only gives this to those who dispose themselves to pray for it. The Church teaches, through St Augustine, that:

Nullum credimus ad salutem, nisi Deo invitante, venire; nullum invitatum salutem suam, nisi Deo auxiliante, operari; nullum, nisi orantem auxilium pro mereri.

(No one believes intowards salvation, except to come to God by [a] calling; no one works out his salvation, except to be worked by [a] helping God; no one, to be merited [this] assistance, except through prayer.)

St Alphonsus also cites Doctor of the Church St John Chrysostom (347-407) who says:

> 'that as the soul is necessary for the life of the body, so is prayer necessary for the soul to preserve it in the grace of God.'

God wills:

> 'that we should ask him for the graces which are necessary for our salvation.'

and St Alphonsus then asks:

> 'Shall we refuse to do such a little thing as this?'

for:

> ***Petite et accipietis*** (Ask and you will receive. *Io* 16:24)

He does not complete this verse from St John's *Gospel*. But it is worth completing:

> ***ut gaudium vestrum sit plenum.***
> (that your joy may be full.)

St James tells us:

> ***Humiliamini in conspectu Domini, et exaltabit vos.***
> (Be humbled! in the sight of [the] Lord, and he will exalt you. *Iac* 4:10)

And how we do that? Christ himself told us in his own words, by our praying:

> ***Confíteor tibi Pater, Dómine caeli et terrae.***
> (I confess to you [O] Father, O Lord of heaven and earth. *Lc* 10:21)

and gave us the very words which, as the Priest at Mass prays, *audémus dícere* (we dare to say). So:

> *Sic ergo vos orabitis: Pater noster, qui es in caelis, sanctificetur nomen tuum.*
> (So therefore you will pray: our Father, who is within heaven, may your name be sanctified. *Mt 6:9*)

The power of prayer (*impetratio*) St Alphonsus tells us repeatedly, 'is grounded in grace', and quotes St Thomas Aquinas teaching us that prayer, 'makes us of the family of God'. One of the earliest of the Christian theologians, Quintus Septimius Florens Tertullianus (Tertullian 155-220) the first writer we know of to use the term ***Trinitas*** (Trinity) in his treatise on prayer (***De Oratione***) and considered to be the Father of Ecclesiastical Latin theology, understood completely that Christ created a new covenant and, therefore, a whole new way of prayer. He writes:

> *Nos sumus veri adoratores et veri sacerdotes, qui, spiritu orantes, spiritu sacrificamus orationem, hostiam Dei propriam et acceptabilem, quam scilicet requisivit, quam sibi prospexit.*
> (We are [the] true worshippers and [the] true Priests, who, praying in spirit, we sacrifice prayer in spirit, [a] sacrifice of God proper and acceptable, which of course he asked for, and which he discerns for himself.)
>
> *Hanc de toto corde devotam, fide pastam, veritate curatam, innocentia integram, castitate mundam, agape coronatam, cum pompa operum bonorum inter Psalmos et hymnos deducere ad Dei altare debemus, omnia nobis a Deo impetraturam.*
> (We ought to bring to [the] altar of God, in [a] procession of good works amongst *Psalms* and hymns, this promise from [the] whole heart, nourished from faith, prepared by truth, completed in

innocence, cleansed in chastity, crowned with love, to obtain all from God for us.)

And the way to that *impetraturam* is to recognise with Tertullian that 'All creation prays' (*orat omnis creatura*). Every beast, bird and flower by their very presence stands before God in permanent prayer. They know no other way. They have not been granted free will. All creation with the exception of humanity are in complete communion with God. Prayer calls us (who have lost this disposition through original sin) back to this communion:

> *Quid ergo amplius de officio orationis? Etiam ipse Dominus oravit, cui sit honor et virtus in saecula saeculorum.*
> (What more is there than [the] obligation of prayer? Even [the] Lord himself prayed, to him be honour and power for ever and ever.)

Tertullian sums it up perfectly here. Unlike the rest of creation, we humans lost communion with God. The sanctification we lost, Christ offers back to us, and the way back is through prayer:

> *Oratio murus est fidei*
> (Prayer is [the] bastion of faith)
> *Arma et tela nostra adversus hostem qui nos undique observat.*
> (our armour and weapons against [the] enemy who is watching us from every side.)
> *Itaque nunquam inermes incedamus: die stationis, nocte vigiliae meminerimus.*
> (So let us never proceed unarmed: by day let us remember [the] station, by night [the] vigil.)
> *Sub armis orationis signum nostri imperatoris custodiamus: tubam angeli exspectemus orantes.*
> (Beneath [the] armour of prayer let us guard our emperor's standard: praying let us wait for the Angel's trumpet.)

Tertullian wrote this almost 2,000 years ago at the very dawn of Christianity. It is as powerful now as it was then, perhaps even more so given all that embattles the Church today, both within and outside it. As St Paul tells the Philippians:

> *cum metu et tremore vestram salutem operamini*
> (work out your salvation with fear and trembling (*Phil* 2:12)

only then might we be able to pray with St Columbanus (540-615):

> *Unde te rogámus, ut sciámus quod amámus, quia nihil áliud praeter te nobis dari postulámus; tu es enim ómnia nostra, vita nostra, lux nostra, salus nostra, cibus noster, potus noster, Deus noster. Inspíra corda nostra, rogo, Iesu noster, illa tui Spíritus aura, et vúlnera nostras tua caritáte ánimas, ut possit uniuscuiúsque nostrum ánima in veritáte dícere: Indica mihi quem diléxit ánima mea, quóniam vulneráta caritáte ego sum.*
>
> (Therefore we ask you, that we may know what we love, for we ask nothing else except yourself to be given to us; you are our all, our life, our light, our salvation, our food, our drink, our God. I ask you, O our Jesus, with that breath of your Spirit, wound our souls with your love, so that each and every one of our souls may be able to say within truth: Show to me what my soul loves, for I am wounded by your love.)

To have our souls 'wounded' with God's love is the ultimate affect of prayer; the ultimate experience. St Augustine calls out to God in the opening invocatory prayer of one of his ***Soliloquia*** (1.1.2-6) praying:

> *Exáudi, exáudi, exáudi me, Deus meus, Dómine meus, rex meus, pater meus, causa mea, spes mea, res mea, honor meus, domus mea, pátria mea, salus mea, lux mea, vita mea. Exáudi, exáudi, exáudi me more illo tuo paucis notíssimo.*

(Heed, heed, heed me, my God, O my Lord, my king, my father, my cause, my hope, my wealth, my honour, my house, my country, my health, my light, my life. Heed, heed, heed me by your custom most well known to [the] few.)

King Alfred of Wessex (848-899, the one supposed to have burnt the cakes and called King Alfred the Great because of his victories over the Viking invasions, and because of his benign treatment of his people) translated this as:

'Gehiere, gehyre me, Drihten, forþam þu eart min God, and min Drihten, and min feder, and mīn sceapen, and min gemetgyend, and min tihopa, and min sped, and min wyrðscipe, and min hus, and min eðel, and min hæle, and min lyf. Gehyre, gehyre me, Drihten, ðine þeawa. Þe feawa ongytað.'

King Alfred was anxious to improve education standards and he advocated for the first stages of education to be in English, and those going onto the Priesthood to then continue their education in Latin. He understood the importance of language and he demonstrated this especially with his own translation (c 890) of Pope St Gregory I's (c 590) **Liber Regulae Pastoralis** (The Book of Pastoral Rule) outlining clerical responsibilities, which he distributed widely within the Church, saying that calling out to God was but the first step. Experiencing God at every stage of our sensory lives, and making every single one of our experiences/customs into a Godward **cultus** (worship) is paramount in our journey to salvation. It is to this sensory and experiential process we now turn in the final *Chapter XIII: Experiential Prayer*.

XIII

EXPERIENTIAL PRAYER

numquid non verba mea sunt quasi ignis dicit Dominus et quasi malleus conterens petram
(are not my words as burning fire says the Lord and as a mallet breaking a stone? *Ier* 23:29)

Sensuality

Richard Rolle of Hampole the 14thC English mystic we saw earlier, sometime hermit and advisor to anchoresses, in his ***Incendium Amoris*** (Fire of Love) calls upon ***Prophetia Ieremiae*** as in the epigraph to this chapter, to make a powerful point. We don't just use words, we *experience* them, and as here, God's words can be as a burning fire and as a hammer smashing stone. Rolle writes:

> 'The psalm (*Ps* 118) also says: ***Ignitum eloquium tuum vehementer***; your speech is hugely burned.'

Language, as this book has emphasised in every chapter, has power, and prayer. It is always sensory. It is about *both* body *and* soul. In his guide to anchoresses *The Form of Perfect Living* Rolle tells them:

'Knawe þat þi lyfe es gyuen to þe seruyce of god. Þan es it schame til þe, bot if þou be als gode, or better, with-in in þi sawle, als þou ert semand at þe syght of men. Turne for-þi þi thoghtes perfitely till god, als it semes þat þou hase done þi body.'

(I know that thy life is given to the service of God. Then is it shame to thee, unless thou beest as good, or better, within thy soul, as thou art seeming in the sight of men. Turn therefore thy thoughts perfectly to God, as it seems that thou hast done thy body. *Hodgson* [1910])

As the Anchoress has committed her body to the eremitical life, so too must she commit her soul. Her spiritual senses are not, as some advisors on prayer might like to think, ready for God only when separated from bodily senses; we bring both body and soul to God, and all the senses that go with them. Dame Julian of Norwich (1342/3-1416) herself an English anchoress, writing of her own revelations wrote:

'The worshipfull cyte that our Lord Jesus sittith in, it is our sensualite, in which He is inclosid; and our kindly substance is beclosid in Jesus with the blissid soule of Criste sitting in rest in the Godhede.'

Mother Julian had 16 mystical visions (shewings) which she described in her *The Shewings of Julian of Norwich* (*Revelations of Divine Love*). In this, the 16th shewing, she grappled with the difficult issue of the relationship between body and soul, talking of it in terms of 'substance' and 'sensuality'. 'Substance' is the higher order, but she did not dismiss sensuality as getting in the way of that higher order, a common theme in Catholic spiritual writings, but recognised the importance of understanding them both as an inescapable unity ('grounded and onyd'). This unity (onyd) she understood as 'the soul'. She accepted that we cannot, as humans, separate our sensual bodily senses from our spiritual senses in our search for the substance of the Divine. This is the powerful message of the Incarnation, and Christ's role in our lives: our soul is both a reflection of God's substance (*gostly*) and sensuality (*bodily*). Prayer involves both experiences. Taken together, we might refer to the relationship between body and soul; the ghostly and the corporeal, as 'sensuality'. Every prayer, wherever it is prayed, is, a sensory experience. It involves our emotions, some of which may well be heightened by the place and atmosphere of where and how we pray, but also our feelings and the histories of those feelings and emotions. Every prayer is an intertextual experience of every other prayer we have prayed, and every time, and in every place, we have prayed those prayers. Every one of our five senses is involved, consciously or unconsciously.

English philosopher and parliamentarian Sir Francis Bacon (1561-1626) referred to this process, in a very different context, using the phrase ***vestigia communis*** (common traces) by which he argued that sensuality is never discrete; every sense holds within it latent traces of all the other senses. So the smell of an extinguished candle, or the lingering fragrance of incense on the air as we enter a church or chapel may bring back to mind a thousand different sensual experiences of prayer. The opening chord on an organ playing before Mass may bring to mind other times when we have heard that melody; other Masses we have participated in; other churches we have been to. The discomfort, perhaps, of kneeling, may sharpen the experience of the prayer or meditation we are engaged in. The dry taste on our lips, and the rumblings of an empty stomach during the traditional 3 hour fast before receiving Communion (it used to be 12 hours and is now generally just 1 hour) or in the abstinences of Advent and Lent, or on the fasts of Vigils, Ember Days and Fridays, or, if still practiced, also on Wednesdays and Saturdays of the week.

The ***usus antiquior*** Octave of Pentecost includes 3 ember days Wednesday, Friday and Saturday. Four times a year the Church sets aside Ember days of fasting and abstinence: in Advent, Lent, Pentecost and After Pentecost (aligning with the natural seasons of the year) to set time aside to reflect upon, and thank God, for the gifts he gives. The name 'Ember Days' has nothing to do with embers or ashes, as might be thought because they are penitential days, but probably derive from the Anglo Saxon 'ymbren' meaning the course (of a year) and was generally known collectively as 'ymbren-tid' (Ember tide) and individually as 'ymbren-dagas' (Ember Days). Traditionally, not a single season goes without fasting and abstinence, but Pope St Paul VI in the 'spirit of *Vatican II*' excluded the Ember Days in his 1966 Apostolic Constitution **Paenitemini** (Be repentant) where he taught that most fasting and abstinence would now be voluntary for Catholics. The official Vatican approved English translation of this Constitution sums up much of what changed at this time in the Church, and the pressures that were put upon Pope St Paul VI in particular to effect that change. Its opening word **Paenitemini** from the verb *paenitere* (to repent/be sorry) is translated by the Vatican as 'be converted', offering up a now somewhat watered down theology of sin and penance. This 'watering down' can be seen in multiple changes that were made in the years after *Vatican II* (and continues today) not least in the theological shifts in many of the 'new' Collects of the ***usus recentior*** Mass and *Office*. For example, at the end of the Octave of Pentecost, but still within the season of Pentecost, the great feast of the Holy Trinity occurs. The ***usus antiquior*** Collect is:

> *Omnípotens sempitérne Deus, qui dedísti fámulis tuis in confessióne verae fídei, aetérnae Trinitátis glóriam agnóscere, et in poténtia maiestátis adoráre unitátem: quǽsumus, ut, eiúsdem fídei firmitáte, ab ómnibus semper muniámur advérsis.*
>
> (O Almighty eternal God, who granted to your servants in confession of true faith, to acknowledge [the] glory of [the] eternal Trinity, and in [the] power of majesty to adore unity: we beseech, that, by firmness in the same faith, we may always be protected from all hostiles.)

This was rewritten in the *usus recentior* to read:

> *Deus Pater, qui, Verbum veritátis et Spíritum sanctificatiónis mittens in mundum, admirábile mysterium tuum homínibus declarasti, da nobis, in confessióne verae fídei, aeternae gloriam Trinitátis agnóscere, et Unitátem adoráre in potentia maiestátis.* (*Missale Romanum, editio typica tertia emendata.* 2008)
> (God our Father, who by sending into the world the Word of truth and the Spirit of sanctification made known to the human race your wondrous mystery, grant us, we pray, that in professing the true faith, we may acknowledge the Trinity of eternal glory and adore your Unity, powerful in majesty. *ICEL, 2011*)

What is immediately obvious is that acknowledgement of the Trinity in the true faith in the *usus recentior* Collect is no longer required for protection against 'hostiles' (those opposed to Catholic beliefs) because acknowledgement of such hostility has been completely excised from the prayer. This happens time and time again in the *usus recentior* Collects. There is a fear of setting Catholicism apart. The 'new' theology is at great pains to reflect the dominant view amongst some theologians (not necessarily the Fathers) of (and after) the Council, which celebrates, at all costs, an ecumenism that equalises everyone and their beliefs. What is perhaps not immediately obvious, however, is the clause in the ICEL English translation above: 'and adore your Unity', where the 'your' is not included in the original Latin, of either the *usus antiquior* (**adorare unitatem**) or its retention in the *usus recentior* version (**Unitatem adorare**). The English Collect is now a prayer addressed to the Father (***Deus Pater***) but Catholic doctrine adores, not the unity of the Father (as it would seem to be in English here) but the unity of the Trinity. This is not linguistic nit-picking. It is a serious theological and doctrinal shift in a post *Vatican II* vernacular prayer, especially when the original (theologically rigorous) Latin text would be rarely, if ever now, prayed, compared to the English vernacular one.

Accuracy is an interesting issue in Latin prayer, given that the very slightest 'mistake' in changing the ending of a word in praying a Pauline *Epistle* at Mass, for example, may completely change the theology involved There is a very old legend where the fictional Titivillus (known by monks since the late 12thC at least) would prowl in the Choir seeking out any monk who made a mistake singing the *Office*, or he would range about in the **Scriptorium** where the copying of texts was carried out by hand. Titivillus would fill his sack a thousand times with errors and mistakes made by the monks and then present these to the Devil, where, the novices would be told, he would enter the mistake and the name of the monk into a book to be read aloud before everyone at the Last Judgement. He featured as a comic character in some of the medieval mystery plays, and when printing arrived, Titivillus became the scourge of those printing the new books. Some versions of the story warn the monks that Titivillus is there to make them make a mistake, rather than to capture the ones they do make, and so they should always be on their guard. Fictional characters aside, mistakes and errors do occur, and there still remains the very laudable monastic practice of 'kneeling out', where, when a monk in choir makes an error, he will kneel for a second during *Office*, to indicate that he has disrespected God and his community with his error, or may simply strike his breast when he makes an error. But this sort of error is of a very different order to the shifting of sound theology to a flawed one as in many of the *usus recentior* Collects.

Comic characters and legends aside, the very heart of our dialogue with God requires both speaking (audibly and silently) but much more importantly: listening, especially to Tradition and the theology and doctrine it has developed over many centuries. Most significantly too, it involves our reason, involving the need to search for theological and doctrinal correctness and accuracy. Meditation, to use St Augustine's words from his **De Civitate Dei** (On the City of God) is both an *exercitatio mentis* (discipline of the mind) and an *exercitatio animi* (discipline of the soul) through which, as people who pray and meditate, we seek to become what the classical philosophers referred to as *exercitati* (well trained, skilled and disciplined people). It is an *exercitatio* not either *mentis* or *animi* but both *mentis* and *animi*, and though often simply translated as 'exercise', it is, perhaps, better understood, and more powerfully in contemporary English, as 'discipline.'

Such discipline was even more important before literacy and printing made texts so easily available. Prayer is essentially oral, even though it may be saturated with the written word in many different forms. Fr Walter Ong SJ (1912-2003) in his now classic 1982 study *Orality and Literacy. The Technologizing of the Word*, makes the important point that we basically understand our relationship with God as an oral, sensory, one. Despite Christianity (like Judaism and Islam) being understood by some as 'a religion of the Book', it is not, and never has been, that. It is a religion of the Word, where we understand the living, speaking, Jesus as Son of God to be that Word. We worship the living Word, not the written word. St Paul tells the Corinthians that:

> *non quod sufficientes simus cogitare aliquid a nobis, quasi ex nobis: sed sufficientia nostra ex Deo est:*
> (not that we are sufficient to think any thing of ourselves, as of ourselves: but our sufficiency is from God. *DR 2 Cor* 3:5)

And God is not a book. Ronald Knox translates *sufficientia* as 'ability', but it is far more than that. Our 'sufficiency', as we saw in an earlier chapter, is far more than just our 'ability'. From the verb *sufficere* (*subficere* - to undermake) it can mean to 'undertake', 'put under', 'supply', 'provide', 'imbue', 'satisfy', 'avail', 'suffice', and from agriculture, to' dip', 'steep' and 'impregnate', all of which, I would suggest, are layered within St Jerome's use of the word *sufficentia* as given to St Paul. We worship God, not the written word. We are 'impregnated' by God, not words. But we use the written word to help us in that worship.

Walter Ong makes the powerful point that even in the most literate of societies we always think of God as 'speaking' to us, not writing to us. And 'memory' and 'meditation' are key to this. In oral cultures, before the widespread advances of the printing press in the 15thC, memory, for example, was, in many ways, the chief disciplinary 'sense' involved in prayer, both public and private. For medieval writers on prayer, **meditatio** was actually an equivalent word for **memoria** (memory). We are not talking about personal memories, but what St John Cassian (360-435) referred to as **sancta memoria** (holy/sacred memory) where the memories of 'self' are sublimated with the collective 'memory of tradition', which replaces that 'self' with an interiority focussed on the meditative remembrance of Christ, in order to then achieve the contemplation of God. Without discipline this becomes just too complicated, and hard to do. So when the medieval monks prayed:

> *Et erunt ut compláceant elóquia oris mei, et meditátio cordis mei in conspéctu tuo semper. Dómine, adiútor meus, et redémptor meus.*
>
> (And [the] words of my mouth will be that they may please, and [the] meditation of my heart always in your sight. O Lord, my helper, and my redeemer. *Ps* 18:15)

at *Prime* on Saturdays (Monday *Prime* in the *PP*) that phrase **meditatio cordis mei** would be saturated with the long year/s of discipline involved in the full memorisation of the entire 150 *Psalms* while still a novice in the monastery, without which they would not be entered into the mainstream community, where they would then pray the *Office*, not usually from books, but from memory, led by a *hebdomadarian* (weekly leader) who may have had the only copy of the full written *Office* before him. The association, therefore of **meditatio** and **memoria** is a very powerful one, and probably made the strongest in Sunday *Lauds*, coming after the night vigil of *Matins*, when we pray:

> *Si memor fui tui super stratum meum, in matutínis meditábor in te.*

(If I have remembered you upon my bed, I will meditate on you in [the] morning *Ps* 62:7)

where ***memor*** (***meminisse***) and ***meditabor*** (***meditare***) both refer to memory and reflection. Both are used variously to mean 'to think', 'reflect upon', 'consider', 'contemplate', 'ponder', 'meditate', 'intend', 'plan', 'contrive', 'devise', 'study', 'remind,' 'bring to mind', 'tell', 'utter', 'recount', 'remember', 'exercise in', 'practice' or 'rehearse', and both have the prefix *me* signalling that any action they signify is always about some sort of reflection on 'self'. Of the eight other times that the noun ***meditatio*** occurs in the *Psalms*, seven are in the longest *Psalm* 118, also prayed at *Prime* and the other minor hours (on Sundays and Feast days) and once in *Psalm* 48 at Tuesday *Matins* (*MP*) and Wednesday (*PP*) where we pray:

> *Os meum loquétur sapiéntiam, et meditátio cordis mei prudéntiam.*
> (My mouth will speak wisdom, and [the] meditation of my heart prudence. *Ps* 48:4)

We have almost forgotten what it is to memorise anything now, but ***meditatio*** as ***memoria*** (and ***memoria*** in ***meditatio***) in prayer must surely be one of the most powerful ways of focussing the mind and heart, and not just upon the words printed in front of us. As an unknown author once wrote:

> ***Bonae autem cogitationes semper a Deo sunt.*** (*PL* 83: LXXXII)
> (For good meditations are always from God)

These ***bonae cogitationes generales modi meditandi*** (good general meditations of the mode of meditating) are recalled and regathered up all the time as we pray, and often from what we may have 'learnt off by heart': a phrase which, when seen in this light, packs a very spiritually powerful experiential and sensory punch.

The Experiential Dynamic

The sight of a bustling family filling an entire pew in front of us at Mass, may bring to mind the busy-ness that is set aside as we bring ourselves to prayer. Every time I see a sanctuary lamp, for example, I remember, as a small child, the fascination of the red sanctuary lamp flickering through the chapel window of the Conventual Franciscan Friary still flanked by barren bombsites from World War II, as I walked alone to my primary school aged 5. No matter where I am, and no matter how many decades have since passed, I remember too that the Friars later moved Friaries from the end of the nearby street, to a park we always played in as children, and so was thus lost to us as a playground, and, when I eventually tried my vocation with them, I remembered all those things. And still do. We bring all of these memories and senses to our prayers, One sense brings to mind all the other senses, and that, in prayer, as the mystics knew so well, is both an absolute joy, but also potentially perilous.

Spanish Carmelite and mystic St John of the Cross, like Richard Rolle before him, talks about the sensory experience of prayer in his poem *O llama de amor viva* as 'the flame of burning love', which 'wounds my soul's deepest centre' (*que tiernamente hieres de mi alma en el más profundo centro*) a recurring theme throughout the history of affective prayer. But such a sensory affect of prayer and meditation, understood in this way, is not given to everyone to experience. But seeking such spiritual knowledge has been a part of the Christian tradition since Apostolic times. We are people with senses: physical and spiritual, and all are involved in our experiences as we pray. As Catholics we bring the full gamut of those senses to the fore as we place our humanity before God. We pray at Wednesday *Compline*:

> *Gustáte et vidéte quóniam suávis est Dóminus; beátus vir qui sperat in eo.*
> (Taste! and see! for [the] Lord is sweet; blessed [is the] man who hopes in him. *Ps* 33:9)

and St Paul declares to the Corinthians:

> ***Deo autem gratias, qui semper triumphat nos in Christo Iesu, et odorem notitiae suae manifestat per nos in omni loco.***
> (For thanks to God, who always triumphs over us in Christ Jesus, and manifests [the] odour of his status through us in every place. *2 Cor* 2:14)

It may seem an odd thing to talk about the 'odour of Jesus' as we nowadays generally tiptoe very cautiously around whatever we say of him, but we *smell* him; we *taste* him; we *hear* him; *touch* him and *see* him, not just spiritually, but as Latin Catholics, physically too; in the lingering smell of incense and extinguished candles when we enter a church to visit him in the most Blessed Sacrament; in the taste of him in the sacred host on our tongues; in the bell that may summon us to prayer - the **vox Dei** (voice of God - as my Jesuit teachers called it) in the prayers we pray *sotto voce* or out loud, and in what Gerard Manley Hopkins called 'the grandeur of God' all around us. As St Paul goes on to say:

> *quia Christi bonus odor sumus Deo in iis qui salvi fiunt, et in iis qui pereunt*
> (for we are [the] good fragrance of Christ to God in those who are to be saved, and in those who perish. *2 Cor* 2:15)

which Knox translates a little more freely as:

'We are Christ's incense offered to God, making manifest both those who are achieving salvation and those who are on the road to ruin.'

Carmelite nun, mystic, and Doctor of the Church, St Teresa of Avila based her own private prayer on forms of mental prayer (*oratio mentalis*) which sought to constantly examine self (*oratio recollectionis*). Known as the 'Doctor of Prayer', St Teresa based her entire spiritual life on seeking ways to ensure the ascent of the soul to God; to withdraw the self from everything and everyone that would prevent this complete submission and surrender of self, in order to achieve a state of perfection. Such an experiential dynamic did not come easily in her life. It is even more difficult now in a world that eschews withdrawal of any kind. But, for St Teresa, this experiential approach to prayer was not 'escape', and did not mean abandoning or denying sensory experience. She wrote that:

Oratio mentalis, meo iudicio, aliud non est quam de amicitia agere, ita ut quis saepe se habeat solitarie agendo cum eo a quo scimus amari.

(Contemplative prayer, in my opinion, is nothing else than to spend [time] between friends, so that [there] may be the frequent taking [time] alone with him by whom we know that we are loved.)

Oratio contemplativa eum quaerit 'quem diligit anima mea'. Iesus, et in eo Pater, quaeritur, quia eum desiderare initium amoris semper est, et ipse quaeritur fide pura, hac fide quae efficit ut ex eo nascamur et in eo vivamus. Etiam in oratione contemplativa potest quis meditari, intuitus tamen in Dominum fertur.

(Contemplative prayer seeks him 'whom my soul loves.' Jesus, and in him [the] Father, is sought, because to desire him is always [the] beginning of love, and [with] himself pure faith is sought, which causes that we may be born from him and we may live in him. Indeed, in contemplative prayer by which it is possible to meditate, yet [our] attention is fixed on [the] Lord.)

Oratio contemplativa is positioned here not as simply a vehicle for withdrawal, but (as the subject of the verb ***quaerit***) as the agent of the action itself; the very 'inscape' of the prayer. Its 'instress' is physical. In effect, it takes on a life of its own in the experiential dynamic of both the body and soul. Meditation is seen here as something that can take place within contemplation, but in the Catholic tradition of meditation, which St Teresa would have been so familiar with, ***contemplatio*** is on an altogether different plane. It involves a level of ***meditatio*** which the ***Catechismus*** separates from ***contemplatio***, seeing it as ***praecipue inquisitio*** (above all a quest §2705) and that quest, more of the mind and reason. Meditation is understood within Catholicism as a form of ***considerationis orantis*** (prayerful reflection §2708) often involving written texts, than it is with the abandonment of mind, as in some other religions. ***Oratio contemplativa***, the ***Catechismus*** tells us: ***est intuitus fidei, in Iesum fixus*** (§2715) (is a gaze of faith, fixed intowards Jesus.) St John Cassian (360-435) refers to it as ***oratio pura*** (pure prayer) and understands it as God's answer to petitionary prayer, not the petition itself, while Pope St Gregory the Great refers to it as the ***donum contemplationis*** (gift of contemplation) that is, a gift from God, and as the ***gratia contemplationis*** (the grace of contemplation). These understandings within the early Church are still with us today, where this 'gaze of faith' is captured most specifically in one of the most frequently occurring prayers in ***usus antiquior*** *Missals* and prayer books, often recommended for praying after Communion or Mass: a prayer prayed before a Crucifix:

DAVID BIRCH

En ego, O bone et dulcíssime Iesu, ante conspéctum tuum génibus me provólvo, ac máximo ánimi ardóre te oro atque obtéstor, ut meum in cor vívidos fídei, spei et caritátis sensus, atque veram peccatórum meórum poeniténtiam, éaque emendándi firmíssimam voluntátem velis imprímere; dum magno ánimi afféctu et dolóre tua quinque vúlnera mecum ipse consídero ac mente contémplor, illud prae óculis habens, quod iam in ore ponébat tuo David prophéta de te, O bone Iesu: Fodérunt manus meas et pedes meos: dinumeravérunt ómnia ossa mea.

(Behold, O good and sweetest Jesus, I cast myself upon my knees in Thy sight, and with the most fervent desire of my soul I pray and beseech Thee to impress upon my heart lively sentiments of faith, hope and charity, with true repentance for my sins and a most firm desire of amendment. Whilst with deep affection and grief of soul I consider within myself and mentally contemplate Thy five most precious wounds, having before my eyes that which David, the prophet, long ago spoke concerning Thee, 'They have pierced my hands and my feet, they have numbered all my bones.' *trad*)

Beginning a prayer with an interjection like *En* in this way might strike us as quite bold, but stylistically it creates an experiential context which demands attention by the pray-er both physically and spiritually casting themselves down on their knees before a Crucifix, and it occurs as a means of providing emphasis like this in Latin, often with imperatives and interrogatives in particular. It is a feature of oral poetry throughout medieval Western Europe, and existed long before these texts were written down. The poet (*scop*) would silence the crowd by a single word at the beginning of his performance, as we saw in an earlier chapter with the *Dream of the Rood*. The West Saxon poem *Beowulf*, for example, which circulated probably for centuries in various oral forms before it was written down by monks (and Christianised to a certain extent as a result) in its first known manuscript (c 975-1025) similarly begins:

Hwaet!
We Gardena in geardagum,
þeodcyninga, þrym gefrunon,
hu ða aeþelingas ellen fremedon.

(Attend!
We have heard in days gone by,
the glory of the kings of spear-Danes,
how the chieftains performed great deeds.)

with the opening *Hwaet!* often interpreted as a way of getting the attention of the listeners, and effectively meaning, as in my translation here, 'Attend!'. It is thought to have been accompanied by a mighty chord struck on the scop's lyre. Similarly, in the early Latin liturgy, one of the tasks (long gone now) of the Deacon was to announce just before Mass began, ***Habete silentium***! to achieve a similar affect. The Irish poet Seamus Heaney (1939-2013) in his translation of *Beowulf* simply translates it as 'So...' which would suggest an already attentive and quiet audience no longer needing a powerful form of address to wake them up. But

| 501 |

attentive audiences for both liturgical and private prayer should not be easily assumed. Prayer is not easy and requires great discipline at every level of our being. And just as Mary stood mourning (**Stabat Mater Dolorosa** - the sorrowful Mother was standing) before the Cross, requiring great discipline on her part, so too praying before a crucifix is especially moving like the prayer that St Francis of Assisi would pray before the now famous crucifix in the chapel at San Damiano, where St Clare (1194-1253) founded her first community of contemplative Franciscan Minoresses (**Ordo sanctae Clarae** which became known world wide as the 'Poor Clares'). St Francis prayed:

> *Summe, glorióse Deus, illúmina ténebras cordis mei, et da mihi fidem rectam, spem certam et caritátem perféctam, sensum et cognitiónem, Dómine, ut fáciam tuum sanctum et verax mandátum. Amen.*
>
> (O highest, glorious God, illuminate! [the] darkness of my heart, and give to me [a] right faith,[a] certain hope, and [a] perfect love, sense and knowledge, O Lord, that I may carry out your holy and true command. Amen.)

This simple and elegant prayer is a full submission to the will of God. When prayed in Passiontide when the Crucifixes are veiled, it brings with it an added mystery, given that the San Damiano crucifix, like so many at that time, were symbols of great joy, and not the stark representations of death that they tend to be today. As such they were, therefore, veiled during passiontide in order to deepen the meditational effect of the penititential prayer before them. The joy of Christ as King, often represented on these earlier crucifixes, would only be revealed once more, as the **Gloria in Exclesis** rings out at the Easter Vigil to herald the Resurrection, and the veils are removed.

The one set of images which are never veiled are the Stations of the Cross: fourteen images depicting the last journey of Christ before his death and being placed in the tomb. Often referred to as the **Via**

Crucis (the Way of the Cross) this was/is a very popular devotion, particularly through Lent and Passiontide. Based on the journey Christ made along what is now called the ***Via Dolorosa*** (the Way of Suffering) in Jerusalem, each image is paused at (often with Priest in violet cope, cross bearer (***crucifer***) and two torchbearers (***luciferi***) and various prayers said before each. There are many variations of this para-liturgical service, but central to them all is a prayerful reflection on the journey Christ made in his passion. Originally 12 stations, Pope Clement XII (1652-1740) added the last two stations in 1731. The last station, where Christ is laid into the tomb, holds with it a beautiful tradition, perhaps long forgotten in contemporary Catholicism, that whatever we pray for before the 14th station will always be granted us. Originally developed as a Franciscan devotion, the Stations of the Cross have many variant forms but it was only in 1686 that Pope Innocent XI (1611-1689) granted permission (at first only to the Franciscans) to erect physical stations within their churches, and then in 1731 Pope Clement XII granted approval for them to be placed in all churches. However we might pray them, when we pray them publicly (para-liturgically) or privately, or indeed when we pray any prayer, we need Christ's power and grace, through the Holy Spirit, to course through us:

> *Obsecro te, dulcíssime Dómine Iesu Christe, ut pássio tua sit mihi virtus, qua múniar, prótegar atque deféndar; vúlnera tua sint mihi cibus potúsque, quibus pascar, inébrier atque delécter; aspérsio sánguinis tui sit mihi ablútio ómnium delictórum meórum: mors tua sit mihi vita indefíciens, crux tua sit mihi glória sempitérna. In his sit mihi reféctio, exsultátio, sánitas et dulcédo cordis mei: Qui vivis et regnas in sǽcula saeculórum. Amen.*

(I beseech you, O most sweet Lord Jesus Christ, that your passion may be to me [a] power, by which I may be strengthened, protected and defended; may your wounds be to me food and drink, by which I may be nourished, inebriated and delighted; may [the] sprinkling of your blood be to me [an] ablution for all my sins: may your death be to me life everlasting, your cross be to me eternal glory. In which be to me refreshment, joy, health and sweetness of my heart: Who lives and reigns in [the] ages of ages. Amen)

This inner reflection on Christ's passion and its potential impact on the individual who is praying this prayer inevitably demands attention, especially by virtue of its emphatic, affective, sensory language, most particularly achieved through the iterative end-rhyme of ***muniar, protegar, defendar, pascar, inebrier*** and ***delecter***, together with the iterative force of the dative ***mihi*** following the subjunctive *sit/sint*. The language is forceful, but is not always enough. All prayer, as we have seen, in one way or another, involves *address, focus* and *force*, but when a community of monks and nuns in choir, or their **Schola Cantorum**, or a similar body of people in a Parish Church, celebrate a ***usus antiquior*** sung *Mass* with Gregorian chant, there is always a sensory *affect*. But neither the words of address, or the melody of the chanted words, are designed to provide an escape from the world, despite all the modern 'new-age' secular appropriations of this type of plainchant as being a way of 'de-stressing' from the world, and 'finding one-self' through the agency of some supposed ethereal 'otherness'. This form of *affective* address through liturgical chanting is designed to heighten the awareness of those praying through it; not to run away from the body and its sensuality, but to use it to its fullest resources. To sing, as St Augustine is quoted in the ***Catechismus*** (§1156) and thought to have said: ***bis orat qui bene cantat*** (who sings well prays twice) though what he actually wrote was *cantare amantis est*. This was cited by Pope Benedict XVI in the homily of the first of his 3 Christmas Masses in 2010 where he taught:

> '*Cantare amantis est*, says Saint Augustine: singing belongs to one who loves. Thus, down the centuries, the angels' song has again and

again become a song of love and joy, a song of those who love. At this hour, full of thankfulness, we join in the singing of all the centuries, singing that unites heaven and earth, angels and men. Yes, indeed, we praise you for your glory. We praise you for your love. Grant that we may join with you in love more and more and thus become people of peace. Amen.' (*Vat*)

This is a beautiful sentiment, but it is more than that. It is a recognition that to sing is what lovers do. And prayer is an act of love. St Augustine writes:

> *Qui enim cantat laudem, non solum laudat, sed etiam hilariter laudat; qui cantat laudem, non solum cantat, sed et amat eum quem cantat. In laude confitentis est praedicatio, in cantico amantis affectio.*
>
> (For who[ever] sings praise, not only praises, but also praises cheerfully; who[ever] sings praise, not only sings, but also loves him whom he sings [for]. In [the] praise of confessing is [a] proclamation, in [the] song of the lover [is] love.)

Plainchant

Plainchant in Latin prayer is an expression of the love of God. Those chanting these prayers actually transform themselves into musical instruments. This is an offering of one's actual body in prayer, through the physical voice of that body. Venerable Pope Pius XII in his 1955 Encyclical ***Musicae Sacrae Disciplina*** ([the] Discipline of Sacred Music) and building upon Pope St Pius X's earlier ***De Musica Sacra***, (On Sacred Music) delivered ***motu proprio*** in 1903, usually referred to by the Italian version of its opening words ***Inter plurimas pastoralis officii sollicitudines*** as *Tra le sollecitudini dell'officio pastorale* (among the solicitudes of the pastoral office) taught:

> *Hominis enim ad finem suum ultimum - qui Deus est - ordinatio ac directio lege absoluta et necessaria, in Dei ipsius natura et infinita perfectione fundata, ita firmatur, ut ne Deus quidem quemquam ab ea possit eximere.*
>
> (The ordination and direction of man to his ultimate end - which is God - by absolute and necessary law based on the nature and the infinite perfection of God Himself is so solid that not even God could exempt anyone from it. *Vat*)
>
> *Qua lege aeterna et immutabili praecipitur, ut et homo ipse et omnes eius actiones Dei infinitam perfectionem, in Creatoris laudem et gloriam, manifestent et pro viribus imitentur. Homo igitur, cum ad hunc supremum finem consequendum natus sit, ad divinum archetypum se conformare omnesque facultates suas cum corporis tum animi recte inter se ordinatas et fini obtinendo debite subiectas, agendo dirigere debet. E sua igitur cum ultimo fine hominis consensione et concordia etiam ars eiusque opera iudicanda sunt; quae ars certe inter nobilissimas humani ingenii exercitationes numeranda est.*
>
> (This eternal and unchangeable law commands that man himself and all his actions should manifest and imitate, so far as possible, God's infinite perfection for the praise and glory of the Creator. Since man is born to attain this supreme end, he ought to conform himself and through his actions direct all powers of his body and his soul, rightly ordered among themselves and duly subjected to the end they are meant to attain, to the divine Model. Therefore even art and works of art must be judged in the light of their conformity and concord with man's last end. *Vat*)

God is our 'ultimate end'. Nothing could be clearer than that. We are born to attain this supreme end, and to do this we should conform ourselves, and through our actions, direct all the powers of our body and soul, to this end. That includes prayer and, where appropriate, it may include *disciplined* music in accordance with the Church's directions. Venerable Pope Pius XII says earlier in this *Encyclical* that:

> *In tot tantisque naturae donis, quibus Deus, in quo perfectissimae concordiae summaeque cohaerentiae est concentus, homines ad suam "imaginem et similitudinem" creatos exornavit, musica profecto est, utpote quae simul cum ceteris liberalibus artibus ad spiritualia pertineat gaudia et ad animi oblectationem.*
>
> (Music is among the many and great gifts of nature with which God, in whom is the harmony of the most perfect concord and the most perfect order, has enriched men, whom he has created in his 'image and likeness'. Together with the other liberal arts, music contributes to spiritual joy and the delight of the soul. *Vat*)

and quotes St Augustine:

> *"Musica, id est scientia sensus bene modulandi, ad admonitionem magnae rei, etiam mortalibus rationales habentibus animas Dei largitate concessa est."*
>
> ('Music, that is the science or the sense of proper modulation, is likewise given by God's generosity to mortals having rational souls in order to lead them to higher things.' *Vat*)

The sensuality of music and chant, therefore, in prayer has one prime purpose: to lead us to God. St Augustine wrote in his **Regula Sancti Augustini** (Rule of Saint Augustine c400AD):

> *Psalmis et hymnis cum oratis Deum, hoc versetur in corde quod profertur in voce.*
>
> (When with *Psalms* and hymns you pray God, may this live in [the] heart which is proffered in [the] voice.)

The monotonic mode of Gregorian chant connects a singer to the liturgical action of the prayer, hymn or *Psalm* in the *Office*/Mass, not by happenstance, but by design. The forms of that chant as a sacramental, far more expertly described by experts like Wili Appel (1893-1988) especially in his 1958 book *Gregorian Chant*, than I would dare try to, are composed to particularly foreground the anagogical sense of the text itself, and not just its literal meaning: to reflect the Catholic way; the journey to St Augustine's **vita beata**. Those forms are liturgical acts in themselves within the larger context of the *Divine Office* in which they are sung. For example:

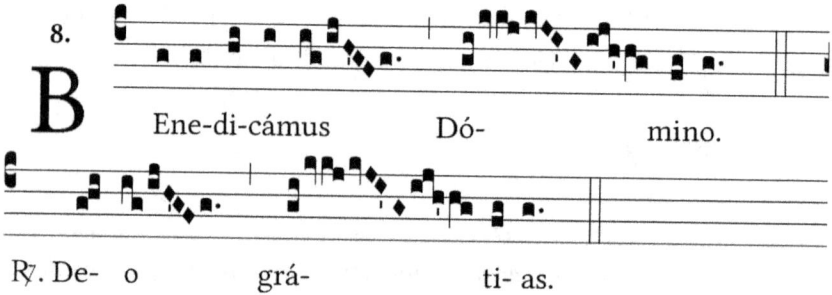

There is a highly complex sensual and spiritual logic to this musical form, regardless of how simple the notation may appear to be compared to polyphonic music. There are no chords indicated, for example, because the human voice is not designed to sing more than one note at a time. The chant is, therefore, monophonic. But consider the journey (informally known as a 'vocal run', but technically known as *melisma* (μέλισμα - μέλος - song/melody) where one syllable runs on more than one note, as here with the sound that the initial 'o' in **Domino** makes before it is resolved at the end of the stave with the final 'mi-no'. This is not just ornamentation, but a prayer in itself, intensifying, in the journey it is making, the focus upon **Dominus**. We are praying: 'Let us give blessings to the Lord', but in this form of the plainsong, we are not just handing the blessing over like a gift from one hand to another, quickly made. We are prolonging the giving of that blessing to the Lord as signified in the chant duration of the initial 'o' of **Domino** itself. Plainchant like this foregrounds the fact that this liturgical action is not the same as our everyday lives. It might perhaps be understood in much the same way as the very slow breathing patterns in some modern meditation techniques. It has physical, experiential, and not just ascetic, affect.

In the *usus antiquior* liturgical year there are many thousands of such chants, some with much more complicated journeys to make across the musical staves than the one illustrated here. For a monastic community celebrating the liturgy through the *usus antiquior* books, the daily rhythm of the Gregorian chant reflects the daily rhythm and harmony of living together in community. This experiential dynamic cannot ever be under estimated as an integral part of the monastic life. As a highly sensual form of prayer it is an experiential and sensory manifestation of love: for God, and for each other in the community. Gregorian chant is, first and foremost, about community participation, especially in an enclosed monastery. It is not passive or individualised consumption-by-listening. In Chapter 19 of his **Regula** (Rule) St Benedict teaches:

> *Ubique credimus divinam esse praesentiam et oculos Domini in omni loco speculari bonos et malos, maxime tamen hoc sine aliqua dubitatione credamus, cum ad opus divinum adsistimus. Ideo semper memores simus quod ait Propheta: Servite Domino in timore, et iterum: Psallite sapienter, et: In conspectu angelorum psallam tibi. Ergo consideremus qualiter oporteat in conspectu Divinitatis et angelorum eius esse, et sic stemus ad psallendum, ut mens nostra concordet voci nostrae.*

(We believe [the] divine to be present everywhere and [the] eyes of the Lord in every place to observe [th]e good and [the] bad, let us firmly believe this without any doubt, when we advance towards divine work. Let us, therefore, always be mindful of what [the] Prophet says: Serve [the] Lord in fear, and again: Sing *psalms* wisely, and: in

[the] sight of [the] angels, I will sing *psalms* to you. Therefore let us consider how it may require to be, in [the] face of [the] Divinity and of his angels, and so may we remain untowards *psalm* singing, that our mind may be in harmony with our voice.)

Just as the form of the chant, although based on speech patterns, is distanced from that speech by its distinctiveness, so too the people chanting it are a part of, but also distanced from, the everyday. Plainchant depersonalises the individual. Just as the ***usus antiquior*** overall is not interested in highlighting the personality of the celebrant and participants, so too plainsong, like Gregorian chant, is not interested in putting a spotlight on individual singers (even though in reality some may stand out and others not).

So, in the 'Alleluia' sung before the *Gospel* on Easter Sunday, despite great technical skill needed to sing this well, the focus is clearly designed for reasons other than as a vehicle for virtuoso performance. The final 'a' of the 'Alleluia' makes a considerable melismatic journey by itself before reaching its final cadence in the words **Pascha nostrum** where the final syllable of **nostrum**, like the final syllables of **immolatus** and **Christus**, make similarly long (and in this case quite complicated) journeys.

The dynamics of chant like this, where its rhythm of rising (ascending) and falling (descending) movements creates a flow of increasing and decreasing melodies, results in a new narrative; a wordless, but complementary, narrative, which means just as much, perhaps experientially more sometimes, than the words themselves; where the dynamics of the rise and fall of the melody signifies the rise and fall of narrative and liturgical action. Anyone who might have witnessed the usually very slight and unobtrusive 'conducting' (known as *chironomy*) of a **Schola Cantorum**, where that narrative and rhythmic flow is captured in the slightest turn of the wrist; the hand rising or falling and moving to the right or left, describing the lightest of curves in the air, not for individual notes on staves, but for groups of those notes, mirrors not just the shape of the chant, its changing volume and transitions, but the spiritual direction and impetus of the chant. There is no urgency in this chironomic direction, just as there is no urgency in the chant itself. The rise/fall dynamic of the melody is in control of the active/restful dynamic of the narrative. This is not an arbitrary collection of notes; nor an arbitrary structure. The stylistics of the music creates its own distinct way of making meanings.

While initially designed as a means of aiding the memorisation of the numerous Latin prayers which, before the age of widespread literacy (and then printing) had to be learnt off by heart for the Mass and *Office*, plainchant developed both a musical and spiritual singularity where the affect, when seen through an anagogical lens, is very striking. With the 'Alleluia' described above, we are waiting for the moment in the Mass when the *Gospel* will be chanted by either the Deacon or the Priest.

This form of liturgical prayer does not just jump in there with: 'Here's the *Gospel*', but prepares us, often over several musical minutes, to pray that *Gospel*. The journey through the 'Alleluia' is designed to be one of considerable expectation. We may be about to hear the words of Christ himself in a particular *Gospel*, or as on Easter Sunday, the announcement of the greatest moment in Christianity: the Resurrection of Christ. This is not something to be rushed into. We need to be properly, and prayerfully, prepared. And the long chant does exactly this. It is, therefore, a time of very deep experiential prayer as the final syllable of these words, all alone as it were, and no longer holding within it specific lexical force or meaning, leads us into the spiritual space ready to pray the *Gospel*. The notes fill this space, descending and rising like musical incense. This is not accidental, nor is it, as some modern ecumenically-minded liturgists would now consider, an unnecessary distraction from the words of the *Gospel* itself. It is a prayerful process that basically says: 'prepare yourselves; look within yourselves and get ready to hear God's word': 'Alleluia. Alleluia. Christ, our Pasch has been sacrificed.'

But this particular Sunday is no ordinary Sunday. Normally the first 'alleluia' would be repeated (signalled in the notation here by *ij*, but this is **Dominica Resurrectionis** (Sunday of the Resurrection) and, as such, the second 'Alleluia' is not repeated (**non repetitur Alleluia**) but instead is added (**sed statim additur**) the **Victimae paschali laudes** (praises to [the] Paschal Victim) a medieval sequence (*sequentia*) which is a hymn thought to have been composed in the 11thC which sings of sacrifice, the tomb, Christ's glory and the Angels:

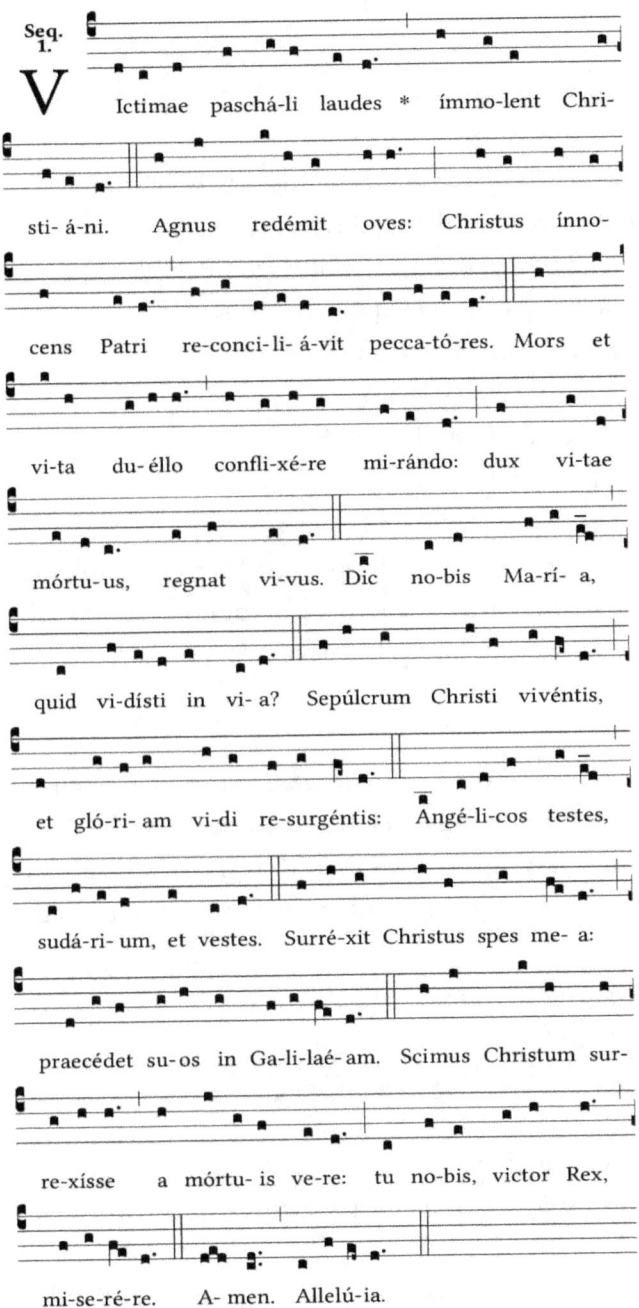

Seq. 1. Victimae pascháli laudes * ímmolent Christiáni. Agnus redémit oves: Christus ínnocens Patri reconciliávit peccatóres. Mors et vita duéllo conflixére mirándo: dux vitae mórtuus, regnat vivus. Dic nobis María, quid vidísti in via? Sepúlcrum Christi vivéntis, et glóriam vidi resurgéntis: Angélicos testes, sudárium, et vestes. Surréxit Christus spes mea: praecédet suos in Galilaéam. Scimus Christum surrexísse a mórtuis vere: tu nobis, victor Rex, miserére. Amen. Allelúia.

DAVID BIRCH

We are praying:

> May Christians sacrifice praises to [the] Paschal victim.
> The lamb has redeemed [the] sheep:
> Innocent Christ has reconciled sinners to [the] Father.
> Death and life to contend in [a] miraculous battle:
> [the] dead leader of life reigns alive.
> Say! to us Mary, what did you see on [the] way?
> I saw [the] tomb of [the] living Christ
> and [the] glory of his rising,
> Angelic witnesses, shroud, and clothes.
> Christ my hope is risen; he will go before his[own] ontowards Galilee.
> We know Christ is truly risen from [the] dead.
> To us, you conqueror, King, be merciful.
> Amen. Alleluia.

The Latin text here is the 1961 *usus antiquior* version reflecting the significant changes that were made (not without considerable controversy and with some lasting concerns even today) to the ceremonies of Holy Week in 1955. The original penultimate verse was removed but reads:

> *Credendum est magis soli*
> *Mariae veraci*
> *Quam Iudaeorum Turbae fallaci.*
> (More is to be believed
> by lone truthful Mary
> than [the] deceitful crowd of [the] Jews.)

thought to be no longer ecumenically appropriate. Similar references were removed elsewhere in the Holy Week ceremonies, and even more significant structural and content changes made. They may still be prayed (though now very rarely) where the pre-1955 books are used. The Sequence ends with:

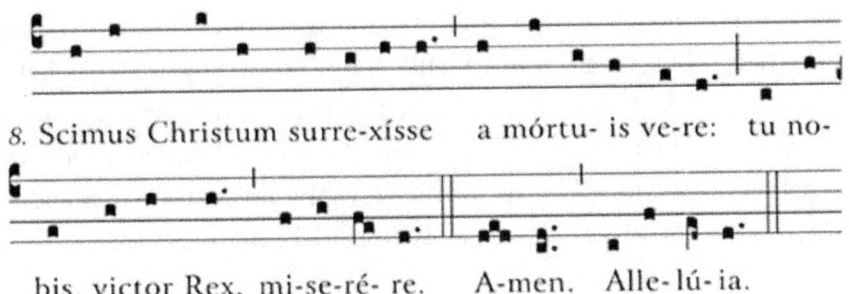

8. Scimus Christum surre-xísse a mórtu- is ve-re: tu no-bis, victor Rex, mi-se-ré- re. A-men. Alle- lú- ia.

And it is this final 'Alleluia' which brings us full circle to the point in the liturgy which may now involve a procession to the Gospel side of the Altar and to the censing of the *Evangelarium* (Gospel book) flanked by acolytes with lighted candles, which, as sacramentals, bring us, like this preparatory plainchant and procession, to the *Gospel* itself. This might be considered sensory overload by some, and it can take some considerable time from the opening 'Alleluia', but sensory and sensual it is, physically and spiritually, and this sensuality is a central part of the way of Latin Catholic prayer and liturgy, which uses every affective force at its disposal to prepare us for meeting with God. Often dismissed as 'bells and smells' by non-Catholics, and now many Catholics as well, together, the words, and all the other tangible, and some often completely intangible things in Latin Catholicism that go with those words, embody the many spiritual and sensory experiences that constitute prayer.

I choose the word 'embody' deliberately here. When we pray; when we chant or sing; when we kneel, sit or stand in prayer, we 'incorporate' (literally we make 'into a body') all of what we are doing. We give it human form, as indeed Christ became 'incarnate', and we 'substantiate' it by seeking the highest substance of all: God. We experience it in body and soul; in spirit and in mind; in the present and in memory; in text and context. As we experience what and how and where we are praying, that experience all contributes to the way we believe, and thus, we hope, the way we live. Our experiences embody that belief and vice versa. In doing so, our prayers are not just of the moment, but position us firmly in the patrimony, legacy, history and Tradition of all prayer. As Latin Catholics we are inculturated into that history and Tradition, just as the smoke of the incense and the smell of burning beeswax candles in church become a tangible part of the very fabric of that church and its expressions of experiential prayer. We pray in Tuesday *Lauds*:

> *Conféssio et pulchritúdo in conspéctu eius; sanctimónia et magnificéntia in sanctificatióne eius.*
> (Praise and beauty in his presence; holiness and majesty in his sanctification. *Ps* 95:6)

But it is a journey of the senses not without difficulty, but always with hope, as Père Jean-Pierre de Caussade in his *Self-Abandonment to Divine Providence*, recognises when he writes:

> 'If the work of our sanctification presents us with difficulties apparently so insurmountable, it is because we do not look at it in the right way. In reality holiness consists in one thing alone, namely, fidelity to God's plan. And this fidelity is equally within everyone's capacity in both its active and passive practice… the divine action is present everywhere and always, although it is only visible to the eye of faith…and 'works unceasingly at the sanctification of souls'.

What Père de Caussade calls here 'divine action', others call 'divine love' and others 'divine majesty' and 'kingdom of God'. Thomas à Kempis in his **De Imitatione Christi** refers to this kingdom of God as being **ad finem ultimum** (the ultimate end-goal) praying through the voice of the Lord:

Fili, ego débeo esse finis tuus suprémus.
(O son, I am obliged to be your supreme end.)

And how do we fulfil that obligation? Thomas à Kempis tells us:

Regnum Dei intra vos est, dicit Dominus. Converte te ex toto corde tuo ad Dominum, et relinque hunc miserum mundum, et inveniet anima tua requiem. Disce exteriora contemnere et ad interiora te dare, et videbis regnum Dei intra te venire. Est enim regnum Dei pax et gaudium in Spiritu Sancto quod non datur impiis. Veniet ad te Christus ostendens tibi consolationem suam, si dignam illi ab intus paraveris mansionem. Omnis gloria eius et decor ab intra est, et ibi complacet sibi. Frequens illi visitatio cum homine interno, dulcis sermocinatio, grata consolatio, multa pax, familiaritas stupenda nimis.

(The kingdom of God is within you, says [the] Lord. Turn! yourself your whole heart intowards [the] Lord, and relinquish! this miserable world, and your soul will find rest. Learn! to condemn external [things] and to give yourself to interior [things]. And then is [the] kingdom of God peace and joy in [the] Holy Spirit, which is not given to [the] wicked. Christ will come towards you showing to you his consolation, if you will have prepared [a] worthy mansion for him inside. All his glory and beauty is from within, and where it is pleasing to him. [A] frequent visit from him with [the] inward man, [a] sweet conversation, [a] pleasing consolation, much peace, friendship exceedingly wonderful.)

Converte te ex toto corde tuo ad Dominum (Turn! yourself your whole heart intowards [the] Lord). The *Catechismus* refers to this as the voices of prayer *cordis recollectio* (compsure of heart). Those voices are summarised in the *Catechismus*:

> *Dominus singulas ducit personas viis et modo quae ei placent. Unusquisque fidelis eidem respondet etiam secundum cordis sui determinationem et expressiones personales orationis suae.*
>
> (The Lord leads all persons by paths and in ways pleasing to him, and each believer responds according to his heart's resolve and the personal expressions of his prayer.)
>
> *Tamen traditio christiana tres expressiones vitae orationis retinuit maiores: orationem vocalem, meditationem et orationem contemplativam. Illis lineamentum fundamentale est commune: cordis recollectio. Haec vigilantia ad Verbum custodiendum et ad permanendum in praesentia Dei efficit ut hae tres expressiones fortia sint vitae orationis tempora.*
>
> (However, Christian Tradition has retained three major expressions of prayer: vocal, meditative, and contemplative. They have one basic trait in common: composure of heart. This vigilance in keeping the Word and dwelling in the presence of God makes these three expressions intense times in the life of prayer *Cat* §2699).

In the words of St John Chrysostom:

> *Ille sine intermissione orat, qui debitis operibus orationem iungit, orationique convenientes actiones; istud enim, sine intermissione orate, hoc uno modo ut praeceptum possibile possumus accipere.*
>
> (Nothing is equal to prayer; for what is impossible it makes possible, what is difficult, easy... For it is impossible, utterly impossible, for the man who prays eagerly and invokes God ceaselessly ever to sin. *Cat* §2744)

For most of us prayer is a spiritual practice that, whilst it may aim for mystical experiences enabling us to actually feel the penetrating presence of God in our souls, tends more towards what the medieval monks referred to as *ruminatio* and *masticatio*: a chewing of the spiritual cud, which nevertheless always provides us with the grace of some 'spiritual knowledge' (γνῶσις - gnosis, which might perhaps be best translated into English as 'insight') even though we may not necessarily experience this physically. Under the umbrella of three forms of prayer: vocal (***oratio vocalis***) meditative (***meditatio***) and contemplative (***oratio contemplativa***) the ***Catechismus*** talks of both ***orationis dimicatio*** (the battle of prayer) and and ***orationis drama*** (the drama of prayer) and summarises various types of prayer as:

- ***Benedictio*** (Blessing)
- ***Adoratio*** (Adoration)
- ***Oratio petitionis*** (The prayer of petition)
- ***Oratio intercessionis*** (The prayer of intercession)
- ***Oratio actionis gratiarum*** (The prayer of thanksgiving)
- ***Laudis oratio*** (The prayer of praise)

all requiring ***humilis vigilantia cordis*** (humble vigilance of heart) and ***filialis fiducia*** (filial piety) ***in amore perseverare*** (to persevere in love). Taken together this is ***orationis drama*** (the drama of prayer).

The Drama of Prayer

St John Baptist de la Salle (1651-1719) talks of our placing ourselves in the presence of God in order for us to become, not just externally subservient, but to be 'penetrated interiorly' by that presence. And to do that we need faith. Blessed Alcuin of York (735-804) recognised this when he included in his works a prayer (set out as a hymn below) which he thought St Benedict of Nursia may have originally composed and which is often referred to as ***Oratio Sancti Benedicti*** (Prayer of St Benedict):

Dignéris mihi donáre,
Pater pie et sancte,
intelléctum qui te intélligat,
sensum qui te séntiat.
(May you deign to give to me
O pious and holy Father,
[the] intellect which may understand you,
[the] sense which may discern you)

Animum qui te sápiat,
diligéntiam quae te quaerat,
sapiéntiam quae te invéniat,
ánimum qui te cognóscat.
([The] spirit which may know you,
[the] diligence which may seek you,
[the] wisdom which may find you,
[the] soul which may know you.)

Víscera quae te ament,
cor quod te cógitet,
actum qui te áugeat,
audítum qui te áudiat.
([The] vitals which may love you,
[the] heart which may know you,
[the] acts which may honour you,
[the] hearing which may hear you.)

Oculos qui te vídeant,
linguam quae te prǽdicet,
conversatiónem quae tibi pláceat,
patiéntiam quae te sustíneat,
perseverántiam quae te exspéctet.

([The] eyes which may see you,
[the] tongue which may declare you,
[the] conversation which may be pleasing to you,
[the] patience which may wait for you,
[the] perseverance which may hope for you.)

Finem perféctum,
praeséntiam tuam sanctam,
resurrectiónem bonam,
retributiónem, vitam aetérnam. Amen.
([A] perfect end,
your holy presence,
[the] blessed resurrection,
reward, eternal life. Amen.)

This beautifully simple, yet dramatic, prayer hinges completely on the opening 2nd pers sg pres subj dep verb *dignari* (to deign/deem worthy) with the infinitive *donare* (to give) followed by a whole series of direct objects (acc) all of which, through a series of subjunctives, become an extended plea to God for the way to sanctification. This prayer has come down to us through the incredible multi-volume ***Patrologia Latina*** edited by Père Jacques Paul Migne (1800-1875) a collection of Latin religious authors he compiled, edited and published in 218 large volumes, and already cited a few times in this book. Père Migne was a French Catholic Priest who aimed to create as complete a library of all Catholic writings from the earliest Fathers as possible. In addition to the 218 volumes of Latin texts, he edited and published 166 volumes of Greek writings (***Patrologia Graeca***) together making up the ***Patrologiae Cursus Completus***. He also translated/edited/compiled the entire Greek Fathers into Latin in an additional 85 volumes, and published a further 349 volumes of other works, in Latin and Greek, mostly theology, and following in his wake, is the now ongoing ***Patrologia Orientalis*** (begun in 1897 as the ***Patrologia Syriaca***) to bring together the writings of the Eastern Fathers with various translations, including Latin. The beauty of this particular prayer included in the *PL* reflects the joy and drama of striving for sanctification. It does not need to be a dark, sombrous, journey of misery and pain. Nor, given the beauty of God in all things, should it be. As a journey it can embrace all our senses.

When Pope Francis completed Emeritus Pope Benedict XVI's unfinished 2013 encyclical **Lumen Fidei** (The Light of Faith) he quoted St Augustine (who clearly understood all about human sensory experiences) from his **Sermo** 229 writing: *Tangere autem corde, hoc est credere* (For to touch [him] with [our] heart: this is to believe). We touch, taste, see, hear and smell in many different ways in prayer. And in Latin prayer, all of those senses may be heightened by the dramatic experience of praying in words, and for some in plainsong chants, which carry with every one of them the rich patrimony of many centuries of prayers in an unchanging form. The *Encyclical* closes with a newly composed Latin prayer, which I have accented below, carrying within it the traditions of over two millennia (§60):

> *Ad Maríam, Matrem Ecclésiae et Matrem fídei nostrae, convértimus nos orántes.*
> *Adiuva, Mater, fidem nostram!*
> *Erige aures nostras ad Verbum, ut vocem Dei agnoscámus eiúsque vocatiónem.*
> *Súscita in nobis desidérium eius vestígia sequéndi, et terram nostram relinquéndo et eius promissiónem excipiéndo.*
> *Adiuva nos ut amóre eius attingámur, ut fide eum attingére valeámus.*
> *Adiuva nos ut nos ipsi plane commendémus, ut eius amóri credámus, potíssimum témpore tribulatiónis et crucis, cum fides nostra ad maturatiónem vocátur. Sémina in fide nostra gáudium Resuscitáti.*

Cómmone nos credéntem numquam solum esse.
Doce nos Iesu óculis contuéri, ut in nostro itínere ille sit lumen; atque hoc fídei lumen in nobis iúgiter augeátur, donec dies ille sine occásu advéniat, qui ipse est Christus, Fílius tuus, Dóminus noster!

(Let us turn in prayer to Mary, Mother of the Church and Mother of our faith. Mother, help our faith!

Open our ears to hear God's word and to recognise his voice and call.

Awaken in us a desire to follow in his footsteps, to go forth from our own land and to receive his promise.

Help us to be touched by his love, that we may touch him in faith.

Help us to entrust ourselves fully to him and to believe in his love, especially at times of trial, beneath the shadow of the cross, when our faith is called to mature.

Sow in our faith the joy of the Risen One.

Remind us that those who believe are never alone.

Teach us to see all things with the eyes of Jesus, that he may be light for our path.

And may this light of faith always increase in us, until the dawn of that undying day which is Christ himself, your Son, our Lord! *Vat*)

Every verb in this very recently composed prayer is about our senses, even those verbs like *esse*, *sit* and *est*, which are about the sensual nature of being. We cannot escape the sensuality of these verbs: they are all about our five bodily senses and how these connect with our spiritual sensibilities. Latin prayer like this is not about escaping from these senses and trying to create an 'other-world', but is a celebration of who we are as human beings. Nor is it just a return to old Latin prayers composed in the mists of time, wonderful though those prayers are. We bring, as modern Latin Catholics, all of those senses to bear in any form of prayer. But regardless of how faltering that prayer may be, like all prayer, it aims to establish a covenant with God which, in the words of the *Catechismus*:

> *Dei et hominis est actio; a Spiritu Sancto et a nobis oritur, prorsus ad Patrem directa, in unione cum voluntate humana Filii Dei hominis facti.*
> (The action is of God and of man, springing forth from both the Holy Spirit and ourselves, wholly directed to the Father, in union with the human will of the Son of God made man. *Cat* §2564)

This is a new Christian covenant where:

> *oratio est viva relatio filiorum Dei cum eorum Patre infinite bono, cum eius Filio Iesu Christo et cum Spiritu Sancto.*
> (prayer is the living relationship of the children of God with their Father who is good beyond measure, with his Son Jesus Christ and the Holy Spirit. *Cat* §2565)

A life of prayer is therefore ***orationis vita est habitualiter esse***, which we might summarise perhaps as 'a habit of being'. William Ewart Gladstone (1809-1898) who served four terms as the British Prime Minister, and while becoming increasingly more 'high church', unlike his sister, he never converted to, but was always generally supportive of, Catholicism, thought of this life of prayer and the love of God as 'the *habit* of my soul'. All of us, ***in Dei indagatione*** (in the search for God §2566) whatever form that search may take, might usefully take Gladstone's words to heart. In Catholic spirituality this 'taking to heart' requires a conversion of heart (***conversio cordis*** §2581) in what St Teresa of Avila called an ***impetus cordis*** (a surge of the heart) in order to enable a one-to-one encounter with God (***solitudine cum Deo*** §2584). The *Catechismus* calls this ***orationis drama*** ([the] drama of prayer §2598) which is:

plene nobis revelatur in Verbo quod caro factum est et quod nobiscum manet.
(fully revealed to us in the Word who became flesh and dwells among us. *Cat* §2598)

In this sense prayer is always *fidei oratio* (a prayer of faith §2611) which:

non in eo solummodo consistit ut dicatur 'Domine, Domine', sed in corde componendo ad faciendam voluntatem Patris.
(consists not only in saying 'Lord, Lord', but in disposing the heart to do the will of the Father. *Cat* §2611)

In other words:

Oratio ad ortum spontaneum interioris impulsus non reducitur: ad orandum, oportet id velle. Scire non sufficit quod Scriptura de oratione revelat: discere oportet etiam orare. Orationis christianae traditio quaedam e formis est incrementi Traditionis fidei, praesertim contemplatione et studio credentium qui eventus et verba Oeconomiae salutis in corde conservant suo, atque profunda penetratione realitatum spiritualium quas experiuntur.
(Prayer cannot be reduced to the spontaneous outpouring of interior impulse: in order to pray, one must have the will to pray. Nor is it enough to know what the Scriptures reveal about prayer: one must also learn how to pray. The tradition of Christian prayer is one of the ways in which the tradition of faith takes shape and grows, especially through the contemplation and study of believers who treasure in their hearts the events and words of the economy of salvation, and through their profound grasp of the spiritual realities they experience. *Cat* §2650-1)

Prayer, then, is:

donum est gratiae et firma responsio e parte nostra.
(both a gift of grace and a determined response on our part. *Cat* §2725)

Nisum semper praesupponit.
(It always presupposes effort. *Cat* §2725)

Orationem dimicationem esse.
(Prayer is a battle *Cat* §2725).

'Spiritualis dimicatio' novae vitae christiani est ab orationis dimicatione inseparabilis.
(The 'spiritual battle' of the Christian's new life is inseparable from the battle of prayer. *Cat* §2725)

Humilitate, fiducia et perseverantia. (Humility, trust and perseverance. *Cat* §2728) are the keys to what the **Catechismus** refers to as **cordis orantis transformatio** (transformation of the praying heart §2739). It is all really summed up when the Church teaches that: **Oratio et vita christianae sunt inseparabiles.** (Prayer and Christian life are inseparable *Cat* §2745) a point well recognised in **Lumen Gentium** promulgated by Pope St Paul VI on November 21, 1964 where the Church teaches:

> *Ideo universi discipuli Christi, in oratione perseverantes et collaudantes Deum, seipsos hostiam viventem, sanctam, Deo placentem exhibeant, ubique terrarum de Christo testimonium perhibeant, atque poscentibus rationem reddant de ea, quae in eis est, spe vitae aeternae.*
>
> (Therefore all the disciples of Christ, persevering in prayer and praising God, should present themselves as a living sacrifice, holy and pleasing to God. Everywhere on earth they must bear witness to Christ and give an answer to those who seek an account of that hope of eternal life which is in them. *LG* §10)

Herein lies the journey to sanctification. It brings with it responsibilities to ourselves, and to others beyond ourselves. But it brings with it joys, dramas and battles as well, as we pray in Tuesday *Compline*:

> *Notas mihi fecísti vias vitae; adimplébis me laetítia cum vultu tuo: delectatiónes in déxtera tua usque in finem.*
> (You have made known to me [the] ways of life; you will fill me [with] joy with your face: at your right hand are delights even ontowards [the] end. *Ps 15*:11)

The presence or absence of this joy (*laetitia*) is a key marker of maturity and growth in the spiritual development of sanctification in the here and now. A joyless prayer life stands absolutely in opposition to the ultimate joy expressed in the Trinity, from which all joy flows. St Paul prays:

> *Deus autem spei répleat vos omni gáudio, et pace in credéndo: ut abundétis in spe, et virtúte Spíritus Sancti.*
> (Also may [the] God of hope fill you with all joy, and peace in believing: that you may overflow in hope, and in [the] goodness of [the] Holy Spirit. *Rom* 15:13)

This is the joy St Peter refers to when talking of Christ:

> *quem cum non vidéritis, diligitis: in quem nunc quoque non videntes creditis: credentes autem exsultabitis laetitia inenarrabili, et glorificata.*
> (whom while having not seen, you love: in whom also now not seeing you believe: and believing thus you will rejoice [with] indescribable, and glorified joy. *1 Pe* 1:8)

and thus:

> *reportantes finem fidei vestrae, salutem animarum.*
> (obtaining [the] end of your faith, the salvation of [your] souls. *1 Pe* 1:9)

St Paul knew this only too well when he similarly wrote to St Timothy saying:

> *pietas autem ad omnia utilis est, promissionem habens vitae, quae nunc est, et futurae.*
> (but godliness is profitable to all things, having promise of [the] life which is now, and to come. *1 Tim* 4:8)

There is joy in that promise of the life to come. But it needs work and discipline. And this book has been about just some of that work and discipline: praying through Latin with faith in order to prepare ourselves for the world to come according to the central axiom of Catholicism:

> *legem credendi lex statuat supplicandi*
> ([the] law of praying may establish [the] law of believing)

or put another way:

> *lex orandi, lex credendi, lex vivendi*
> ([the] law of praying, [is the] law of believing, [is the] law of living)

The Latin gerunds say it all: ***orandi***, ***credendi*** and ***vivendi*** are not just nouns referring to 'things', they are verbal nouns requiring action; these actions involve our *addressing* God, *focussing* on God and doing that *forcefully* that we might be *affected* by God. Pope Francis' Papal motto, which he also used as his Episcopal motto, is made up of two gerunds: ***Miserando atque Eligendo***. *Miserando* - abl sg m gerund of the deponent verb ***miserari*** (to lament/pity) and as a verbal noun might be translated into English as 'for the lamentable/wretched one' or 'by taking pity', and **Eligendo** - abl sg m gerund of *eligere* (to choose/elect) which, as a verbal noun, might be translated into English as 'by electing/choosing; or 'by/for the chosen/elected one'. There are a number of ways of translating this motto, and some who do not favour Pope Francis, have picked variations of 'miserable' and 'pitiful', in some quite uncharitable and mischievous ways, for example 'miserable yet chosen', implying the choice was a bad one. Despite the negative connotations in modern English, though, at the heart of the motto, actually borrowed from the Venerable Bede, 'wretched/miserable' and 'chosen/elect' (or something similar) should lie at its very core, as, for example in 'pitiable and yet chosen', to signal the heavy burden of high office. As Latin gerunds they may be easily manipulated in English to signal whether one likes Pope Francis ('lowly and so chosen') or dislikes him ('pitiful nevertheless chosen') but there are enough scriptural precedents about the paths of wretchedness which Christians (especially those chosen for leadership) have to take, as indeed Christ as the chosen one, took himself. Context (favourable or otherwise towards a person or idea) will always colour our reading of a text. It is for that very reason that the Church has, for most of its history, sought to protect revealed truths, in Scripture and Tradition, from wayward interpretations. So, St. Paul:

> **Tu es sacerdos in aeternum, secundum ordinem Melchisedech.**
> (You are [a] priest for ever, according to [the] order of Melchisedech. (*Heb* 5:8)
> **De quo nobis grandis sermo, et ininterpretabilis ad dicendum: quoniam imbecilles facti estis ad audiendum.**
> (About whom [there is] great talk by us, and inexplicable [*for the purpose*] in [the] saying: because you have become weak [*for the purpose*] to [the] hearing. *Heb* 5:11).

The *DR* translates this last part as:

'Of whom we have much to say, and hard to be intelligibly uttered: because you are become weak to hear.'

and the *Knox* version as:

'Of Christ as priest we have much to say, and it is hard to make ourselves understood in the saying of it, now that you have grown so dull of hearing.'

Both aim to capture the purpose involved in the Latin gerund **dicendum** (**dicere** - to say) by using an English infinitive 'to be uttered' (*DR*) and 'to make understood' (*Knox*) because to translate **audiendum** as 'the hearing' in English loses most, if not all, of its purposive sense, and certainly does not work well as an English text. The key, in Latin prayer, however, is to be able to capture this purposiveness in the Latin, and not just to translate the text so it works well in English. Latin meaning must always be the main goal in Latin prayer, not just workable English translations, or, indeed, translations that suit particular political ends.

As Catholics we are part of a long intellectual tradition that has framed its forthright theological interpretations, determinations, and dynamics, through a pre-Christian Platonic and Aristotelian way of thinking about the world in terms of the contrast (and relationship between) action and contemplation. Meditation, as a form of mental prayer within that frame, is understood within Catholicism as an 'interior' activity designed to be, as St John Baptist de la Salle put it, 'an application of the soul to God'. Such an application (St John Baptist's *l'oraison*) requires a 'readiness' to apply oneself to a process of **recollectio** (**recolligere** - literally, to 'gather', 'draw', 'bring' or 'collect together again', and so meaning to 'think upon', 'weigh', 'consider'; 'deduce', 'conclude', 'infer' and 'gather'). One book, written when Leo XIII was Pope, to help students with such **recollectio** is ***Medulla Pietatis Christianae sive Libellus Precum pro Adolescentibus Litterarum Studiosis*** (*The Pith of Christian Piety or A Little Book of Common Prayer for*

Young Students of Letters) by Fr Joseph Schneider SJ and suggests the following themes for meditation beginning with the directive:

Memento tuum esse hodie (Call yourself to mind this day):

Deum glorificare - to glorify God
Iesum imitari - to imitate Jesus
Beatissimam Virginem et Sanctos venerari - to venerate [the] Blessed Virgin and [the] Saints
Angelos invocare - to invoke [the] Angels
animam salvare - to save [the] soul
corpus mortificare - to mortify [the] body
virtutes a Deo exorare - to acquire virtues from God
peccata expiare - to expiate sins
Paradisum comparare - to gain Paradise
Infernum evitare - to avoid Hell
aeternitatem considerare - to consider eternity
tempus bene applicare - to apply time well
proximum aedificare - to edify [a] neighbour
mundum formidare - to fear [the] world
daemones impugnare - to overcome demons
passiones frenare - to restrain passions
mortem semper exspectare - to always expect death
ad iudicium te praeparare - to prepare yourself towards judgement

These suggestions not only provide topics for **recollectio**, but also provide a disciplinary frame for some of the traditional Catholic sensibilities which together might form a Catholic Rule of Life. Such topics help determine who we are as Catholic Christians, unpopular, and unfashionable some of them may be today. The **Septem opera misericordiae corporalia** (Seven corporal works of mercy) do the same:

Cibum praebere esurientibus - to provide food for the hungry
Potum praebere sitientibus - to offer drink to the thirsty
Nudos cooperire - to clothe the naked
Hospites excipere - to welcome strangers
Infirmos visitare - to visit the sick
Carcere clausos invisere - to visit [those] locked up in prison
Mortuos sepelire - to bury the dead

and the:

Septem opera misericordiae spiritualia (Seven spiritual works of mercy):

Dubitantibus consilia dare - to give counsel to the doubtful
Ignorantes instruere - to instruct the ignorant
Peccatores monere - to warn sinners
Afflictos solari - to comfort the afflicted
Offensas remittere - to forgive offences
Molestos patienter sustinere - to bear troubles patiently
Pro vivis et defunctis Deum orare - to pray God for the living and the dead

These are not just things to be done, but core Catholic precepts to be prayed and meditated on, because they too frame who we are as Catholics, where, reflecting upon their history, tradition and impacts and affects upon ourselves as individuals, and societies in general, they may provide many opportunities for ***cordis recollectio***. ***Recollectio*** like this, involving Catholic narrative, theology, spirituality and Tradition becomes ***meditatio*** (a process of mental prayer) and not just ***cogitatio*** (thinking about something). St John Baptist de la Salle was not content at leaving it there though. To complete meditative prayer satisfactorily also involves 'thanksgiving' to God; a powerfully Christian recognition that meditation as an 'interior activity' is not simply about self and ego, as it may be in other religions and spiritualities, but is, as we have talked about throughout this book, an act of submission to a higher Being than ourselves or the world we live in. One central way of submission is through *Lectio Divina*.

Lectio Divina

Carthusian monk Guigo II (1140-1193) 9th Prior of the Grande Chartreuse monastery in France, in his ***Scala Claustralium: Epistola de Vita Contemplativa*** (Ladder of the Little Cloister: Letter on the Contemplative Life) often referred to as *The Ladder of Monks* and thought to have been written in 1188, describes *lectio divina* (spiritual reading) as ***quatuor spirituales gradus animo*** (four spiritual rungs for the soul). This has been at the very heart of Catholic spirituality for over 2,000 years in which St Benedict's much earlier four steps of prayer: ***lectio, meditatio, oratio,*** and ***contemplatio***) together form the very powerful, and now many centuries old, practice of ***Lectio Divina***. The ***Catechismus*** quotes Guigo paraphrasing *Mt 7:7*:

> ***Quaerite legendo, et invenietis meditando: pulsate orando, et aperietur vobis contemplando.***
> (Seek in reading and you will find in meditating; knock in mental prayer and it will be opened to you by contemplation. *Cat* §2654)

as ***Lectio Divina*** this is not always an easy process, especially in its later stages. St Ambrose of Milan is quoted by St Alphonsus de Liguori in his still influential *The Importance of Spiritual Reading* as saying of God that:

'We address him when we pray; we hear him when we read'.

Thought to have been first developed at the very dawn of Christianity by Origen of Alexandria a highly influential (but at times contested) theologian, and first introduced into monastic practice by St Gregory of Nyssa (335-395) and St John Cassian, and then more rigorously by St Benedict of Nursia, **Lectio Divina** is generally structured as follows:

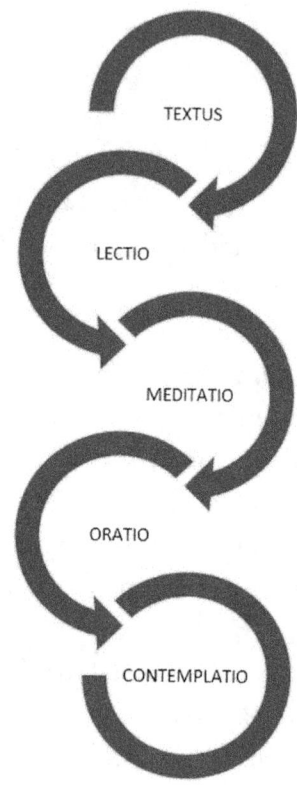

Throughout its development over many centuries this was first and foremost a community practice with times set aside for religious communities to collectively read scripture closely and deliberately, as if Jesus himself was reading it, in order to become more Christ-like. The first step (*lectio*) is to read: principally a text of Scripture often up to four times or more and best read *sotto voce*. Reading in this step, therefore, is really all about listening. This 'reading' in the early days of monasticism was usually a memorising of a particular text; memorisations which, in fact, continued well into the 19thC as the Most Reverend Archbishop William Bernard Ullathorne OSB (1806-1899) a Benedictine monk of Downside Abbey, describes in his autobiography where, in his formation as a Priest, he was required to learn all the Sunday Gospel *pericopes* off by heart. One time Vicar-General to Bishop William Placid Morris (1794-1872) in the early days of the Australian missions, and later, on his return to England, after a second stay in Australia, with the re-establishment of the hierarchy in England and Wales (1850) he became the first Roman Catholic Bishop of the Diocese of Birmingham, and was close to St John Henry Cardinal Newman who lived out the rest of his life in Birmingham, after he had founded the Oratory there.

Both men would have been very familiar, in their different ways, with **lectio divina**, the second step of which (***meditatio***) is to meditate upon the text just read (by memory or otherwise). The classic form of Catholic meditation is to go through the text and to think it through in every way possible. This is not meditation as, say, understood in Buddhist, or contemporary 'new age' circles, but is a step by step textual consideration and reflection of the whole or of parts, but always, as a Christian meditation, involving our listening to the words we have slowly read or recalled, and analysing them to redefine them perhaps, and in that redefining to give ourselves space to listen to the Holy Spirit. Unlike many forms of meditation, traditional Christian meditation like this is not a stepping outside of ourselves; a 'transcendental' clearing of the mind, so to speak, but is a stepping *into* the *inside* of a text. It is about listening to the text; listening to ourselves; listening to the histories of the reception and use of this text, not, as in the first step of *lectio*, specifically to the sound of the words of the text, or to its grammatical elements, but listening to what the text reveals anagogically, concentrating on what I have referred to in this book as the dynamics of *address*, *focus*, *force* and *affect*, which the language of the text opens up when we listen, as St Benedict says, **aure cordis nostri** (with the ear of our heart). St Matthew tells of Christ famously teaching:

> *Omnis enim qui petit, accipit: et qui quaerit, invenit: et pulsanti aperietur. Aut quis est ex vobis homo, quem si petierit filius suus panem, numquid lapidem porriget ei? Aut si piscem petierit, numquid serpentem porriget ei?*
>
> (For every one who asks, receives: and who[ever] seeks, finds: and [by] knocking [it] will have been opened. Or what man is from you, who if his son will have asked for bread, will he surely offer to him [a] stone? Or if he will have asked for [a] fish, will he surely offer to him [a] serpent? *Mt* 7:8-10)

While Scripture is essential in this process of prayer, 'it is necessary to learn to pray' (***discere oportet etiam orare*** *Cat* §2650) and the *Catechism* teaches Catholics that the best way to do that is from the Holy Spirit who teaches us, as we saw earlier:

> *Nunc vero, Spiritus Sanctus, per transmissionem vivam (sanctam Traditionem) Dei filios in credenti et oranti Ecclesia orare docet.*
>
> (Now truly through a living transmission (Sacred Tradition) within "the believing and praying Church," the Holy Spirit teaches the children of God how to pray. *Cat* §2650)

Catholic Tradition considers that 'prayer is a gift of grace', but a gift which the *Catechism* tells us 'presupposes a determined response on our part': a ***cordis recollectio*** (composure of the heart *Cat* §2699). French philosopher Simone Weil (1909-1943) referred to this ***recollectio*** (though not with direct reference to the *Catechism*) in her book *La Pesanteur et la Grâce* (*Gravity and Grace* published posthumously in 1947) writing that:

> 'La purification est la séparation du bien et de la convoitise.'
> (Purification is the separation of good from covetousness.)

In other words, meditation (***recollectio***) is about pure attention; it needs the good to be separated from the bad. German Lutheran theologian Rudolf Otto (1869-1937) who helped develop the concept of the *numinous* as referred to in this book, talks of religious experience as both a ***mysterium tremendum*** (an awe-inspiring mystery) often translated as a mystery that terrifies, and a ***mysterium fascinosum*** (a mystery that fascinates) and often put together in the phrase ***mysterium tremendum et fascinans*** which Otto thought of as a universal transcendent force beyond specific religions, that both repels and attracts. From a Catholic point of view that means that we stand in awe of that mystery, and as such, may also be frightened by it, but at the same time, are always fascinated by it. St Columbanus (540-615) says of a soul that seeks Christ as the fountain of all life, that such a soul (***anima***):

> ***semper tamen sitit bibendo, semper haurit desiderando, quae semper bibit sitiendo.***
> (although always thirsts with drinking, always consumes with desiring, which always drinks with thirsting.)

In other words, seeking Christ is, like St Teresa of Avila's meditation of one single book that took her over 17 years, and was a task never fully completed; it always demands more; but always gives more. As the world we know today replaces much religious ceremony with secularised ritual (witness the fictions of the opening and closing ceremonies of the Olympic Games) the ***mysterium tremendum et fascinans*** is still clearly a central part of what it means to be human. Thomas Merton (1915-1968 in religion Fr Mary Louis OCSO) advised us in his 1961 book *Seeds of Contemplation*:

> 'learn to take the risks implied by faith, to make the choices that deliver us from our routine self and open to us the door of a new being, a new reality.'

That he tended in his later years, before his untimely death in Thailand, to take perhaps more risks than Catholic Tradition might approve of, and was very much a sign of the reformist times in which he lived, some of his insights remain enormously valuable for us. Whatever risks he did take in the practice of his faith, he did so because he genuinely sought to be holy, an unfashionable thing to say now in a world that has tended to restrict ideas of what it is to be 'holy' to little more than 'morality' or the ***summum bonum*** we saw earlier. Latin Catholicism, for all its marginalisation now, seeks (and has always sought) an understanding (through the original Jewish linguistic roots) of what it really is to be holy: that is 'to be set apart'.

The third step of **lectio divina** (***oratio***) is to pray what we have learnt from **meditatio**. That is not an easy step, by any stretch of the imagination. We may repeat the thoughts we had when listening in our **meditatio**; we may invest them with our own intentions, or with those of the people we may be praying for. We may try to think through what we think might have been the intentions of the writers of our texts, and the contexts in which they wrote by our highlighting in our minds certain parts of the text. We may repeat them in many different ways, investing them with different emphases and foregrounding particular elements. But in doing so we 'run the risk' of simply repeating our **meditatio**. The overall (and very difficult) aim of ***oratio*** is to pray in a new space from the one where we have spent time reading (***lectio***) and meditating (***meditatio***) in order to enter into a listening (wordless) dialogue with God; to create a radically new context; to let the spiritual (numinous) affects of our meditation become the source of that dialogue. That is not an easy process either to do, or to explain. It is always highly personal. St Francis de Sales taught us in his 1609 *Introduction à la vie dévote* (*Introduction to the Devout Life*):

> 'The work of the soul's purification neither may, nor can end, save with life itself; do not then let us be disheartened by our imperfections,

our very perfection lies in diligently contending against them, and it is impossible so to contend without seeing them, or to overcome without meeting them face toe face. Our victory does not consist in being insensible to them, but in not consenting to them.' (Part I:5)

And so:
'All our devout exercises must sink into the heart, and when we come forth from our meditation and retirement it behoves us to tread warily in business or society, lest the wine of our good resolutions be heedlessly spilt; rather let it soak in and penetrate every faculty of the soul, but quietly, and without bodily or mental excitement.' (Part V:16)

This is not easy. But what is even more difficult is the fourth step (***contemplatio***) which is to take those spaces we have opened up, and without any words or reflections at all, and in the total quiet of our heart and mind, to become silent before God. As John the Solitary (John of Apamea, d 394) an early Syriac Christian put it so well: our aim should be to create a *noetic* (νοητικός - *noetikós* - see/understand) space in which:

'there is a silence of the tongue, there is a silence of the whole body, there is a silence of the soul, there is the silence of the mind, and there is the silence of the spirit.'

where, within this *noetic* space, silence itself becomes the prayer, as inscribed in various places, including upon some High Altars around the world:

Lingua fundamentum sancti silentii.
(Language [is the] foundation of holy silence.)

I cannot begin to explain what this might mean for those able to achieve this fourth step: the *contemplatio* of *lectio divina*; to pray silently without praying in words, where those words are replaced by the silence of resting quietly in the presence of God. In 1864 (aged just 19 and a student at Oxford and before he became a Catholic) Gerard Manley Hopkins was translating some of Christina Rossetti's (1830-1894) poems into Latin elegiacs (only fragments of which are left to us) and was writing in his own poetry about seeing what is here 'but with a holier mind'. He was later to understand this through the Latin writings of Duns Scotus and St Thomas Aquinas. Aquinas had been strongly influenced by much of the spiritual philosophy of the Jewish philosopher and scholar Maimonides (Rabbi Moshe ben Maimon 1135-1204) himself, as was Aquinas, heavily influenced by the writings of Aristotle, and doing much the same through Aristotle for Judaism as Aquinas did for Catholicism. Central to much of Maimonides' thinking was that God's creation (the natural world) was not just to be lived in, but to be reflected upon, and through that reflection a true love for God would be achieved based on a recognition of the insignificance of humanity before God (a view Rossetti often wrote about and which Hopkins also adopted). As Aquinas was to make so clear for the Catholic world in which he lived (and which has been heavily influenced by his thought ever since) there is no useful separation to be made between the truths of God and the valid results of human reasoning, because that reasoning, like the fallen leaf or snowflake contemplated for hours at a time by Hopkins, is God-given. Seen through a Catholic lens this effectively enables us to consider that all things are *referenced* and themselves *reference* God.

Prayer, and the liturgy of the Church focuses the mind on this single truth in a world where now *self* and the natural world, are promulgated as the only movers through the pages and screens of the world we live in; as being the only worthwhile referent. Individual personality - the *ego perspective* - now dominates. Materiality dominates. Hopkins' fallen leaf now references only itself and the materiality in which it has lived and fallen. Prayer, if it is considered at all, is seen as inconsequential and peripheral to the real business of being human; acknowledged, usually grudgingly, as a necessary belief for some on the fringes, perhaps, but with no substance, because the only real substance in this way of thinking is the material.

Aldous Huxley (1894-1963) perhaps not the first person one might think of to counter this celebration of the material, talked in his 1954 book *The Doors of Perception* about the 'incompatibility between man's egotism and the divine purity; between 'man's self-aggravated separateness and the infinity of God'. It is against the predominance of this 'self-aggravated separateness' that this book on Latin prayer stands. Fr Erich Przywara SJ (1889-1972) in his inspiring 1925 **Maiestas Divina** (trs 1944 by Fr Thomas Corbishley SJ (1903-1976 as *The Divine Majesty*) for example, meditating on the *Spiritual Exercises of St Ignatius*, wrote:

> Plunge in
> till you lose the last traces
> of self-sufficiency insensibility ungenerous reserve
> all notion of 'mine' and 'own'
> that you may be ready for unconditional surrender
> to him
> 'a giving up of yourself and all that is yours
> to God
> like a snowflake falling from the sky'

And St María Rafael Arnáiz Báron (1911-1938) a Trappist Oblate who, because of illness was never able to solemnly profess monastic vows, said most hauntingly:

> 'It is not the silence of one who has nothing to say, but the silence of one, who, having many and very beautiful things within,

keeps quiet in order that mere words, which are always soiled, may not adulterate one's dialogue with God. In a word: silence is all in the contemplative life.'

This is *numinous affect* of God's infinity, the like of which may seem unattainable to many of us, but which this book has sought to show glimpses of in a Latin Catholic context, through a way of Latin prayer that might seem to be all about words, grammar and syntax, but which we might pray with Isaiah, as we do in the glorious *Introit* of the Mass of the Feast of the Immaculate Conception of Our Lady (8th December):

> *Gaudens gaudébo in Dómino, et exsultábit ánima mea in Deo meo, quia índuit me vestiméntis salútis, et induménto iustítiae circúmdedit me, [quasi sponsum decorátum coróna,] et quasi sponsam ornátam monílibus suis.*
> (Rejoicing I will rejoice in [the] Lord, and my soul will rejoice in my God, because he clothed me with [the] clothes of salvation, and with [the] robe of justice he has surrounded me, [as a bridegroom decorated with [a] crown,] and as [a] bride adorned with her jewels.
> *Is* 61:10)

The power of the prayer, therefore, lies not just in the concrete words being used, or the tangible grammatical function they are performing, but also in the intangible forms, gaps and spaces between and behind those words and grammatical functions and structures in the silences. Swiss Philosopher and convert from Judaism to Roman Catholicism, Max Picard (1888-1965) in his 1948 book *Die Welt des Schweigens* (*The World of Silence*) wrote:

> 'Silence contains everything within itself. It is not waiting for anything; it is always wholly present in itself and it completely fills out the space in which it appears.'

Aiming for this in prayer, as this book has shown, is not an easy process. Aiming to achieve what Picard says:

> 'In every moment of time, man through silence can be with the origins of all things.'

is even harder. The 15thC Indian poet Kabir wrote:

> still the body
> still the mind
> still the voice inside
>
> in silence
> feel the stillness move
>
> friends
> this feeling
> cannot be imagined

Kabir Das (1398/1440-1448/1518) a Sufi, sought sanctification in his own way. Latin Catholics, as this book has shown, seek it in other ways, but what he said about silence is still powerfully resonant as long as the voice we 'still inside' us is ours and not God's. Danish philosopher Søren Kierkegaard (1813-1855) born to a Lutheran (and troubled) family, and often stridently anti-formal/institutionalised Christianity, once insightfully wrote:

> 'The function of prayer is not to influence God, but rather to change the nature of the one who prays.'

Silence, as well as words can help a lot in that. In Pope St Paul VI's 1971 *Apostolic Exhortation* on the renewal of the religious life ***Evangelica Testificatio*** ([The] Evangelical Witness) advocating considerable, and not always welcome, change in Religious Orders following *Vatican II*, he teaches that people need 'a certain solitude' in order 'to hear God "speaking to his heart."' (*Hos* 2:16). He continues:

> 'silence which is a mere absence of noise and words, in which the soul cannot renew its vigour, would obviously lack any spiritual value. On the contrary, the search for intimacy with God involves the truly vital need of a silence embracing the whole being, both for those who must find God in the midst of noise and confusion and for contemplatives. Faith, hope and a love for God which is open to the gifts of the Spirit, and also a brotherly love which is open to the mystery of others, carry with them an imperative need for silence.' (*Vat* §46)

It may seem odd to talk about **silentium** (silence) at the end of a book that has seemingly been all about words, and Latin ones at that. But for most us this may perhaps be the only way we have of approaching the 4th step of **Lectio Divina - contemplatio**. In prayer, with words or silence, we become *supplicant-worshippers* of the origin of all creation, because we recognise, acknowledge, name and call out to this origin as Divine. We call out to someone other than (and beyond) ourselves and the world we live in. This makes what we do with the language, grammar, structures and silences of prayer quite different from how we use language in our ordinary lives.

When we learn Latin in order to pray, we are not learning or reading Latin as an exercise in 'blackboard linguistics'. Latin lives as a language in Latin Catholicism because it is *prayed*. It lives not as an exercise in digging up a long-dead text, or long-gone empire and culture, but as an active, vibrant *calling out* and *turning* to God, recognising and seeking, by the discipline of that *turning*, to participate in *theosis*; to be affected by the *numinous*; to experience prayer and thus, we hope, to experience God. Italian born Priest and academic, Servant of God (**Servus Dei**) Romano Guardini (1885-1963) probably most famous for his book, originally written in German in 1937 and translated into English in 1954 as, *The Lord*, summed it all up quite simply when he said:

> '...reverently pause before this or that word or act, ready to learn, adore, obey.'

When he was Prefect of the Congregation for the Doctrine of Faith Joseph Cardinal Ratzinger introduced a new edition of this most famous book (1982) writing:

> 'For Guardini the first step is always attentive listening to the message of the [scriptural] text... But in this attentiveness to the text, the listener, according to Guardini's understanding, does not make himself to be master of the Word. Rather the listener makes himself the believing disciple who allows himself to be led and enlightened by the Word.'

Regardless of the difficulties that may be involved in that 'believing discipline' and in prayer (in general) and in the steps of **Lectio Divina** (in particular) there is a very ancient extra-liturgical tradition in the Church of praying a very simple, repeated, set of prayers, one of which is the *Jesus Prayer* (also known as 'The Prayer of the Heart') which predates the popularising of the *Rosary* (formally approved in 1569) by many centuries:

> *Iesu*
> *Iesu Christe*
> *Dómine Iesu*
> *Dómine miserére,*
> *Dómine Iesu Christe, Fili Dei, miserére mei.*
> *Dómine Iesu Christe, Fili Dei, miserére mei, peccatóris* [m]/*peccatrícis* [f]. *Amen.*

(O Jesus

O Jesus Christ

O Lord Jesus

O Lord, have mercy

O Lord Jesus Christ, Son of God, have mercy on me

O Lord Jesus Christ, Son of God, have mercy on me [a]sinner. Amen.)

This prayer is very popular in Eastern Catholic and Orthodox traditions, much more so than in western Roman rite cultures. There are many versions of the *Jesus Prayer* but perhaps the best known is the simpler:

Dómine Iesu Christe, Fili Dei, miserére mei, peccatóris [m]/*peccatrícis* [f]. *Amen.*
(Lord Jesus Christ, Son of God, have mercy on me, a sinner.'

There is a long history to the idea of the power of prayer in the repetition of a name, and while the Western rite has tended to give prominence to that repetition through *Aves* and *Paters*, the Eastern rite often retains the centrality of the repetition of the name *Jesus*, and, as such, the *Jesus Prayer* is often repeated first thing in the morning every day for ten or fifteen minutes at a time using a prayer rope (in the Greek Orthodox Church known as a κομποσκοίνι - *komboskini* and in the Russian Orthodox Church as a чётки - *chotki*) which may be made with 100 knots or with just 33 knots representing the lifespan of Christ on earth. Simple prayers like this are easy to learn in Latin, but powerful in affect. Gerard Manley Hopkins perfectly captures this simplicity in the first stanza of his poem 133, *Summa:*

The best ideal is the true
And other truth is none,
All glory be ascribèd to

> The holy Three in One.

This is the the simple summation of all that is Christian - to give glory to and for God the Trinity. Over the two millennia of Catholic life within the Church, much has been written on prayer, as we have seen to some extent in this book, and many of the types now summarised in the *Catechism* have become the life of many people seeking sanctification. Some few become Saints, to become part of what the *Catechism* refers to as the **nubes testium** (the cloud of witnesses) - the Saints in Heaven - who 'contemplate God, praise him and constantly care for those whom they have left on earth. *Cat* §2683). They all prayed, of course, and they all prayed in different ways. Some chose/choose the hesychast way (ἡσυχασμός - *hesychasmos* - stillness/silence) sometimes within an eremitical (ἐρημίτης - *eremites* - hermit) way of life, other times within a cenobitic (κοινοβιακός - *koinobiakos* - communal) monastic way of life; but most times simply as people seeking as best a way we can of living a life of prayer in our usually busy and crowded lives.

But however we live those lives, and wherever we may be on this journey of **devotio**, we all of us who pray, are seeking to pray with words (**lectio/meditatio**) but also in the silence of our hearts, striving as best we can for affective prayer (**oratio/contemplatio**). In sometimes very different and varying ways, we seek the numinous, and even, perhaps, the mystical *theosis* hinted at in this book. Many writers on prayer have determined a threefold path: the 'Purgative Way'; the 'Illuminative Way' and the 'Unitive Way', signalling a journey of steady perfection in prayer. But however we live our lives, and wherever we may be on this journey of prayer, we all of us who seek to pray with our mind (*noesis*) and with our heart (*cardiognosis*) very few of us will 'withdraw' from the world to do it. Even fewer of us will enter the consecrated life, in any of its institutional forms. We will do it as best we can, in the context, and calling, in which we live. St Paul summed it up perfectly for the Ephesians when he wrote to them:

> *State ergo succincti lumbos vestros in veritate, et induti loricam iustitiae, et calceati pedes in praeparatione Evangelii pacis, in omnibus sumentes scutum fidei, in quo possitis omnia tela nequissimi ignea extinguere: et galeam salutis assumite, et gladium Spiritus (quod est verbum Dei) per omnem orationem et obsecrationem orantes omni tempore in Spiritu: et in ipso vigilantes in omni instantia et obsecratione pro omnibus sanctis.*
>
> (Stand therefore your loins readied in truth, and clothed with [the] breastplate of justice, and your feet shod in preparation of [the] Gospel of peace, in all claiming [the] shield of faith, with which you may be able to extinguish all fiery weapons: and take up [the] helmet of salvation, and [the] sword of [the] Spirit (which is [the] word of God) through all prayer and supplication praying at all times in [the] Spirit: and in this same watching on all occasions and with supplication for all [the] saints. *Eph* 6:14-18)

And for us to do that, the prayer of the Psalmist, as always, is invaluable:

> *vocem meam audi secúndum misericórdiam tuam, Dómine: et secúndum iudícium tuum vivífica me.*
> (hear! my voice according to your mercy, O Lord: and according to your justice enliven! me. *Ps* 118:149)

XIV

AFTERWORD

Et nunc in omni corde et ore collaudate, et benedicite nomen Domini.
(So now within the whole heart and by mouth praise, and bless the name of the Lord. *Ecc* 39:41)

Pope Leo XIII in his 1889 *Encyclical* on the Holy Spirit, ***Divinum Illud Munus*** (That Divine Office) teaches:

Divinum illud munus quod humani generis causa a Patre acceptum Iesus Christus sanctissime obiit, sicut eo tamquam ad ultimum spectat, ut homines vitae compotes fiant in sempiterna gloria beatae, ita huc proxime attinet per saeculi cursum, ut divinae gratiae habeant colantque vitam, quae tandem in vitam floreat caelestem.

(That divine office which Jesus Christ received from his Father for the welfare of mankind, and most perfectly fulfilled, had for its final object to put men in possession of the eternal life of glory, and proximately during the course of ages to secure to them the life of divine grace, which is destined eventually to blossom into the life of heaven. *Vat*)

I have sought to show throughout this book that the ***divinum munus*** this great Pope is talking about has one sole purpose:

> *ut homines vitae compotes fiant in sempiterna gloria beatae.*
> (to put men in possession of the eternal life of glory. *Vat*)

And to achieve that he further teaches:

> ***Spiritum Sanctum exorari et obsecrari oportet, quippe cuius praesidio adiumentisque nemo unus non egeat maxime. Ut enim quisque est inops consilii, viribus infirmus, aerumnis pressus, pronus in vetitum, ita ad eum confugere debet, qui luminis, fortitudinis, consolationis, sanctitatis fons patet perennis.***
> (We ought to pray to and invoke the Holy Spirit, for each one of us greatly needs his protection and his help. The more a man is deficient in wisdom, weak in strength, borne down with trouble, prone to sin, so ought he the more to fly to him who is the never-ceasing fount of light, strength, consolation, and holiness. *Vat*)
>
> ***Demum hoc est fidenter assidueque supplicandum, ut nos quotidie magis et luce sua illustret et caritatis suae quasi facibus incendat; sic enim fide et amore freti acriter enitantur ad praemia sempiterna, quoniam ipse est pignus hereditatis nostrae.***
> (Lastly, we ought confidently and continually to beg of him to illuminate us daily more and more with his light and inflame us with his charity: for, thus inspired with faith and love, we may press onward earnestly towards our eternal reward, since he is the pledge of our inheritance. *Vat*)

'Pressing onward' is not always easy. But we always have the Liturgical Year to both comfort us, and to guide us, in the joys, and sorrows, of prayer. This is expressed well by a contemporary of St John Henry Newman, John Keble (1792-1866) a Minister of the Anglican church and early stalwart of the Oxford Movement, like Newman, but who never converted to Roman Catholicism. The journey from *chronos* to *kairos* is captured well by Keble, as he talks elegantly in his 1827 book of verse, *The Christian Year*, of the seasons that lead us 'through time to timeless glory':

Sounding the Seasons

> Tangled in time, we live with hints and guesses
> Turning the wheel of each returning year,
> But in between our failures and successes
> We sometimes glimpse the Love that casts out fear,
> Sometimes the heart remembers its own reasons
> And breathes a *Sanctus* as we tell our story,
> Tracing the tracks of grace, sounding the seasons
> That lead at last through time to timeless glory.
> From the first yearnings for a Saviour's birth
> To the full joy of knowing sins forgiven
> We gather as His church on Gods's good earth
> To share an echo of the choirs of heaven
> I share these hints, returning what was lent,
> Turning to praise each 'moment's monument.

'Tracing the tracks of grace' in our prayer life is often a journey of one step forward and two steps back. There are the dark, barren times. There are the uninspired and arid times; the times of empty heads and hearts; the times of heads and hearts filled with nonsense; the times of seeming to seek but seeming never to find; of sometimes not even having the spiritual energy to knock on the door. But all of humanity is in God's hands. No matter how difficult our prayer life may be, or how much we might, at times, want to run away from it all, as perhaps all seeming far too difficult. But there is no hiding, even if we do run away. Victorian Catholic poet Francis Thompson understood this well writing in his 1890 poem *The Hound of Heaven*:

> 'I fled Him, down the nights and down the days;
> I fled Him, down the arches of the years;
> I fled Him, down the labyrinthine ways
> Of my own mind; and in the mist of tears
> I hid from Him, and under running laughter.
> Up vistaed hopes I sped;
> And shot, precipitated,
> Adown Titanic glooms of chasmèd fears,
> From those strong Feet that followed, followed after.
> But with unhurrying chase,
> And unperturbèd pace,
> Deliberate speed, majestic instancy,
> They beat—and a Voice beat
> More instant than the Feet—
> "All things betray thee, who betrayest Me."'

But to no avail.

> 'Fear wist not to evade as Love wist to pursue.
> Still with unhurrying chase,
> And unperturbèd pace,
> Deliberate speed, majestic instancy,
> Came on the following Feet,
> And a Voice above their beat—
> 'Naught shelters thee, who wilt not shelter Me.'

God's love relentlessly pursues.

'Lo! naught contents thee, who content'st not Me.'

Submission to God's will is inescapable:

'Ah, fondest, blindest, weakest,
I am He Whom thou seekest!

Catholic convert Eric Gill (1882-1940) a modernist sculptor and typographer, responsible for the Stations of the Cross and the altarpiece of the Chapel of St George and the English Martyrs in the Catholic Cathedral of the Most Precious Blood of Our Lord Jesus Christ in Westminster, London (started in 1895 and opened in 1903 and still far from complete inside). Regardless of Gill's somewhat dubious lifestyle, he nevertheless recognised within Catholicism an opportunity to put into practice what he had believed for many years, that:

'without philosophy man cannot know what he makes; but without religion he cannot know why.'

If this book has been about anything, it has been about the importance of religion in our lives, and expressed in this book through the discipline of Latin prayer and liturgy. St Augustine, which this book has referred to many times, as always, captures this sensibility perfectly, saying:

Constanter Deo crede, eique te totum committe quantum potes. Noli esse velle quasi proprius et in tua potestate, sed eius clementissimi et utilissimi Domini te servum esse profitere. Ita enim te ad se sublevare non desinet, nihilque tibi evenire permittet, nisi quod tibi prosit, etiam si nescias.

(Constantly believe in God, and commit yourself wholly to him as much as you are able. Wish not to be as though special and under your [own] control, but promise yourself to be [a] servant to that most clement and most valuable Lord. For he will thus not hesitate to lift you to himself, and may permit nothing to befall you, unless what may do good to you, even though you may not know it. *Soliloquia* 15:30)

I have not attempted to present a unique case for praying in Latin; nor to suggest that vernacular prayer is any the less for not being Latin. But I have tried to present a view that suggests we lose a great deal, and not just of the patrimony and Tradition of the Church, if we no longer include Latin in our prayer (public and private) as Catholics. I am by profession (or was before retirement) an academic linguist, and this book is, in effect, the extended meditation of a linguist thinking about, reflecting upon, and praying Latin prayer, not simply as a scholarly exercise, but as a sustained (if only ever partial) *lectio divina.* This extended meditation is offered in the same spirit that Pope Leo XIII taught in his *Encyclical* on the 'Restoration of Christian Philosophy' issued on August 4, 1879 *Aeterni Patris,* (of the Eternal Father') in which he celebrated the medieval scholastic philosophy of St Thomas Aquinas:

> *Igitur hac quoque in re exempla sequamur Doctoris angelici, qui numquam se lectioni aut scriptioni dedit, nisi propitiato precibus Deo; quique candide confessus est, quidquid sciret, non tam se studio aut labore suo sibi peperisse, quam divinitus accepisse: ideoque humili et concordi obsecratione Deum simul omnes exoremus, ut in Ecclesiae filios spiritum scientiae et intellectus emittat, et aperiat eis sensum ad intelligendam sapientiam. Atque ad uberiores percipiendos divinae bonitatis fructus, etiam B. Virginis Mariae, quae sedes sapientiae appellatur, efficacissimum patrocinium apud Deum interponile; simulque deprecatores adhibete purissimum Virginis Sponsum B. Iosephum, et Petrum ac Paulum Apostolos maximos, qui orbem terrarum, impura errorum lue corruptum, veritate renovarunt, et caelestis sapientiae lumine compleverunt.*

(Therefore in this also let us follow the example of the Angelic Doctor, who never gave himself to reading or writing without first begging the blessing of God, who modestly confessed that whatever he knew he had acquired not so much by his own study and labour as by the divine gift; and therefore let us all, in humble and united prayer, beseech God to send forth the spirit of knowledge and of understanding to the children of the Church and open their senses for the understanding of wisdom. And that we may receive fuller fruits of the divine goodness, offer up to God the most efficacious patronage of the Blessed Virgin Mary, who is called the seat of wisdom; having at the same time as advocates St Joseph, the most chaste spouse of the Virgin, and Peter and Paul, the chiefs of the Apostles, whose truth renewed the earth which had fallen under the impure blight of error, filling it with the light of heavenly wisdom. § 33 *Vat*)

And it is within that spirit that I close this book:

Ad glóriam ígitur omnipoténtis Dei et Dómini nostri Iesu Christi, spectántes fidúciam in auxílio Sanctíssimae Vírginis Maríae et beatórum Petri et Pauli Apostolórum habéntes ánimum ad utilitátem spiritualémque progressiónem Ecclésiae attendéntes.
Benedictus Deus sanctus, sanctus, sanctus. Amen

(To the glory therefore of God most holy and of our Lord Jesus Christ, trusting in the aid of the Blessed Virgin Mary and of the holy Apostles Peter and Paul paying attention to the value of the soul and preserving the spirit and growth of the Church.
Blessed God, holy, holy, holy Amen.
(Pope St Paul VI: *Credo of the People of God*, 1968)

DAVID BIRCH

APPENDIX: ACCENTING AND PRONUNCIATION

Unus Cultus Unus Cantus Una Lingua
(One Worship One Chant One Language)

Accenting

In Liturgical Latin stress in 2 syllable words is always on the first syllable, though this is not marked as such in writing (but may be marked in chant notation) but in words longer than 2 syllables it is marked, and appears as: á, é, í, ó, ú, ý, ǽ, and more rarely ë (usually on proper nouns like **Israël**, but also as the equivalent of é in the digraph æ to distinguish it from the unaccented diphthong ae eg aërem (acc sg - air) and œ (usually from Greek loan words) Where *oe* is meant to be accented it is sometimes written as the digraph œ usually without an accent (eg *obœdiens*) but may often be replaced with ǽ. Overall, the acute accent indicates where the vowel should be stressed, as in **Dóminus** (Lord) or **Beátus** (Blessed) where ó should be pronounced - *or* as in English *daughter* and not as in English *mop* and á should be pronounced as English *father* and not as in English *cat*. In a word of 3 or more syllables the penultimate (next to the last) syllable is marked with an accent if it has a long vowel sound, and if it has a short vowel sound then the syllable before that (the last but two [antepenultimate]) is marked with an accent. For example:

Ave, María, grátia plena; Dóminus tecum

where the penultimate vowel 'i' of *grátia* is short (grar - tsee - a) and so the antepenultimate vowel is accented á (ar) So:

á as in English *father* not *fat* - ***pátria*** *(*par - tree - ar*)* - country
é as in English *fate* not *felt* - ***régula*** (ray - goo - lar) - rule
é as in English *fair* not *fur* - ***aspérgere*** (as - pair -ge - ray) - to sprinkle
í as in English *feet* not *fit* - ***discípulus*** (di - sheep - u - loos) - disciple
í as in English *fear* not *fit* - ***vírgine*** (vear - gin - ay) - virgin
ó as in English *for* not *fob* - ***Dóminus*** (dor - min - oos) - Lord
ú as in English *food* not *foot* - ***secúndum*** (se - koon - doom) - following
ý as in English *machine* not *bit* - ***týmpanum*** (teem - par - noom) - drum
ǽ as in English *pay* not *pet* - ***quǽrere*** (kway - re -ray) - to seek
œ as in English *pay* not *pet* - ***prœmium*** (pror - ay - mee - oom) - preface

So:

Aspérges me Dómine, hyssópo, et mundábor; lavábis me et super nivem dealbábor.

where each of the accented vowels is long:

as - ***pér*** - *ges* as in *fair* not as in *fur*
Dóm - *i* - *ne* as in *for* not *fob*
hys - ***só*** - *po* as in *for* not *fob*
mun - ***dá*** - *bor* as in *father* not *fat*
la -***vá*** - *bis* as in *father* not *fat*
de - *al* - ***bá*** - *bor* as in *father* not *fat*

Latin prayer is only accented in this book where it is designed to be prayed, even when the source text may not be accented, for example prayers included in Encyclicals. It is not accented in this book where it is used for illustrative or other purposes, and this short guide is meant for speaking the Latin prayer sotto voce or out loud. Stricter rules may sometimes apply more rigorously in plainchant. Capital letters are not marked with an accent in this book, and the letters *AE/Ae/ae* are written in full throughout this book except where an accent is required and then an accented digraph is used *ǽ*. *OE/Oe/oe* are written in full, but where an accent is required, the unaccented digraph *œ* is used.

For a comprehensive account of accenting in Liturgical and Ecclesiastical Latin see: https://github.com/gregorio-project/latin-ecclesiastic-accents/blob/master/doc/accentuation-rules.md

Pronunciation

The pronunciation of Liturgical Latin for most of the Church's long history was subject to often considerable regional variation; variations which may still be heard to day, though more rarely now, following the instructions given *motu proprio* in *Litterae Encyclicae Musica Sacrae Disciplina* in 1903 by Pope St Pius X, who sought to standardise pronunciation to what we now tend to call the 'Italian' or 'Roman' usage (*more Romano*; see: http://www.pronunciationguide.info/Latin.html) Every letter is pronounced in Liturgical Latin, so when there are 2 vowels together (except *ae* and *oe*) each is pronounced and not elided (run together) as in English - e.g. *suávis* (sweet) has 3 syllables (soo/ar/vis) not 2 as in English (swa/vis) *Aaron* has 3 syllables (A/a/ron) and not 2 as in English (air/on) where *A* and *a* are both pronounced separately as in English *cat*.

Where there are 2 consonants together, both are pronounced, for example *occísor* (killer) which is pronounced (*ok/cee/sor*) and not (*och/i/sor*)

Pronunciation generally follows a so-called 'Italian' pronunciation which began with various vowel and consonant shifts evident in late Antiquity rather than the assumed classical Latin pronunciation, as in the accented vowels above, and the following:

a (unaccented) is pronounced as in English *cat*, not as *father* or *fate* so each *a* in **Abraham** is pronounced as in English *cat* (*a/bra/ham*)

c (before e, i, ae, oe) is pronounced *ch* as in English *church* and elsewhere as *k* as in English *carrot*. May also replace *ti* (*solacium/solatium*) and be pronounced *tsee*

ch is pronounced *k* as in English **Christ**

g (before e, i, ae, oe) is pronounced as a 'soft' *g* as in English **gentle**) and elsewhere as a 'hard' *g* as in English **garden**

gn is pronounced as in English *canyon*

h may or may not be aspirated as in English - its use varies according to individual, Religious Community or regional preference - but in **mihi** it is usually pronounced with a *k* (*mi/ki*)

j/J is written as *i/I* in some books as in **Iesus**, but this is not a rigid rule, and both versions are used, though generally consistently as one type or another. *i/I* is used in this book and pronounced *yes* not *jam*

r is generally rolled a little as in French

s is always pronounced unvoiced, that is as in English *sweet* and not voiced (*z*) as in English *raise*

-as/-es/-is/-os/-us at the end of words especially at the end of a line may often be purposefully faded out altogether in the chanting by some Religious Orders, and is often lost all together without any fading out at all

sc (before a, o, u or a consonant) as in English *scatter*

sc (before e, i, oe, ae) as in English *shoot*

ti before a vowel and after any letter except s, t, or x is pronounced *tsee*

th as in English *trip* never as in English *think*

Latin prayer lives in many different ways across the world, and is always going to be subject to regional variation in its pronunciation, despite written guidance from Rome. From the sometimes English precision of the Latin of the Brompton Oratory in London, for example, to the often heavily Italianate accents; the distinctive Parisian uvular 'r trill' of some French monasteries streaming online; some strong American rhotic accents and some Australian non-rhotic ones. Interestingly, St John Henry Cardinal Newman, when he began praying the Latin Office with his brethren at their house in Littlemore (Oxford) before he became a Roman Catholic, used the English (Classical) pronunciation of Latin (rarely found now in churches and religious orders in England, but still to be heard in some Anglo-Catholic services and in some Oxbridge colleges when Latin grace is said) for the two years before he was converted to Catholicism, immediately after which Newman and the Littlemore community then prayed the Office, still in Latin, but now according to Roman pronunciation usage. For example, they would have classically prayed **Regina Caeli** with a hard 'g' and 'k' and then ecclesiastically with a soft 'j' and 'ch', and initially the 'ae' as a long 'i' and then as a long 'ay'. In **Vox Dei**, 'v' would have been prayed classically with a 'w' and then ecclesiastically with a soft 'v'.

For a comprehensive guide to Liturgical Latin pronunciation see: de Angelis (1937) and for a shorter guide see: https://www.siue.edu/MUSIC/CHOIR/LatinPronunciation.pdf.

For a contrasting guide to pronunciation in Classical Latin see: https://orbilat.com/Languages/Latin/Grammar/Latin-Pronunciation-Syllable-Accent.html

BIBLIOGRAPHY: REFERENCES

Ergo qui multa legit et intelligit, impletur
(Therefore who[ever] reads and understands much, is fulfilled)
St Ambrose

A Carthusian Monk (1996) *They Speak by Silence*, Darton, Longman & Todd: London

A Carthusian Monk (1998) *The Spirit of Place: Carthusian Reflections*, Darton, Longman & Todd: London

à Kempis, Thomas (1959/1963) *The Imitation of Christ*, English trs by Ronald Knox, completed by Michael Oakley with editorial input from Evelyn Waugh, Burns & Oates: London

à Kempis, Thomas (c1436) *De Imitatione Christi : Libri Quatuor*, Desclée et Socii edition: Paris, 1948

Allen, Rosamund S (1988) trs & ed *Richard Rolle: The English Writings*, New York: Paulist Press: New York

Abercrombie, Nigel (1936) *The Origins of Jansenism*, Clarendon Press: Oxford

Abbott, Walter (gen ed) (1966) *The Documents of Vatican II. All Sixteen Texts Promulgated by the Ecumenical Council 1963-1965*, ed Joseph Gallagher, Geoffrey Chapman: London

Ælfric of Eynsham (990-992) *Sermones Catholici*, First Series see: Clemoes (1997) Second Series (containing the Sermon on Job) see: Godden (1979) See also: www.oldenglishaerobics.net/aelfric_job.html

Alfred, King of Wessex see: Hargrove (ed 1902)

Allen, Paul, Raymond Canning & Lawrence Cross (eds) (1998) *Prayer and Spirituality in the Early Church*, Centre for Early Christian Studies, Australian Catholic University: Everton Park, Queensland

Alphonsus, St Mary de Liguori (1759) *A short treatise on prayer; the great means of obtaining from God eternal salvation, and all the graces of which we stand in need,* John Coyne: Dublin

Alphonsus, St Mary de Liguori (1767) *The Way of Salvation and of Perfection, Meditations - Pious Reflections - and Spiritual Treatises by St Alphonsus de Liguori* ed Fr Eugene Grimm CSSR (1926) St Louis Redemptorist Fathers: Brooklyn. See also Jones (1836)

Altizer, Thomas JJ & William Hamilton (1966) *Radical Theology and the Death of God,* Bobbs-Merrill: Indianapolis

Ambrose, of Milan St (c388) *Enarrationes in XII Psalmos Davidicos*, see: *PL* 14.963-1238 and Ní Riain (2000)

Ambrose, of Milan St (c388) *Expositio Psalmi CXVIII*, see Ní Riain (1998)

Ancrene Wisse / Ancrene Riwle) (early 13[th]C): https://d.lib.rochester.edu/teams/text/hasenfrantz-ancrene-wisse-part-one

Anon (13[th]C) *Fioretti di San Francesco*: https://www.ccel.org/ccel/ugolino/flowers.html

Anselm, of Canterbury St (1077/8) *Proslogion*: http://www.thelatinlibrary.com/anselmproslogion.html see also: https://jasper-hopkins.info/proslogion.pdf

Anselm, of Canterbury St (c1094) *Cur Deus Homo*: https://archive.org/details/sanselmicantuar04laemgoog see also: https://en.wikisource.org/wiki/Cur_Deus_Homo

Anselm, of Canterbury St (1103/5) *Ad Deum*: https://operaantiqua.blogspot.com/p/sancti-anselmi-orationes-sive.html

Anselm, St (early 12[th]C) *Ave Crux Sancta*: https://www.preces-latinae.org/thesaurus/Filius/AveCrux.html

Apel, Willi (1958) *Gregorian Chant,* Burns & Oates: London.

Aquinas, St Thomas (1264) *The Office of Corpus Christi*, see Moser ed (1993)

Aquinas, St Thomas (1252?) *De Ente et Essentia*, see: https://isidore.co/aquinas/DeEnte&Essentia.htm

Aquinas, St Thomas (1961-1965 edition) *Summa Theologiae*, Biblioteca de Autores Christianos: Madrid, Latin text 5 vols & see: https://aquinasinstitute.org/operaomnia/

Arnáiz, Maria Rafael Barón St (2002) *Rafael Obras Completas*. Preparadas por Friar Maria Alberico Feliz Carbajal (Rafael Complete works. Compiled by Friar Maria Alberico Feliz Carbajal) 4 ed Burgos: Editorial Monte Carmelo. See also: *Saint Rafael Arnáiz: Collected Works* (2022) trs Catherine Addington with an introduction by Sr María Gonzalo OCSO, Cistercian Publications: Kalamazoo

Athanasian Creed: www.todayscatholicworld.com/athanasian-creed.htm

Atkinson, James (1968) *Martin Luther and the Birth of Protestantism*, Penguin: Harmondsworth

Auerbach, Erich (1953) *Mimesis. The Representation of Reality in Western Literature*, trs Willard R Trask, Princeton University Press: Princeton, New Jersey

Augustine, St (416?) *Sermones*: https://thelatinlibrary.com/augustine/serm.shtml

Augustine, St (426) *De Civitate Dei Contra Paganos*: https://www.thelatinlibrary.com/august.html

Augustine, St (416?) *In Iohannis Epistulam ad Parthos Tractatus*: https://www.newadvent.org/fathers/1702.htm

Augustine, St (1912) *Augustine Confessions*, Latin/English Parallel texts, 2 vols Loeb Classical Library, Harvard UP: Cambridge Mass, English trs vol 1 & 2 William Watts https://faculty.georgetown.edu/jod/latinconf/latinconf.html; see also: https://www.newadvent.org/fathers/110102.htm

Augustine, St (5th C) *Augustine Select Letters*, Latin/English Parallel texts, Loeb Classical Library, Harvard UP: Cambridge Mass (1930) English trs James Houston Baxter

Augustine, St (c397) *Confessions*, Latin text ed James O'Donnell, Clarendon Press: Oxford; English trs H Chadwick (1991) OUP: Oxford

Augustine, St (5th C) *Enarratio in Psalmum 72*: http://www.augustinus.it/latino/esposizioni_salmi/esposizione_salmo_091_testo.htm

Augustine, St (5th C) *Sermo* 117 in *PL* 38: 661-671

Augustine, St (5th C) *Sermones*, see: *Sancti Aurelii Augustini Hipponensis Episcopi Opera Omnia*, caput III *Sermo CL*, ed JP Migne (1841): https://archive.org/details/sanctiaureliia05augu/page/404/mode/2up

Augustine, St (5th C) *St Augustine. Two Books of Soliloquies*, trs Rev Charles C Starbuck AM, Nicene and Post-Nicene Fathers: Series I (1885) eds Alexander Roberts and James Donaldson vol VII

Bacon, Francis (1605) *The Advancement of Learning*: https://archive.org/details/advancementofl00baco

Bacon, Francis (1620) *Novum Organum*: https://archive.org/details/advancementoflea0000baco_wr33

Bacon, Roger (1267) *De Utilitate Grammaticae*: http://capricorn.bc.edu/siepm/DOCUMENTS/BACON/Bacon_Opus%20Majus%20III.pdf

Baker, Augustine Dom (1657) *Sancta Sophia, or, Directions for the Prayer of Contemplation &c. : Extracted out of more then [sic] XL Treatises, written by the late Ven. Father F Augustin Baker, a monke of the English congregation of the Holy Order of S. Benedict, and methodically digested by the R.F. Serenvs Cressy of the same order and congregation*, John Patte and Thomas Fievet: Douai. Trs Dom Norbert Sweeney (1876) and reissued (1911) as *Holy wisdom or, Directions for the Prayer of Contemplation, Extracted out of more than Forty Treatises*, Burns Oates & Washbourne: London, see also: https://web.archive.org/web/20080511191124/http://www.ccel.org/ccel/baker/holy_wisdom.html

Bede, the Venerable (c731) *Historia Ecclesiastica Gentis Anglorum*: http://www.thelatinlibrary.com/bede.html. For AM Sellar's 1907 translation into modern English see: https://www.gutenberg.org/files/38326/38326-h/38326-h.html

Bellarmine, Robert St (1611) *In omnes Psalmos Dilucida Expositio (Explanatio in Psalmos)*: https://archive.org/details/bub_gb_7j0Mm5XItI4C; see also O'Sullivan (2020) and https://www.ecatholic2000.com/bell/psalms.shtml#_Toc417747179

Benedict XVI, Pope (2008) *Message of his Holiness Benedict XVI for the Sixteenth World Day of the Sick*: https://www.vatican.va/content/benedict xvi/en/messages/sick/documents/hf_ben-xvi_mes_20080111_world-day-of-the-sick-2008.html

Benedict XVI, Pope (2009) *Caritas in Veritate*: http://w2.vatican.va/content/benedict-xvi/en/encyclicals/documents/hf_ben-xvi_enc_20090629_caritas-in-veritate.html

Benedict XVI, Pope (2010) 'Christmas Homilies': https://www.vatican.va/content/benedict-xvi/en/homilies/2010/documents/hf_ben-xvi_hom_20101224_christmas.html

Benedict, St (516?) *Regula Sancti Benedicti*, see Fry et al (1980) See also: http://www.thelatinlibrary.com/benedict.html & https://e-benedictine.com/rule/

Benedictine of Stanbrook Abbey (1954) *Medieval Mystical Tradition and St John of the Cross,* Burns & Oates: London

Benedictine Monastery of Solesmes eds (1938) *Graduale Romanum*, 1961 edition Desclée & Co: Tournai, see also: https://archive.ccwatershed.org/media/pdfs/13/08/14/13-43-42_0.pdf

Bernanos, George (1936) *Journal d'un Curé de Campagne,* Librairie Plon: Paris

Biblia Sacra iuxta Vulgatam Clementinam (1592) *Nova Editio,* 1965, Biblioteca de Autores Christianos: Madrid

Birch, David (1978) 'Sense and Word in Liturgical Language', *New Blackfriars*, 59/695, 176-183

Birch, David (1983) *Early Reformation English Polemics* (Elizabethan and Renaissance Studies, 92:7) Salzburg: Universität Salzburg: Institut für Anglistik und Amerikanistik

Birch, David (1989) *Language, Literature and Critical Practice. Ways of Analysing Text*, Routledge, London, Interface Series

Birch, David (1991) *The Language of Drama: Critical Theory and Practice*, Macmillan, London, The Language of Literature Series

Birch, David (2005) 'What does it mean to be a Catholic? Has this changed since Vatican II?' *AD 2000 A Journal of Religious Opinion*, 18/4 May 16-18

Birch, David (2006) '*Deus Caritas Est* - More Than Papal Lyricism', *The Priest. The Journal of the Australian Confraternity of Catholic Clergy*, 10/1, 30-32, 37

Birch, David (2006) 'Updating the Principles of the Liturgical Movement. A translation from the original French (Dom Charbel de Lys OSB)', *The Priest. The Journal of the Australian Confraternity of Catholic Clergy*, 10/2, 24-28

Birch, David (2008) 'No Smoke Without Fire: Benedict XVI and True Liturgical Reform', *AD2000 A Journal of Religious Opinion*, 21/8, 12-13

Birch, David (2008) '"Catholic Literature": What Does This Mean?' *AD2000. A Journal of Religious Opinion*, 21/11, 12-13

Birch, David (2008) 'Catholic Books: Catholic Minds', *Kairos: Catholic Journal* 19(20) 8-9

Birch, David (2009) 'John Henry Newman: A Conversion to Die For', *L'Osservatore Romano*, Weekly Edition in English, no 38 (2112) 4

Blowers, Paul M & Peter W Martens (2019) eds *The Oxford Handbook of Early Christian Biblical Interpretation*, Oxford University Press: Oxford

Boehner, Philotheus OFM (1956) trs (rev ed Zachary Hayes OFM 2002) *The Journey of the Mind into God* (St Bonaventure: *Itinerarium mentis in Deum*) Franciscan Institute: New York

Boulding, Maria (2002-4) trs & ed *Expositions of the Psalms* 6 volumes in *The Works of Saint Augustine A Translation for the 21st Century*, New City Press: New York

Bowden, JE (1869) *The Life and Letters of Frederick William Faber*, John Murphy & Co: Baltimore

Breviarium Romanum (Pius V revised Pius X) (1943) *editio XX*, Pustet: Ratisbon, 4 Vols

Breviarium Romanum, cum Textu Psalmorum e Versione Pii Papae XII (1960) Marietti: Rome, 2 Vols

Bridges, Robert (1918) *Poems of Gerard Manley Hopkins*, Oxford University Press: Oxford

Britt, Dom Matthew OSB (1922) trs *The Hymns of the Breviary and Missal*, Benziger Brothers: New York. See also: https://kp-shaw.blogspot.com/2013/05/latin.html

Brock, SP (1987) trs *The Syriac Fathers on Prayer and the Spiritual Life*, Cistercian Publications: Kalamazoo Michigan: https://archive.org/details/syriacfathersonp1987unse/page/n9/mode/2up

Buber, Martin (1923) *I and Thou*, trs Ronald Gregor Smith, 1937, T & T Clarke: Edinburgh, see also: https://www.burmalibrary.org/docs21/Buber-c1923-I_And_Thou-ocr-tu.pdf

Bugnini, Annibale (1983) *The Reform of the Liturgy, 1948-1975*, trs Matthew J O'Connell, The Liturgical Press edition 1990: Collegeville, Minnesota

Burton-Christie, D (1993) *The Word in the Desert: Scriptures and the Quest for Holiness in Early Christian Monasticism*, Oxford University Press: Oxford

Campbell, Nathaniel M (2018) trs *Hildegard of Bingen. The Book of Divine Works*, The Catholic University of America Press: Washington DC

Campos, Miguel & Michael Sauvage (1995) trs Oswald Murdoch, *Encountering God in the Depths of the Mind and Heart. A Commentary on John Baptist de la Salle's Explanation of the Method of Mental Prayer*, Brothers of the Christian Schools: Rome

Carpenter, Humphrey (1981) ed *The Letters of J R R Tolkien*, George Allen & Unwin, Houghton Mifflin: London

Cassian, John (4thC) *Conferences*, Latin text (1886) M Petschenig ed, Tempsky: Vienna; English trs (1997) B Ramsey, Paulist Press: New York

Caswall, Rev Edward (1851) trs *Lyra Catholica: Containing All the Hymns of the Roman Breviary and Missal*: https://archive.org/details/lyracatholicaco00caswgoog/page/n38/mode/2up.

Catéchisme de l'Église Catholique (1992) Mame/Plon:Tours/Paris

Catechismus Catholicae Ecclesiae (1997 *editio typica*): https://www.vatican.va/archive/catechism_lt/index_lt.htm

Catechism of the Catholic Church (1994) Libreria Editrice Vaticana. 2nd edition 2019: https://www.vatican.va/archive/ENG0015/_INDEX.HTM

Catechismus Romanus: Ex Decreto Concilii Tridentini ad Parochos (1567): https://archive.org/details/ita-bnc-ald-00000512-001; see also: https://www.catholicsociety.com/documents/Catechism_of_the_Council%20of_Trent.pdf

Catherine, of Siena (1378) *Catherine of Siena: The Dialogue* (Classics of Western Spirituality) 1980, Paulist Press: New York. See also: http://catholicplanet.com/ebooks/Dialogue-of-St-Catherine.pdf

Catholic Encyclopedia: https://www.newadvent.org/

Chesterton, GK (1908) *Orthodoxy*, 1967 edition Collins: London

Chesterton, GK (1926) *The Collected Poems of G K Chesterton*, 1954 Methuen: London

Chesterton, GK (1929) 'Some of Our Errors,' in *The Thing: Why I Became a Catholic*, Sheed and Ward, London

Chesterton, GK (1986-2021) *Collected Works*, 37 vols ongoing Ignatius Press. See also: https://www.gutenberg.org/files/58032/58032-h/58032-h.htm

Chiffolo, Anthony (2013) *Padre Pio: In My Own Words*, Liguori Publications: Liguori Missouri

Clement, XI Pope (1713) *Unigenitus. Condemnation of the Errors of Paschasius*: https://www.papalencyclicals.net/clem11/c11unige.htm

Clement XI Pope (1721) 'The Universal Prayer for All Things Necessary to Salvation': http://blog.adw.org/wp-content/uploads/2011/03/Universal-prayer-in-columns.pdf

Clemoes, P (1979) ed *Ælfric's Catholic Homilies: The First Series: Text*, Early English Text Society, s.s. 17, Oxford University Press: Oxford & London

Cloude of Unknowynge (14[th]C) see Hodgson (1944) see also: https://archive.org/details/cloudofunknowing00wolt_0/page/n211/mode/2up

Colledge, Edmund & James Walsh (1978) eds & trs *The Ladder of Monks and Twelve Meditations by Guigo II*, Image Books: New York

Collins, Joseph B (1939) (trs) *The Catechetical Instructions of St Thomas Aquinas*, Joseph Wagner: New York

Columbanus, St (543-615) see Walker (1957)

Compendium of the Catholic Church (2005) Libreria Editrice Vaticana: Rome

Congregatio de Cultu Divino et Disciplina Sacramentorum (2001) *De Usu Linguarum Popularium in Libris Liturgiae Romanae Edensis* (*Liturgiam Authenticam* (Authentic Liturgy. On the Use of Vernacular Languages in the Publication of the Books of the Roman Liturgy) See: https://www.vatican.va/roman_curia/congregations/ccdds/documents/rc_con_ccdds_doc_20010507_liturgiam-authenticam_lt.html

Connelly, Joseph Fr (1957) *Hymns of the Roman Liturgy*, Longmans Green: London

Constitutio de Sacra Liturgia. Sacrosanctum Concilium (1963) (Constitution on the Sacred Liturgy. Sacred Council) See: https://www.vatican.va/archive/hist_councils/ii_vatican_council/documents/vat-ii_const_19631204_sacrosanctum-concilium_lt.html

Conte Jr, Ronald L (2009) trs *The Holy Bible. Catholic Public Domain Version:* https://www.acatholic.org/wp-content/uploads/2013/07/Catholic-Public-Domain-Bible.pdf

Crampton, GR (1994) ed *The Shewings of Julian of Norwich*, Medieval Institute Publications: Kalamazoo Michigan

Crystal D (1990) 'Liturgical Language in a Sociolinguistic Perspective' in: Jasper & Jasper (eds) 120-146

Crystal, David (1964) 'A Liturgical Language in a Linguistic Perspective', *New Blackfriars*, 46/534, 148-156

Cunliffe, Charles A ed (1956) *English in the Liturgy A Symposium*, Burns & Oates: London

Cunningham, Lawrence S (1989) *Catholic Prayer*, Crossroad: New York

Curtius, Ernst Robert (1953) *European Literature and the Latin Middle Ages*, trs WR Trask, Routledge: London & New York

Cyprian of Carthage (3rdC) *Opera & Epistola*, PL vols 3 & 4; see also Karpov (2015)

Davies, JG (1972) *A New Dictionary of Liturgy and Worship*, new edition 1986, SCM Press: London

de Caussade, Jean-Pierre SJ (posthumous 1861) *L'Abandon à la Divine Providence*, ed Fr H Ramière, SJ. See Olphe-Gallard (1966) See also: http://livres-mystiques.com/partieTEXTES/Caussade/Abandon.html. Also published as *The Sacrament of the Present Moment*, see Thorold (1933) & Foster (1982): https://www.ccel.org/ccel/decaussade/abandonment.toc.html & https://www.catholicspiritualdirection.org/abandonment.pdf

de Chardin, Pierre Teilhard SJ (1926-7) *Le Milieu Divin*, Editions du Seuil: Paris trs Bernard Wall *The Divine Milieu. An Essay on the Interior Life* (1960) Harper & Row: New York

de Lubac, Henri (1965) *Teilhard de Chardin The Man and his Meaning*, Mentor-Omega: New York

de Lubac, Henri (1970) *Christian Faith The Structure of the Apostles' Creed*, trs Illtyd Trethowan and John Saward, Geoffrey Chapman: London 1986

de Montfort, St Louis Marie Grignon (1712 first published 1843) *Treatise on the True Devotion to the Blessed Virgin*, English trs Malachy Gerard Carroll, St Paul Publications: Langley, Bucks. 1962.

de Montfort, St Louis Marie Grignon: *Oeuvres Complètes de Saint Louis-Marie Grignion de Montfort* (1966) Editions du Seuil: Paris

Demeulenaere, Roland (1985) ed *Commononitorium* in *Corpus Christianorum*. Series Latina Vol 64, Brepols: Turnholti

Denis, the Carthusian St see: Ní Riain (2005)

Denis, the Carthusian St (1896-1935) *de Contemplatione* vol 41, *Doctoris ecstatici D. Dionysii Cartusiani Opera Omnia*, ed M Leone, 42 vols, Typis Cartusiae Sanctae Mariae de Pratis: Montreuil, Tournai, Parkminster

Denzinger, Heinrich JD (1854) ed *Enchiridion Symbolorum, Definitionum et Declarationum de Rebus Fidei et Morum*. See Huenermann ed (2012) see also: http://catho.org/9.php?d=g1; http://patristica.net/denzinger/

de Sales, Francis St (1609) *Introduction à la Vie Dévote* ed & trs JK Ryan as *Introduction to the Devout Life*, MH Gill & Son, Dublin, see: https://archive.org/details/anintroductiont00salegoog/page/n4/mode/2up

de Villiers, Henri (2011) trs Shawn Tribe, 'The *Sub Tuum Praesidium*', *New Liturgical Movement*: https://www.newliturgicalmovement.org/2011/02/sub-tuum-praesidium.html#.YlMH_ZFBzIU

di Pippo, Gregory (2009) 'Compendium of the 1955 Holy Week Revisions of Pius XII' in 9 parts *New Liturgical Movement*: https://www.newliturgicalmovement.org/2009/05/compendium-of-1955-holy-week-revisions_11.html#.Yif4rHxBzIU

Dickins, Bruce & Alan SC Ross (1954) eds *Dream of the Rood* 4th ed, Methuen: London

Didache, Greek text and English trs by A Milavec, *The Didache, Faith, Hope and Life in the Earliest Christian Communities, 50-70 CE*, Newman Press; New York; see also: http://www.greekdoc.com/early/didache.html

Dillistone, FW (1990) 'Liturgical Forms in Word and Act' in Jasper & Jasper (1990) 3-25

Divine Office, The Liturgy of the Hours According to the Roman Rite, Approved for use in Australia, England etc (1974) 3 Vols, approved by the Episcopal Conferences of Australia, England and Wales, Ireland and Scotland, Harper Collins: London. Reissued 2006

Divinum Officium: https://www.divinumofficium.com/cgi-bin/horas/officium.pl

Dix, Dom Gregory (1945) *The Shape of the Liturgy*, Dacre Press: London

Douay Rheims Bible. The Holie Bible Faithfvlly Translated into English out of the Avthentical Latin (1582-1609 revised in 1749-1752) See: http://www.catholicbible.online/

Donovan, J (1829) trs *Catechism of the Council of Trent*, James Duffy: Dublin

Doyle, William (2000) *Jansenism: Catholic Resistance to Authority from the Reformation to the French Revolution*, Macmillan: London

Dream of the Rood, see Dickins & Ross (1954) see also : http://www.apocalyptic-theories.com/literature/dor/oeodora1.html.
See also:
https://www.yorku.ca/inpar/Dream_Rood_Kennedy.pdf

Duchesne, Mgr L trs ML McClure (1903) 5th edition (1927) *Christian Worship. Its Origin and Development. A Study of the Latin Liturgy up to the Time of Charlemagne*, SPCK: London

Dudley, Will (2007) *Hegel, Nietzsche, and Philosophy: Thinking Freedom*, Modern European Philosophy series, Cambridge University Press: Cambridge

Eishenhofer, Ludwig & Joseph Lechner trs AJ & EF Peeler ed by HE Winstone (1961) *The Liturgy of the Roman Rite*, Nelson: Edinburgh

Evans, Christopher (2007) *Explanatio Symboli Sancti Athanasii* in *Hildegard Opera Minora* (gen ed P Dronke et al) Brepols: Turnhout, 99-193

Evans, E (1953) *On the Lord's Prayer* (Tertullian) Latin text and English translation, SPCK: London

Faber, Frederick Fr (1863) trs *Treatise on the True Devotion to the Blessed Virgin* with commentary see: https://www.ecatholic2000.com/montfort/true/devotion.shtml

Faber, Frederick Fr see Bowden (1869) See also: http://www.traditionalmusic.co.uk/faber-hymns/

Faustus, of Riez St: see Smith (1970) and **Opera Omnia**: *PL* Vol 58: http://www.documentacatholicaomnia.eu/30_10_0425-0490_Faustus_Rhegiensis_Episcopus.html

Fenton, Ferrar (1903) *The Holy Bible in Modern English*, SW Partridge: London

Fitzgerald, Allan D ed (1999) *Augustine Through the Ages. An Encyclopedia,* William B Erdmans: Grand Rapids, Michigan

Foster, Richard J (1966) *The Sacrament of the Present Moment*, trs Kitty Muggeridge, Harper Collins: San Francisco, 1982

Fourth Lateran Council (1215) See: http://www.internetsv.info/Archive/CLateranense4.pdf; see also: http://www.legionofmarytidewater.com/faith/ECUM12.HTM

Francis, de Sales St (1609) *Introduction to the Devout Life* (trs & ed John K Ryan) Doubleday: New York, 1989; see also: https://www.philothea.de/philothea_FR.pdf

Francis, de Sales St (posthumous) *Lettres de François de Sales adressées à des gens du monde,* see: https://archive.org/details/lettresde-saintfr00fran. See also https://archive.org/details/letterstopersons00franuoft/page/n3/mode/2up

Francis, Pope (2013) *Litterae Encyclicae Lumen Fidei*: https://www.vatican.va/content/francesco/la/encyclicals/documents/papa-francesco_20130629_enciclica-lumen-fidei.html

Francis, Pope (2016) *Constitutio Apostolica. De vita contemplativa mulierum* [*Vultum Dei quaerere*] (Apostolic Constitution. On Women's Contemplative Life [To seek the Face of God]:

https://www.vatican.va/content/francesco/la/apost_constitutions/documents/papa-francesco_costituzione-ap_20160629_vultum-dei-quaerere.html

Francis, Pope (2020) *Epistola Apostolica: Patris Corde*: https://www.vatican.va/content/francesco/la/apost_letters/documents/papa-francesco-lettera-ap_20201208_patris-corde.html

Francis, Pope (2020) *Traditiones Custodes*. Apostolic Letter issued *Motu Proprio* 'On the Use of the Roman Liturgy Prior to the Reform of 1970': https://www.vatican.va/content/francesco/en/motu_proprio/documents/20210716-motu-proprio-traditionis-custodes.html

Fry, Timothy, Timothy Horner & Imogene Baker (1980) eds *The Rule of St Benedict in Latin with English Notes*, Liturgical Press: Collegeville, Minnesota

Fry, Timothy, Timothy Horner & Imogene Baker (1981) eds *The Rule of St Benedict in English*, Liturgical Press: Collegeville, Minnesota

Gardner, WH & NH MacKenzie (1967) eds *The Poems of Gerard Manley Hopkins*, OUP: Oxford revised 1970

Gaston, Robert W (1998) 'Attention and Decorum in Early Christian Prayer' in Allen et al (1998) 81-96

Gingrich, F Wilbur (1957/1965) *Shorter Lexicon of the Greek New Testament*, Chicago UP, Chicago

Glunz, H (1933) *History of the Vulgate in England from Alcuin to Roger Bacon*, CUP: Cambridge

Godden, M (1979) ed *Ælfric's Catholic Homilies: The Second Series: Text*, Early English Text Society, s.s. 5, Oxford University Press: Oxford

Gower, John see: Macaulay (1901) and Peck (2005)

Gregorian chant notation summary see: https://maternalheart.org/resources/gregorian_chant_notation/

Gregory I, Pope St (6thC) *Liber Regulae Pastoralis*: https://www.newadvent.org/fathers/36011.htm. See also: http://cudl.lib.cam.ac.uk/view/MS-II-00002-00004/1

Gregory I, Pope St (6thC) *Moralia in Job*, see Parker (1844)

Greenberg, M (1983) *Biblical Prose Prayer* Berkeley: Los Angeles & London

Guardini, Romano (1937) *Der Herr*, trs Elinor C Briefs as *The Lord*, 1954. Reissued with an Introduction by Joseph Cardinal Ratzinger (1996) Regnery Publishing: Chicago

Guardini, Romano (1943) *The Art of Praying: The Principles and Methods of Christian Prayer*, 1994 edition, Sophia Institute Press: Manchester New Hampshire

Guigo, II the Angelic (12thC) *Scala Claustralium*: https://www.com/scalaclaustralium.html. See also: http://www.umilta.net/ladder.html

Hamman, A (1952) *Prières des Premiers Chrétiens* (Fayard: Paris) trs W Mitchell, *Early Christian Prayers* (1961) Longmans: London

Happold, FC (1971) *Prayer and Meditation. Their Nature and Practice*, Penguin: Harmondsworth

Hart, Columba & Jane Bishop (1990) trs *Scivias*, Paulist Press: New York

Hargrove Henry Lee (1902) ed *King Alfred's Old English Version of St. Augustine's Soliloquies*, Yale Studies in English vol XIII, Henry Holt & Co: New York

Hazell, Matthew P (2013) *Scripture Index of Chants and Readings in the 1962 Missale Romanum*: https://www.scribd.com/document/152413656/Scriptural-Index-of-Chants-and-Readings-in-the-Missale-Romanum-1962

Hazell, Matthew P (2016) & Peter A Kwasniewski (Foreword) *Index Lectionum: A Comparative Table of Readings for the Ordinary and Extraordinary Forms of the Roman Rite*, Vol I (Lectionary Study Press, 2016)

Heather, Noel (2000) *Religious Language and Critical Discourse Analysis: Ideology and Identity in Christian Discourse Today*, Peter Lang: Bern

Henry, of Ghent (late 13thC) *Summae Quaestionum Ordinarium*, multiple vols, see: *Henrici de Gandavo Opera Omnia* (1979-2011 et seq) EJ Brill: Leiden & Leuven University Press: Leuven

Hettinger, Franz Fr (1863 *et seq*) *Apologie des Christenthums*, 2 vols 5 parts; English trs Fr Henry Sebastian Bowden CO as *Revealed Religion* (Burns and Oates, 1895) and *Natural Religion* (Burns and Oates, 1890)

Hilary, of Poitiers St (c 315-367) *Tractatus Super Psalmos*, in Migne (1844) *PL* 9:890-916. see: https://archive.org/details/shilariiepiscopi22hilauoft/page/n7/mode/2up. See also: https://archive.org/details/shilariiepiscopi22hilauoft/page/n31/mode/2up

Hildegard, of Bingen St (1142 *et seq*) *Scivias* (*Sci vias Domini*) see Hart & Bishop (1990)

Hildegard, of Bingen St (1158 *et seq*) *Liber Vitae Meritorum*, see Hozeski (1997)

Hildegard, of Bingen St (1163 *et seq*) *Liber Divinorum Operum*, see Campbell (2018)

Hildegard, of Bingen St (1170?) *Explanatio Symboli Sancti Athanasii*, see: Evans (2007) & http://www.clerus.org/bibliaclerusonline/de/evd.htm

Hiley, David (1993) *Western Plainchant. A Handbook*, Clarendon Press: Oxford

Hiley, David (2009) *Gregorian Chant*, Cambridge University Press: Cambridge

Hodgson, Phyllis (1944 for 1943) ed *The Cloud of Unknowing and The Book of Privy Counselling*, Early English Text Society by Oxford University Press: Oxford

Hoffman, Alexius OSB (1928) *Liturgical Dictionary*, The Liturgical Press: Collegeville Minnesota, for a PDF online see: https://babel.hathitrust.org/cgi/pt?id=mdp.39015011274423&view=1up&seq=1

Hozeski, Bruce (1997) trs *The Book of the Rewards of Life*, Oxford University Press: New York

Huenermann, Peter ed (2012) *Enchiridion Symbolorum*, Ignatius Press: San Francisco

Huxley, Aldous (1954) *The Doors of Perception*, Chatto & Windus: London

Ignatius, of Loyola St (1548) *Exercitia Spirituali* (*Vulgata*): http://www.raggionline.com/saggi/scritti/es/ejercicios.pdf. See also: https://www.catholicspiritualdirection.org/spiritualexercises.pdf, and: https://www.ccel.org/ccel/ignatius/exercises.html

Innocent, III Pope (1198) *De Sacro Altaris Mysterio*, see: *Opera Omnia* in *PL*: http://www.documentacatholicaomnia.eu/01_01_1198-1216-_Innocentius_III.html

Irenaeus, of Lyons (2ndC) *Adversus haereses*, see Unger (2012) and also: http://www.prudencetrue.com/images/Irenaeus_Against_Heresies_Book_III.pdf

Jasper, David & Ronald Jasper (eds) (1990) *Language and the Worship of the Church*, Macmillan: London

John, St Cassian (360-435) *Opera Omnia*, *PL*: http://www.documentacatholicaomnia.eu/30_10_0360-0435-_Cassianus_Ioannes.html

John, St of the Cross (16thC) *Poems*, see: Nims (1959) &: https://www.jesus-passion.com/John_of_the_Cross.htm

John, Damascene St *Writings* (1958) trs Frederic H Chase, *Fathers of the Church* vol 37, Catholic University of America Press: Washington, DC

John Paul II, Pope St (1979) *Constitutio Apostolica Scriptutarum Thesaurus*:
https://www.vatican.va/archive/bible/nova_vulgata/documents/nova-vulgata_index_lt.html

John Paul II, Pope (1989) *Redemptoris Custos*: https://www.vatican.va/content/john-paul-ii/la/apost_exhortations/documents/hf_jp-ii_exh_15081989_redemptoris-custos.html

John Paul II, St Pope (1992) *Constitutio Apostolica Fidei Depositum*: https://www.vatican.va/content/john-paul-ii/la/apost_constitutions/documents/hf_jp-ii_apc_19921011_fidei-depositum.html

John Paul II, St Pope (1997) *Litterae Apostolicae Laetamur Magnopere*: https://www.vatican.va/content/john-paul-ii/la/apost_letters/1997/documents/hf_jp-ii_apl_15081997_laetamur.html

John Paul II, Pope St (2002) *Epistula Apostolica Rosarium Virgines Mariae*: https://www.vatican.va/content/john-paul-ii/la/apost_letters/2002/documents/hf_jp-ii_apl_20021016_rosarium-virginis-mariae.html

John XXIII, Pope (1962) *Constitutio Apostolica Veterum Sapientia*: https://www.vatican.va/content/john-xxiii/la/apost_constitutions/1962/documents/hf_j-xxiii_apc_19620222_veterum-sapientia.html. See also: https://adoremus.org/2007/12/veterum-sapientia/

John XXIII, Pope (posthumous 1964/5) *Journal of a Soul 1895-1962,* McGraw Hill: New York

John, the Solitary (John of Apamea 5thC) see Brock (1987)

Jones, Cheslyn, Geoffrey Wainwright & Edward Yarnold (eds) (1980) *The Study of Liturgy*, London

Jones, Rev James (1836) trs *The Way of Salvation. Meditations for Every Day of the Year by Blessed Alphonsus Liguori* , Keating and Brown: London

Juliana, of Norwich *The Shewings of Julian of Norwich*: https://www.catholicspiritualdirection.org/revelations.pdf. See also: https://d.lib.rochester.edu/teams/text/the-shewings-of-julian-of-norwich-part-3

Kabir, Das (1915) *One Hundred Poems of Kabir*. Trs Rabindranath Tagore, ed Evelyn Underhill. University of Toronto Press: Toronto.

Karpov, Kirill V (2015) 'Lectio Divina, *Meditatio, Oratio, Contemplatio* as Basic Categories of Medieval Spirituality', *European Journal For Philosophy of Religion* 7/2 (Summer) 125-136 see: https://philarchive.org/archive/KARLDM-3

Keating, Thomas OCSO Fr (1994) *Intimacy With God. An Introduction to Centering Prayer*, Crossroad: New York

Keble, John (1827) *The Christian Year,* see Christian Classics Ethereal Library: https://www.ccel.org/ccel/keble/year.html

Kelly, JND (1950) *Early Christian Creeds* (1967 edition) Longmans: London

Kennedy, George A (1980) *Classical Rhetoric and its Christian and Secular Traditions*, Croom Helm: London

Kennedy, George A (1984) *New Testament Interpretation Through Rhetorical Criticism*, UNC Press Books: Chapel Hill, NC

Kennedy, George A (1990) 'The Rhetoric of the Early Christian Liturgy' in Jasper & Jasper (eds) 26-43

Ker, Ian (1994) ed *John Henry Newman Apologia pro Vita Sua*, Penguin Books: London

Kierkegaard, Søren (1938) *The Journals of Soren Kierkegaard: A Selection*, ed and trs by Alexander Dru, London: Oxford University Press: London

Kierkegaard, Søren (1941) *Training in Christianity*, trs Walter Lowrie, Oxford University Press: Oxford

Kierkegaard, Søren (1956) *The Prayers of Kierkegaard*, ed Perry Lefevre. University of Chicago Press: Chicago

King James Bible (1611) *The Holy Bible Conteyning the Old Testament and the New.*
See: https://www.kingjamesbibleonline.org/1611-*Bible*/

Klarmann, Andrew F (1945) *Gregorian Chant. A Textbook for Seminaries, Novitiates and Secondary Schools*, Gregorian Institute of American: Toledo, Ohio

Knox Bible (1945-1950) *The Holy Bible: A Translation From the Latin Vulgate in the Light of the Hebrew and Greek Originals* (by Monsignor Ronald Knox)
See: http://www.catholicbible.online/

Koloiejchuk, Brian Fr MC (2007) *Mother Teresa: Come be my Light: The Private Writings of the Saint of Calcutta*, Doubleday: New York

Kwasniewski, Peter (2016) 'The Law of Liturgical Entropy':
https://www.newliturgicalmovement.org/2016/05/the-law-of-liturgical-entropy.html#.YSQIZ0vivIU

La Bible de Jérusalem (1945-1955 in sections and in full in 1956 and revised in 1961) For the full 1966 text see: https://archive.org/details/thejerusalembible1966/page/n5/mode/2up

Lass, FB & A Debrunner (1896/1902) *A Greek Grammar of the New Testament and Other Early Christian Literature*, University of Chicago Press: Chicago, revised edition Robert W Funk (1961)

Le Clercq, Jean (1961) trs Catherine Misrahi, *The Love of Learning and the Desire of God A Study of Monastic Culture*, Fordham University Press: New York

Lefebvre, Dom Gaspar ed (1956) *The Saint Andrew Daily Missal*, Abbey of St Andre: Bruges. Partial parallel Latin/English text

Leo XIII, Pope (1879) *Epistola Encyclica Aeterni Patris* (Encyclical Letter Of the Eternal Father): https://www.vatican.va/content/leo-xiii/la/encyclicals/documents/hf_l-xiii_enc_04081879_aeterni-patris.html

Leo XIII, Pope (1889) *Quamquam pluries*: https://www.vatican.va/content/leo-xiii/la/encyclicals/documents/hf_l-xiii_enc_15081889_quamquam-pluries.html

Leo XIII, Pope (1891) *Litterae Encyclicae Rerum Novarum Sanctissimi D.N. Leonis Papae XIII de Conditione Opificum*: https://www.vatican.va/content/leo-xiii/la/encyclicals/documents/hf_l-xiii_enc_15051891_rerum-novarum.html

Leo XIII, Pope (1893) *Litterae Encyclicae de Studiis Scripturae Sacrae* (*Providentissimus Deus*): https://www.vatican.va/content/leo-xiii/en/encyclicals/documents/hf_l-xiii_enc_18111893_providentissimus-deus.html

Leo XIII, Pope (1897) *Epistola Encyclicae Divinum illud munus*: https://www.vatican.va/content/leo-xiii/la/encyclicals/documents/hf_l-xiii_enc_09051897_divinum-illud-munus.html

Levi, Peter (1987) *The Frontiers of Paradise: a study of monks and monasteries*, Collins Harvill: London

Liber Precum Publicarum seu Ministerii Ecclesiasticae Administrationis Sacramentorum, Aliorumque Rituum et Caeremoniarum in Ecclesia Anglicana (1847) Parker Society: London. See: http://justus.anglican.org/resources/bcp/Latin1560/BCP_Latin1560.htm

Liber Usualis Missae et Officii (1930) Desclée: Paris. For English rubrics and explanations see: https://archive.org/details/TheLiberUsualis1961/page/n37/mode/2up

Litaniae ad Deum Patrem (Litanies to God the Father): http://www.preces-latinae.org/thesaurus/Pater/LitaniaePatris.html

Litaniae de Sanctissimo Sacramento (Litanies concerning the Most Holy Sacrament): http://www.preces-latinae.org/thesaurus/Euch/LitDeSS.html

Litaniae de Sancto Patre Nostro Francisco (Litanies concerning Our Holy Father Saint Francis): http://www.preces-latinae.org/thesaurus/Sancti/SFranciscusAssisiensis/Litaniae.html

Litaniae de Sacratissimo Corde Iesu (Litanies concerning the Sacred Heart of Jesus): http://www.preces-latinae.org/thesaurus/Filius/LitSCI.html

Litaniae Dominae nostrae Dolorum (Litanies of Our Lady of Sorrows): http://www.preces-latinae.org/thesaurus/BVM/Dolorum.html

Litaniae ad Beatam Mariam Virginem [*Litaniae Lauretanae*] (Litanies to the Blessed Virgin Mary [Litanies of Loreto]): http://www.preces-latinae.org/thesaurus/BVM/Laurentanae.html

Litaniae de Sancto Spiritu (Litanies Concerning the Holy Spirit): http://www.preces-latinae.org/thesaurus/Spiritus/LitDeSanctoSpiritu.html

Litaniae Pretiosissimi Sanguinis Domini Nostri Iesu Christi: http://www.preces-latinae.org/thesaurus/Filius/LitPSDNIC.html

Litaniae Sancti Ioseph (Litanies of St Joseph): http://www.preces-latinae.org/thesaurus/Ioseph/LitStIoeseph.html

Litaniae Sanctissimi Nominis Iesu (Litanies of the Most Holy Name of Jesus): http://www.preces-latinae.org/thesaurus/Filius/LitSNI.html

Litaniae Sanctorum (Litanies of Saints): http://www.preces-latinae.org/thesaurus/Sancti/LitSanctorum.html

Litaniae Vitae et Passionis Domini Nostri Iesu Christi (Litanies of the Life and Passion of Our Lord Jesus Christ): http://www.preces-latinae.org/thesaurus/Filius/LitVitaePass.html

Liturgia Horarum Iuxta Ritum Romanum (1971) *Ex Decreto Sacrosancti Oecumenici Concilii Vaticani II Instauratum Auctoritate Pauli PP VI Promulgatum, Editio Typica Altera* (2nd Typical Edition) Libreria Editrice Vaticana: Rome, 4 vols, revised *Editio Typica Tertia* 1985; *Editio Typica Altera* 2000 & 2003

Liturgy of the Hours (1975) approved by the International Commission on English in the Liturgy (ICEL) *Novus Ordo Officium Divinum* in English (2005 ICEL edition) Catholic Book Publishing: New York

Logan, Stephen (1998) *William Wordsworth*, Everyman's Poetry, JM Dent: London

Lumen Gentium, Constitutio Dogmatica de Ecclesia (1964): http://www.vatican.va/archive/hist_councils/ii_vatican_council/documents/vat-ii_const_19641121_lumen-gentium_lt.html

Macaulay, GC (1901) ed *The Works of John Gower*, Clarendon Press:Oxford

Manasseh, Prayer see: *Prex Manasse* at preces-latinae.org

Manley Hopkins SJ, Gerard Fr see Bridges (1918) and Gardner & MacKenzie (1967)

Maritain, Jacques (1947) *Art and Scholasticism with other essays*, Sheed and Ward: London

Maritain, Jacques & Raïssa Maritain (1933) *De La Vie d'Oraison*, L'Art Catholique: Paris

Maritain, Jacques & Raïssa Maritain (1938) *Situation de la Poésie*, Desclée: Paris, trs *The Situation of Poetry* (1955) Philosophical Library: New York

Maritain, Jacques & Raïssa Maritain (1982-2007) *Oeuvres Complètes*, Editions Saint-Paul: Paris, 17 vols

Maritain, Raïssa (1963) *Le Journal de Raïssa par Raïssa Maritain*, ed Jacques Maritain, Desclée de Brouwer: Paris

Maritain, Raïssa (1965) *Patriarch Tree. Thirty Poems by Raïssa Maritain*, trs by a Benedictine of Stanbrook, Stanbrook Abbey Press: Worcester

Maritain, Raïssa (1968) *Poemes et Essais* Desclée de Brouwer: Paris

Maritain, Raïssa (1974) *Raïssas Journal*, ed Jacques Maritain, Magi Books: Albany, NY

Martin, Michael (1998 -) *Thesaurus Precum Latinarum*: https://www.preces-latinae.org/index-3.html

McGinn, Bernard (1991) *The Presence of God: A History of Western Christian Mysticism. A History of Western Christian Mysticism. The Foundations of Mysticism: Origin to the Fifth Century*, Crossroad: New York

McGinn, Bernard (1994) *The Growth of Mysticism*. New York: Crossroad. *The Flowering of Mysticism: Men and Women in the New Mysticism 1200-1350*, Crossroad: New York

McGinn, Bernard (2005) *The Harvest of Mysticism in Medieval Germany 1300-1500*, Crossroad: New York

McGinn, Bernard (2013) *The Varieties of Vernacular Mysticism 1350-1550*, Crossroad: New York

McGinn, Bernard (2017) *Mysticism in the Reformation 1500-1650*, Crossroad: New York

McGinn, Bernard (2017) *Mysticism in the Golden Age of Spain 1500-1650*,Crossroad: New York

McGinn, Bernard (2020) *The Persistence of Mysticism in Catholic Europe: France, Italy, and Germany 1500-1675*, Crossroad: New York

Merleau-Ponty, Maurice Jean Jacques (1942) *La Structure du comportement*, Presses Universitaires de France: Paris, trs as *The Structure of Behavior* Alden Fisher (1965) Methuen: London

Merleau-Ponty, Maurice Jean Jacques (1945) *Phénoménologie de la Perception* Gallimard: Paris, trs as *Phenomenology of Perception* Colin Smith (1962) Routledge & Kegan Paul: London

Merton, Thomas (1949) *Seeds of Contemplation*, New Directions: Norfolk Connecticut

Merton, Thomas (1957) *The Silent Life*, Farrar, Straus & Giroux: New York

Merton Thomas (1960) *The Wisdom of the Desert*, New Directions, New York

Merton, Thomas (1997) *Dancing in the Waters of Life*, vol 5 (1963-65) *The Journals of Thomas Merton* ed Robert E Daggy, Harper Collins, New York

Metzer, Bruce (1965) ed *The Oxford Annotated Apocrypha*. Oxford University Press: New York

Metzger, Marcel (1994) *History of the Liturgy. The Major Stages*, trs Madeleine M Beaumont, 1997, Liturgical Press: Collegeville, Minnesota

Meynell, Wilfrid ed (1913) *The Poems of Francis Thompson*, 1937 edition, OUP: Oxford & London

Migne, JP (1841-1865) ed *Patrologiae Cursus Completus. Series Latina.* 217 volumes plus 4 volumes of *Indices*, Paris: Garnier Fraters. See also: https://www.patristica.net/latina/

Patrologia Graeca: http://www.patristica.net/graeca

See also: *Patrologia Orientalis*: https://www.roger-pearse.com/weblog/patrologia-orientalis-po-pdfs/

Miller, PB (1994) *They Cried to the Lord: The Form and Theology of Biblical Prayer*, The Liturgical Press: Collegeville, Minnesota

Missale Romanum ex Decreto Concilii Tridentini Restitutum (1634) *Typica Editio* 1920, reissued as the *Typica Iuxta* in 2004 see: http://media.musicasacra.com/pdf/romanmissal_classical.pdf. Revised 1951 & 1955 by Pope Pius XII. In 1962 Pope John XXIII issued *Missale Romanum, ex decreto Ss. Concilii Tridentini restitutum, editio typica*, Typis Polyglottis Vaticanis: Rome see: http://media.musicasacra.com/pdf/missale62.pdf

Missale Romanum ex decreto Sacrosancti Oecumenici Concilii Vaticani II instauratum (1970) *Typica Editio* approved by Pope Paul VI. 2nd typical edition 1975 and 3rd typical edition 2002 approved by Pope John Paul II further revised in 2008 as *Missale Romanum, editio typica tertia emendata*, Libreria Editrice Vaticana: Rome

More, St Thomas (1963 *et seq*) *The Yale Edition of The Complete Works of St Thomas More*, 15 vols, Yale University Press: New Haven

Moser, Johann M (1993) ed *Devoutly I Adore Thee: The Prayers and Hymns of Saint Thomas Aquinas*, Sophia Institute Press: Manchester New Hampshire

Neufeld, Vernon (1963) *The Earliest Christian Confessions*, EJ Brill: Leiden

Newman, John Henry (1836) *Lyra Apostolica*, Rivingtons: London, Oxford & Cambridge. See also: https://archive.org/details/lyra00newmuoft

Newman, John Henry (1864) *Apologia Pro Vita Sua*, Longman, Green, Longman, Roberts & Green: London

Newman, John Henry (1893) *Meditations and Devotions of the Late Cardinal Newman,* Longmans Green & Co : London and New York (1907 edition) published posthumously and edited by Fr W P Neville, see: https://www.newmanreader.org/works/meditations/

Nicholls, Aidan OP (1996) *Looking at the Liturgy A Critical View of its Contemporary Form*, Ignatius Press: San Francisco

Nims, John Frederick ed (1959) *The Poems of St John of the Cross*, Chicago University Press: Chicago, 3rd edition 1979

Ní Riain, Íde M Sr (1998) trs *Homilies of Saint Ambrose on Psalm 118 (119)* Halcyon Press: Dublin

Ní Riain, Íde M Sr (2000) trs *Commentary of Saint Ambrose on Twelve Psalms*, Halcyon Press: Dublin

Ní Riain, Íde M Sr (2005) trs *The Spiritual Writings of Denis the Carthusian: contemplation, meditation, prayer, the fountain of light and the paths of life, monastic profession, exhortation to novices*, Four Courts: Dublin

Nova Vulgata. Bibliorum Sacrorum (1979) *editio typicia altera maior*, 1986, Libreria Editrice Vaticana: Vatican City

O'Connell J & HPR Finberg (eds) (1949) *The Missal in Latin and English*, 5th edition 1962, Burns & Oates: London. Scripture translations Mgr RA Knox, Latin & English parallel text

Officium Parvum Beatae Mariae Virginis (1925) Pustet: Ratisbon, see also: https://archive.org/details/officiumparvumbe00cath/page/n6/mode/2up

Olphe-Gallard, Fr Michel SJ (1966) ed *L'abandon à la Divine Providence*. Desclée Brouer: Paris

Origen, *On Prayer* (1899) Greek text eds P Koetschau et al, JC Hinrichs: Leipzig; English translation (1979) *Origen*, Paulist Press: New York

O'Sullivan, John Ven (2020) trs *A Commentary on the Book of Psalms. Translated From the Latin of St Robert Bellarmine*, Sophia Institute Press: Manchester NH

Otto, Rudolf (1917) *Das Heilige. Über das Irrationale in der Idee des Göttlichen und sein Verhältnis zum Rationalen* (The Sacred. On the Irrational in the Idea of the Divine and its Relationship to the Rational) trs JW Harvey as *The Idea of the Holy*, Oxford University Press: Oxford & New York (1923; 2nd edition, 1950; re-isssued 1970)

Otto, Rudolf (1930) 'The *Sensus Numinis* as the Historical Basis of Religion', *Hibbert Journal* 29, 1-8

Paine, Scott Randall (2018) 'The Language that Rose from the Dead': https://www.memoriapress.com/articles/language-rose-dead/

Parker, John Henry (1844) *Gregory the Great. Moralia in Job*, trs 3 vols, JGF & J Rivington: Oxford

Paul VI, Pope St (1971) *Constitutio Apostolica De Sacramento Confirmationis Divinae Consortium Naturae*: https://archive.org/details/paulvisapostolic00cath

Paul VI, Pope St (1974) *Adhortatio Apostolica Marialis Cultus*: https://www.vatican.va/content/paul-vi/la/apost_exhortations/documents/hf_p-vi_exh_19740202_marialis-cultus.html

Paul VI, Pope St (1968) *Motu Proprio Sollemni hac Liturgia* ('Creed of the People of God'): https://www.vatican.va/content/paul-vi/la/motu_proprio/documents/hf_p-vi_motu-proprio_19680630_credo.html

Peck, Rusell A (2005) ed *Confessio Amantis,* Medieval Institute Publications:Kalamazoo:

Pennington, Basil OCSO (1998) *Lectio Divina. Renewing the Ancient Practice of Praying the Scriptures*, Cross Road Publishing: New York

Picard, Max (1948) *Die Welt des Schweigens*, trs Stanley Godman as *The World of Silence* (1988) Gateway Editions: Washington DC

Pio, Padre see Chiffolo (2013)

Pius V, Pope (1569) *Consueverunt Romani Pontifices*: https://www.papalencyclicals.net/Pius05/p5consue.htm

Pius IX, Pope (1854) *Constitutio Apostolica Ineffabilis Deus*: https://www.papalencyclicals.net/pius09/p9ineff.htm

Pius IX, Pope (1870) *Quemadmodum Deus*: https://osjusa.org/st joseph/magisterium/quemadmodum-deus/ msclkid=bb35ff-bfbb7411ecb94720cd55191646

Pius, X Pope (1903-4) *Motu Proprio De Musica Sacra*:https://www.vatican.va/content/pius-x/it/motu_proprio/documents/hf_p-x_motu-proprio_19031122_sollecitudini.html

Pius XI, Pope (1922) *Litterae Apostolicae Officiorum Omnium*: https://www.vatican.va/content/pius-xi/la/apost_letters/documents/hf_p-xi_apl_19220801_officiorum-omnium.html

Pius XII, Pope (1945) *Psalterium Pianum*: http://liberpsalmorum.info/Psalterium%20Pianum.html

Pius XII, Pope (1947) *Litterae Encyclicae Mediator Dei Hominum*: https://www.vatican.va/content/pius-xii/la/encyclicals/documents/hf_p-xii_enc_20111947_mediator-dei.html

Pius XII, Pope (1950) *Constitutio Apostolica Munificentissimus Deus*: https://www.vatican.va/content/pius-xii/la/apost_constitutions/documents/hf_p-xii_apc_19501101_munificentissimus-deus.html

Pius XII, Pope (1955) *Litterae Encyclicae Musicae Sacrae Disciplina*: https://www.vatican.va/content/pius-xii/la/encyclicals/documents/hf_p-xii_enc_25121955_musicae-sacrae.html

Pius XII, Pope (1955) *Breviarium Romanum, ex Decreto Sacrosancti Concilii Tridentini Restitutum Summorumque Pontificum Cra Recognitium cum Nova Psalterii. Versione PII Papae XII Iussu Edita.* Libreria Editrice Vaticana: Vatican City (*editio typica* 1961)

Plus, Raoul SJ Fr (1927) *How to Pray Always. Principles and Practices for Attaining to Union with God*, Benziger Bros, New York. 2004 edition Sophia Institute Press

Plus, Raoul SJ Fr (1956) *How to Pray Well*, Newman Press edition, Westminster: MD

Price, Simon & Emily Kearns (2003) *The Oxford Dictionary of Classical Myth and Religion*, Oxford University Press: Oxford

Prostas, Lauren (2013) *The Collects of the Roman Missal*, Bloomsbury: London

Protoveangelium, of James (1[st]C): http://www.sthermanoca.org/documents/The%20Orthodox%20Faith/Protoevangelium%20of%20James.pdf

Quigley, EJ (1920) *The Divine Office: A Study of the Roman Breviary*, MH Gill: Dublin

Raccolta. Preces et pia opera in favorem omnium christifidelium vel quorumdam coetuum personarum indulgentiis ditata et opportune recognita (1938) (*Prayers and pious works, for the sake of all the Christian faithful or certain groups of persons, enriched with Indulgences and opportunely recognized*) reissued as *Enchiridion Indulgentiarum* (*Handbook of Indulgences*) 1950. For the Fr Ambrose St John English translation, *The Raccolta or Collection of Indulgenced Prayers and Good Works*, 1910 ed) see: http://www.saintsbooks.net/books/The%20Raccolta%20-%201910.pdf

Ratzinger, Joseph Cardinal (2000) *The Spirit of the Liturgy*, Ignatius Press: San Francisco

Robertson, Duncan (2011) *Lectio Divina: The Medieval Experience of Reading*, Liturgical Press: Collegeville Minnesota

Robinson, John AT Bishop (1963) *Honest to God*, SCM Press: London

Rolle, Richard of Hampole (c 1330) *The Incendium Amoris of Richard Rolle of Hampole,* trs ed Margeret Deanesly, Manchester at the University Press, Longmans, Green & co, London, Manchester 1915; see also Allen (1988) & also: https://lollardsociety.org/pdfs/Rolle_IncendiumAmoris.pdf. See also: https://www.ccel.org/r/rolle/incendium/incendium.htm, and: https://biblehub.com/library/rolle/the_fire_of_love/prologue_of_richard_rolle.htm

Rolle, Richard of Hampole (c1330s/1910) *The Form of Perfect Living and Other Prose Treatises,* trs Geraldine E Hodgson, Thomas Baker: London. See also: https://archive.org/details/formofperfectliv00roll

Schilderman, Hans ed (2007) *Discourse in Ritual Studies,* Brill: Leiden

Schneider, Joseph SJ (1876) *Medulla Pietatis Christianae sive Libellus Precum pro Adolescentibus Litterarum Studiosis*: https://www.preces-latinae.org/thesaurus/Numeri/Meditatio.html

Schuster, Cardinal Illdefonso (1924) *The Sacramentary: Historical and Liturgical Notes on the Roman Missal* (*Liber Sacramentorum*) English trs in 5 vols, Burns, Oates and Washboume: London

Silva, Mpoises (1983) *Biblical Words and Their Meaning An Introduction to Lexical Semantics,* Zondervan Publishing House: Grand Rapids Michigan (revised edition 1994)

Simon Mary of the Cross MCarm, Fr (2021) *Mary, Summa Contemplatrix in Denis the Carthusian,* International Marian Research Institute: Dayton Ohio: https://www.academia.edu/48803101/Mary_Summa_Contemplatrix_in_Denis_the_Carthusian

Smith, Thomas A (1990) *De Gratia: Faustus of Riez's Treatise on Grace and Its Place in the History of Theology,* University of Notre Dame Press: Notre Dame, IN

Socias, James Rev (gen ed) (1992) *Handbook of Prayers* (Latin and English) Scepter Publishers: Princeton New Jersey

St John, Ambrose (1857) ed *The Raccolta or Collection of Indulgenced Prayers & Good Works*, Latin and English, Burns & Oates: London. For a 1910 edition online see: http://www.saintsbooks.net/books/The%20Raccolta%20-%201910.pdf

Steiner, George (1975) *After Babel. Aspects of Language and Translation*, Oxford University Press: Oxford.

Steinsaltz, Adin Even-Israel (2012) ed *Koren Talmud Bavli Noé Edition*, 42 volumes, Hebrew/English, Koren: Jerusalem

Stewart, Columba OSB (2008) 'Prayer' in *The Oxford Handbook of Early Christian Studies* eds Susan Ashbrook Harvey and David G Hunter, ch 36: 744-763, Oxford University Press: Oxford & New York

Studzinski, Raymond OSB (2009) *Reading to Live: The Evolving Practice of Lectio Divina*, Liturgical Press: Collegeville Minnesota

Swann, L (2007) *The Benedictine Tradition: Spirituality in History*, Liturgical Press: Collegeville

Talmud, see Steinsaltz (2012) &: https://www.jewishvirtuallibrary.org/babylonian-talmud-full-text

Taunton, Ethelred L Fr (1903) *The Little Office of Our Lady. A Treatise Theoretical, Practical and Exegetical*, John Ball, Sons & Danielson Ltd & R & T Washbourne: London

Teresa of Avila, St (1921) *The Interior Castle* (*or The Mansions*) trs The Benedictines of Stanbrook, rev edition Fr Benedict Zimmerman OCD, Thomas Baker: London

Teresa, of Calcutta St see: Koloiejchuk (2009)

Tertullianus, Quintus Septimius Florens (Tertullian c200) *De Oratione* (On Prayer) see Evans (1953) and: https://www.tertullian.org/articles/evans_orat/evans_orat_03latin.htm, and: https://www.newadvent.org/fathers/0322.htm

The Greek New Testament (1966) 4th revised edition, 1993/4, Deutsche Bibelgesellschaft/United Bible Societies: Stuttgart

The Holy Bible (1611/1881-1885/1901) *Revised Standard Version*, revised edition 1952 Thomas Nelson: London, 1957/1964 editions

The Holy Bible, A Translation from the Latin Vulgate in the Light of the Hebrew and Greek Originals, by Ronald Knox, one volume edition 1955, School Edition 1957/1965, Burns & Oates/Macmillan, London

The Holy Bible, Authorised King James Version (1611) Collins: London, 1958 edition

The Holy Bible, Douay Version (1956) trs from the Vulgate 1609, Rheims 1582, with notes by Bishop Challoner (1691-1781) Preface Bernard Cardinal Griffin,1955, CTS: London

The Holy Bible. English Standard Version (2002) Collins: London

The Holy Bible. New International Version (1973/1978) *Fully Revised Zonderman NIV Study Bible (*2002) gen ed Kenneth I. Barker, Zondervan, Grand Rapids, Michigan

The Holy Bible. New International Version (1973/1978) Hodder & Stoughton, London, 1979/1983

The Holy Bible. The New Testament of Our Lord and Saviour Jesus Christ, Newly Translated from the Latin Vulgate and Authorized by the Archbishops and Bishops of England and Wales (1945) trs Ronald Knox, Burns & Oates: London

The Holy Bible. The Old Testament Genesis-Esther, Newly Translated from the Latin Vulgate and Authorized by the Archbishops and Bishops of England and Wales (1953) trs Ronald Knox, Burns & Oates: London

The Holy Bible. The Old Testament Job-Machabees with Appendix (Alternative version of the Psalms) Newly Translated from the Latin Vulgate and Authorized by the Archbishops and Bishops of England and Wales (1949) trs Ronald Knox, for private use only, Burns & Oates: London

The Jerusalem Bible. New Testament (1966) gen ed Alexander Jones, standard edition (Complete) Darton, Longman & Todd: London

The Missal (1912) Burns Oates & Washbourne, 6th edition (1928) parallel Latin & English, London

The New English Bible (New Testament (1st edition 1961) 2nd edition 1970, *Old Testament,* 1970, One Volume Bible, OUP & CUP: Oxford & Cambridge, 1970

The New Testament of Our Lord and Saviour Jesus Christ According to the Received Greek Together with the English Authorised Version. Arranged in Paragraphs (parallel Greek/English text) CUP: Cambridge, for the British and Foreign Bible Society: London, 1899

The NKJV Greek English Interlinear New Testament (1994) Thomas Nelson: Nashville, Trethowan & John Saward, Geoffrey Chapman: London 2nd edition (1986)

The Psalms. A Prayer Book, also the Canticles of the Roman Breviary, New English Translation Including the New Latin Version from the Hebrew by the Professors of the Pontifical Biblical Institute Authorised by Pope Pius XII (1945/1947) 4th edition, Benziger Bros: New York, Parallel Latin and English text, with various English commentaries

The Roman Breviary (Pius V revised Pius X) (1936) *An English version compiled by the Benedictine Nuns of the Abbey of Our Lady of Consolation at Stanbrook*, Burns Oates & Washbourne: London, 4 Volumes

Thorold, Algar (1933) trs *Self-Abandonment to Divine Providence* (1971 edition) Collins, Fontana: London.

Tolkien, JRR see Carpenter (1981)

Torkington, David (2018) *Wisdom from the Christian Mystics. How to Pray the Christian Way*, Circle Books: London

Turner, Nigel (1965) *Grammatical Insights into the New Testament*, T & T Clark: Edinburgh

Ullathorne, William Bernard Archbishop (1868) *The autobiography of Archbishop Ullathorne : with selections from his letters*, revised edition (1891) Burns & Oates: London, and reissued with an Introduction by Shane Leslie as *From Cabin Boy to Archbishop. The Autobiography of Archbishop Ullathorne*, Burns Oates: London (1941)

Unger, Dominic J (2012) ed *St Irenaeus of Lyons: Against the Heresies III*. Ancient Christian Writers: The Works of the Fathers in Translation, trs MC Steenberg, The Newman Press: New York

Van Campenhausen, Hans (1959) trs Stanley Godman, *The Fathers of the Greek Church*, Pantheon, New York

Van Campenhausen, Hans (1964) trs Manfred Hoffman, *The Fathers of the Latin Church*, Stanford U.P. Stanford

Vatican II (1962-1965) Second Ecumenical Council of the Vatican: https://www.vatican.va/archive/hist_councils/ii_vatican_council/index.htm

Villon, François (15th C): https://www.gutenberg.org/files/12246/12246-h/12246-h.htm

von Balthasar, Hans Urs (1989) *Christian Meditation*, Ignatius Press: San Francisco

Vincent, St of Lerins (5th C) *Commonitorium.* See Demeulenaere (1985) and: https://www.newadvent.org/fathers/3506.htm

Vulgate (1592) *Biblia Sacra Vulgata* (late 4th century revised as the *Vulgata Clementina* in 1592): http://www.catholicbible.online/

Walker, GSM (1957) ed *Columbani Opera*. The Dublin Institute for Advanced Studies:Dublin

Walsh, James (1981) trs *The Cloud of Unknowing*, Paulist Press, New York

Watson, G (1990) *Augustine: Soliloquies and Immortality of the Soul*, Aris & Phillips: Cambridge

Weil, Simone (1947) *La Pesanteur et la Grâce*, Librairie Plon: Paris, see also: http://palimpsestes.fr/textes_philo/weil/pesanteur_et_grace.pdf

Werner, Eric (1959) *The Sacred Bridge Liturgical Parallels in Synagogue and Early Church*, Columbia UP: New York

Wicks, Robert J (2016) ed *Prayer in the Catholic Tradition. A Handbook of Practical Approaches*, Franciscan Media: Cincinatti, Ohio

Wordsworth, William see: Logan (1998)

Zerwick, Max (1966) *A Grammatical Analysis of the Greek New Testament*, trs Mary Grosvenor, unabridged 5th revised edition, 1996, Editrice Pontifico Istituto Biblico, Rome

Verba volant, scripta manent. (Words fly, writings remain.)

BIBLIOGRAPHY: LITURGICAL LATIN

Bene orasse est bene studuisse.
(To have prayed well is to have prepared well. Ovid)

Adams, JN (2016) *An Anthology of Informal Latin, 200 BC-AD 900*, Cambridge University Press: Cambridge

Baumeister, Edmund J (1941) *The New Missal Latin. A Two-Year Course Based on the Sunday Missal*, 2 vols, Mount St John Press: Dayton Ohio. See also: vol 1 1996; vol 2 1998, *The New Missal Latin*, St Mary's Publishing Company: St. Mary's, Kansas:http://www.traditio.com/feature/newmiss.txt

Birch, David (2007) 'The Place of Latin in the Church'. *The Priest. The Journal of the Australian Confraternity of Catholic Clergy*, 11/1, 16-18 republished in *Mass of Ages*, Latin Mass Society, London, vol 155 February 2008, 26-28

Blaise, Albert (1955) *Manuel du Latin Chrétien*, trs as *A Handbook of Christian Latin: Style, Morphology, and Syntax* trs G Roti, Brepols, Georgetown University Press: Washington DC, 1994

Bourgain, Pascale with Marie-Clotilde Hubert (2005) *Le Latin Médiéval*, L'Atelier du Médiéviste, vol 10, Brepols: Turnhout

Bretzke, James T (1998) *Consecrated Phrases A Latin Theological Dictionary. Latin Expressions Commonly Found in Theological Writings*, The Liturgical Press: Collegeville, Minnesota

Britt, Dom Matthew OSB ed (1928) *A Dictionary of the Psalter Containing the Vocabulary of the Psalms, Hymns, Canticles, and Miscellaneous Prayers of the Breviary Psalter*, Benziger Brothers: New York

Brittain, F (1934) *Latin in Church. Episodes in the History of its Pronunciation Particularly in England*, Cambridge University Press: Cambridge

Bugnolo, Alexis Bro (2002/2007) *Ecclesiastical Latin Grammar*, a 14 week course (28 DVDs) 'to prepare the student or Priest to read and understand the Traditional Latin Mass': https://www.franciscan-archive.org/latin.html

Byrne, Carol (1999) *Simplicissimus. An Entirely New Approach to Learning the Latin of the Traditional Roman Mass*, Latin Mass Society, London

Caswall, Rev Edward (1868) *The Catholic's Latin Instructor in the Principal Church Offices and Devotions*, Burns & Oates: London

Collins, John F (1985) *A Primer of Ecclesiastical Latin*, revised edition 1988, Catholic University of America Press: Washington DC

Corbett, P (1970) 'Christian Latin' in *The Oxford Classical Dictionary* 2nd edition OUP: Oxford, 579-580

Corpus Scriptorum Ecclesiasticorum Latinorum: Critical editions of Latin works by late-antique and early-medieval Christian authors. See: http://csel.sbg.ac.at/en/

Daniel, HA (1841-56) *Thesaurus Hymnologicus*. 5 vols, E Anton: Halle and Leipzig

de Angelis, Michael Rev (1937) *The Correct Pronunciation of Latin According to Roman Usage*, St Gregory Guild: Philadelphia

Deferrari, Roy J (1921) *A First Latin Book for Catholic Schools*, The Catholic Education Press, Washington DC: https://archive.org/details/AFirstLatinBookForCatholicSchools

Deferrari, Roy J (1960) *A Latin-English Dictionary of St Thomas Aquinas, Based on the Summa Theologica and Selected Passages of his Other Writings*, St Paul Editions: Boston, MA (1986)

Diamond, Wilfrid (1941) *Diamond's Liturgical Latin: A Simple Method of Learning the Latin of the Missal*, Benziger Brothers, New York. Published (on demand) as *Liturgical Latin. Church Latin and your Missal*, Church Latin Publishing Company, 2021: https://www.churchlatin.com/liturgical-latin

Diamond, Wilfrid (1961) *Dictionary of Liturgical Latin,* Bruce Publishing: New York. See also: https://www.churchlatin.com/liturgical-latin

Distler, Paul F SJ (1962) *Teach the Latin. I Pray You,* Loyola University Press: Chicago

Ecclesiastical Latin blogspot (2018/2022 online): https://ecclesiasticallatin.blogspot.com/

Ecclesiastical Latin. Learn to Read the Bible in Latin (2009-2020 online): https://ecclesiasticallatin.com/ecclesiasticallatin_home.php

Elliott, Alison Goddard (1997) 'A Brief Introduction to Medieval Latin Grammar', in Harrington,1997 (2nd edition) pp 1-51

Foster, Reginald Fr (online) *First Experience Latin* see: https://frcoulter.com/latin/First_Experience.pdf. There is no second experience online as this was a conversation class.

Foster, Reginald Fr (online) *Third Experience Latin* see: see:https://frcoulter.com/latin/third/index.html

Foster, Reginald & Daniel P McCarthy (2016) *Ossa Latinitatis Sola Ad Mentem Reginaldi Rationemque: The Mere Bones of Latin According to the Thought and System of Reginald,* Catholic University Press of America: Washington DC

Foster, Reginald & Daniel P McCarthy (2021) *Ossium Carnes Multae e Marci Tullii Ciceronis epistulis: The Bones' Meats Abundant from the Epistles of Marcus Tullius Cicero,* a sequel to *Ossa Latinitatis* (2016) Catholic University Press of America: Washington DC

Gildersleeve, R and Lodge, G (1992) *Gildersleeve's Latin Grammar,* 3rd edition, Thomas Nelson and Sons: Edinburgh

Grandgent, CH (1907) *An Introduction to Vulgar Latin,* Tiger Xenophon: Richmond UK, reprint 2009

Harden, JM (1921) *Dictionary of the Vulgate New Testament,* reprinted 1975, second edition, 2007, Simon Wallenberg Press: London

Harkins, Franklin T (2019) 'Medieval Latin Reception' in Blowers & Martin eds (2019) pp 651-66

Harrington, KP (ed) (1925) *Medieval Latin*, revised second edition by Joseph Pucci, 1997, with a Grammatical Introduction by Alison Goddard Elliott, University of Chicago Press: Chicago

Henle, Robert SJ (1945) *Henle Latin Series*, see: https://www.memoriapress.com/curriculum/latin/henle-latin

Huber, Vincent Abbot OSB (1931) *Latin for Sisters: a Practical Guide to Breviary-Latin for Sisterhoods who Recite the Divine Office or the Little Office of the Blessed Virgin,* Tabernacle & Purgatory Press: Clyde, Missouri

Janson, Tore (2004) *A Natural History of Latin, The Story of the World's Most Successful Language* OUP: Oxford

John XXIII, Pope St (1962) *Constitutio Apostolica Veterum Sapientia de Latinitatis Studio Provehendo* (Apostolic Constitution on the Promotion of the Study of Latin) see:

https://www.vatican.va/content/johnxxiii/la/apost_constitutions/1962/documents/hf_j-xxiii_apc_19620222_veterum-sapientia.html; for an English translation see: https://adoremus.org/2007/12/veterum-sapientia/

Jones, PV & KC Sidwell (1986) *Reading Latin*, CUP: Cambridge

Jones, PV & KC Sidwell (2000) *An Independent Study Guide to "Reading Latin", Cambridge University Press: Cambridge*

Kennedy, Benjamin Hall (new edition 1930) *The Revised Latin Primer*, revised edition James Mountford, 1962, Longman: London

Konus, William J (1959) *Dictionary of the New Latin Psalter of Pope Pius XII,* Newman Press: New York

Kuhnmuench SJ, Otto J (1939) *Liturgical Latin*, Loyola University Press: Chicago

Lang, Uwe Michael (2007) trs Fr Anthony Forte 'Latin: vehicle of unity between peoples and cultures', *L'Osservatore Romano*, November 15

Latham, RE (1965) ed *Revised Medieval Latin Word-List from British and Irish Sources,* British Academy: London

Latinum: https://www.latinum.org.uk/resources/grammars

Lewis, CT and Short, C (1879) eds *A New Latin Dictionary founded on the Translation of Freund's Latin-German Lexicon,* trs Ethan Allen Andrews, Clarendon Press: Oxford See: http://www.perseus.tufts.edu/hopper/text?doc=Perseus:text:1999.04.0059

Lewis, CT (1891) *An Elementary Latin Dictionary*, revised edition 1963, Clarendon Press: Oxford

Lowe, JE (1924) *Church Latin for Beginners: An Elementary Course of Exercises in Ecclesiastical Latin* Foreword by Ronald Knox, Burns, Oates & Washbourne: London

Manning, Lloyd R (1928) *Church Latin: An Aid to the Appreciation of Our Lady's Little Office,* privately published: New York, see: https://learnchurchlatin.files.wordpress.com/2021/01/church-latin-pp.-1-67-copy.pdf https://learnchurchlatin.files.wordpress.com/2021/07/church-latin-pp.-67-135-copy.pdf

Mantello, FAC & AG Rigg eds (1996) *Medieval Latin An Introduction and Bibliographical Guide*, Catholic University of America Press: Washington DC

Martin, Michael (1998 *et seq*): www.preces-latinae.org/index.htm

Martin, Michael (nd) 'What the Church says on the Latin Language': http://www.preces-latinae.org/thesaurus/Introductio/Popes.html

Martin, Michael (nd) 'The Pronunciation of Latin': http://www.preces-latinae.org/thesaurus/Introductio/Pronunciatio.html

Martindale, CC (1932) *The Words of the Missal*, Sheed & Ward: London

McInerny, Ralph (1995) *Let's Read Latin Introduction to the Language of the Church*, Dumb Ox Books: South Bend, Indiana

Merrill, William A (1904) *Latin Hymns*, 1917 edition reprinted by Lightning Source: Milton Keynes

Messenger, Ruth Ellis (1953) *The Medieval Latin Hymn*, Capital Press: Washington DC

Mohrmann, Christine (1957) *Liturgical Latin: Its Origins and Character. Three Lectures,* The Catholic University of America, Washington DC reprinted 1959 Burns & Oates: London

Most, William Fr (1957-1961) *Latin by the Natural Method,* 3 vols, Henry Regnery Press: Chicago

Neale, J M (1851)*Hymni Ecclesiae e Breviariis,* John Henry Parker: London

Newman, J H (1865) *Hymni Ecclesiae.* Macmillan: Oxford and London

Niermeyer, JF & C van deKieft (1976) eds *Mediae Latinatis lexicon minus,* 2nd rev edition by J W J Burgers, 2vols, Brill: Leiden 2002

Nunn, HPV (1922) *An Introduction to Ecclesiastical Latin,* CUP: Cambridge. For a PDF online see: http://www.liberius.net/livres/An_introduction_to_ecclesiastical_latin_000000433.pdf

O'Brien, RJ (1965) *A Descriptive Grammar of Ecclesiastical Latin Based on Modern Structural Analysis,* Georgetown University Latin Series, Loyola University Press: Chicago

Ostler, Nicholas (2007) *Ad Infinitum. A Biography of Latin and the World it Created,* Harper Press: London 2009

Palmer, LR (1954) *The Latin Language,* Faber & Faber: London

Perkins, Mary (1942) *Your Catholic Language Latin from the Missal,* Sheed & Ward: London

Perseus Latin Word Study Tool: https://www.perseus.tufts.edu/hopper/morph?l=Cedant&la=la

Plater, WE & HJ White (1926) *A Grammar of the Vulgate. Being an Introduction to the Study of the Latinity of the Vulgate Bible,* Clarendon Press: Oxford

Pontificia Academia Latinitatis (Pontifical Academy for Latin) see: https://www.vatican.va/roman_curia/pontifical_academies/latinitatis/index.htm

Raby, FJE (1927) *A History of Christian Latin Poetry from the Beginnings to the Close of the Middle Ages,* Clarendon Press: Oxford, 2nd edition 1953

Scanlon, Cora Carroll & Charles L Scanlon (1944) *Latin Grammar. Grammar, Vocabularies, and Exercises in Preparation for the Reading of the Missal and Breviary*, ed Rev Newton Thompson, reissued 1976, Tan Books: Rockford Illinois

Scanlon, Cora Carroll & Charles L Scanlon (1948 2nd ed 1963) *Second Latin Grammar, Vocabularies, and Exercises in Preparation for the Reading of Philosophy, Theology and Canon Law*, reissued 1976, Tan Books: Rockford Illinois

Scarre, AM (1831 rev 2nd rev edition 1938) *An Introduction to Liturgical Latin*, Geo EJ Coldwell: London

Sidwell, Keith (1995) *Reading Medieval Latin*, CUP: Cambridge

Simpson, DP (1968) ed, *Cassell's New Latin-English, English-Latin Dictionary* (1854) 5th edition Cassell, London

Sleumer, Albert & Josef Schmidt (1926) *Kirchenlateinisches Wörterbuch*, 2nd edition, Steffen: Limburg a.d. Lahn, reprinted: G Olms: Hildesheim, 1996

Solodov, Joseph B (2010) *Latin Alive The Survival of Latin in English and the Romance Languages*, Cambridge University Press: Cambridge

Souter, A (1949) *A Glossary of Later Latin to 600 AD*, new edition 1957, Clarendon Press: Oxford

Spencer, Matthew (online) *Latin for Clergy, Religious and Laypeople in association with the Latin Mass Society of England and Wales*, see: https://lms.org.uk/sites/default/files/resource_documents/Latin_Courses_LMS_2022.pdf

Stelten, Leo F (1995) *Dictionary of Ecclesiastical Latin with an Appendix of Latin Expressions Defined and Clarified*, Hendrickson: Peabody, Mass

Strecker, Karl (1939 3rd edition) *EinführungindasMittellatein*, trs Robert B Palmer, *Introduction to Medieval Latin*, 1968, Weidmann: Dublin & Zurich

The Latin Library, online early Christian Latin texts, see: https://thelatinlibrary.com/christian.html

The Oxford Latin Dictionary (2012) 2nd edition, 2 vols, Oxford University Press: Oxford

Townsend, Cora I (1892) *Mantrina. A Latin Primer Especially Adapted to the Missal and Breviary,* Ariston Book Company: New York

Tribe, Shawn (2008) 'Ecclesiastical Latin Resources', *New Liturgical Movement:* https://www.newliturgicalmovement.org/2008/01/ecclesiastical-latin-resources.html

Usarium, A Digital Library and Database for the Study of Latin Liturgical History in the Middle Ages and Early Modern Period: https://usuarium.elte.hu/origins

Vulgate Lexicon: http://www.intratext.com/IXT/LAT0001/_FA2.HTM

Vulgate search facility: http://vulsearch.sourceforge.net/cgi-bin/vulsearch

Vulgate, Douay Rheims & Knox Bible (Parallel Versions): http://www.catholicbible.online/

Waddell, Helen (1927) *The Wandering Scholars* (The 'Vagantes', Latin Poets of the Middle Ages) 1954 Pelican edition based on the revised and enlarged 6th edition 1932, Penguin, Harmondsworth

Walker, John (1830) *A Key to the Classical Pronunciation of Greek, Latin, and Scripture Proper Names,* T Cadell, CJG & F Rivington: London

Wilson, W Michael (1968) *Essentials of Latin Grammar. A Practical Guide to the Mastery of Latin,* Passport Books: Chicago

Abeunt studia in mores.
(Studies transform into habits. Ovid)

www.ingramcontent.com/pod-product-compliance
Lightning Source LLC
Chambersburg PA
CBHW050257010526
44107CB00055B/2078